SOUL MUSIC A–Z

Hugh Gregory

BLANDFORD

A BLANDFORD BOOK

First published in the UK 1991
by Blandford
(a Cassell imprint)
Villiers House
41/47 Strand
LONDON
WC2 5JE

Distributed in the United States
by Sterling Publishing Co., Inc.
387 Park Avenue South, New York, NY 10016–8810

Distributed in Australia
by Capricorn Link (Australia) Pty Ltd
P.O. Box 665, Lane Cove, NSW 2066

British Library Cataloguing in Publication Data
Gregory, Hugh
  Soul music A–Z.
I. Title
782.4216440922

ISBN 0–7137–2179–0 Hardback
ISBN 0–7137–2183–9 Paperback

(Compiled on an Apple Macintosh)
Typeset by August Filmsetting, Haydock, St Helens
Printed and bound by Courier International Limited
East Kilbride

CONTENTS

INTRODUCTION

One of the many problems in attempting to compile a reference book is the quest for objectivity; and when that reference book is dealing with a somewhat minor, but influential aspect of creative endeavour that objectivity comes under serious stress. When I embarked on the research and the collation of material for a book on Soul Music, I had certain key themes, primarily to provide a book that actually took account of the influence of session musicians, producers, label owners and writers. It seemed to me that, in pursuing this particular avenue, I would be providing some sort of insight into an area that has traditionally recieved scant attention.

It was at this point that the first major stumbling block occurred: can white men sing soul? They can sing soulfully, certainly, but where should the line be drawn? The influence of white musicians and businessmen upon the development of soul has been immense. Therefore, the inclusion of musicians like Steve Cropper is fundamental to the understanding of the early days of Stax. Nothing wrong with that at all. Where my original precepts went awry, was in supposing blithely that, there would be little reason for including white artists who have been more readily associated with rock like Robert Palmer, for instance: to exclude Palmer, who has worked with The Meters (see Neville Brothers) and Bernard Edwards and whose style has been moulded by the great Soul Singers of the sixties, would be like trying to exclude Ray Charles on the grounds that, for the last twenty years or so, most of Charles' records have been out and out country. Thus the parameters of the book had changed before I had even started. It was going to be intensely subjective because I was compelled to establish my own criteria for inclusion, as opposed to any perceived notion of what generic category any specific artist belonged to.

With that consideration firmly in mind, I set about my research with renewed fervour, until the next stumbling block arrived: the distinction between soul and blues and rhythm and blues. In this area, the dividing line has been murky and controversial: John Lee Hooker and Muddy Waters have been excluded, because they belong to the rural traditions of the blues and have not adjusted their style with the passage of time. John Lee Hooker's acclaimed LP, *The Healer* of 1989, was a moving testament to the spirit of the blues, there was not a note of compromise; in much the same way Muddy Waters' later LPs with Johnny Winter were reaffirmations of his commitment to the blues. However, B. B. King has been included: there is no doubt that King is one of best blues guitarists of all time, but in recent years, his studio LPs have seen him broadening his scope by using session men like Joe Sample and Wilton Felder. His repertoire has broadened to encompass songs by artists like Stevie Wonder. The arrangements have completed the gradual departure from being regarded purely as a blues musician, although his best performances are reserved for the blues.

The big band vocalists of the forties have been excluded for similar reasons: the phrasing of singers like Big Joe Turner and Sarah Vaughan are firmly entrenched in the traditions of jazz whereas Ruth Brown, whose career started with a big band, moved away from the styles of a big band vocalist to embrace the more populist traditions of rhythm and blues.

Another area that requires explanation is disco. Soul from its earliest days has thrived on the dance-floor: Motown, Stax, Atlantic and James Brown all depended upon exposure on local radio stations for their records to be successful locally, the next step to a national hit was "Can you dance to it?". In the seventies, the dance-floor began to dictate more openly what could and couldn't be done; Stevie Wonder's use of the synthesizer opened up the door for a whole host of technicians only too eager to experiment with repetitive rhythmic patterns. Much of what materialised during those years was, ultimately, forgettable; throughout the world, groups and singers were signed up by producers and writers with the sole objective of creating hit records. However, it should be emphasized that not every disco record was so cynically produced: Motown, TK and Brown proved to be adept at combining the energy of the dance-floor with a creative urgency that was totally lacking in much of what came out of Europe in the name of disco.

Similarly, rap and hip hop quickly absorbed some of the more facile elements of disco: an apparent need on the part of producers to come of with anything that might have dancefloor appeal. Having said that, it should be emphasized that, the need to generate fresh sounds for the dancefloor, has enabled a large number of people with no formal training or musical background to experiment with sound and rhythms by sampling and re- mixing. But it is a completely separate area and needs to be appraised as such. As a result groups like Public Enemy, De La Soul, sampling DJs and MCs have been excluded. All of these qualifications might appear pedantic, but to even attempt to compile a book that covers all the hybrids of soul would ultimately devalue any inherent thematic development. To have been influence by soul has been insufficient in itself to justify inclusion.

With these criteria in mind, one of the most contentious issues – certainly among purists – is "What is Soul?". Soul is a synthesis of R&B and Gospel: the testifyin' traditions of gospel fused with the secular traditions of R&B. The hybrid is soul. Thus one of the first soul records was "I Gotta Woman" by Ray Charles: the call-and-response style of Charles' vocals can be traced back to gospel, while the lyrical imagery dealt with the minutiae of everyday life. Sam Cooke was Soul's first true sex symbol. When he was a member of The Soul Stirrers the adulation his performances inspired had little or nothing to do with religious zeal: his ability to work a congregation up into a frenzy was born out of his awareness of his own sexuality and his instinctive showmanship. Some members of the Soul Stirrers were ashamed of his ability to manipulate the congregations so blatantly, believing his act to be sacrilegious. However, Cooke never forgot the lessons he learnt in church: when he left The Soul Stirrers to become a "pop singer" he took the inflections and intonations with him. The relationship between soul and gospel remains symbiotic: some performers return to the church abandoning the secular for good, others periodically record gospel LPs. The only way to differentiate between the two styles now is in the lyrical imagery. Solomon Burke being a prime example: having sung and preached from the age of four, he had a very successful career as a soul singer in the 1960s and then returned to the church in the 1970s. During the1980s he has recorded gospel and soul LPs.

Many purists would argue that Motown had very little to do with soul. Their arguments miss a vital point though: soul embraces the secular in equal measure. It's not just about the trials and tribulations of everyday life, it also celebrates the emotional achievements and successes of everyday life. Just because a record is good to dance to doesn't invalidate its artistic merits. While Motown tended to borrow freely from the Chicago and Detroit-based traditions of urban R&B, so Stax borrowed liberally from the country music of the Deep South. In its own way, each is just as potent an expression of soul – it's just that the terms of reference differ.

"Northern Soul" is another generic term that has gained currency among aficionados in the last twenty-five years,or so. Its roots and derivations remain something of an enigma to most, mainly because there is a widely held assumption that "Northern Soul" is intrinsically different from any other type of soul. If one makes a direct comparison between the Soul music of the Northern and Southern States of the US the differences are immediately apparent. However, the term "Northern Soul" denotes a certain elitism, referring to records that have gained popularity on the UK Northern club circuit. Initially, the criteria of a "Northern Soul Classic" meant that it was seriously obscure: often there were examples of a record ceasing to be popular because it had been reissued! However, it is still governed by the dictates of the dance-floor: the most execrable bit of rubbish can still end up being a "Northern Soul Classic" by being a barn-storming stomper or good to dance to, in other words.

In the final analysis, the term "soul" is perjorative and perceptual: this book represents an attempt to come to terms with some of the major reference points. The discographies refer to LPs, Cassettes and Compact Discs and, theoretically, are available in the UK as of time of going to press. There are many who will find errors and omissions. I claim sole ownership of my mistakes. For those who feel disposed to put me right, I will be delighted to receive any correspondence: reference books of this nature are organic, and need to mutate and grow.

Hugh Gregory
London, 1991

SOUL MUSIC A–Z

ABBOTT, GREGORY There can be few careers that have had more auspicious beginnings than Abbott's. In the early 1980s, having first obtained degrees from the Universities of Boston and Stanford, he moved, without bothering to complete his doctorate at the University of California, to Los Angeles, where he met and married Freda Payne. By 1984, having moved to New York, he had started to work on Wall Street as a researcher. Then he was given the opportunity by some friends to build his own recording studio. In 1986 the fruits of his labours materialized in the shape of the single, *Shake You Down* (USA#1; UK#6.1986), the LP of the same name was moderately successful, peaking at #16 in the USA. His most recent LP, *I'll Prove it to You*, showed that he had a lot of promise but lacked any sort of clear identity of his own.

SHAKE YOU DOWN, CBS, 1986
I'LL PROVE IT TO YOU, CBS, 1988

ABNER, EWART During the fifties, Ewart Abner was instrumental in bringing soul and R&B to a much wider audience from his native Chicago working with a number of independent labels. After joining Chance in 1950 he wrote and produced for The Moonglows (see FUQUA, Harvey), he founded the Veejay label with Jimmy Bracken and Vivian and Calvin Carter in 1954. From then until the collapse of the company in 1965, through bankruptcy, he developed the careers of artists like The DELLS, The IMPRESSIONS, Gene CHANDLER, John Lee Hooker and Jimmy Reed. Furthermore, when a group from Liverpool called The Beatles were turned down by Capitol, Abner picked up their earliest releases and broke them in the USA. After the disintegration of Veejay, he ran his own label, Constellation, before joining Motown. At Motown, he supervised the company's transition from independent to major status; he was rewarded by being appointed President in 1973. In 1975, he became Stevie WONDER's business consultant.

ABRAMSON, HERB Herb Abramson's career in the music business has been dogged by missed opportunities, but his clearsighted understanding and genuine affection for music has been instrumental in bringing to black popular music the credibility it enjoys to this day.

In 1945, while he was working as a producer and A&R man for Al Greene's National label, he and Jesse STONE, a fellow employee, concluded that Greene hadn't the faintest idea what he was doing and decided to launch their own label. This ambition was not realized until 1947 when they met Ahmet ERTEGUN, who was prepared to finance the company, it was called Atlantic Records. Abramson was installed as president and he, Ertegun and Stone started a tradition of venturing down to the Southern states in search of new artists. One of his earliest signings was Ruth BROWN; her influences were Billie Holiday and Sarah Vaughan but, under the auspices of Abramson, she was transformed into 'Miss Rhythm'. In 1953 he was drafted into the army and left his wife Miriam to monitor his interests. When he returned two years later, not only had he lost touch with new developments in music and separated from his wife, but also Jerry WEXLER had joined the company: Abramson sold out his shares for $300,000.

After his departure from Atlantic, he launched a series of labels in an effort to get back into the music business: Triumph, Blaze and Festival. Despite the fact that he signed artists like Solomon BURKE, Don COVAY and Gene Pitney, who would enjoy considerable success later in their careers, none of these ventures was remotely successful. In 1964 he discovered Tommy TUCKER in Asbury Park, New Jersey and began to manage him. Tucker recorded the self-composed *Hi-Heel Sneakers* with Abramson producing; leased out to the Chess subsidiary, Checker, it became an international hit. Since then, Abramson has retired from the business, returning briefly towards the end of the sixties with a set of Louisiana Red tapes, which he leased to Atlantic, only to disappear from sight once again. According to Charlie Gillett, he still harbours plans for a return, one day.

ACE, JOHNNY Johnny Ace was born in Memphis on June 9, 1929, as John Marshall Alexander. After graduating from the Booker T. Washington High School, he enlisted in the navy (although under age) and served World War Two. At the end of the war he returned to Memphis, where he joined Adolph Duncan's Band as a pianist for a spell before joining up with B. B. KING, who had his own show on the local radio station, WDIA. When King left to go on a nationwide tour, Ace took over the show. In 1952, he signed with Don ROBEY's label, Duke, where his first recording, the rather lugubrious, *My Song*, topped the R&B charts. By 1954, he had established a reputation as one of the few black artists to break out of the restricting "race" market; the same year he was voted Most Programmed R&B Artist in the Cashbox DJs Poll. It was

unfortunate that he was unable to perpetuate his success; on Christmas Eve 1954 at the Civic Auditorium in Houston, Texas, he killed himself while playing Russian roulette, it was an ignominious end to a promising career. After his death *Pledging My Love* (USA#17.1955) was a modest hit. Posterity will mark him as the first casualty of the rock'n'roll era.

MEMORIAL ALBUM, Ace, 1981

ACKLIN, BARBARA Barbara Acklin was born on February 28, 1943 in Chicago, Illinois. She gained experience initally by singing in the local gospel choir and then doing a stint with the locally based St Lawrence label, where she provided back-up vocals and issued a couple of rather undistinguished records under the pseudonym of Barbara Allen. In 1967 she signed with the Brunswick label and in 1968, she scored with *Love Makes a Woman* (USA#15.1968), which prompted Brunswick to team her up with Gene CHANDLER for a series of duets including *From The Teacher To The Preacher*; her other recordings included *Just Ain't Love* and *Am I the Same Girl*, which were regional hits but failed to cross over into the national charts. Her real bid for stardom came through the songwriting partnership she forged with her future husband Eugene Record of The CHILITES. This produced, among others, the seminal *Have You Seen Her*, a #3 hit in both the USA and the UK in 1971. More recently she has recorded for Capitol and Chi-Sounds, the latter being part-owned by her husband, and has re-established her connection with Gene Chandler. However, due to the unwillingness of record companies to release her records with any degree of consistency in the UK or, indeed, to promote them properly in the USA, she has been unable to attract anything other than a small coterie of committed admirers.

GROOVY IDEAS, Kent, 1987

ADAMS, JOHNNY In his native New Orleans, where he was born in 1932, Adams has always enjoyed the respect of his contemporaries, but beyond "The Crescent City" he has been hard put to make an impression.

His career started in 1959, when he recorded a series of songs for the local Ric label. These sold reasonably well locally, and he was dubbed "The Tan Canary". His earlier training in gospel groups enabled him to extract "just that little bit extra" from material that was mainstream at best, substandard at worst. Throughout the 1960's, his career was in the doldrums until it was revived by Shelby SINGLETON, who issued a number of records on his SSS International label. These included *Release Me, I Can't Be All Bad* and his most successful record, *Reconsider Me* (USA-#28.1969). After this his career slipped back into the doldrums until 1984, when he was offered a contract with the Rounder label. Since then he has recorded three LPs for Rounder, although none have sold in vast quantities they have drawn words of approval from a growing number of devotees.

RECONSIDER ME, Charly, 1969
FROM THE HEART, Demon, 1984
AFTER DARK, Rounder, 1986,
ROOM WITH A VIEW OF THE BLUES, Rounder, 1989

ADAMS, OLETA One day in 1985 Oleta Adams, having played the club and hotel bar circuit since leaving school, was performing in the bar of the Hyatt Regency Hotel in Kansas City when she was spotted by Roland Orzabal

and Curt Smith of the group Tears for Fears. Two years later they gave her her first break by recruiting her to sing on their LP *The Seeds Of Love*. In 1990, her first LP, *Circle of One* (UK #1.1991), was produced by Orzabal and released on the Fontana label in the UK, where it was greeted with critical acclaim, many likening her style to that of Anita BAKER.

CIRCLE OF ONE, Fontana, 1990

ADEVA Adeva was born Patricia Daniels in New Jersey; she had four brothers and one sister. Raised in the gospel tradition, on leaving school she obtained a degree in psychology and started to teach handicapped and disturbed children. In 1988 she approached Mike Cameron, the president of the New Jersey production company, Smack; after a brief audition he signed her. Her first LP, *Warning*, collected her four hit singles: *Respect, Musical Freedom, Warning* and *I Thank You*. While, it would be easy to credit her success to the continuing power of the dance-floor to create hits, her gospel roots have given her the ability to outlast volatile fads of fashion.

WARNING, Chrysalis, 1988

ALEXANDER, ARTHUR Arthur Alexander was born on May 10, 1940, in Florence, near Sheffield, Alabama. On leaving school he met and started to collaborate with lyricist Tom Stafford, who introduced him to Rick HALL. Hall was so enthusiastic about Alexander's songs that he took Alexander straight into the makeshift studios above the drugstore belonging to Stafford's father; the result was *You Better Move On* (USA#24.1962). The track was hawked around until the Dot label picked it up and put him under contract: in 1962, it became Alexander's first and biggest hit and provided Hall with enough money from his percentage to set up the Fame Studios.

At Dot his style of music wasn't really appreciated, the company was more accustomed to selling Pat Boone records and so they marketed him in exactly the same way. Initially, nevertheless, he was moderately successful with records like *Anna, Go Home Girl* and *Where Have You Been* all making small dents in the US charts; in the UK, he was very with popular groups like The Beatles and The Rolling Stones, who brought his material to a much wider audience by recording their own versions. Eventually, in 1965, he parted company with Dot, and signed with the Monument subsidiary, Sound Stage 7, but found that he was being given less control over his career than at Dot, and gradually he stopped recording altogether. In 1972, however, with a fresh contract from Warner Bros. under his belt, he recorded the LP, *Arthur Alexander*. Produced by Tommy COGBILL, it was as close a representation of his true abilities as anything he had done since his earliest recordings. However, it failed to sell and he slipped back into obscurity, where he has remained ever since, apart from a brief excursion for Buddah in 1975, when he recorded the self-penned *Every Day I Have To Cry* (USA#45.1975). Over the years, he has been showered with praise from those in the know but major success has eluded him.

ARTHUR ALEXANDER, Ace, 1972
A SHOT OF RHYTHM AND SOUL, Ace, 1985
SOLDIER OF LOVE, Ace, 1987
THE GREATEST, Ace, 1989

ALEXANDER, J.W. "WOODY" The career of "Woody" Alexander was inextricably entangled with the development of Sam COOKE. He was raised in Independence,

Kansas, where he held down a number of jobs, working for the Civilian Conservation Corps, playing baseball professionally for the Ethiopian Clowns amongst other things. By 1948 he had become the manager of and tenor in a gospel group, The Pilgrim Travellers and had succeeded in procuring for them a contract with Art RUPE's Specialty label in Los Angeles; they were the second gospel group to be signed to the label. In 1949, in his new capacity as chief scout, he signed The Soul Stirrers, whom Sam Cooke joined in 1950, following the departure of the lead singer, Rebert Harris. Although they were in rival groups, Alexander monitored Cooke's career avidly and so when, in 1956, Cooke had tired of singing gospel, it was Alexander, who put Cooke's case to Rupe.

In 1957, Alexander and his group, The Travellers (they had dropped the adjective "Pilgrim") were signed by Andex, a subsidiary of Cooke's new label, Keen. Later the same year, Alexander set up his own publishing company, Kags Music; within the year, Cooke had become his partner. In 1960, following a dispute over royalties with Keen, Cooke signed with RCA. Throughout, Alexander had maintained his ties with Specialty, but by 1959 Rupe had lost interest in the music business; he allowed Alexander to record The Soul Stirrers independently, and the result was the formation of the Sar label with The Soul Stirrers the first signing. Other contracted artists included Johnnie TAYLOR, the lead singer of The Soul Stirrers, The Sims Twins and The Valentinos (see WOMACK, Bobby). Perhaps the biggest irony was the fact that, while Cooke's recordings for RCA were overproduced, the recordings of his material by other artists for Sar were significantly grittier than the originals, because of Alexander's influence as co-producer. The death of Sam Cooke in 1964 was such a shock to Alexander that he shut down Sar and, effectively, ceased to play an active part in the music business, although he dabbled occasionally by helping Lou RAWLS in his quest for stardom and in 1965 producing for the Veejay label a number of LITTLE RICHARD sessions who was trying to stage a comeback.

ALLEN, BARBARA See ACKLIN, Barbara

ALLEN, LEE In 1958, an instrumental, *Walkin' with Mr. Lee*, featuring the saxophone of Lee Allen reached #11 in the US R&B charts. It was only fitting that a measure of individual recognition should be accorded to a man whose solos had lifted records by artists like LITTLE RICHARD, Fats DOMINO, Amos Milburn, Etta JAMES and Roscoe Gordon from the merely good to the memorable. In the 1960s his style of playing fell out of favour and he worked in an aircraft factory for a period until moving to California, where he has started to play once again on the club circuit.

ALLMAN, DUANE Duane Allman was born in Nashville on November 26, 1946, but moved with his family to Florida during the 1950s. In 1967, having played guitar in local groups like The House Rockers and Allman Joys with his brother, Gregg; he formed Hourglass, they recorded two LPs for Liberty before splitting up, having had its third LP rejected by the record company. They had been recording it at Rick HALL's Fame Studios and Hall was sufficiently impressed by Allman's guitar work to offer him session work at the studio. Throughout 1968, Allman was featured prominently on sessions by Clarence CARTER, KING CURTIS, Wilson PICKETT and Aretha FRANKLIN. In 1969 he and his group, The Allman Brothers Band, were signed to Atlantic; they were managed by Otis REDDING's former manager, Phil WALDEN, who would later sign them to his recently established Capricorn label. The success of the group came gradually and Allman continued playing sessions, contributing to Eric Clapton's *Layla* among others. On October 29, 1971, he was killed when his motorbike crashed while trying to avoid a lorry in Macon. The group's most successful record to feature his playing was the live recording *At The Fillmore East* (USA#13.1971); the follow-up, *Eat A Peach* (USA#4.1972), included three tracks which Allman had recorded before he died.

AT THE FILLMORE EAST, (The Allman Brothers Band), Polydor, 1971
EAT A PEACH, (The Allman Brothers Band), Polydor, 1972 BEGINNINGS, (The Allman Brothers Band), Polydor, 1973

ALSTON, GERALD Gerald Alston was born in North Carolina; his father was a preacher and his uncle was Johnny Fields of the gospel group, The Blind Boys. After singing with gospel groups through his adolescence he was invited to join The Manhattans, with whom he remained until 1988. While never desperately successful, the group had a few hits in the mid-1970s and early 1980s: *Don't Take Your Love* (USA#37.1975), *Kiss and Say Goodbye* (USA#1; UK#4.1976), *Hurt* (UK#4. 1976), *It's You* (UK#43.1977), *Shining Star* (USA#5; UK#45.1980) and *Crazy* (UK #63.1983).

When he left to pursue a solo career he was signed by the Taj label. His debut, *Gerald Alston*, was not especially distinguished in itself, but it did show that he had the temperament to rub shoulders with other artists of the same ilk, like Luther VANDROSS, Alexander O'NEAL and Freddie JACKSON. His second LP *Open Invitation* (1990) went a long way towards vindicating the promise of his debut.

MANHATTANS, CBS, 1976
AFTER MIDNIGHT, (Manhattans), CBS, 1980
FOREVER BY YOUR SIDE, (Manhattans), CBS, 1983
BEST OF THE MANHATTANS, CBS, 1984
BACK TO BASICS, (Manhattans), CBS, 1986
GERALD ALSTON, Motown, 1989
OPEN INVITATION, Motown, 1990

ASHFORD & SIMPSON   Of all the song-writing parnerships to be nurtured at Motown, none has proved to be as enduring or versatile as Ashford & Simpson. Nicky Ashford was born in Fairfield, South Carolina on May 4, 1943, and Valerie Simpson was born in the Bronx, New York City on August 26, 1948. They met at the White Rock Baptist Church in Harlem, where they belonged to the same gospel group, and decided to form a songwriting partnership. They got jobs as staff writers for the Wand and Scepter labels, where they wrote for Maxine BROWN and Chuck JACKSON; in 1966, Ray CHARLES picked up and recorded one of their songs, *Let's Go Get Stoned*. It reached #31 in the USA.

As a result, they joined the publishing arm of Motown, Jobete Music, in 1967 as writers and producers. Their songs were recorded at first by the duo, Marvin GAYE and Tammi TER-RELL, and included hits like *Ain't No Mountain High Enough, You're All I Need To Get By, Ain't Nothing Like The Real Thing* and *The Onion Song*. With Terrell's increased incapacity due to illness – indeed, according to Marvin Gaye, Simpson herself sang some of Terrell's parts in the later recordings – they started to write for Diana ROSS, who had just embarked upon a solo career. Writing for and producing Diana Ross proved even more successful for them with hits like *Remember Me, Reach Out (and Touch Somebody's Hand)* and a reworking of *Ain't No Mountain High Enough*.

In 1964, as Val and Nick, they had recorded *I'll Find You* for the Glover label and so it was inevitable that they should wish to perform themselves. Despite GORDY's reluctance, Simpson's solo career was launched in 1971 with the LP, *Exposed*, followed by *Valerie Simpson* in 1972. In 1973 they signed with Warner Bros. as artists, although they continued to work for Motown on a freelance basis. They remained with Warner Bros. for eight years and established a reputation for themselves as purveyors of classy soul, with their LPs selling consistently well: *Is It Still Good To Ya* (USA#20.1978), *Stay Free* (USA#23.1979) and *A Musical Affair* (USA#38.1980). In 1981 they signed with Capitol, where they had their biggest hit to date with *Solid* (USA#12; UK#3. 1985). While they have grown in stature as performers, they have continued to work with other artists like Diana Ross, Gladys KNIGHT, Chaka KHAN and Quincy JONES.

A MUSICAL AFFAIR, Warner Bros., 1980
SOLID, Capitol, 1985
REAL LOVE, Capitol, 1986
LOVE OR PHYSICAL, Capitol, 1989

ATLANTIC STARR   Atlantic Starr was formed in New York in 1976 by brothers David (guitar and vocals), Jonathan (trombone) and Wayne Lewis (keyboards) as a soul/funk outfit; they recruited Sharon Bryant (vocals), Clifford Archer (bass), Porter Carroll (drums), Koran Daniels (saxes), Joseph Phillips (percussion and flute) and William Sudderth (trumpet) to complete the line-up. They secured a recording contract with A&M, where they remained until 1987 and developed a reputation for consistency with a succession of singles that included *Gimme Your Lovin'* (UK#66.1978); *Circles* (UK#38.1982); *Silver Shadow* (UK#41.1985); *One Love* (UK

#58.1985); *Secret Lovers* (USA#3;UK #10.1986) and *If Your Heart isn't in It* (UK #48.1986) and a pair of LPs, *Brilliance* (USA#18.1982) and *As the Band Turns* (USA#17; UK#64.1986). In 1985, Sharon Bryant left the group to pursue a solo career and was replaced by Barbara Weathers; in 1987, the group signed with Warner Bros. The debut LP for their new label, *All in the Name of Love* (UK#48.1987), included their biggest hit in the UK, *Always* (UK#3.1987), which was followed by *One Lover at a Time* (UK #57.1987). In 1989, Sharon Bryant released her own debut LP for Polydor.

YOURS FOREVER, A&M, 1983
AS THE BAND TURNS, A&M, 1985
SECRET LOVERS: THE VERY BEST OF ATLANTIC STARR, A&M, 1986
ALL IN THE NAME OF LOVE, Warner Bros., 1987
SHARON BRYANT, Polydor, 1989

AUSTIN, PATTI Patti Austin was born in New York City on August 10, 1948. She has sung professionally since she was five years old, when she was a protege of Dinah Washington and Sammy Davis, Jr. In 1976 she issued her first LP, *End of a Rainbow*, for Creed Taylor's label, CTI. It was followed by *Havana Candy* (1977) and *Body Language* (1980). None of these made any significant impression. In 1981 she sang some of the vocal parts for the Quincy JONES LP, *The Dude*, including the hit single *Razzamatazz*, and then signed with his label Qwest.

Her first Qwest LP, *Every Home Should Have One*, included a duet with James INGRAM, *Baby Come To Me* (USA#1.1982; UK #11.1983), which was featured prominently in the TV series *General Hospital*. Since then she has failed to make any impression upon the charts, but she has fully vindicated Jones'

assessment of her as one of the best vocalists in the USA, by recording a succession of critically well received LPs.

EVERY HOME SHOULD HAVE ONE, Warner Bros., 1981
PATTI AUSTIN, Qwest, 1984
GETTIN' AWAY WITH MURDER, Qwest, 1985

AVERAGE WHITE BAND The Average White Band was formed in 1972 by bassist Alan Gorrie (born July 19, 1946, in Perth, Scotland), who recruited Robbie McIntosh (drums), Hamish Stuart (guitar/ vocals), Roger Ball (alto/baritone saxes), Malcolm Duncan (tenor/soprano saxes) and Onnie McIntyre (guitar). After playing at the Lincoln Festival and then at the Rainbow, supporting Eric Clapton, they were offered a contract by MCA. Their debut for MCA *Show Your Hand* (1973) gained little more than interest. On September 23, 1974, McIntosh died from a heroin overdose, his replacement was Steve Ferrone. They signed with Atlantic and their second LP, *Average White Band* (USA#1; UK#6.1975), proved to be more viable; produced by Arif MARDIN, it included the single, *Pick Up The Pieces* (USA#1; UK#5.1975). As a result, MCA re-issued the group's first LP as well as a single, *Put It Where You Want It* (USA#39.1975), a cover of The CRUSADERS composition. Their second LP for Atlantic was *Cut The Cake* (USA#4; UK#28.1975), the title track (USA#10; UK#37.1975) *If I Ever Loose This Heaven* (USA#39.1975) and *School Boy Crush* (USA#33.1975) were released as singles. It was followed by the LPs, *Soul Searching* (USA#8.1976), featuring the single *Queen of My Soul* (USA#40; UK#22.1976), and *Person to Person* (USA#28.1976). In 1977, they teamed up with Ben E. KING for the LP *Benny and Us* (USA#33.1977), which was moderately successful, commercially; more significantly it generated interest among black performers, keen to utilise the group's abilities as backing musicians.

After signing with RCA in 1978, they appeared to lose interest: although the LP *Feel No Fret* (UK#15.1979) gave them their biggest seller in the UK since their debut for Atlantic, it was a lack-lustre affair, as was the follow-up, *Shine* (UK#14.1980), which included the single, *Let's Go Round Again* (UK#12.1980). After the release of the LP *Cupid's in Fashion* they went their separate ways, each concentrating upon session work; in 1988, Stuart was enlisted by Paul McCartney.

SHOW YOUR HAND, Fame, 1973
AVERAGE WHITE BAND, Fame, 1974
CUT THE CAKE, Atlantic, 1975
SOUL SEARCHING, RCA, 1976
PERSON TO PERSON, Atlantic, 1977
BENNY AND US, (with Ben E. King), Atlantic, 1977
FEEL NO FRET, RCA, 1979
CUPID'S IN FASHION, RCA, 1982
THE BEST OF THE AVERAGE WHITE BAND, RCA, 1984

BABYFACE See LA & BABYFACE

BAILEY, PHILIP Philip Bailey was born in Denver, Colorado on May 8, 1951. He was recruited to EARTH, WIND & FIRE by Maurice White in 1972 as a vocalist and percussionist and has remained with the group ever since, providing the soaring vocals that have become characteristic of its recorded output, and playing centre-stage in its live performances. In 1983 he embarked upon a parallel solo career with the LP *Continuation*, produced by George DUKE and featuring contributions from Deniece WILLIAMS and Jeffrey OSBORNE. The following year, he released the LP *Chinese Wall* (USA#22; UK

#29.1985), which included the singles, *Easy Lover* (USA#2.1984; UK#1.1985), a duet with Phil Collins, and *Walking on the Chinese Wall* (USA#46; UK#34.1985). The same year saw the release of the gospel LP, *The Wonders of His Love*, which sold over a quarter of a million copies in the USA. In 1986, he recorded two more LPs, *Inside Out* and *Triumph*, the latter being another gospel LP. In 1987 he returned to Earth, Wind & Fire, when White re-formed the group.

CONTINUATION, CBS, 1983
CHINESE WALL, CBS, 1984
THE WONDERS OF HIS LOVE, Myrrh, 1985
INSIDE OUT, CBS, 1986
TRIUMPH, Myrrh, 1986

BAKER, ANITA Of the soul singers to emerge in the 1980s, Anita Baker, born in Detroit, conforms more than most to the traditions of the genre. In 1980 she became lead singer of the group Chapter 8, which disbanded after the commercial failure of their first LP, although the single, *I Just Want To Be Your Girl*, was lionised critically. After a three-year lay-off, during which she worked in an office, she was given the opportunity by the Beverly Glen label to record a solo album. The result was *The Songstress*: three singles, including *Angel*, were released but, although they sold well, they failed to set the national charts alight. However, the LP provided further proof that Baker was an artist of the very highest calibre, prepared to draw her inspiration from artists like Dinah Washington, Sarah Vaughan and Aretha FRANKLIN, that she was able to write her own material was a considerable bonus.

In 1985, after severing her connections with Beverly Glen, she signed with Elektra. Her first release was the LP, *Rapture* (USA#12; UK #13.1986), produced and co-written by

Michael Powell. It was a spare, but slinky production, harnessing Baker's vocals with simple arrangements that allowed her voice to shine. That she chose to eschew the gadgetry of synthesizers and drum machines, preferring the traditional methods, was indicative of her general stance. A single, *Sweet Love* (USA#8; UK#13.1986) was released, which provided her with the crossover success that had previously eluded her. In 1986 she toured the UK, where her performances were greeted with unanimous approval. In April the following year she won a Grammy as Best Newcomer. The follow-up to *Rapture*, *Giving You The Best I Got* (USA#2; UK#9.1988), was once again produced and co-written by Powell. It consolidated her reputation as one of the best stylists to emerge since Aretha Franklin's debut; the next LP, *Compositions* (USA#9; UK#20.1990), featured substantially the same team.

THE SONGSTRESS, Beverly Glen, 1983
RAPTURE, Elektra, 1986
GIVING YOU THE BEST I GOT, Elektra,1988
COMPOSITIONS, Elektra, 1990

BAKER, ARTHUR Arthur Baker was born on April 22, 1955 in New York City. He came to prominence in the early 1980s under the auspices of the independent, yet wildly influential Tommy Boy label, which specialised in rap and hip-hop, *Planet Rock* being a "classic of the genre". His earliest associations were with Afrika BAMBAATAA. His pioneering mixing technique came to the attention of rock artists like Bruce Springsteen and Cyndi Lauper, and he was called upon to treat some of their recordings. While he has remained just beyond the mainstream, his version of *A Love Supreme* by Will DOWNING has become a dance classic. His production of

the Artists Against Apartheid record, *Sun City*, was a rare example of a charitable motivation resulting in a creative success.

His own forays into individual label ownership have been beset by myriad problems. In 1986, he signed with A&M and formed The Backbeat Disciples. The ensuing LP *Merge*, featured guest vocalists like Al GREEN, Martin Fry and Jimmy Somerville; a single from it, *Love Is The Message*, featuring Al Green, was released and became a minor hit in the UK.

MERGE, A&M, 1989

BAKER, LaVERN LaVern Baker was one of the torch bearers of the soul era. At the time her style was regarded as a raucous synthesis of gospel and jump. Although she was bracketed with Ruth BROWN by her label, Atlantic, her style was much less bluesy, and became a source of inspiration to artists like Esther PHILLIPS and Etta JAMES. She was born in Chicago on November 11, 1929. When she was twelve she made her debut in the local church choir; by the time she was seventeen, she had become known as "Little Miss Sharecropper" at the various clubs at which she performed like the DeLisa. After being spotted by jazz musician Fletcher Henderson, she was signed to Columbia and then to King.

In 1953, she was signed by Ahmet ERTEGUN and Jerry WEXLER to the Atlantic label. Over the next ten years she recorded a string of hit singles: *Tweedlee Dee* (USA#14.1955), *I Can't Love You Enough* (USA#22.1956), *Jim Dandy* (USA#17.1956), *I Cried a Tear* (USA#6.1958), *I Waited Too Long* (USA#33.1959), *Saved* (USA#37.1961) and *See See Rider* (USA#34.1963). Many of these were covered by white artists like Georgia Gibbs, thus depriving Baker of the degree of success that was rightfully hers – indeed, such was her irritation that she wrote to a congressman drawing his attention to the situation. By the mid-1960s, her charting days were over, despite cutting some sides for Brunswick, which failed to capture the attention of the public and she moved into retirement in Japan. However, tracks like *Soul on Fire* and *I Cried a Tear* were the spiritual ancestors of *I Never Loved a Man* and *Respect* by Aretha FRANKLIN, and it was a great shame that Baker was never given the benefit of recording at Muscle Shoals.

REAL GONE GAL, Charly, 1984

BAKER, MICKEY See ROBINSON, Sylvia

BALLARD, HANK Hank Ballard was born in Detroit on November 18, 1936. His musical career started in 1953, when he left his job at the Ford Car Factory to become lead singer of the doo-wop group, The Royals, who were signed to Federal Records. Shortly after he joined the group they changed their name to The Midnighters. Their first hit came in 1954, when *Work with me Annie* topped the R&B charts, it was followed in July by *Sexy Ways*, which climbed to #3 in the R&B charts. However, both records failed to chart nationally because they were banned by some radio stations for their "sexually explicit language".

In 1959, after a prolonged period without hits, they signed with the King label and changed their billing to Hank Ballard & The Midnighters. Their first release was *Teardrops On Your Letter*, the B-side was Ballard's song *The Twist*. In May, their version of *Kansas City* climbed to #72, and in July, following the success of Chubby CHECKER's cover version, *The Twist* was reissued and reached #28 in the USA. Their first major hit was *Finger Poppin'*

Time (USA#7.1960), it was followed by *Let's Go, Let's Go, Let's Go* (USA#6.1960). They continued to record songs about dance crazes throughout the next year. By 1962 the record-buying public's appetite for new dance crazes had been sated: *Do You Know How To Twist* peaked at a lowly #87. In February Ballard parted company with The Midnighters and started a solo career. He remained signed to King, where he began working with James BROWN.

For the next ten years, he performed regularly with The James Brown Revue while continuing to record as a solo artist. He failed, however, to arrest his continuing decline into obscurity. From 1972, he toured the USA constantly, reworking his old hits with creditable fervour. In 1986 he toured the UK and recorded a live LP; it was so well received by the critics that he was dubbed the "legendary" Hank Ballard.

LIVE AT THE PALAIS, Charly, 1986
THEIR GREATEST JUKE BOX HITS, Sing, 1988
HANK BALLARD AND THE MIDNIGHTERS, Sing, 1988
SINGIN' AND SWINGIN', Sing, 1988
THE ONE AND ONLY, Sing,1988
DANCE ALONG, Sing, 1989 24 SONGS, Sing, 1989
LET 'EM ROLL, Charly, 1990

BAMBAATAA, AFRIKA One of the primary forces in making rap and sampling fashionable in the early 1980s with the seminal Tommy Boy label, Bambaataa started as a lieutenant in a street gang called The Black Spades in the Bronx, New York City in 1974. By 1976 he had formed The Zulu Nation, a curious hybrid of a culturally and politically motivated group, who focussed their attention on the burgeoning activity in clubs and warehouses. In 1980 he teamed up with producer Paul Winley for two separate versions of *Zulu Nation Throwdown*, neither of which were great successes.

By 1982 he had met up with Tom Silverman, who was putting together the dance oriented Tommy Boy label. At Tommy Boy, he met up with producer Arthur BAKER, and together they produced the first release, *Jazzy Sensation* by The Jazzy Five, although it failed to sell as many as they would have liked, it created a buzz about Bambaataa. Later that year, with Soul Sonic Force and Baker producing, he released *Planet Rock* (USA#48; UK#53.1982), drawing extensively upon the music of electro-groups like Kraftwerk and Can, it sold over a million, despite its lowly chart-placing. The follow-up, *Looking for the Perfect Beat* was a great example of how microchip technology need not be boring. In 1984 he parted company with Baker, after *Renegades Of Funk* (UK #30.1984), and joined the Celluloid label, where he was teamed with producer and bassist Bill Laswell. His parting gesture for Silverman was a collaboration with James BROWN entitled *Unity: The Third Coming* (UK #49.1984), which led to collaborations with Public Image Ltd. for *World Destruction* (UK #44.1985) and UB40 for *Reckless* (UK #17.1988). He broke up The Soul Sonic Force in 1986 to concentrate upon his solo projects.

BEWARE (THE FUNK IS EVERYWHERE), WEA, 1986
DEATH MIX THROWDOWN, Blatant, 1987

BANKS, DARRELL The career of Darrell Banks was tragically short, due to being a late starter, as well as being stopped when he was shot in a "duel" with a policeman, who had been having an affair with his girl friend. However, the few sides he did cut showed a great sense of timing, combined with a flair for choosing appropriate material.

He was born in Buffalo in 1938. After moving to Detroit he worked as a cement finisher and played local clubs in his spare time until he was signed to the local Revilot label. His first record, *Open the Door to Your Heart* (USA#27.1966), prompted Atlantic to lease enough material to issue the LP, *Darrell Banks is Here*, on the subsidiary Atco label in 1967. After recording some sides for another subsidiary, Cotillion, including *I Wanna Go Home*, he was signed to Stax. His debut LP *Here To Stay*, in 1970, included *No One Blinder than a Man who can't See* and a cover version of Jerry BUTLER's *Only the Strong Survive*.

Unfortunately, he was unable to reap the benefits as the altercation, resulting in his death, intervened.

BANKS, HOMER The songwriting team of Homer Banks, Bettye Crutcher and Raymond Jackson was known collectively as We Three; they provided much of the material for the Stax roster after the arrival of Al BELL in 1968. Banks was born in Memphis on August 2, 1941. He became a regular at Stax, working in the record shop at the front of the studios, until making his debut as a performer for the Genie label, recording *Little Lady Gone* with Isaac HAYES and David PORTER producing in 1964. It was followed by another Hayes and Porter composition, *60 Minutes Of Your Love* (1966) for the Minit label.

When Bell arrived he was given an opportunity to write, his first success being *Who's Making Love* in 1968 for Johnnie TAYLOR. Over the next eight years, Banks with Crutcher and Jackson – until Jackson's death in a road accident in 1971 – penned songs for artists like Johnnie Taylor, The Soul Children and The STAPLE SINGERS making them one of the most successful songwriting teams to emerge from Stax. He also collaborated Mack Rice, co-writing Luther INGRAM's best known song, *(If Loving You Is Wrong) I Don't Want To Be Right*. After the demise of Stax, Banks, in common with Crutcher, Frederick KNIGHT and George JACKSON has providing material for independent labels like TK in Florida and Malaco in Jackson. More recently, he and Lester Snell have formed the partnership Two's Company.

BARKAYS The Barkays were the second unit backing band at Stax, they were comprised of Ronnie Caldwell, Ben Cauley, Carl Cunningham, Phalin Jones and Jimmy King. In 1967, they scored with the instrumental *Soul Finger* (USA#17; UK#33.1967). Their success was shortlived: at 3:28 pm on Saturday, December 9, 1967, the plane in which they were travelling with Otis REDDING crashed into Lake Monona on the outskirts of Madison. The only survivor was Ben Cauley: the fact that the hopes for Stax's continued prosperity had revolved around Redding has often obscured the equally important fact that, with the wiping out of The Barkays, a whole generation of Memphis musicians perished.

After the group reformed in the 1970s, they signed with the Mercury label and had another hit with *Shake Your Rump To The Funk* (USA #23.1976; UK#41.1977), which was a far cry from the promise of their earlier material. They had to wait another eight years before their next hit, *Sexomatic* (UK#51.1985), by which time they had become just another proficient funk outfit, their popularity being due to their ability to make good dance-oriented records like *Freakshow on the Dance Floor*. To this day, they have continued to tour the USA and Europe on the lucrative club circuit.

PROPOSITIONS, Mercury, 1983
DANGEROUS, Mercury, 1984
BANGING THE WALL, Mercury, 1985
MONEY TALKS, Stax, 1990

BARNUM, H.B Since the early 1960s, H.B. Barnum has exerted a considerable influence upon those whom he has worked with, whether it be as a writer, arranger, producer or pianist. He was brought up in Los Angeles. After having a hit in his own right with the instrumental, *Lost Love* (USA#35.1961), he became an arranger and producer for the Imperial label, working with artists like Irma THOMAS. After Imperial, he moved to Capitol, where he worked with artists like Lou RAWLS and The Gentrys. In the early 1970s he started to work for Motown, where he collaborated with Stevie WONDER, Diana ROSS and Marvin GAYE amongst others. In addition to his work for Motown, he continued to arrange on a freelance basis for artists like O. C. Smith and Boz SCAGGS. To this day, he remains as sought after as he ever was.

BARRETT, RICHARD Richard Barrett was born in Philadelphia in 1936. His career started in 1954, following his discharge from the army, when he was recruited as lead singer for The Valentines. Despite their lack of major success, he met up with George GOLDNER and from then until 1963, when Goldner's penchant for gambling got the better of his empire, Barrett was an integral part of the organisation, writing for and producing groups like Frankie LYMON & The Teenagers, The CHANTELS and LITTLE ANTONY & THE IMPERIALS. In 1963, he returned to Philadelphia where he recorded Harold MELVIN & The Blue Notes, as well as discovering an early lineup of The Three Degrees. His association with The Three Degrees spanned their hit-making days, and it would not be unreasonable to say that he taught them everything he knew. In 1982 he parted company with the group, who had become fixtures on the international cabaret circuit, and since then he has appeared to play little part in the music business.

BARRY, JEFF With his wife Ellie GREENWICH, Jeff Barry formed just one of the many songwriting partnerships working out of New York's Brill Building. Together with Phil SPECTOR, they penned hits for groups like The CRYSTALS, The RONETTES, Ike and Tina TURNER, The RIGHTEOUS BROTHERS and many others. Although they had a stab at their own career, with the group The Raindrops, they moved more towards production – initially with LEIBER & STOLLER and producer Shadow Morton – until the breakdown of their marriage. Although Barry has continued to write and produce under his own name since then, he has failed to strike the rich vein of former years.

BARRY, LEN Len Barry was born Len Borisoff in Philadelphia on June 12, 1942. After forming The Dovells, the group was signed to the Parkway label. At Parkway the group had a series of dance-oriented novelty hits like *Bristol Stomp* (USA#2.1961), *Do the New Continental* (USA#37.1962), *Bristol Twistin' Annie* (USA#27.1962) and *Hully Gully Baby* (USA#25.1962). However, their most durable hit was a version of *You Can't Sit Down* (USA#3.1963), which had been a hit as an instrumental for Phil UPCHURCH; their version included lyrics written by Parkway owner, Kal Mann.

In 1964 Barry left the group for a solo career and signed with American Decca, where his first release, *Lip Sync*, was a modest hit, mainly because it was aimed squarely at the flourishing club market. It was followed by *1-2-3* (USA#2; UK#3.1965), which was co-written by

HOLLAND, DOZIER & HOLLAND, it big became an international dance-floor hit. His chart success encouraged him to start performing live. Another hit, *Like a Baby* (USA#27; UK#10.1966) followed, but when he issued his version of *Somewhere* (USA#26.1966) from the Leonard Bernstein musical, *West Side Story*, the formula showed signs of wear and tear. Two more singles, *It's that Time of Year* and *I Struck it Rich*, were both minor hits in the USA, but his recording career gradually petered out and he started to write and produce. Under the guise of The Electric Indian, he scored in 1969 with *Keem- O-Sabe*. Since then he has been notably quiet, making the odd contribution to film soundtracks like *Bob, Carol, Ted and Alice*, although he still performs on the international cabaret circuit.

MORE FROM THE 1-2-3 MAN, Bulldog, 1982

BARTHOLOMEW, DAVE Dave Bartholomew was born in Edgard, Louisiana, on December 24, 1920. After serving in the army he became one of the pioneering figures on the New Orleans scene in the 1940s and 1950s as a writer, producer, arranger and A&R man for Imperial. The inventiveness of his productions on Fats DOMINO's major hits changed the face of music in New Orleans. Furthermore, he assembled the house band – pianist Allen TOUSSAINT, bassist Frank Fields, drummer Earl PALMER, saxophonists Lee ALLEN, Herb Hardesty and Alvin Tyler – that was to grace most of the sessions in the "Crescent City" backing artists like LITTLE RICHARD, Lloyd PRICE and Smiley LEWIS. Although he recorded under his own name, his real achievement lay in his ability to extract the best from others. After Domino's departure from Imperial in 1963,

Bartholomew moved into semi-retirement, although they hooked up for the occasional tour, with Bartholomew leading the band.

JUMP CHILDREN, Pathe Marconi, 1984
THE MONKEY, Pathe Marconi, 1985
THE BEST OF DAVE BARTHOLOMEW, Stateside, 1989

BASS, FONTELLA Fontella Bass was born in St. Louis, Missouri, on July 3, 1940. Her mother, Martha Bass, was a member of the gospel group The Clara Ward Singers. Her career started as pianist in the LITTLE MILTON Band, where she came to the attention of Ike TURNER, who signed her to the Chess label. Under the direction of Oliver Sain, she was teamed with Bobby McClure, their most successful collaboration was *Don't Mess Up A Good Thing* (USA#33.1965). Such was its success that Chess launched her as a solo artist; her debut *Rescue Me* (USA#4; UK #11.1965) did much to restore the reputation of Chicago after years of chart domination by Memphis and Detroit. The follow-up, *Recovery* (USA#37; UK#32.1966), attempted to repeat the formula, but was marginally less successful. After her marriage to Lester Bowie, the trumpeter with The Art Ensemble of Chicago, she returned to the club circuit but quickly abandoned that particular avenue. During the 1970s she recorded the odd single for Stan LEWIS' Jewel label, but concentrated upon collaborations with her husband, most notably in 1983 on the LP *All The Magic* for ECM, which featured her brother, vocalist David PEASTON.

ALL THE MAGIC, with Lester Bowie and David Peaston, ECM, 1983

BASS, RALPH Ralph Bass' pre-eminence has always been based upon his association with Syd NATHAN's King label and his signing of James BROWN, but he started his career in the the late 1930s as a producer and talent scout, principally for the jazz label Black & White. Born in New York on May 1, 1911, he was at first a violinist before he moved to the West Coast and produced Charlie Parker, Dizzy Gillespie and Erroll Garner. In 1949, he made the transition from jazz to R&B by producing Johnny OTIS. The following year he returned to New York and joined King as head of A&R; apart from discovering and producing James Brown's early hits like *Please, Please, Please,* he worked also with Hank BALLARD, The FIVE ROYALES and Billy WARD & The Dominoes. In 1960 he moved to Chicago, where he joined Chess as a staff producer and worked with Etta JAMES among others. By the mid-1970s he had effectively retired, although he has produced the odd blues record from time to time since then.

BECKETT, BARRY When Spooner OLDHAM was lured to the American Studios in Memphis by Dan PENN in 1967, Barry Beckett moved in to play keyboards for the house band at Rick HALL's Fame Studios. Born in Birmingham, Alabama in 1944, Beckett moved to Pensacola, Florida, where he teamed up with DJ Papa Don Schroeder, who had started to put together his own roster of artists like Oscar TONEY, MIGHTY SAM and James and Bobby PURIFY. Beckett started playing keyboards on sessions. In 1966, Schroeder began to bring some of his roster to record at Fame in Muscle Shoals; with Oldham's departure, Beckett was quickly ensconced. He remained at Fame for two years leaving to set up the rival Muscle Shoals Sound Studios with Roger HAWKINS, David HOOD and Jimmy JOHN-

SON. Since 1969, he has been an integral part of the studio house band, recording with artists like The Rolling Stones, The STAPLE SINGERS, Paul Simon, Millie JACKSON, Etta JAMES, Willie Nelson and Bobby WOMACK. After the studios were sold to Malaco in 1985, he concentrated upon production, his finest achievement being his work with Etta James.

BELL, AL In 1965, Al Bell joined Stax as head of promotion. His credentials for the job were impeccable. He had been involved, as a minister, in Dr Martin Luther King's Civil Rights Movement and then, as a DJ, at WLOK in Memphis and WUST in Washington. Prior to joining Stax, he had also operated his own record label, Safice, with Eddie FLOYD, who came to Stax with him as a songwriter. At the behest of Bell, "package tours" featuring Stax artists toured the USA, the UK and the rest of Europe incessantly throughout the mid-1960s, bringing performers like Otis REDDING, Eddie Floyd, SAM & DAVE and Carla THOMAS into the heartlands of the record-buying public. In 1967 Redding appeared at the Monterey Pop Festival alongside Jimi HENDRIX and The Who; for Bell the exposure of Redding to a predominantly white, rock-oriented audience represented a major achievement. The death of Redding later the same year was a watershed for Stax, but his posthumous appearance at the top of the US charts indicated that Stax had indeed succeeded in crossing over into the mainstream without sacrificing any of its ideals.

In 1968, Jerry WEXLER drew the attention of Bell and Jim STEWART to a clause in their original distribution contract with Atlantic which enabled the latter to retain control of all of the Stax masters. They panicked and promptly signed a new deal with Gulf & Western for approximately $3 million and some Gulf & Western stock. As a result Bell became the executive vice-president of Stax. Reverting to the dicta of his former mentor, the late Martin Luther King, who had been assassinated earlier that year, Bell set about increasing the political profile of Stax by donating funds to and organising benefits for operations like Jesse Jackson's "People United To Save Humanity". In 1972, he funded the annual festival in the Watts District of Los Angeles; entitled Wattstax '72, this featured an impressive array of Stax recording artists. The motives for these gestures were genuinely altruistic, but they did not make sound economic sense. Moreover, he and Stewart wanted to extricate themselves from the Gulf & Western deal as Stewart wanted to sell his shares for cash. All in all, Bell was faced by a serious cash-flow problem, which he endeavoured to rectify by doing another deal, this time with Clive DAVIS at CBS. Ostensibly it was a good one, as Stax received an advance of $6 million and retained complete creative control, but unfortunately the whole deal was sealed with an "handshake", which made the situation acutely embarrassing when Davis was fired by CBS for "expense account violations". As a result, all Davis' transactions and deals were examined in the minutest detail by CBS, who began to alter the agreed payments to Stax. This, in turn, affected Stax's loan repayments to the Union Planters National Bank in Memphis. In 1973, Stax and Bell were investigated by the Internal Revenue Service, and were jointly sued by CBS and the Union Planters National Bank; in 1975 Isaac HAYES sued them for non-payment of royalties. In 1976, Stax went out of business for good. Bell, despite being exonerated of all wrong-doing, was subjected to a vitriolic witch-hunt within the music business and failed to get a job commensurate with his ability until 1988, when he was appointed vice-president of A&R at Motown.

BELL, ARCHIE, & THE DRELLS

Archie Bell & The Drells were Bell, Lee Bell, James Wise and Willie Pernell. The group formed while still at school in Houston, Texas in 1965. In 1967, they were spotted by DJ Skipper Lee Frazier, who became their manager and got them a recording contract with the Atlantic label. By the time their first single, *Dog Eat Dog*, was released in 1968, Bell had been called up for military sevice in Vietnam. Local DJs were unimpressed by the A- side, but started to play the B-side, *Tighten Up* (USA #1.1968), written by Bell. The follow-up, *I Can't Stop Dancing* (USA#9.1968), saw them joining forces with the writing and production partnership of GAMBLE & HUFF, who would continue to shape their career. In 1969, with Bell back from the army, they recorded *There's Gonna be a Showdown* (USA#21.1969; UK#35.1973), it failed to chart first time around in the UK, but became a dancefloor hit when it was re-released as the follow-up to *Here I Go Again* (UK#16.1972).

When their contract with Atlantic was up, they signed with the Miami-based label, Glades, which resulted in a minor hit, *Dancing to Your Music* . This was their final hit until 1976, when they signed up with the Philadelphia International label, which was owned by Gamble & Huff. *Soul City Walk* (UK#13.1976) was taken from the debut LP with their new label. In 1977 they had another minor hit in the UK, *Everybody have a Good Time* (UK #43.1977), and participated in another minor hit, *Let's Clean Up the Ghetto*, which was credited to The Philadelphia All Stars. In 1986 *Don't Let Love Get You Down* (UK#49.1986) was re-issued in the UK, focusing the spotlight upon the group once again despite Bell having left in 1981 to pursue a solo career.

I NEVER HAD IT SO GOOD, Beckett, 1981
WHERE WILL YOU GO WHEN THE PARTY'S OVER, Portrait, 1986

BELL, MADELEINE

Despite the excellence of her voice, Madeleine Bell is a very good example of someone's whose abilites as a soul-singer have been consistently overshadowed. After moving to the UK in the sixties, she became a session singer contributing backing vocals for artists like Dusty Springfield. As a result she was given the opportunity to record in her own right for Springfield's record label, Philips. She had one hit, *I'm Gonna Make You Love Me* (USA #26.1968), a cover of the song first recorded by Dee Dee WARWICK in 1967. In 1969, she was approached by writers Roger Cook and Roger Greenaway to provide vocals for the single, *Melting Pot*, which had started as an instrumental by a group session musicians, recording under the name of Blue Mink. Over the next four years, the group were seldom far from the UK charts, the less said about the records the better, as they were just ordinary "middle of the road" pop songs. In 1975 the group disbanded and Bell returned to session work, as well as singing on jingles and TV commercials. In 1981 she was used by the BBC for a spell as a DJ. Since then she has continued to do sessions as well as theatrical work.

BELL, THOM

When GAMBLE & HUFF set up first the Gamble label and then Philadelphia International Records, one of their collaborators at the Sigma Sound studios was Thom Bell. Bell was born in Philadelphia in 1941, and got to know Gamble during his adolescence, becoming a member of Gamble's group, The Romeos. After collaborating with Brenda & The Tabulations, The Showstoppers and Dusty Springfield, he worked with The DELFONICS writing songs like *La La Means I Love You* and *Didn't I Blow Your Mind This Time* for the independent Philly Groove Label. By the time Gamble & Huff were ready to start operating Bell had developed his own sound, based on a melodic lightness. From 1971 until 1973, in partnership with writer Linda Creed, The STYLISTICS notched up a string of hits under his supervision. Similarly, whereas The DETROIT SPINNERS had been almost completely ignored when they were signed to Motown, after they were signed by Atlantic, Bell transformed them into one of the better examples of the Philadelphia Sound, with a succession of hits between 1971 and 1979 including *I'll be Around, Could it be I'm Falling in Love* and *Rubber Band Man.* In 1974 Bell suggested a duet between Dionne WARWICK and The Detroit Spinners, and the result was the single *Then Came You.* The popularity of the Sigma Sound studios during the 1970s became comparable to that of Muscle Shoals and Stax during the 1960s, and both Elton John and David Bowie used Bell as an arranger. In 1980, ill health persuaded him to move to Seattle for a spell, where he produced and arranged two LPs for Deniece WILLIAMS. In 1987 he arranged *Let me Touch You* for The O'JAYS, which reunited him with Gamble & Huff.

BELL, WILLIAM William Bell was the archetypal journeyman. While other artists on the Stax roster were vying with one another, he was content to pursue his own career with a singular lack of histrionics.

He was born in Memphis on July 16, 1939 as William Yarborough, and his early ambition was to be a doctor. At school he became a member of The Del Rios, who won a talent contest in 1956. This gave them the opportunity to record a single, *Alone on a Rainy Night,* for the Meteor label; they were backed by Rufus THOMAS' group, The Bearcats. Although the single bombed it attracted sufficient interest for Bell to be invited to join Phineas

Newborn's Band as a vocalist. After touring with Newborn, he returned to Memphis in 1962 and signed with Stax.

At the insistence of producer Chips MOMAN, Bell recorded the self-written, *You Don't Miss Your Water (Til The Well Runs Dry)*; the simple homespun philosophy of the lyrics were typical of Bell's demeanour and his delivery was reminiscent of Sam COOKE's, but lacked the histrionics that characterised the work of so many other performers. The success of *You Don't Miss Your Water* was certainly a financial fillip for Stax, but, more importantly, it defined the company's artistic parameters, providing a blueprint for future releases. In 1963 his career was interrupted for two years when he was drafted into the army; by the time he returned Otis REDDING had replaced him as Stax's main artist. Bell continued to record and formed a songwriting partnership with BOOKER T, which provided him with a string of minor hits like *Everybody Loves A Winner, Share What You Got* and *Everyday will be Like a Holiday.* They also wrote *Born under a Bad Sign* for Albert KING which, despite its failure to chart, has since been covered by a variety of artists in varying styles. In 1968 he recorded *Tribute to a King* (UK#31.1968), which was dedicated to the recently deceased Otis Redding; its success in the UK was indicative of the esteem in which Redding was held there. It was followed by a duet, *Private Number* (UK #8.1968), with session singer Judy Clay, who sang with Cissy HOUSTON and Doris TROY.

After the closure of Stax in 1976, Bell – who had continued to tour despite his lack of chart success – signed with Mercury for whom he recorded *Trying to Love Two* (USA#10.1977), his biggest hit in the USA. In 1980 he established his own production company, Peach Tree, in Atlanta, and then his own label, Wilbe. In 1985 he recorded the LP *A Passion,* which provided him with the minor hit, *Headline News*

(UK#70.1986): the LP was a revelation in that it showed that his talent had matured and that he had grown in stature as a performer. His most recent outing was the LP *On A Roll* in 1989.

DO RIGHT MAN, Charly, 1984
A PASSION, Tout Ensemble, 1986

BELLE, REGINA Regina Belle has the potential to become one of the most important soul singers of her generation. She made her debut in 1987, after signing with CBS. Her first LP *All by Myself* showed that she has the ability to become a fine interpreter of other people's songs. However, her second LP *Stay with Me*, produced by Narada Michael WALDEN and Nick Martinelli, showed a tendency towards rather middle-of-the-road material, which, combined with a penchant for duets with singers like Peabo BRYSON and James Taylor (see KOOL & THE GANG), have made her highly susceptible to the high profile packaging of the music industry.

ALL BY MYSELF, CBS, 1987
STAY WITH ME, CBS, 1989

BELVIN, JESSE Jesse Belvin was born on December 15, 1933, in Texarkana, Arkansas. After moving to south Los Angeles in his childhood, he joined Big Jay McNeely's Band in 1949 as a vocalist. Throughout the 1950s, except for a spell in the army, he worked as a performer, writer and arranger, recording for Specialty, Kent, Federal and Modern, among others. In 1954 he wrote *Earth Angel* for The Penguins, and in 1956 he recorded *Goodnight My Love* for Modern. Both songs were watersheds: the former has come to represent the embodiment of doo-wop and was the first record on an independent R&B label to

make the US charts, while the latter established Belvin as Nat "King" Cole's heir apparent. He was never to realise the full potential of the two records: he did not receive the royalties that were his due for *Earth Angel* and he was killed in a road accident on February 6, 1960, having secured his first contract with a major label, RCA, in 1959. His driver, Charles Shackleford, fell asleep at the wheel of his Cadillac and ploughed into an oncoming car on Route 67, just outside Fairhope, Arkansas. Belvin and Shackleford were killed immediately, and Belvin's wife, Jo Ann died two days later.

MEMORIAL ALBUM, Ace, 1984
JUST JESSE BELVIN, RCA, 1985
THE BLUES BALLADEER, Ace, 1990

BENJAMIN, BENNY Under Maurice King, the musical director of Motown, The Funk Brothers came into being. The rhythm section of drummer Benny "Papa Zita" Benjamin and bassist James JAMERSON was the foundation of the Motown Sound. Throughout the 1960s, their inventive backbeat distinguished Motown from all its imitators, with a string of hits for artists like Marvin GAYE, The SUPREMES and The TEMPTATIONS. It was Berry GORDY's great good fortune to secure the services of musicians that, not only knew their job inside out and enjoyed it, but also didn't appear to mind that they got little or no credit.

BENTON, BROOK Brook Benton was born Benjamin Franklin Peay on September 19, 1931, in Camden, South Carolina. In 1953, he signed with the Okeh label as a solo artist, having cut his teeth in a variety of gospel groups, but by 1957 he had temporarily abandoned his singing career in favour of being a truck driver. Then he met Clyde Otis, a music publisher, and they formed a songwriting partnership with the arranger Belford Hendricks. The venture struck gold when Nat "King" Cole and Clyde McPHATTER recorded *Looking Back* and *A Lover's Question* , respectively. In 1959 Benton was signed by Mercury Records. His first release, *It's Just a Matter of Time* (USA#3.1959), was followed by *Endlessly* (USA#12; UK#28.1959), both records were ballads and they established the pattern of his career. *Thank You Pretty Baby* (USA#16.1959) and *So Many Ways* (USA#6.1959) consolidated his position still further and led to a couple of duets with Dinah Washington: *Baby(You Got What It Takes)* (USA#5.1960) and *A Good Rockin' Way (to Mess Around and Fall in Love)* (USA#7.1960), which were followed by *Kiddio* (USA#7; UK#29.1960) and *Fools Rush In* (USA#24.1960; UK#50.1961). *The Boll Weevil Song* (USA#2; UK#30.1961) was his final success in the UK, and the follow-up was a revival of another traditional song, *Frankie and Johnny* (USA#20.1961), both continued his run of hit singles in the USA. Throughout 1962 he notched up one hit after another, although the quality of much of the material was doubtful, to say the least: his success was due more to the insatiable appetite of US audiences for maudlin ballads than to his ability to convey a strong song. *Hotel Happiness* (USA#3.1963), his biggest hit since *The Boll Weevil Song*, was also his final appearance in the top ten for seven years.

In 1965 he left Mercury as his popularity had dwindled. RCA, with whom he now signed, were unable to arrest his declining sales. In 1967 he was signed by Frank Sinatra's label, Reprise, but it was just as unsuccessful at reviving his flagging career as RCA had been. In 1968 he moved to Cotillion, a subsidiary of Atlantic, and started to record more soulful material, adapting his style accordingly. In 1970 his LP *Brook Benton Today* (USA #27.1970). His version of the Tony Joe White composition *Rainy Night in Georgia* (USA #4.1970) was his final significant hit, but it clearly indicated that, given suitable material, his style would always find a niche for itself. The follow-up, *My Way* , showed what little grasp he had over the selection of suitable material. However, he returned to form when he recorded the Joe SOUTH song, *Don't it Make You Want to Go Home* , which gave him his last appearance in the top fifty. Since 1971 he has recorded sporadically with Stax, MGM and All Platinum, but none of these records sold in any quantity, despite the fact that he retained his popularity on the club circuit. On April 9, 1988, he died in hospital in New York City, aged 56.

SPOTLIGHT ON BROOK BENTON, Philips, 1977
BACK TO BACK, (with Dinah Washington), Mercury, 1978
THE TWO OF US, (with Dinah Washington), Mercury, 1978
BEST OF BROOK BENTON, VOLUME I, Phoenix, 1982
BEST OF BROOK BENTON, Mercury, 1984
BROOK BENTON SINGS THE STANDARDS, RCA, 1984
TWENTY GOLDEN PIECES, Bulldog,1984
MAGIC MOMENTS, RCA, 1985
16 GOLDEN CLASSICS, Castle, 1986
HIS GREATEST HITS, Mercury, 1987
A RAINY NIGHT IN GEORGIA, Mainline, 1988

BERNS, BERT If there is one single record that has become identified with Bert Berns it is The ISLEY BROTHERS' version of *Twist and Shout,* which he co-wrote under his original name of Bert Russell with Phil Medley. He was born in 1929 in New York, where he attended The Juilliard School Of Music. After working as an A&R man, a plugger and composer, he came up with *Twist and Shout,* which enabled him to continue working as a freelance, producing records like *A Little Bit of Soap* for The Jarmels among others. In 1963 he became a staff producer at Atlantic, where he produced records like *Everybody Needs Somebody To Love*, which he wrote himself and was revived in the 1980s by The Blues Brothers, and *If You Need Me* for Solomon BURKE, *Make Me Your Baby* for Barbara LEWIS and *Under The Boardwalk* for The DRIFTERS.

His association with Van MORRISON started in 1964, when he was enlisted by Decca to produce the group Them, which was fronted by Morrison; among his contributions was *Here Comes the Night*. After BERNS had set up his own labels, Bang and Shout, in 1965, Morrison was signed as a solo artist. Morrison's first single for the label was the timeless *Brown Eyed Girl* . Among the other artists signed by Berns were The McCoys, Erma FRANKLIN, Freddie Scott and Neil Diamond. Tragically, he died on December 31, 1967, of a heart attack just as he was beginning to take advantage of the increased musical awareness in audiences.

BERRY, CHUCK Charles Berry was born in San Jose, California, on October 18, 1926. He formed a trio with drummer Ebby Harding and pianist Johnnie Johnson in St Louis, Missouri, in 1952, while employed as a hairdresser. They worked the club circuit in 1955, winding up in Chicago, where Berry met Muddy Waters, who suggested that he contact Chess Records. His debut, *Maybelline* (USA #5.1955), contained all the ingredients that were to characterise his style and sound for years to come. In 1956 he charted again with *Roll Over Beethoven* (USA#29.1956); it was followed by *School Days* (USA#3; UK#21.1957), and then, after the less successful *Oh Baby Doll, Rock And Roll Music* (USA#8.1957). Throughout 1958 he continued to make waves as one of the most popular live performers in the USA, particularly when his performance of *Sweet Little Sixteen* (USA#2; UK#13.1958) at the Newport Jazz Festival was filmed for inclusion in the Bert Stern film *Jazz on a Summer's Day*. Other singles included *Johnny B. Goode* (USA#8; UK#27.1958), *Carol* (USA#18.1958), *Almost Grown* (USA#32.1959) and *Back in the USA* (USA#37.1959).

In July 1959 he was arrested and charged with violating the Mann Act. He had brought a girl from Texas to work at his night club in St Louis as a cloakroom attendant, but fired her when he was lead to believe she was working as a prostitute as well. She went to the police and confessed to them that she was only fourteen: Berry was charged under the Mann Act for transporting a minor over a state line for immoral purposes. At first the charge was quashed, but the prosecutors hounded him until they secured a conviction in 1962, when he was sentenced to two years in prison. While he was in prison his name and reputation were kept alight by Chess, who released *Memphis Tennessee* (UK#6.1963), and by the growing number of UK and US groups who covered his songs and attempted to emulate his style of playing.

When he emerged from the Indiana Federal prison in 1964, he picked up where he had left off, recording *Nadine (Is It You?)* (USA#23; UK#27.1964), *No Particular Place to Go* (USA#10; UK#3.1964) and *You Never Can Tell* (USA#14; UK#23.1964). Throughout the latter half of the 1960s his records failed to sell as consistently as they had done in the past, but he continued touring. In 1972 he teamed up with The Faces for a concert at The Lanchester Arts Festival in the UK, as well as recording some tracks in the studio with them. The resulting LP, *The London Chuck Berry Sessions* (USA#8.1972), included the novelty single *My Ding-a-Ling* (USA/UK#1.1972), which became, commercially, his most successful single. It was followed by *Reelin' and Rockin'* (USA#27; UK#18.1973).

Since 1973 he has recorded the occasional LP but has tended to concentrate more upon his business interests, notably Berry Park, an amusement park in Wentzville, Missouri, which he acquired in 1961. In 1978 he appeared in the film biography of the DJ Alan Freed, *American Hot Wax*. The following year he was sentenced to four months in prison for income-tax evasion. In 1986, Keith Richard of The Rolling Stones organised a concert at the Fox Theatre in St Louis celebrating Berry's 60th birthday; the concert was filmed for inclusion in the Tayor Hackford documentary, *Hail! Hail! Rock'n' Roll*. In 1988 *Chuck Berry: An Autobiography*, written during his impris onment, was published. However, his later years have been marred by his extraordinary notion that everyone is trying to take advantage of him, and as a result his concerts have included some bizarre spectacles.

ST LOUIS TO LIVERPOOL, Chess, 1965
THE LONDON CHUCK BERRY SESSIONS, Chess, 1972
BIO, Chess, 1973
PROFILE OF CHUCK BERRY, Teldec, 1981
ROCKIN' WITH CHUCK BERRY, Mercury, 1981
THE MOTIVE SERIES, Mercury, 1982
CHESS MASTERS, Chess, 1983
DUCKWALKING, Chess, 1983
GREATEST HITS LIVE!, Pickwick, 1983
REELIN', ROLLIN' AND ROCKIN', Bulldog, 1983
ROCK 'N' ROLL HITS, Mercury, 1983
THE BEST OF CHUCK BERRY, Creole, 1984
LIVE!, Premier, 1984
REELIN' AND ROCKIN', Magnum Force, 1984
SWEET LITTLE ROCK 'N' ROLLER, Mercury, 1984
20 SUPER HITS, Chess, 1985
THE CHUCK BERRY COLLECTION, Deja Vu, 1986
GREATEST HITS, Chess, 1986
GREATEST HITS, Showcase, 1986
NEW JUKE BOX HITS, Chess, 1986

16 GREATEST HITS, Bescol, 1987
BERRY IS ON TOP, Chess, 1987
ROCKIN' AT THE HOPS, Chess, 1987
ROCK 'N' ROLL RARITIES, Chess, 1987
HAIL! HAIL! ROCK 'N' ROLL, Chess, 1988
THE CHESS BOX, Chess, 1990
THE GREAT TWENTY EIGHT, Chess, 1990

BEVERLY, FRANKIE   See MAZE

BIG APPLE BAND   See CHIC

BIG MAYBELLE   Big Maybelle was born Mabel Louise Smith on May 1, 1924, in Jackson, Mississippi. A shouter in the style of the jump-band vocalists of the 1940s, she suffered in that her records never matched her live performances due to an inability on the part of her various record labels to partner her with sympathetic producers. Her biggest successes came during the 1950s when she was signed to the Columbia subsidiary Okeh, with the R&B hits *Grabbin' Blues* and *Way Back Home* . By the 1960s, she had been dubbed "the Mother of Soul", and recorded for Epic and Scepter, among others. Just when she was beginning to achieve wider acceptance her career was cut short by her death on January 23, 1972.

THE OKEH SESSIONS, Charly, 1988

BLACKMON, LARRY   See CAMEO

BLACKWELL, BUMPS   Robert A. Blackwell was born in Seattle, Washington, on May 23, 1922. He has always been associated primarily with his role in developing the career of LITTLE RICHARD but, within the wider context of soul, it is more important that he was ultimately responsible for persuading Sam COOKE to change his style from gospel to soul.

His own career started during the 1940s when he played with Ray CHARLES. After studying composition in Hollywood, he got a job at Specialty as an arranger, where he produced Larry WILLIAMS, Lloyd PRICE and Little Richard. His contribution to Specialty cannot be underestimated, as he not only produced and arranged he also co-wrote – with John Marascalco – songs like *Good Golly Miss Molly* and *Rip it Up* and – with Little Richard – *Long Tall Sally*. When Art RUPE, the owner of Specialty, showed disquiet at the notion of Sam Cooke singing pop, Blackwell took Cooke over to the Keen label, where he was promptly signed up. This marked the end of Blackwell's association with Specialty. He remained with Keen for even less time, leaving to become head of A&R at Mercury on the West Coast. When Little Richard's contract with Specialty expired he signed with Mercury, teaming up with Blackwell once again. Although, Little Richard had left rock'n'roll behind in favour of gospel, Blackwell showed his versatility by cutting gospel records that were bang up-to-date in arrangement and production. As a result Blackwell became Little Richard's manager, a position he held until 1973. Towards the end of his association with Little Richard, Blackwell produced the LP *The Rill Thing* on Reprise. Despite its lack of commercial success it showed that Little Richard could cut up-to-date soul albums as well as anybody. On March 9, 1985, Blackwell died, aged 62.

BLAND, BOBBY Robert Calvin Bland was born in Rosemark, Tennessee on January 27, 1930. During the 1940s, he moved to Memphis, where he sang in the gospel group, The Miniatures. In 1949, he joined The Beale Streeters, which had included in its lineup at one time or another, B. B. KING, Johnny ACE and Roscoe Gordon. After a stint as King's driver, he started to record for the Modern label, which was owned by the Bihari Brothers. In 1953 he signed with the Duke label, where he recorded a string of singles which included: *Lead Me On, Farther up the Road* (USA #34.1957), *Cry Cry Cry* (USA#71.1960), *I Pity the Fool* (USA#46.1961), *Turn on Your Lovelight* (USA#28.1962), *Call on Me* (USA #22.1962), *Ain't Nothing You Can Do* (USA #20.1964) and *If You Could Read My Mind*.

In 1962 he recorded the LP*Two Steps from the Blues*, which, despite its title, is the embodiment of soul: the marriage between the gospel and the secular traditions. Throughout his career with Duke, it was his very good fortune to be in the hands of the musical director and producer, Joe Scott, who allowed the soulfulness of Bland's voice to carry the records, rather than swamping them with over elaborate arrangements. After Don ROBEY sold Duke to ABC, Bland's career went into a decline during the latter half of 1960s, although he continued to tour regularly with King.

In 1972 he recorded the LP *The California Album*, with the cream of the West Coast session musicians. It was followed by the LP *The Dreamer*; in the same way as *Two Steps from the Blues* had been before, this was a blueprint for what a soul LP should be: the arrangements embellishing the voice. While neither of these records were huge commercial successes, they established him as one of the great vocalists of the period. Throughout the 1970s, he continued to record and tour. A double LP *Together Again – Live!* , with B. B. King, was released in 1976. It was followed by the LPs, *Reflections In Blue* (1977) and *Come Fly With Me* (1978), which were marred by some indifferent material.

In 1983, he signed with the Jackson-based label, Malaco, for whom he has recorded a succession of LPs: *Members Only* (1985), *After All*

(1986), *Blues You Can Use* (1988), *Midnight Run* (1989) and *First Class Blues* (1989). The empathetic productions by Tommy COUCH and Wolf Stephenson underline Bland's ability to leave most performers standing in their tracks when he has good material to play with.

TWO STEPS FROM THE BLUES, Duke, 1962
THE CALIFORNIA ALBUM, BGO, 1972
THE DREAMER, BGO, 1974
TOGETHER AGAIN – LIVE!, (with. B. B. King), Impulse, 1976
THE BAREFOOT ROCK, (with Junior Parker), Duke, 1977
LIKE 'ER RED HOT, Duke, 1977
HERE'S THE MAN, Duke, 1977
CALL ON ME, Duke, 1977
AIN'T NOTHING YOU CAN DO, Duke, 1977
THE SOUL OF THE MAN, Duke, 1977
TOUCH OF THE BLUES, Duke, 1977
SPOTLIGHTING THE MAN B. B, Duke, 1977
INTROSPECTIVE OF THE EARLY YEARS, Duke, 1977
REFLECTIONS IN BLUE, ABC, 1977
WOKE UP SCREAMING, Ace, 1981
THE BEST OF BOBBY BLAND, ABC, 1982
THE SOULSIDE OF BOBBY BLAND, Kent, 1985
MEMBERS ONLY, Malaco, 1985
BLUES IN THE NIGHT, Ace, 1985
AFTER ALL, Malaco, 1986
BLUES YOU CAN USE, Malaco, 1988
SOUL WITH A FLAVOUR, Charly, 1988
MIDNIGHT RUN, Malaco, 1989
FIRST CLASS BLUES, Malaco, 1989
THE "3 B" BLUES BOY, Ace, 1991

BLOODSTONE Bloodstone were formed as a vocal group, The Sinceres, in Kansas City, during the 1960s.
They were comprised of Charles McCormick, Willis Draffen, Charles Love, Henry Williams and Roger Durham. Initially they failed to make any headway until they changed their name in 1971 and became an instrumental funk outfit. They were booked by Al GREEN to open for him on a tour of the UK; in the course of the tour they were signed to the Decca label by Mike Vernon. Their debut LP *Natural High* (USA#30.1973) was recorded in the UK at the Chipping Norton Studios; consequently they were signed to the London label for the USA.

It was peculiar that a group from Kansas should travel all the way to Chipping Norton to record an LP that was so similar in the arrangements and vocal harmonies to those that were being cut in Philadelphia by GAMBLE & HUFF and Thom BELL. The title track *Natural High* (USA#10; UK #40.1973) became a big hit internationally. It was followed by another hit, *Outside Woman* (USA#34.1974). In 1975, they financed the film *Train to Hollywood*; it wasn't particularly memorable however. In recent years they have been unable to make any waves, despite contracts with Motown and Epic.

NATURAL HIGH, Decca, 1972

BLOW, KURTIS Kurt Walker was born in New York City on August 9, 1959. He studied voice at the High School Of Music and Art and Communications at the New York City College. In 1976 he adopted the name Kurtis Blow and started rapping as a DJ in assorted New York clubs, joining GRANDMASTER FLASH and The Furious Five for a short time. In 1979, he left The Furious Five and signed with Mercury. His debut was a seasonally inspired offering, *Christmas Rappin'* (UK#30.1979). The following year, he teamed up with Davy D for *The Breaks* (UK#47.1980), although it failed to make any significant inroads into the US charts it sold over a million copies, peaking at #4 in the R&B charts. After touring the US extensively, he toured the UK and Europe and then released the LP*Deuce*. In 1985, he resumed recording with *Party Time* (UK#67.1985), it was followed by *If I Ruled The World* (UK #24.1986) and *I'm Chillin'* (UK#64.1986). The LP *Kingdom Blow* featured contributions from a galaxy of stars like Bob Dylan, George CLINTON and Trouble Funk. Since that time he has continued to tour, although he hasn't recorded recently.

TOUGH, Mercury, 1982
THE RAPPER IN TOWN, Mercury, 1984
EGO TRIP, Mercury, 1984
AMERICA, Club, 1985
KINGDOM BLOW, Club, 1986
BEST OF....... RAPPIN', Mercury, 1991

BLUE NOTES   See MELVIN, Harold, & The Blue Notes

BOB & EARL   In 1956, Earl Lee Nelson Jr moved from his home town, Lake Charles, Louisiana, to Los Angeles, where he joined The Hollywood Flames, which comprised Bobby Byrd, Dave Ford and Clyde Tillys. They secured a contract with a local label, Ebb, which was owned by Mrs Lee Rupe, the wife of Art RUPE, the owner of Specialty Records. Their first and only hit was *Buzz-Buzz-Buzz* (USA#11.1957), after which they gradually went their separate ways. Byrd left to pursue a solo career, adopting the pseudonym of Bobby DAY; he was replaced by Bobby Garrett, also known as Bobby Relf. In 1959 Tillys and Ford left to further their careers in New York. After four years of performing as a duo, Nelson and Garrett recorded *Harlem Shuffle* (UK#7.1969) for the Class label. It was arranged by Barry WHITE and was a minor hit in the USA and a club hit in the UK, initially; but when it was reissued in 1969 in the UK it became a top-ten hit. In 1965 Nelson,

having been bitten by the pseudonym bug, released *The Duck* (USA#14.1965) under the name of Jackie Lee. Since the late 1960s both Bob & Earl have disappeared from sight.

HARLEM SHUFFLE, Line (West Germany), 1984

BOOKER T & THE MGs   In May, 1962, at the end of a recording session, Booker T. Jones (keyboards, born on December 11, 1944 in Memphis), Steve CROPPER (guitar), Lewis Steinberg (bass) and Al JACKSON, Jr (drums) were jamming in the studio, where they were employed as session musicians in the Stax house band The MARKEYS. By the end of the session they had recorded two instrumentals, *Behave Yourself* and *Green Onions*. Jim STEWART liked what he heard and decided to release the tracks as a single, with the former as the A-side, under the name of Booker T & The MGs (MG being an acronym for Memphis Group). The local radio stations were unimpressed by the A-side, but started to plug the B-side, *Green Onions* (USA #3.1962; UK#7.1979); as a result Stewart reissued the record with reversed priorities. The record was a major hit in the USA but in the UK, despite attracting a lot of attention in the clubs, it failed to chart until 1979, when it was included in the soundtrack of the film, *Quadrophenia*. Over the next ten years, Booker T & The MGs continued to record as a separate entity, gaining hits with titles like *Hip Hug Her* (USA#37.1967), *Soul Limbo* (USA#17.1968; UK#30.1969), used by the BBC as the theme to the television cricket broadcasts, *Hang 'Em High* (USA#9.1969), the theme to the film of the same name, starring Clint Eastwood, and *Time is Tight* (USA#6; UK#4.1969). Throughout, they continued also to be the crack session squad at the Stax studios, backing artists like Otis REDDING, SAM & DAVE, Eddie FLOYD and Wilson PICKETT, creating the sound that fully vindicated the epithet "Soulsville USA" emblazoned over the front entrance to the studios. It was a measure of the professionalism in that the only change in the line-up came in 1964, when Steinberg was replaced by Donald "Duck" DUNN, a former member of The Royal Spades.

In 1970, Booker T left the group and moved to Los Angeles, where he married Priscilla Coolidge and started a solo career as well as his own production company, which involved producing Bill WITHERS and Earl Klugh, among others. Later the same year Steve Cropper left Stax. In 1973 Bobby Manuel (guitar) and Carson Whitsett (keyboards) were recruited by Dunn and Jackson to record an LP entitled *The MGs*. It was a pale imitation of their former days. The murder of Jackson in 1975, followed by the closure of Stax in 1976, appeared to finish the group for good, but in 1977, Booker T, Cropper and Dunn reunited to participate in the 25th Anniversary programme of *American Bandstand*. They stayed together to record an LP for Asylum entitled *Universal Language*; it failed to sell and they disbanded once again. Since then they have tended to tour periodically, most recently in the UK and Europe in 1990.

UPTIGHT, Stax, 1969
BOOKER T SET, Stax, 1969
GREEN ONIONS, Atlantic, 1962
McLEMORE AVENUE, Stax, 1970
UNIVERSAL LANGUAGE, Asylum, 1977
THE BEST OF BOOKER T & THE MGS, Atlantic, 1984

BOOTSY William "Bootsy" Collins became a member of James BROWN's backing band, The JBs, in 1970; as bassist, he contributed the thrust to records like *Get Up, I Feel Like Being A Sex Machine*. In 1971, he left The JBs and joined the George CLINTON combine, Parliament/Funkadelic, as a bassist, guitarist and vocalist, and quickly established himself as one of the lynchpins of the entire operation, cowriting with Clinton and Jerome Brailey, *Tear the Roof Off the Sucker (Give up the Funk)*. As he was such a dominant personality within this group, Clinton suggested that he form his own.

Bootsy's Rubber Band was formed in 1976. It was comprised of other members of the P-Funk family, including Bootsy's brother Catfish, Gary Cooper, Rick Gardner, Richard Griffiths, Joel Johnson, Maceo Parker and Fred Wesley. Their first LP *Stretchin' Out* was as uncompromising as anything that either of his erstwhile employers had put their name to, and the follow-up, *Ahhh...... the Name is Bootsy, Baby!* (USA#16.1977), almost succeeded in eclipsing both Brown and Clinton. In 1978 he released the LP *Bootsy: Player of the Year* (USA#16.1978); it yielded his only UK hit, *Bootzilla* (UK#43.1978). The next LP *This Boot is Made for Funk* (1979) marked the end of their brief pre-eminence. Throughout, Bootsy had continued to record with Clinton –which he does to this day despite his involvement with the occasional one-off project like the celebrated *5 Minutes (C-C-C-Club Mix)* in 1984, in which he collaborated with Jerry Harrison of Talking Heads under the name of Bonzo Goes To Washington: a backing track to a Reagan speech announcing an impending nuclear attack upon the Soviet Union! In 1990 he signed with the Island subsidiary, 4th & Broadway, and toured the UK with Maceo Parker and Fred Wesley.

STRETCHIN' OUT, Warner Bros., 1976
AHH! ......THE NAME IS BOOTSY, BABY!, Warner Bros., 1977
BOOTSY: PLAYER OF THE YEAR, Warner Bros., 1978

BRASS CONSTRUCTION This group was formed in Brooklyn by Randy Muller in 1968 as Dynamic Soul. By 1975, after some chopping and changing of personnel, the line-up was Muller, Sandy Billups, Michael Grudge, Wayne Parris, Larry Payton, Morris Price, Jesse Ward, Wade Williamson and Joseph Arthur Wong, and the group had changed its name to Brass Construction. They were signed by United Artists and their first LP, *Brass Construction* (USA#10; UK#9.1976) established their reputation as one of the leading exponents of jazz-oriented funk. It included the single, *Movin'* (USA#14; UK#23.1976), the first of a string of hit singles that included *Ha Cha Cha (Funktion)* (UK#37.1977), *Music Makes You Feel Like Dancing* (UK#39.1980), *Walkin' The Line* (UK#47.1983), *Partyline* (UK#56.1984) and *Movin' 1988* (UK#24.1988). After this initial success, *Brass Construction 2* (USA#26.1976) consolidated their reputation. Although their subsequent LPs have failed to sell in quite the same quantity, they have continued to record and tour regularly, with Muller writing and producing. In 1977 Muller masterminded the comeback of Garnett MIMMS with a degree of success.

CONQUEST, Capitol, 1985
MOVIN': THE BEST OF BRASS CONSTRUCTION, EMI, 1988

BRIGGS, DAVID Pianist and guitarist David Briggs was one of the founder members of the group The Mark Vs, which gradually metamorphosed into the first house band at the Fame Studios in Muscle Shoals. He was featured on the early hits recorded at Fame by artists like Arthur ALEXANDER, Jimmy HUGHES, Tommy Roe and The TAMS. While recording at Fame, he toured with The Mark Vs, now renamed Dan PENN & The Pallbearers. In 1964 he left Muscle Shoals for Nashville, where he recorded with Elvis Presley among others and was a member of the group, Area Code 615. By the early 1970s, he had set up the formidably successful Quadrafonic Studios in Nashville with Jerry CARRIGAN and Norbert PUTNAM, backing artists like Charlie Rich and Dobie GRAY.

BRISTOL, JOHNNY Johnny Bristol was one of Berry GORDY's multi-talented honchos, who could turn his hand to production, arrangement and composition. He was born in Morgantown, North Carolina, and made his recording debut in 1961 with Jackie Beavers for Harvey FUQUA's label, Tri-phi. Although they failed to achieve any success, their ability as composers was evident in songs like *Someday We'll be Together*.

In 1962 he spotted Junior WALKER & The All Stars, whom he recommended to Fuqua, and they were signed to the Harvey label. When Fuqua's labels were absorbed into Motown in 1964, Bristol took over as Walker's principal producer. Quite apart from his work with Walker, he cowrote or coproduced songs like *If I Could Build My Whole World Around You* and *Your Precious Love* for Marvin GAYE and Tammi TERRELL, *Yester-Me, Yester-You, Yesterday* for Stevie WONDER, *My Whole World Ended* for David RUFFIN and *Daddy Could Swear, I Declare* for Gladys KNIGHT & The Pips.

When Motown relocated to Hollywood, Bristol left the company to produce TAVARES before becoming a producer at CBS, where he worked with Boz SCAGGS and others. However, when they rejected his proposals to record a solo LP he approached MGM. His first single, *Hang on in There Baby* (USA#8; UK #3.1974), was a massive international hit; the LP of the same name (UK#12.1974) included *Love Me for a Reason*, which was covered by The Osmonds.

Since then he has continued to record occasionally, but with little success.

THE BEST OF JOHNNY BRISTOL, Polydor, 1988

BROTHERS JOHNSON George Johnson was born on May 17, 1953, and his brother, Louis was born on April 13, 1955. Their musical career started in the early 1970s when they started to play the club circuit of their native Los Angeles. By 1975 they had played with David RUFFIN, The SUPREMES, Billy PRESTON and Quincy JONES; in that year Jones featured them on his LP *Mellow Madness*, enabling them to secure a recording contract with A&M. Their debut LP *Look Out For #1* (USA#9.1976) was produced by Jones and included the singles *I'll be Good to You* (USA#3.1976) and *Get the Funk Outta Ma Face* (USA#30.1976). The follow-up, *Right on Time* (USA#13.1976), likewise produced by Jones, yielded the single *Strawberry Letter 23* (USA#5; UK#35.1977). Their next LP *Blam!* (USA#7; UK#48.1978) was followed by *Light Up the Night* (USA#5; UK#22.1980), which included the singles *Stomp* (USA#7; UK#6.1980) and *Light up The Night* (UK#47.1980).

Flushed with success they took over the production chores themselves for their next LP *Winners,* but it failed to sell in any great quantity – as have their subsequent outings. While they have continued to tour and record, clearly they need a producer of Jones' calibre to maximise their potential.

LOOK OUT FOR #1, A&M, 1976
STOMP: GREATEST HITS, A&M, 1984

BROWN, BOBBY Bobby Brown formed New Edition in 1983, in Boston, Massachussetts, with Ralph Tresvant, Ronald DeVoe, Michael Bivins and Ricky Bell. He

remained with the group for three years. Initially they were signed to London, where they scored with *Candy Girl* (UK#1.1983) and *Popcorn Love* (UK#43.1983), but were lured away to MCA. At MCA they notched up a series of hits, which included *Cool it Now* (USA#4.1984), *Mr Telephone Man* (USA#4; UK#19.1985), *Lost in Love* (USA#35.1985), *A Little Bit of Love (is all it Takes)* (USA #38.1986) and *Earth Angel* (USA#21.1986). Their arrival launched intense speculation that they would take over from where the JACKSONS had left off; (this speculation was only caused by the members' extreme youth). However, both Tresvant and Brown's replacement, Johnny GILL, have subsequently launched highly successful solo careers of their own

After Brown left the group to launch his own solo career his solo debut LP, *King of Stage*, included the single *Girlfriend*. His second LP *Don't be Cruel* included the singles *Don't be Cruel* (UK#42.1988), *My Prerogative, Roni* and *Every Little Step*; it was produced and co-written by LA & BABYFACE and launched him into the big league along with Michael JACKSON and PRINCE. Whether he has the ability to sustain this momentum and develop what he has begun remains to be seen. However, on the evidence of his live performances, he certainly seems to possess the charisma of greatness.

NEW EDITION, MCA, 1984
ALL FOR LOVE, (New Edition), MCA, 1986
EARTH ANGEL, (New Edition), MCA, 1987
KING OF STAGE, MCA, 1987
DON'T BE CRUEL, MCA, 1988
DANCE ....YA KNOW IT!, MCA, 1990
RALPH TRESVANT, MCA, 1990

BROWN, JAMES On December 17, 1988, a South Carolina judge sentenced James Brown, "the Hardest Working Man in Show

Business", to six years in prison on a variety of charges, including resisting arrest and carrying firearms without a licence, and thus a career that has spanned 33 years came to a halt. However, as a visit to any club in any town in any part of the world will quickly demonstrate, Brown's influence remains just as strong as it ever has. In purely statistical terms, he has notched up 114 appearances in the US charts, which is more than any other black artist.

He was born in Augusta, Georgia on May 3, 1933. In 1954, The Famous Flames were formed out of The Gospel Starlighters, of which Brown was a member; Bobby Byrd was in its lineup. In 1956 Brown signed with the Federal label, a subsidiary of King, and recorded *Please Please Please*; that it was described by the owner of King, Syd NATHAN, as "a piece of shit" said more about Nathan than it did about the record. Although it was a very minor hit in the USA, it possessed the dramatic sense of timing that was to become Brown's hallmark. In 1959, having signed with the booking agency, Universal Attractions, he took the James Brown Show out on the road and began a practice that would earn him a reputation as one of the most exciting performers in the world. His shrewd business acumen enabled him to take this step: he ensured that, whenever he was to play a new venue, the local radio stations and record shops knew well in advance, so that his records were promoted remorselessly. Throughout this period he released new singles every couple of months. Although most were only minor hits – the biggest was *Think* (USA#33.1960) – he managed to maintain an unflagging momentum that generated continued interest, and he was constantly attracting fresh audiences. In 1962 he released *Night Train* (USA#35.1962), in which he listed the regular stop-overs on his tour schedule. The culmination of this process was the recording of a live LP at Harlem's Apollo

Theatre in 1962 entitled *Live at the Apollo (USA#2.1963), this LP went a long way towards capturing the bare excitement of his stage show and is still considered one of the best live LPs ever recorded. Its release coincided with that of Prisoner of Love* (USA #18.1963), which became his first top twenty hit.

In 1964, eager to capitalize upon the success of *Live at the Apollo*, Brown formed his own production company, Fair Deal, with Ben Bart, owner of the booking agency Universal Attractions, and sent some new recordings to the Smash label, a subsidiary of Mercury. The first two releases on Smash were very minor hits, penetrating the lower reaches of the top hundred, but the third, *Out Of Sight* (USA #24.1964), clearly indicated the direction Brown was taking: the juddering bass line punctuated by staccato blasts from the horns and the extraordinary rhythmic intensity pioneered a dance-oriented funk that would prepare the ground for countless imitators. Nathan, who had instituted legal action against Brown for breach of contract, issued another live LP: recorded at the Royal Theater in Baltimore, Maryland, this was called *Pure Dynamite! Live At The Royal* (USA#10.1964). Nathan also finally acceded to Brown's demands for a higher royalty rate and greater artistic control. His first record under his new contract with King was *Papa's Got A Brand New Bag* (USA#8; UK#25.1965); it continued where *Out Of Sight* had left off and won him a Grammy, as well as providing him with his first hit in the UK. The follow-up, *I Got You (I Feel Good)* (USA#3.1965; UK#29.1966), was still further proof that the lessons in "emoting" that he had learnt while he was a member of The Gospel Starlighters had not been wasted. The release in 1966 of *It's A Man's, Man's, Man's World* (USA#8; UK#13.1966) showed that, although he had pioneered a sound of his own, he was more than a match for the balladeers who were beginning to make an impact. In 1967, following the replacement of Nat Jones by Alfred "Pee Wee" Ellis as Brown's chief musical collaborator, he recorded *Cold Sweat* (US#7.1967); this provided another example of Brown's pioneering instincts by using the vocal track to supplement the rhythm,

As Ray CHARLES had done in the 1950s, so Brown was to do in the 1960s by being both a catalyst and a commentator upon the growing Civil Rights Movement. Although Martin Luther King was quoted as saying that he viewed Brown's support as potentially hazardous, this did not stop Brown from appearing to appeal for calm on national TV following King's assassination on April 4, 1968, and the ensuing rioting in over thirty cities. The same year saw the release of *I Got the Feelin'* (USA #6.1968) and *Say it Loud - I'm Black and I'm Proud* (USA#10.1968), the latter encapsulating a political sentiment that sent tidal waves through the music industry, so that black artists across the country began to record songs with socially aware lyrics. In 1969, ever eager to blaze new trails he developed a new dance, *The Popcorn*. The first composition promulgating it was *Mother Popcorn (You Got to Have a Mother for Me)* (USA#11.1969) and the dance provided him with countless opportunites for reworking the same theme into new formats, a practice which has since become standard among DJs and remix engineers.

In 1970, he disbanded The Famous Flames and replaced them with The JBs. Although he retained seasoned professionals like Ellis and Fred Wesley, he brought in younger players like BOOTSY; the benefits of the reorganization were quick to materialize when *Get Up I Feel Like Being A Sex Machine* (USA#15; UK #32.1970/#45.1985/#46.1986) restored him to the UK charts; it has become one of the lynchpins of his live act and has become such a staple for DJs that it has been re-issued twice in the

UK, charting on each occasion. Later the same year *Super Bad* (USA#13.1970) was released, while the double live LP *Sex Machine* (USA #29.1970), showed no indication of any lessening of his ability to whip up an audience into a frenzy. The following year he parted company with King and set up his own record label, People, which he licensed to Polydor for worldwide distribution. The change gave him the chance to record other artists like Bobby Byrd and Lyn Collins. At this point various members of The JBs left to join George CLINTON's Parliament-Funkadelic group.

After the release of another double live LP *Revolution of the Mind* (USA#39.1972) and a series of modest hits, Brown released *Get on the Good Foot* (USA#18.1972). In 1973 he duetted with protege, Lyn Collins, and collaborated with Wesley in the scoring of the films *Black Caesar* and *Slaughter's Big Rip-Off*; on the sleeves he was dubbed "the Godfather of Soul". The next year he had another major success with *The Payback* (USA#26.1974): although the single never got higher than #26, it remained in the charts for over three months, as did the double LP of the same name (USA #34.1974). Throughout the latter half of the 1970s the number of hit records decreased, but Brown's influence continued to exert a strong hold upon audiences, and nowhere was this influence more keenly felt than in the volatile atmosphere of clubland, where by the 1980s his earlier records were being sampled and remixed by DJs. This prompted electro-rapper Afrika BAMBAATAA to collaborate with Brown; the result was *Unity (The Third Coming)* (UK#49.1984), which was released on the independent label Tommy Boy. In 1986 Brown was asked by Sylvester Stallone to record the theme to the film *Rocky 4: Living in America* (USA#4; UK#5.1986); it gave him his biggest hit for thirteen years. In 1988 the single *The Payback Mix* (UK#12.1988), a sampled re-mix by Coldcut of his earlier material, showed how strong his influence continued to be. *I'm Real* (UK#31.1988) was produced by Full Force, as was the ensuing LP of the same name, which reached #27 in the UK. In April 1991, he was released from gaol and by May the same year he was back on the road.

EXCITEMENT, Polydor, 1962
LIVE AT THE APOLLO, VOLUME I, Polydor, 1962
PRISONER OF LOVE, Polydor, 1963
PLEASE PLEASE PLEASE, Polydor, 1964
UNBEATABLE SIXTEEN HITS, Polydor, 1964
PAPA'S GOT A BRAND NEW BAG, Polydor, 1965
I GOT YOU, Polydor, 1966
IT'S A MAN'S, MAN'S, MAN'S WORLD, Polydor, 1966
COLD SWEAT, Polydor, 1967
JAMES BROWN'S FUNKY PEOPLE, People, 1973
DEAD ON THE HEAVY FUNK, 1974-76 , Polydor. 1977
BODY HEAT, Polydor, 1977
SOLID GOLD, Polydor, 1977
TAKE A LOOK AT THOSE CAKES, Polydor, 1979
SPECIAL, Polydor, 1981
SOUL SYNDROME, RCA, 1981
BEST OF JAMES BROWN, Polydor, 1982
MEAN ON THE SCENE, Phoenix, 1982
SOUL CLASSICS, Polydor, 1983
ROOTS OF A REVOLUTION, Polydor, 1984
FEDERAL YEARS, VOLUME I, Solid Smoke, 1984
FEDERAL YEARS, VOLUME 2, Solid Smoke, 1984
COMPACT DISC OF JAMES BROWN, Polydor,1985
GREATEST HITS, Polydor, 1985
GRAVITY, Scotti Brothers, 1986
IN THE JUNGLE GROOVE, Polydor, 1986
LP OF THE JB, Polydor, 1986
SEX MACHINE AND OTHER SOUL CLASSICS, Polydor, 1988
I'M REAL, Scotti Brothers, 1988
DUETS, Urban, 1990
MESSING WITH THE BLUES, Polydor, 1990
SOUL JUBILEE, Blue Moon, 1990
STAR TIME, Polydor, 1991

BROWN, MAXINE   Despite her fine voice Maxine Brown has never been accorded the success, which is her due. Usually this can be attributed to a dearth of reasonable material, in her case she has had writers like GOFFIN & KING and ASHFORD & SIMPSON writing for her, but somehow she has never been able to pull all the strands together to build a solid career.

She was born in Kingstree, South Carolina. She moved to New York in the early 1960s where she worked as a model and sang with gospel groups like The Royaltones until she was spotted by Tony Bruno, who signed her to his Nomar label. She scored immediately with *All In My Mind* (USA#19.1961) and *Funny* (USA#25.1961). After leaving Nomar, she was signed by ABC for a brief spell, and from ABC she moved to Wand. At Wand, with Luther DIXON producing, she recorded tracks like *Oh No Not My Baby* (USA#25.1964), the Goffin & King composition, and *If You Gotta Make a Fool*. She was teamed with fellow Wand artist Chuck JACKSON for a number of duets like *Something You Got, Daddy's Home* and *Hold On We're Comin*. Although, she managed to crack the R&B charts with considerable regularity, her output was often overlooked by her record label, who were enjoying considerable success with Dionne WARWICK. In 1968 she left Wand and although she has recorded for labels like Epic, Commonwealth United and Avco, her visits to the studios have been less frequent in recent years.

ONE IN A MILLION, Kent, 1984
LIKE NEVER BEFORE, Kent, 1985

BROWN, ROY   Roy Brown was born in New Orleans on September 10, 1925. He sang gospel at his local church until, in 1945, he won a talent contest in Los Angeles. At first he sang ballads, but in 1947 he recorded *Good*

Rockin' Tonight. The track marked a radical change of style, being reminiscent of jump-band vocalists like Eddie "Cleanhead" Vinson and Wynonie Harris, but Brown never became a "shouter": there was always a hint of gospel in his phrasing, and this was to influence artists like Clyde McPHATTER and Jackie WILSON. *Good Rockin' Tonight* was followed by self-penned compositions like *Mighty Mighty Man*, *Boogie at Midnight* and *Hard Luck Blues*, the latter climbing to #1 on the R&B charts in 1949.

In 1952 he was signed to Syd NATHAN's King label, where he remained until 1955, when he was signed by Imperial. Although he was based in Los Angeles, his version of *Let the Four Winds Blow* (USA#29.1957) showed the influences of his early years in New Orleans. He gradually dropped out of sight, although returning to tour on odd occasions. In 1970 Johnny OTIS persuaded him to appear at the Monterey Jazz Festival, which was recorded and released by Epic. Throughout the next ten years, he toured the USA and Europe regularly until, on May 25, 1981, he died of a heart attack, aged 55.

CHEAPEST PRICE IN TOWN, Faith, 1979
LAUGHING BUT CRYING, Route 66, 1980
GOOD ROCKIN' TONIGHT, Magnum Force, 1984
BOOGIE AT MIDNIGHT, Charly, 1985
THE BLUESWAY SESSIONS, Charly, 1988

BROWN, RUTH Ruth Weston was born in Portsmouth, Virginia, in 1928; in the mid-1940s she married trumpeter Jimmy Brown. In 1949 she was signed by Herb ABRAMSON to the fledgling Atlantic label. After making a verbal agreement with Abramson she was involved in a car accident in Chester, Pennsylvania, which set her career back by a year. After her hospitalisation she cut a series of records including *So Long, Teardrops from My Eyes, 5-10-15 Hours* and *(Mama)He Treats Your Daughter Mean* (USA#23.1953), all of which were monster R&B hits. As a result she was dubbed "Miss Rhythm" and Atlantic was nicknamed "the House that Ruth Built". In 1957 she recorded the LEIBER & STOLLER song, *Lucky Lips* (USA#25.1957), which was followed by *This Little Girl's Gone Rockin'* (USA#24.1958). By 1961 her hard rockin' style had become unfashionable, and in 1962 she parted company with Atlantic.

From 1962 until 1976 she raised her children and worked in a variety of jobs including driving school buses and cleaning. Since then she has begun to accrue some of the credit due to her, principally in the form of royalties back-dated from her years with Atlantic; her quest to retrieve those royalties led to the formation of the non-profit making Rhythm & Blues Foundation. In the 1980s, she has appeared variously in Allen TOUSSAINT's off-Broadway musical *Staggerlee*, in John Waters' film *Hairspray* as Motormouth Mabel and hosting *Harlem Hit Parade* and *Blues Stage*. In 1989 she won a Tony Award for her performance in the Broadway play *Black and Blue*, and her most recent LP, *Blues on Broadway*, has earned her a Grammy.

SUGAR BABE, President, 1977
BLACK IS BROWN, BROWN IS BEAUTIFUL, President, 1981
TAKING CARE OF BUSINESS, Stockholm, 1984
BROWN SUGAR, Charly, 1986
BLUES ON BROADWAY, Fantasy, 1989
THE HITS, Official, 1989

BROWN, SHIRLEY Shirley Brown was one of the many artists whose career went into decline as a result of the demise of Stax. She was born in West Memphis on January 6, 1947. She came to prominence with the single *Woman to Woman* (USA#22.1974), released on the Stax affiliate label Truth; it was similar in style to much of Millie JACKSON's material, but seemed to have more humour in it. Throughout the latter half of the 1970s her career went into the doldrums and she recorded the LP *Shirley Brown* (1977) for Arista. By the mid-1980s she had been signed to the Island subsidiary 4th & Broadway, where she recorded the LP *Intimate Storm* (1985); two singles were released, *Boyfriend* and *Love Fever*, but both failed to make any impression on either the US or the UK charts. By 1989 she had been signed by Malaco, where she recorded the LP *Fire and Ice*, coproduced by Jim STEWART.

WOMAN TO WOMAN, Stax, 1974
INTIMATE STORM, 4th & Broadway, 1985
FIRE AND ICE, Malaco, 1989

BRYANT, SHARON See ATLANTIC STARR

BRYSON, PEABO Bryson has succeeded in carving a niche for himself in potentially the most lucrative corner of the market as a concert and cabaret performer for the affluent middle classes. He was born on April 13, 1951, in Greenville, South Carolina, as Robert Peabo Bryson, and made his debut in 1971 as a member of the R&B group Moses Dillard & The Tex-Town Display while working for the Bang label as a producer and session singer. In 1976 he was featured as the lead vocalist on a minor disco hit, *Do It With Feeling* by The Michael Zager Band. This exposure enabled him to gain a contract as a solo artist with Capitol.

His debut LP, *Reaching for the Sky* (USA #49.1978), established him as a skilful interpreter of ballads, although the two singles taken from the LP failed to make any significant impression. His career was boosted by his

collaboration with Natalie COLE: a joint tour was followed by an LP, *We're the Best of Friends* (USA#44.1980). This was the first of a number of duets he would record with different artists, the most successful being his partnership with Roberta FLACK: the LP *Born to Love* (USA#25; UK#15.1983) brought him to a new audience in the UK, while the single, *Tonight I Celebrate My Love for You* (USA#16; UK#2.1983)was a major hit in that country. In 1984 he signed with Elektra. His debut LP for his new label, *Straight from the Heart* (USA #44.1984) provided the source for his biggest US hit, *If You're Ever in my Arms* (USA #10.1984). Since 1984 the competition in his corner of the market has been stiff, with performers like Freddie JACKSON, Alexander O'NEAL and Luther VANDROSS attracting considerable attention, but he has continued to record consistently well crafted LPs. In 1988, he recorded another duet, this time with Regina BELLE for the LP *Positive*.

BORN TO LOVE, (with Roberta Flack), Capitol, 1983
STRAIGHT FROM THE HEART, Elektra, 1984
TAKE NO PRISONERS, Elektra, 1985
QUIET STORM, Elektra, 1986
POSITIVE, Elektra, 1988

BURKE, SOLOMON The style of Solomon Burke has always owed more to his gospel roots than is the case with many of his contemporaries; indeed the debt is such that, were it not for the subject matter of many of his records, the difference would be imperceptible.

He was born in 1936 in Philadelphia, where his family had their own church – the House of God for All People – at which, as a boy, he would frequently preach. Initially he recorded for specialist gospel labels like Apollo until, in 1960, he was signed by Jerry WEXLER to the Atlantic label, where he remained for the next eight years. Although his style had been moulded in the histrionic "testifying" tradition of gospel, his second release for Atlantic, *Just out of Reach (of My Two Empty Arms)* (USA #24.1961), was the embodiment of country-soul at its very best with the Muscle Shoals studio band defining the sound that was to become synonymous with the name Atlantic. The follow-up, *Cry to Me* (USA#44.1962), teamed him with producer Bert BERNS. They collaborated on two more singles which were minor hits. The following year at Wexler's suggestion, he recorded the Wilson PICKETT composition, *If You Need Me* (USA#37.1963); it stopped the Pickett original in its tracks. He continued to notch up minor hits with great regularity, *Got to Get You Off My Mind* (USA #22.1965) being his biggest hit. It was followed by *Tonight's the Night* (USA#28.1965).

In 1966 the idea was mooted of a collaboration between all the major male Atlantic artists under the collective name The Soul Clan; apart from Burke, it was to include Otis REDDING, Joe TEX, Don COVAY and Wilson Pickett. By the time the record, *Soul Meeting*, was made in 1968, Redding was dead and Pickett had dissociated himself from the project; they were replaced by Arthur CONLEY and Ben E. KING. For Burke, the failure of the project marked the end of his tenure with Atlantic.

He next signed with Larry Utall's Bell label, where he had his final hit, *Proud Mary* (USA #45.1969), a cover of the John Fogerty composition. It was recorded at Fame with Barry BECKETT producing and was extracted from the LP of the same name, which featured a marvellous version of the Chuck WILLIS song, *What am I Living For*. The sessions were significant for a couple of reasons: they were some of the final sessions at Fame for the house band, who were about to set up the rival Muscle Shoals Sound studios; and for Utall, who was about to turn his back on soul in

favour of pop like The Partridge Family. In 1971 Burke signed with MGM, for whom he released the LP *We're Almost Home*; it was another perfect example of country-soul, but failed to sell. In 1975, he released the LP *Music to Make Love by* on Chess and then retired from the music business to run the family church, of which he had become Bishop.

In 1981, The Soul Clan reformed with Pickett in the lineup. Its one concert, played in New York, was by all accounts a fiasco. Burke, however, recorded a double live LP in Washington, *Soul Alive!*, which was commercially successful. The 1980s have seen him recording with much greater frequency. Rather than attempting to update his sound, he has relied upon the gospel-traditions for inspiration, recording LPs like *Lord I Need a Miracle Right Now, Into My Life You Came, Take Me Shake Me* and *This is His Song* for the Savoy label

SOUL ALIVE!, Rounder, 1984
THE BEST OF SOLOMON BURKE, Atlantic, 1985
A CHANGE IS GONNA COME, Rounder, 1986
LOVE TRAP, Polygram, 1987

BUTLER, JERRY Jerry Butler, born in Sunflower, Mississippi on December 8, 1939, moved to Chicago when he was three years old. In 1957, he joined the R&B group The Roosters with his close friend, Curtis MAYFIELD. The group was renamed The IMPRESSIONS and, following an audition, signed with Ewart ABNER's Falcon label, a subsidiary of Veejay. The following year they scored with *For Your Precious Love* (USA #11.1958), written by Butler and Arthur Brooks; there was considerable dissent within the group over the fact that it was credited to Jerry Butler and The Impressions. At the end of the year Butler went his own way.

He had to wait two years for his next hit, *He will Break Your Heart* (USA#7.1960), featuring his former colleague, Curtis Mayfield, who also cowrote the song. Over the next four years he had a string of hits, many featuring Mayfield, including *Find Another Girl* (USA#27.1961), *I'm a-Tellin' You* (USA#25.1961), *Moon River* (USA#11.1961), *Make it Easy on Yourself* (USA#20.1962), *Need to Belong* (USA #31.1964) and *I Stand Accused*. The last has become a standard of sorts, and provided Isaac HAYES with a modest hit in 1970. In November 1964 he teamed up with Betty EVERETT for a number of duets, including *Let it be Me* (USA#5.1964) and *Smile* (USA#42.1965); the LP *Delicious Together* just failed to crack the top hundred. These were the first of many such collaborations with female artists.

After Veejay went bankrupt in 1966, Butler signed a fresh contract with Mercury and became known as the "Iceman", a nickname coined by the Philadelphia DJ George Woods. His second record for Mercury was *Mr. Dream Merchant* (USA#38.1967). The following year he met and teamed up with the production and writing partnership of GAMBLE & HUFF. The collaboration was immediately successful, producing a sequence of hits that lasted for two years: *Never Give You Up* (USA#20.1968), *Hey, Western Union Man* (USA#16.1968), *Are You Happy?* (USA#39.1969), *Only the Strong Survive* (USA#4.1969), *Moody Woman* (USA #24.1969) and *What's the Use of Breaking Up* (USA#20.1969). Two LPs were released, *The Iceman Cometh* (USA#29.1969) and *Ice on Ice* (USA#41.1969), which served to emphasise his reputation as an all-round performer. The partnership was dissolved in 1970, when Gamble & Huff left to start their own record label in Philadelphia. Butler, with the backing of the music publishers Chappell's, set up the Songwriter's Workshop to encourage the development of young writers.

In 1975, having had several lean years during which he had recorded a series of duets with Gene CHANDLER and then Brenda Lee

Eager, and three LPs including *The Sagittarius Movement*, which sold consistently but never got any higher than #123, Butler parted company with Mercury. He was approached by Ewart Abner, by now the president of Motown, and offered a contract. His first LP for Motown, *Love's On The Menu*, was a commercial failure. The second, *Thelma and Jerry*, teamed him up with Thelma HOUSTON. By 1979 he had moved on once more, this time renewing his partnership with Gamble & Huff; however, they were unable to emulate their former achievements. Throughout the 1980s he has continued to perform regularly. A reunion with Curtis Mayfield in 1983 to commemorate the 25th anniversary of the formation of The Impressions was so successful that the group reforms periodically for touring purposes only.

ONLY THE STRONG SURVIVE, Club, 1985
THE LEGENDARY PHILADELPHIA HITS, Mercury, 1987

CAIN, KENNY See PORTER, David

CALHOUN, CHARLES See STONE, Jesse

CAMEO Cameo was formed in 1976 by Larry Blackmon in New York City, when he was studying at the Juillard School of Music. Initially they were known as The New York City Players, the group had a lineup that could include anything up to thirteen members; however, its nucleus has revolved around Blackmon and vocalists Thomas Jenkins and Nathan Leftenant. In 1977 they signed to a subsidiary of Casablanca, Chocolate City, for whom they recorded their first LP, *Cardiac Arrest*. This led to an invitation from George CLINTON to support his group, Parliament-

Funkadelic, on their forthcoming tour. Over the next five years, with an ever-changing line-up, the group notched up a string of highly successful LPs including *Knights of the Sound Table* (USA#44.1981), the first LP of theirs to be released in the UK (although their previous LPs had all been available as imports). It was followed by the LP *Alligator Woman* (USA #23.1982).

In 1983, Blackmon formed his own record company, Atlanta Artists. Although their first LP on this label, *Style* (USA#53.1983), was not quite as commercially successful as their previous efforts, it showed that he was beginning to emerge as a stylist in his own right. The next LP, *She's Strange* (USA#27.1984), consolidated their reputation as arch- exponents of dance-oriented funk; the single, *She's Strange* (USA#47; UK#37.1984), became their first hit single. The following year they released the LP *Single Life* (USA#58; UK#66.1985); the single of the same name (UK#15.1985) gave their following in the UK a huge boost and prompted a tour, which was a sell-out. Four singles – *Word Up* (USA#6; UK#3.1986), *Candy* (USA #21.1987; UK#27.1986), *Back And Forth* (UK #11.1987) and *She's Mine* (UK#35.1987) – were taken from their next LP, *Word Up* (USA#8; UK#7.1986), which established the group as a major international act, not least because of their proficiency as performers. Their most recent LPs, *Machismo* (1988) and *Real Men ......Wear Black* (1990), have served to consolidate what *Word Up* had started, despite a slight suspicion that they are becoming formulaic. Blackmon has also contributed to LPs by Ry Cooder and Miles Davis, as well as producing Chaka KHAN.

ALLIGATOR WOMAN, Casablanca, 1982
STYLE, Casablanca, 1983
SHE'S STRANGE, Club, 1984
SINGLE LIFE, Club, 1985
WORD UP, Club, 1986

MACHISMO, Club, 1988
REAL MEN...... WEAR BLACK, Atlanta Artists, 1990

CAMPBELL, BARBARA See COOKE, Sam

CAREY, MARIAH Mariah Carey was born in New York in 1970; her mother, Patricia Carey, sang with the New York City Opera before becoming a vocal coach. In 1988 Mariah was introduced to Tommt Mottola, the president of CBS, who was sufficiently impressed by a demo tape she had cut to sign her. Her debut single, *Vision Of Love* (USA #1.1990), immediately established her in the vanguard of female US vocalists. She has been likened to Whitney HOUSTON, among others, but the fact that *Vanishing*, the most artistically successful track on her debut LP, *Mariah Carey* (USA#1; UK#6.1991) was self-produced and eschews theatricality in a very reassuring way indicates that, potentially, she is more self-contained. Provided that she is allowed to choose her own material and take an active role in the production chores, she has the ability to knock most of the competition out of the window.

MARIAH CAREY, CBS, 1990

CARLTON, CARL Carl Carlton was born in Detroit in 1953. He started to record in the late 1960s as Little Carl Carlton, having a couple of minor hits with *Don't Walk Away* and *Competition Ain't Nothing*. He had to wait until 1974, when he covered the Robert KNIGHT song *Love On A Mountain Top* (USA#6.1974), for his first major success. His next hit, *She's A Bad Mama Jama (She's Built, She's Stacked)* (USA#22; UK#34.1981), was little more than a rather daft novelty item. Throughout his career he has had a following among the Northern Soul fraternity in the UK, but he has never managed to establish large scale acceptance due to his inability to create a style of his own.

CARL CARLTON, 20th Century, 1981

CARLTON, LARRY Larry Carlton has long been regarded as the doyen of Los Angeles session guitarists, recording with artists like Bill WITHERS, Joni Mitchell, Steely Dan, Bobby BLAND, B. B. KING, Randy CRAWFORD and Quincy JONES. He was born on March 2, 1948, in Torrence, California. After years of session work he joined The CRUSADERS in 1975, with whom he has remained on a part-time basis ever since. From 1979 onwards he recorded a slew of solo LPs. While none have been huge commercial successes, they have shown him to be a virtuoso of the highest calibre who is quite prepared to experiment. In purely commercial terms, his biggest success to date has been as the featured guitarist on the single of the theme of the TV series, *Hill Street Blues* (USA #10.1981; UK#25.1982).

LARRY CARLTON, Warner Bros., 1979
LIVE IN JAPAN, Flyover, 1979
SLEEPWALK, Warner Bros., 1982
FRIENDS, Warner Bros., 1983
LAST NITE, MCA, 1986
ALONE BUT NEVER ALONE, MCA, 1987

CARR, JAMES James Carr was born in Memphis on June 13, 1942. Throughout his adolescence he sang in a variety of gospel groups until he hooked up with O. V. WRIGHT in The Harmony Echoes, where he met his future mentor and manager, Roosevelt Jamison. In 1963 Jamison introduced both Carr and Wright to Quinton CLAUNCH, the Goldwax supremo. Carr's career at Goldwax was short and eventful: were it not for the extreme gravity of his psychological condition he would have become one of the great soul singers, such was the strength and range of his voice. From 1964 until 1970, when Goldwax folded, he recorded a slew of great tracks: *Dark End of the Street; That's How Strong My Love Is; Pouring Water on a Drowning Man* and *That's the Way Love Turned Out for Me*. The fact that material was provided by any combination of Chips MOMAN, Dan PENN and Spooner OLDHAM among others was certainly no hindrance for him! After the disintegration of Goldwax Carr was totally unable to cope and went to pieces, becoming increasingly reliant on drugs to get him through. In 1977, he recorded briefly for the River City label, including *Let me be Right*. After an abortive tour of Japan in 1979, he returned to gospel – a field which, perhaps, he should never have left. In 1991 he made a comeback with the LP *Take Me to the Limit* on which he was teamed with Claunch and Jamison once again.

TAKE ME TO THE LIMIT, Ace, 1991

CARRIGAN, JERRY Until his departure with David BRIGGS and Norbert PUTNAM to Nashville in 1964, Jerry Carrigan was the drummer in The Mark Vs, which gained wider currency as the house band at the Fame Studios in Muscle Shoals. He was featured on the earliest records to emanate from that studio by artists like Arthur ALEXANDER, Jimmy HUGHES, Tommy Roe and The TAMS. He became like many of the other session musicians, who customised the great soul records of the early sixties, one of the stalwarts of the Nashville Sound. With Briggs and

Putnam, he runs the Quadrafonic studios, where he has backed artists like Elvis Presley and Charlie Rich and worked with producers like Billy Sherrill and Chips MOMAN.

CARTER, CLARENCE Clarence Carter was born in 1936 in Alabama. He attended the Taladega School for the Blind, learning to play the guitar and the piano. At first he was one half of the duo Clarence & Calvin (Scott). They recorded for the Duke label until being dropped in 1965, when they moved to Rick HALL's Fame label and recorded *Step by Step*.

After Scott's injury in an accident, Carter started to record as a soloist, becoming one of Hall's most successful artists with several hit records: *Slip Away* (USA#6.1968), *Too Weak To Fight* (USA#13.1968), *Snatching It Back* (USA#31.1969), *Patches* (USA#4; UK#2.1970) and *Sixty Minute Man* (USA#65.1973). During his tenure at Fame he married Candi STATON. After Hall closed the label in 1974, Carter's recording career went into a decline and he was compelled to rely on touring. The resurgence of interest in soul in the 1980s has enabled him to record more frequently for independent labels. Singles like *Messin' with my Mind* (1985) and *I Was in the Neighbourhood* (1986) have enjoyed moderate success, while the 1986 LP *Doctor C C* has shown that his blues-oriented style has not escaped him.

SOUL DEEP, Edsel, 1984
DOCTOR C C, Ichiban, 1986

CASH, ALVIN Alvin Cash was born in St. Louis, Missouri, on September 15, 1939. After moving to Chicago, he formed The Crawlers, which included his brothers, Robert and George. After signing with the Mar-V-Lus label, a subsidiary of One-Der-Ful, they had a hit with the instrumental, *Twine Time* (USA #14.1965). This success prompted him to form a backing band, The Registers, and he began to tour the USA and Europe. A series of dance floor hits like *Alvin's got a Boogaloo, Philly Freeze* and *Funky Washing Machine* were all firm indications of his inability to take anything remotely seriously, but their very quirkiness ensured that he remained in the public eye. In recent years, he has not been quite so active, but his tours of the UK are greeted with much anticipation by adherents of Northern Soul.

CASTOR, JIMMY Jimmy Castor was born on June 22, 1943, in New York City. He made his debut as a member of Lewis Lymon's group, The Teenchords (Lewis was the brother of Frankie LYMON). After a spell with them he started to play saxophone on sessions until, in 1967 he had a hit on the Smash label with the instrumental, *Hey, Leroy, Your Mama's Calling You* (USA #31.1967). Unable to sustain this momentum he went back to session work until 1972, when he was signed by CBS and then RCA, as The Jimmy Castor Bunch, comprising Gerry Thomas (keyboards), Doug Gibson (bass), Harry Jensen (guitar), Lenny Fridie (congas) and Bobby Manigault (drums). With this line-up he had his biggest hit, *Troglodyte (Cave Man)* (USA#6.1972), taken from the LP *It's Just Begun* (USA#27.1972). Although it was a novelty item, it succeeded in arousing the attention of Atlantic, who signed him upon expiry of his RCA contract. Another novelty item followed, *The Bertha Butt Boogie* (USA#16.1975). The same year he was included on an Atlantic package tour of the UK with SISTER SLEDGE, Ben E. KING and The DETROIT SPINNERS. However, once more his career slipped into the doldrums until, in 1982 he was signed to the Salsoul label. Of late his career has generated little enthusiasm with the result that he has had to return to playing sessions, as well as touring regularly.

CHAIRMEN OF THE BOARD Chairmen of the Board was the brainchild of Norman "General" Johnson, who was born in Norfolk, Virginia, on May 23, 1943. His first commercial success came in 1961, when, as a member of The Showmen, he recorded *It Will Stand* and *Country Fool* for the Minit label, both were produced by Allen TOUSSAINT. The group released a few more singles before breaking up the following year. Little was heard from Johnson until 1969, when he formed Chairmen of the Board with Eddie Curtis, Harrison Kennedy and Danny Woods. They were signed by HOLLAND, DOZIER & HOLLAND to their fledgling Invictus label, and over the next two years notched up a string of hits like *Give me Just a Little More Time* (USA/UK#3.1970); *(You've Got me) Dangling on a String* (USA#38; UK#5.1970); *Everything's Tuesday* (USA#38.1970; UK#12.1971); *Pay to the Piper* (USA#13.1970; UK#34.1971); *Chairman of the Board* (UK#48.1971); *Working on a Building of Love* (UK#20.1972); *Elmo James* (UK#21.1972); *I'm on My Way to a Better Place.* (UK#30.1973) and *Finder's Keepers* (UK#21.1973). Quite apart from the group's success, Johnson produced and contributed songs for other Invictus artists like Freda Payne – who had monster hits with *Band of Gold* (USA#3; UK#1.1970) and *Bring the Boys Home* (USA#12.1971) – and HONEY CONE, as well as *Patches* for Clarence CARTER. By the end of 1973 the hits had dried up and the group split, with Johnson embarking upon a solo career. His first LP, *General Johnson*, released on Arista in 1978, failed to arouse much more than passing interest. In 1986, he reformed the group for the single *Loverboy* (UK#56.1986).

THE SKIN I'M IN, CBS, 1974
YOU'VE GOT ME DANGLING ON A STRING, HDH, 1984
SALUTE THE GENERAL, HDH, 1984
AGM, HDH, 1985
LOVERBOY, EMI, 1986
SOUL AGENDA, HDH, 1989
SOME FOLKS DON'T UNDERSTAND IT (The Showmen), Charly, 1989

CHANDLER, GENE Gene Chandler was born Eugene Dixon in Chicago on July 6, 1937. In 1957 he was conscripted for National Service; on his return two years later he joined the R&B group, The Dukays. They signed up with the Nat label and had a hit with *The Girl's a Devil*. The follow-up was going to be *Duke of Earl* (USA#1.1962), but Nat sold it to the Veejay label, who signed Dixon as a solo artist. It was at this stage that he changed his name to Chandler, after the actor Jeff Chandler. The single went straight to the top of the charts and remained there for three weeks. In May 1964, following a string of minor hits, he moved from Veejay to Ewart ABNER's newly established Constellation label, where he notched up a succession of hits including *Nothing Can Stop Me* (USA#18.1965; UK#41.1968), which three years later, when it was leased to the Soul City label, became his first hit in the UK.

In 1967 he changed label once again, this time signing a three-year contract with Brunswick. However, apart from a series of duets with Barbara ACKLIN including *From the Teacher to the Preacher* (USA#57.1968), he enjoyed only very modest chart success. In 1969 he produced *Backfield in Motion* for Mel & Tim; this went to #10, selling over a million copies. (They went on to have another hit this time on Stax in 1972 with *Starting All Over Again*, which climbed to #19). His contract with Brunswick having expired, he signed with Mercury and recorded *Groovy Situation* (USA

#11.1970) which gave rise to an LP of duets with Jerry BUTLER that failed to make the top hundred.

When Eugene Record of The CHI-LITES established Chi-Sound Records and enlisted his services as vice-president, Chandler was prompted to record again. The resulting LP, *Get Down* (USA#47.1979), was in the charts for over six months and the title track (USA#53; UK#11.1979), gave him his biggest UK hit. He had two more chart successes in the UK with *When You're Number One* (UK#43.1979) and *Does She Have a Friend* (UK#28.1980). Throughout the 1980s, he has continued to record and to tour, while also devoting considerable energy to the affairs of Chi-Sound.

SIXTIES SOUL BROTHER, Kent, 1986

CHANGE Change was a group formed by the producer Jaques Fred Petrus in the late 1970s. Initially it comprised Timmy Allen, Jeff Bova, Rick Brennan, Michael Campbell, Deborah Cooper, Vince Henry and Toby Johnson. They scored their first hit with *A Lover's Holiday* (USA#40; UK#14.1980), it was followed by *Searching* (UK#11.1980), which featured Luther VANDROSS as lead vocalist. In 1982 they released the LP *Sharing Your Love*, which featured the single, *Very Best in You*.

Despite the fact that their singles always fared well on the black charts, they didn't pick up again until 1984, when they were teamed with producers Jimmy JAM & Terry Lewis for the LP, *Change Of Heart* (UK#34.1984), which included the singles *Change of Heart* (UK#17.1984) and *You Are My Melody* (UK#48.1984), and was the first recording by the recently recruited lead vocalist James Robinson. In 1985 they scored again with the LP *Turn on the Radio* (UK#39.1985), which featured the singles *Let's Go Together* (UK#37.1985), *Oh What A Feeling* (UK#56.1985) and *Mutual Attraction* (UK#60.1985). Since the mid-1980s, the group has shown little inclination to make its presence felt.

SHARING YOUR LOVE, London, 1982
CHANGE OF HEART, WEA, 1984
TURN ON THE RADIO, Chrysalis, 1985

CHANTELS The significant thing about The Chantels was that they were one of the first all-girl groups to write most of their own material, using doo-wop groups like The Cadillacs and Otis WILLIAMS & The Charms as role models. The group was formed in New York in 1956 and comprised Arlene Smith, Sonia Goring, Jackie Landry and Rene Minus. They were signed by Richard BARRETT to the End label, where they recorded a number of singles including *He's Gone, Maybe* (USA#15.1958) and *Every Night (I Pray)* (USA#39.1958). In 1959, Arlene Smith left to be replaced by Annette Smith from The Veneers. The group changed labels, moving to Carlton, while retaining Barrett as producer. *Look in My Eyes* (USA#14.1961) and *Well I Told You* (USA#29.1961) were their final hits. Arlene Smith launched out on her own, signing with the Big Top label, where she worked with Phil SPECTOR; despite her considerable prowess as a writer and arranger, her solo career never took off. Since then she has been teaching in a primary school in New York and performing in aid of under-privileged children.

THE CHANTELS, End, 1979

CHARLES, RAY The career of Raymond Charles Robinson is inextricably interwoven with the beginnings of soul music. He was born in Albany, Georgia, on September 23,

1930. When he was seven he contracted glaucoma and became blind; he was sent to study piano and clarinet at the Deaf and Blind School in Florida. By the time he was sixteen he was earning his living playing in various bands in and around Florida. In 1948, he moved to Seattle, where his next-door neighbour was Quincy JONES, and formed The Maxim Trio with guitarist G. D. McGhee and bassist Milton Gerred. In 1949, they signed with Downbeat Records, who releasd his first published composition, *Confession Blues*; the same year he changed his name to Ray Charles, while Downbeat changed their name to Swingtime. With Swingtime, he released a spate of singles, most of which were covers of standards and blues classics, but they were good enough to persuade the owners of Atlantic – Herb ABRAMSON and Ahmet ERTEGUN – to buy out his contract from Swingtime for $2,500 in 1952.

Overnight, the emphasis in his repertoire changed from a jazz-tinged flavour to a much harder R&B Sound. One of the earliest recordings was *Mess Around*, written by Ahmet Ertegun, which has since become a classic of the genre. In 1954 he notched up his first hit single, *It Should Have Been Me*; it went to #7 in the R&B charts. It was followed by a string of R&B hits over the next three years including *I've Got A Woman* and *Hallelujah! I Love Her So*. In 1957 his first LP, *Ray Charles*, was released; it was followed in November by his first major hit, *Swanee River Rockin' (Talkin' 'Bout that River)* (USA#34.1957). The next year he appeared at the Newport Jazz Festival, and his performance was recorded and released on an LP, *Ray Charles at Newport*. Then came the release of *What'd I Say* (USA#6.1959), which has become synonymous with Charles and been covered by a variety of artists. In 1959, he signed a three-year contract with ABC- Paramount, although Atlantic retained the rights to his recordings, which enabled them to reissue his material at whim, most notably the two LPs, *The Genius of Ray Charles* (USA#17.1960) and *Ray Charles in Person* (USA#13.1960).

The only reason he recorded *Georgia On My Mind* (USA#1; UK#24.1960) was because his chauffeur was always singing it. The LP, *The Genius Hits the Road* (USA#9.1960) was his first for ABC; all the song titles related to place names in the USA. In 1961 he won four Grammy Awards; in May the LP *Genius + Soul = Jazz* (USA#4.1961) was released and contained the single *One Mint Julep* (USA #8.1961): the arrangements had been written by Quincy Jones. The LP gave a clear indication that while he was happy playing soul, he certainly intended to keep alive the traditions of the big band sound that were just as much a part of his musical heritage as anything else. In September he released *Hit the Road Jack* (USA#1; UK#6.1961), written by Percy MAYFIELD. The following year he sparked considerable controversy by recording the LP *Modern Sounds in Country & Western* (USA#1; UK #6.1962), which included two singles, *I Can't Stop Loving You* (USA/UK#1.1962) and *You Don't Know Me* (USA#2; UK#9.1962). The sequel, *Modern Sounds in Country & Western, Volume 2* (USA#2; UK#15.1963), spawned a pair of hit singles: *Your Cheating Heart* (USA#29; UK#13.1963) and *Take these Chains from my Heart* (USA#8; UK#5.1963).These two LPs highlighted his strong associations with and affection for country music.

In March 1962 he set up his own record label, Tangerine, and in March 1963 he opened the offices and studios in Los Angeles: it was another typical gesture of independence, consolidating his position as a member of the black community who was not going to be subjugated by the predominantly white-owned music business. The release of the LP *Ingredients In A Recipe For Soul* (USA#2.1963) gave him yet another hit single, *Busted* (USA#4;

UK#21.1963), which won a Grammy the following year for Best R&B Record. His final top-ten LP, *Sweet And Sour Tears* (USA #9.1964), produced a couple of minor hits but lacked the verve and imagination of his earlier records. In recent years his records have been marred all too often by an apparent lack of interest or by indifferent material. Every so often, however, he has released an LP – like *The Volcanic Action of my Soul* in 1971 – which has recaptured some of the visceral energy of the Atlantic material. Latterly, his better performances have been in supporting roles: a duet with Aretha FRANKLIN at the Fillmore West in 1971; the recording of George Gershwin's *Porgy & Bess* with Cleo Laine in 1976 for RCA; his performance in the USA for Africa record, *We are the World*, in 1985; in the same year, an LP, *Friendship*, featured him duetting with a different country artist on each track; in 1989, a contribution to the Quincy Jones LP, *Back on the Block*. All these outings show him at his most imaginative and powerful; however, such is his charisma that he could probably set a railway timetable to music and it would be worth listening to. His status as a "living legend" has enabled him to mine a rich vein in cameo roles for both film and television.

SOUL MEETING, (with Milt Jackson), Atlantic, 1959
GENIUS + SOUL = JAZZ, Castle, 1961
COME LIVE WITH ME, London, 1974
TRUE TO LIFE, London, 1978
EVERYTHING, President, 1980
RAY OF HOPE, President, 1980
SIMPLY RAY, President, 1980
IF I GIVE YOU MY LOVE, Polydor, 1982
20 GOLDEN PIECES, Bulldog, 1982
HERE I AM, Barclay (France), 1983
WHAT IS LIFE, Barclay (France), 1983
DO I EVER CROSS YOUR MIND, CBS, 1984
FRIENDSHIP, CBS, 1984
GOIN' DOWN SLOW, Magnum, 1984
RAY CHARLES BLUES, Astan, 1984

SEE SEE RIDER, CBS, 1984
CAN'T STOP LOVING YOU, Platinum (W.Germany), 1985
THE FANTASTIC RAY CHARLES, Musidisc (France), 1985
HIT THE ROAD JACK, Platinum (W.Germany), 1985
RAY CHARLES COLLECTION, Deja Vu, 1985
THE SPIRIT OF CHRISTMAS, CBS, 1985
THE COUNTRY SIDE OF RAY CHARLES, Arcade, 1986
FROM THE PAGES OF MY MIND, CBS, 1986
THE RIGHT TIME, Atlantic, 1987
JUST BETWEEN US, CBS, 1988
THE COLLECTION, Castle, 1990.

CHARMS   See WILLIAMS, Otis

CHASE, LINCOLN   See ELLIS, Shirley

CHECKER, CHUBBY   Ernest Evans was born in South Carolina on October 3, 1941. On the strength of his impressions of artists like LITTLE RICHARD he was signed to the Cameo-Parkway label in 1958, following an introduction to the owner Kal Mann. His name was changed to Chubby Checker at the suggestion of Bobby Clark, the wife of the host of the TV show, *American Bandstand*, Dick Clark; she thought that he bore a marked resemblance to Fats DOMINO, and thus "Fats" became "Chubby" and "Domino" became "Checker". His first record, *The Class* (USA#38.1959), was followed by his version of the Hank BALLARD composition, *The Twist* (USA#1.1960/#1.1961; UK#44.1960/#14.1962/ #5.1975); when this record and the twist were first featured on *American Bandstand*, a wave of enthusiasm for new dances surged across the country.

Over the next five years Checker recorded a series of dance-inspired tracks for Parkway: *Pony Time* (USA#1; UK#27.1961), *Let's Twist Again* (USA#8; UK#2.1961/#5.1975), *The Fly* (USA#7.1961), *Slow Twistin'* , a duet with Dee Dee SHARP (USA#3; UK#23.1962), *Limbo Rock* (USA#2; UK#32.1962), *Popeye the Hitchhiker* (USA#10.1962) and *Do the Freddie* (USA#40.1965). In 1966 he parted company with Parkway, and remained silent for the next three years until he signed with Buddah in 1969. However, he was unable to revive his flagging career even though he had by now become a fixture on the oldies circuit. His status was temporarily revived by renewed interest in *The Twist* in discotheques in 1975; and again in 1988 when he re-recorded *The Twist (Yo Twist)* (UK#2.1988) with The Fat Boys, which was followed by an appearance at the Nelson Mandela Concert in London in 1988.

LET'S TWIST AGAIN, K-Tel, 1983
THE BEST OF CHUBBY CHECKER, Creole, 1984
16 GREATEST HITS, Bescol, 1987
GREATEST HITS, K-Tel, 1987

CHESS, LEONARD In 1947, Leonard and Phil Chess set up Aristocrat Records. Polish immigrants, they had arrived in Chicago in 1938, and by the early 1940s had established a network of clubs and bars; the main attraction was the Mocamba Club, which regularly featured artists like Ella Fitzgerald and Billy Eckstine. Establishing their own record label was a logical progression for them. The first record, *I Can't Be Satisfied* by Muddy Waters, was an R&B hit, and for the next three years they recorded predominantly local artists. In 1950, they placed an announcement in Billboard saying that they were forming a new label, Chess, that all of their existing artists under contract would be recording for

the label, and that they would also be looking for fresh talent. During the 1950s, they set about building a roster of artists that changed the face of contemporary music: Chuck BERRY, Bo DIDDLEY, Buddy Guy, Howlin' Wolf, Etta JAMES, LITTLE MILTON, Little Walter, The Moonglows (See FUQUA, Harvey) and Sonny Boy Williamson. Although, most of the records credited Leonard Chess as the producer, the man who was inspirational to the records the company released was bassist and songwriter Willie Dixon.

As styles and tastes became more sophisticated with the dawning of the 1960s, Chess rather lost its way, failing to appreciate the impact of Motown and Stax until Marshall Chess took over in the mid-1960s and the arrival of house producer Cash McCall. After the release of *Rescue Me* by Fontella BASS they sent contract artists like Laura LEE, Etta James and Irma THOMAS to the Fame Studios in Muscle Shoals in 1967. However, before Rick HALL's team could complete the transformation, Leonard Chess died of a heart attack. Phil promptly sold the label to GRT, manufacturers of pre-recorded tape. By the mid-1970s, GRT had run into financial difficulties and in 1985, MCA acquired the Chess catalogue.

CHIC The nucleus of Chic was formed in 1972 by guitarist Nile RODGERS and bassist Bernard EDWARDS. They had met at odd intervals since 1970 in various New York clubs and had started to play together. They added drummer Tony Thompson and became The Big Apple Trio; initially they toured the clubs backing artists like New York City and Carol Douglas. In 1976, Norma Jean Wright joined as lead singer. The following year, they changed their name to Chic and produced a number of demos in a bid to obtain a recording contract. In September, 1977, they signed with Atlantic.

In 1978 their first record, *Dance, Dance, Dance (Yowsah, Yowsah, Yowsah)* (USA/UK #6.1978) was an immediate hit; the parenthetic "Yowsah, Yowsah, Yowsah" was latched upon by DJs throughout the world became a sort of disco war-cry. The debut LP, *Chic* (USA #27.1978) showed that they were not just one-hit wonders capitalising upon the disco-boom. Wright left the group, being replaced by Alfa Anderson and Luci Martin. The follow-up single, *Everybody Dance* (USA#38; UK #9.1978), lost a lot of its impact through its inclusion on the debut LP. In December, they released *Le Freak* (USA#1.1978; UK#7.1979). The LP, *C'est Chic* (USA#4; UK#2.1979), included *Le Freak* as well as another hit single, *I Want Your Love* (USA#7; UK#4.1979). With their success, Edwards and Rodgers were becoming highly sought-after as producers, calling themselves the Chic Organization. Their next record was *Good Times* (USA#1; UK#5.1979), and such was its influence that it became a blueprint for the constituents of a good dance record; it was taken from the LP, *Risque* (USA#5; UK#29.1979), as were *My Forbidden Lover* (USA#43; UK#15.1979) and *My Feet Keep Dancing* (UK#21.1980). From the beginning of the 1980s, the star of Chic went into decline and by 1983, they had gone their separate ways although the production arm of The Chic Organization continued to flourish for a period of time.

GREATEST HITS, Atlantic 1979
GREATEST HITS, (with Sister Sledge), Telstar, 1987
MEGACHIC, Atlantic, 1990

CHIFFONS The Chiffons comprised Judy Craig, Barbara Lee, Patricia Bennett and Sylvia Peterson. They came together in New York in 1960 while they were still at school. After meeting Ronnie Mack, a local musician and songwriter, they began to sing some of his songs for a demo. He sold one of the songs, *Tonight's the Night* (USA#76.1960), to the Big Deal label, who turned it into a minor hit. Eventually, Mack succeeded in persuading The Tokens, who had opened their own production company, Bright Tunes, to sign both himself and The Chiffons. The first product of this deal was *He's So Fine* (USA#1; UK#16.1963), featuring The Tokens as the backing group; although it was turned down by Capitol it was snapped up by the independent Laurie label. However, later the same year, Mack died of Hodgkinson's disease. The follow-up, *One Fine Day* (USA#5; UK #29.1963), was written by GOFFIN & KING and featured LITTLE EVA, however The Tokens erased Little Eva's vocal part and substituted The Chiffons. It was their final major hit for three years, despite recording briefly for the Rust label as The Four Pennies.

In 1964, the group sued The Tokens to extricate themselves from their contract with Bright Tunes and, after shopping around, re-signed with Laurie. Their final hit, *Sweet Talking Guy* (USA#10; UK#31. 1966/#3.1972), gave them a brief further lease of life. Since 1966 the group has continued to tour on the oldies circuit, although Judy Craig left in 1969. In 1976, they recorded *My Sweet Lord*, the George Harrison song in which he had subconsciously plagiarised their 1963 hit, *One Fine Day*. However their version sank without trace.

EVERYTHING YOU WANTED TO HEAR BUT COULDN'T GET, Laurie, 1984
DOO-LANG DOO-LANG DOO-LANG, Ace, 1985
FLIPS, FLOPS AND RARITIES, Ace, 1986
GREATEST RECORDINGS, Ace, 1990

CHI-LITES The Chi-Lites comprised Eugene Record, Marshall Thompson, Robert

Lester, Creadel Jones and Clarence Johnson. The group were formed in Chicago in 1960 as The Hi-Lites. A rival group claimed origination of the name and threatened legal action if they didn't change it, so they added a c as a prefix.

They did not achieve any measurable success until 1969, when they signed with the Brunswick label and had a minor hit with *Give it Away* (USA#88.1969). The song had been written by Record, who had established himself as the group's leader and started a songwriting partnership with fellow Brunswick artist and future wife, Barbara ACKLIN. Major success continued to elude them until the release of *(For God's Sake) Give More Power to the People* (USA#26; UK#32.1971); the LP of the same name (USA#12.1971) consolidated their success. The follow-up was *Have You Seen Her* (USA/UK#3.1972), a slow part-spoken, part-sung narrative that teetered on the brink of banality without ever quite toppling over it. In the same year, they scored with *Oh Girl* (USA#1; UK#14.1972) and the LP *A Lonely Man* (USA#5.1972), which established them as arch- exponents of soft-soul. They were unable to sustain their winning form in the USA, but in the UK they continued to notch up hits with considerable frequency: *Homely Girl* (UK#5.1974), *Too Good to be Forgotten* (UK#10.1974), *It's Time for Love* (UK #5.1975) and *You Don't Have to Go* (UK#3.1976).

Record, though, was disappointed with their sales in the USA and left the group to pursue a solo career; the rest attempted to carry on without him by signing a fresh contract with Mercury, but their records were all commercial failures. Record, who had retained an executive role at Brunswick, signed a solo contract with Warner Bros. in 1979. An LP, *Welcome to my Fantasy* , was his only release apart from a single, *Magnetism*; both were moderately successful in the disco market. In 1980 Record re-formed The Chi-Lites and set up the Chi-Sound label, enlisting the services of Gene CHANDLER as vice-president. Since then they have toured and recorded frequently enough to satisfy their deeply loyal band of followers, particularly in the UK, but they have been unable to recapture their glory of the mid-1970s.

HEAVENLY BODY, 20th Century, 1980
ME AND YOU, 20th Century, 1981
CHANGING FOR YOU, Red Bus, 1983
CHI-LITES CLASSICS, SMP, 1983
20 GOLDEN PIECES: THE CHI-LITES, Bulldog, 1984
BEST OF THE CHI-LITES, Kent, 1987

CHIMES The Chimes' versatility has established them, after only one LP, *The Chimes*, as one of the brighter prospects of the 1990s. The group was formed by James Locke and Michael Paden, who had both worked with Bernie Worrell from George CLINTON's Parliament, and they recruited vocalist Pauline Henry, whose reading of the U2 composition, *I Still Haven't Found What I'm Looking For* (UK #6.1990) gave them their first major hit. However, their adaptability lies in their ability to combine the traditional styles of soul with the values of deep house, as in *1-2-3* and *Underestimate*, which were produced by Nellee Hooper and Jazzie B of SOUL II SOUL.

THE CHIMES, CBS, 1990

CLARENCE AND CALVIN See CARTER, Clarence

CLARK, DEE Delecta Clark was born in Blythville, Arkansas, on July 11, 1938. After moving to Chicago he performed on the Red

Saunders hit, *Hambone*, in 1952. This resulted in the formation of the gospel group The Hambone Kids, who were signed to the Okeh label. However, he was quickly encouraged to leave gospel for R&B, when he was asked to join The Goldentones and then The Kool Gents. His career prospered with neither group, until Ewart ABNER gave him the chance to record as a solo artist. After signing with the Veejay subsidiary, Abner, he notched up a string of hits that included *Nobody but You* (USA #21.1959), *Just Keep it Up* (USA#18; UK #26.1959), *Hey Little Girl* (USA#20.1959) and *How About That* (USA#33.1960). In 1961, he was moved onto the main Veejay label, where he continued his run of hits with *Your Friends* (USA#34.1961) and *Raindrops* (USA#2.1961). The changes in musical tastes left him high and dry and, by the time Veejay had gone out of business, he had slipped into obscurity sustained only by touring, playing US Airforce bases throughout the world. He re-emerged in 1975 with a disco hit in the UK, *Ride a Wild Horse* (UK#16.1975), it proved to be a temporary respite, as his career slipped back into the doldrums.

CLARKE, STANLEY See DUKE, George

CLAUNCH, QUINTON Quinton Claunch was born in Tishomingo, Mississippi, in 1922. In the 1940s he was a guitarist in a country group, that included Bill Cantrell and Dexter Johnson. After obtaining a slot on Sam Phillips' afternoon show for the radio station WLAY, they were invited to record some tracks for the fledgling Hi label. This involvement with Hi galvanised Claunch into forming his own label, Goldwax, in the second half of 1963 with his erstwhile partner and co-producer "Doc" Russell, who put up some money.

Although the label lasted only until 1970, during that time it issued a series of records by artists like James CARR, The Ovations and Spencer Wiggins, as well as one-offs by artists like O. V. WRIGHT. Through his connection with Sam Phillips most of the Goldwax tracks were cut at his studio on Madison Avenue, with Stan KESLER engineering or at the Hi studios with Kesler or Chips MOMAN; the backing band, assembled by Moman as the house band at his own neighbouring American Studios, consisted of Reggie Young (guitar), Tommy COGBILL (bass), Bobby Emmons (keyboards) and Gene Chrisman (drums). Since the end of Goldwax, Claunch has remained peripherally involved in the music business, but with little actual success other than an Al GREEN LP, *Precious Lord*, which he co-produced with Bill Cantrell.

CLAY, JUDY See BELL, William

CLAY, OTIS Otis Clay was born and brought up in Gunnerson, Mississippi. When his family moved to Muncie, Indiana, he formed a gospel group, The Morning Glories. In 1957, having sung with an assortment of gospel groups, he settled in Chicago, where he eventually joined another, The Sensational Nightingales. In 1963 he made the quantum leap from gospel to R&B and signed with the One-Der-Ful label, and then with Cotillion, Dakar and Hi.

During his tenure at Hi, under the watchful eye of Willie MITCHELL, he recorded a bunch of tracks like *Trying to Live my Life without You* and *Home is Where the Heart Is*, that established his reputation as one of the better journeyman Southern soul singers.

When Mitchell sold Hi in 1980, Clay concentrated on touring and became one of the first signings to Mitchell's new label, Waylo. In 1985 he recorded the LP *Live in Japan*, which was followed by the studio LPs, *The Only Way is Up* and *Watch Me Now*.

LIVE IN JAPAN, Blue Sting, 1985
TRYING TO LIVE MY LIFE WITHOUT YOU, Hi, 1987
THE ONLY WAY IS UP, Waylo, 1988
WATCH ME NOW, Waylo, 1989

CLINTON, GEORGE George Clinton was born in Plainfield, New Jersey on July 22, 1940. He formed his first version of The Parliaments in 1955 as a doo-wop vocal group. Their first single *Poor Willie*, released by ABC in 1956, failed to attract much attention. After a two-year hiatus they released their second single on the local label, New; like its predecessor, *Lonely Island* failed to cause any waves in the charts. In 1959 Clinton uprooted the group and moved to Detroit, where they auditioned for Motown and recorded several tracks for them, but nothing was ever released. For the next six years, they played the clubs in and around Detroit. In 1965, they released *My Girl* on another small independent label, Golden World; yet again the single was a commercial failure. At last, in 1967, The Parliaments broke through with *(I Wanna) Testify* (USA #20.1967). It was followed by four more singles, all of which failed to chart.

In 1969 Clinton temporarily lost the right to use the name The Parliaments as a result of a contract he had signed with Motown and the Invictus label, which was owned by former Motown employees, HOLLAND, DOZIER & HOLLAND. Clinton's reaction was to change the name of the group to Funkadelic and sign a contract with Westbound Records. It was the beginning of an empire that Clinton had been gradually building ever since he had arrived in Detroit, and which was to become comparable in size to that of James BROWN's operation. In 1970, having regained the rights to the name The Parliaments, he changed it to Parliament and signed up with Invictus; their first LP was *Osmium*. Later the same year, keyboardist Bernie Worrell joined the Parliament-Funkadelic combine; other recruits included former JBs bassist BOOTSY in 1972 and guitarist Gary Shider in 1973. In 1974, Clinton signed a contract for Parliament with Casablanca, Invictus having gone out of business, and in 1976 the group released the LP *Mothership Connection* (USA#13.1976), which included the single, *Tear the Roof off the Sucker (Give up the Funk)* (USA#15.1976). The follow-up LP, *The Clones of Dr Funkenstein* (USA#20.1976), consolidated his reputation still further as one of the most experimental exponents of funk. Throughout, Clinton used Parliament-Funkadelic as an umbrella, encouraging various units within the organization to pursue solo projects: the horn section, known as The Horny Horns, which included in its lineup Fred Wesley, Maceo Parker, Rick Gardner and Richard Griffith; Bootsy and his group Rubber Band; the vocalists, Parlet & The Brides of Dr Funkenstein – all recorded solo projects with varying degrees of success. Clinton's practice has been emulated in recent years by PRINCE, who has groomed many young artists in much the same way.

In 1977, Parliament's LP *Funkentelechy vs. the Placebo Syndrome* (USA#13.1977) was released; it contained the single *Flash Light* (USA#16.1978). Clinton signed Funkadelic to Warner Bros., for whom the first LP *One Nation Under a Groove* (USA#16; UK #56.1978) provided them with the long-awaited breakthrough in the UK, when the title track (USA#28; UK#9.1978) was released as a single; this one LP has subsequently become one of the key records of the era. In 1980, Clinton became embroiled once again in a series of legal wrangles with various record companies, and so he was unable to use the names Parliament or Funkadelic. The following year, he collaborated with Sly Stone (see SLY & THE FAMILY STONE) on the Funkadelic LP *The Electric Spanking of War Babies*. In 1982, he signed another contract as a solo artist with Capitol; his first LP for them, *Computer Games* (USA#40; UK#57.1982), included the single *Atomic Dog*, which was a major club hit in both the USA and the UK. In 1984, he released the LP *You Shouldn't Nuff Bit, Fish*; it was followed by another LP in 1985, *Some of my Best Friends are Jokes*, and in 1989 he released *The Cinderella Theory* on Paisley Park, Prince's label.

Clinton's dogged disregard for the orthodox has enabled him to remain close to the top of tree. In the process he has carved out a unique niche for himself and influenced a generation of artists, not only musically, but also in the way he has provided an object lesson in how to deal with record companies.

FUNKADELIC, Westbound, 1970
FREE YOUR MIND.... , (Funkadelic), Westbound, 1971
AMERICA EATS ITS YOUNG, (Funkadelic), Westbound, 1972
COSMIC SLOP, (Funkadelic), Westbound, 1973
MOTHERSHIP CONNECTION, (Parliament), Casablanca, 1976
THE CLONES OF DR FUNKENSTEIN, (Parliament), Casablanca, 1976
MOTOR BOOTY AFFAIR, (Parliament), Casablanca, 1978
HARDCORE JOLLIES, (Funkadelic), Warner Bros., 1978
GLORYHALLASTOOPID, (Parliament), Casablanca, 1980
TROMBIPULATION, (Parliament), Casablanca, 1981
COMPUTER GAMES, Capitol, 1982
SOME OF MY BEST JOKES ARE FRIENDS, Capitol, 1985

UNCUT FUNK-THE BOMB: THE BEST OF PARLIAMENT, Club, 1986
THE CINDERELLA THEORY, Paisley Park, 1989

CLOVERS The Clovers were one of the most influential of all the early signings to the Atlantic label, insofar as they helped to establish the R&B vocal group as a highly commercial medium of expression. The group was scouted by Lou Krefetz in 1949 in Washington; the nucleus was formed by Charles White and John Bailey, who hired additional members as necessary, including Bill Harris, Harold Lucas, Billy Mitchell, Harold Winley and Thomas Woods. After initially recording for the Rainbow label, they were signed by Ahmet ERTEGUN to Atlantic. Over the next ten years their idiosyncratic synthesis of R&B and gospel provided them with a string of hits including *Don't You Know I Love You, One Mint Julep, Ting-a-Ling, Good Lovin', Little Mama, Your Cash Ain't Nothing but Trash, Blue Velvet, Devil or Angel, Love, Love, Love* (USA #30.1956) and *Love Potion #9* (USA#23.1959). It was measure of their influence that white artists like Kay Starr, Bobby Vee and Bobby Vinton covered their material and got bigger hits – indeed, as recently as 1990 Bobby Vinton scored yet again with his version of *Blue Velvet*. Their final – and biggest national- hit, *Love Potion #9* , was their first for United Artists. As their style of delivery slipped out of vogue they split up, only to reform some years later for the benefit of the oldies circuit. It is highly debatable as to how many members of the re-formed versions of the group had any entitlement to the name.

FIVE COOL CATS, Edsel, 1986

CLOWNS See SMITH, Huey "Piano"

COASTERS In 1949 The Robins were formed in Los Angeles by Johnny OTIS. Having seen the potential of vocal groups, Otis added the bass voice of Bobby Nunn (born in Birmingham, Alabama, in 1925) to The A Sharp Trio, which included Carl Gardner (born in Tyler, Texas, on April 29, 1928) in its line-up. Over the next two years the group recorded titles like *If it's so Baby* and *Double Crossin' Blues*, until in 1951 they teamed up with LEIBER & STOLLER, recording titles like *That's What the Good Book Says, Riot in Cell Block #9* and *Smokey Joe's Cafe*. Their style was to become the blueprint for the later success of The Coasters.

The Coasters were formed in 1956 when Gardner and Nunn left The Robins. They recruited Leon Hughes and Billy Guy (born in Attasca, Texas, on June 20, 1936). Hughes did not last long and was replaced by Young Jessie in 1957. After moving to New York, Jessie and Nunn were replaced by Cornel Gunter (born in Los Angeles on November 14, 1938) and Will Jones, respectively. They had been signed to the Atlantic subsidiary, Atco, following a production deal with Leiber & Stoller. From 1957, under the auspices of Leiber & Stoller, they notched up a whole string of hits: *Searchin'* (USA#3; UK#30.1957), *Young blood* (USA #8.1957), *Yakety Yak* (USA#1; UK#12.1958), *Charlie Brown* (USA#2; UK#6.1959), *Along Came Jones* (USA#9.1959), *Poison Ivy* (USA#7; UK#15.1959) and *Little Egypt* (USA#23.1961). While some of their records were regarded as novelty songs, there can be little doubt that their success lay in Leiber & Stoller's ability to get straight to the heart of black American music by utilising the vernacular of the streets in their lyrics.

By the end of 1961 their major chart successes were behind them, mainly because Leiber & Stoller were in considerable demand and had little time to spend with the group. In 1967, they signed with CBS subsidiary, Date, where they had a couple of minor hits. Since then they have had no chart success, although they have become fixtures on the oldies circuit and performed at the Atlantic 40th Anniversary Birthday Concert in 1988. On February 26, 1990, Gunter was found shot dead in his car in Las Vegas; he was 51.This was the second time a member of the group had been murdered: in 1980 an erstwhile member, Nathaniel Wilson, was found dead in California, his body dismembered.

20 GREAT ORIGINALS, Atlantic, 1978
JUKE BOX GIANTS, Audio Fidelity, 1982
THUMBING A RIDE, Edsel, 1985
WHAT IS THE SECRET OF YOUR SUCCESS?, Mr R&B, 1991

COGBILL, TOMMY Tommy Cogbill was raised in Memphis and became bassist in Bill Black's Combo, the group formed by Elvis Presley's former bassist. After Chips MOMAN left Stax in 1962, Cogbill was enlisted as part of the house-band at the embryonic American studios. In 1966, Moman and Cogbill were recruited by Jerry WEXLER to play on the Aretha FRANKLIN sessions at Muscle Shoals. As a result Cogbill was hired to do more sessions for Atlantic, with artists like Wilson PICKETT and KING CURTIS. Furthermore, Quinton CLAUNCH used him on most of the Goldwax sessions, featuring James CARR and O.V. WRIGHT Throughout, he continued to be involved with Moman's American Studios, playing on a host of sessions not just by soul singers but also by pop artists like Sam the Sham and The Box Tops. 1n 1972 he produced the comeback LP by Arthur ALEXANDER and in the following year he participated in the final LP by Ivory Joe HUNTER, which was recorded in Nashville, where Cogbill continued to work until his death in 1983.

COLE, NATALIE Natalie Cole was born in Los Angeles on February 6, 1950, the second daughter of pianist Nat 'King' Cole, with whom she made her debut in 1962. Before becoming a professional performer she obtained a degree in child psychology at the University of Massachusetts in 1972, supplementing her income at college by singing in clubs. After meeting the Canadian promoter Kevin Hunter (who was to become her manager), she began to get work on TV and at larger venues and as a result was approached by Chuck JACKSON and Marvin Yancy (her future husband), who wanted her to cut an LP. It was recorded at Curtis MAYFIELD's Curtom studios and, after it had been rejected by a number of companies, Capitol picked it up. The LP, *Inseparable* (USA#18.1975), provided her with the hit single *This Will Be* (USA#6; UK#32.1975), and the following year she won two Grammies for Best New Artist and Best R&B Vocalist. In 1976 the follow-up LP *Natalie* (USA#13.1976) was released; it included the single *Sophisticated Lady* (USA #25.1976), for which she won another Grammy, this time for Best R&B Vocal Performance. Her next two LPs were *Unpredictable* (USA#8.1977), which contained *I've Got Love on my Mind* (USA#5.1977), and *Thankful* (USA#16.1977). In 1978, she released a double live LP, *Natalie.....Live!* (USA#31.1978), which was to be her last commercially successful LP for almost ten years.

During this decade-long hiatus she participated in duets with Peabo BRYSON on the LP *We're the Best Of Friends* in 1980 and with Johnnny Mathis on the LP *Unforgettable: A Tribute to Nat "King" Cole* in 1983. In 1982 she moved from Capitol to Epic and, in 1985 she signed with the Modern label. The LP *Dangerous* failed to make any waves, peaking at #140. In September 1986 she signed with the EMI subsidiary, Manhattan, and the ensuing LP, *Everlasting*, marked a return to hit-making

form with no fewer than four hit singles including *Jump Start* (USA#13; UK#36.1987), *Pink Cadillac* (USA/UK#5.1988), *Everlasting* (UK #28.1988) and *I Live For Your Love* (USA#13; UK#34.1988). Part of the success of the LP can be attibuted to her appearance in June 1988 at the Nelson Mandela Concert in London, which had the effect of galvanizing record sales throughout the UK, but also her choice of material represented a great improvement on her previous outings. The next LP *Good to be Back* teamed her up once again with the writers and producers, Dennis LAMBERT and Narada Michael WALDEN, both of whom had contributed to her previous effort. The LP provided her with her biggest hit to date, *Miss You Like Crazy* (USA#3; UK#2.1989).

Although, her records have always been aimed at the MOR market, her phrasing and timing have managed to transcend the ordinariness of much of her material. While she will probably never become a soul singer with gut-wrenching capabilities, she will certainly continue to outdistance most of her contemporaries through her sheer professionalism and verve.

THANKFUL, Capitol, 1978
NATALIE ...LIVE!, Capitol, 1978
I'M READY, Epic, 1982
THE UNFORGETTABLE: A TRIBUTE TO NAT "KING" COLE, (with Johnny Mathis), Epic, 1983
EVERLASTING, Manhattan, 1987
GOOD TO BE BACK, Manhattan, 1989

COLLIER, MITTY Mitty Collier was born in Birmingham, Alabama. After being signed to Chess in 1961, she recorded a string of singles up until 1968, when she was dropped by the label. Why she never achieved any degree of lasting success is a mystery. The LP *Shades of a Genius*, which collected her singles, contained some fine examples of soul singing in the gospel tradition with songs like *I Had A Talk With My Man Last Night*, *No Faith, No Love* and *Got to Get Away from it All*. The expiry of her contract pushed her into obscurity, where she has remained ever since, despite the high regard in which she is held by serious soul buffs.

SHADES OF A GENIUS, Chess, 1988

COLLINS, LYNN   See BROWN, James

COLLINS, WILLIAM   See BOOTSY

COMMODORES The Commodores came together in 1967 in Tuskegee, Alabama, as the result of the merging of two groups, The Mighty Mystics and The Jays. By 1971, the line-up of the group was established: Lionel RICHIE (vocals and keyboards), William King (trumpet); Thomas McClary (guitar); Milan Williams (keyboards, trombone and drums); Ronald LaPraed (bass) and Walter Orange (vocals and drums). They were spotted performing by the creative vice- president of Motown, Suzanne De Passe, at the Turntable Club in New York, and they were immediately signed to Motown. They continued to tour for the next three years, honing their act. In 1974 they recorded the instrumental *Machine Gun* (USA#22; UK#20.1974), which has subsequently become a classic of the genre. They consolidated this success with the follow-up, *The Zoo (Human Zoo)* (UK#44.1974).

Over the next seven years they had a string of hits: *Slippery When Wet* (USA#19.1975), *Sweet Love* (USA#5.1976; UK#32.1977), *Just to be Close to You* (USA#7.1976; UK#62.1978), *Easy* (USA#4; UK#9.1977), *Brick House* (USA#5; UK#32.1977), *Three Times a Lady* (USA/UK #1.1978), *Sail On* (USA#4; UK#8.1979), *Still*

(USA#1; UK#4.1979), *Lady (You Bring me Up)* (USA#8; UK#56.1981) and *Oh No* (USA#4; UK#44.1981). If their singles were models of consistency, their LPs were equally successful: *Commodores* (USA#3.1977), *Live!* (USA#3; UK#60.1977), *Natural High* (USA#3; UK#8.1978), *Midnight Magic* (USA#3; UK #15.1979), *Heroes* (USA#7; UK#50.1980) and *In the Pocket* (USA#13; UK#69.1981). It was this consistency that enabled them to become one of the biggest draws on the US and European concert circuit. In 1982 Lionel Richie, who had been largely responsible for the group's image through writing most of their biggest hits left to pursue a solo career. On August 17, 1982, their manager, Benny Ashburn, died of a heart attack. In 1983, Thomas McClary left the group to start a solo career. In 1985, following a period of re-assessment and having recruited former HEATWAVE singer, J. D. Nicholas, they released *Nightshift* (USA/ UK#3.1985), written by Orange with producer Dennis LAMBERT as a tribute to Marvin GAYE and Jackie WILSON. It has become the one song that is most readily associated with The Commodores. The LP *Nightshift* (USA#12; UK#13.1985) proved that they were still a force to be reckoned with, despite Richie's absence. In 1986 they signed with Polydor, for whom their first single was *Goin' To The Bank* (USA#65; UK#43.1986). Although they have not been able to maintain the chart consistency of former years, their sheer professionalism as a touring group will continue to ensure them audience as long as they want one.

MACHINE GUN, Motown, 1974
CAUGHT IN THE ACT, Motown, 1975
MOVIN' ON, Motown, 1975
HOT ON THE TRACKS, Motown, 1976
ZOOM, Motown, 1977
LIVE!, Motown, 1978
NATURAL HIGH, Motown, 1978

MIDNIGHT MAGIC, Motown, 1979
HEROES, Motown, 1980
GREATEST HITS, Motown, 1981
IN THE POCKET, Motown, 1981
ALL THE GREATEST LOVE SONGS, Motown, 1982
LOVE SONGS, K-Tel, 1982
13, Motown, 1983
14 GREATEST HITS, Motown, 1984
NIGHTSHIFT, Motown, 1985
THE BEST OF THE COMMODORES, Telstar, 1985
UNITED, Polydor, 1986
ROCK SOLID, Polydor,1988

CONLEY, ARTHUR Arthur Conley was born in 1946 in Atlanta, Georgia. His career started in 1965, when he was discovered by Otis REDDING, who became his mentor and producer. After a number of flops, he recorded *Sweet Soul Music* (USA#2; UK#7.1967); plainly derivative of the Sam COOKE song, *Yeah Man*, it became an anthem of sorts for the growing body of Southern soul aficionados. Of course there were those who scoffed at it, but in the main it was perceived as a celebration of soul. After the death of Redding, Conley recorded *In the Same Old Way* and *(Take Me) Just as I Am* for the Fame label before signing with Atco, where he had a couple of hits: *Shake, Rattle and Roll* (USA#31.1967) and *Funky Street* (USA#14; UK#46.1968). He became Redding's replacement in the much-vaunted Soul Clan (see BURKE, Solomon). He recorded two LPs *Sweet Soul Music* (1967) and *Soul Directions* (1968), both of which were testaments to the moving spirits of his heroes, Redding and Cooke. In the early 1970s he recorded briefly for Phil WALDEN's Capricorn label, but none of his output could match the success of his earlier work. In recent years he has been a regular on the European club circuit.

CONTOURS To some critics the slickness of Berry GORDY's operation was a reason for dismissing much of the Motown product as soulless pop music, lacking in any real bite. The Contours disproved this theory out of hand: their lack of enduring popularity was due to the fact that their style was pure unadulterated R&B, comparable to anything that Wilson PICKETT was to record during the latter half of the 1960s.

They were formed in 1958 in Detroit and recommended to Gordy by Jackie WILSON, the cousin of founder member, Hubert Johnson, who had formed the group with Billy Gordon. Later incarnations of the group included Joe Stubbs, the brother of Levi Stubbs, lead singer of The FOUR TOPS, and Dennis EDWARDS, a future member of The TEMPTATIONS. After signing with the Gordy label, they recorded titles like *Do You Love Me* (USA#3.1962), *Shake Sherrie* (USA #43.1962), *Can You Jerk like Me, Baby Hit and Run, Just a Little Misunderstanding* (UK #31.1970) and *It's so Hard being a Loser*. However, their rough-hewn style proved to be too unsophisticated for most audiences, despite the fact that their records were powered by the omni-present house band, who contributed some of the most startling settings to emerge from Studio A. In 1968, the group disbanded, but reformed in 1987, following the inclusion of *Do You Love Me* on the film soundtrack *Dirty Dancing*.

COOKE, SAM Sam Cooke was born in Chicago on January 22, 1931. His career started in church when he was aged nine: he formed The Singing Children with two of his sisters and a brother. By 1950 he had become lead tenor of the celebrated gospel group The Soul Stirrers, who had a recording contract with Art RUPE's Specialty label. In 1956 Bumps BLACKWELL, the head of A&R at

Specialty, encouraged him to record some 'pop songs'. Initially he did so under the pseudonym of Dale Cook, so as to avoid offending his fervent gospel devotees, but he quickly reverted to plain Sam Cooke. In 1957, he recorded *You Send Me* (USA#1.1957; UK#29.1958), in which Blackwell added a white female chorus to broaden its appeal; Rupe was clearly unimpressed as he allowed them to pull out of their contracts and take the tape elsewhere. Eventually it was released on a small Los Angeles label, Keen; it sold over a million copies and was the first of eight consecutive hits for the label, including *(I Love You) For Sentimental Reasons* (USA#17.1958), *Only Sixteen* (USA#2; UK#23.1959) and *Wonderful World* (USA#12; UK#27.1960/#2.1986), the latter being written by Cooke, under his wife's name, Barbara Campbell, with Lou Adler and Herb Alpert.

Although these pop songs were distinguished by a lyrical purity and strongly oriented in the gospel tradition, the overt sentimentality of the lyrics were too much at odds with the image The Soul Stirrers wished to project and so, in 1958, they went their separate ways. Cooke, however, continued to exert a strong influence on the career of The Soul Stirrers both by selecting his own replacement, Johnnie TAYLOR, and by signing them to his own record label, Sar, which he started with J. W. ALEXANDER in 1961.

In 1960, his contract with Keen expired and he signed with RCA for a guaranteed $100,000. He was teamed with producers HUGO & LUIGI. He continued to notch up hits including *Chain Gang* (USA#2; UK#9.1960), *Cupid* (USA#17; UK#7.1961), *Twistin' the Night Away* (USA#9; UK#6.1962), *Bring it on Home to Me* (USA#13.1962), *Another Saturday Night* (USA#10; UK#23.1963), *Frankie and Johnny* (USA#14; UK#30.1963) and *Little Red Rooster* (USA#11.1963). Most of the songs that he recorded with Hugo & Luigi were lavishly orchestrated and overproduced, but he was always able to overcome the mawkish sentimentality of the material; in so doing he established a tradition for the "sweet soul ballad" that influenced artists like Otis REDDING, Al GREEN, Luther VANDROSS and Bob Marley, to name but a few.

On December 11, 1964, Cooke was shot and killed in Los Angeles by the manageress of the motel in which he was staying. His final hit, *Shake* (USA#7.1965), was released posthumously. The poignant B-side, *A Change is Gonna Come*, chronicled the changing attitude towards black people. Its evocativeness was not lost on Otis Redding, who recorded his own version months before his own death in 1967. Since Cooke's death, his reputation has continued to grow and, although James BROWN may well be the "Godfather Of Soul", Sam Cooke remains the archetypal "Soul Man".

TWISTIN THE NIGHT AWAY, CBS, 1962

MR SOUL, RCA International, 1963

LIVE AT HARLEM SQUARE, RCA, 1963

THE GOLDEN AGE, RCA, 1976

HIS GREATEST HITS, RCA, 1983

THE BEST OF SAM COOKE, RCA, 1983

THE FABULOUS SAM COOKE, Cambra, 1985

SOLITUDE, Cambra, 1985

THE MAN AND HIS MUSIC, RCA, 1986

SAM COOKE, Deja Vu, 1987

20 GREATEST HITS, Conifer, 1987

WHEN I FALL IN LOVE, Arena, 1987

SAM COOKE AND THE SOUL STIRRERS, Ace, 1990

COOKIES The Cookies were formed by Earl-Jean McCrae, Dorothy Jones and Margaret Ross. Initially they got work singing backing vocals for Aldon, the label owned by music publisher Don Kirshner. After the success of LITTLE EVA, songwriters GOFFIN

& KING wrote a number of hits for The Cookies: *Chains* (USA#17.1962; UK#50.1963), *Don't Say Nothin' Bad (about my Baby)* (USA #7.1963) and *Girls Grow Up Faster than Boys* (USA#33.1964). Although, a solo career was launched by the lead vocalist under the name of Earl-Jean, she had just the one hit, *I'm into Something Good* (USA#38.1964). Once the fad for girl groups had been eclipsed by the British invasion, both she and the remainder of the group began the long descent into obscurity. Now they are probably best known for the fact that The Beatles covered *Chains*, and Herman's Hermits covered *I'm into Something Good*.

COUCH, TOMMY With the Malaco label Tommy Couch, Wolf Stephenson and Stewart Madison have achieved the unthinkable by bringing southern soul back into prominence. There are those who would contend that what Malaco produces today lacks the passion and excitement of its 1960s counterparts like Stax. The point is that Malaco has managed to achieve a level of consistency, in terms of quality of performance, of material and of commitment that has been absent since the demise of Stax, thereby creating a sympathetic environment for artists like Bobby BLAND, LITTLE MILTON, Johnnie TAYLOR and Shirley BROWN.

Couch was born in Tuscumbia, Alabama. He grew up around Muscle Shoals and went to the University of Mississippi to study pharmacology. He started to book local groups like Dan PENN's Mark Vs, Jimmy JOHNSON's Del-Rays and David HOOD's Mystics for fraternity parties. Upon graduation in 1965 he moved to Jackson, where he set up a booking agency, later to be known as Malaco, with his brother-in-law Mitch Malouf. The success of the agency enabled him to purchase a nightclub and start a record company, under the guidance of Johnny VINCENT. He acquired a disused warehouse and set about installing a four-track studio. Their first recordings were *Simon Says* by Eddie Houston, which was written by George Soule and Paul Davis, and the LP, *I Don't Play No Rock 'N' Roll* for Mississippi Fred McDowell; both were leased to Capitol. In 1969 Stephenson, a fellow pharmacology graduate, started to undertake more and more of the engineering chores.

In 1970 they were approached by Wardell QUEZERGUE who, with his partner Elijah Walker, had built up a roster of artists that included Jean KNIGHT and KING FLOYD. The first single under the new arrangement was *What Our Love Needs* by Floyd. Although, Don Davis at Stax refused to issue it, they decided at the suggestion of DJ Joe Lewis to release the record themselves on their own Chimneyville label. At first it failed to sell, but when Lewis flipped it over and started to play the B-side, *Groove Me*, they achieved their first hit, with Atlantic taking out a licensing deal. FLOYD continued to have hits, but their next smash was *Mr Big Stuff* by Jean Knight. In 1975 Malouf and the musical director, Jerry Puckett, left the company and the deal with Atlantic expired, but Eddie FLOYD heard session singer Dorothy MOORE cutting a demo of *Misty Blue* and encouraged Couch to issue it. After it was rejected by Henry STONE's TK label, Couch decided to issue it himself on his own Malaco label, although Stone acquired distribution of Malaco.

Since 1975 the label has gone from strength to strength. A gospel division was started in 1976, and in 1979, Stewart Madison joined the label to take care of business. Just before the collapse of TK, the label went out on its own. Gradually it has built up a roster of artists that would have been the envy of Stax in its heyday. In 1985 Malaco acquired Muscle Shoals Sound studios, including the house band of Roger HAWKINS, David Hood and Jimmy Johnson in the deal, and in 1987, they bought the Savoy

Gospel Catalogue. The key to Malaco's success has been the ability to gather a team of writers and musicians and to keep them.

COVAY, DON Don Covay was born in Orangeburg, South Carolina, in March, 1938, but his family soon moved to Washington DC, where he became a member of a gospel group, The Cherry-Keys while still at school. In 1958, he joined The Rainbows, which included Marvin GAYE and Billy STEWART in its line-up. They were signed to Bobby ROBINSON's Red Robin label and then, George Wein's Pilgrim label. After meeting LITTLE RICHARD, he cut his first solo record, *Bip Bop Bip*, which was released by Atlantic. He then moved to New York and got work as a songwriter for Roosevelt Music in the Brill Building on Broadway; those who recorded his songs included Jerry BUTLER and Gladys KNIGHT.

He obtained a recording contract with Rosemart, distributed by Atlantic, which enabled him to meet Jerry WEXLER of Atlantic. He was signed up as a solo artist, backed by The Goodtimers, and recorded *Mercy, Mercy* (USA#34.1964) and *See Saw*. As a writer he provided material for Solomon BURKE, *Chain Of Fools* for Aretha FRANKLIN and *I Don't Know What You Got (But it's Got Me)* for Little Richard. In 1966, with Burke, he set the wheels in motion for The Soul Clan (see BURKE, Solomon); the plan failed to come to fruition for two years, and proved to be a pale imitation of what they had intended .

In 1969, he cut a very bluesy LP *House of Blue Lights*. This was followed by the didactic *Different Strokes* LP; neither, however, caused punters to beat a path to their nearest record shop. In 1973, after a hiatus in his career, he signed with Mercury as an A&R man as well as an artist. He had two hit singles, *I was Checkin' Out, She was Checkin' In* (USA#29.1973) from the LP *Super Dude One* and *It's Better to Have (and Don't Need)* (UK#29.1974) from the LP *Hot Blood*. Since those two slices of fortune little has been heard of him, apart from the LP *Travellin' in Heavy Traffic* (1976) for the Philadelphia International label and a disastrous reunion of The Soul Clan in 1981. In 1986, he re- emerged to collaborate with The Rolling Stones on their LP *Dirty Work*.

HOUSE OF COVAY, Atlantic, 1976
MERCY, Edsel, 1984

CRAWFORD, RANDY Veronica Crawford was born in Macon, Georgia, in 1952. From 1967 until 1976 she performed regularly on the club circuit in the USA and Europe. In 1975 she was featured in a tribute concert to the jazz musician Cannonball Adderley, alongside Quincy JONES and George Benson.

Her first LP, *Everything Must Change*, was released by Warner Bros. in 1976; it featured Joe SAMPLE and Wilton FELDER of The CRUSADERS. The next two LPs, *Miss Randy Crawford* (1978) and *Raw Silk* (1979), attracted good reviews but were commercial failures. In 1979, she was asked by Sample to provide the vocal for the title track of The Crusaders' LP *Street Life*; the single *Street Life* reached #5 in the UK. As a result The Crusaders helped her to produce her fourth LP, *Now we May Begin* (UK#10.1980); a single from it, *One Day I'll Fly Away* (UK#2.1980), provided the foundation for her popularity in the UK, where she has continued to be more successful than in her native USA. Since 1980, with the success in the UK of her LPs *Secret Combination* (UK #2.1981),*Windsong* (UK#7.1982), *Nightline* (UK#37.1983) and *Abstract Emotions* (UK #14.1986) and her singles *You Might Need Somebody* (UK#11.1981), *Rainy Night in Georgia* (UK#18.1981), *Nightline* (UK#51.1983) and *Almaz* (UK#4.1987), she has established a reputation that culminated in an invitation to perform with the London Symphony Orchestra at the Barbican in London in 1988.

EVERYTHING MUST CHANGE, Warner Bros., 1976
RAW SILK, Warner Bros., 1979
NOW WE MAY BEGIN, Warner Bros., 1980
SECRET COMBINATION, Warner Bros., 1981
WINDSONG, Warner Bros., 1982
NIGHTLINE, Warner Bros., 1983
GREATEST HITS, Telstar, 1984
ABSRTACT EMOTIONS, Warner Bros., 1986
LOVE SONGS, Telstar, 1987

CRAY, ROBERT Robert Cray was born in Columbus, Georgia on August 1, 1953. His career started when he formed his first band, One Way Street, while still at school. He joined Albert Collins' touring band in 1973 after meeting Richard Cousins, Collins' bass player. In 1975 Cray and Cousins left to form their own group, The Robert Cray Band, bringing in Peter Boe on keyboards and David Olson on drums. They recorded their first LP, *Who's Been Talkin'?*, in 1978 in between tours, although it wasn't released for two years. In 1983, after almost a decade of touring, they recorded the LP *Bad Influence*, which was released by Hightone in the USA and Demon in the UK. In 1984, they toured the UK and Europe, where they were greeted with tumultuous acclaim. Their third LP, *False Accusations* (UK#68.1985), won the Best Blues Album Award from the National Association of Independent Record Distributors. Cray's collaboration with Albert Collins and Johnny Copeland on the LP *Showdown* for the Alligator label won a Grammy.

In 1986 the group signed to Mercury and recorded the LP *Strong Persuader* (USA#13; UK#34.1987). Two singles from it – *Smoking Gun* (USA#22.1987) and *Right Next Door* (UK#50.1987) – were released. In 1986 Cray was featured in the Chuck BERRY 60th Birthday Concert, as well as appearing in the film, *Hail! Hail! Rock'n'Roll*. In 1987 the group played support for Eric Clapton and Tina TURNER. The following year, Cray released the LP *Don't Be Afraid of the Dark*, which consolidated his position as one of the most influential musicians currently working. In 1990, he augmented his band with Wayne JACKSON and The Memphis Horns for the LP *Midnight Stroll*; it saw him combining the twin elements of blues and soul without any loss of potency. Cray's greatest contribution has been his unswerving devotion to the blues, highlighting the often ignored fact that blatant commercialism is not the only way to sell records.

WHO'S BEEN TALKIN'?, Charly, 1980
BAD INFLUENCE, Demon, 1983
FALSE ACCUSATIONS, Demon, 1985
STRONG PERSUADER, Mercury, 1987
DON'T BE AFRAID OF THE DARK, Mercury, 1988
MIDNIGHT STROLL, Mercury, 1990

CREATORE, LUIGI See HUGO & LUIGI

CROPPER, STEVE Steve Cropper was born in Willow Springs in the Ozark Mountains on October 21, 1941. He was employed by Jim STEWART at Stax in 1961 as a guitarist in the house band, The MARKEYS, which had formed when he was at school under the name of The Royal Spades. In 1962, as a result of a late-night jam-session, during which *Green Onions* was recorded he became a founder member of BOOKER T & THE MGs, who were formed out of The Markeys. His contribution to the Stax sound cannot be over emphasised: not only did he play guitar on most of the Otis REDDING sessions, he also produced and cowrote many of Redding's finest records including *(Sittin' on the) Dock of the Bay, Fa-Fa-Fa-Fa-Fa (Sad Song)* and *I Can't Turn You Loose*. Furthermore he collaborated with Wilson PICKETT and Eddie FLOYD in the writing of *In the Midnight Hour* and *Knock on Wood*, respectively.

In 1971, having been replaced by Don Davis as chief producer, he left Stax and The MGs to set up his own studio and production company, TMI. In 1977, he rejoined a re-formed Booker T & The MGs for the 25th Anniversary Show of US TV's *American Bandstand*. They stayed together long enough to record an LP, *Universal Language*, for Asylum. In 1980 he was featured with "Duck" DUNN as a member of the rhythm section in the film *The Blues Brothers*. Such was the film's popularity that a group called The Blues Brothers was formed and has toured the USA with considerable success. Booker T & The MGs have also once again re-formed, with Cropper, and toured the UK and Europe. In 1990, The Blues Brothers, featuring Cropper, had a hit with *Everybody Needs Somebody to Love*, a revival of the Solomon BURKE hit from 1964.

CROWNS See DRIFTERS

CRUSADERS In 1956 Joe SAMPLE (keyboards), Wilton FELDER (tenor sax and bass) and Nesbert "Stix" Hooper (percussion), having played in a marching band at school in Houston, Texas, formed The Nite Hawks; they were later joined by trombonist Wayne Henderson. In 1958 they moved to Los Angeles where they worked the club circuit and played sessions. In 1961 they changed the name of the group to The Jazz Crusaders and were signed by the Pacific Jazz Label.

Throughout the 1960s, they recorded a slew of jazz LPs, as well as developing strong individual reputations as session musicians. In 1966, they recorded their version of the Stevie WONDER hit, *Uptight* (USA#95.1966); not only was it their first hit, but it gave an indication of the direction in which they were heading. After more jazz LPs, they parted company with Pacific Jazz and signed with the Chisa label.

In 1970 they released the LP *Old Socks, New Shoes ...... New Socks, Old Shoes* (USA #90.1970). The success of the record caused them to drop "Jazz" from their name to become The Crusaders. They recorded one further LP for Chisa, *Pass The Plate*, before signing to the ABC subsidiary, Blue Thumb. Their first release for Blue Thumb, the double LP *Crusaders 1* (USA#90.1972), set the seal on their position as one of the premier jazz-funk outfits in the country. A single from it, *Put It Where You Want It* (USA#52.1972), became a massive turntable hit in clubs all over the UK and Europe. Throughout the 1970s, they continued to record an LP a year, despite Blue Thumb being absorbed into the parent company ABC; these included *Southern Comfort* (USA#31.1974), *Chain Reaction* (USA #26.1975), *Those Southern Knights* (USA #38.1976) and *Images* (USA#34.1978). Additionally, each member embarked upon solo careers. In 1975, they were joined by the guitarist Larry CARLTON; the following year Henderson left the group to devote more time to his solo work.

In 1979 they were signed by MCA. Their first LP on their new label was *Street Life* (USA#18; UK#10.1979); the title track of which was released as a single (USA#36; UK#5.1979), featuring vocalist Randy CRAWFORD. Such was the success of the collaboration with Crawford that subsequent LPs have featured guest vocalists like Bill WITHERS, Joe Cocker, Siedah GARRETT and Nancy Wilson. In

1982, they recorded *Royal Jam* with B. B. KING and the Royal Philharmonic Orchestra; the following year Hooper left the group, and was replaced by Leon "Ndugu" Chancler. In 1986, to celebrate their 30th anniversary, they released the LP *Good Times and Bad Times*, which was a reaffirmation of their jazz roots. It featured erstwhile Crusader, Larry Carlton and vocalist Nancy Wilson. In 1988 they released the LP *Life in the Modern World*. Throughout their career their sheer professionalism has enabled them always to remain close to the top. Furthermore their various collaborations have provided cachet for those with whom they have worked.

SCRATCH, ABC, 1974

CHAIN REACTION, ABC, 1975

THOSE SOUTHERN KNIGHTS, ABC, 1976

FREE AS THE WIND MCA, 1977

IMAGES, ABC, 1978

STREET LIFE, MCA, 1979

RHAPSODY AND BLUES, MCA, 1980

THE BEST OF THE CRUSADERS, ABC, 1981

ROYAL JAM, MCA, 1982

THE VOCAL TAPE, MCA, 1983

THE GOOD TIMES AND THE BAD TIMES, MCA, 1986

LIFE IN THE MODERN WORLD, MCA, 1988

CRUTCHER, BETTYE See BANKS, Homer

CRYSTALS Barbara Alston, Mary Thomas, Dee Dee Kennibrew, Lala Brooks and Pat Wright were formed as The Crystals in 1961 by their first manager, Benny Wells, while they were still at school in Brooklyn, New York City. In May 1961, they were signed to his label, Philles, by Phil SPECTOR who had overheard them rehearsing. Their first record was *There's no Other (Like my Baby)* (USA#20.1961); the follow-up, *Uptown* (USA#13.1962), was written by Barry MANN and Cynthia Weil. After recording *He Hit Me (and it Felt Like a Kiss)*, which bombed because nobody would play it because of its apparently masochistic lyrics, Spector released *He's A Rebel* (USA#1; UK#18.1962), which was credited to The Crystals, but was in fact recorded by a substitute group composed of Darlene LOVE, Fanita James and Gracia Nitzsche. The next record, *He's Sure the Boy I Love* (USA #11.1962), was also by the surrogate group.

In 1963 the original group, now a quartet due to the departure of Mary Thomas to get married, recorded *Da Doo Ron Ron* (USA#3; UK#5.1963/#34.1974), it was followed by *Then He Kissed Me* (USA#6; UK#2.1963); while both records were instrumental in establishing the Phil Spector and the "Wall of Sound", the relationship between the group and Spector was becoming increasingly strained. In October 1963 Wright left to get married and was replaced by Frances Collins; the same year, they contributed to the Phil Spector Christmas LP, *A Seasonal Gift for You*. In 1965, they bought themselves out of their contract with Philles and signed with United Artists, but after a year they were dropped. In 1971, they re-formed and started to tour on the oldies circuit, where they have remained ever since. The only original member still in the group is Kennibrew.

PHIL SPECTOR WALL OF SOUND, Phil Spector International, 1975

CYMONE, ANDRE Andre Anderson first teamed up with PRINCE in 1970, while they were both at school. The friendship resulted in Prince, who had run away from home, moving into the Anderson household. As bassist in Grand Central, Champagne and then the early versions of The Revolution,

Anderson (who had changed his name to Cymone), was one of Prince's longest- serving collaborators, until he left the group in 1981 to concentrate upon a solo career.

He obtained a recording contract with CBS, for whom he cut two LPs, *Survivin' in the Eighties* (1983) and *A C* (1985), which included *The Dance Electric*; the fact that neither record made much impression commercially has probably been to Jody WATLEY's advantage, as Cymone has been concentrating upon production since 1985, in addition to collaborating with Ray PARKER.

SURVIVIN' IN THE EIGHTIES, CBS, 1983
A C, CBS, 1985

D'ARBY, TERENCE TRENT Terence Trent D'Arby was born in New York City on March 15, 1962. After leaving the University of Central Florida in 1980, he joined the army, enlisting in Elvis Presley's former regiment, the Third Armoured Division, and was posted to West Germany. In 1982 he joined a local funk outfit, Touch, as a vocalist; in 1983 he left the army and remained with the group until 1984, when he moved to London. For the next two years, he concentrated upon setting his solo career in motion by writing material and recording demos.

In 1987, having obtained a recording contract with CBS, he released his first single, *If You Let Me Stay* (UK#7.1987); it was followed by *Wishing Well* (USA#1.1988; UK#4.1987). His debut LP, *Introducing the Hardline According to Terence Trent D'Arby* (USA#4.1988; UK#1.1987) included the first two singles, as well as *Dance Little Sister* (UK#20.1987) and *Sign Your Name* (USA#5; UK#2.1988). In 1989, he released the follow-up LP, *Neither Fish Nor Flesh*. Although he has never been reticent about his talent, he has already shown that, unlike so many of his contemporaries, he is always prepared to experiment rather than take an easy option.

INTRODUCING THE HARDLINE ACCORDING TO TERENCE TRENT D'ARBY, CBS, 1987
NEITHER FISH, NOR FLESH, CBS, 1989

DAVIS, CLIVE Clive Davis has managed to combine the business side of running a record company with the creative, although he has seldom been credited as anything more than being Executive Producer. His intuition has enabled him to create conducive environments for even the most difficult artists.

He joined Columbia Records as a lawyer straight from law school in 1960; by 1967 he had become president. By the time of his departure in 1973, he had turned Columbia into one of the more far-seeing companies, with a roster of artists that included Bruce Springsteen, Barbra Streisand, Janis Joplin, SLY & THE FAMILY STONE, EARTH, WIND & FIRE and Santana; furthermore through a series of distribution deals, CBS had stakes in Stax, The ISLEY BROTHERS's T-Neck label and GAMBLE & HUFF's Philadelphia International label, which made them one of the major distributors of soul worldwide. After his dismissal, he set up the Arista label in 1974, and his flair has enabled him to revive the careers Dionne WARWICK and Aretha FRANKLIN and launch that of Whitney HOUSTON. This has all been achieved by the simple knack of knowing which producer to match to which artist, and being able to spot talent.

DAVIS, MARY See S O S BAND

DAVIS, TYRONE Throughout his career, Tyrone Davis has been widely regarded as a fine interpreter with his bluesy vocals and his fine arrangements, but for far too long he has been allowed to languish in semi-obscurity.

He was born in Greenville, Mississippi in 1938. After moving to Chicago, he was signed by Ray CHARLES to his Tangerine label, where he cut *Can I Change My Mind*. It failed to make any impression, but he built up his reputation throughout the Northern States until he was signed by Carl Davis to the Dakar label. His first release was a re-recording of *Can I Change my Mind* (USA#5.1969); it was the first of a number of hits for the label: *Is it Something you've Got* (USA#34.1969), *Turn Back the Hands of Time* (USA#3.1970) and *There It Is* (USA#32.1973). He remained with Dakar until 1975, when he was signed by CBS, where he had another hit with *Give it Up (Turn it Loose)* (USA#38.1976). The disco explosion eclipsed later offerings and although he has continued to record occasionally, most notably with a version of *How Sweet it is (to be Loved by You)* in 1980, he has had to depend upon the club circuit and his committed band of followers.

THE TYRONE DAVIS STORY, Kent, 1985
MAN OF STONE, Timeless, 1987

DAY, BOBBY Robert Byrd was born on July 1, 1932 in Fort Worth, Texas. His career started when, having moved to Watts in Los Angeles in the early 1950s, he began working for Johnny OTIS. He joined The Hollywood Flames as a singer and songwriter and in 1957, they released *Little Bitty Pretty One* on the Class label under the name of Bobby Day & The Satellites. In 1958, he left the group and embarked upon a solo career. Later that year he released *Rockin' Robin* (USA#2; UK #29.1958). In January, 1959, he perpetuated the ornithological metaphor with *The Bluebird, the Buzzard and The Oriole* (USA#59.1959), and then promptly declined into obscurity,

although his songs have continued to be covered to very successful effect by artists like The Dave Clark Five, Clyde McPHATTER, The JACKSONS and Michael JACKSON. He died in 1990, aged 58.

DeBARGE This group was formed in 1978 by four brothers (Eldra, Mark, James and Randy) and a sister (Bunny) from the DeBarge family of ten as a gospel group in Grand Rapids, Michigan. In 1979, having moved to Los Angeles, they auditioned for Jermaine JACKSON, who recommended them to Berry GORDY. They were signed by him immediately. Their first LP, *DeBarge*, was released in 1980, but failed to attract much attention. Their next, *All this Love* (USA #24.1982), broke the ice for them and featured two hit singles, *I Like It* (USA#31.1983) and *All this Love* (USA#17.1983). Their third LP, *In a Special Way* (USA#36.1983) provided them with a further two hit singles: *Time Will Reveal* (USA#18.1984) and *Love Me in a Special Way* (USA#45.1984). Later the same year they appeared in Gordy's first film, *The Last Dragon*, as well as contributing to the soundtrack with the title track of the LP, *Rhythm of the Night* (USA#44; UK#94.1985). When released as a single, this track (USA#3; UK#4.1985) gave the group their first hit in the UK. The follow-up, *Who's Holding Donna Now?* (USA#6.1985) was also featured on the LP.

In 1986, Eldra left the group, although remained with Motown as a solo artist and recorded under the name of El DeBarge; his first single, *Who's Johnny?* (USA#3; UK #60.1986), was included on his debut LP *El DeBarge* (USA#24.1986). Another member of the DeBarge family, Chico, signed to Motown, his eponymous first LP sold moderately and included the single, *Talk to Me* (USA#12.1987). In 1987, Bunny left the group and recorded a solo LP for Motown. By 1988, the group had effectively ceased to function, added to which two members of the family, Chico and Robert were charged with trafficking cocaine.

IN A SPECIAL WAY, Gordy, 1984
RHYTHM OF THE NIGHT, Gordy, 1985
GREATEST HITS, Motown, 1986
EL DeBARGE, Gordy, 1986
CHICO DeBARGE, Motown, 1986

DEEE-LITE Every so often there arrives on the scene a group that seems to have its fingers on the pulse and with unerring accuracy delivers a record to match the mood of the time. When this happens, the group is lionised by the press as "the next big thing". However, when the group's tongue appears to be lodged firmly in its cheek, the immediate reaction is to discount their impact, ascribing the success to the susceptibility of the general public. Deee-Lite provides a case in point.

The group members are Super DJ Dmitry (born in Kiev, Russia), Jungle DJ Towa-Towa (born in Tokyo, Japan) and Lady Miss Kier (born in Pittsburg, Philadelphia). The group came into being on the New York club circuit in 1989. Their debut LP, *World Clique*, featuring their debut single *Groove is in My Heart* (UK#1.1990), borrowed liberally from the styles of the 1970s, revelled in the tackiness of the whole disco period, but setting it within the context of the 1990s. While the influence of SLY Stone and George CLINTON is apparent, particularly in the witty use of language in the lyrics, contributions from Maceo Parker, Fred Wesley, BOOTSY and Q Tip from A Tribe Called Quest have imbued their debut efforts with a visceral urgency that brims with energy.

WORLD CLIQUE, Elektra, 1990

DEES, SAM Despite having recorded extensively for a variety of labels, Sam Dees has never enjoyed far reaching popularity as a performer. As a writer, however, he has exerted a considerable influence upon the repertoires of others like Clarence CARTER, Z. Z. HILL, Tyrone DAVIS, The Persuaders, Loleatta Holloway and Ted TAYLOR.

He was born in Birmingham, Alabama, but moved to Rochester, New York. After recording tracks like *Maryanna, Can You be a One Man Woman* and *Love Starvation* for Chess he was signed by Shelby SINGLETON to his Nashville based SSS International label. While his records were fine examples of the country-soul genre, little stuck and he tended to provide material for others, which compensated for the lack of interest in his own output. After Singleton's decision to stop recording soul in the mid-1970s, he was signed by Atlantic for a spell. In recent years, the emphasis has been on writing, apart from the occasional single like *Survive* (1986).

DELFONICS When Thom BELL started to produce The Delfonics in 1967 he created a sound that was to become synonymous with Philadelphia, in much the same way as Motown did for Detroit and Stax for Memphis. The group – consisting of Randy Cain (born in Philadelphia on May 2, 1945), Wilbert Hart (born in Washington on October 19, 1947), William Hart (born in Washington on January 17, 1945) and Ritchie Daniels – was called The Four Gents until in 1967, when Stan Watson, a former member of The Del-Vikings, discovered them and changed their name .

At first they recorded for Cameo and Moonshot; this was where they met Thom Bell, who was a producer, session musician, arranger and all-purpose factotum for the labels. Their early records, like *He Don't*

Really Love You and *You've been Untrue,* were enough to convince Watson to set up the Philly Groove label. Although Watson was credited with the production of their first single for the label *La La Means I Love You* (USA#4.1968; UK#19.1971), Bell and lead singer William Hart cowrote it (as indeed they did all the subsequent hits); perhaps, Watson was adopting a tactic that had always been prevalent: he owned the label, thus he claimed the production credits. However, on the remainder of their hits production was credited to Bell: *Break Your Promise* (USA#35.1968), *Ready or not Here I Come (Can't Hide from Love)* (USA #35.1969; UK#41.1971), *You Got Yours and I'll Get Mine* (USA#40.1969), *Didn't I (Blow your Mind This Time)* (USA#10.1970; UK#22.1971) and *Trying to Make a Fool of Me* (USA #40.1970).

In 1971 Bell started to produce The STYL-ISTICS, thus severing his connections with the group. William Hart became the creative impetus behind the group, but proved unable to match up to the high standards set by Bell. The same year, Cain left the group and was replaced by Major Harris, who remained until 1973, when he left to start a solo career; eventually this was to bear fruit, with the single *Love Won't Let Me Wait* (USA#5; UK#37.1975), and he has continued recording intermittently ever since, scoring with *All My Life* (UK#61.1983). The Delfonics were signed by Curtom, where they recorded a number of unsuccessful singles before disappearing into the relative safety of the cabaret circuit.

SUPER HITS, Arista, 1972

DELLS For over thirty years, The Dells have been regarded by critics and fellow musicians as exemplars of their craft, but their sales have never been commensurate with this high standing. The group was formed in 1952 by Vern Allison, Chuck Barksdale, Marvin Junior, John Funches, Lucius and Micky McGill, all of whom were still at school in Chicago. They cut their debut, an "acapella" called *Darling, Dear I Know* in 1953 for the Checker label, a subsidiary of Chess, before signing with VeeJay, where they scored their first R&B hit, *Oh What a Night* in 1956. Their follow-ups failed to sustain interest and so they consolidated their reputation on the nightclub circuit. However, there had been changes in the line-up: Lucius McGill left in 1955 and John Funches was injured in a road accident in 1958; the latter's replacement was former FLAM-INGO Johnny Carter.

In 1962 they rejoined Chess, where they remained until 1973 (apart from another brief spell in the mid-1960s with Veejay), and were teamed with producer Bobby Miller and arranger Charles Stepney. In 1968 they were assigned to the Chess subsidiary Cadet, where they hit their chart-making peak with *There Is* (USA#20.1968), *Stay in my Corner* (USA #10.1968), *Always Together* (USA#18.1968), *Does Anybody Know I'm Here* (USA#38.1969), *I Can Sing A Rainbow/ Love Is Blue* (USA #22.1969), *Oh What A Night* (USA#10.1969) – a remake of their 1956 hit, *The Love We Had (Stays on my Mind)* (USA#30.1971) and *Give Your Baby A Standing Ovation* (USA#34.1973).

In 1973 they moved to Mercury, where they recorded the LPs *We Got to Get Our Thing Together* (1974) and *No Way Back* (1976). More recently they have recorded for 20th Century. Despite the changes in style and fashion, they have kept their following and managed to remain a going concern by touring constantly.

WHATEVER TURNS YOU ON, 20th Century, 1981
BREEZY BALLADS & TENDER TUNES, Solid Smoke, 1985

DeSANTO, SUGARPIE Sugarpie De-Santo was born, of Filipino extraction, Peylia Balington in Brooklyn, New York City. During her childhood, she moved to San Francisco where she was brought up and she started to perform on the club circuit. After being spotted by Johnny OTIS, she was signed first to the King subsidiary, Federal, and then to the Aladdin label. Unable to get a break, she signed to the Chess subsidiary, Checker. Between 1960 and 1966, she recorded a string of singles for Checker, which included *It Won't be Long, So What, Never Love a Stranger, Soulful Dress* and *In the Basement*; the latter being a magnificent duet with Etta JAMES. However, her contract was allowed to expire and she slipped into obscurity.

LOVIN' TOUCH, Diving Duck, 1987
DOWN IN THE BASEMENT, Chess, 1988

DETROIT EMERALDS The Detroit Emeralds were formed in 1968 by Abe and Ivory Tillman and James Mitchell. At first they recorded for Eddie Wingate's Ric Tic label, but were not retained when it was bought out by Motown. After working on their live act in their native Detroit, they were signed to the Westbound label: the smooth harmonies combined with tuneful melodies were reminiscent of the Motown of the mid-1960s, unfortunately the arrangements lacked the flair of Motown. Be that as it may, they had a few decent sized hits: *You Want It, You Got It* (USA#36.1972; UK#12.1973), *Baby Let me Take You (in my Arms)* (USA#24.1972), *Feel the Need in Me* (UK#4.1973) and *I Think Of You* (UK#27.1973). In 1974 Mitchell and Ivory Tillman left the group only to rejoin three years later, when they were signed for a short spell to Atlantic. At Atlantic, they re-recorded another version of *Feel the Need in Me* (UK #12.1977), which was followed by the LP *Let's*

Get Together. Despite their lack of success recently they have carved a niche for themselves on the international cabaret circuit.

LET'S GET TOGETHER, Atlantic, 1978

DETROIT SPINNERS After Harvey FUQUA moved to Detroit, one of the labels he set up in conjunction with Motown was Tri-Phi. It was to this label that he signed The Spinners in 1961. The group comprised Bobbie Smith, Billy Henderson, Henry Fambrough and Pervis Jackson. Their first two records, *That's What Girls are Made for* and *Love, I'm so Glad I Found You,* featured Fuqua on lead vocals. For four years they were becalmed, touring and releasing the odd record, until they released *I'll Always Love You* (USA#35.1965). Another five years passed during which time G. C. Cameron joined as lead vocalist and they were transferred to the subsidiary VIP label. With Stevie WONDER producing, they scored with *It's a Shame* (USA#14; UK#20.1970); the follow-up, *We'll Have it Made*, also produced by Wonder, failed to consolidate their advantage and they left Motown, signing with Atlantic on the recommendation of Aretha FRANKLIN. G. C. Cameron left the group for a solo career and was replaced by Phillipe Wynne.

At Atlantic, they were put in the hands of arranger, producer and long-time admirer, Thom BELL. Under Bell's direction, they notched up a string of hits including *I'll be Around* (USA#3.1972), *Could it be I'm Fallin' in Love* (USA#4; UK#11.1973/#32.1977), *One of a Kind (Love Affair)* (USA#11.1973), *Ghetto Child* (USA#29; UK#7.1973), *Mighty Love, Part 1* (USA#20.1974), *I'm Coming Home* (USA#18.1974), *Love Don't Love Nobody* (USA#15.1974), *Living a Little, Laughing a Little* (USA#37.1975), *They Just Can't Stop it the Games People Play* (USA#5.1975), *Love or*

Leave (USA#36.1976), *The Rubber Band Man* (USA#2; UK#16.1976) and *Wake Up Susan* (UK#29.1977). They were teamed with Dionne WARWICK for the single *Then Came You* (USA#1; UK#29.1974), which did a great deal to revive Warwick's fortunes. Under Bell's direction, the LPs were as successful as the singles: *Spinners* (USA#8.1973), *Mighty Love* (USA#16.1974), *New and Improved* (USA #9.1974), *Pick of the Litter* (USA#8.1975), *Spinners Live!* (USA#20.1976), *Happiness is Being with the Detroit Spinners* (USA#25.1976) and *Yesterday, Today and Tomorrow* (USA #26.1977).

In 1977 Wynne left the group (he died, aged 43, in 1984), being replaced by John Edwards. Two years later Bell left and they were teamed with producer Michael Zager for a number of dance-oriented medleys: *Working my Way Back to You/Forgive Me Girl* (USA#2; UK #1.1980) and *Cupid/I've Loved You for a Long Time* (USA/UK#4.1980). Although, these were commercially successful they were a far cry from the haunting lyricism of Bell. Over the last ten years, despite their absence from the charts, their popularity has remained intact, culminating in an appearance at the Atlantic 40th Anniversary concert in 1988.

DETROIT SPINNERS, Atlantic, 1973
SMASH HITS, Atlantic, 1977
DANCIN' AND LOVIN', Atlantic, 1980
20 GOLDEN CLASSICS, Motown, 1980
LABOUR OF LOVE, Atlantic, 1981
CAN'T SHAKE THIS FEELING, Atlantic, 1981
GRAND SLAM, Atlantic, 1983
GOLDEN GREATS, Atlantic, 1985
LOVIN' FEELING, Atlantic, 1985

DIDDLEY, BO Bo Diddley was born Elias Bates on December 30, 1928, in McComb, Mississippi. In 1933, his family moved to the South Side of Chicago, where his career started in 1951. In 1955 he signed to the Chess subsidiary, Checker. His first release was the self-penned *Bo Diddley*, which peaked at #2 in the R&B charts. His band comprised his half-sister, "The Duchess" (guitar and vocals), Otis Spann (piano), Jerome Green (bass), Frank Kirkland (drums) and Billy "Boy" Arnold (harmonica). Over the next ten years he recorded a string of singles and LPs, which were to prove inspirational to many groups from the UK in the early to mid-1960s. Many of the tracks released as singles were his own compositions, including *Who Do You Love, Say Man* (USA#20.1959) – arguably the prototype "rap" record – *Roadrunner* (USA#75.1960) and *Pretty Thing* (UK#34.1963). Throughout, he toured constantly, developing a reputation for his live act, and as a result his LPs tended to be more successful than the singles: *Bo Diddley* (UK#11.1963), *Bo Diddley is a Gunslinger* (UK#20.1963), *Bo Diddley Rides Again* (UK #19.1963) and *Bo Diddley's Beach Party* (UK #13.1964). While he could never have been accused of profundity, he wrote a number of songs that have become classics of the genre, and his influence upon groups like The Rolling Stones has been incalculable. Although he seldom records now, he continues to tour and is a much sought-after "special guest" at rock 'n' roll revival shows.

CHESS MASTERS, Chess, 1981
I'M A MAN, Black Lion, 1982
AIN'T IT GOOD TO BE FREE, New Rose, 1984
ROAD RUNNER, Black Lion, 1984
HAVE GUITAR WILL TRAVEL, Chess, 1986
HEY, Conifer, 1986
HEY BO DIDDLEY, Magnum Force, 1986
HIS GREATEST SIDES, VOLUME 1, Chess, 1986
BO DIDDLEY, Chess, 1987
GO BO DIDDLEY, Chess, 1987
IN THE SPOTLIGHT, Chess, 1987

DIXIE CUPS The Dixie Cups were formed in 1963 and comprised Joan Johnson, Rosa Lee and Barbara Ann Hawkins. They were spotted at a talent contest in their native New Orleans by their future manager, Joe Jones, who took them to New York to audition for George GOLDNER at the newly established Red Bird label. The names of the writers (Jeff BARRY, Ellie GREENWICH and Phil SPECTOR) and producers (LEIBER & STOLLER, with Barry and Greenwich) of their first single, *Chapel Of Love* (USA#1; UK#22.1964), read like a who's who of early sixties pop, and not surprisingly, the single stayed at the top of the US Charts for three weeks, selling over a million copies. Their subsequent successes – *People Say* (USA #12.1964), *You Should Have Seen the Way He Looked at Me* (USA#39.1964), *Little Bell* (USA#51.1965) and *Iko, Iko* (USA#20; UK #23.1965) – established a commendable pattern of consistency but, after they separated from Red Bird and signed with ABC and then RCA, they gradually slipped from sight and eventually broke up.

THE DIXIE CUPS MEET THE SHANGRI-LAS, Charly, 1986

DIXIE FLYERS In 1970 Jerry WEXLER, having tired of spending his winters in New York, decided to purchase Criteria Studios, so that he could pass the winter months in the warmth of Miami. His first move was to ask Jim Dickinson to assemble a house band. The band was dubbed The Dixie Flyers. They comprised Dickinson (keyboards), Charlie Freeman (guitar; a founder member of The MARKEYS), Mike Utley (keyboards), Tommy McClure (bass) and Sammy Creason (drums). This amalgam had been first used in 1965 by Stan KESLER at Sam Phillips'

studios; they replaced the original group, which had defected to Chips MOMAN's American studios.

Wexler's decision to partially relocate was instrumental in the establishment of Miami as a recording mecca in the early 1970s. The presence of a house band of such a calibre as The Dixie Flyers was one of the reasons for the exodus to Miami. However, as BOOKER T and Steve CROPPER had left The MGs and Rick HALL and Moman were working more and more in the country and pop markets, it meant that there were fewer studios left able to keep the flag of southern soul flying. Despite backing artists like Aretha FRANKLIN, SAM & DAVE and Brook BENTON, they also worked with Delaney & Bonnie, which encouraged other white bands like Derek & The Dominoes to record at the studios. This was to render The Dixie Flyers superfluous ultimately, and as a result the group disintegrated in the wake of Charlie Freeman's death in the early 1970s.

DIXON, LUTHER Luther Dixon was one of the first and most effective of the production-line producers, much as were HOLLAND, DOZIER & HOLLAND and GAMBLE & HUFF. He began his career as a vocalist in the quartet The Four Buddies before moving into writing and publishing. When Florence Greenberg started the Scepter label, she recruited him to guide the career of The SHIRELLES and to develop a roster of artists. His production of their early records had a profound influence on the whole girl-group genre and on popular music in general: *Will You Love Me Tomorrow* still stands as definitive of the genre; and his production of *Dedicated to the One I Love*, the first record he cut with The Shirelles, showed just what could be done with a cover version. In addition, to his work with The Shirelles, he signed Chuck

JACKSON and Maxine BROWN, both of whom he produced, before leaving Scepter in 1963 to set up his own label, Ludix. In 1969, he married Inez FOXX.

DOCTOR JOHN Malcolm John Rebennack was born on November 21, 1941 in New Orleans. By 1957, he had established a reputation for himself as a session musician, working for labels like Ace, Rex, Ric and Ebb. In 1958, he issued his first LP, *Storm Warning*, after co-writing *Lights Out* for Jerry Byrne (1958). In 1962, he went to Los Angeles and became highly sought after as a session musician by producers like Phil SPECTOR, H. B. BARNUM and Harold Battiste, the latter being a former acquaintance from New Orleans. Over the next three years, he established a fresh identity as Dr John Creaux, The Night Tripper, fusing the traditional sounds of New Orleans R&B with West Coast rock. In 1968 he released the LP *Gris Gris* for the Atlantic subsidiary, Atco, although it failed to sell in large quantities it attracted a substantial following among the cognoscenti. Over the next three years he released three more LPs: *Baylon, Remedies* and *Dr. John, The Night Tripper (The Sun, Moon and Herbs)*, the latter featuring an all-star cast of admirers, including Eric Clapton and Mick Jagger.

In 1972 he returned to his roots, recording the LP *Gumbo*; it consisted of R&B standards, mostly originating from New Orleans, and was produced by Jerry WEXLER. From it, he got his first hit single, *Iko Iko* (USA#71.1972). The next LP, *In the Right Place* (USA#24.1973), included the singles *Right Place Wrong Time* (USA#9.1973) and *Such a Night* (USA #42.1973); the follow up, *Desitively Bonnaroo* (1974), was his final offering for Atco. Both LPs were produced by Allen TOUSSAINT. Since 1974, despite being plagued by ill-health, he has continued to record; although the sales of his records have been poor, their eclecticism has guaranteed interest from his long-term admirers. In 1976 he appeared in the Martin Scorsese film of The Band's final concert, *The Last Waltz*, which led to him joining The RCO All Stars, the group formed by The Band's ex-drummer Levon Helm. In 1985, he collaborated with the saxophonist Hank Crawford on the LP *Roadhouse Symphony*, which featured celebrated session men like Bernard Purdie and David 'Fathead' Newman. Throughout his career he has toured constantly, and his extensive knowledge of R&B makes his live performances a treat to behold. In 1989, he released the LP *In a Sentimental Mood*, which featured a duet with Rickie Lee Jones.

TRIUMVIRATE, (with Mike Bloomfield and John Paul Hammond), Edsel, 1971
HOLLYWOOD BE THY NAME, BGO, 1975
DR JOHN PLAYS MAC REBENNACK, Demon, 1981
THE BRIGHTEST SMILE IN TOWN, Demon. 1982
LOSER FOR YOU BABY, Fontana, 1982
TAKE ME BACK TO NEW ORLEANS, (with Chris Barber), Black Lion, 1983
I BEEN HOODOOD, Edsel, 1984
SUCH A NIGHT: LIVE IN LONDON, Spindrift, 1984
ROADHOUSE SYMPHONY, (with Hank Crawford), Fantasy, 1985
IN A SENTIMENTAL MOOD, Warner Bros., 1989

DOMINO, FATS Antoine "Fats" Domino was born on February 26, 1928, in New Orleans; he was taught to play the piano as a teenager. In 1949 he was discovered, while playing with Billy Diamond's Combo, by producer and arranger Dave BARTHO-LOMEW, who was talent-scouting for Imperial. It was the beginning of a relationship that would encompass the most successful years of Domino's recording career. In

1950, he entered the J&M Studios in New Orleans and recorded *The Fat Man*, a reworking of *Junkers Blues,* backed by Bartholomew's band. By 1953, it had sold over a million copies. It was followed by *Rockin' Chair* (1951), *Goin' Home* (1952), *Goin' to the River* and *Please Don't Leave Me* (1953) and *You Done me Wrong* (1954). In 1951 he had formed his own touring band and started to tour, beating a trail from coast to coast.

In 1955, he scored with his first national hit, *Ain't that a Shame* (USA#10.1955), over the next six years he notched up another 35 top-forty Hits, including *I'm in Love Again* (USA#3; UK#12.1956), *Blueberry Hill* (USA #2; UK#6.1956), *Blue Monday* (USA#5; UK#23.1957), *I'm Walkin'* (USA#4; UK #19.1957), *Valley of Tears* (USA#6; UK #25.1957), *Whole Lotta Loving* (USA#6.1958), *I Want to Walk You Home* (USA#8; UK #14.1959), *Be my Guest* (USA#8; UK#11.1959) and *Walkin' To New Orleans* (USA#6; UK #19.1960). Throughout the 1950s he appeared in a variety of films including *The Girl Can't Help It, Shake, Rattle and Roll, Jamboree* and *The Big Beat.* In 1963, his recording contract with Imperial expired and he signed to ABC, with whom he had his final top-forty Hit, *Red Sails in the Sunset* (USA#35; UK#34.1963). In 1965 he signed with Mercury and in 1968 with Reprise. Since the 1960s, he has tended to record less and less, concentrating more on touring and personal appearances in Las Vegas. Perhaps, the most significant aspect of his career was his ability to commercialise his own style of New Orleans R&B and, in the process, develop a sound that has been much emulated by other New Orleans musicians like DOCTOR JOHN, Smiley LEWIS and Allen TOUSSAINT.

TWENTY GREATEST HITS, United Artists, 1977
SLEEPING ON THE JOB, Sonet, 1979
FATS IS BACK, Mercury, 1981
LET'S DANCE WITH DOMINO, EMI (France), 1981
KINGS OF ROCK, (with Bill Haley), Polydor, 1982
20 ROCK 'N' ROLL HITS, EMI (Germany), 1983
THE FABULOUS MR D, Imperial (France), 1983
HERE STANDS FATS DOMINO, EMI (France), 1983
I MISS YOU SO, Imperial (France), 1983
A LOT OF DOMINOS, EMI (France), 1983
MILLION RECORD HITS, Imperial (France), 1983
ROCK AND ROLLIN', EMI (France), 1983
THIS IS FATS, Imperial (France), 1983
THIS IS FATS DOMINO, EMI (France), 1983
THE VERY BEST OF FATS DOMINO, Liberty (Germany), 1983
JAMBALAYA, Astan, 1984
MY BLUE HEAVEN, Astan, 1984
WHAT A PARTY, Pathe Marconi (France), 1984
THE BEST OF FATS DOMINO, Liberty, 1985
BOOGIE WOOGIE BABY, Ace, 1985
FATS DOMINO, Mercury (Holland),1985
THE FATS DOMINO COLLECTION, Deja Vu, 1985
NEW ORLEANS ROCK 'N' ROLL, Pathe Marconi (France), 1985
BE MY GUEST, Bulldog, 1986
THE COLLECTION, Spectrum, 1986
THE FAT MAN: LIVE!, Magnum Force, 1986
ROCK 'N' ROLL GREATS, MFP, 1986
16 GREATEST HITS, Bescol, 1987

DOMINOES See WARD, Billy & The Dominoes

DORSEY, LEE Irving Lee Dorsey was born in New Orleans on December 4, 1926. His records were to be pivotal in the redevelopment of New Orleans as a recording centre. During the 1950s he had a moderately successful career as a boxer, fighting as Kid Chocolate, before joining the Navy. In 1961, he recorded *Ya Ya* (USA#7.1961) for Bobby

ROBINSON's Fury label; it was produced by Harold Battiste. The following year he released *Do Re Mi* (USA#27.1962), his last record for three years due to the dissolution of Fury.

In 1965 he made his comeback with *Ride Your Pony* (USA#28.1965); it was written and produced by Allen TOUSSAINT with the nucleus of The Meters (see NEVILLE BROTHERS) providing the backing. This combination would feature on most of his records for the remainder of his career. The following year he scored with *Get out of my Life Woman* (USA#44; UK#22.1966), *Confusion* (UK#38.1966), *Working in a Coalmine* (USA/UK#8.1966) and *Holy Cow* (USA#23; UK #6.1966). From 1967, his records became increasingly less successful commercially, but his reputation as a performer continued to flourish and the few records he made were highly regarded by fellow artists and critics alike. After the release of the LP *Yes We Can Can* in 1970, he went into semi-retirement and looked after his car-repair shop until 1980, when The Clash persuaded him to tour with them in the USA.

He died of emphysema on December 1, 1986, aged 59. Although his career was comparatively short, the few records he cut have been very influential, with Robert PALMER, The Judds, Little Feat and The Band, among others recording their own versions of his songs.

CAN YOU HEAR ME?, Charly, 1987

DOVELLS See BARRY, Len

DOWD, TOM Tom Dowd was one of the reasons for the astonishing success of Atlantic during the 1950s, as he was able to engineer a clarity of sound that made most contemporary recordings sound as if there was glue in the equipment. He was born in 1925 in New York, and graduated in Natural Sciences before joining the Apex studios in 1946. When Atlantic was set up, Dowd was brought in to engineer the earliest records by artists like Ruth BROWN, The CLOVERS, The DRIFTERS, Joe Turner, LaVern BAKER and Ray CHARLES. With Nesuhi Ertegun, the director of the jazz repertoire for the label, Dowd engineered The Modern Jazz Quartet and John Coltrane.

During the mid-1960s, when Atlantic were recording artists like Solomon BURKE, Otis REDDING, Aretha FRANKLIN and Wilson PICKETT at the Stax, Fame and American studios, Dowd - in association with Jerry WEXLER – supervised the recordings. When arranger Arif MARDIN joined the label in 1967, the combination of the three of them arguably did more to advance the progress of recording techniques in popular music than anyone had done before. In 1966 Dowd became the producer for The Young Rascals. Since then he has produced a wide range of artists including KING CURTIS, Dusty Springfield, The Allman Brothers Band (See ALLMAN, Duane), Derek & The Dominoes, DOCTOR JOHN and Rod Stewart. Although he became a freelance in 1972, he has tended to work from Atlantic South (Criteria studios) in Florida. His more recent productions have included FINE YOUNG CANNIBALS and Diana ROSS.

DOWNING, BIG AL Al Downing was born in Oklahoma in 1940. Throughout his childhood, he was raised on country music until in 1956, he joined a rockabilly outfit The Poe-Kats, led by Bobby Poe, playing the local club circuit. By 1959 he had been discovered by Lelan Rogers, who took him to the J&M studios in New Orleans, where he recorded a series of country-ish sides like *Story Of My Life*, a Marty Robbins composition. In 1963 he was teamed with Esther PHILLIPS for *You Never Miss Your Water*. It was followed by a solo side, *Mr Hurt Walked In* for the Lenox label. Throughout his dealings with Rogers he continued to play the club circuit with The Poe-Kats, until they decided to revamp their image by dropping Downing from the line-up and adopting a more rock-oriented approach. They promptly disappeared into obscurity, Downing continued to play the club circuit, backed by pick- up bands.

In 1969, he teamed up with Rogers once again, who had formed the Silver Fox label, and recorded tracks like *I'll Be Your Fool Once More* for the House Of The Fox label, on which he was backed by Maceo Parker and All The King's Men. Another hiatus in his career occurred until he linked up with Tony Bongiovi (he had been instrumental in developing Gloria GAYNOR's career) for *I'll Be Holding On* in the mid-1970s. In 1979, he was signed by Warner Bros. and recorded *Mr Jones*; it was followed in 1982 by the LP *Big Al Downing*; although the overt country influences were a welcome departure from the disco-oriented *I'll Be Holding On* the material represented the prosaic side of country. In recent years, he has recorded little, but at least he seems to have realized that country music is his metier.

DOWNING, WILL Will Downing was born in New York. At first he worked as a session vocalist backing artists like Jennifer HOLLIDAY, Billy OCEAN, Nona HENDRYX and ROSE ROYCE; then he was enlisted by producer Arthur BAKER to work with Jeff Beck in the UK. His association with Baker enabled him to obtain a recording contract with the Island subsidiary, 4th & Broadway. The ensuing debut LP included the singles, *A Love Supreme* (UK#14.1988); *In My Dreams* (UK#34.1988) and *Free* (UK #58.1988). In 1989, he collaborated with Mica

PARIS in a reworking of the Donny HATHAWAY and Roberta FLACK duet, *Where Is The Love*. In 1989 he released the follow-up LP, *Come Together as One*, most of which he cowrote; it was followed in 1991 by *A Dream Fulfilled*. Much of it was recorded live in the studio and emphasised the strong jazz influence in his work; in many ways his work is too imaginative for general audiences and, consequently, he has never been unable to reap the bounty that is his due.

WILL DOWNING, 4th & Broadway, 1988
COME TOGETHER AS ONE, 4th & Broadway, 1989
A DREAM FULFILLED, 4th & Broadway, 1991

DOZIER, LAMONT See HOLLAND, DOZIER & HOLLAND

DRAMATICS The Dramatics were formed in Detroit as The Dynamics. Initially, they recorded for Eddie Wingate's Wingate label, part of his Ric Tic group of labels. When the labels were sold to Motown, The Dynamics were left high and dry. However, when producer Don Davis moved from Motown to Stax in late 1968, he took The Dynamics with him (in the interim they had changed their name to The Dramatics) and they were signed to the Volt label. By this time the lineup, having undergone many changes, had settled with Ron Banks, William Howard, Larry Demps, Willie Ford and Elbert Wilkins. In 1971 the LP *Whatcha See Is Whatcha Get* (USA#20.1972) gave them two massive hits with the title track (USA#9.1971) and *In The Rain* (USA#5.1972). This success prompted more changes in the line-up with Wilkins and Howard leaving in 1973, they were replaced by L. J. Reynolds and Lenny Mayes.

No more hits were immediately forthcoming and with Stax falling into a state of disarray they left the label and were signed by ABC.

Their first LP for the new label, *The Dramatic Jackpot* (USA#31.1975), re-established their credentials. After the assimilation of ABC into MCA, they recorded *Music Is For The People*, but they were dropped by MCA shortly afterwards. In 1982, they were signed by Capitol, their debut LP, *New Dimensions*, was produced by lead vocalist, Ron Banks. L. J. Reynolds left the group to concentrate upon a solo career, signing with Phonogram, where he had a minor hit with *Don't Let Nobody Hold You Down* (UK#53.1984), and then in 1987, with Fantasy. In 1989, The Dramatics regrouped after a three year hiatus and signed with Fantasy subsidiary, Volt, cutting the LP *Positive State of Mind*. Despite their lack of chart success for some years now, The Dramatics are such seasoned performers that they can tour indefinitely

WHATCHA SEE IS WHATCHA GET, Stax, 1971
A DRAMATIC EXPERIENCE, Stax, 1973
THE BEST OF THE DRAMATICS, London, 1987
TELL ME YOU WILL, (L. J. Reynolds), Fantasy, 1987
POSITIVE STATE OF MIND, Volt, 1989

DRELLS   See BELL, Archie, & The Drells

DRIFTERS   The Drifters were formed in 1953 by Clyde McPHATTER, who had been fired as lead singer of Billy WARD and The Dominoes. After a few changes in line-up, the group comprised McPhatter, Bill Pinckney and Andrew and Gerhart Thrasher. Their first record was *Money Honey*, written by Atlantic producer and A&R man Jesse STONE. It topped the R&B Charts for eleven weeks and was the first of a series of R&B hits including *Such a Night, Lucille, Bip Bam* and *Whatcha Gonna Do?*. However, in 1954 McPhatter was drafted into the army to be replaced by David Baughan, who remained with the group until 1955, being in turn replaced by Johnny Moore.

In 1955 Andrew Thrasher was fired by their manager, Bill Treadwell, and replaced by Charlie Hughes. After another spate of changes in personnel, including the departure of Johnny Moore, who was drafted, the whole group was fired by Treadwell. Claiming ownership of the name, he hired another group, The Crowns, and rechristened them The Drifters. In 1959, with Ben E. KING taking the lead vocal, they started to record under the guidance of LEIBER & STOLLER.

Over the next five years, despite occasional changes in personnel, most notably the resignation of Ben E. King in 1961, they recorded a string of hits: *There Goes my Baby* (USA #2.1959), *Dance with Me* (USA#15.1959; UK #14.1960), *This Magic Moment* (USA#16. 1960), *Save the Last Dance for Me* (USA#1; UK#2.1960), *I Count the Tears* (USA#17.1960; UK#28.1961), *Some Kind of Wonderful* (USA #32.1961), *Please Stay* (USA#14.1961), *Sweets for my Sweet* (USA#16.1961), *When my Little Girl is Smiling* (USA#28; UK#31.1962), *Up on the Roof* (USA#5.1962), *On Broadway* (USA #9.1963), *I'll Take you Home* (USA#25; UK #37.1963), *Under the Boardwalk* (USA#4; UK#45.1964), *I've Got Sand in my Shoes* (USA #33.1964) and *Saturday Night at the Movies* (USA#18.1964; UK#3.1972). Their success was primarily due to the excellence of the material which came from Brill Building writers like Doc POMUS, Mort SHUMAN and GOFFIN & KING, as well as Leiber & Stoller. In 1963, Bert BERNS took over from Leiber & Stoller as their producer; he remained at the helm until 1966. In 1964 Johnny Moore returned to the line-up, following the death of Rudy Lewis, who had replaced Ben E. King. Throughout the 1960s, the group continued to chart. Although their popularity was on the wane, their well rehearsed stage show ensured that they were constantly in demand on the club circuit, particularly in the UK and Europe.

In 1973, they signed a fresh contract with Bell in the UK. Over the next four years they had a succession of hits: *Like Brother and Sister* (UK#7.1973), *Kissin' in the Back Row of the Movies* (UK#2.1974), *Down on the Beach Tonight* (UK#7.1974), *Love Games* (UK #33.1975), *There Goes my First Love* (UK #3.1975), *Can I Take You Home Little Girl?* (UK#10.1975), *Hello Happiness* (UK #12.1976), *Every Night's a Saturday Night with You* (UK#29.1976) and *You're More than a Number in my Little Red Book* (UK#5.1976). These songs were by a variety of writers including Roger Cook, Roger Greenaway, Tony Macauley, Les Reed, Bary Mason and Geoff Stephens. Since 1977 The Drifters have toured the UK and Europe constantly but, as is so often the case, there have been so many different line- ups of the group over the years that any number of people can lay, and have laid claim to the name.

GOLDEN HITS, Atlantic, 1974

24 ORIGINAL HITS, Atlantic, 1975

JUKE BOX GIANTS, Audio Fidelity, 1982

GREATEST HITS: LIVE!, Astan, 1984

THIS MAGIC MOMENT, Astan, 1984

BIP BAM, (with Clyde McPhatter), Edsel, 1984

GREATEST HITS, MFP, 1985.

LIVE AT HARVARD UNIVERSITY, Showcase, 1986

THE VERY BEST OF THE DRIFTERS, Telstar, 1986

THE COLLECTION, Castle, 1987

SOME KIND OF WONDERFUL, Meteor, 1987

SAVE THE LAST DANCE FOR ME, Atlantic, 1987

1959 – 1965: ALL TIME GREATEST HITS, Atlantic, 1991

DUKE, DORIS She was born Doris Curry in Sandersville, Georgia. Her career started singing in her local church after which she moved into a succession of gospel groups like The Raspberry Singers and The Evangelistic Gospel Singers. On moving to New York, she began to work as a session singer, backing artists like Aretha FRANKLIN, Frank Sinatra, Junior WALKER and Dusty Springfield. This enabled her to record some sides under her married name of Doris Willingham for the independent Hy-Monty label in 1967; after which she toured in Europe briefly with Nina SIMONE as a backing vocalist.

In 1969, having returned to the South and changed her name to Doris Duke, she hooked up with Jerry Williams for the LP, *I'm a Loser*, for the Canyon label; it was one of the great expositions of country-soul, that it failed commercially was, perhaps, no great surprise, the combination of Williams' idiosyncratic production with Duke's achingly soulful voice seemed to reflect the passing of an era. The follow-up, *A Legend In Her Own Time*, continued the partnership with Williams, but lacked the impact of its predecessor. After the demise of Canyon, she recorded the LP *Mankind* in London for the Contempo label; however, the inexorable rise of disco left her out in the cold. In recent years, she has been active on the gospel circuit.

DUKE, GEORGE The career of George Duke has fallen into two distinct categories: as a musician, he has become one of the chief keyboard jazz session musicians in the USA; as a producer he has worked with a variety of performers like Philip BAILEY, Al JARREAU, Jeffrey OSBORNE, Smokey ROBINSON and Deniece WILLIAMS.

He was born on January 12, 1946, in San Rafael, California. After playing with Cannonball Adderly's group, he joined Frank Zappa's outfit, The Mothers of Invention, in 1970, where he teamed up with violinist Jean-Luc Ponty. After his spell with Zappa he left to continue session work and to launch his own career. His LPs, *Reach For It* (USA

#25.1977), *Don't Let Go* (USA#39.1978) and *A Brazilian Love Affair* (UK#33.1980), the title track (UK#36.1980) was released as a single, have always owed a lot to Miles Davis and he was well-placed to capitalize upon the vogue for jazz/funk during the late1970s, in much the same way as former Davis alumni, Herbie Hancock and Stanley Clarke were able to do. Collaborations with bassist Stanley Clarke resulted in the LPs, *The Clarke-Duke Project* (USA#33.1981), which included the single *Sweet Baby* (USA#19.1981),*The Clarke- Duke Project 2* (1983) and *The Clarke-Duke Project 3* (1988). His talent as a musician has been his foremost asset in his production work, since he is able to relate to projects as a musician would, rather than just as a technician. In recent years he has been increasingly in demand for these very reasons.

THE CLARKE-DUKE PROJECT II, Epic, 1983
I LOVE THE BLUES, Polydor, 1984
THIEF IN THE NIGHT, Elektra, 1985
GEORGE DUKE, Elektra, 1986
THE CLARKE-DUKE PROJECT 3, Epic, 1988

DUNN, DONALD "DUCK" After Lewis Steinberg was sacked from BOOKER T & THE MGs in 1964, Donald "Duck" Dunn was hired to replace him. He was born in Memphis on November 24, 1941. He had joined Stax as a bassist in the house band, The MARKEYS, after leaving school, where he had been a member of The Royal Spades, and so his promotion to The MGs was a relatively short step. His partnership with drummer Al JACKSON set fire to a whole crop of records throughout the 1960s and early 1970s by artists like Otis REDDING, Wilson PICKETT, Eddie FLOYD, Johnnie TAYLOR and Carla THOMAS, imbuing them with an inventive solidity matched only

by James JAMERSON and Benny BENJA-MIN at Motown and the team at Rick HALL's Fame Studios.

After both Booker T and Steve CROPPER left Stax, The MGs effectively disbanded. In 1973, at the behest of Stax, Dunn and Jackson recruited Carson Whitsett and Bobby Manuel to record the LP, *The MGs*, it was a lack-lustre affair by comparison with their former work. Since the demise of Jackson in 1975, Dunn has continued to do session work and has participated in the occasional tour or recording with the re-formed Booker T & The MGs. In 1980, he and Cropper were featured as backing musicians in the film, *The Blues Brothers*, which was such a success that a group was formed to tour the USA. In 1989, The Blues Brothers, featuring Dunn on bass, recorded their version of the Solomon BURKE hit from 1964, *Everybody Needs Somebody to Love*.

E, SHEILA One of PRINCE's particular talents has been his undoubted ability to single out potential in his female collaborators; Sheila E, like Cat Glover and WENDY & LISA, launched a solo careers after being nurtured by Prince, while much of her achievements are directly traceable to Prince's influence she has in her time penned some pretty nifty tunes.

Sheila Escovedo was born in San Francisco on December 12, 1959; her father, Pete Escovedo, was percussionist in Santana. In 1984, having recorded her debut LP, *Sheila E In The Glamorous Life* (USA#28.1984), with Prince, she joined his group The Revolution; the LP featured two singles, *The Glamorous Life* (USA#7.1984) and *The Belle Of St. Mark* (USA#34; UK#18.1984). She has remained one of the key figures in the group, despite occasionally leaving. In 1985 she recorded the LP, *Romance 1600*. It included the single, *A Love Bizarre* (USA#11.1985), which was featured in the film, *Krush Groove*. Her next solo LP, *Sheila E*, made with assistance from the Paisley Park retinue, was released in 1987, and it was followed by the rather dubious sounding *Sex Cymbal* LP in 1991, which did little to enhance her reputation.

SHEILA E IN THE GLAMOROUS LIFE, Warner Bros., 1984
ROMANCE 1600, Warner Bros., 1985
SHEILA E, Paisley Park, 1987
SEX CYMBAL, Warner Bros., 1991

EARL-JEAN   See COOKIES

EARTH, WIND & FIRE   Earth, Wind & Fire was formed in 1970 by Maurice White (born in Memphis, Tennessee on December 19, 1944). While he was still at school White learnt to play the drums and teamed up with Booker T. Jones (see BOOKER T & THE MGs). In 1960 he started to attend the Chicago Conservatory of Music, where he studied composition and percussion. By 1963, he was working as a drummer at the Chess Studios, where he backed Chuck BERRY, Fontella BASS, Mitty COLLIER, The DELLS and Etta JAMES, among others. In 1966 he joined The Ramsey LEWIS Trio with whom he remained until 1969, when he formed The Salty Peppers and had a local hit with *La La Time* for Capitol. In 1970 he changed the name of the group to Earth, Wind & Fire and signed with Warner Bros., for whom they recorded two LPs, *Earth, Wind & Fire* and *The Need of Love*. In 1972 the group signed to CBS and White dismissed the existing line-up, retaining his brother, bassist Verdine White, and recruiting Philip BAILEY (vocals and percussion), Jessica Cleaves (vocals), Roland Bautista

(guitar), Larry Dunn (keyboards), Ronnie Laws (sax and flute) and Ralph Johnson (drums and percussion).

In the course of the next twelve years they established themselves as one of the most successful black groups in the world with a string of hit singles: *Mighty Mighty* (USA#29.1974), *Shining Star* (USA#1.1975), *That's the Way of the World* (USA#12.1975), *Sing a Song* (USA #5.1975), *Getaway* (USA#12.1976), *Saturday Nite* (USA#21.1976; UK#17.1977), *Serpentine Fire* (USA#13.1977), *Fantasy* (USA#32.1977; UK#14.1978), *Got to Get You into my Life* (USA#9; UK#33.1978), *September* (USA#8; UK#3.1978), *After the Love Has Gone* (USA#2; UK#4.1979), *Boogie Wonderland* with The EMOTIONS (USA#6; UK#4.1979), *Let's Groove* (USA/UK#3.1981) and *Fall In Love With Me* (USA#17; UK#47.1983). Although the singles were succesful by anyone's standards the LPs proved even more so, with all but four selling over a million copies: *Head to the Sky* (USA#27.1973), *Open Our Eyes* (USA #15.1974), *That's the Way of the World* (USA #1.1975), *Gratitude* (USA#1.1975), *Spirit* (USA#2.1976), *All 'n' All* (USA#3.1977; UK #13.1978), *I Am* (USA#3; UK#5.1979), *Faces* (USA/UK#10.1980), *Raise!* (USA#5; UK #14.1981) and *Powerlight* (USA#12; UK #22.1983).

In 1979 White established his own record label, The American Recording Company, and signed artists like The Emotions, Weather Report, D. J. Rogers and Deniece WILLIAMS, many of whose careers he supervised personally. As a producer he was much sought after by artists like Barbra Streisand and Jennifer HOLLIDAY. In 1984, White disbanded the group once again, this time to rest and to concentrate upon his production company, Kalimba. In 1985, he released his first solo LP *Maurice White*. In 1987, he re-formed the group for a world tour with Philip Bailey, Verdine White, Andrew Woolfolk and Sheldon

Reynolds to promote the LP, *Touch The World.* In 1990 the LP *Heritage* was released, featuring contributions from Sly Stone (see SLY & THE FAMILY STONE) and MC Hammer, but it failed to match up to the standards of the group's previous outings.

LAST DAYS AND TIME, CBS, 1972
HEAD TO THE SKY, CBS, 1973
THAT'S THE WAY OF THE WORLD, CBS, 1975
GRATITUDE, CBS, 1975
SPIRIT, Hallmark, 1976
ALL 'N' ALL, CBS, 1977
THE BEST OF EARTH, WIND & FIRE, VOLUME1, CBS, 1978
I AM, CBS, 1979
FACES, CBS, 1980
RAISE!, CBS, 1981
COLLECTION, K-Tel, 1984
MAURICE WHITE, CBS, 1986
TOUCH THE WORLD, CBS, 1987
HERITAGE, CBS, 1990

EDWARDS, BERNARD Bernard Edwards was born on October 31, 1952, in Greenville, North Carolina. He and Nile RODGERS formed The Big Apple Band in 1972; in 1977 they changed the name to CHIC. Throughout the late 1970s, Chic were the most successful dance-oriented group in the world. The expertise of Rodgers and Edwards, the creative force behind the Chic Organization, enabled them to revive the career of SISTER SLEDGE, galvanize the career of Diana ROSS and launch the solo career of Debbie Harry. As the popularity of Chic declined, they were each able to move into separate careers as producers.

After the demise of Chic, Edwards started the apparently obligatory solo career by releasing an LP, *Glad to be Here.* Although it failed to sell in the quantities he had become accustomed to, it led to an invitation to join and produce The Power Station. This group consisted of Robert PALMER (lead vocals), John Taylor (bass), Andy Taylor (guitar) and former Chic drummer Tony Thompson. The debut LP, *The Power Station,* provided them with two hit singles, *Some Like It Hot* and *Get It On.* After Palmer left the group, Edwards continued to work with him, producing his solo albums.

EDWARDS, DENNIS When David RUFFIN left The TEMPTATIONS in July 1968, Dennis Edwards (born on February 3, 1943, in Birmingham, Alabama) had the perfect credentials to fill the vacant role. He had sung in the gospel group, The Golden Wonders, and in fellow Motown group, The CONTOURS. For ten years, he contributed the lead vocals to some of The Temptations most powerful songs including *Cloud Nine, Psychedelic Shack, Runaway Child Running Wild* and *Papa was a Rolling Stone:* with his gospel roots, he was able to extract every ounce of emotion from the social comment of the lyrics. In 1978, he made the first of several attempts at pursuing a solo career. By 1980, he had returned to The Temptations, where he remained for a further three years. In 1984, having restarted his solo career, he released the LP, *Don't Look any Further,* it failed to sell well despite being very well received critically and the title track (UK#45.1984/#55.1987) charting on two separate occasions. The follow-up, *Coolin' Out* (1985) attracted even less attention despite the obvious perk of his collaborating with producer Dennis LAMBERT. In 1987 he rejoined The Temptations once again, following revived interest in the group. The fact that his solo career has failed to ignite must remain one of the great enigmas: on the evidence of his two outings to date, he suffers no shortage of either ability or suitable material.

DON'T LOOK ANY FURTHER, Gordy, 1984
COOLIN' OUT, Gordy, 1985

ELBERT, DONNIE Donnie Elbert's career started in 1954 in his native Chicago. By 1957, he had obtained his first recording contract with the De-Luxe label, where he cut *What Can I Do* among others. In 1958 Ewart ABNER signed him to Veejay, where he cut *Will You Ever Be Mine*, which was a minor hit. In 1961, he was drafted into the US Army. After his discharge he recorded briefly in Philadelphia for the Parkway label, and for Checker in Chicago. Then, he founded his own label, Gateway, recording his most well known hit, *A Little Piece Of Leather* (UK#27.1972), as well as *Run Little Girl*, both of which became turntable hits in the clubs in the UK; the former was reissued in 1972 when it finally became a hit. In 1964 he moved to the UK, where he got married. For the next six years he was a regular on the European club circuit. However, in 1970 he moved back to the USA and was signed by Sylvia ROBINSON to the All Platinum label, where he recorded versions of songs like *Where Did our Love Go* (USA#15.1971; UK#8.1972), *I Can't Help Myself* (USA#22; UK#11.1972) and *Can't Get over Losing You*. Throughout the latter half of the 1970s he recorded little, touring on the chitlin' circuit constantly, interspersed with occasional European tours. He resumed recording in 1981 with *You Don't Have To Be A Star* for Sylvia Robinson's Sugarhill label, but its lack of success was sufficient for him to concentrate his energies upon touring.

ELGINS The Elgins were a very good example of a perfectly sound vocal group, who, because they were signed to Motown, never got a look in on a regular basis as there were so many other acts competing for attention and material. The group was formed as The Downbeats in 1962, it comprised Cleo Miller, Johnny Dawson and Robert Fleming. After Sandra Edwards joined the group in 1964, they changed their name to The Elgins. They were signed to the Motown subsidiary, VIP, where they were assigned to the writer/production team of HOLLAND, DOZIER & HOLLAND. Between 1965 and 1966, they cut tracks like *Heaven Must Have Sent You* (UK #3.1971), *Darling Baby, Put Yourself In My Place* (UK#28.1971) and *Stay In My Lonely Arm*: the very fact that their biggest hit was *Heaven Must Have Sent You*, which only reached #50 in the USA when it was first released, was in itself a reflection of the amount of talent that Motown had at its disposal and was in no way an indication of the group being palmed off with sub-standard material. Their lack of success caused the group to break up in 1968. Subsequently, the group charted in the UK, when their singles were reissued.

ELLIS, SHIRLEY Shirley Ellis was born in the Bronx, New York, in 1941. After joining The Metronomes she started to write. One of her first compositions was *One, Two, I Love You*, which was recorded by The Heartbreakers. In 1958, she teamed up with her future husband Lincoln Chase, composer of titles like *Jim Dandy* and *Jim Dandy Got Married*, the LaVern BAKER hits, to write titles like *The Nitty Gritty* (USA#8.1963), *The Name Game* (USA#3.1965) and *The Clapping Song* (USA#8; UK#6.1965), all of which she performed herself. Although they were nominally novelty items, they proved immensely popular in the clubs. However, their success typecast her and she was unable to break the pattern. In 1967, she retired from the music business.

ELLISON, LORRAINE Until she was discovered by Jerry RAGAVOY, Lorraine Ellison was a member of the gospel group, The Golden Chords. Her overwrought, dramatic style was perfectly complemented by Ragavoy's penchant for lavish orchestral arrangements. This penchant achieved its ultimate expression with her rendition of the Ragavoy and George Weiss composition, *Stay with Me*. Although it failed to climb any further than #64 in 1966, it was a benchmark for later female soul singers of the seventies with less intrinsic ability, and they were able to get away with inferior material, swamped by lavish arrangements. Ragavoy's association with Ellison lasted until 1969, during which time they recorded the LPs, *Heart and Soul* and *Stay with me Baby*. Although, these records are much sought after and Ellison's standing remains high among aficionados, she has recorded little since then.

EMOTIONS The Emotions were a trio of sisters from Chicago; Wanda (born on December 17, 1951), Sheila (born on January 17, 1953) and Jeanette Hutchinson (born in February, 1951). When they were children they formed a gospel group called The Hutchinson Sunbeams. Under the eagle eye of their father, they developed their act until "Pops" Staples of the STAPLE Singers suggested they should go to Stax in Memphis. From 1968, with the writing and production partnership of Isaac HAYES and David PORTER, they recorded a string of singles including *So I Can Love You* (USA#39.1969), *Stealin' Love* and *When Tomorrow Comes*. In 1970, Jeanette left the group and was replaced by Teresa Davis (born August 22, 1950). When Stax folded they were left without a recording contract and so continued to tour until, in 1976, they were teamed up with Maurice White of EARTH, WIND & FIRE. Their first LP with White was *Flowers* (1976). It was followed by the LPs *Rejoice* (USA#7.1977), which included the singles, *Best Of My Love* (USA#1; UK#4.1977) and *I Don't Wanna Lose Your Love* (UK #40.1977), and then by *Sunbeam* (USA #40.1978). The following year they featured with Earth, Wind & Fire on the single *Boogie Wonderland* (USA#6; UK#4.1979). During the 1980s, they toured with Earth, Wind & Fire and The COMMODORES among others and recorded briefly for Motown, before retiring to concentrate on raising their families. More recently plans have been mooted of a return to live work, but nothing has materialised so far.

IF I ONLY KNEW, Motown, 1985

ENCHANTERS See MIMMS, Garnett

ERTEGUN, AHMET Apart from Motown, Atlantic has been the one label that has exerted the strongest influence upon the popularisation of black music – be it jazz, soul or R&B. It was founded in 1947 by Ahmet Ertegun and Herb ABRAMSON. Ertegun was the son of the former Turkish Ambassador to the USA. He was approached by Abramson and Jesse STONE, who were looking for backing to set up their own label to record black music. Ertegun was not simply a money man: much as did Berry GORDY, he had the creative vision to harness the direction the company would take by visiting the deep South with Abramson and Stone to root out talent at source.

Throughout the 1950s, Ertegun – with Stone and Abramson, and then with Jerry WEXLER – signed up a whole crop of artists like Ruth BROWN, LaVern BAKER, Big Joe Turner, The DRIFTERS, The COASTERS, Ray CHARLES, Chuck WILLIS and The CLOVERS. His sphere of influence didn't stop there: his production credits included *Shake, Rattle And Roll* for Big Joe Turner, *What'd I Say* for Ray Charles, *Money Honey* for The Drifters, *One Mint Julep* and *Blue Velvet* for The Clovers, *Since I Met You Baby* for Ivory Joe HUNTER , *I Cried A Tear* and *Soul On Fire* for LaVern Baker, *A Lover's Question* for Clyde McPHATTER and *Don't Play That Song* for Ben E. KING. By the dawning of the 1960s, while he remained firmly in control, producers like Tom DOWD, Jerry Wexler and Arif MARDIN were tending to oversee most of the production chores, leaving Ertegun free to preside over a company that had, increasingly, embraced all facets of popular music. While the signing of Aretha FRANKLIN, Wilson PICKETT, Joe TEX and Percy SLEDGE, and the close association with Jim STEWART's Stax label certainly endorsed Atlantic's position as one of the major independent soul labels, the company began to sign rock acts like Vanilla Fudge, The Young Rascals, Buffalo Springfield and Led Zeppelin. This enabled Atlantic to consolidate themselves as one of the major forces in contemporary music; their linking up with Warner Bros. for over $15 millions in 1967 served only to emphasise this claim. In 1970 they acquired the Criteria studios in Florida, which have come to be known as Atlantic South. The 1970s and 1980s have seen the total assimilation of Atlantic into Warner Bros. (now owned by Time Inc.), but Ertegun has remained with the company and has become, in the process, a guru-like figure in the music business.

EVERETT, BETTY Betty Everett was born on November 23, 1939, in Greenwood, Mississippi. In 1956 she moved to Chicago where, having sung gospel in church choirs, she turned her attention to R&B. In 1963, after performing on the local club circuit and recording for small local labels like Cobra, she was signed to Veejay, where she had a number of hits: *You're No Good, The Shoop Shoop Song (It's in his Kiss)* (USA#6.1964; UK#34.1968); *I Can't Hear You* and *It's Getting Mighty Crowded* (UK#29.1965). As duos were in vogue, she was teamed with Jerry BUTLER for *Let it be Me* (USA#5.1964) and *Smile*. However, she moved labels, signing with ABC and then with Uni, where she had a hit with *There'll Come a Time* (USA#26.1969). Then she was signed by Fantasy where she had a modest hit with *I Got to Tell Somebody*. Throughout the 1970s, she continued to be a strong draw on the club circuit in the USA and Europe, but her records have tended to miss the mark despite working with prestigious arranger Gene PAGE on the LPs *Love Rhymes* (1974) and *Happy Endings* (1975).

BETTY EVERETT 1957-1961, Flyright, 1986

EXCITERS The nucleus of The Exciters revolved around the husband and wife team of Herb Rooney and Brenda Reid, the line-up was completed by Carol Johnson and Lilian Walker until 1966, when they were replaced by Ronnie Pace and Skip McPhee. They were formed and based in New York from 1961, but were unfortunate in that their most well-known records *Tell Him* (USA#4.1962), a Bert BERNS composition, and *Do Wah Diddy*, a Jeff BARRY and Ellie GREENWICH composition, produced by LEIBER & STOLLER, were covered by other artists, who rather stole their thunder. In 1964, they recorded *He's Got the Power* and The Jarmels' *A Little Bit Of Soap*, another Bert Berns composition. However, they were unable to make an indelible impression in their own right.

FALCONS The Falcons are significant for three reasons: first, they recorded *You're So Fine* (USA#17.1959); second, they recorded *I Found A Love* in 1962 and, third, they provided such an admirable education for would-be writers and performers like Eddie FLOYD, Wilson PICKETT and Mack Rice (songwriter and, on occasions, Luther INGRAM's co-writer). Even Joe Jackson, father of the JACK-SONS used to play guitar for them. Furthermore The OHIO PLAYERS (as The Ohio Untouchables) were the group's backing band in the early 1960s.

I FOUND A LOVE, Relic, 1985
YOU'RE SO FINE, Relic, 1985

FELDER, WILTON Wilton Felder (tenor sax and bass) was born on August 31, 1940 in Houston, Texas. While he was still at school he was a founder member of what would become The CRUSADERS. As a session musician, he has worked with B. B. KING, Bobby BLAND, Randy CRAWFORD, Quincy JONES and many others. His solo career started in 1978 with the release of the LP, *We All Have a Star*. It was followed in 1980 by the LP *Inherit the Wind*; the title track featured a vocal by Bobby WOMACK and was an international turntable hit (UK #39.1980) in the clubs. The LP *Gentle Fire* was released in 1983, being followed by the LP *Secrets* (USA#81.1985), with Bobby Womack once again providing the vocal parts. Throughout, Felder has continued to be an integral part of The Crusaders and to work on sessions.

WE ALL HAVE A STAR, ABC, 1978
GENTLE FIRE, MCA, 1983
SECRETS, MCA, 1985

FINE YOUNG CANNIBALS After the break-up of The Beat in 1983, guitarist Andy Cox (born in Birmingham, UK, on January 25, 1956) and bassist David Steele (born in Birmingham, UK, on September 8, 1960) enlisted vocalist Roland Gift, who had been brought up in Hull. They called themselves Fine Young Cannibals, after the Robert Wagner and Natalie Wood film, *All the Fine Young Cannibals*. They were signed by London. Their eponymous debut LP (UK#11.1985), included the singles *Johnny Come Home* (UK #8.1985) and *Suspicious Minds* (UK#8.1986). After the success of the LP, they got involved in separate projects: Gift costarred in the film, *Sammy and Rosie Get Laid*, and also had a cameo role in the film dramatization of the Profumo Affair, *Scandal*. Steele and Cox recorded the single *Tired of Getting Pushed Around* (UK#18.1988) under the name of Two Men, A Drum Machine and A Trumpet, and then collaborated with Wee Papa Girl Rappers on their single, *Heat It Up*. Both singles established a much greater collective credibility for the group with the increasingly influential club set.

In 1986 the group contributed four songs to the soundtrack of the Barry Levinson film, *Tin Men*, starring Danny DeVito. Their idiosyncratic version of The Buzzcocks' composition, *Ever Fallen in Love* (UK#9.1987), was included on the soundtrack of another highly successful film, *Something Wild*. In 1989 they released that difficult second LP, *The Raw and the Cooked* (USA/UK#1.1989), which included the singles *She Drives Me Crazy* (USA#1; UK#5.1989), *Good Thing* (UK#7.1989) and *Not the Man I Used to Be* (USA#1.1989). After a period of touring to promote the LP, Gift returned to acting, appearing in the Hull Truck Theatre Group's production of *Romeo & Juliet* in 1990. Cox and Steele worked with Moni Love on her debut LP. The same year they re-grouped, contributing their version of *Love For Sale* to the

LP of Cole Porter songs, *Red Hot and Blue*: a compilation assembled to promote awareness of AIDS and the HIV virus.

FINE YOUNG CANNIBALS, London, 1985
THE RAW AND THE COOKED, London, 1989

FIVE ROYALES In 1952 Lowman Pauling, the leader of the gospel group, The Royal Sons, changed its musical direction and renamed it The Five Royales. The group had been formed in 1942 in Winston, North Carolina, and in 1948 had started to record for Apollo, where they had a string of R&B hits including *Baby Don't Do It, Too Much Lovin', Help Me Somebody, Crazy Crazy Crazy* and *Laundromat Blues*. In 1954, they signed with the King label and, in an occasional partnership with Ralph BASS, the A&R supremo at King, Pauling wrote some of the most potent R&B compositions of the 1950s, including *Dedicated to the One I Love, Think, Tell the Truth* and *The Slummer the Slum*, in which his technique as a guitarist was inspirational. Despite their inability to crack the national top forty, by the time they stopped recording in 1966 the influence of their records had percolated through into all idioms of contemporary music: girl groups of the early sixties like The SHIRELLES; harmony groups of the mid-1960s like The Mamas and The Papas; guitarists like Eric Clapton and Steve CROPPER and, of course, architects of soul like Ray CHARLES, James BROWN and Aretha FRANKLIN.

THE ROOTS OF SOUL, Charly, 1987
DEDICATED TO YOU, King, 1988
SING FOR YOU, King, 1988
THE FIVE ROYALES, King, 1988

FIVE SATINS In 1953, while still at school in New Haven, Connecticut, Fred Parris formed The Scarlets comprising Bill Baker, Al Denby, Jim Freeman, Ed Martin and pianist Jesse Murphy. In the mid-1950s, they recorded four singles for the Red Robin label, none of which made any appreciable inroads. By 1956, Parris, who had been conscripted, wrote *In the Still of the Nite* (USA #24.1956) during his guard duty. Upon his return on leave he re-formed the group as The Five Satins and cut his composition in a church basement, leasing it to Ember Records via the Standard label. Since its release it has become one of the epochal doo-wop records and, although the subsequent *To the Aisle* (USA #25.1957) was a far more intriguing record with lyrics that were straight out of a slushy romantic novel, it has eclipsed The PLATTERS' many offerings to become one of the most celebrated record of the genre, returning to the lower echelons of the US Charts on several further occasions. After these successes, the group was unable to match them with later releases. Despite various attempts by Parris to relaunch the group under fresh guises, they have still had to resort to the comparative security of the oldies circuit. In 1982, under the name Fred Parris & The Five Satins, they returned briefly to the US charts with *Memories of Days Gone By*, which peaked at #71.

FLACK, ROBERTA Roberta Flack was born in Asheville, North Carolina, on February 10, 1939. She studied music at Howard University in Washington DC., and then taught music. In 1968 she started to perform in clubs in Washington when she was spotted by Les McCann. He arranged an audition for her with Ahmet ERTEGUN which resulted in a contract with Atlantic. Her first LP, *First Take* (USA#1; UK#47.1972), was produced by Joel Dorn in 1970, and included the Ewan

MacColl song *The First Time Ever I Saw Your Face* (USA#1; UK#14.1972), which was featured in the Clint Eastwood film *Play Misty for Me* two years after its initial release. Her second LP, *Chapter Two* (USA#33.1970), was followed by a duet with Donny HATHAWAY on a cover version of the Carole King (see GOFFIN & KING) song *You've Got A Friend* (USA#29.1971). This was the beginning of a liaison that lasted until Hathaway's death in 1979. Their first LP together, *Roberta Flack And Donny Hathaway* (USA#3.1972), featured the single *Where is the Love?* (USA#5; UK#29.1972).

Her third LP, *Quiet Fire* (USA#18.1972), was followed in 1973 by her version of the Lori Leiberman composition, *Killing me Softly with his Song* (USA#1; UK#6.1973). The LP of the same name (USA#3; UK#40.1973) proved to be her final full collaboration with producer Joel Dorn, who parted company with Atlantic midway through the recording of her next LP, *Feel Like Making Love* (USA#24.1975), the title track of which (USA#1; UK#34.1974) was released as a single and sold over a million copies. In 1975 she reverted to her former occupation, teaching, concentrating particularly upon the plight of the under privileged. Then, in 1978, she released the LP *Blue Lights in the Basement* (USA#8.1978), which included the single *The Closer I Get To You* (USA#2; UK#42.1978), a duet with Hathaway. In 1979 she embarked upon another LP with Hathaway, but recording was halted by his sudden death and she ended up finishing it alone as a tribute to him. Called *Featuring Donny Hathaway* (USA#25; UK#31.1980), It included *Back Together Again* (USA#56; UK#3.1980). In 1981, she teamed up with Peabo BRYSON for a series of live performances which gave birth to a double live LP, *Live and More* (USA #52.1981). This was the beginning of a collaboration that was to become as successful as that with Hathaway. It included the LP *Born*

To Love (USA#25; UK#15.1983), featuring *Tonight I Celebrate my Love for You* (USA#16; UK#2.1983). In 1988, after a lengthy absence from recording during which she had both toured and been involved in educational projects, she released the LP *Oasis*.

KILLING ME SOFTLY WITH HIS SONG, Atlantic, 1973
FIRST TAKE/CHAPTER TWO, Atlantic, 1975
BLUE LIGHTS IN THE BASEMENT, Atlantic, 1978
ROBERTA FLACK, Atlantic, 1978
FEATURING DONNY HATHAWAY, Atlantic, 1980
THE BEST OF ROBERTA FLACK, Atlantic, 1981
LIVE AND MORE, (with Peabo Bryson), Atlantic, 1981
BORN TO LOVE, (with Peabo Bryson), Capitol, 1983
GREATEST HITS, K-Tel, 1984
OASIS, Atlantic, 1988

FLAMINGOS The Flamingos were formed in 1952 in Chicago and comprised, initially, Terry Johnson (born in Baltimore on November 12, 1935), Ezekiel Carey (born in Bluefield, West Virginia, on January 24, 1933), Paul Wilson (born in Chicago on January 6, 1935), Jacob Carey (born in Pulaski, Virginia, on September 9, 1926), Sollie McElroy and John Carter (both McElroy and Carter only remained with the group for a short time). Although their career lasted into the seventies, they were at the pinnacle of their influence during the 1950s, when they recorded a number of doo-wop records that managed to appeal to the gospel market as well as the pop market. In 1953 they were picked up by the Chance label and had an R&B hit with *Golden Teardrops*. From Chance they moved to Checker, via Parrot, where they recorded *Kokomo*; at Checker they had minor hits with *I'll Be Home*, which was written by Stan

LEWIS and Fats Washington, and *The Vow*. However, McElroy had left – his replacement was Nathaniel Nelson (born in Chicago on April 10, 1932) – as had John Carter, who had joined The DELLS and been replaced by Tommy HUNT. After a brief stint with Decca and Checker once again, they were signed by George GOLDNER to the End label, where they achieved national recognition with *I Only Have Eyes For You* (USA#11.1959) and *Nobody Loves Me Like You* (USA#30.1960). Both were sentimental ballads with lavish arrangements and featured the lead vocal of Tommy Hunt. Throughout the 1960s, having adapted to the burgeoning soul market, they recorded periodically without any great degree of success for a variety of labels, mostly small independents.

FLOYD, EDDIE Superficially, the career of Eddie Floyd has revolved around one record, *Knock On Wood*, but he typified the artisan quality of many of the backroom boys who played such a prominent role in the formative years of Stax. He was born in Montgomery, Alabama, on June 25, 1935, and moved to Detroit during his teens, where he became a founder member of The FALCONS with whom he had two chart successes – *You're So Fine* and *I Found A Love* – before the group disbanded in 1962. He moved to Washington DC and set up Safice Records with Al BELL, but the venture was unsuccessful and so, when Bell was hired by Jim STEWART of Stax, Floyd was taken on as a staff songwriter. At Stax, he teamed up with Steve CROPPER to write *634-5789, Ninety Nine And a Half* for former Falcon, Wilson PICKETT, and *Knock On Wood* (USA#28; UK#19.1966) for Otis REDDING. After hearing Floyd's demo of the latter, Stewart decided to release it. Quite apart from its chart success, *Knock On Wood*, became one of the definitive Stax records with Cropper, "Duck" DUNN and Al JACKSON

all playing as if their lives depended on it. Over the next two years he had a succession of hits including *Raise Your Hand* (UK#42.1967), *Things Get Better* (UK#31.1967), *I've Never Found a Girl (to Love me Like You Do)* (USA #40.1968) and *Bring it on Home to Me* (USA #17.1968), although none of them matched the immediacy of *Knock On Wood*. Since 1970, when the supply of even very minor hits dried up, he has concentrated on touring and writing, providing material for artists like SAM & DAVE, Rufus THOMAS and Eric Clapton. In recent years, he has been recording for William BELL's Wilbe label. His performances have, on occasion, tended to veer more in the direction of self-parody than is entirely desirable, but his contribution to the development of Stax has been of the highest order.

FORD, FRANKIE Apart from the three years he spent in the Army, when from 1962 to 1965, he toured South East Asia as part of an entertainment unit, Frankie Ford has been a fixture on the New Orleans club circuit. He was born Frank Guzzo on August 4, 1940 in Gretna, Louisiana and formed his first group, The Syncopators, while he was still at school. In 1959 he started to record for Johnny VINCENT's Ace label with Huey 'Piano' SMITH and The Clowns. His first two records, *Sea Cruise* (USA#14.1959) and *Alimony*, had his vocal overdubbed onto The Clowns' backing track after the original lead vocal by Bobby MARCHAN had been erased. In 1960 he signed with Imperial, but was unable to repeat the success of *Sea Cruise*, although he had modest hits with *You Talk too Much* and *Seventeen*. After his stint in the army, he returned to New Orleans, buying a club in 1971 and recording occasionally for Stan LEWIS' Paula label.

LET'S TAKE A SEA CRUISE WITH FRANKIE FORD, Ace, 1983

NEW ORLEANS DYNAMO, Ace, 1984

FOSTER, FRED Fred Foster was born in Rutherford, North Carolina. In 1954 he joined Mercury to work in field promotion; in 1956 he joined ABC-Paramount, where he signed Lloyd PRICE. In 1958 he set up the Monument label in Nashville and struck gold immediately when he signed Roy Orbison. In 1963 he established the subsidiary label Sound Stage Seven, which was devoted to soul and R&B. In 1965, he enlisted the services of John RICHBOURG to produce some of the artists in the growing roster, which included Roscoe Shelton, Arthur ALEXANDER, Joe SIMON, Fenton Robinson, Ann Sexton and Ella Washington. Richbourg set up a connection with the Stax studios in Memphis, and most of the records were cut there until Monument set up its own house band, which comprised bassist Tim Drummond, guitarists Troy Seals, Wayne Moss and Mac Gayden, pianist Bob Wilson, drummer Kenny Buttrey and Charlie McCoy on harmonica. In 1970 Foster signed a distribution deal with CBS/Columbia; this marked the end of Richbourg's association with Monument and also the end of the Sound Stage Seven label, as Foster thereafter concentrated on his roster of country artists.

FOUR PENNIES See CHIFFONS

FOUR TOPS Initially this group was known as The Four Aims. The line-up comprised Levi Stubbles, Renaldo Benson, Abdul Fakir and Lawrence Payton, all of whom were born and brought up in Detroit. Their career started in 1953, when they performed at parties and church events; after several auditions they were taken on by a talent agency which secured work further afield for them. By 1956 the group's name had been changed to The Four Tops and Stubbles had shortened his name to Stubbs. They had started to obtain work singing back-up or opening for artists like Brook BENTON and Billy Eckstine, and got their first opportunities to record: a one-off deal with Chess was followed by another one-off deal with Red Top, neither record attracting much attention. In 1960 they were signed by John Hammond to Columbia, but were dropped by the label after just one release. In 1963 they met Berry GORDY, who signed them to the fast-developing Motown label; after a year of singing back-up on sessions they were called upon by the Motown producers and writers HOLLAND, DOZIER & HOLLAND to record a demo of *Baby I Need Your Loving* (USA#11.1964). It was an association that would last until late 1967.

Over the next eight years, they became one of Motown's most consistent acts, releasing a string of hit singles: *I Can't Help Myself* (USA#1; UK#23.1965/#10.1970), *It's the Same Old Song* (USA#5; UK#34.1965), *Reach Out I'll be There* (USA/UK#1.1966), *Standing in the Shadows of Love* (USA#6.1966; UK#6.1967), *Bernadette* (USA#4; UK#8.1967), *Seven Rooms of Gloom* (USA#14; UK#12.1967), *Walk Away Renee* (USA#14.1968; UK#3.1967) – a cover of the 1966 hit by The Left Banke – *If I Were a Carpenter* (USA#20; UK#7.1968) – a re-working of the Tim Hardin song – *It's all in the Game* (USA#24; UK#5.1970), *Still Water (Love)* (USA#11; UK#10.1970) and *Simple Game* (UK#3.1971). In 1971 they were teamed with The SUPREMES for the first of three LPs, *The Magnificent Seven*, which included their version of *River Deep, Mountain High* (USA#14; UK#11.1971). Initially their LPs mirrored the success of the singles: *Four Tops on Top* (USA#32; UK#9.1966), *Four Tops Live!*

(USA#17; UK#4.1967) and *Reach Out* (USA#11; UK#4.1967).

In 1972 Motown relocated to Los Angeles. The Four Tops decided to remain in Detroit, signing with Dunhill, where they were teamed with the staff writers and producers Dennis LAMBERT and Brian Potter. They remained with Dunhill until 1976, their principal hits for the label being *Keeper of the Castle* (USA#10; UK#18.1972), *Ain't No Woman (Like the One I Got)* (USA#4.1973) and *Are You Man Enough?* (USA#15.1973). In 1981 they signed with the Casablanca label, where they stayed for one year before resigning with Motown; in that short time they scored with *When She was my Girl* (USA#11; UK#3.1981) and *Don't Walk Away* (UK#16.1982).

Their renewed association with Motown failed to recapture their former glories and, in 1988, they signed with Arista. Their debut LP for Arista, *Indestructible*, featured contributions from artists like Kenny G, Aretha FRANKLIN, Phil Collins and Narada Michael WALDEN and included the single *Goin' Loco in Acapulco* (UK#9.1989), featured in the film, *Buster*, which starred Phil Collins and Julie Walters. In 1987 the group was honoured by the Michigan State Governor, James Blanchard, for their contribution to American Music and to Civic Events; the upshot was the declaration of "Four Tops Day" on July 29. Throughout their career, they have toured constantly, like The O'JAYS, and their live act remains an object lesson in professionalism.

FOUR TOPS, Motown, 1965
FOUR TOPS SECOND ALBUM, Motown, 1965
LIVE!, Motown, 1967
REACH OUT, Motown, 1967
STILL WATERS RUN DEEP, Motown, 1970
MAGNIFICENT SEVEN, (with The Supremes), Motown, 1970
KEEPER OF THE CASTLE, ABC, 1972

IT'S ALL IN THE GAME, MFP, 1979
FOUR TOPS STORY, Motown, 1981
20 GOLDEN GREATS, Motown, 1981
SUPER HITS, Motown, 1981
TONIGHT, Casablanca, 1981
BEST OF THE FOUR TOPS, K-Tel, 1982
HITS OF GOLD, Motown, 1982
ONE MORE MOUNTAIN, Casablanca, 1982
BACK WHERE I BELONG, Motown, 1983
FOUR TOPS, (with The Supremes), Motown, 1983
COMPACT COMMAND PERFORMANCE, Motown, 1984
THE FABULOUS FOUR TOPS, Motown, 1984
GREATEST HITS, Motown, 1985
MAGIC, Motown, 1985
ANTHOLOGY, Motown, 1986
HOT NIGHTS, Motown, 1986
INDESTRUCTIBLE, Arista, 1988

FOXX, CHARLIE & INEZ Charlie and Inez Foxx were born in Greensboro, Carolina, Charlie on October 29, 1939, and Inez on September 9, 1944. They made their debut in the Greensboro Gospel Tide Choir; the experience encouraged them to move to New York, where they worked the club circuit. In 1963 they recorded *Mockingbird* (USA#7.1963; UK#34.1969) for Juggy Murray's Symbol label; they had to wait until 1969, when it was re-issued, for it to become a hit in the UK, although on its first outing in 1963, it had caused quite a ripple on the club circuit. It was followed by two formulaic novelty numbers, *Hi Diddle Diddle* and *Ask Me*. Apart from *Hurt by Love* (UK#40.1964) and another novelty item, *Count the Days* , they failed to have any more hits. By the end of the 1960s, Charlie had moved into production and Inez had married producer Luther DIXON. In 1973 she went to Memphis to record the LP *Inez in Memphis*, for the Stax subsidiary Volt.

MOCKINGBIRD, Stateside, 1986

FRANKLIN, ARETHA Given her upbringing, it is inconcievable that Aretha Franklin could have done anything other than becoming a singer. She was born in Memphis on March 25, 1942. Her parents separated and she was brought up in Detroit by her father, the Reverend C. L. Franklin, pastor of the New Bethel Church. She was taught to sing by family friends like the gospel stars, Mahalia Jackson, Clara Ward and Marion Williams. Her first record was issued in 1956 on the Checker label; recorded live at the New Bethel Church, it featured her singing some Clara Ward hymns. In 1960 she moved to New York, where she recorded four songs including *Today I Sing the Blues*, these came to the attention of John Hammond at Columbia Records, and he put her under contract. Her first LP, *The Great Aretha Franklin*, was released in October, 1960. Apart from the single *Today I Sing the Blues*, which reached #10 in the R&B charts, it failed to generate much enthusiasm. She remained with Columbia for six years, during which time she recorded some estimable tracks, but major success eluded her, partly because Hammond, convinced that he had discovered Billie Holiday's successor, had her working with inappropriate material. Jerry WEXLER showed just how much of an error this had been, when he signed her to Atlantic in 1966.

In January, 1967, Wexler took Franklin to Rick HALL's Fame Studios in Alabama and recorded *I Never Loved a Man (the Way I Love You)* (USA#9.1967); the B-side was the Chips MOMAN and Dan PENN composition, *Do Right Woman*. Both featured the Muscle Shoals house band comprising Chips Moman, Tommy COGBILL, Jimmy JOHNSON, Spooner OLDHAM and Roger HAWKINS. The follow-up was a reworking of the Otis REDDING hit, *Respect* (USA#1; UK #10.1967). It demonstrated just how adept she had become at combining her gospel training with an intuitive flair for popular music that she was able (with the assistance of Wexler and her sister, Carolyn FRANKLIN) to even consider lifting the entire bridge from SAM & DAVE's hit, *When Something is Wrong with my Baby* and re- arranging the whole song accordingly to accommodate it. This indicated a grasp of technique that would have eluded many more seasoned performers. Her first LP *I Never Loved a Man* (USA#2; UK#36.1967) was the first of a series which were not only commercial successes but also artistic triumphs: *Aretha Arrives* (USA#5.1967), *Lady Soul* (USA#2; UK#25.1968), *Aretha Now!* (USA#3; UK #6.1968), *Aretha in Paris* (USA#13.1968), *Soul '69* (USA#15.1969), *This Girl's in Love with You* (USA#17.1970), *Spirit in the Dark* (USA #25.1970) and *Young, Gifted and Black* (USA #11.1972). Throughout the late 1960s she notched up a series of hit singles that were models of economy and phrasing: *Baby I Love You* (USA#4; UK#39.1967), *(You Make me Feel Like) A Natural Woman* (USA#8.1967), *Chain of Fools* (USA#2; UK#43.1967), *Think* (USA#7; UK#26.1968), *I Say a Little Prayer* (USA#10; UK#4.1968), *Don't Play that Song* (USA#11; UK#13.1970) and *Spanish Harlem* (USA#2; UK#14.1971).

In March 1971 she performed for three nights at the Fillmore West in San Francisco with Ray CHARLES, KING CURTIS and The Tower of Power. An LP, *Aretha Live at the Fillmore West* (USA#7.1971), was released, featuring a duet with Ray Charles; it showed that the gospel traditions of her upbringing were still just as potent as ever. Further proof materialized in the form of another live LP, *Amazing Grace* (USA#7.1972), recorded at a church in the Watts District of Los Angeles and featuring James Cleveland and the Southern California Community Choir. This LP was her final collaboration with Wexler. From 1973 until she left Atlantic, she recorded with a number of different producers: Quincy

JONES, Lamont Dozier (see HOLLAND, DOZIER & HOLLAND), Curtis MAYFIELD and Arif MARDIN. The results were somewhat mixed. The LPs, *Hey Now Hey (The Other Side of the Sky)* (USA#30.1973), produced by Jones, and *Let Me In Your Life* (USA #14.1974), produced by Mardin and Tom DOWD, each included a hit single: *Angel* (USA#20; UK#37.1973) and *Until You Come Back to Me (That's what I'm Gonna Do)* (USA#3; UK#26.1974), respectively.

In 1980 she left Atlantic and signed with Arista under the auspices of Clive DAVIS. This was the beginning of a new phase in her career, which would bring her to a significantly wider and younger audience. Her first LP for Arista, *Aretha*, produced by Mardin, included her version of *What A Fool Believes* (UK#46.1980). Part of the credit for the dramatic increase in her popularity must go to Davis, who has teamed her with producers like Luther VANDROSS and Narada Michael WALDEN, both of whom have written material specifically for her. Furthermore, he instigated duets with artists like George Benson – *Love All the Hurt Away* (USA#46; UK#49.1981) – Annie Lennox and The Eurythmics – *Sisters are Doing it for Themselves* (USA#18; UK #9.1985) – Keith Richard – *Jumpin' Jack Flash* (USA#21; UK#58.1986) and George Michael – *I Knew You Were Waiting (for Me)* (USA/UK #1.1987). In 1985 the LP *Who's Zoomin' Who?* (USA#13; UK#49.1985), produced by Walden became her first million-selling LP. It included the singles, *Who's Zoomin' Who?* (USA#7; UK#11.1985), *Freeway Of Love* (USA#3; UK #51.1985) and *Another Night* (USA#22; UK #54.1986). Despite the strongly commercial slant to her records, in 1988 she recorded the double live LP *One Lord, One Faith*, at the New Bethel Church as a tribute to her father, who had died the previous year.

Doubtless there are those that would contend that her recent material could not hold a light to the early Atlantic records which Wexler produced for her. However, "The Voice" - once described by the state governor as "one of Michigan's natural resources" – has retained its strength and her phrasing and timing are unimpaired by the passage of time.

GREATEST HITS, Atlantic, 1975
TEN YEARS OF GOLD, Atlantic, 1976
ALMIGHTY FIRE, Atlantic, 1978
ARETHA, Arista, 1980
LOVE ALL THE HURT AWAY, Arista, 1981
JUMP TO IT, Arista, 1982
GET IT RIGHT, Arista, 1983
WHO'S ZOOMIN' WHO?, Arista, 1985
FIRST LADY OF SOUL, Stylus, 1985
SOUL SURVIVOR, Blue Moon, 1986
ARETHA, Arista, 1986
GREATEST HITS: 1960-65, CBS, 1987
NEVER GROW OLD, (with. Rev. C. L. Franklin), Chess, 1987
20 GREATEST HITS, Atlantic, 1987
ONE LORD, ONE FAITH, Arista, 1988
THROUGH THE STORM, Arista, 1989
THE GREAT ARETHA FRANKLIN, CBS, 1990

FRANKLIN, CAROLYN Carolyn Franklin was born in 1945, the younger sister of Aretha FRANKLIN. While she has never been accorded the respect that is her due, she exerted a considerable influence upon the career of her sister as a motivator, writer and backing vocalist. Among her compositions were *Ain't no Way* and *Angel* and *Without Love*, which she co-wrote with Ivy Hunter. Her own recording career was overshadowed by that of Aretha and it never fulfilled its her early promise; it was cut short in 1988, when she died of cancer, aged 43.

FRANKLIN, ERMA Erma Franklin was Aretha FRANKLIN's youngest sister. Her career started singing gospel with Aretha and another sister, Carolyn FRANKLIN at her father's church in Detroit. Erma, like Carolyn, has always been over-shadowed by Aretha. After recording R&B songs like *Baby What You Want Me to Do* and *Big Boss Man*, she achieved her biggest success in 1967 with *Piece of My Heart*. It was produced and cowritten by Jerry RAGAVOY with Bert BERNS and released on the Shout label, it has become a classic of the genre and illustrated her ability to stamp a song with her own imprimatur. After the death of Berns in 1967, his wife, Ilene, attempted to keep the Shout label going, but Franklin moved to the Brunswick label, where she cut a version of the Isaac HAYES and David PORTER composition, *Hold on I'm Coming*, as well as a version of *Son of a Preacher Man*. However, by the end of the 1960s, she had semi-retired, apart from occasional backing vocals for Aretha.

FREEMAN, BOBBY Bobby Freeman was born in San Francisco on June 13, 1940. He made his debut in 1955 as the pianist in The Romancers, who recorded for Dootone Records. In 1958 he was signed to the Josie label and recorded the self-penned *Do You Wanna Dance?* (USA#5.1958), which has become a standard, with a variety of artists recording their own versions. It was followed by *Betty Lou Got a New Pair of Shoes* (USA #37.1958) and *Need Your Love*. In 1959 he graduated from college and became a professional musician. In 1960, after two more singles for Josie, he signed with the King label and scored with *(I Do The) Shimmy Shimmy* (USA #37.1960); after three years in the wilderness he was signed by the San Francisco DJ Tom Donahue to his record label Autumn. Freeman's first single, *Let's Surf*, flopped, but the follow-up, *C'mon And Swim* (USA#5.1964), was a monster; it was produced by another

local DJ, Sylvester Stewart, who achieved recognition in his own right as Sly of SLY & THE FAMILY STONE. The next release, *S-W-I-M*, proved to be his final hit – and a modest one at that. Since then he has become something of a fixture on the club circuit in San Francisco and has recorded intermittently for small local labels.

FRITTS, DONNIE Donnie Fritts was born and brought up in Florence, Alabama, where he met local songwriter Tom Stafford. In 1959 Stafford set up the publishing outlet, Spardus, and in 1960 he invited Fritts and David BRIGGS to become partners in it. After Rick HALL set up Fame, Fritts became one of Dan PENN's songwriting partners, as well as playing drums in a local R&B group, Hollis Dixon. By the mid-1960s Fritts had joined the growing body of writers and musicians migrating to Nashville. In 1974, he recorded an LP, *Prone To Lean*, for Atlantic; recorded at Muscle Shoals sound studios and produced by Jerry WEXLER and Kris Kristofferson. Since then he has continued to play sessions and write for the country music fraternity.

FUQUA, HARVEY Perhaps Berry GORDY's most singular talent was his ability to recognize talent in others. Harvey Fuqua, born on July 27, 1928 in Kentucky, was one of his earliest recruits to Motown as a staff writer and producer. Throughout the 1950s, Fuqua and his group The Moonglows recorded a succession of singles for Chess including *Sincerely* (USA#20.1955), *See Saw* (USA #25.1956) and as Harvey & The Moonglows, *The Ten Commandments of Love* (USA #22.1958), all of which he had written with DJ Alan Freed. While at Chess, he started to work as an A&R man and as a producer, discovering

Etta JAMES and The Marquees, whose lead singer was Marvin GAYE. In 1959, Marvin Gaye joined The Moonglows; it was the beginning of an association with Fuqua that would span Gaye's career. By 1960 Fuqua had formed his own record label, Harvey; among the artists under contract were Gaye and Junior WALKER. Through his association with Gordy's sister, Gwen, he sold his roster of artists to Gordy. He remained with Motown for over ten years, writing and producing with Johnny BRISTOL. In the early 1970s, he left Motown for RCA, with whom he had a production contract. Among the groups he produced were New Birth and The Nite-Liters. Towards the end of the decade, he produced a number of disco hits by Sylvester for the Fantasy label, including *You Make Me Feel (Mighty Real)*. In 1982, he teamed up with Gaye once again for the LP *Midnight Love*, which he produced.

GAMBLE & HUFF During the mid-1960s lyricist Kenny Gamble, who had had his own group The Romeos, which included Thom BELL, met up in Philadelphia with Leon Huff, a pianist and arranger, who had formerly been a staff writer at Cameo Records. They decided to start producing records, one of the earliest examples being *Expressway To Your Heart* by The Soul Survivors. They started to gather about them a nucleus of musicians and technicians including Ronnie Baker (bass), Norman Harris (guitar), Earl Young (drums), engineer Joe Tarsia and producer Thom Bell. In 1968 Tarsia took over a local studio called Sound Plus and changed the name to Sigma Sound; it became the base for the Gamble label, to which one of the first signings was The INTRUDERS. Distribution through Chess was confirmed, but the death of Leonard CHESS, and the subsequent sale of the company to GRT, threw all of their plans

awry and so they had to undertake freelance work. One of the first arrivals was Jerry BUTLER, whose career needed revitalising. Moreover Atlantic started to send artists like Wilson PICKETT to Sigma Sound. In 1970, with funding from CBS, they set up Philadelphia International Records and started to build a roster of artists including The O'JAYS, Harold MELVIN & The Blue Notes, The Three Degrees and Billy PAUL. Throughout the 1970s the Sound of Philadelphia was characterised by the percussive dance rhythms offset by lush, swirling string arrangements. Although Gamble & Huff wrote a percentage of the material themselves, writers like Gene McFadden and John Whitehead and Bunny Sigler were also key contributors.

By 1975 the Sound of Philadelphia had been reduced to a formula for the dance-floor, although it would still generate a number of fine records like McFadden & Whitehead's *Ain't No Stoppin' Us Now*. By the middle of the 1980s, Gamble & Huff had returned to their former independent status as Gamble & Huff Records, with The O'Jays under contract and a distribution deal with EMI. It was ironic that the sound they had done so much to develop should become their nemesis.

GAP BAND The eldest of three brothers, Ronnie Wilson formed this group in 1967 in Tulsa; the name was derived from the initials of Tulsa's three main streets – Greenwood, Archer and Pine. By 1978, after years of chopping and changing personnel, the group had narrowed down to include younger brothers, Charles and Robert, and had signed with Mercury Records. Their first LP, *The Gap Band*, locked them firmly into the disco-oriented mould of funk; the follow-up, *The Gap Band II* (USA#42.1980), established them internationally by spawning two hit singles, *Oops Upside your Head* (UK#6.1980/#20.1987) and *Party Lights* (UK#30.1980). Their third LP, *The Gap Band III* (USA#16.1980), consolidated their reputation still further with another brace of hit singles, *Burn Rubber on Me (Why you Wanna Hurt Me?)* (UK#22.1980) and *Humpin'* (UK#36.1981).

In 1982 they were signed by the Los Angeles entrepeneur Lonnie Simmons, to his label, Total Experience. He took over production duties for their next LP, *The Gap Band IV* (USA#14.1982), his influence was detectable in the change of direction with a proportion of the LP being devoted to ballads while the dance-oriented track *You Dropped The Bomb On Me* (USA#31.1982) was a foretaste of the transformations that would be wrought by PRINCE. *The Gap Band V – Jammin'* (USA#28.1983) included the single, *Someday* (UK#17.1984), and marked the beginning of their decline in popularity in the USA, where their brand of funk was starting to date – although they continued with each successive single to prop up the R&B Charts. In the UK, by contrast their singles continued to be popular: in 1987 they had their biggest hit with *Big Fun* (UK #4.1987), it was followed by a re-mixed version of the 1980 hit, *Oops Upside your Head*, which peaked at #20. *The Gap Band VIII* (UK#47.1987) became their most commercially successful LP in the UK. Their most recent LP, *Round Trip* (1990) has shown that they are still capable of knocking out good reliable soul-funk in a George CLINTON vein, but they are going to need to rethink their strategy if they are going to set the world on fire.

THE GAP BAND IV, RCA, 1982
THE BEST OF THE GAP BAND, Mercury, 1985
THE GAP BAND VII, Total Experience, 1986
THE GAP BAND VIII, RCA, 1987
STRAIGHT FROM THE HEART, RCA, 1988
ROUND TRIP, Capitol, 1990

GARRETT, SIEDAH Siedah Garrett was born in Los Angeles in 1963. To date her career has revolved around an unimpeachable reputation as a session singer and a burgeoning renown as a songwriter. She was discovered in 1978 by vocalist D. J. Rogers, who enlisted her to sing on his LP, *Love, Music and Life*. Over the next five years she played the club circuit, until in 1983 she was auditioned by Quincy JONES for the vocal group, Deco, who had a hit on the US Dance Charts with *Do You Want it Right Now?*. Her association wth Jones prompted considerable interest in her vocal attributes, and she was recruited by The CRUSADERS, Donna SUMMER, The COMMODORES, Madonna and Dennis EDWARDS to provide backing vocals. Furthermore, her material was used by Kenny Loggins, The POINTER SISTERS, Aretha FRANKLIN and Michael JACKSON. Her involvement with Jackson resulted in a duet on *I Just Can't Stop Loving You* (USA/UK#1.1987) and in cowriting *Man In The Mirror*, both of which were featured on Jackson's LP *Bad*. The success of her collaborations with Jackson enabled her to get a solo deal with Quincy Jones' Qwest label. Her debut LP, *Kiss of Life*, materialised in 1988, it was produced by Rod Temperton (see HEATWAVE) and included contributions from LA & BABYFACE, as well as some self-penned material.

KISS OF LIFE, Qwest, 1988

GAYE, MARVIN Marvin Gaye was born in Washington DC on April 2, 1939. He joined The Rainbows in 1955, which included Billy STEWART and Don COVAY in its lineup. After a spell in the US Navy from which he obtained an honourable discharge in 1957 he joined the doo-wop group The Marquees, who had gained an opportunity to record some tracks for the Columbia subsidiary

Okeh as a result of an introduction from Bo DIDDLEY. Although, these tracks failed to ignite popular enthusiasm, they struck a chord with Harvey FUQUA, who was in the process of re-forming The Moonglows. In 1959, The Moonglows, now called Harvey & The Moonglows, had relocated to Chicago and revived their contract with Chess; by 1960 both Fuqua and Gaye had left, moving to Detroit, where Fuqua set up his own record company and Gaye signed to the Motown subsidiary, Anna, run by Berry GORDY's sister, Gwen. After working as a drummer and a backing vocalist, Gaye signed to Motown as a solo artist. His first LP, *The Soulful Moods of Marvin Gaye*, was a collection of ballads in jazz-tinged settings owing more to the style of Nat "King" Cole and Billy Eckstine than to the R&B of The Moonglows. In 1962, he was teamed with producer William STEVENSON for the single *Stubborn Kind Of Fellow*, which was followed by *Hitch Hike* (USA#30.1963).

His next record was *Pride and Joy* (USA #10.1963), and over the succeeding five years he notched up a succession of hits that included *Can I Get aWitness* (USA#22.1963), *You're a Wonderful One* (USA#15.1964), *Try it Baby* (USA#15.1964), *Baby Don't You Do It* (USA #27.1964), *How Sweet it is to be Loved by You* (USA#6; UK#49.1964), *I'll Be Doggone* (USA #8.1965), *Pretty Little Baby* (USA#25.1965), *Ain't That Peculiar* (USA#8.1965), *One More Heartache* (USA#29.1966), *Little Darlin'* (UK#50. 1966), *Your Unchanging Love* (USA #33.1967), *You* (USA#34.1968) and *Chained* (USA#32.1968). In 1964, he was teamed with Mary WELLS to record an LP, *Together*; a single, *Once Upon A Time* (USA#19; UK #50.1964), was taken from it. When Wells left Motown later the same year, he was teamed with Kim Weston. Their first single together was a comparative failure, but in 1967 *It Takes Two* (USA#14; UK#16.1967), from the LP, *Take Two*, provided sufficient encouragement

for him to be teamed with Tammi TERRELL. His partnership with Terrell lasted for two years, during that time they recorded a string of hits, most of which were written and produced by ASHFORD & SIMPSON: *Ain't No Mountain High Enough* (USA#19.1967), *Your Precious Love* (USA#5.1967), *If I Could Build my Whole World around You* (USA#10; UK #41.1967), *Ain't Nothing Like the Real Thing* (USA#8; UK#34.1968), *You're All I Need to Get By* (USA#7; UK#19.1968), *Keep on Loving Me Honey* (USA#24.1968), *You Ain't Livin' till You're Lovin'* (UK#21.1969), *Good Lovin' ain't Easy to Come By* (USA#30. UK#26.1969) and *The Onion Song* (UK#9.1969).

In 1968 Gaye recorded *I Heard it Through the Grapevine* (USA#1.1968; UK#1.1969/#8.1986), written by Norman WHITFIELD and Barrett STRONG for Gladys KNIGHT & The Pips, who had turned it into a million-seller. Gaye's version turned the song on its head, making it a tale of brooding suspicion and jealousy. It sold more copies than any other Motown record and gave Gaye the requisite leverage to pursue and develop his own style separately from the remainder of the Motown organization. This achieved its perfect expression in 1971, when the self-penned and self-produced LP, *What's Going On* was released. In the interim, his popularity flourished with the singles *Too Busy Thinking about My Baby* (USA#4; UK #5.1969), *That's the Way Love Is* (USA#7.1969) and *Abraham, Martin and John* (UK#9.1970). With the release of *What's Going On* (USA #6.1971) the public perception of Motown altered: the company previously dismissed as being concerned solely with the making of hit records was now seen as addressing the social problems endemic in US society. Furthermore, Gaye's creative independence was the catalyst which allowed other Motown artists like Stevie WONDER and, to a lesser extent, Diana ROSS to gain their liberty within the structure of the company. In purely commercial terms, three hit singles were taken from the LP – *What's Going On* (USA#2.1971), *Mercy Mercy Me (The Ecology)* (USA#4.1971) and *Inner City Blues (Makes Me Wanna Holler)* (USA #9.1971) – all of which have subsequently been covered by other artists. In 1972, as a result of this new creative freedom, Gaye wrote the score for the film *Trouble Man*; the soundtrack was released as an LP (USA#14.1973), whose title track was in turn released as a single (USA#7.1973). The next LP, *Let's Get It On* (USA#2; UK#39.1973), written and co-produced by Gaye with Ed Townsend included three singles: *Let's Get It On* (USA#1; UK #31.1973), *Come Get To This* (USA#21.1973) and *Distant Lover* (USA#28.1974). The same year he teamed up with Diana Ross for the LP *Diana And Marvin* (USA#26.1973; UK #6.1974); three singles were extracted from it, including *You Are Everything* (UK#5.1974). Next came the LP, *Marvin Gaye Live!* (USA #8.1974), which had been recorded at Oakland, California.

In 1976 he released the LP *I Want You* (USA#4; UK#22.1976), the title track of which was released as a single (USA#15.1976). The same year he visited London for a series of concerts, which were recorded and released on a double LP, *Live At The London Palladium* (USA#3.1977); the only studio track was *Got To Give It Up* (USA#1; UK#7.1977). In 1979 another double LP followed: *Here, My Dear* (USA#26.1979), represented the settlement for his recently divorced wife, Anna, who would recieve the royalties. His final LP for Motown, *In Our Lifetime*, was released without his permission and sold disappointingly by comparison with his previous work. After his departure from Motown he signed with CBS and recorded the LP, *Midnight Love* (USA#7; UK#10.1982), with Harvey Fuqua in attendance; the title track (UK#10.1982) and *(Sexual) Healing* (USA#3.1982) were issued as singles.

On April 1, 1984, Gaye was shot dead by his father during a violent quarrel. His mental condition had become increasingly unstable through years of extended drug abuse and the stress imposed by financial pressures. He was interred at Forest Lawn Cemetery in Los Angeles on April 5, 1984. In November, his father was sentenced to five years' imprisonment for voluntary manslaughter.

THAT STUBBORN KINDA FELLOW, Motown, 1963

HOW SWEET IT IS, Motown, 1964

MARVIN GAYE AND HIS GIRLS, (with Mary Wells, Kim Weston and Tammi Terrell), Motown, 1969

M.P.G., Motown, 1969

GREATEST HITS, (with Tammi Terrell), Motown, 1970

WHAT'S GOING ON, Motown, 1971

TROUBLE MAN, Motown, 1973

DIANA AND MARVIN, (with Diana Ross), Motown, 1973

LET'S GET IT ON, Motown, 1973

LIVE!, Motown, 1974

I WANT YOU, Motown, 1976

LIVE AT THE LONDON PALLADIUM, Motown, 1977

HERE, MY DEAR, Motown, 1979

IN OUR LIFETIME, Motown, 1981

EARLY YEARS 1961–64, Motown, 1981

ANTHOLOGY, Motown, 1981

HITS OF MARVIN GAYE, Motown, 1981

BEST OF MARVIN GAYE, Motown, 1981

THE MAGIC OF MARVIN GAYE, Motown, 1982

UNITED, (with Tammi Terrell), Motown, 1982

GREATEST HITS, (with Tammi Terrell), Motown, 1982

MIDNIGHT LOVE, CBS, 1982

GREATEST HITS, Telstar, 1983 15

GREATEST HITS, Motown, 1984

ROMANTICALLY YOURS, CBS, 1985

THE VERY BEST OF MARVIN GAYE, Telstar, 1986

MOTOWN REMEMBERS MARVIN GAYE, Motown, 1986
COMPACT COMMAND PERFORMANCES, Motown, 1987

GAYNOR, GLORIA Gloria Gaynor was born in Newark, New Jersey, on September 7, 1949. Her career started in 1965 when she was signed by the Jocinda label, for whom she recorded just the one single, which failed to attract any attention. After singing in nightclubs for eight years she was teamed up with engineer Tony Bongiovi and arranger Meco, the resulting *Honey Bee* and *Never Can Say Goodbye* (USA#9; UK#2.1974) slotted into the emergent disco boom. They were followed by a reworking of The FOUR TOPS hit, *Reach Out I'll be There* (UK#14.1975), *All I Need is Your Sweet Lovin'* (UK#44.1975) and *How High the Moon* (UK#33.1976). After a fallow period she returned with *I Will Survive* (USA/UK#1.1979) and *Let Me Know (I Have A Right)* (UK #32.1979), only to slip out of sight once more. During the 1980s, her one contribution was a cover of *I Am What I Am* (UK#13.1983) from the musical, *La Cage aux Folles*, although she has recorded regularly for a succession of labels.

NEVER CAN SAY GOODBYE, MGM,1975
I KINDA LIKE ME, Polydor, 1981
GREATEST HITS, Polydor, 1982
GLORIA GAYNOR, Ectasy, 1983
I AM GLORIA GAYNOR, Chrysalis, 1984
THE POWER OF GLORIA GAYNOR, Stylus, 1986

GEORGE, BARBARA Barbara George was one of the first beneficiaries of the All For One collective formed by Harold Battiste with session musicians like Allen TOUSSAINT and Red Tyler. Although, the collective never really emerged as the force it was intended to be, George, who was born in Louisiana, had a monster hit with the self-penned *I Know (You Dont Love Me No More)* (USA#3.1961), that it was her only hit doesn't alter the fact that it was a sublime slice of New Orleans R&B at its pokiest. Its success encouraged Juggy Murray, the owner of the Sue label, to buy her contract, but she never had another hit even after recording tracks like Chris KENNER's *Something You Got* and she gradually slipped into obscurity.

GILL, JOHNNY When Bobby BROWN left New Edition, Johnny Gill became his eventual replacement. He remained with the group for two years. His career started when, aged eight, he became a member of the gospel quartet Gill Special, which included his three brothers. As a result of his friendship with Stacy Lattishaw he made a demo which she took to the president of Atlantic. Gill was signed to the subsidiary, Cotillion. His first solo LP, *Johnny Gill*, released in 1983, was followed by an LP of duets with Lattishaw, *Perfect Combination*, another solo LP, *Chemistry*, followed in 1985, but then he joined New Edition. During his career with the group, he provided the lead vocals on *Can You Stand The Rain* and *Boys To Men*. In 1990, he relaunched his own solo career, this time with Motown. His debut LP for them, again called *Johnny Gill*, was variously produced by Jimmy JAM & Terry Lewis and LA & BABYFACE. It included the singles *Rub You The Right Way* and *My, My, My*. While adhering to certain stereotypes too strictly, it certainly augured well for his future.

CHEMISTRY, Cotillion, 1985
JOHNNY GILL, Motown, 1990

GLOVER, HENRY It was Syd NATHAN's extreme good fortune that in 1947 he was able to attract someone of Henry Glover's ability to become house producer and arranger for the King label, which Nathan had founded in 1944. Glover, who held the post for ten years, was born in Hot Springs, Arkansas, in 1922. During the 1940s, he was a member of Lucky Millinder's band where he wrote the arrangements and played the trumpet. Before he joined King, the emphasis in its repertoire had leaned heavily towards country music – even R&B artists like Wynonie Harris had performed cover versions of country songs like *Bloodshot Eyes*. With Glover's arrival, in tandem with Ralph BASS, the label's growing roster of artists – James BROWN, Little Willie JOHN, Hank BALLARD & The Midnighters, The FIVE ROYALES, Bill Doggett, Roy BROWN, Otis WILLIAMS & The Charms and Billy WARD & The Dominoes and others – was able to put out some of the most memorable records of the 1950s. Glover's background in jazz enabled him to call upon musicians from both the Count Basie and the Duke Ellington bands. After joining Roulette in 1956, where he remained for seven years, he rejoined King in 1963 and eventually was made a vice-president of the company.

GOFFIN & KING During the 1960s one of the most prolific and successful songwriting partnerships to emanate from New York's Brill Building was that of Gerry Goffin (born February 11, 1939, in Queens, New York) and Carole King (born Carole Klein; February 9, 1942, in Brooklyn, New York). The partnership was formed when both joined music publisher Don Kirshner. Between 1961 and 1968 they wrote a succession of hits for a variety artists: *Oh No Not My Baby* by Maxine BROWN, *One Fine Day* by The CHIFFONS, *Chains* and *Don't Say Nothing Bad about My Baby* by The COOKIES, *Some Kind of Wonderful*, *When My Little Girl is Smiling* and *Up on*

the Roof by The DRIFTERS, *I'm into Something Good* by Earl-Jean, *(You Make me Feel Like) A Natural Woman* (with Jerry WEXLER) by Aretha FRANKLIN, *The Locomotion* by LITTLE EVA and *Will You Love me Tomorrow?* by The SHIRELLES.

In 1968 they went their separate ways. Goffin began to collaborate with keyboardist Barry Goldberg, penning *I've Got to Use My Imagination* (1974) for Gladys KNIGHT & The Pips, and King moved to Los Angeles. King, having had a hit in her own right with *It Might as Well Rain Until September* in 1962, signed a recording contract with Lou Adler's Ode label. The first LP *Carole King: Writer* failed to make any significant waves; the follow-up, *Tapestry* (1970), however, became one of the most important LPs of the era, selling in excess of 15 million copies. While none of her later LPs could match the success of *Tapestry* they were all very well-crafted, using some of the most respected session musicians Los Angeles could offer. During the 1980s they have occasionally written together again, but their output lacks the sparkle of former years.

GOLDNER, GEORGE George Goldner, one of the great record-men of the 1950s, was born in New York in 1918. He had an intuitive flair for picking up a song and turning into a hit for whoever might be around to sing it. Thus the groups he was involved with tended to be curious amalgams of session singers or "serious wannabes". However, he was perpetually broke, because he was also a keen gambler, and so the labels he started were constantly being sold to finance his habit: Rama, Gee, Gone, End, Cindy, Roulette, Juanita, Tee-Gee, Mark-X, Casino and Goldisc. Many of the names were indications of his obsession. Among the artists, he produced were Frankie LYMON & The Teenagers, The FLAMINGOS, LITTLE ANTHONY & The

Imperials, The Cleftones, The Crows and The Wrens. Through his dealings with DJ Alan Freed he was in a good position to make his records hits. In 1964 he helped to found the Red Bird label with LEIBER & STOLLER, and discovered the labels first group, The DIXIE CUPS. He sold up his share in the label soon after their initial success, due to personal bankruptcy. His final venture was Firebird in 1969. He died on April 15, 1970.

GOODMAN, SHIRLEY See SHIRLEY & LEE

GORDY, Jr, BERRY When Berry Gordy set up Motown Records in 1959, his determination for it to succeed was such, that it was as if he had some foreknowledge that, by the end of the 1960s, he would be in control of the largest black-owned corporation in the USA. He was born on November 28, 1929 and by 1950, had already completed a successful career as a boxer. After three years in the army in Korea, he returned to the USA in 1953 and opened the 3-D Record Mart; by 1956 the shop had been forced into bankruptcy. In 1957, after a spell working for General Motors, he formed a songwriting partnership with Billy Davis, the boyfriend of his sister Gwen, and they started to write for one of his former boxing colleagues, Jackie WILSON. In 1958 they had their first hit, *To be Loved;* it was followed by *Lonely Teardrops, I'll Be Satisfied* and *Reet Petite*. With the royalties he earned from Wilson's records, he set up his own record company, Motown. His motives for this step were undoubtedly governed by a desire to make money, but also he had taken exception to the way Brunswick had produced the songs he had written for Wilson, swamping them with lavish string arrangements. By 1960 Gwen had set up her own label, Anna, which

had Barrett STRONG, Joe TEX, Lamont Dozier (see HOLLAND, DOZIER & HOLLAND) and The Spinners (see DETROIT SPINNERS) all under contract. In addition, she had met Harvey FUQUA, whose own label, Harvey, had Junior WALKER and Marvin GAYE under contract. Fuqua sold Harvey to Gordy, and in March 1960 Motown had its first hit, *Money* by Barrett Strong, written by Gordy, it climbed to #23.

While there can be little doubt about Gordy's business acumen – the voracity with which he set about accumulating publishing rights was breathtaking – he had a remarkable nose for talent and, like all good managers, the ability to delegate. He set about employing under contract teams of musicians, writers, producers, engineers and arrangers to service the requirements of his fast-developing roster of artists; it was they who pioneered the Motown Sound. A former friend, Smokey ROBINSON, who with his group The Miracles gave Motown its first million-seller, was the only artist initially afforded any latitude within the strict hierachy, although Marvin Gaye and Stevie WONDER were later allowed to break the mould, after Gaye's phenomenal success with *I Heard it Through the Grapevine*. By the mid-1960s, he had assembled a roster of artists like The SUPREMES, The FOUR TOPS, The MARVELLETTES, Gaye, Wonder, The TEMPTATIONS and many more who regularly slugged it out in the charts. Although some critics maintained that Gordy tailored the Motown Sound to the requirements of the white middle-class, and although some of the Motown acts were indeed much more pop-orientated than others, a large percentage of Motown's output was just as feisty and raw as anything that came out of the Stax or Fame studios.

In 1971 Gordy relocated Motown to Los Angeles. Some artists like The Four Tops chose to remain behind in Detroit. Furthermore, artists and technicians who had become increasingly resentful over his niggardly rates of pay and lack of credit drained gradually away to other labels where – or so they thought – they would be better rewarded. However, unlike its main competitor of the 1960s Stax, Motown has continued to thrive throughout the 1970s and 1980s, signing artists like The Jackson Five (see JACKSONS), Lionel RICHIE, The COMMODORES, DeBARGE, Johnny GILL and Gerald ALSTON. In 1982 Gordy signed a distribution deal with MCA, which culminated in the selling of the entire company to an entertainment conglomerate, Boston Ventures, with MCA acquiring 20 percent of it.

GRAHAM, LARRY Larry Graham was born in Beaumont, Texas on August 14, 1946, but his family moved to Oakland, California, in 1948. In 1966 he was enlisted to join SLY & THE FAMILY STONE as bassist, and he remained with them until 1972 when he left to form Graham Central Station. Throughout the mid-1970s he released a succession of soul/funk LPs, that were some of the better examples of the genre: *Graham Central Station* and *Release Yourself* in 1974 and *Ain't no 'Bout-a-Doubt-it* (USA#22.1975); the latter included the single *Your Love* (USA#38.1975). The disco-boom of the mid-1970s did not help the cause of these records as they lacked the crassness necessary to real success, but the group's next LPs, *Mirror* (1976) and *Now do U Want to Dance* (1977), were both modestly successful. The following year the LP, *My Radio Sure Sounds Good to Me*, was credited to Larry Graham and Grand Central Station; it was eclipsed by lesser efforts, as was the follow-up in 1979, *Star Walk*. This lack of success caused him to disband the group and concentrate upon a solo career. His debut LP, *One in a Million You* (USA#27.1980), provided him

with his first top ten single, *One in a Million You* (USA#9.1980), but the follow-up, *When We Get Married*, failed to consolidate his position. His later LPs – *Just be my Lady* (1981), *Sooner or Later* (1982), *Victory* (1983) and *Fired Up* (1985) – have not been sufficiently distinctive to set them apart from the efforts by other members of the super-slick, sophisticated soul brigade.

JUST BE MY LADY, Warner Bros., 1981
FIRED UP, Warner Bros., 1985

GRAND CENTRAL STATION See GRAHAM, Larry

GRANDMASTER FLASH Joseph Saddler was born in the Bronx, New York City, on January 1, 1958. In 1977 he started to work as a DJ for a mobile disco, where he started to develop scratching and mixing techniques. In 1978 he formed Grandmaster Flash & The Three MCs (Cowboy, Kid Creole and MELLE MEL) and then added two other rappers, Kurtis BLOW and Duke Bootee, to make The Furious Five. In 1979, after a brace of commercially unsuccessful but influential singles for minor labels, he signed with Sylvia ROBINSON's fledgling Sugarhill label. In 1980 their first single, *Freedom* , sold in sufficient quantity in New York to qualify for a gold disc, although it failed to crack the national charts; the following year a similar fate befell the single, *The Adventures of Grandmaster Flash on Wheels of Steel*, which was dubbed by some "the definitive rap record". In 1982, they recorded *The Message* (UK#8.1982), which was part-written by Sylvia Robinson; despite its success in the UK and the fact that, like its predecessors, it achieved a gold disc, it only peaked at #62 in the USA. The following year, Melle Mel started to break out in his own right and Flash implemented legal proceedings against Sugarhill to retain the rights to the name, The Furious Five, although the anti-cocaine track, *White Lines (Don't Do It)* (UK #7.1984), was released in the interim. In 1985 Flash signed a solo deal with Elektra; the four LPs he has released since then have failed to achieve any notable popularity. It is unfortunate that, since signing to a major label, he has sacrificed the rawness of his earlier records in favour of slick productions – a treatment which is surely in contradiction to the basic premises of rap.

THE MESSAGE, Sugarhill, 1982
GREATEST MESSAGES, Sugarhill, 1984
THEY SAID IT COULDN'T BE DONE, Elektra, 1985
THE SOURCE, Elektra, 1986
BA DOP BOOM BANG, Elektra, 1987
ON THE STRENGTH, Elektra, 1988

GRAY, DOBIE Dobie Gray was born Leonard Victor Ainsworth on July 26, 1942, in Brookshire, Texas. Although his claim to fame was *Drift Away* (1973), he came to prominence as early as 1965 with the dance-floor classic *The In Crowd* (USA#13.1965), which was later covered by The Ramsey LEWIS Trio. After this brief spell of celebrity, his musical career slipped into the doldrums and he turned to acting. In 1969, however he joined the group Pollution, with whom he made an LP; then, in 1971, he met Mentor Williams, the brother of the songwriter, Paul Williams. Over the next three years he recorded three LPs for MCA – *Drift Away*, *Loving Arms* and *Hey Dixie* – that embodied the rock-inflected "country-soul"; the fact that they were recorded in Nashville with old stalwarts like David BRIGGS, Reggie Young, Charlie McCoy and Troy Seals, illustrated the deeply rooted ties between soul and country. Although the single *Drift Away*

(USA#5.1973) was a big international hit, both *Loving Arms* and *Hey Dixie* suffered from poor promotion and a general lack of understanding. As a result Gray was dropped by MCA. He was signed by Capricorn for the 1975 LP, *New Ray Of Sunshine*, which was produced by Seals, but it too sunk without trace. After a few years of obscurity, he returned with the disco-oriented single *You Can Do It* (USA#37.1979), produced by Rick HALL; more years of obscurity followed, during which he cut the odd single for independent labels like Inferno until in 1986, with Seals collaborating, he recorded *The Dark Side of Town* for Capitol; this LP gave him a minor hit in the country charts. Since then he has continued to play around the South.

DOBIE GRAY SINGS FOR IN CROWDERS THAT GO-GO, Kent, 1987

GREAVES, R.B. R. B. Greaves was born Ronald Bertram Aloysius Greaves of Indian extraction on a US Air Force Base on November 28, 1944, in Georgetown, Guyana. As a result of being the nephew of Sam COOKE, he managed to obtain a recording contract with Atlantic in 1969. He was sent down to the newly established Muscle Shoals Sound studios where he recorded tracks like *Home to Stay, Take a Letter, Maria* (USA#2.1969), *A Whiter Shade of Pale* and *Always Something there to Remind Me* (USA#27.1970). At the end of his contract with Atlantic he moved to the UK where he recorded briefly under the pseudonym of Sonny Childe for Polydor. However, after his return to the USA he quickly disappeared into obscurity.

GREEN, AL Al Greene was born on April 13, 1946, in Forrest City, Arkansas. As a teenager he formed a gospel quartet with his three brothers, Walter, William and Robert. In 1964, after moving with his family to Michigan, he formed The Creations with school friends Palmer James, Curtis Rogers and Gene Mason. They signed with Zodiac, a local label, and played on the chitlin' circuit. By 1967 the group had been renamed Al Greene & The Soulmates and had formed their own record label, Hot Line Music Journal, to release a single, *Back Up Train* (USA#41.1968). The success of the single prompted an invitation to perform at the Apollo in Harlem, but the follow-up, *Don't Hurt Me No More*, failed to sell and the group disbanded. Green started a solo career and dropped the final letter from his surname.

In 1969 he met Willie MITCHELL, the moving force behind the Memphis-based Hi label, who signed him up. It was the beginning of an association that would last until 1978. Backed by the Hi house band, Green recorded a string of hits that gave the studios a reputation comparable to that of the Stax, Fame and the Muscle Shoals Sound studios. His first LP, *Green is Blues* (USA#19.1973), set the pattern for his future records, combining standard cover versions with original material. The distinctive timbre of his voice and the imaginativeness of the arrangements enabled him to get away with things that few other performers could. In 1971 he started his run of hits with *Tired of Being Alone* (USA#11; UK#4.1971) from the LP *Al Green Gets next to You;* it was followed by the LP *Let's Stay Together* (USA#8.1972), whose title track was released as a single (USA#1; UK#7.1972). His next LP, *I'm Still in Love with You* (USA#4.1972), included the singles *Look What You Done for Me* (USA#4; UK#44.1972) and the title track (USA#3; UK#35.1972). It was followed by the LP, *Call Me* (USA#10.1973), from which were taken the singles *You Ought to be with Me* (USA#3.1972), *Call Me (Come back Home)* (USA#10.1973) and *Here I Am (Come and Take Me)* (USA#10.1973). The following year he released the LP *Livin' for You* (USA #24.1973), which included the singles *Livin' for You* (USA#19.1974) and *Let's Get Married* (USA#32.1974). On October 25 he was hospitalised with second-degree burns after a former girl-friend, Mary Woodson, stormed into his house while he was having a shower and hurled boiling grits all over him before shooting herself. His next LP, *Al Green Explores Your Mind* (USA#15.1975), featured the single *Sha-La-La (Make me Happy)* (USA#7; UK#20.1974). It was followed by the gospel-flavoured LP, *Al Green is Love* (USA#28.1975), from which the single *L-O-V-E (Love)* (USA#13; UK #24.1975) was taken.

In 1976, he bought a church in Memphis, having been ordained as a minister of the Full Gospel Tabernacle. Over the next few years or so, the gospel influences in his recorded output became ever more pronounced, until by 1979 he had eschewed the secular in favour of gospel. In 1977 he parted company with Mitchell, forming his own backing group and taking over the production duties himself. The first product of this new arrangement was *The Belle Album*, his final secular LP. After a string of gospel LPs through the 1980s, he signed with A&M in 1985. He has recorded three LPs for them, as well as collaborating with Annie Lennox on *Put a Little Love in Your Heart* (UK#28.1988) and in 1989 with the Arthur BAKER Project on *The Message is Love*. In 1988 he appeared at the Nelson Mandela Birthday Concert in London, and in 1990 he performed in the John Lennon Memorial Concert at Pier Head, Liverpool.

GREEN IS BLUES, Hi, 1969
AL GREEN GETS NEXT TO YOU, Hi, 1971
LET'S STAY TOGETHER, Hi, 1972
I'M STILL IN LOVE WITH YOU, Hi, 1972
CALL ME, Hi, 1973
LIVIN' FOR YOU, Hi, 1973

AL GREEN EXPLORES YOUR MIND, Hi, 1974
AL GREEN'S GREATEST HITS, Hi, 1975
AL GREEN IS LOVE, Hi, 1975
FULL OF FIRE, Hi, 1976
HAVE A GOOD TIME, Hi. 1976.
GREATEST HITS, VOLUME 2, Hi, 1977
THE BELLE ALBUM, Hi, 1978
THE LORD WILL MAKE A WAY, Myrrh, 1980
TOKYO- LIVE!, Hi, 1981
HIGHER PLANE, Hi, 1982
PRECIOUS LORD, Hi,1982
TRUST IN GOD, Hi, 1985
GOING AWAY, A&M, 1985
THE LIGHT, A&M. 1985.
SOUL SURVIVOR, A&M, 1987
HI-LIFE: THE BEST OF AL GREEN, K-Tel, 1988
LOVE RITUAL, Hi, 1989
I GET JOY, A&M, 1989

GREENE, MARLIN When Quin IVY set up Quinvy in 1965, he was recommended by Rick HALL to approach Marlin Greene as his "in house all rounder". Greene like Jimmy JOHNSON and Dan PENN could turn his hand to anything: playing guitar, arranging, designing, writing, producing or engineering. A vital person to have around, in other words. He had recorded a bit himself for RCA, but with little success before playing occassionally with The Mark Vs. The most successful signing at Quinvy was Percy SLEDGE. Greene contributed to that success in no small way by providing material like *Cover Me* and *You're all Around Me* , which was written in partnership with Eddie HINTON. However, Greene's contribution crystallised with his co-production (with Ivy) of Sledge's *When A Man Loves A Woman*. While much has been written here and elsewhere about the impact of this one song, Greene's contribution was a significant factor in its success. In 1969 he co-produced, with Jann Wenner, the editor of Rolling Stone

magazine, the Boz SCAGGS LP for Atlantic. Throughout the 1970s and 1980s, he continued to write with Hinton and to play on sessions at Muscle Shoals Sound, Atlantic South and Capricorn.

GREENWICH, ELLIE In the early 1960s the Brill Building on New York's Broadway was the centre of the songwriting business: there hordes of producers like LEIBER & STOLLER, George GOLDNER and Phil SPECTOR would flock in the hope of picking up some tune or another that they could bang out onto the market with their latest discovery. Ellie Greenwich was one of these writers. She was born in New York in 1940. After recording as a member of The Raindrops, she formed a partnership with Jeff BARRY, whom she married, and Phil Spector, and wrote songs like *Be my Baby* and *Baby I Love You* for The RONETTES, *Da Doo Ron Ron* and *Then He Kissed Me* for The CRYSTALS, *Today I Met the Boy I'm Gonna Marry* for Darlene LOVE, *Chapel of Love* for The DIXIE CUPS, *Do Wah Diddy* for The EXCITERS and *Leader of the Pack* for The Shangri-Las. In the early 1970s, she had stab at a solo career with the LP, *Let it be Written, Let It be Sung*; although it was a fine record, she was unable to emulate the success of former Brill Building incumbent, Carole King (see GOFFIN & KING). Since the 1960s, she has had difficulty in harnessing her talents with the same degree of success as before. In 1985 a musical loosely based on her life story, *Leader Of The Pack*, starring herself and Darlene Love, opened on Broadway.

HALE, WILLIE "BEAVER" See STONE, Henry

HALL, DARYL, & JOHN OATES
Daryl Franklin Hohl was born on October 11, 1949, in Pottstown, Pennsylvania, and John Oates on April 7, 1949, in New York City. Both were raised in the Philadelphia suburbs. They met in 1967 at the Adelphi Ballroom, leading their own groups, Hall with The Temptones and Oates with The Masters; Hall had also recorded a single as a member of Kenny Gamble & The Romeos (see GAMBLE & HUFF). After their meeting Hall joined the group Gulliver, and two years later, having finished college, Oates did likewise, but it broke up soon after. Hall started to do session work, singing backing vocals for groups like The STYLISTICS and The DELFONICS. In 1972, he and Oates having teamed up as a duo, were signed to Atlantic and recorded their debut LP, *Whole Oats*, which was produced by Arif MARDIN. Two years later they released the follow-up, *Abandoned Luncheonette* (USA#33.1974); once again produced by Mardin, it included *She's Gone* (USA#7; UK#42.1976), which peaked at #60 in the USA first time around but became a big hit when it was reissued two years later. Their next LP, *War Babies*, was produced by Todd Rundgren and was a stylistic departure from their previous outings: it led to their contract with Atlantic being terminated.

In 1975 they signed with RCA. Their debut LP for the label, *Daryl Hall & John Oates* (USA#17; UK#56.1976), included *Sara Smile* (USA#4.1976). Later that year the LP *Bigger than Both of Us* (USA#13; UK#25.1976) spawned three singles: *Do What you Want, Be What you Are* (USA#39.1976), *Rich Girl* (USA#1.1977) and *Back Together Again* (USA#28.1977). Their next LP, *Beauty on a Back Street* (USA#30; UK#40.1977), was followed by the live LP *Livetime*, which featured their touring band of guitarist Caleb Quaye, bassist Kenny Passarelli, drummer Roger Pope, keyboardists David Kent and Charles DeChant .

Over the next three years, they continued to knock out LPs: *Along the Red Ledge* (USA #27.1978), *X-Static* (USA#33.1979) and *Voices* (USA#17.1980); the latter included the singles *Kiss on my List* (USA#1.1981; UK#33.1980) and *You Make My Dreams* (USA#5.1981).

Their next LP, *Private Eyes* (USA#5.1981; UK#8.1982), represented something of a watershed in their career: not only did it include four hit singles – *Private Eyes* (USA #1.1981; UK#32.1982), *I Can Go for That (No Can Do)* (USA#1; UK#8.1982), *Did It In A Minute* (USA#9.1982) and *Your Imagination* (USA#33.1982) – but *I Can Go for That (No Can Do)* topped the R&B charts for one week, something extremely rare for a white group. The next LP, *H2 O* (USA#3; UK#24.1982), provided them with another three singles: *Maneater* (USA#1; UK#6.1982), *One on One* (USA#7; UK#63.1983) and *Family Man* (USA#6; UK#15.1983). It was followed by the compilation LP, *Rock 'n' Soul (Part 1)* (USA#7; UK#16.1983), which included two previously unreleased tracks that were issued as singles: *Say it Isn't So* (USA#2; UK #69.1983) and *Adult Education* (USA#8; UK #63.1984). After a brief rest, during which Hall duetted with Elvis Costello and produced the LP *Swept Away* for Diana ROSS the LP, *Big Bam Boom* (USA#5; UK#28.1984) was released with producer Arthur BAKER assisting in the mixing. Once again it included a slew of hit singles: *Out of Touch* (USA#1; UK#48.1984), *Method Of Modern Love* (USA#5; UK #21.1985), *Somethings are Better Left Unsaid* (USA#18.1985) and *Possession Obsession* (USA#30.1985).

In May 1985 they invited Eddie KENDRICKS and David RUFFIN, formerly of The TEMPTATIONS, to participate in a concert performance at the Apollo in Harlem to celebrate its reopening. The concert was recorded for the LP, *Live at the Apollo with David Ruffin and Eddie Kendricks* (USA#21;

UK#32.1985), and a single, *A Night at the Apollo Live!* (USA#20; UK#58.1985). In 1986, Hall resumed his solo career with the LP, *Three Hearts in the Happy Ending Machine* (USA#29; UK#26.1986); it was produced by Dave Stewart and proved to be more commercial than his earlier solo LP, *Sacred Songs*, which had been produced by Robert Fripp, and provided him with a brace of hit singles: *Dreamtime* (USA#5; UK#28.1986) and *Foolish Pride* (USA#33.1986). In the mean time, Oates took on outside production work. In 1988 they reunited for the LP, *Ooh Yeah!* (USA#24.1988), having parted company with RCA and signed with Arista. Since then they have both been working on independent projects. In 1990 they resumed their partnership, cutting the LP, *Change Of Season*, and touring the UK.

WHOLE OATS, Atlantic,1972
ABANDONED LUNCHEONETTE, Atlantic, 1974
DARYL HALL & JOHN OATES, RCA, 1976
NO GOODBYES, Atlantic, 1977
PAST TIMES BEHIND, Chelsea, 1977
BEAUTY ON A BACK STREET, RCA, 1977
LIVETIME, RCA, 1978
ALONG THE RED LEDGE, RCA, 1978
X-STATIC, RCA, 1979
SACRED SONGS, (Daryl Hall), RCA, 1980
VOICES, RCA, 1980
PRIVATE EYES, RCA, 1981
H2O, RCA, 1982
ROCK 'N' SOUL (PART 1), RCA, 1983
THE PROVIDER, Thunderbolt, 1984
LIVE AT THE APOLLO WITH DAVID RUFFIN AND EDDIE KENDRICKS, RCA, 1985
20 CLASSIC TRACKS, Meteor, 1986
THE EARLY YEARS, Showcase, 1986
THREE HEARTS IN THE HAPPY ENDING MACHINE, (Daryl Hall), RCA, 1986
OOH YEAH!, Arista, 1988
CHANGE OF SEASON, Arista, 1990

HALL, RICK Rick Hall was born in Franklin County, Alabama on January 31, 1932. In 1957 he joined the country group, Carmol Taylor & The Country Pals, where he met Bily Sherrill. By 1958 both he and Sherrill had left their respective groups to form The Fairlanes, which featured vocalist Dan PENN. In 1959, Fame (Florence Alabama Music Enterprises) was launched. At first it was sited above a drugstore belonging to the father of a local songwriter, Tom Stafford. Word got around, and local and aspiring musicians gravitated quickly to the studios: David BRIGGS, Norbert PUTNAM, Jerry CARRIGAN, Spooner OLDHAM, Donnie FRITTS, Roger HAWKINS, David HOOD, Jimmy JOHNSON and, of course, Penn. In 1961, Hall had his first hit, *You Better Move On* by Arthur ALEXANDER. With the royalties Hall set up the Fame studios in new premises in neighbouring Muscle Shoals. From this assortment of inexperienced musicians, he assembled the first of several versions of the house band. Furthermore, he was the catalyst for the songwriting partnerships Penn formed with Fritts and with Oldham. After the first hit and the establishment of the new studio, music publisher Bill Lowery brought Tommy Roe and The TAMS to Fame to record. It was Lowery who was in part responsible for the first hit on the newly formed Fame label, *Steal Away* by Jimmy HUGHES; a blueprint if ever there was one for the emergent sound of Fame.

In 1964, following the departure of the nucleus of the first house band – Briggs, Carrigan and Putnam – for Nashville, Hall put in place Mark 2; it consisted of drummer Roger Hawkins, guitarist Jimmy Johnson, bassist Junior Lowe and Spooner Oldham on keyboards. It was this combination that put Muscle Shoals on the international map; although in 1967 Lowe was replaced first by Tommy COGBILL and then, David Hood. Over the next four years a steady stream of artists and producers

came to Hall's front door: Aretha FRANK-
LIN and Wilson PICKETT with Jerry
WEXLER and Tom DOWD, Joe TEX with
Buddy KILLEN, MIGHTY SAM and James
& Bobby PURIFY with Papa Don Schroeder,
as well as artists that Hall was producing him-
self, like Clarence CARTER, Etta JAMES,
Irma THOMAS, Ted TAYLOR, Candi
STATON and Laura LEE.

In 1969, Johnson, Hood, Hawkins and
Barry BECKETT left Fame to set up their own
operation, Muscle Shoals sound studios in
Sheffield. Beckett had been Spooner Oldham's
replacement when he joined Dan Penn at Chips
MOMAN's American studios. After their
departure, Junior Lowe moved back into the
frontline, supplemented by guitarist Travis
Wammack, drummer Freeman Brown, bassist
Jesse Boyce and keyboardist Clayton Ivey.
This combination proved to be less durable
than its predecessor, as in 1972 Ivey and Terry
Woodford – formerly of David Hood's old
group, The Mystics – set up the Wishbone
studios, which played host to Motown artists
like The SUPREMES, The TEMPTATIONS
and The COMMODORES. Hall, however,
had increasingly begun to devote more and
more of his energy to recording pop and country music by artists like Mac Davis, The
Osmonds, Paul Anka, Bobbie Gentry. In 1974,
he closed the Fame label for good. By the end
of the seventies, Hall had all but given up the
practical side of recording and was concentrating upon his publishing interests.

HARRIS, BETTY Betty Harris was
another great underrated songstress, whose
soulful vocals were overtly rooted in the
gospel traditions. She was born in Alabama
but relocated to New Orleans after scoring
with the Bert BERNS composition, *Cry To
Me* (USA#23.1963) for the Jubilee label. In
New Orleans she was teamed with Allen

TOUSSAINT at Marshall Sehorn's Sansu
studios, where she recorded sides like *Ride Your
Pony, Nearer To You, What'd I Do Wrong* and *I
Can't Last Much Longer*. In addition to her solo
recordings she was also teamed with Lee
DORSEY for duets like *Take Good Care Of
Our Love*. By 1968 she had moved to Shelby
SINGLETON's SSS International label,
where she recorded some great examples of
country soul like *There's A Break In The Road*.
However, since the late 1960s she has tended to
concentrate on playing the club circuit in New
Orleans.

HARRIS, MAJOR   See DELFONICS

HARRISON, WILBERT   Wilbert Harrison was born in Charlotte, North Carolina,
on January 6, 1929. Having left the navy in
1954 he embarked upon a recording career,
cutting singles on a one-off basis with a variety
of independent labels. In 1958, he recorded
the LEIBER & STOLLER composition
Kansas City (USA#1.1959) for Bobby
ROBINSON's Fury label. He was unable to
consolidate its phenomenal success. The
follow-up, *C. C. Rider*, was an idiosyncratic
version of a standard and failed to sell.
Throughout the 1960s he toured regularly,
recording sporadically for small labels. In 1970
he re-recorded *Let's Work Together* (USA
#32.1970), which he had originally recorded as
Let's Stick Together for the Fury label. The LP
Let's Work Together included versions of standards like *Stagger Lee* and *What Am I Living
For?*. It was one of those rare records where the
mood reflected the period in which it was
made: introspective and slightly paranoid.
Since its modest success, he has reverted to
type: touring constantly and recording singles
or LPs on a one-off basis with quite obscure
specialist labels, although he has reaped con-

siderable benefits from the accrued royalties of *Let's Work Together*, which has been covered by artists like Canned Heat and Bryan Ferry.

LOVIN' OPERATOR, Charly, 1985
SMALL LABELS, Krazy Kat, 1986
WILBERT HARRISON, Ace, 1989

HARVEY & THE MOONGLOWS See FUQUA, Harvey

HATHAWAY, DONNY Donny Hathaway was born on October 1, 1945, in Chicago. He was raised in St. Louis and sang in church choirs throughout his adolescence before going to Howard University in Washington DC, where he met his future collaborator, Roberta FLACK. Having majored in music theory, he returned to Chicago in 1968, there meeting Curtis MAYFIELD, who enlisted him as a producer for the newly established Curtom label. From Curtom he moved to Stax, *via* Chess, and produced Carla THOMAS. Through the Stax connection, he got to know KING CURTIS, who suggested that he get his own contract with Atlantic. In 1970, he cut his debut LP, *Everything is Everything*, from which was taken the single, *The Ghetto*; in 1971 he teamed up with Flack for a cover version of *You've Got a Friend* (USA #29.1971). The following year, he recorded a live LP, *Donny Hathaway Live!* (USA#18.1972) and duetted with June Conquest and Flack; the duet with Flack, *Where is the Love?* (USA#5; UK#29.1972), was taken from the LP, *Roberta Flack and Donny Hathaway* (USA#3.1972). It was followed by the LP, *Extension of a Man*, from which the single, *Love, Love, Love,* was taken. During the mid-1970s, he was preoccupied with his own production company, working with Aretha FRANKLIN among others. In 1978 he teamed up with Flack once

again for the duet, *The Closer I Get to You* (USA#2; UK#42.1978). On January 13, 1979, he plunged to his death from the fifteenth floor of a New York Hotel; he had been working with Flack on the LP, *Roberta Flack Featuring Donny Hathaway* (USA#25; UK#31.1980), from which another duet was taken, *Back Together Again* (USA#56; UK#3.1980). His daughter, Lalah HATHAWAY, has taken up his mantle to impressive ends.

ROBERTA FLACK FEATURING DONNY HATHAWAY, Atlantic, 1980

HATHAWAY, LALAH Lalah Hathaway, the daughter of Eulalah and Donny HATHAWAY, was born in New York. After graduating from the Berklee School Of Music in Boston, she made her debut with an eponymously titled LP for AVL in 1990. A debut of great maturity, it combined her late father's knack for melody with an intuitive ability to get the best out of her material. Among the producers involved were Angela Winbush, Chucki Booker and Gary Taylor. The single *Heaven Knows* failed to make appreciable waves in national charts.

LALAH HATHAWAY, AVL, 1990

HAWKINS, ROGER From the inception of the Fame studios, Roger Hawkins was a key component, although he didn't become a member of the house band until 1964: when David BRIGGS, Norbert PUTNAM and Jerry CARRIGAN all defected to Nashville, he was waiting there as the reserve drummer from the local Hollis Dixon group. For five years, Hawkins backed most of the principal artists to record at Fame, including Aretha FRANKLIN, James & Bobby PURIFY,

Wilson PICKETT and Clarence CARTER; in addition he played on sessions at other studios, backing artists like Percy SLEDGE.

In 1969, he left Fame to set up the rival Muscle Shoals Sound studios with Barry BECKETT, David HOOD and Jimmy JOHNSON. Although the new studios were very successful with artists like The STAPLE SINGERS, Clarence Carter and Millie JACKSON recording there, the greatest triumphs were with white artists like The Rolling Stones, Traffic, Boz SCAGGS, Rod Stewart and Paul Simon. In 1985, they sold the studios to the independent Malaco label, but Hawkins remained and is still plying his trade backing artists like Johnnie TAYLOR, Dorothy MOORE, Shirley BROWN and Bobby BLAND.

HAWKINS, SCREAMIN' JAY One of the great eccentrics of R&B was born on July 18, 1929, in Cleveland, Ohio, as Jalacy Hawkins. In 1954, having distinguished himself as a boxer, he retired from the ring to focus his energies upon a career in music, adopting the name Screamin' Jay Hawkins. After recording for the Apollo label among others, he released *I Put a Spell on You* on the Okeh label, it became a major R&B hit in 1956. Since then he has had a number of local hits like *I Hear Voices* and *Poor Folks*, but has been able to base his career upon his solitary major success. He tours the USA and Europe constantly with a stage act that falls just short of kitsch. *I Put a Spell on You* has been covered by a wide range of artists, from Arthur Brown to Alan Price.

FRENZY, Edsel, 1982
SCREAMIN' THE BLUES, Red Lightnin', 1982
LIVE, Midnight, 1986
I I's, Official, 1989
THE FEAST OF THE MAU MAU, Edsel, 1989
BLACK MUSIC FOR WHITE PEOPLE, Demon, 1991

HAYES, ISAAC Isaac Hayes has been underrated over the years. *Hot Buttered Soul* (1969) was an inspiration for artists like Barry WHITE, Curtis MAYFIELD and, to some extent, Marvin GAYE. Without Hayes having led the way, it is debatable whether soundtracks by black artists would have enjoyed the same degree of acceptance that they do today. Furthermore, the length of his records contributed to the need for the twelve-inch single. However, his penchant for the grandiose has made him increasingly susceptible to the fickle finger of fashion.

Hayes was born on August 20, 1942, in Covington, Tennessee. In 1964 he was introduced to Jim STEWART by Floyd Newman, who played baritone sax in the Stax house band, The MARKEYS. As a result of the meeting he started to do session work playing keyboards for the cream of the Stax crop like Otis REDDING, Carla THOMAS and William BELL, although he continued to work also as a packer at a meat plant. While at the meat plant he met David PORTER, who was trying to sell him life insurance; out of this meeting was formed one of the most successful songwriting and production partnerships to emanate from Stax. They were responsible for all of SAM & DAVE's hits, as well as collaborating with other artists like Carla Thomas, The Soul Children and Eddie FLOYD.

His career as a solo performer started by accident in 1968 when the result of a late-night session with "Duck" DUNN and Al JACKSON was considered to be sufficiently good to release. Entitled *Presenting Isaac Hayes*, it failed to sell in any quantity, but the following year he was given the opportunity to record a follow-up LP as part of the link-up with Gulf & Western. *Hot Buttered Soul* (USA#8.1969) was released on the new Stax subsidiary, Enterprise; the eulogistic "raps" that featured so prominently on it set a pattern that would be repeated time and again. In 1971 he recorded the soundtrack for the film *Shaft*, whose title-song, *Theme from Shaft* (USA#1; UK#4.1971), established him in the UK. There was an element of self-indulgence about some of his work, particularly *Black Moses* (USA #10.1971), which depicted him on the cover as some sort of evangelical refugee from a Cecil B. De Mille epic. In August 1972 he played at the Seventh Annual Watts Festival in Los Angeles, Wattstax '72, featuring a variety of fellow Stax artists. However, the writing was on the wall for Stax, who were undergoing major financial problems (mostly of the self-inflicted variety) and for Hayes, whose days of supremacy as a major stylist were effectively over. Nevertheless, Hayes continued to issue LPs like *Live At The Sahara Tahoe* (USA#14.1973) – a double LP featuring his full orchestra – and *Joy* (USA #16.1974). These were commercially very successful but artistically full of cliches and overblown.

In 1975 he left Stax after a disagreement over royalties and set up his own record company, Hot Buttered Soul, with a distribution arrangement with ABC: the move prompted him to tailor his sound to the prevailing disco fashion. He recorded three LPs in swift succession: *Chocolate Chip* (USA#18.1975), *Disco Connection* and *Groove-a-Thon*; a single, *Disco Connection* (UK#10.1976), was extracted, but later the same year he filed for bankruptcy. In March 1977 he recorded a double live LP with Dionne WARWICK, it was the final release on the Hot Buttered Soul label. In June he was declared bankrupt with six million dollars' worth of debts; he moved to Atlanta and signed a fresh deal with Polydor. His most successful LP for Polydor, *Don't Let Go* (USA#39.1979), provided him with his last gold disc to date and, although he has continued to tour and record, he has been unable to recapture his former standing. Latterly he has been much sought-after as an actor, contributing a number of "cameos" to both films and television.

HOT BUTTERED SOUL, Stax, 1969
ISAAC HAYES MOVEMENT, Stax, 1970
TO BE CONTINUED, Stax, 1971
SHAFT, Stax, 1971
BLACK MOSES, Stax, 1972
LIVE AT THE SAHARA TAHOE , Stax, 1973
HIS GREATEST HITS, Stax, 1974
A MAN AND A WOMAN, (with Dionne Warwick), ABC, 1977
THE BEST OF SHAFT, Stax, 1981
U-TURN, CBS, 1986
THE BEST OF ISAAC HAYES, VOLUME 2, London, 1987

HEAD, ROY Roy Head's flirtation with stardom lasted approximately six months in 1965, when he was widely touted as being the definitive "blue-eyed soul boy". He was discovered and produced by Huey MEAUX in his native Texas, where he recorded the singles *Treat Her Right* (USA#2; UK#30.1965) and *Apple of My Eye* (USA#32.1965) for Don ROBEY's Back Beat label. After recording for Scepter briefly, cutting *Just A Little Bit* (USA #39.1965), he returned to playing the club circuit where his energetic live act had its admirers. However, by the end of the decade and an even briefer spell with Steve CROPPER's production company TMI, he stopped singing soul and started to sing country, recording for Dot and Elektra.

HEATWAVE Heatwave were formed in Germany in 1975 by Johnny and Keith Wilder, who had both served in the US Army. Their first recruit was Rod Temperton, who had been playing sessions; he was followed by guitarist Eric Johns, bassist Mario Mantese from Spain, percussionist Ernest Berger from Czechoslovakia and guitarist Jesse Whitten from Chicago completed. Throughout 1976 they toured the European club circuit, until they came to the attention of Dick Leahy, the owner of the GTO label, who signed them and partnered them with producer Barry Blue. They struck gold immediately with *Boogie Nights* (USA/UK#2.1977); it was followed by the LP (USA#11; UK#46.1977) and single *Too Hot to Handle* (UK#15.1977). In November 1977 one of the first of many tragedies befell the group: Whitten was stabbed to death while visiting his home in Chicago. He was replaced by Roy Carter, who had been a member of The Foundations in the late 1960s.

In 1978 Temperton stopped touring to devote his energies to songwriting: over the years he would write for Aretha FRANKLIN, George Benson and Michael JACKSON, including the title track of the LP, *Thriller*. Despite his departure from the group, he continued to write for it, contributing to hits like *The Groove Line* (USA#7; UK#15.1978), *Always and Forever* (USA#18; UK#9.1978) and *Mind Blowing Decisions* (UK#12.1978), as well as the LP *Central Heating* (USA#10; UK#26.1978). In July 1978 Mantese was partially paralysed in a car crash, so that he had to leave the group. This prompted the enlistment of Calvin Duke (keyboards), Derek Bramble (bass) and Keith Harrison (guitar and vocals), who had all been members of the funk outfit, Fatback Band, and guitarist William Jones, a cousin of the Wilder brothers. In 1979 *Razzle Dazzle* (UK#43.1979), from the LP *Hot Property* (USA#38.1979), was produced by Phil Ramone. In June Johnnie Wilder was involved in a car crash which totally paralysed him. Although he subsequently managed, with the help of a fully modified wheel chair, to resume his role in the group for studio work, his position in the touring unit was taken by J. D. Nicholas. In 1981, the Temperton compositions *Gangsters Of The Groove* (UK#19.1981) and *Jitterbuggin'* (UK#34.1981) marked their return to the charts; both were taken from the LP *Candles* (UK#29.1981). In 1982 Nicholas joined The COMMODORES

as the replacement for Lionel RICHIE. Since then the group has continued to tour throughout the US and Europe regularly, while Temperton has continued producing and writing for artists like Jeffrey OSBORNE.

CENTRAL HEATING, GTO, 1978
HOT PROPERTY, GTO, 1979
MAXIMUM HEAT, Hallmark, 1983
GREATEST HITS, Epic, 1984

HEBB, BOBBY Bobby Hebb was born in Nashville in 1941. His career started in 1953, playing the spoons in Roy Acuff's Smokey Mountain Boys, who were frequently featured at the Grand Ole Opry. In 1955 after being spotted by John RICHBOURG, who signed him to his Rich label, he recorded *Night Train to Memphis*. He continued to play in and around Nashville until in 1961, he teamed up with Sylvia Shemwell (see HOUSTON, Cissy), recording as Bobby & Sylvia. In 1966 he signed with Philips and scored with *Sunny* (USA#2; UK#12.1966); it wasn't a particularly distinguished item, but managed to cross over into all three charts – National, R&B and Country. It was followed by a rendering of the Porter Wagoner composition, *A Satisfied Mind* (USA #39.1966), although it failed to match the success of its predecessor, it showed quite precisely that Hebb's metier was country. In the early seventies, having concentrated upon country-ish material, he scored again with *Love Love Love* (UK#32.1972). Recent years have seen him move closer to the middle of the road, where his popularity on the cabaret circuit is unswerving.

HENDRIX, JIMI Of all the performers to emerge during the 1960s, James Marshall Hendrix was one of the most influential. His technical prowess as a guitarist far exceeded the flamboyant showmanship for which he was mostly known. His style broke many of the ground rules, opening up fresh vistas for artists like James BROWN, Sly Stone (see SLY & THE FAMILY STONE), The ISLEY BROTHERS, George CLINTON, The TEMPTATIONS and, more recently, PRINCE. He was born in Seattle, Washington, on November 27, 1942. In 1954, he was given an electric guitar, and he taught himself how to play it by listening to records by blues artists like Muddy Waters, B. B. KING and Elmore James. After a spell in the army with the 101st Airborne Division – from 1959 until his discharge due to injuries sustained during parachute training in 1961- he became a session guitarist, adopting the pseudonym Jimmy James and backing artists like Sam COOKE, B. B. KING, Jackie WILSON, LITTLE RICHARD and Ike & Tina TURNER. In 1964 he moved to New York, where he joined The Isley Brothers' touring band, and also played sessions with KING CURTIS and Curtis Knight; he started to write his own material with the latter. By 1965 Hendrix had launched out on his own, forming Jimmy James & The Blue Flames. He performed regularly on the club circuit, where he started to develop a strong local following. In 1966, following a recommendation from Linda Keith, Keith Richards' girlfriend, Chas Chandler, the former bass-player of The Animals, who had now formed his own management company, went to see Hendrix performing at a New York club, and suggested that he should go to London and form a new group. In September 1966 Hendrix and Chandler arrived in London and recruited drummer Mitch Mitchell and bassist Noel Redding to form the Jimi Hendrix Experience. Their first single was a cover of The Leaves' hit *Hey Joe* (UK#6.1967); as a result of this success the group was booked to support The Who at The Saville Theatre; following their performance there they were signed by Kit Lambert to

his fledgling Track label. Their first release for Track was *Purple Haze* (UK#3.1967); it was followed by the debut LP *Are You Experienced?* (USA#5; UK#2.1967). The next single was *The Wind Cries Mary* (UK#6.1967). On June 18, 1967, the group appeared at the Monterey Pop Festival on the same bill as Otis REDDING; both performances were recorded but were not released until 1970 under the title of *The Monterey International Pop Festival* (USA#16.1970) by which time Redding was dead and Hendrix did not have long to live – he was to die while it was still in the US charts. Their next single, *Burning of the Midnight Lamp* (UK#18.1967), was recorded in New York and featured The Sweet Inspirations (see HOUSTON, Cissy), providing the backing vocals. It was followed by the LP, *Axis: Bold As Love* (USA#3.1968; UK#5.1967), which prompted extensive tours throughout the USA and Europe, although there were frequent ructions within the group. Their next LP, a double, *Electric Ladyland* (USA#1; UK#6.1968), included contributions from Stevie Winwood and from bassist Jack Casady of Jefferson Airplane. It contained the single, *All Along The Watchtower* (USA#20; UK#5.1968). At the end of 1968, the group parted company with their manager, Chandler. His replacement, Mike Jeffrey, persuaded the group to undertake a series of concerts in the UK and the USA, including the Woodstock Festival, before the group split up permanently.

Hendrix then formed The Band of Gypsys with Buddy Miles, previously the drummer for The Electric Flag, and bassist Billy Cox, a former colleague from his army days. However, his relationship with Miles was extremely tempestuous from day one and, after their second concert together, Miles left the group – only to be replaced by Mitch Mitchell! The Band of Gypsies released an eponymous LP (USA#5; UK#6.1970) recorded live at their first concert. With the disintegration of The

Band of Gypsies, Hendrix played a series of concerts and festivals, backed by Cox and Mitchell, including the Isle of Wight Festival in the UK. His appearance at the Islwe of Wight Festival proved to be his final major performance: on September 18, 1970, Hendrix was found dead, he was 27. His death had been caused by choking on his own vomit while sleeping under the influence of barbiturates.

Since his death, the haphazard nature of his various contractual agreements with record companies and individuals has become painfully evident, with almost anybody being able to issue posthumous records of Hendrix, regardless of their quality. His final official LP, *The Cry of Love* (USA#3; UK#2.1971), contained material for a concept LP *The First Rays of the Rising Sun*, which he had been working on up to the time of his death. However, throughout the 1970s a slew of LPs materialised, most live recordings or studio out-takes: *Experience* (UK#9.1971), *Rainbow Bridge* (USA#15; UK#16.1971), *Jimi Hendrix at the Isle of Wight* (UK#17.1971), *Hendrix in the West* (USA#12; UK#7.1972), *War Heroes* (USA#48; UK#23.1972), *Soundtrack Recordings from the Film Jimi Hendrix* (UK#37.1973), *Jimi Hendrix* (UK#35.1975) and *Crash Landing* (USA#5; UK#35.1975), to name but a few. In 1990, the 20th. anniversary of his death was commemorated in London by the screening at the National Film Theatre of a film of his performance at the Isle of Wight Festival in 1970. Despite his premature death, he managed to cram enough into his comparatively short career to last most people a lifetime. Had he lived, there is no telling what he might have done.

ARE YOU EXPERIENCED?, Polydor, 1967
AXIS: BOLD AS LOVE, Polydor, 1968
SMASH HITS, Track, 1968
ELECTRIC LADYLAND, Polydor, 1968

BAND OF GYPSIES, Polydor, 1970
THE CRY OF LOVE, Polydor, 1971
RAINBOW BRIDGE, Reprise, 1971
JIMI HENDRIX AT THE ISLE OF WIGHT, Polydor, 1971
HENDRIX IN THE WEST, Polydor, 1972
WAR HEROES, Polydor, 1972
SOUNDTRACK RECORDINGS FROM THE FILM JIMI HENDRIX, Reprise, 1973
FRIENDS FROM THE BEGINNING, (with Little Richard), Ember, 1974
CRASH LANDING, Polydor, 1975
RARE EXPERIENCE, Enterprise, 1976
THE ESSENTIAL JIMI HENDRIX, Polydor, 1978
10th ANNIVERSARY BOX, Polydor, 1980
FREE SPIRIT, Phoenix, 1981
JIMI HENDRIX: PROFILE, Teldec, 1981
COSMIC TURNAROUND, Audio Fidelity, 1982
20 GOLDEN PIECES, VOLUME 1, Bulldog,1982
20 GOLDEN PIECES, VOLUME 2, Bulldog, 1982
EXPERIENCE, Bulldog, 1982
MORE EXPERIENCE, Bulldog, 1982
THE LEGENDARY JIMI HENDRIX, Polydor, 1982
MOODS, Phoenix, 1982
VOODOO CHILE, Polydor, 1982
WOKE UP THIS MORNING AND FOUND MYSELF DEAD, Red Lightnin', 1982
HEY JOE, Polydor, 1983
RE-EXPERIENCED, Polydor, 1983
THE JIMI HENDRIX ALBUM, Contour, 1983
THE SINGLES ALBUM, Polydor, 1983
STONE FREE, Polydor, 1983
IN THE BEGINNING, Premier, 1984
LEGENDS OF ROCK, Telefunken, 1984
KISS THE SKY, Polydor, 1984
TOMORROW NEVER KNOWS, Happy Bird (Germany), 1984
JIMI PLAYS MONTEREY, Polydor, 1986
JOHNNY B. GOODE, Fame, 1986
REPLAY ON, Sierra, 1986
STRANGE THINGS, Showcase, 1986
THE BEST OF JIMI HENDRIX, EMI, 1987
LIVE AT WINTERLAND, Polydor, 1987

THE JIMI HENDRIX CONCERTS, Media Motion, 1990
CORNERSTONES: 1967–1970, Polydor, 1990
NIGHT LIFE, Thunderbolt, 1990

HENDRYX, NONA   The career of Nona Hendryx has, like those of her former colleagues Sarah Dash and Patti LaBELLE, been full of troughs. She was born in Trenton, New Jersey, on August 18, 1945. From 1962 until 1976, she was a member of the various incarnations of LaBelle (first The Bluebelles, then Patti LaBelle & The Bluebelles and finally LaBelle). When she left to go it alone she seemed to have all the credentials for a long and very successful solo career: that this success has not been forthcoming can only be attributed to bad luck, as her style is comparable to those of Patti LaBelle (not unreasonably) and Tina TURNER, both of whom have experienced similar troughs in their careers but gone on to achieve massive success. With a series of labels, she has released a string of LPs including: *The Art Of Defence* (1983), *The Heat* (1985), *Female Trouble* (1987) and *Skindiver* (1989).

THE ART OF DEFENCE, RCA, 1983
THE HEAT, RCA, 1985
FEMALE TROUBLE, EMI America, 1987
SKINDIVER, Private, 1989

HEWETT, HOWARD   See SHALAMAR

HILL, JESSE   See SHIRLEY & LEE

HILL, Z.Z.   Arzell Hill was born in Naples, Texas on September 30, 1935. His career began with the gospel group, The Spiritual Five. In the early sixties he became Z. Z. Hill and started a solo career in R&B. In 1963 he signed with his elder brother's label, MHR, and recorded *Tumbleweed,* which prompted the Kent label to sign him. At Kent he gained a reputation for being a fine singer, but the prosaic productions militated against mainstream success. In 1969 he recorded two singles with producer Quin IVY at Muscle Shoals. In 1971 he recorded *Don't Make me Pay for this Mistake* for the Hill label (owned by his brother), which reached #18 in the R&B charts. In 1972 he signed with United Artists, where he remained until signing with CBS in 1977. Throughout, both Kent and Hill continued to issue singles with great regularity.

In 1980 he signed with the independent Malaco label, where his blues-tinged R&B style was in its element. His second LP for Malaco, *Down Home*, stayed in the charts for almost two years. It was the first time in a career spanning over twenty years that his easy soulful style had been produced sympathetically. His later LPs, *The Rhythm & the Blues* and *I'm a Bluesman* continued the process: strong material with neat unfussy productions. On April 27, 1984, at the age of 49 he died from a blood clot, having been involved in a road accident two months before. His fifth LP for the label, *Bluesmaster*, which he had just finished, was released posthumously and provided an excellent epitaph for a career that was nearing its peak.

Z. Z. HILL, Malaco, 1981
DOWN HOME, Malaco, 1982
THE RHYTHM & THE BLUES, Malaco, 1982
I'M A BLUESMAN, Malaco, 1983
DUES PAID IN FULL, Kent, 1984
BLUESMASTER, Malaco, 1984
IN MEMORIAM, Malaco, 1985
GREATEST HITS, Malaco, 1986
WHO'S THRILLING YOU, Stateside, 1986
BEST OF Z. Z. HILL, Malaco, 1987

HINTON, EDDIE One of the great unsung heroes of Muscle Shoals was guitarist Eddie Hinton. He was brought up in Tuscaloosa, Alabama. While he was still at college he became a member of a local group, The Minutes. On moving to Muscle Shoals he became a session musician and formed a songwriting partnership with Marlin GREENE. Together they penned hits for artists like Aretha FRANKLIN, Percy SLEDGE and Dusty Springfield. In 1977 he was signed by Phil WALDEN to his Capricorn label. His debut LP, *Very Extremely Dangerous*, was recorded at Muscle Shoals Sound studios with Barry BECKETT, Roger HAWKINS, David HOOD and Jimmy JOHNSON. Unfortunately Capricorn went bust, leaving Hinton high and dry. After several years of obscurity, during which he had serious drug and alcohol problems, he started to write and perform once again.

LETTERS FROM MISSISSIPPI, Line/Zane, 1986
CRY AND MOAN, Rounder 1990

HOLLAND, DOZIER & HOLLAND
The songwriting and production partnership of Brian Holland (born on February 15, 1941, in Detroit), Lamont Dozier (born on June 16, 1941, in Detroit) and Eddie Holland (born on October 30, 1939 in Detroit) was one of many such partnership that thrived at Motown during the early 1960s. Eddie Holland was one of the first artists to be signed by Berry GORDY: they met in 1957 when Gordy was writing songs for Jackie WILSON and Eddie Holland sang on the demos. As a performer Eddie's biggest hit was *Jamie* (USA#30.1962), but his main contribution to Motown in its earliest days was his knowledge of phrasing and inflexion; this proved invaluable when working with some of the younger artists. Dozier had released a couple of unsuccessful singles for

United Artists as Lamont Anthony and then be signed to the Motown subsidiary Anna. Brian Holland had achieved some success, producing *Please Mr Postman* for The MARVELETTES.

Inevitably, partnerships were forged between artists and production teams. In the case of Holland, Dozier & Holland, they provided hits for The ELGINS *(Heaven Must Have Sent You)*, The FOUR TOPS *(Baby I Need Your Loving, I Can't Help Myself, Reach Out I'll be There, Standing in the Shadows of Love* and *Bernadette)*, Marvin GAYE *(Can I Get a Witness* and *How Sweet it is (To be Loved by You)*, The ISLEY BROTHERS *(This Old Heart Of Mine)*, MARTHA & THE VANDELLAS *(Come and Get these Memories, Nowhere to Run* and *Heat Wave)*, Smokey ROBINSON & The Miracles *(Micky's Monkey)*, The SUPREMES *(When the Lovelight Starts Shining through His Eyes, Where Did Our Love Go?, Baby Love, Back in my Arms Again, Stop! In the Name of Love, Love is Like an Itching in my Heart, You Can't Hurry Love* and *You Keep me Hangin' On)* and Mary WELLS *(You Lost the Sweetest Boy)*.

When they left Motown in 1967 to found their own labels, Invictus and Hot Wax, they set about building a roster of artists including Freda Payne, The CHAIRMEN OF THE BOARD, HONEYCONE and Laura LEE. By 1974, the label and the partnership had collapsed, and they signed independent production deals with Buddah and Capitol. In 1977 Dozier produced the Aretha FRANKLIN LP *Sweet Passion*; he went on to produce LPs by Eric Clapton, Ben E. KING, Phil Collins and Simply Red. He revived his own career as an artist, recording for Invictus and, when it closed down, for CBS, ABC and Warner Bros; among the LPs he cut were *Right There* (1976), *Peddlin'* (1977) and *Bittersweet* (1979). In the early 1980s Dozier started up his own label Megaphone and reunited with Eddie and Brian

Holland to work with The Four Tops at Motown.

BIGGER THE LIFE, (Lamont Dozier), Demon, 1983

HOLLIDAY, JENNIFER Jennifer Holliday shot to prominence in 1982 as a member of the cast of the Broadway musical, *Dreamgirls*; such was the quality of her performance that she won a Tony Award for Best Actress. She was born in Houston, Texas on October 19, 1960. After singing gospel as a child she enrolled in drama school, which enabled her to get selected for a part in *Dreamgirls;* her biggest hit *And I Am Telling You I Am Not Going* (USA #22.1982) was extracted from the show. In the wake of this success, she was signed as a solo artist by the Geffen label. However, her solo career has failed to live up to the high early expectations because, although her first solo LP *Feel My Soul* (USA#31.1983), produced by Maurice White of EARTH, WIND & FIRE, was a moderate hit, she has become far too theatrical in her delivery: perhaps her aspirations are theatrical.

DREAMGIRLS, (Original Cast Recording), Geffen, 1982
FEEL MY SOUL, Geffen, 1983

HOLLOWAY, BRENDA Unusually, for a Motown signing Brenda Holloway didn't come from Detroit, she was born in Atascadero, California on June 21, 1946. She was spotted and signed by Berry GORDY at a DJ's convention in Los Angeles in 1963. Her first hit, *Every Little Bit Hurts* (USA#13.1964), was written by Ed Cobb. The follow-up was *I'm Gone* (USA#25.1965); this was followed by *You've Made Me So Very Happy* (USA #39.1967), which she cowrote and it was subsequently a hit for the jazz-rock group, Blood, Sweat & Tears. As a result of being spotted by Brian Epstein she was booked to appear on The Beatles US Tour. In 1967 she left the music industry as she had become a born-again christian. In later years she has made a comeback as a session singer for artists like Joe Cocker.

HONEY CONE Honeycone comprised Edna Wright, the sister of Darlene LOVE and a former member of the gospel group The Children of God in Christ Singers, Carolyn Willis and Shellie Clark. They were spotted by Eddie Holland of HOLLAND, DOZIER & HOLLAND in 1969 when they were working as backing vocalists. He signed them to his Hot Wax label, where they recorded a succession of hits including *While You're Looking out for Sugar, Want Ads* (USA#1.1971), *Stick Up* (USA#11.1971), *One Monkey Don't Stop no Show* (USA#15.1971) and *The Day I Found myself* (USA#23.1972). While they were signed by Holland the bulk of their material was written and produced by Norman Johnson and Greg Perry of CHAIRMEN OF THE BOARD, due to contractual problems. Despite their success the group folded in 1973.

GIRLS IT AIN'T EASY, HDH, 1984

HOLLYWOOD FLAMES See BOB & EARL

HOOD, DAVID When Rick HALL's first house band left Fame, there were any number of willing recruits to fill the vacant slots. In 1967 David Hood, who had been a member of a local group The Mystics took over from Junior Lowe as the regular bassist at Fame, backing artists like Clarence CARTER, Candi STATON, Wilson PICKETT and Solomon BURKE. In April 1969 Hood left Fame with Roger HAWKINS, Barry BECK-

ETT and Jimmy JOHNSON to set up Muscle Shoals Sound studios, where he backed a variety of artists – black and white – like Millie JACKSON, The Rolling Stones, Traffic, Paul Simon, Joe Cocker, Boz SCAGGS, Eddie HINTON and Bobby WOMACK. By 1985 the studios had been sold to Tommy COUCH at Malaco, but Hood has remained, playing sessions for artists like Bobby BLAND and Johnnie TAYLOR.

HOUSTON, CISSY Cissy Houston was born Emily Drinkard in Newark, New Jersey in 1932. As a member of the gospel group, The Drinkard Sisters, which included Dee Dee WARWICK and Dionne WARWICK, she recorded for the Savoy label before forming a pool of session vocalists that included Judy Clay (see BELL, William), Doris TROY, Dee Dee Warwick and Myrna Smith. Throughout the late 1950s and early 1960s, they backed artists like Solomon BURKE, Wilson PICKETT, Garnet MIMMS and The DRIFTERS. In 1967 she formed The Sweet Inspirations with Sylvia Shemwell, who had been in the duo Bobby & Sylvia with Bobby HEBB, at the suggestion of Jerry WEXLER. Wexler had been so impressed by the calibre of their back-up vocals for Aretha FRANKLIN that he booked them into Chips MOMAN's American studios, where they recorded the Dan PENN and Spooner OLDHAM composition, *Sweet Inspiration* (USA#18.1968). It was followed by versions of *Knock On Wood, To Love Somebody* and *Unchained Melody*. Despite the success of the record, they continued to work primarily as back-up vocalists for Elvis Presley and Dusty Springfield, among others. By 1971 the group had separated, with Houston concentrating on a solo career. She was signed by Janus, where she recorded songs like *Midnight Train to Georgia* and *The Long and Winding Road*, but by the mid-1970s she had semi-retired, breaking her silence only to pro-

vide back-up vocals for artists like her cousin, Dionne Warwick. In 1980 she recorded the LP *Step Aside for A Lady*, since when she has recorded as a backing vocalist for her daughter Whitney HOUSTON.

MAMA'S COOKIN', Charly, 1986

HOUSTON, THELMA Thelma Houston was born in Leland, Mississippi, the sister of Cissy HOUSTON. As an occasional member of The Drinkard Sisters, a family concern, she started to sing gospel from an early age. She made her recording debut for Dunhill in 1969 with the LP *Sunshower*, which was produced by Jim Webb. After signing with Motown, she had her first hit with the GAMBLE & HUFF composition, *Don't Leave me this Way* (USA#1; UK#13.1977). The success of the LP *Any Way You Like It* (USA#11.1977) encouraged Motown to team her with Jerry BUTLER for the LP *Thelma and Jerry*. She scored her next hit with *Saturday Night, Sunday Morning* (USA#34.1979). After a spell with RCA, where she had a minor hit with *If You Feel it* (UK #48.1981), she was signed to MCA, where she had another minor hit with *You Used to Hold me so Tight* (UK#49.1984). Throughout her career, she has always managed to get the best out of sometimes rather undistinguished material. In addition to singing she has had a parallel career as a film actress.

SUNSHOWER, Motown, 1969
ANY WAY YOU LIKE IT, Motown, 1977
BREAKWATER CAT, RCA, 1980
NEVER GONNA BE ANTHER ONE, RCA, 1981
I'VE GOT THE MUSIC IN ME, (with Pressure Cooker), Sheffield Treasury, 1982

HOUSTON, WHITNEY Whitney Houston was born in New Jersey on August 9,

1963. From a very tender age she was encouraged by her mother Cissy HOUSTON to sing. She made her debut when she was eleven in the New Hope Baptist Junior Choir. Through her well placed connections, she was encouraged to sing back-up vocals for artists like her aunt, Dionne WARWICK, and Chaka KHAN. In 1981 she obtained work as a model and in 1983 she was signed by Clive DAVIS to the Arista label. Her debut LP *Whitney Houston* (USA#1; UK#2.1985) was produced by a combination of Michael Masser, Narada Michael WALDEN and Kashif. It included four hit singles: *You Give Good Love* (USA#3.1985), *Saving All my Love for You* (USA/UK#1.1985), *How Will I Know?* (USA#1; UK#5.1986) and *The Greatest Love of All* (USA#1; UK#8.1986). After extensive touring in the UK and Europe, she released her next LP *Whitney* (USA/UK #1.1987); as with her debut it featured a variety of producers, and included several hit singles: *I Wanna Dance with Somebody* (USA/UK #1.1987), *Didn't We Almost Have it All* (USA#1; UK#14.1987); *So Emotional* (USA#1; UK #5.1987); *Where Do Broken Hearts Go* (USA#1; UK#14.1988) and *Love Will Save the Day* (USA#9; UK#10.1988). Her next venture was to record *One Moment In Time* (USA/UK #1.1988), the theme for a collaboration between a number of artists celebrating the Olympic Games. Since then film producers have been blazing a trail to her front door, offering her all sorts of roles. In 1990 she released the LP *I'm Your Baby Tonight*, featuring a cast of thousands; it was characteristically slick and polished.

WHITNEY HOUSTON, Arista, 1985
WHITNEY, Arista, 1987
I'M YOUR BABY TONIGHT, Arista, 1990

HUFF, LEON See GAMBLE & HUFF

HUGHES, JIMMY Jimmy Hughes was born in Leighton, Alabama. He was a member of a local gospel group, The Singing Clouds, when he met Rick HALL while both were working for the Robbins Rubber Company. After Hall set up the Fame studios he was approached by Hughes, who wanted to record some demos. In 1963 he cut *I'm Qualified*, which became a small local hit. The following year, he scored with *Steal Away* (USA #17.1964), it was the second hit for Hall and was released on his own Fame label. It provided the blueprint for the country-soul style that was to become emblematic of the sound of Fame and was a perfect example of Dan PENN's craftmanship when combining the imagery of country music with the punchy immediacy of R&B. The follow-up, *Try Me*, a James BROWN song, failed to capture the resonance of *Steal Away* and bombed commercially. Although Hughes had a number of modest local hits like *A Shot of Rhythm and Blues*, he was never able to recapture the glory of *Steal Away*. He remained at Fame until 1966 and was active on the chitlin' circuit until his retirement in 1974.

HUGO & LUIGI Hugo Peretti was born the son of a violinist in New York in 1918. By the early 1940s when he met up with Luigi Creatore, he had been variously employed as a trumpeter and an arranger for Guy Lombardo and Charlie Barnet. After working in A&R for Mercury, they bought the Roulette label from George GOLDNER, which they kept for two years (they sold it to Henry GLOVER and Morris Levy). In 1959, they joined RCA, where they became the joint-heads of A&R. Their biggest coup was to secure a contract with Sam COOKE's independent Sar label to produce and arrange all his records for RCA. Although Cooke's records during this period tended to be overproduced – a regular failing of Hugo & Luigi productions – they were perfectly suited to the pop market and thus made the predominantly white-run record business a lot more aware of the potential marketability of black music. However, their production of *Shout* for The ISLEY BROTHERS showed that they were quite capable of cutting records that were good basic R&B: no gloss, just a barn-storming stomper.

Their role as true all-rounders was consolidated by their composition for Elvis Presley, *Can't Help Falling in Love*, for the film *Blue Hawaii*. As a result of this connection with the film business, they set up the Avco label with producer Joseph E. Levine; their most notable signings were The STYLISTICS, whom they started to produce once Thom BELL had left the company, but their recruitment of producer and arranger Van McCOY was a masterstroke as his extensive musical background and vision enabled them to breast the disco explosion with comparative ease. After McCoy's death in 1979 they parted company with Avco and composed the score for the Broadway musical *Maggie Flynn*, but gradually moved into retirement. On May 1, 1986, Hugo died after a protracted illness.

HUNT, TOMMY Tommy Hunt was born in a tent in Pittsburg, on June 18, 1933. His father worked in vaudeville, travelling the Northern states until settling in Chicago. Hunt's career started as a gospel singer in The Echoes, until in 1958 he joined The FLAMINGOS, where he contributed the lead vocal to titles like *I Only Have Eyes for You* among others. After leaving The Flamingos, he embarked upon a solo career with the Scepter label. However, his career hardly flourished and he was compelled to resort to providing backing vocals for artists like Chuck JACKSON and Maxine BROWN. In 1968 he moved to the UK, settling in Wales as Scepter sides like *Human* had attracted much enthusiasm on the UK Northern soul circuit. Consequently, he was signed to the UK-based Spark label where in the mid-1970s he had three hits: *Crackin' Up* (UK#39.1975), *Loving on the Losing Side* (UK#28.1976) and *One Fine Morning* (UK#44.1976). Since then he has continued to work in Europe and the UK, touring the club circuit and US Airforce bases.

HUNTER, IVORY JOE Ivory Joe Hunter was born and brought up in Kirbyville, Texas in 1914. During the 1930s he performed gospel in and around his native Texas. By the 1940s he had gravitated to the West Coast, where he put out records on his own Ivory label. In 1947 he signed to the Cincinnatti-based King label, recording country songs like *Jealous Heart*; by 1949, he had moved once again, this time to MGM, the home of Hank Williams, where he stayed for the next five years, recording his own compositions like *I Almost Lost my Mind* and *I Need You So*. In 1954 he signed with Atlantic, where he continued writing and recording his own compositions, scoring with *Since I Met You Baby* (USA#12.1956). Throughout the 1960s he continued to record for a series of labels: Capitol, Veejay, Stax, Goldwax, Sound Stage Seven and Epic. In 1970 he appeared with The Johnny OTIS Show in Monterey; the concert was recorded and issued as a double live LP. In 1973 his final LP, *I've Always Been Country*, was recorded with Reggie Young and Tommy COGBILL among others. On November 8, 1974, he died of cancer, aged 60. Shortly before his death a benefit concert was staged at the Grand Ole Opry in Nashville.

77th STREET BOOGIE, Route 66, 1980
THE ARTISTRY OF IVORY JOE HUNTER, Bulldog, 1982

THIS IS IVORY JOE, Ace, 1984
THE HITS, Official, 1988
SIXTEEN ALL-TIME HITS, King, 1989

IN TUNE, Whitfield, 1979
IN AND OUT, Motown, 1983
MAKING A GAME OUT OF LOVE, Motown, 1985

HUTCH, WILLIE Willie Hutch has spent most of his career at Motown, as a cornerstone to their operation since their move to Hollywood. He has also contributed much in his own right. After a stint in the marines in the early 1960s he played on the chitlin' circuit with groups like The Phonetics and The V-Notes. In 1967 he was given a break as a songwriter by Lamonte McLemore of The Fifth Dimension – they were in the Marines together – when they recorded his song, *I'll be Loving You*. This stroke of good fortune enabled him to get an introduction to Johnny Rivers, who owned the Soul City label. Consequently, Hutch started to write and arrange for the label on a regular basis, working with Rivers, Al Wilson and The Friends of Distinction until Motown arrived in Los Angeles.

At Motown he has written for Smokey ROBINSON, The Jackson Five (see JACKSONS), Diana ROSS, Marvin GAYE and Junior WALKER as well as coproducing Smokey Robinson's first solo LP *Smokey*. In 1971 he launched his own solo career. A succession of LPs like *Mark of the Beast, Fully Exposed* and *Ode to My Lady* followed. In 1973 he wrote the soundtrack for the film *The Mack* and contributed to the soundtrack of the Motown-produced film *The Last Dragon*. In 1979 he moved to Norman WHITFIELD's label, recording the LP *In Tune*, but returned to Motown when Whitfield closed the label down. On his return he scored immediately with the single *In and Out* (UK#51.1982), from the LP of the same name. In 1985 he released the LP *Making a Game out of Love,* which had the distinction of featuring Berry GORDY as executive producer; it included the single *Keep On Jammin'* (UK#73.1985).

HUTSON, LEROY See IMPRESSIONS

IKETTES See TURNER, Ike & Tina

IMPRESSIONS In 1957 three of the five members of the Tennessee group, The Roosters (Sam Gooden and the brothers, Arthur and Richard Brooks, who had been raised in Chattanooga) moved to Chicago, where they were joined by Jerry BUTLER and Curtis MAYFIELD. After recording a couple of singles for local Chicago labels, they signed with Veejay and changed their name to The Impressions. Their first success was *For Your Precious Love* (USA#11.1958), written by Arthur Brooks and Jerry Butler; it was credited to Jerry Butler & The Impressions, there was some ill-feeling towards Butler, who left to pursue a solo career. He was replaced by Fred Cash – a former member of The Roosters. With Butler out of the picture, the group slipped gradually into obscurity until 1959, when Mayfield re-formed them and moved to New York, where he secured a contract with ABC/Paramount. In 1961, they scored with *Gypsy Woman* (USA#20.1961). The next three singles got no further than the lower reaches of the charts, and so Mayfield, Gooden and Cash returned to Chicago, retaining the name of the group and leaving the Brooks brothers behind. As a trio, they had to wait until the end of 1963 before they achieved the big breakthrough with *It's All Right* (USA#4.1963). This was the first of many hits including *Talkin' about my Baby* (USA#12.1964), *I'm so Proud* (USA#14.1964), *Keep on Pushin'* (USA#10.1964), *You Must Believe Me* (USA#15.1964), *Amen* (USA

#7.1965), *People Get Ready* (USA#14.1965), *You've Been Cheatin'* (USA#33.1966) and *We're a Winner* (USA#14.1968). Their LPs, *Keep on Pushin'* (USA#8.1964) and *People Get Ready* (USA#23.1965), sold equally well. With the completion of their contract with ABC, Mayfield set up his own record label, Curtom, although ABC continued to release old material.

Their first single for Curtom was *Fool for You* (USA#22.1968); it was followed by *This is my Country* (USA#25.1968) and *Choice of Colours* (USA#21.1969). In 1970 Mayfield left the group to pursue a solo career; despite his departure he continued to write and produce for the group and even recruited his successor, Leroy Hutson. Hutson remained with the group until 1973, during which time their biggest hit was *Check out Your Mind* (USA#28.1970). As a solo artist Hutson remained with Curtom until 1981, when he was signed by Elektra; however his style of delivery has been faced by stiff opposition, which has militated against any great degree of success. Hutson's successors were Reggie Torian and Ralph Johnson; with this line-up The Impressions achieved their one and only hit in the UK, *First Impressions* (UK#16.1975). In 1976 Johnson left to form Mystique, being replaced by Nate Evans. Since the late 1970s they have continued to record occasionally. In 1983 Mayfield and Butler rejoined the group for a reunion tour, which proved to be enormously successful.

THE IMPRESSIONS, Kent, 1963
THE NEVER ENDING IMPRESSIONS, Kent, 1964
KEEP ON PUSHIN', Kent, 1964
PEOPLE GET READY, Kent, 1965
WE'RE A WINNER, ABC, 1968
BEST OF THE IMPRESSIONS, ABC, 1968
FINALLY GOT MYSELF TOGETHER, Buddah, 1974
ORIGINALS, ABC, 1976

16 GREATEST HITS, ABC, 1977
FAN THE FIRE, 20th Century, 1981
PARADISE, (Leroy Hutson), Elektra, 1982

INGRAM, JAMES In 1973, having been a member of Revelation Funk, James Ingram moved from his home town of Akron, Ohio, to Los Angeles, where he joined the Ray CHARLES Orchestra. By 1975 he had joined Leon Haywood as his musical director and was providing vocals for demos at a publishing company. In 1980 Quincy JONES was played one of the demos by producer Russell Titelman. It was the beginning of a fruitful association between Jones and Ingram. Ingram added the vocals to *Just Once* and *One Hundred Ways* on Jones' LP *The Dude*; as a result, he was signed to Jones' label Qwest. In 1982 he teamed up with Patti AUSTIN for a duet, *Baby Come to Me* (USA#1; UK #11.1983), which was featured as the theme for the soap opera *General Hospital*. The same year he recorded his debut LP *It's Your Night* (USA #46.1983; UK#25.1984), produced by Jones and featuring the cream of the Los Angeles session musicians, including guitarist Larry CARLTON, reedman Tom Scott and drummer Harvey Mason. A duet with Michael McDonald, *Ya Mo B There* (USA#19.1984; UK#12.1985), was followed by *What About Me?*, featuring Kenny Rogers and Kim Carnes. His second LP *Never Felt So Good* was only modestly successful, due to a blandness that seemed to suffuse the whole affair. In 1987 he was teamed with Linda Ronstadt for a duet, *Somewhere out There* (USA#2; UK#8.1987), which was included in the Steven Spielberg film, *An American Tail*. In 1989 he released the LP *It's Real*, but like its predecessor it was slightly characterless. The following year he topped the charts with *I Didn't Have the Heart* (USA#1.1990).

IT'S YOUR NIGHT, Qwest, 1984
NEVER FELT SO GOOD, Qwest, 1986
IT'S REAL, Qwest, 1989

INGRAM, LUTHER When Luther Ingram joined Stax in 1968, *via* a distribution deal with Koko, the label to which he was signed, it was unfortunate that Stax was beginning its long descent into the mire of avarice and suspicion that culminated in its eventual closure in 1976. It was equally unfortunate that Johnny Baylor, the owner of Koko, was also Ingram's manager. Baylor was a pistol-packin' strong-arm man, who contributed through his unwholesome methods to the demise of Stax. However, his protege, Ingram was a different matter altogether.

Ingram (born in Jackson on November 30, 1944) was raised singing gospel in church choirs. He moved to New York where he was signed by the Mercury subsidiary, Smash; his first success was *I Spy for the FBI*, later a hit for Jamo Thomas. After hooking up with Baylor, he cut a string of R&B hits, including *Pity for the Lonely* (1969), *My Honey and Me*, *To the Other Man* (1970) and *Missing You* (1971). In 1971 he contributed as a writer to The STAPLE SINGERS' LP, *Bealtitude: Respect Yourself*, including the title track *Respect Yourself*, cowritten with Mack Rice. The following year he scored on his own account with *(If Loving You is Wrong) I Don't Want to be Right* (USA#3.1972) and *I'll be Your Shelter (in Times of Storm)* (USA#40.1973) from the LP *If Loving You is Wrong I Don't Want to be Right* (USA#39.1972). The same year he appeared in the film *Wattstax*. Since the demise of Stax, Ingram has continued to release LPs, like *Luther Ingram* (1986), for the Profile label, but with limited success.

INTRUDERS The Intruders, like The O'JAYS, have been stalwarts of GAMBLE & HUFF ever since the latter's earliest days as independent producers. They were formed in 1960 by Samuel "Little Sonny" Brown, Eugene Daughtry, Robert Edwards and Phil Terry, cutting their first records for the Gowen and Musicor labels: *All the Time* was produced for Musicor by Leon Huff. In 1966, they were signed to the Gamble label. After a number of R&B hits like *(We'll be) United, Together* and *Baby I'm Lonely*, they broke into the mainstream with *Cowboys to Girls* (USA#6.1968), followed by *(Love is Like a) Baseball Game* (USA#26.1968), *Slow Drag, When We Get Married, I Bet He Don't Love You, I'll Always Love My Mama* (USA#36.1973; UK#32.1974) and *(Win Place or Show) She's a Winner* (UK #14.1974). Since the mid- 1970s they have had little commercial success, apart from *Who Do You Love?* (UK#65.1984), but they have continued to tour and to work with Gamble & Huff.

ISLEY BROTHERS The Isley Brothers, born in Cincinnatti, Ohio, were Rudolph (born April 1, 1939), Ronald (born May 21, 1941) and O'Kelly (born December 21, 1937). During the early 1950s they performed in local churches with another brother, Vernon, but disbanded when he was killed in a road accident. Within the year, at the request of their parents, the three had re-formed . They went to New York in 1957 and recorded a number of singles for small independent labels, but these failed to make any impression. However, in 1959 they were spotted by Howard Bloom of RCA records during a performance at the Howard Theatre in Washington DC, and he promptly signed them. Their first record, *Turn to Me*, was produced by HUGO & LUIGI but failed to sell; the follow-up, *Shout* (USA#47.1959), sold over a million and is as close to being a perfect slice of R&B as one could hope to find. In 1960 they signed with Atlantic, where they were teamed with LEIBER & STOLLER, but after four singles that went nowhere fast they signed with Wand in 1962.

Their second record for Wand was *Twist and Shout* (USA#17.1962; UK#42.1963), written and produced by Bert BERNS. Like *Shout* it has become a standard, with artists like The Mamas & The Papas, Bruce Springsteen and The Beatles covering it. However, they were unable to sustain this level of success and therefore changed record label once again, this time for United Artists, although they retained the services of Berns. Their relationship with United Artists was never harmonious and, after being told to record *Surf and Shout*, they formed their own label, T-Neck. Their first record, *Testify*, was another commercial failure despite the presence of guitarist Jimi HENDRIX. In 1964, they re-signed with Atlantic, but Atlantic dropped them after a year and so they signed with Motown, where they remained for three years. In that time they created a sound that would characterise their records throughout the rest of their career. This sudden change of fortune was due, in part, to the songwriting and production partnership of HOLLAND, DOZIER & HOLLAND, who provided them with material of a consistently high quality: *This Old Heart of Mine* (USA#12; UK#47.1966/#3.1968), *I Guess I'll Always Love You* (USA#61; UK#45.1966/#11.1969) and *Behind a Painted Smile* (UK#5.1969). Their success in the UK prompted them to re-establish T-Neck, the first release was *It's Your Thing* (USA#2; UK#30.1969). The LP *It's Our Thing* (USA#22.1969) sold over two million copies. As a result, they expanded the lineup to include Ernest Isley (guitar), Marvin Isley (bass and percussion) and Chris Jasper (keyboards). The influences of James BROWN, Sly Stone (see SLY & THE FAMILY STONE) and Hendrix

became ever more apparent. In 1973, after four comparatively lean years during which time they tended to cover songs by white rock artists, they recorded the soulful *That Lady* (USA#6; UK#14.1973), written by Chris Jasper and Ernest and Marvin Isley and taken from the LP *3 + 3* (USA#8.1973).

The most important aspect of the success of *That Lady* was that it finally established their style. No longer were they "just another soul band": their sound was instantly recognisable. This new found individuality generated a string of hit singles: *Highways of my Life* (UK #25.1974), *Summer Breeze* (UK#16.1974), *Fight the Power* (USA#4.1975), *For the Love of You* (USA#22.1975), *Harvest for the World* (UK#10.1976), *Livin' in the Life* (USA #40.1977), *It's a Disco Night (Rock don't Stop)* (UK#14.1979) and *Don't Say Goodnight (It's Time for Love)* (USA#39.1980). During the same period, nine successive LPs achieved gold or platinum status in the USA.

In 1984, Chris Jasper and Ernest and Marvin Isley left to form their own group – ISLEY JASPER ISLEY – amid considerable acrimony. The following year The Isley Brothers signed with Warner Bros. Since 1985 their records have had only moderate success, the most notable achievements being a collaboration with Angela Winbush , the LP *Smooth Sailin'* and a duet, *This Old Heart of Mine* (USA#9.1990), between Ronald Isley and Rod Stewart in 1989. On March 31, 1986, Kelly Isley died of a heart attack at the age of 48.

3 + 3, Epic, 1973
LIVE IT UP, Epic, 1974
THE HEAT IS ON, Epic, 1975
HARVEST FOR THE WORLD, Epic, 1976
FOREVER GOLD, Epic, 1977
WINNER TAKES ALL, Epic, 1979
GO ALL THE WAY, Epic, 1980
GRAND SLAM, Epic, 1981

SUPER HITS, Motown, 1981
BETWEEN THE SHEETS, Epic, 1983
20 GOLDEN PIECES, Bulldog, 1983
GREATEST HITS: VOLUME I, Epic, 1984
MASTERPIECE, Warner Bros., 1985
LET'S GO, Stateside, 1986
GREATEST MOTOWN HITS, Motown, 1987
SMOOTH SAILIN', Warner Bros., 1987
THE SOUND OF SOUL, Blatant, 1989
SPEND THE NIGHT, Warner Bros., 1989
THE COMPLETE VICTOR SESSIONS, RCA, 1991
GREATEST HITS AND RARE CLASSICS, Motown, 1991

ISLEY JASPER ISLEY Ernest Isley, Chris Jasper and Marvin Isley left The ISLEY BROTHERS to form Isley Jasper Isley in 1984 and signed with Epic. However, their subsequent claim that they were responsible for the success of The Isley Brothers has not been borne out by their achievements. Their most notable hit, *Caravan of Love* (USA#51; UK#52.1985), was covered by The Housemartins, whose "acapella" treatment of the song gave them a #1 hit in the UK in 1986. Despite the release of three LPs, they have been unable to achieve the same degree of success that they had as members of The Isley Brothers. In 1988, Jasper released a solo LP, *Superbad*, which peaked at #182 in the USA.

BROADWAY'S CLOSER TO SUNSET BOULE-VARD, Epic, 1985
CARAVAN OF LOVE, Epic, 1985
DIFFERENT DRUMMER, Epic, 1987
SUPERBAD, (Chris Jasper), Epic, 1988

IVY, QUIN Quin Ivy was born in Oxford, Mississippi, in 1937. In 1965, he approached Rick HALL about the possibility of setting up his own studio, Quinvy, as a means of tracking down fresh local talent. His association with Hall stemmed from his position as the main DJ at the local radio station, WLAY, and from the fact that he had collaborated as a lyricist with Hall on a number of demos in the early 1960s. Although Ivy attempted to lure Dan PENN into his new operation, he was persuaded by Hall to approach the trumpeter and guitarist, Marlin GREENE. Their first independent production was with an unknown hospital orderly, Percy SLEDGE: the record was *When a Man Loves a Woman*. Ivy and Greene produced it and the nucleus of the Fame house band provided the backing. A distribution and publishing deal was struck with Jerry WEXLER at Atlantic. Ivy became Sledge's manager and attempted to mastermind his career, a position that he would hold for thirteen years before retiring from the music business to become a professor of business studies at the University of North Alabama. During this time the Quinvy studios played host to an array of artists like Bill Brandon, Z. Z. HILL and June Edwards. Perhaps, Ivy's most significant contribution, quite apart from producing a record that is to this day as fresh as a daisy, was that it proved to Wexler that Muscle Shoals was the place to be and brought Aretha FRANKLIN and Wilson PICKETT to the studios.

JACKSON, Jr, AL Al Jackson was born on November 27, 1935 in Memphis, Tennessee. In 1962, as the drummer in Willie MITCHELL's band, he was brought to Stax by Booker T (see BOOKER T & THE MGs) to play on what proved to be the famous *Green Onions* session. Jackson remained at Stax for the next ten years. The partnerships that he formed with the bassists Lewis Steinberg and, later, "Duck" DUNN provided the bedrock for artists like Otis REDDING, Wilson PICKETT, Eddie FLOYD and SAM & DAVE who created some of the definitive soul hits of the 1960s. Following the departures of

Booker T and Steve CROPPER, The MGs effectively disbanded until, in 1973, Jackson and Dunn recorded the LP *The MGs* with new recruits Bobby Manuel (guitar) and Carson Whitsett (keyboards). It failed to sell and Jackson continued to do session work first at Stax and, then at Mitchell's Hi studios, where he backed artists like Al GREEN, Ann PEEBLES, O. V. WRIGHT and Otis CLAY. On October 1, 1975, the career of one of USA's best drummers was brought to a premature close when, aged 39, he was shot dead in his house when he disturbed a burglar.

JACKSON, CHUCK   Chuck Jackson has never hit the high-spots, being a singer more of the journeyman variety. He was unfortunate in that his heyday was the early 1960s, when soul had not achieved the high profile of later years. He was born in Winston Salem, South Carolina, on July 22, 1937. At first he was a member of the gospel group, Raspberry Singers, leaving to join The Del-Vikings. When they split up in 1958, Jackson started a solo career. Initially he recorded for the independent Clock and Beltone labels; then he was spotted by Luther DIXON and signed to the Wand label. Throughout the early 1960s he had a string of hits, particularly on the R&B charts, written by teams like Burt Bacharach & Bob Hilliard, ASHFORD & SIMPSON, GOFFIN & KING and LEIBER & STOLLER: *I Don't Want to Cry* (USA #36.1961), *I Wake up Crying, Any Day Now* (USA#23.1962), *I Keep Forgettin', Tell Him I'm not Home, Beg Me* (USA#45.1964) and *I Need You*. Additionally he formed a successful duo with Maxine BROWN, cutting *Something You Got* (1965) and *Daddy's Home* (1967). In 1967, he joined Motown; then he went to ABC for *I Only Get The Feeling* (1973); then on to All Platinum for *I'm Needing You, Wanting You* (1975), and in 1980 he was to be found on the

EMI America label where he had a very minor hit with *I Wanna Give You Some Love*. He has continued to have a large following on the UK's Northern Soul circuit and constant touring have ensured that his performances are always well attended.

THE GREAT CHUCK JACKSON, Bulldog, 1982
MR EMOTION, Kent, 1985
A POWERFUL SOUL, Kent, 1988

JACKSON, FREDDIE   As a child, Freddie Jackson (born on October 2, 1956) started to sing in his local church, the White Rock Baptist Church in Harlem, where he met ASHFORD & SIMPSON. When he left school he worked in a bank and then formed the group LJE; in 1983, he moved to California and joined another group, Mystic Merlin. The following year, he returned to New York and became a backing vocalist for artists like Evelyn KING and Melba Moore; the latter promptly recommended him to her management company, who secured him a recording contract with Capitol. His first LP *Rock me Tonight* (USA#10; UK#73.1985) included a bunch of singles that slotted very neatly into the super-slick supper club soul category: *Rock me Tonight (for Old Times' Sake)* (USA #18.1985; UK#18.1986), *You are my Lady* (USA#12; UK#49.1985) and *He'll Never Love You (like I Do)* (USA#25.1986). After a tour and a duet with Melba More, he released his second LP *Just Like the First Time* (USA#23; UK#30.1986), which included the singles, *Have You Ever Loved Somebody* (UK#33.1987) and *Jam Tonight* (USA#32.1987). His third LP, *Don't Let Love Slip Away* (USA#48; UK #24.1988), was produced by Paul Laurence, a former colleague in LJE; it bore an uncanny resemblance to its predecessors. His fourth LP *Do Me Again* was undistinguished but successful.

ROCK ME TONIGHT, Capitol, 1985
JUST LIKE THE FIRST TIME, Capitol, 1986
DON'T LET LOVE SLIP AWAY, Capitol, 1988
DO ME AGAIN, Capitol, 1990

JACKSON, GEORGE George Jackson is one of a handful of writers, who has done much to contribute to the success of the Malaco label in the 1980s. He was born in Memphis. After recording briefly for Quinton CLAUNCH's Goldwax label in the mid-1960s and writing for James CARR, he moved to Rick HALL's Fame studios. At Fame he provided material for Clarence CARTER, Candi STATON and Wilson PICKETT. In 1981 he wrote *Down Home Blues* for Z. Z. HILL for the LP, *Down Home*; this one LP was perhaps more responsible for the success of Malaco in eighties than any other LP. Since then Jackson has contributed regularly to the repertoires of the entire Malaco roster.

JACKSON, JANET Janet Jackson was born in Gary, Indiana, on May 16, 1966; she was the youngest of nine siblings, who included The Jackson Five (see JACKSONS). She made her debut when she was seven in one of The Jackson Five's concerts at the Grand Hotel in Las Vegas. By 1977 she had become an actress, appearing in *Good Times* and *Fame*. In 1982 she signed a recording contract with A&M. Her debut LP, *Janet Jackson*, included a pair of minor hits. It was followed in 1984 by the LP *Dream Street*, which also sold modestly well. In 1986, having teamed up with Minnesota producers JAM & LEWIS, she released the LP *Control* (USA#1; UK#8.1986), which included six hit singles: *What Have You Done for me Lately* (USA#4; UK#3.1986), *Nasty* (USA#3; UK#19.1986), *When I Think of You* (USA#1; UK#10.1986), *Control* (USA#5.1987; UK#42.1986), *Let's Wait Awhile* (USA#2; UK

#3.1987) and *The Pleasure Principle* (USA#14; UK#24.1987). This LP was successful not only commercial in terms but also artistically, as Janet jettisoned all the trappings and encumbrances of being one of the Jackson siblings, in favour of a rough-tough mix aimed firmly at the dance-floor, while retaining a lyrical and melodic flavour reminiscent of PRINCE. An invitation to sing *Diamonds* (USA#5; UK#27. 1987) on the Herb Alpert LP, *Keep Your Eye on Me*, with Jam & Lewis producing, followed as a result. In 1988 she recorded the follow-up, *Janet Jackson's Rhythm Nation 1814* (USA/UK#1.1989), which included another slew of hit singles including *Miss You Much* (USA #1.1989). In 1990 she undertook a world tour.

JANET JACKSON, A&M, 1982
DREAM STREET, A&M, 1984
CONTROL, A&M, 1986
CONTROL – THE RE-MIXES, A&M, 1987
JANET JACKSON'S RHYTHM NATION 1814, A&M, 1989

JACKSON, JERMAINE After the success of Michael JACKSON's solo career, his brother Jermaine (born December 11, 1954) was the next member of The JACKSONS to start a solo career. His first LP *Jermaine* (USA#27.1972) included the singles, *That's How Love Goes* (USA#46.1972) and *Daddy's Home* (USA#9.1973). In 1973, he married Berry GORDY's daughter Hazel, driving a wedge between him and the rest of the group, which culminated in his departure when the group signed with Epic in 1975. Throughout the latter half of the 1970s his records were marred by humdrum material, but in 1980, he teamed up with Stevie WONDER to record the LP *Let's Get Serious* (USA#6; UK#22.1980), which included the singles, *Let's Get Serious* (USA#9; UK#8.1980) and *You're Supposed to Keep your Love for Me* (USA#34.1980). It was followed by another LP called *Jermaine* (USA #44.1981), which included the single *You Like Me, Don't You?* (USA #50; UK#41.1981). The title track of his final LP for Motown was released as a single, *Let Me Tickle Your Fancy* (USA#18.1982).

In 1984 he signed with Arista. His debut LP for the label, *Dynamite* (USA#19.1984), featured contributions from Michael Jackson and Whitney HOUSTON and was coproduced by Michael Omartian and Jackson himself; it included the singles, *Dynamite* (USA#15.1984) and *Do What You Do* (USA#13.1984; UK #6.1985). The same year he was teamed with actress Pia Zadora for a duet, *When the Rain Begins to Fall* (USA#54; UK#68.1984). In 1986 *I Think it's Love* (USA#16.1986) became his final hit single to date, extracted from the LP *Precious Moments*. His most recent LP was *Don't Take it Personal* in 1989.

LET'S GET SERIOUS, Motown, 1980
JERMAINE, Motown, 1981
I LIKE YOUR STYLE, Motown, 1981
DYNAMITE, Arista, 1984
PRECIOUS MOMENTS, Arista, 1986
DON'T TAKE IT PERSONAL, Arista, 1989

JACKSON, MICHAEL In 1971 Michael Jackson (born August 29, 1958) signed to Motown as a solo artist, although he remained lead vocalist of The JACKSONS. His early records as a soloist laid the groundwork for the formidable degree of success he has achieved in later years. Most of the material he recorded at Motown as a soloist was derivative, but the range of his voice imparted a special quality to even the most hackneyed songs: *Got to be There* (USA#4.1971; UK #5.1972), *Rockin' Robin* (USA#2; UK#3.1972), *Ain't no Sunshine* (UK#8.1972), *I Wanna be Where You Are* (USA#16.1972), *Ben* (USA#1; UK#7.1972), *Just a Little Bit of You* (USA

#23.1975) and *One Day in Your Life* (UK #1.1981). After his departure from Motown in 1975 for Epic, he played the part of the "Scarecrow" in the film *The Wiz.*, a remake of the *The Wizard Of Oz*. While the film itself was no great shakes, Jackson met Quincy JONES who was supervising the score. From this meeting, he was able to move up several gears; under the guidance of Jones, he issued three LPs which proved that he was not only a great performer but also a great songwriter.

The first LP for Epic, *Off The Wall* (USA#3; UK#5.1979), featured four hit singles: *Don't Stop 'Til You Get Enough* (USA#1; UK #3.1979), *Rock with You* (USA#1.1979; UK #7.1980), *Off the Wall* (USA#10.1980; UK#7.1979) and *She's out of My Life* (USA#10; UK#3.1980). In 1982 Jackson and Jones started work on the follow-up LP, *Thriller* (USA/UK#1.1982), which contained an unprecedented seven hit singles: *The Girl is Mine* (USA#2.1983; UK#10.1982), *Billie Jean* (USA/UK#1.1983), *Beat It* (USA#1; UK #3.1983), *Wanna be Startin' Something* (USA#5; UK#8.1983), *Human Nature* (USA #7.1983), *P.Y.T (Pretty Young Thing)* (USA #10.1983; UK#11.1984) and *Thriller* (USA#4.1984; UK#10.1983), the last being written by Rod Temperton (see HEATWAVE). In 1983 *Say Say Say* (USA#1; UK#2.1983), a duet with Paul McCartney, which had been recorded as a sequel to their former duet, *The Girl is Mine,* continued Jackson's monopoly of the international charts. The following year he participated in the reunion tour of The Jacksons to promote their LP, *Victory*, which featured him duetting with Mick Jagger on *State of Shock*; and in 1985, he cowrote, with Lionel RICHIE, *We are the World* for USA for Africa, which had been organised by Quincy Jones to raise funds for famine relief in Africa.

In 1987 he released his third LP for Epic, *Bad* (USA/UK#1.1987). Once again, it was produced by Quincy Jones, and once again seven singles were taken from it: *I Just Can't Stop Loving You* (USA/ UK#1.1987), a duet featuring Siedah GARRETT, *Bad* (USA#1; UK #3.1987), *The Way you Make me Feel* (USA#1; UK#3.1987), *Man in the Mirror* (USA#1; UK #21.1988), *Dirty Diana* (USA#1; UK#4.1988), *Another Part of Me* (USA#11; UK#15.1988) and *Smooth Criminal* (UK#8.1988). After its release, he embarked upon a world tour that became the biggest grossing tour of all time (until 1990, when it was eclipsed by The Rolling Stones' world tour). In 1988 his autobiography, *Moonwalk,* was published, it was followed by the film *Moonwalker*.

GOT TO BE THERE, Motown, 1972

BEN, Motown, 1973

OFF THE WALL, Epic, 1979

THE BEST OF MICHAEL JACKSON, Motown, 1981

ONE DAY IN YOUR LIFE, Motown, 1981

AIN'T NO SUNSHINE, Motown, 1982

FOREVER MICHAEL, Motown, 1983

THRILLER, Epic, 1983

18 GREATEST HITS, (with The Jackson Five), Telstar, 1983

FAREWELL MY SUMMER LOVE, Motown, 1984

MUSIC AND ME, Motown, 1984

GREAT LOVE SONGS OF MICHAEL JACKSON, Motown, 1984

LOOKING BACK TO YESTERDAY, Motown, 1986

ANTHOLOGY, Motown, 1987

BAD, Epic, 1987

JACKSON, MILLIE In 1957 Millie Jackson ran away from home in Thompson, Georgia, where she had been born on July 15, 1943. She settled in New York and worked first as a model and then as a singer at the Palm Cafe in Harlem and, later, at Club Zanzibar in New Jersey. In 1969, having honed her live act, she recorded a single for MGM, but it failed to sell

and she had to wait another three years before she got the opportunity to record again. In 1972, she was signed by the Spring label. Her debut for them, *A Child of God (It's Hard to Believe)*, was a minor hit; the follow-up, *Ask Me what You Want* (USA#27.1972), was followed by *My Man, A Sweet Man* (USA#42; UK#50.1972). The same year she recorded her first LP, *Millie Jackson*, written by Raeford Gerald. In 1973 the single *Hurts so Good* (USA #24.1973), extracted from the LP *It Hurts so Good,* was featured in the film *Cleopatra Jones*.

The following year she recorded the concept LP *Caught Up* (USA#21.1974), contemplating the eternal triangle between men and women (husbands, wives and mistresses); it was a highly successful example of its kind. It was produced by Brad Shapiro and Jackson herself at the Criteria studios (Atlantic South) in Florida and Muscle Shoals sound studios. The incisiveness of the respective house bands made for a cohesive offering combining self-written material with standard pop songs like Bobby Goldsboro's *Summer the First Time*. She followed it with the LP *Still Caught Up*, an elaboration of the themes of its predecessor, revolving around a revival of the Luther INGRAM hit, *(If Loving You is Wrong) I Don't Want to be Right* (USA#42.1975); furthermore, she integrated the trademark rap into the song, which had become a pivotal part of her live act developed through years of working the club circuit. Soon after the LP *Lovingly Yours* (1977), she released *Feelin' Bitchy* (USA #34.1977), which was marketed on the strength of its provocative language.

Since 1978 she has continued to release LPs at regular intervals, including an LP of duets with Isaac HAYES entitled *Royal Rappin';* in 1985 she duetted with Elton John on the single, *Act of War* (UK#32.1985). In 1979 she set up her own music publishing company, Double Ak-Shun Music, as well as managing the group Facts Of Life. It is to her detriment that successive record companies have been constrained to market her records on the strength of the "explicit" nature of the language contained instead of the quality of the music.

MILLIE JACKSON, Southbound, 1972
IT HURTS SO GOOD, Southbound, 1973
CAUGHT UP, Important, 1975
STILL CAUGHT UP, Important, 1976
THE BEST OF MILLIE JACKSON, Spring, 1976
FREE AND IN LOVE, Spring, 1976
LOVINGLY YOURS, Spring, 1977
FEELIN' BITCHY, Spring, 1977
GET IT OUT CHA SYSTEM, Spring, 1978
A MOMENT'S PLEASURE, Spring, 1979
LIVE AND UNCENSORED, Important, 1980
FOR MEN ONLY, Spring, 1980
I HAD TO SAY IT, Spring, 1981
HARD TIMES, Spring, 1982
E.S.P, Sire, 1984
AN IMITATION OF LOVE, Jive, 1987
THE TIDE IS TURNING, Jive, 1988
BACK TO THE SHIT, Jive, 1989

JACKSON, RAYMOND See BANKS, Homer

JACKSON, WALTER After contracting polio during his adolescence Walter Jackson overcame his crippling disability to become a performer of considerable courage and stature, needing the help of a walking stick while performing. He was born in Pensacola, Florida in 1939. After partially recovering from polio he was signed by the CBS subsidiary, Okeh, where he recorded sides like *It's All Over, Speak her Name* and *Uphill Climb from the Bottom*. His career was interrupted by illness until the late 1970s, when, having relocated to Chicago, he was signed to the Chi-Sound label, where he had a minor hit with a reworking of the Peter Frampton composition,

Baby I Love Your Way. After more spells in hospital he was signed to the independent Bluebird label for the single, *Touching in the Dark* (1984).

A PORTRAIT OF WALTER JACKSON, Bluebird, 1984

JACKSON, WAYNE When The Royal Spades were formed at Messick High School in Memphis during the late 1950s, one of the earliest recruits was trumpeter Wayne Jackson, born the son of a sharecropper in Arkansas in 1944. As The Royal Spades gradually metarmorphosed into The MARKEYS, the first house band at Stax, so Jackson's reputation picked up. By the time BOOKER T & THE MGs had superseded The Markeys, Jackson had been joined by saxophonist Andrew Love, and together they had become known as The Memphis Horns. After Stax went into decline they played more regularly on sessions at Willie MITCHELL's Hi Studios. Since then they have carved a reputation for being one of the most proficient horn sections in the business, recording with just about everybody at one time or another. In 1990 they were enlisted to augment Robert CRAY's band, and were featured on his *Midnight Stroll* LP, participating in the subsequent "Midnight Stroll" Tour.

JACKSON FIVE See JACKSONS

JACKSONS In 1963, in Gary, Indiana, the three oldest sons, Jackie (born May 4, 1951), Tito (born October 15, 1953) and Jermaine JACKSON, of crane driver Joe Jackson, formed The Jackson Family with their cousins, pianist Johnny Jackson and drummer Ronnie Rancifier. By 1964 the two cousins had been relegated to being backing musicians. They were replaced by two younger brothers, Marlon (born March 12, 1957) and Michael JACKSON, and the group was renamed The Jackson Five. After winning a local talent contest, they took part in another at the Apollo in Harlem, which they also won. In 1967 they supported Motown group Gladys KNIGHT & The Pips, at a concert in Indiana. Knight recommended them to Motown boss, Berry GORDY. The following year they recorded *Big Boy* for the local Steeltown label and in 1969 they performed at a benefit concert for the Mayor of Gary, Gordy was in the audience with Diana ROSS, he signed them immediately and packed them off to the West Coast to rehearse. The entire family moved with them.

In late 1969 the group debuted at the Hollywood Palace with Diana Ross & The SUPREMES. This was followed by their first single *I Want You Back* (USA#1; UK#2.1970); featuring Michael as lead vocalist, it was the perfect debut for him, combining innocence with urgency, an extraordinary feat for a twelve-year old. Their first LP was *Diana Ross Presents The Jackson 5* (USA#5; UK#16.1970): the misleading implication that Diana Ross had discovered the group was another of Gordy's publicity gambits. Over the next six years the group notched up a series of hit singles: *ABC* (USA#1; UK#8.1970), *The Love You Save* (USA#1; UK#7.1970), *I'll Be There* (USA#1; UK#4.1970), *Mama's Pearl* (USA#2; UK#25.1971), *Never Can Say Goodbye* (USA#2; UK#33.1971), *Maybe Tomorrow* (USA#20.1971), *Sugar Daddy* (USA#10.1971), *Little Bitty Pretty One* (USA#13.1972), *Lookin' Through The Windows* (USA#16; UK#9.1972), *Corner of the Sky* (USA#18.1972), *Doctor My Eyes* (UK#9.1973), *Hallelujah Day* (USA#28; UK#20.1973), *Skywriter* (UK#25.1973), *Get it Together* (USA#28.1973), *Dancing Machine* (USA#2.1974), *Whatever You Got I Want*

(USA#38.1974) and *I am Love, Parts 1 & 2* (USA#15.1975). It was a measure of their popularity that, while they were primarily a singles group, their LPs also sold consistently well: *ABC* (USA#4; UK#22.1970), *Third Album* (USA#4.1970), *Maybe Tomorrow* (USA#11.1971), *Goin' Back to Indiana* (USA#16.1971), *Lookin' Through the Windows* (USA#7; UK#16.1972), *Dancing Machine* (USA#16.1974) and *Moving Violation* (USA#36.1975).

In 1971 Motown launched Michael Jackson's solo career. Jermaine Jackson followed suit in 1972 and Jackie Jackson in 1973. An animated cartoon series based on the group was launched by ABC Television in 1971. In 1973 Jermaine married Berry Gordy's daughter Hazel; in 1975, when they signed with Epic, he left the group and remained with Motown. Gordy sued the group for breach of contract, a dispute that wasn't resolved until 1980. Jermaine was replaced by another sibling, Randy (born October 29, 1962), and the line-up was further augmented by the inclusion of two sisters, LaToya (born May 29, 1956) and Maureen (known as Rebbie; born March 29, 1950). The departure of The Jackson Five from Motown heralded a new era in the group's development, as they were given creative control over their career; furthermore, their royalty rate became significantly higher. However, as Motown owned the name The Jackson Five, they became The Jacksons. Since signing with Epic they have continued to notch up hits, although not with the same degree of consistency: *Enjoy Yourself* (USA#6.1976; UK#42.1977), *Show You the Way to Go* (USA#28; UK#1.1977), *Dreamer* (UK#22.1977), *Goin' Places* (UK#26.1977), *Even Though You've Gone* (UK#31.1978), *Blame it on the Boogie* (UK#8.1978), *Destiny* (UK#39. 1979), *Shake Your Body (Down to the Ground)* (USA#7; UK#4.1979), *Lovely One* (USA#12; UK#29.1980), *Heartbreak Hotel* (USA#22.1981;

RAY CHARLES: The man who, arguably, cut the first soul record *I Gotta Woman* (courtesy Columbia Records).

Above
BERRY GORDY brought back black music out of the ghettoes and into the homes of the white middle classes with his Mowtown label (courtesy Motown Records).

Opposite
CLIVE DAVIS built an impressive roster of soul artists at Columbia in the late 1960s and early 1970s; at Arista he has continued to do the same thing in the 1980s and 1990s (courtesy Arista Records/Adrian Boot).

THE MIRACLES, with writer and producer SMOKEY ROBINSON, were responsible for Motown's first million-seller *Shop Around* (courtesy Motown Records).

MARVIN GAYE acknowledges the plaudits of an unseen audience (courtesy Motown Records).

THE CONTOURS (*top left*), THE MARVELETTES (*top right*), THE FOUR TOPS (*bottom left*) and THE SUPREMES (*bottom right*) all contributed to the early success of Motown (all courtesy Motown Records).

Above
LITTLE STEVIE WONDER, once the *wunderkind* of Motown, and still a world superstar (courtesy Motown Records).

Opposite
IKE AND TINA TURNER whip it up on stage (courtesy A.I.P.).

ARETHA FRANKLIN — the Queen of Soul (courtesy Arista Records).

WILSON PICKETT tells it like it is in Black Star Square, Accra, Ghana (from the film *Soul to Soul*).

UK#44.1980), *Can You Feel It?* (UK #6.1981),*Walk Right Now* (UK#7.1981), *State of Shock* (USA#3; UK#14.1984) and *Torture* (USA#17; UK#26.1984). The LPs have tended to be more accurate reflections of their abilities as they contain a large percentage of their own material: *The Jacksons* (USA#36; UK #54.1977), *Goin' Places* (UK#45.1977), *Destiny* (USA#10; UK#33.1979), *Triumph* (USA#10; UK#13.1980), *Jacksons Live* (USA#30; UK #53.1981) and *Victory* (USA#4; UK#3.1984).

Since 1979 there has been a general tendency to downgrade the work of the group as a whole as the phenomenal success of Michael's solo career has quite unjustly eclipsed the contributions of the others. In 1984 the group, including both Michael and Jermaine, started a forty-date concert tour of the USA; this was the first time the group had performed publicly since 1976. After the tour, they disbanded to concentrate upon solo careers. In addition to Michael and Jermaine, LaToya, Rebbie and Marlon all recorded their own LPs with varying degrees of success. In 1989, various members of the group reformed for the LP *2300 Jackson Street*.

DIANA ROSS PRESENTS THE JACKSON FIVE, Motown, 1970

ABC, Motown, 1970

THE JACKSON FIVE CHRISTMAS ALBUM, Motown, 1970

THIRD ALBUM, Motown, 1972

GREATEST HITS, Motown. 1972.

LOOKIN' THROUGH THE WINDOWS, Motown, 1972

SKYWRITER, Motown, 1973

ANTHOLOGY, Motown, 1976

DESTINY, Epic, 1979

TRIUMPH, Epic, 1980

20 GOLDEN GREATS, Motown, 1981

THE JACKSON FIVE, Motown, 1984

GREAT LOVE SONGS, Motown, 1984

VICTORY, Epic, 1984

REACTIONS, (Rebbie Jackson), CBS, 1986

THE VERY BEST OF MICHAEL JACKSON & THE JACKSON FIVE, Telstar, 1986

2300 JACKSON STREET, Epic, 1989

JAM, JIMMY, & TERRY LEWIS

Although PRINCE has been the apex of the Minneapolis Sound, the production team of keyboardist Jimmy Jam and bassist Terry Lewis has done almost as much to galvanise that sound so that it has become a commercial property. As members of Flyte Tyme with drummer Jesse "Jellybean" Johnson and vocalist Alexander O'NEAL, they (and Prince) had developed the sound as early as 1978. In 1981 Flyte Tyme became Time; Warner Bros. released an eponymous LP featuring keyboardist Monte Moir and vocalist Morris Day singing Prince's compositions; it was followed by the LPs, *What Time Is It?* (USA#26.1982) and *Ice Cream Castle* (USA #24.1984). However, the group disbanded in 1984 when Day and Johnson left to start solo careers, although later two tracks, *Jungle Love* (USA#20.1985) and *The Bird* (USA#36.1985), were featured in the film *Purple Rain*.

In 1980 Jam and Lewis formed their own record label Tabu. It was crucial to their success, as it enabled them to develop their own roster of artists. Their earliest success was with The SOS Band, a funk outfit from Atlanta fronted by lead vocalist Mary Davis, who continued to have hits throughout the 1980s. Jam & Lewis continued writing and producing other acts like CHANGE. In 1986 they started to produce Janet JACKSON, having worked with Alexander O'Neal, Cherrelle and Force MDs. The first LP with Janet Jackson, *Control,* included five hit singles; the follow-up, *Janet Jackson's Rhythm Nation 1814,* proved to be equally successful. In 1990 Time was re-formed for the LP *Pandemonium*, released on Prince's Paisley Park label and featuring the single, *Jerk*

Out (USA#16.1990). Unfortunately, it all sounded as if it had been locked in a time-warp since 1978.

TIME, Warner Bros., 1981
WHAT TIME IS IT, (Time), Warner Bros., 1982
ICE CREAM CASTLE, (Time), Warner Bros., 1984
PANDEMONIUM, (Time), Paisley Park, 1990

JAMERSON, JAMES While Berry GORDY may have created the backdrop for Motown, it was the musicians who filled in all the detail. James Jamerson was the bassist in The Funk Brothers, the house band at Motown. In tandem with drummer Benny BENJAMIN, he created the liquid backbeat for scores and scores of hits by everyone from Mary WELLS right through to Diana ROSS. Jamerson died in 1983 of a heart attack.

JAMES, ETTA Etta James Hawkins was born in Los Angeles on January 25, 1938. She was discovered by Johnny OTIS in 1951 when she was singing in the vocal group Peaches; he booked her into his club, the Barrelhouse. As a result she was signed by the Bihari Brothers to the Modern label in 1955, for whom she recorded *Roll with Me Henry* and *Good Rockin' Daddy*. At the end of her contract with Modern in 1959, she was signed to the Chess subsidiary, Argo. With Ralph BASS producing, she notched up a succession of hits: *All I Could do was Cry* (USA#33.1960), *My Dearest Darling* (USA#34.1960),*Trust In Me* (USA#30.1961), *Don't Cry Baby* (USA#39.1961), *Something's Got a Hold on Me* (USA#37.1962), *Stop the Wedding* (USA#34.1962) and *Pushover* (USA #25.1963). During the mid-1960s, the hits came to an end; her increasing reliance upon heroin didn't help. In November 1967, however, she was packed off to the Fame studios in Muscle Shoals where, with Rick HALL producing, she recorded songs like *I'd Rather Go Blind, Tell Mama* (USA#23.1967), *Steal Away* and *Security* (USA#35.1968). Although, these records failed to generate the same degree of interest that Aretha FRANKLIN's had, they substantially increased her reputation; were it not for the death of Leonard CHESS in 1969, and the subsequent sale of the Chess label, she would undoubtedly have achieved the success that was her due.

As it was, the end of Chess left her without a recording contract, and she didn't cut another record until 1978, when Jerry WEXLER signed her to Warner Bros. and produced the LP *Deep in the Night*. Quite why it failed to work is one of the great enigmas of our time. She had to wait another two years before recording again. This time it was for MCA, with Allen TOUSSAINT producing; entitled *Changes*, it was recorded in New Orleans and featured an array of crack session musicians. Another hiatus ensued, during which she toured the USA and Europe. In 1986 she teamed up with Eddie "Cleanhead" Vinson for the LP *Blues in the Night*, which featured Shuggie Otis, Brother Jack McDuff and Paul Humphrey and was recorded live at a club in Los Angeles. In 1989 she was signed by Island and teamed with producer Barry BECKETT for the LP *Seven Year Itch*. It was followed by *Sticking To My Guns* in 1990 with the same producer and session musicians like Reggie Young, Roger HAWKINS and the the Muscle Shoals Horn Section under Harrison Calloway. Both LPs showed that her phrasing and timing are unimpaired and that, given the right circumstances, she is still one of the finest natural soul singers around.

TELL MAMA, Chess, 1967
DEEP IN THE NIGHT, Warner Bros., 1978
CHESS MASTERS, Chess, 1981
GOOD ROCKIN' MAMA, Ace, 1981
TUFF LOVER, Ace, 1983

BLUES IN THE NIGHT, (with Eddie "Cleanhead" Vinson), Fantasy, 1986
R&B QUEEN, Crown, 1986
AT LAST, Chess, 1987
R&B DYNAMITE, Ace, 1987
HER GREATEST SIDES, VOLUME 1, Chess, 1988
ROCKS THE HOUSE, Chess, 1988
COME A LITTLE CLOSER, Chess, 1988
JUICY PEACHES, Chess, 1988
SEVEN YEAR ITCH, Island, 1989
STICKING TO MY GUNS, Island, 1990

JAMES, RICK James Johnson was born on February 1, 1952, in Buffalo, New York. He joined the navy but deserted to settle in Toronto , where he formed The Mynah Birds and became known as Rick James. Then they moved to Detroit and signed with Motown, but nothing was released and so he moved to London, where he formed another group, The Main Line. By 1977 he had returned to the USA and formed The Stone City Band, who were signed to the Motown subsidiary, Gordy. His debut LP, *Come Get It* (USA #13.1978), exhibited the influence of James BROWN and George CLINTON; it included the single, *You and I* (USA#13; UK#46.1978). His second LP, *Bustin' out of L Seven* (USA #16.1979), was followed by a US tour with The Stone City Band and The MARY JANE GIRLS; the same year he produced the debut LP by Motown artist Teena Marie; over the years each would contribute to one another's records. In 1981, after releasing two more LPs, *Fire It Up* (USA#34.1979) and *Garden Of Love*, he released *Street Songs* (USA#3.1981), which included the singles *Give it to me Baby* (USA#40; UK#47.1981) and *Super Freak (Part 1)* (USA#16.1981). Since 1981 he has continued to issue LPs at regular intervals, including *Throwin' Down* (USA#13.1982) and *Cold Blooded* (USA#16.1983), as well as producing artists such as The Stone City Band, The Mary

Jane Girls and comedian Eddie Murphy; he has collaborated with other Motown artist like Smokey ROBINSON and The TEMPTATIONS. However, in 1985 his contract with Motown ended and, for a while, he recorded at his own studio in Buffalo. In 1987 he signed with Reprise; his debut LP *Wonderful* featured Roxanne Shante on the extracted single *Loosey's Rap*.

COME GET IT, Motown, 1978
BUSTIN' OUT OF L SEVEN, Motown, 1978
GARDEN OF LOVE, Motown, 1980
STREET SONGS, Motown, 1981
THROWIN' DOWN, Motown, 1982
COLD BLOODED, Motown, 1983
REFLECTIONS, Motown, 1984
GLOW, Gordy, 1985
THE FLAG, Gordy, 1985
GREATEST HITS, Motown, 1986
WONDERFUL, Reprise, 1988

JARREAU, AL Al Jarreau was born in Milwaukee on March 12, 1940. Although his interest in music stemmed from his childhood, his career didn't get under way until 1968, when he started to work the West Coast club circuit. By 1975, he had established a thorough-going reputation for himself as one of the more stylish vocalists on the circuit, which encouraged Warner Bros. to give him a recording contract.

His first LP *We Got By* didn't sell in vast quantities; the follow up *Glow* consolidated his reputation and prompted a world tour in 1977, during which the double live LP *Look to the Rainbow* was recorded. Such was its success that he won a Grammy for Best Jazz Vocalist. He followed it with the LP *This Time* (USA #27.1980). After winning another Grammy, this time as Best R&B Vocalist, he embarked upon another world tour. Then came the LP *Breakin' Away* (USA#15; UK#60.1981), which included the single *We're in this Love Together* (USA#15; UK#55.1981). After winning another Grammy, he released *Jarreau* (USA#13; UK#39.1983); three singles were extracted, including *Mornin'* (USA#21; UK #28.1983).

Since 1984 his records have been consistent rather than interesting, settling for the safeness of his known formula; this has made him a far more marketable commodity: the success of his title theme to the television series *Mooonlighting* (USA#23; UK#8.1987) exemplifies this acceptance. In 1988 he released the LP *Heart's Horizon*, produced by George DUKE.

WE GOT BY, Reprise, 1975
GLOW, Reprise, 1976
LOOK TO THE RAINBOW, Warner Bros., 1977
ALL FLY HOME, WEA, 1978
THIS TIME, WEA, 1980
BREAKIN' AWAY, Warner Bros., 1981
JARREAU, WEA, 1983
THE MASQUERADE IS OVER, Happy Bird, 1983
HIGH CRIME, WEA, 1984
SPIRITS AND FEELINGS, Happy Bird, 1984
IN LONDON, WEA, 1985
REPLAY OF AL JARREAU, Sierra, 1985
YOU, Platinum, 1985
L IS FOR LOVER, WEA, 1986
HEARTS HORIZON, WEA, 1989

JENKINS, JOHNNY It was through the offices of guitarist Johnny Jenkins that Otis REDDING's career took off in earnest. Jenkins and his group The Pinetoppers, of which Redding was an occasional member, played the club circuit around Macon and Dawson. In 1962 he had a local hit with the instrumental *Love Twist*. It led to a session at Stax, set up by Joe Galkin from Atlantic, to record the follow-up. The follow-up never materialised, but Redding recorded *These Arms of Mine*, featuring Jenkins playing the guitar. Although

Jenkins continued to play local clubs, his career gradually slipped into the doldrums until the late 1960s when he recorded the LP *Ton Ton Macoute* for Capricorn, which was owned by his manager Phil WALDEN. It was a curious affair combining rock with soul, featuring the nucleus of The Allman Brothers Band. It failed to sell and Jenkins promptly disappeared into obscurity.

JOHN, LITTLE WILLIE Throughout the mid-1950s Little Willie John carved a reputation for himself as being one of the first soul singers with a succession of records that owed as much to the blues as to gospel, but his vocal style was completely out of kilter with the contemporary popularity of the doo-wop groups.

He was born in Lafayette, Arkansas, on November 15, 1937. After being discovered by Johnny OTIS in 1953 he was signed to Syd NATHAN's King label where, under the watchful eye of producer Henry GLOVER, he recorded his first single *All Around the World*. It was followed by a number of records like *Fever* (USA#24.1956), *Need Your Love so Bad* – featuring guitarist Mickey Baker (see ROBINSON, Sylvia) – *Talk to Me, Talk to Me* (USA#20.1958), *Let them Talk*, *Heartbreak (It's Hurtin' Me)* (USA#38.1960) and *Sleep* (USA#13.1960). His career was brought to a premature close when he was imprisoned for murder, after stabbing a railway official. He died on May 26, 1968, aged 30, at Walla Walla Prison in Washington.

FEVER, Sing, 1989
TALK TO ME, TALK TO ME, Sing, 1989
MISTER LITTLE WILLIE JOHN, Sing, 1989

JOHNSON, JIMMY From the late 1950s, Jimmy Johnson was the rhythm guitarist in The Del-Rays, who played the club circuit and high school balls in and around

Muscle Shoals. When Rick HALL set up Fame, Johnson was one of the first of many to join the studios. Initially he played the odd session as well as performing the engineering duties. After David BRIGGS and the rest of the first house band left, Johnson became the guitarist in the second band with Roger HAWKINS, Spooner OLDHAM and Junior Lowe. In 1969 Johnson, with Hawkins, David HOOD and Barry BECKETT left Hall to open the Muscle Shoals Sound studios. Johnson continued in his former capacity as guitarist, although he engineered some of the sessions, much as he had done at Fame and at Quin IVY's Quinvy studios, where he had engineered Percy SLEDGE's *When a Man Loves a Woman*. In 1985, when the studios were sold to Malaco, Johnson remained as a session musician, contributing to LPs by Bobby BLAND and Johnnie TAYLOR.

JOHNSON, JOHNNY, & THE BAND-WAGON During the mid-1960s, a large number of Americans and West Indians started to develop a Soul Scene in the UK. It came about through the fast-growing interest in soul on the club circuit. Johnny Johnson & The Bandwagon came to the UK from the USA in 1967 where they hadn't managed to break through. While their efforts were spirited they tended to lack distinctiveness, mainly because they seemed to equate soul music with histrionic emoting. However, they managed to carve a small niche for themselves with a series of hits: *Breakin' Down the Walls of Heartache* (UK#4.1968), *You* (UK#34.1968), *Let's Hang on* (UK#36.1969), *Sweet Inspiration* (UK#10.1970) and *Blame it on the Pony Express* (UK#7.1970). These hits have guaranteed them work for as long as they want on the club circuit throughout Europe and the UK, as well as being hardy perennials on the Northern Soul circuit.

JOHNSON, MARV One of the first bright stars in the Motown firmament was Marv Johnson. This was in the days when Berry GORDY was leasing his material to any takers. Johnson was born in Detroit on October 15, 1938. His earliest records like *Come to Me* (USA#30.1959), *You Got What it Takes* (USA#10.1959; UK#5.1960), *I Love the Way you Love* (USA#9; UK#35.1960), *Ain't Gonna be that Way* (UK#50.1960) and *(You've Got to) Move Two Mountains* (USA#20.1960) were instrumental in providing Gordy with the cashflow and credibility to set the wheels of Motown properly in motion, as they were all leased out to United Artists. By the time Motown was up and running smoothly, Johnson had been eclipsed by others. However, despite having had very limited success with Motown itself, apart from occasional reissues in the UK like *I'll Pick a Rose for my Rose* (UK#10.1969) and *I Miss you Baby* (UK#25.1969), he has been able to ply his trade on the club circuit ever since and has become a journeyman in the truest sense of the word. Since joining Motor City records, he has been able to extend his reputation among the cognoscenti by touring constantly.

MOTOR CITY ROOTS: THE ROOTS OF DETROIT SOUL, Stateside, 1986

JOHNSON, NORMAN "GENERAL" See CHAIRMEN OF THE BOARD

JOHNSON, PAUL Paul Johnson has always been touted as one of the most promising of the new young UK soul stars, but he has consistently failed to make the quantum jump into the front-line of international performers. He has one of the finest voices to emerge in recent years, but the productions have been less than sympathetic. He made his debut in 1987 with the LP *Paul Johnson* (UK #63.1987), from which included the single *When Love Comes Calling* (UK#52.1987). The second LP *Personal* was a seamless production, but unfortunately it suffered from a common failing: undistinguished material. Since then he has contributed to LPs by other UK-based artists like Mica PARIS.

PAUL JOHNSON, CBS, 1987
PERSONAL, CBS, 1989

JONES, BOOKER T   See BOOKER T & THE MGs

JONES, GRACE
One of the less flattering aspects of the career of Grace Jones has been her unflinching propensity for controversy: whether this is due to her enormous success as a fashion model or merely to a desire to court publicity for its own sake is a question that only she can answer. The fact remains that her talent as a performer is sufficient in itself: the controversial publicity is entirely superfluous.

She was born in Jamaica on May 15, 1953. In 1976 she started to record a series of disco-oriented tracks which became immensely successful on the New York club circuit. The following year she was signed by Island and over the next three years she recorded three disco-oriented LPs *Portfolio*, *Fame* and *Muse*, all of which consolidated her growing reputation on the club circuit. In 1980, with Island owner Chris Blackwell producing and the crack rhythm section of Sly & Robbie backing her, she recorded the LP *Warm Leatherette* (UK #45.1980), which included the single *Private Life* (UK#17.1980). Her next LP, *Nightclubbing* (USA#32; UK#35.1981), repeated the same formula with the same producer and musicians and included the single *Pull up to the Bumper* (UK#53.1981/#12.1986). The following year,

she released the LP *Living my Life* (UK #15.1982). This was to be her final LP for three years, during which time she concentrated upon her acting career appearing in the films, *Conan the Destroyer* and *A View to a Kill*.

On her return to the music scene she released the LP *Slave To the Rhythm* (UK#12.1985) with Trevor Horn taking care of the production duties. The title track (UK#12.1985) was released as a single. It was followed by her version of The Roxy Music song, *Love is the Drug* (UK#35.1986). Her contract with Island expired and she signed with the EMI subsidiary, Manhattan. Her first LP for the new label, *Inside Story* (UK#61.1986), was produced by Nile RODGERS. In 1989, having signed with Capitol, she released the LP *Bulletproof Heart*, after which she undertook a European tour.

PORTFOLIO, Island, 1977
FAME, Island, 1978
WARM LEATHERETTE, Island, 1980
NIGHTCLUBBIN', Island, 1981
LIVING MY LIFE, Island, 1982
SLAVE TO THE RHYTHM, Island, 1985
ISLAND LIFE, Island. 1985.
INSIDE STORY, Manhattan, 1986
BULLETPROOF HEART, Capitol, 1989

JONES, LINDA
One of the great forgotten soul singers, Linda Jones had a painfully short career. She was signed initially to the Atlantic subisidiary, Atco, where she recorded *Take the Boy out of the Country* (1964). In 1967, she released *Hypnotised* (USA#21.1967) and *What Have I Done to Make you Mad?* for the independent Loma label, with producer George Kerr and arranger Richard Tee. After this her career hit the doldrums. In 1971 she signed with the Turbo label, but on March 24, 1972, aged 26, she died from a diabetic attack after a performance at the Apollo in Harlem. After her death, All Platinum released her ver-

sion of the Jerry BUTLER and Arthur Brooks composition, *For Your Precious Love*. Although it became a minor hit, it signally failed to stop her from becoming yet another singer destined for obscurity.

JONES, QUINCY Quincy Jones was born on March 14, 1933, in Chicago. His career started in 1949 when he was asked by the jazz bassist Oscar Pettiford to arrange a song for him. In 1950 he joined the Lionel Hampton Orchestra as a trumpeter; he remained there for three years contributing arrangements as well as performing. By 1956 he was recording under his own name. His first LP, *This is How I Feel about Jazz*, was credited to Quincy Jones & The All Stars: among The All Stars were Charlie Mingus and Milt Jackson. The following year saw the release of *Go West Man*, which featured, among others, Art Pepper and Shelley Manne. Over the next ten years, he produced and wrote arrangements for a wide diversity of artists including The Count Basie Orchestra, Ray CHARLES, Peggy Lee, Dinah Washington and Sarah Vaughan. In 1961 he was appointed musical director of Mercury records and, in 1963, he had a foretaste of the success he would later achieve with Michael JACKSON, when he produced the single *It's My Party* for Lesley Gore which went to #1. in the USA. As a reward for this he was appointed vice-president of Mercury in 1964. In 1967 he composed and arranged the soundtrack for the film, *In the Heat of the Night*; the title-song was a modest hit for Ray Charles. Jones also composed and arranged the soundtracks of the films *For Love of Ivy* in 1968 and *The Heist* in 1971, which featured songs by artists like B. B. KING, LITTLE RICHARD and Roberta FLACK.

In 1971 a collaboration with Ray Charles, entitled Black Requiem, was performed by the Houston Symphony Orchestra with an eighty-voice choir.

In 1972 having signed with A&M, he recorded *Smackwater Jack*. This LP represented a slight change of direction in as much as it contained versions of material by contemporary writers like Carole King (see GOFFIN & KING) as well as self-composed material. The arrangements were less jazz oriented than those in his previous work. As if to consolidate this change of emphasis, he produced the Aretha FRANKLIN LP, *Hey Now Hey (The Other Side of the Sky)*, which included her version of the Jimi HENDRIX composition, *Angel* (USA#20; UK#37.1973). In 1974, he released the LP, *Body Heat*, (USA#6.1974). It was followed by the LP, *Mellow Madness* (USA #16.1975), which featured The BROTHERS JOHNSON, whose debut LP he produced the following year. In 1977, he scored the soundtrack for the TV series *Roots* (USA #21.1977). In 1978 came his production and scoring of the Motown-backed film *The Wiz*, which included Michael JACKSON among its cast. The same year saw the release of the LP, *Sounds ..... And Stuff Like That* (USA#15; UK #34.1978); a single, *Stuff Like That* (USA #21.1978), was released that featured vocals by ASHFORD & SIMPSON and Chaka KHAN.

In 1979, he started to produce Michael Jackson for Epic. The first LP *Off The Wall* spawned a slew of international hit singles. In 1982, he produced the follow-up *Thriller*, which was to become the best selling LP of all time. 1981 saw the formation of his own record label, Qwest; signings to the label included Patti AUSTIN, Siedah GARRETT and James INGRAM, all of whom achieved a measure of success under his tutelage. The same year saw the release of his own LP, *The Dude* (USA#10; UK#19.1981). Two singles, *Ai No Corrida* (USA#28; UK#14.1981) and *Razzamatazz*

(UK#11.198I), were released; they featured vocals by the group Dune and Patti Austin, respectively. In 1984 The Quincy Jones Orchestra recorded *LA is my Lady*, featuring Frank Sinatra. In 1985 he produced the US contribution to Live Aid, *We are the World*. Credited to USA For Africa, the single featured a veritable who's who of the music business; that the song itself succeeded in plumbing new depths of mawkish sentimentality was no fault of Jones's. It remained at the top of the US charts for four weeks and generated millions of dollars for the starving in Africa. In 1987 he coproduced *Bad*, Michael Jackson's follow-up to *Thriller*, it failed to sell in quite the same quantity as its predecessor (by the odd million or so). In 1989 he released *Back on the Block* (USA#7.1990). Its guest list was almost as compendious and diverse as the cast of USA For Africa had been and offered further proof – if any were necessary – that Quincy Jones remains one of the staunchest and most inventive upholders of the traditions of contemporary US Music. Towards the end of 1990 a documentary film entitled *Listen Up*, chronicling his life and times was released.

THIS IS HOW I FEEL, Jasmine, 1956

QUINTESSENCE, Jasmine, 1957

THE GREAT WIDE WORLD, Mercury, 1959

BOSSA NOVA, Mercury, 1961

BIRTH OF A BAND, Mercury, 1963

I HAD A BALL, Philips, 1964

WALKING IN SPACE, A&M, 1969

SMACKWATER JACK, A&M, 1972

MELLOW MADNESS, A&M, 1975

SOUNDS ..... AND STUFF LIKE THAT!, A&M, 1978

THE DUDE, A&M, 1981

THE BEST OF QUINCY JONES, A&M, 1982

THE QUINCY JONES ALL STARS, Esquire, 1986

BACK ON THE BLOCK, Qwest, 1989

LISTEN UP, Warner Bros., 1991

KC & THE SUNSHINE BAND In 1973 Harold Wayne Casey (born January 31, 1951, in Hialeah, Florida) met up with the bassist and engineer at TK Records, Richard Finch (born January 25, 1954, in Indianapolis, Indiana) through his job in a record shop. Between them, they decided to form a group. Although the line-up was flexible – ranging from nine to eleven members – they started to build up a strong local following. The following year, they were signed to Henry STONE'S Florida-based TK label.

Their first single, *Blow Your Whistle*, was a dance-floor smash and provided the blueprint for the sound of their records in years to come. At TK they notched up a string of hits including *Queen of Clubs* (UK#7.1974), *Sound Your Funky Horn* (UK#17.1974), *Get Down Tonight* (USA#1; UK#21.1975), *That's the Way (I Like it)* (USA#1; UK#4.1975), *I'm So Crazy* (UK-#34.1975), *(Shake Shake Shake) Shake Your Booty* (USA#1; UK#22.1976), *Keep it Comin' Love* (USA#2.1977; UK#31.1976), *I'm Your Boogie Man* (USA#1; UK#41.1977), *Boogie Shoes* (USA#35; UK#34.1978), *It's the Same Old Song* (USA#35; UK#49.1978) and *Please Don't Go* (USA#1; UK#3.1979). Their LPs, *KC & The Sunshine Band* (USA#4; UK#26.1975), *Part 3* (USA#13.1976) and *Who Do Ya (Love)* (USA#36.1978), were all excellent examples of undemanding dance music.

In their capacity as house band at TK, they wrote for and produced other artists like George and Gwen McCRAE and Betty WRIGHT. In 1979 Casey duetted with Teri DeSario on a revival of Barbara MASON song, *Yes I'm Ready* (USA#2.1979). In 1981 the group disbanded when TK went bankrupt and Casey signed with Epic; the following year he was seriously injured in a car crash near his house. After a lengthy period of convalescence he recorded the LP *All in a Night's Work* (UK#46.1983), featuring the singles *Give it Up* (USA#18.1984; UK#1.1983) and *(You Said)*

You'd Gimme Some More (UK#41.1983). Since 1984, when he formed his own label, Meca, he has continued to record and tour, although he hasn't been able to recapture his former success.

DO YOU WANNA GO PARTY, TK, 1979
GREATEST HITS, Epic, 1983
THE BEST OF KC & THE SUNSHINE BAND, CBS, 1990

K-DOE, ERNIE Ernest Kador, Jr, was born in New Orleans on February 22, 1936. His father was a minister in a Baptist Church, and Ernest sang gospel there in his youth. After moving to Chicago briefly, where he recorded for the United label, he returned to New Orleans as a member of The Blue Diamonds, recording *Honey Baby* for the Savoy label. He left The Blue Diamonds for a solo career in 1955 and signed for Specialty where he became a LITTLE RICHARD imitator with *Do Baby Do*. In 1960 he was signed to Minit by Allen TOUSSAINT. His first records for Minit failed, but with *Mother-in-Law* (USA#1; UK#29.1961) he struck gold, although all the credit doesn't belong to K-Doe: the bass repetitions from Benny Spellman were the distinguishing feature. However, it wasn't entirely one way traffic as, in 1962 K-Doe played on Spellman's hit, *Lipstick Traces*. Spellman went on to have another other minor hit with the Allen Toussaint composition *Fortune Teller* (1962). K-Doe proved to be a one hit wonder, as subsequent releases like *I Cried my Last Tear*, *Popeye Joe*, *A Certain Girl* and *Waiting at the Station* failed to generate the interest of *Mother-in Law*. He recorded briefly for the Duke label in the mid-1960s with Willie MITCHELL producing, and in 1970 he was reunited with Toussaint. In recent years he has concentrated upon live work.

MOTHER IN LAW, Stateside, 1986
FORTUNE TELLER, (Benny Spellman), Charly, 1988

BURN, K-DOE, BURN!, Charly, 1990

KENDRICKS, EDDIE Eddie Kendricks was born in Birmingham, Alabama, on December 17, 1939. His career is inextricably interwoven with that of The TEMPTA-TIONS, his involvement spanning the years when they were, arguably, the most significant black vocal group in the USA. His departure in June 1971 for a solo career said more about timing than anything else: while his career prospered at first, that of his former colleague, David RUFFIN, foundered. It was his good fortune or, indeed, astuteness that he was able to record two songs that were the embodiment of the fast-developing disco-fever: *Keep on Truckin'* (USA#1; UK#18.1973) and *Boogie Down* (USA#2; UK#39.1974). Although these records were monsters, he was unable to sustain the momentum and, by the mid-1970s his supply of good material was exhausted. In 1981 he re-emerged with an LP for Atlantic, which suffered from the perennial problem: indifferent material. In 1982 he particpated in The Temptations' reunion celebrations, which led to an invitation from Daryl HALL and John Oates to appear with them and David Ruffin at the reopening of the Apollo. An LP, *Live at the Apollo with David Ruffin and Eddie Kendricks* (USA#21; UK#32.1985), generated sufficient interest for RCA to sign them as a duo. Their debut LP, *Ruffin and Kendricks*, showed that given half-decent material they can knock spots off most of their contemporaries.

LOVE KEYS, Atlantic, 1981
LIVE AT THE APOLLO WITH DAVID RUFFIN AND EDDIE KENDRICKS, RCA, 1985
RUFFIN AND KENDRICKS, RCA, 1987

KENNER, CHRIS A veteran of the New Orleans recording scene Chris Kenner was born in New Orleans in 1929. His vocal style was developed initially through singing gospel; although he later broadened his scope to encompass R&B, the gospel- tinged inflections of his phrasing were characteristic of all his records. His recording career, which started in 1957, was frequently interrupted by visits to Louisiana penitentiaries. When he did get round to cutting records he came up with classics like *Land of a 1000 Dances, Something you Got, How Far?* and *I Like it Like That* (USA#2.1961). The former was adapted from the gospel song, *Children Go where I Send You*, although Wilson PICKETT had the bigger hit with it, in 1966, Allen TOUSSAINT'S production of Kenner's original established it as one of the real landmark records of the Crescent City. After years of playing the local club circuit in and around, New Orleans, Kenner died on January 25, 1976.

I LIKE IT LIKE THAT, Charly, 1990

KESLER, STAN   Stan Kesler's career started as a steel guitarist in the house band at the Sun studios on Madison Avenue in Memphis; it included Quinton CLAUNCH in its lineup. However, he stopped playing sessions in favour of engineering them, and became a dab hand at assembling house bands: the first comprised Reggie Young (guitar), Tommy COGBILL (bass), Bobby Emmons and Bobby Woods (keyboards) and Gene Chrisman (drums). When this section defected to Chips MOMAN's American studios, after working on some of the Goldwax sessions for Claunch, he assembled another band. This band comprised Charlie Freeman (guitar), Jim Dickinson and Mike Utley (keyboards), Tommy McClure (bass) and Sammy Creason (drums). This band was used by Lelan Rogers of Silver Fox for some Betty LaVETTE sessions, but was pinched by Jerry WEXLER,

when he set up Atlantic South, where they became known as The DIXIE FLYERS. After The Dixie Flyers defection, Kesler assembled another short-lived band; this was pinched by Chips Moman's erstwhile partner, Seymour Rosenberg, Charlie Rich's manager, for his new studio. Kesler went to work for Chips Moman, who was to set up new studios in Atlanta; it was short-lived as Moman left the music industry altogether for a while and Kesler returned to Memphis, where he has gone back to working for Sam Phillips.

KHAN, CHAKA   Yvette Marie Stevens was born in Great Lakes, Illinois, on March 23, 1953. In 1969, she adopted the moniker Chaka Khan as a result of attending the Yurbiba Tribe African Arts Centre in Chicago. After singing with a number of groups she joined Ask Rufus which had been formed out of the remnants of The American Breed. In 1973 the group shortened its name to Rufus and signed with ABC; the line-up was Andre Fischer (drums), Tony Maiden (guitar), Nate Morgan, Kevin Murphy (keyboards) and Bobby Watson (bass).

Their debut LP, *Rufus*, sold only modestly but it generated considerable interest in the group, prompting Stevie WONDER to contribute *Tell Me Something Good* (USA#3.1974) to their next LP, *Rags to Rufus* (USA#4.1974), which also included *You Got the Love* (USA #11.1974). The following year they released the LP *Rufusized* (USA#7; UK#48.1975), featuring *Once You Get Started* (USA#10.1975). Their next LP, *Rufus Featuring Chaka Khan* (USA #7.1976), included the single *Sweet Thing* (USA#5.1976) and marked the emergence of Khan as the star of the group. *Ask Rufus* (USA#12.1977) became their biggest selling LP; it included the singles *At Midnight (My Love Will Lift You Up)* (USA#30.1977) and *Hollywood* (USA#32.1977). In 1978, Khan's solo career began to take shape with a couple of collaborations with other artists: she duetted with Joni Mitchell on the LP *Don Juan's Restless Daughter* and sang the lead vocal on the Quincy JONES single *Stuff Like That*. The same year Rufus issued the LP *Street Player* (USA#14.1978) and Khan signed with Warner Bros. as a solo artist, although still remaining in the group.

Her first solo LP *Chaka* (USA#12.1978), was produced by Arif MARDIN and featured contributions from George Benson and The AVERAGE WHITE BAND; it included the ASHFORD & SIMPSON composition, *I'm Every Woman* (USA#21; UK#11.1979). Her profile as a soloist continued to rise with her contribution to the Ry Cooder LP *Bop 'Til You Drop*. The next Rufus LP *Masterjam* (USA #14.1980) featured *Do You Love what you Feel?* (USA#30.1980). The solo LPs *Naughty* (USA-#43.1980) and *What 'Cha Gonna Do for Me?* (USA#17.1981) followed.

The next year she reunited with Rufus for a concert at the Savoy Theatre in New York; this was recorded and released on a double LP as *Live – Stompin' at the Savoy* (USA#50; UK #64.1983), which featured *Ain't Nobody* (USA #22.1983; UK#8.1984). Another solo LP, *Chaka Khan*, followed. Her real breakthrough came with the LP, *I Feel for You* (USA#14; UK#15.1984), it was produced by Arif Mardin again; it included the singles, *I Feel for You* (USA#3; UK#1.1984), written by PRINCE and featuring Grandmaster MELLE MEL and Stevie Wonder, *This is My Night* (UK #14.1985) and *Eye to Eye* (UK#16.1985). What really set it apart from other LPs of the period was that, while stylistically the embodiment of soul, it had the contemporary sound of the electro-funk that was bouncing off every wall of every club the world over.

Since then she has continued recording, with the LPs *Destiny* (1986) and *CK* (1988), and collaborated with Robert PALMER, David Bowie and Steve Winwood. However, the most interesting development has been the issue of the double LP, *Life Is A Dance,* which was a collection of ten of her choicest cuts remixed by producers like Paul Simpson, Shocklee & Sadler of Public Enemy and Danny D; it illustrated just how successfully she has managed to marry the traditions of soul with the sound of rap and deepest house.

NAUGHTY, Warner Bros., 1980
WHAT CHA GONNA DO FOR ME, Warner Bros., 1981
LIVE – STOMPIN' AT THE SAVOY, (with Rufus), Warner Bros., 1983
I FEEL FOR YOU, Warner Bros., 1984
DESTINY, Warner Bros., 1986
CK, Warner Bros., 1988
LIFE IS A DANCE, Warner Bros., 1989

KILLEN, BUDDY In 1961 Buddy Killen founded the Dial label to record the output of his recently discovered protege Joe TEX. Killen was born in Florence, Alabama, and secured session work as a bassist at the Grand Ole Opry in Nashville until he joined Jack Stapp, who had recently founded the publishing company, Tree; they became partners in 1957. Killen was an old associate of Rick HALL's, having been born in Muscle Shoals; and so, although he hooked up with Chips MOMAN first, it was at the Fame studios that he got his first hit with Tex, *Hold What You Got,* before linking up with Moman once again in the latter part of the1960s. The success of Tex prompted Killen to expand his roster of R&B artists to include the veteran Clarence "Frogman" Henry, Paul Kelly and Bobby MARCHAN. However, Tex remained his principal source of contact with the soul and R&B markets. After Dial's distribution deal with Atlantic had expired, he signed a fresh deal with Mercury; when that in turn expired he did another deal, this time with Epic. When Tex died in 1982, Killen reverted to overseeing his substantial publishing interests that have exceeded those of Acuff-Rose, the best known country-music publisher of all.

KING, ALBERT While the name Albert King has, largely because of his virtuoso guitar work, always been associated with the blues, his vocals and arrangements seem to be influenced more by Bobby BLAND than by, say, B. B. KING.

He was born Albert Nelson in Indianola, Mississippi, on April 25, 1923. The early part of his career was devoted to playing in Arkansas, with a short spell in Chicago. In 1956 he relocated to St Louis, where he played the club circuit and recorded for the occasional independent label. In 1966 he was signed by Stax. His first LP, *Born Under a Bad Sign* (1967), featured BOOKER T & THE MGs and was produced by Jim STEWART; the title track was written by Booker T. Jones and William BELL. The LP as a whole confirmed his status as a vocalist. It was followed in 1968 by a live LP, recorded at the Fillmore in San Francisco: *Live Wire/Blues Power*. He remained with Stax until their demise, recording LPs like *King Does the King's Things* in 1969 (a tribute to Elvis Presley), *Lovejoy* in 1971, *I'll Play the Blues for You* in 1972 and *I Wanna Get Funky* in 1974. Throughout, he toured regularly on the festival and college circuits, often backed by The BARKAYS and The Memphis Horns (see JACKSON, Wayne). After signing with Utopia, he recorded LPs like *Truckload Of Lovin'* and *Albert* (1976) and *King Albert* (1977). In 1978, he teamed up with Allen TOUSSAINT for the LP, *New Orleans Heat*.

Although, he has frequently been accused of being "too poppie" by blues purists, he has regained some of his former followers with the LPs, *San Francisco '83* and *I'm in a Phone-Booth, Baby*

in 1986. His willingness to tour regularly has ensured a strong loyal following in the USA and Europe encouraging interest in the blues, with young adherents like Larry McCray, Robert CRAY and the late Stevie Ray Vaughn taking up the guitar and following in his footsteps, adapting the blues to contemporary settings.

LIVE WIRE/BLUES POWER, Mobile Fidelity, 1968
DOOR TO DOOR, (with Otis Rush), Chess, 1969
LOVEJOY, Stax, 1971
I'LL PLAY THE BLUES FOR YOU, Stax, 1972
TRUCKLOAD OF LOVIN', Charly, 1976
ALBERT, Charly, 1976
KING ALBERT, Charly, 1977
NEW ORLEANS HEAT, Charly, 1978
SAN FRANCISCO '83, Fantasy, 1983
LAUNDROMAT BLUES, Edsel, 1984
THE LAST SESSION, Stax, 1986
I'M IN A PHONE-BOOTH, BABY, Fantasy, 1986
THE BEST OF ALBERT KING, London, 1987
RED HOUSE, Essential, 1991

KING, B. B. Of all the bluesmen to cross over into R&B and soul, few have managed to be as resilient and as impervious to the fickleness of passing fads as B. B. King. He was born Riley King on September 16, 1925 at Itta Bena, Mississippi. After working as a sharecropper and tractor driver, he made his bid for fame in 1948 when he moved up to Memphis. His big break came when Sonny Boy Wiliamson, whom he knew through Williamson's guitarist Robert Lockwood, gave him an opportunity to play on one of his programmes for the radio station KWEM. As a result he began to secure work on the club circuit and, by 1949, had his own show on another radio station, WDIA, where Rufus THOMAS was employed as a DJ. It was at this time that King became known as the "Beale Street Blues Boy", a nickname eventually reduced to "Blues Boy" – hence the acronym B. B . With his popularity on the up, he formed a band which included Lockwood and John Alexander (who would achieve popularity in his own right as Johnny ACE). The same year he cut his first singles for the Bullet label. They attracted the attention of Ike TURNER, who recommended him to the Bihari Brothers, the owners of the Modern label in Los Angeles; in 1950 he was signed by Modern and started an association that lasted until 1962.

In 1951, he scored a #1 R&B hit with *Three O'Clock Blues*, the first of a series of R&B hits. Throughout the 1950s he toured continually and built his reputation with a live act that would remain essentially unchanged for the rest of his career. In 1962 he was given an advance of $25,000 to join ABC – this was prompted by Modern's inability to sell his records beyond the "race" market. His first records for ABC were overproduced, but in 1965 they released *Live at the Regal*; this was the first time that the raw excitement of one of his concerts had been successsfully captured on record. Its success was part of a process that would culminate in his decision in 1969 to aim at white rock- oriented audiences instead of continuing to play the chitlin' circuit.

His attraction for white audiences was based upon the large number of US and UK blues musicians like John Mayall, Eric Clapton, Mike Bloomfield, Paul Butterfield, Bob Hite of Canned Heat and Alexis Korner, among others – who had consistently championed his work by recording their own versions of his material. It was through this avenue that he had his biggest hits: *Rock me Baby* (USA #34.1964) and *The Thrill is Gone* (USA #15.1970). The LP *Completely Well* (USA#38.1970), included string arrangements, notably on the single, *The Thrill is Gone;* later the same year, he teamed up with white musicians like Leon Russell and Joe Walsh for the LP *Indianola Mississippi Seeds* (USA#26.1970); three singles were extracted, including *Ask Me*

no Questions (USA#40.1971). After another live LP, *Live in Cook County Jail* (USA #25.1971), he teamed up with what amounted to a who's who of British R&B for the LP *B. B. King in London*. In 1973 he released the Stevie WONDER composition, *To Know You is to Love You* (USA#38.1973), from the LP of the same name; another single, *I Like to Live the Love* (USA#28.1973) was also extracted. Throughout the latter half of the 1970s his most consistent records featured him in partnership with artists like Bobby BLAND and The CRUSADERS; with The Crusaders, he recorded the LP *Midnight Believer* in 1978.

During the 1980s, he has continued recording and touring. Although he won a Grammy in 1987 for his lifetime achievements, the extent of his reputation and the degree of his contribution to contemporary music have never been reflected in his record sales. It is a measure of his influence, however, that groups like U2 have continued to champion his influence upon them, by featuring him as a guest artist on their world tour in 1989-90.

LIVE AT THE REGAL, Ace, 1964
LUCILLE, BGO, 1968
COMPLETELY WELL, MCA, 1970
INDIANOLA MISSISSIPPI SEEDS, Castle, 1970
IN LONDON, BGO, 1971
THE INCREDIDIBLE SOUL OF B. B. KING, Musidisc, 1970
MIDNIGHT BELIEVER, MCA, 1978
TAKE IT HOME, MCA, 1979
NOW APPEARING AT OLE MISS, MCA, 1980
THE BEST OF B. B. KING, MCA. 1983
ROCK ME BABY, Ace, 1984
20 BLUES GREATS, Deja Vu, 1985
KING OF THE BLUES GUITAR, Ace, 1985
SIX SILVER STRINGS, MCA, 1985
AMBASSADOR OF THE BLUES, Crown, 1986
THE BEST OF B. B. KING, VOLUME 1, Ace, 1986
SPOTLIGHT ON LUCILLE, Ace, 1986
THE BEST OF B. B. KING, VOLUME 2, Ace, 1987

LIVE, Kingdom, 1987
ONE NIGHTER BLUES, Ace, 1987
RAREST B. B. KING, Blues Boy, 1987
KING OF THE BLUES, MCA, 1989
LUCILLE HAD A BABY, Ace, 1989
B.B BOOGIE, Blue Moon, 1990
LIVE AT SAN QUENTIN, MCA, 1990

KING, BEN E. Although the career of The DRIFTERS has been chequered, they have recorded some of the finest and earliest examples of smooth sophisticated soul, characterised by lush arrangements and memorable melodies from the pens of some of New York's finest songwriting partnerships. The voice of lead singer Ben E. King was, from 1958 until 1960, the trademark of their sound.

King was born Benjamin Earl Nelson on September 23, 1938 in Henderson, North Carolina, where he sang in church choirs before moving to Harlem. He joined The Crowns in 1957, after an unsuccessful audition for The Moonglows (see FUQUA, Harvey). In 1958 the manager of The Drifters, George Treadwell, having fired the original group, hired The Crowns to become The Drifters. In 1960, despite their success, the group were still being poorly paid by Treadwell. King complained and offered his resignation, which was promptly accepted. He signed with Atlantic subsidiary Atco and started a solo career with LEIBER & STOLLER producing.

His first records as a soloist were *Spanish Harlem* (USA#10.1961) and *Stand by Me* (USA#4.1961/#9.1986; UK#27.1961/#1.1987), both of which formed the bedrock of his career. They were followed by *Amor* (USA#18; UK #38.1961), *Don't Play that Song (You Lied)* (USA#11.1962) and *I (Who Have Nothing)* (USA#29.1963), which proved to be his final hits until the mid-1970s. Throughout the late 1960s and early 1970s, his career was in decline due to unsuitable material and arrangements:

had he been packed off to Muscle Shoals or Stax the story might have been different, but instead he was left to ply his trade on the cabaret and club circuit. However, when the much vaunted Soul Clan (see BURKE, Solomon) finally recorded a single in 1968, he was featured instead of Wilson PICKETT, who had become a star in his own right. In 1975 he was re-signed to Atlantic and recorded the LP *Supernatural* (USA#38.1975). The single from it, *Supernatural Thing* (USA#5.1975), proved to be a big dance-floor filler, slotting neatly into the pervasive disco mode.

In 1977 he teamed up with The AVERAGE WHITE BAND for the LP *Benny and Us* (USA#33.1977), after which he suffered more lean years and reverted to the omnipresent club circuit. His career was revitalised in 1986 by the film *Stand by Me*, which featured his song as the theme, and in 1987 the UK advertising agency Bartle, Bogle & Hegarty featured the same song in a commercial for jeans. That year his revived fortunes prompted EMI to sign him to their subsidiary, Manhattan. The ensuing LP, predictably titled *Save the Last Dance for Me* featured a variety of producers, including Mick Jones and Lamont Dozier (see HOLLAND, DOZIER & HOLLAND).

STREET TOUGH, Atlantic, 1981
GREATEST HITS, Dynamic, 1984
HERE COMES THE NIGHT, Edsel, 1984
STAND BY ME: THE ULTIMATE COLLECTION, Atlantic, 1987
SAVE THE LAST DANCE FOR ME, Manhattan, 1987

KING, CAROLE See GOFFIN & KING

KING, EARL Despite his eminence as a session guitarist and the consistently high standard of his material, Earl King's records have remained well-kept secrets. He was raised in New Orleans and became an integral part of the New Orleans club scene. He was signed to Specialty, where he recorded tracks like the self-composed *Trick Bag* and *Let the Good Times Roll*. In 1955 he was signed by Johnny VINCENT, his producer at Specialty, to the newly established Ace label. Over the next few years he cut a string of records including *Those Lonely Lonely Nights, It must have been Love* and *My Love is Strong*. Although many credited Vincent as joint composer, it seems likely that Vincent was following the old principle that putting up the money for the session warranted a slice of the composer's royalty. After parting company with Vincent he was signed to Imperial by Dave BARTHO-LOMEW in 1959, where he recorded an immaculate version of the Guitar Slim composition, *The Things that I Used to Do*. However, he stopped recording under his own name to concentrate on writing and session work for artists like DOCTOR JOHN, Lee DORSEY and The Meters (see NEVILLE BROTHERS). He returned to recording in 1986, backed by the group Roomful Of Blues, cutting the excellent LP *Glazed* for the New Orleans label, Black Top.

LET THE GOOD TIMES ROLL, Ace, 1983
GLAZED, (with Roomful Of Blues), Demon, 1986
TRICK BAG, Stateside, 1987
STREET PARADE, Charly, 1990

KING, EVELYN 'CHAMPAGNE'

Evelyn 'Champagne' King was born in the Bronx, New York City, on June 29, 1960. During the 1950s, her father had been a member of groups like The Orioles and The Harptones, and so her musical aspirations were encouraged from an early age. Her family moved to Philadelphia in 1970, and in 1976 she turned professional playing the thriving club circuit.

In 1977, while filling in for her sister, who was a cleaner at the Sigma sound studios, she was heard singing by the writer and producer, T. Life. In 1978 she was signed by RCA, for whom she recorded a string of hits over the next eight years: *Shame* (USA#9; UK #39.1978), *I Don't Know if it's Right* (USA#23; UK#67.1979), *I'm in Love* (USA#40; UK #27.1981), *If You Want my Lovin'* (UK #43.1981), *Love Come Down* (USA#17; UK #7.1982), *Back to Love* (UK#40.1982), *Get Loose* (UK#45.1983), *Your Personal Touch* (UK#37.1985) and *High Horse* (UK#55.1986). Her style was tailored to the dance-floor, which ensured that her LPs – often containing extended versions of the singles – sold consistently well: *Smooth Talk* (USA#14.1978), *Music Box* (USA#35.1979), *I'm in Love* (USA #28.1981) and *Get Loose* (USA#27; UK #35.1982).

In 1987 she changed record companies, signing with the Manhattan label. Her next LP *Flirt* was produced by, among others, Leon Sylvers and "Wah Wah" Watson, who conspired to give her a tougher, yet more sophisticated sound, which did not depend exclusively upon the volatile trends of the dance-floor for its appeal.

I'M IN LOVE, RCA, 1981
GET LOOSE, RCA, 1982
CHAMPAGNE, RCA, 1983
SO ROMANTIC, RCA, 1984
LONG TIME COMING, RCA, 1985
FLIRT, Manhattan, 1988
THE BEST OF EVELYN "CHAMPAGNE" KING, RCA, 1990

KING CURTIS

Curtis Ousley was born in Fort Worth, Texas in 1934. When he was sixteen he moved to New York and started to play saxophone in Lionel Hampton's Band. By 1953 he had started to record in his own jazz group; however, with Sam "The Man" Taylor, his robust style of playing quickly secured him work on the burgeoning session circuit. From 1956 until 1971 he backed just about everyone from The COASTERS through Jimi HENDRIX to Aretha FRANKLIN. In 1962 he had his first hit in his own right, *Soul Twist* (USA#17.1962), with his group The Noble Knights for Bobby ROBINSON'S Enjoy label. In 1967 he had another two hits with The Kingpins, which featured Tommy COGBILL, Donny HATHAWAY, Cornell Dupree and Chuck Rainey, among others: *Memphis Soul Stew* (USA#33.1967) and *Ode to Billie Joe* (USA#28.1967). On August 14, 1971, he died of stab wounds sustained in a street fight in New York, aged 37. It was a tragic end to a career which, at the time of his death, seemed destined to go through the roof in his new capacity as leader of Aretha Franklin's backing band.

JAZZ GROOVE, Prestige, 1980
20 GOLDEN PIECES, Bulldog, 1982
KING CURTIS, Red Lightnin', 1983
LIVE IN NEW YORK, JSP, 1985
SOUL GROOVE, Blue Moon, 1987
DIDN'T HE PLAY, Red Lightnin', 1989
INSTANT GROOVE, Edsel, 1990

KING FLOYD In 1970 Wardell QUEZERGUE arrived at Malaco in Jackson to record *Funky Thing* by The Uunemployed. Such was its success, that the next time he came, he brought a bus load of artists he'd been working with in New Orleans. One of them was King Floyd. Under the aegis of Tommy COUCH and Quezergue, Floyd cut *What Our Love Needs* and *Groove Me* for Couch's Chimneyville label. Initially it failed, until DJs started to play the B-side, *Groove Me* (USA #6.1970). Floyd was to have one more sizable hit, *Baby Let me Kiss You* (USA#29.1971), before disappearing into obscurity.

KINGS OF RHYTHM See TURNER, IKE

KNIGHT, FREDERICK Frederick Knight was born on August 15, 1944, in Birmingham, Alabama. Before joining Stax, among his better known titles were *Throw the Switch* on Mercury, with Buddy KILLEN producing, and *Have a Little Mercy* for Capitol. At Stax his reputation as a performer was based on one notable hit, *I've Been Lonely for so Long* (USA #27.1972). From performing he began to establish a reputation as a writer and producer. After the Stax's collapse he moved to Henry STONE'S TK label in Miami, where he produced the novelty hit *Ring my Bell* for Anita Ward in 1979. However, with the gradual decline of TK because of financial problems, he moved to the Malaco label in Jackson, where he has collaborated with Bobby BLAND, Dorothy MOORE and LITTLE MILTON, among others.

KNIGHT, GLADYS, & THE PIPS When she was seven, Gladys Knight won $2,000 for her rendition of *Too Young* on US TV's *Ted Mack's Original Amateur Hour*. She was born in Atlanta, Georgia on May 28, 1944. In 1952, with her brother Merald (born September 4, 1942 in Atlanta) and her sister Brenda, she formed a vocal group with their cousins William (born June 2, 1941 in Atlanta) and Eleanor Guest, and they started to perform at the local church, singing gospel. By 1957 they had turned professional at the suggestion of another cousin James "Pips" Wood; they called themselves The Pips after him and he became their manager. They secured a one-off contract with Brunswick and recorded *Whistle My Love*. It failed to sell, but it enabled them to obtain work supporting established performers like Sam COOKE and Jackie WILSON. In 1959 Langston George and

Edward Patten (born August 2, 1939 in Atlanta) joined the group to replace Brenda Knight and Eleanor Guest, both of whom left to get married. The group continued touring, building up their reputation and developing their live act.

In 1960 they recorded *Every Beat of my Heart* (USA#6.1961) for the local Huntom label, who sold it to VeeJay. The following year they were signed to Bobby ROBINSON's Fury label, where they re-recorded *Every Beat of my Heart*. Curiously, both versions charted separately. The next year they recorded *Letter Full of Tears* (USA#19.1962), which was followed by the less successful *Operator*, after which George left the group; Gladys herself left to get married and start a family. The remainder of the group concentrated upon session work until Gladys rejoined them in 1964.

Her return was marked by a new contract, this time to the independent Maxx label. The debut single, *Giving Up* (USA#38.1964), was written by Van McCOY; after another single the label went bankrupt. They remained without a recording contract for two years, during which time they toured incessantly. In 1966 they were signed to the Motown subsidiary Soul, where they remained until 1973. At Motown, despite the comparative lack of attention they were accorded they still managed to make some of the best records to come out of the label; this was due to producers and songwriters like Johnny BRISTOL, Norman WHITFIELD and ASHFORD & SIMPSON, who were part of the Motown furniture and knew how to get the best out of far lesser voices than Knight's – and succeeded, with hits like: *Take Me in Your Arms and Love Me* (UK#13.1967), *Everybody Needs Love* (USA#39.1967), *I Heard it Through the Grapevine* (USA#2; UK#47.1967), *The End of Our Road* (USA#15.1968), *It Should Have Been Me* (USA#40.1968), *The Nitty Gritty* (USA#19.1969), *Friendship Train* (USA#17.1969),

You Need Love Like I Do (Don't You?) (USA#25.1970), *If I Were Your Woman* (USA#9.1970), *I Don't Want to Do Wrong* (USA#17.1971), *Make Me the Woman that You Go Home to* (USA#27.1972), *Just Walk in My Shoes* (UK#35.1972), *Help Me Make it Through the Night* (USA#33; UK#11.1972), *Look of Love* (UK#21.1973), *Neither One of Us (Wants to be the First to Say Goodbye)* (USA#2; UK#31.1973) and *Daddy Could Swear I Declare* (USA#19.1973).

At the end of their contract with Motown, The Pips were signed to Buddah, where they remained until 1977. Unlike most Motown defectors, they sustained their success, although their records were, superficially, rather tame and cliche-ridden; however, such was the quality and range of Gladys Knight's voice that even the most banal lyric became affecting: *Where Peaceful Waters Flow* (USA#28.1973), *Midnight Train to Georgia* (USA#1.1973; UK#10.1976), *I've Got to Use my Imagination* (USA#4.1974), *Best Thing that Ever Happened to Me* (USA#3.1974; UK#7.1975), *On and On* (USA#5.1974), *I Feel a Song (In My Heart)* (USA#21.1974), *The Way We Were/Try to Remember* (USA#11; UK#4.1975), *Part Time Love* (USA#22; UK#30.1975), *Make Yours a Happy Home* (UK#35.1976), *So Sad the Song* (UK#20.1976), *Nobody but You* (UK#34.1977), *Baby Don't Change Your Mind* (UK#4.1977), *Home Is Where the Heart Is* (UK#35.1977), *The One and Only* (UK#32.1978), *Come Back and Finish what You Started* (UK#15.1978) and *It's a Better Than Good Time* (UK#59.1978).

In 1977 they tried to sign with CBS but became embroiled in a legal tussle with Motown over unpaid royalties. For three years they were unable to record together and, although they recorded separately, they lost their momentum. By 1980, having resolved their contractual problems, they signed with CBS, where they stayed until 1985. Although they had few hits at CBS, they were teamed with Ashford & Simpson and produced some of the best work of their career. In 1985 they moved to MCA and Knight teamed up with Dionne WARWICK, Stevie WONDER and Elton John for the single, *That's what Friends are For*. In 1988, they had their biggest hit for over ten years with *Love Overboard* (USA#13; UK#42.1988). The same year Gladys recorded the theme for the James Bond film *Licence to Kill*.

NITTY GRITTY, Motown, 1969
HELP ME MAKE IT THROUGH THE NIGHT, Motown, 1972
NEITHER ONE OF US, Motown, 1973
IMAGINATION, Buddah, 1974
THE BEST OF GLADYS KNIGHT & THE PIPS, Buddah, 1976
STILL TOGETHER, Buddah, 1977
THE ONE AND ONLY, Buddah, 1978
AT LAST .... THE PIPS, Casablanca, 1978
CALLIN', (The Pips), Casablanca, 1978
MEMORIES OF THE WAY WE WERE, Buddah, 1979
MISS GLADYS KNIGHT, Buddah, 1979
ANTHOLOGY, Motown, 1981
20 GOLDEN GREATS, Motown, 1981
TEEN ANGUISH, Charly, 1981
EVERY BEAT OF MY HEART, Motown, 1982
JUKE BOX GIANTS, Audio Fidelity, 1982
LOOKING BACK: THE FURY YEARS, Bulldog, 1982
THE TASTE OF BITTER LOVE, Hallmark, 1983
BEFORE NOW AFTER THEN, Cambra, 1984
BLESS THIS HOUSE, Buddah, 1984
ALL THE GREATEST HITS, Motown, 1985
COLLECTION, Starblend, 1985
GLADYS KNIGHT & THE PIPS, Cambra, 1985
REPLAY ON, Sierra, 1986 17
GREATEST HITS, Motown, 1986
THE CBS YEARS: 1980-85, CBS, 1988
THE SINGLES ALBUM, Polygram, 1990
THE WAY WE WERE, Music Club, 1991

KNIGHT, JEAN A veritable one-hit wonder, Jean Knight hit the big time in 1971 with *Mr Big Stuff* (USA#2.1971). It was produced by Wardell QUEZERGUE for the fledgling Malaco label, who leased it out for distribution by Stax. Prior to her success with this one single, she had recorded with Huey P. MEAUX in New Orleans, where she had originally met up with Quezergue. Although, she continued to record for a while she could not repeat her former success, and she disappeared from sight.

MR BIG STUFF, Stax, 1971

KNIGHT, ROBERT In 1967 the British group The Love Affair had a monster hit with a cover version of the Robert Knight original *Everlasting Love* (USA#13; UK#40.1967/ #19.1974), which promptly generated interest in the original version and in Knight himself. He was born in Nashville in 1945. He formed The Paramounts in 1961 with drummer Kenny Buttrey, who has become one of Nashville's crack session musicians. They were signed to Dot; although they had a slight success, Knight gave up the music business in preference to chemical research at Tennessee University. However, in 1967 he was heard singing at a party by Mac Gayden, who signed him to the Rising Sons label, which was distributed by Monument. In 1973 *Love on a Mountain Top* (UK#10.1973) became a big hit for him in the UK, due to its popularity on the Northern Soul circuit, and *Everlasting Love* was reissued for a renewed run in the charts. Since these slices of good fortune he has slipped from sight, although both records have become Northern Soul Classics.

KOOL & THE GANG This group was formed by Robert "Kool" Bell in 1964 in New

Jersey while he was still at school. At first it was known as The Jazziacs, through the influence of Bell's father, who had played with Thelonius Monk. The line-up was Bell (bass; born October 8, 1950, in Youngstown, Ohio), his brother, Ronald (saxophones; born November 1, 1951, in Youngstown), George Brown (drums; born January 5, 1949, in New Jersey), Dennis Thomas (saxophones; born February 9, 1951, in New Jersey), Rick Westfield (keyboards), Robert Mickens (trumpet) and Woody Sparrow (guitar); in 1967, Claydes Smith (guitar; born September 6, 1948, in New Jersey) replaced Sparrow. Although the group continued playing jazz, gradually their style moved more towards R&B and Soul. By 1968, they had changed their name to The New Dimension; they then became The New Flames before eventually adopting Kool & The Gang as their name. The next year they met the owner of the recently formed De-Lite label, Gene Redd, who was sufficiently impressed with their act to offer them a recording contract.

Their earliest singles showed their strong jazz influence and established them as one of the earliest purveyors of jazz-funk: *Kool and the Gang*; *The Gang's Back Again*; *Let the Music Take Your Mind* and *Funky Man*. Their first major breakthrough came with *Funky Stuff* (USA#29.1973). From the LP, *Wild and Peaceful* (USA#33.1973), it has remained a cornerstone of their act and become one of the stock records of the funk era. The same LP provided them with their next single, *Jungle Boogie* (USA#4.1974). Throughout the latter half of the 1970s, their blend of jazz-funk was eclipsed by the disco fad, but in 1978 they teamed up with producer Eumir Deodato and enlisted vocalist James Taylor (born August 16, 1953 in South Carolina).

The arrival of a vocalist enabled them to expand their horizons; furthermore, Deodato's influence, which was based upon a strong jazz-oriented sensibility, enabled them to develop a style that was more commercial and accessible. The chemistry worked with the first LP, *Ladies Night* (USA#13.1979), which included the singles *Ladies Night* (USA#8; UK#9.1979) and *Too Hot* (USA#5; UK#23.1980). Their next LP, *Celebrate!* (USA#10.1981), included three singles – *Celebration* (USA#1.1981; UK#7.1980), *Jones vs. Jones* (USA#39; UK#17.1981) and *Take it to the Top* (UK#15.1981) – as did the LP *Something Special* (USA#12; UK#10.1982) – *Steppin' Out* (UK#12.1981), *Take my Heart (You Can Have it if You Want it)* (USA#17.1981; UK#29. 1982) and *Get Down on It* (UK#3; UK#10.1982). The LP *As One* (USA#29; UK#49.1982) was their final collaboration with Deodato. It included the statutory three singles: *Big Fun* (USA#21; UK#14.1982), *Oooh La La La (Let's Go Dancing)* (USA#30.1983; UK#6.1982) and *Hi De Hi, Hi De Ho* (UK#29.1983).

With Deodato's departure they took over the production chores themselves for the LP *In the Heart* (USA#29; UK#18.1984). Another four singles were extracted: *Straight Ahead* (UK#15.1983), *Joanna* (USA#2.1983; UK #2.1984), *Tonight* (USA#13.1984) and *(When You Say You Love Somebody) In the Heart* (UK#7.1984). After Bell and Taylor's participation in the Band Aid single, *Do They Know it's Christmas?*, they released the LP *Emergency* (USA#28; UK#47.1984), which featured the singles: *Misled* (USA#10; UK#28.1985), *Fresh* (USA#9.1985; UK#11.1984), *Cherish* (USA#2; UK#4.1985) and *Emergency* (USA#18; UK #50.1985). In 1987 Curtis Williams joined the group on keyboards, as did trombonist Clifford Adams and trumpeter Michael Ray. Their final LP with vocalist James Taylor, who was to leave in 1988 for a solo career, was *Forever* (USA#25.1987); it included the singles, *Victory* (USA#10.1987; UK#30.1986) and *Stone Love* (USA#10; UK#45.1987). Taylor's replacements were Dean Mays and two former members of the Dazz Band, Gary Brown and Skip Martin. In 1989 they released the LP *Sweat*, which failed to impress record buyers as much as their previous offerings.

LADIES NIGHT, De-Lite, 1979
CELEBRATE, De-Lite, 1981
SOMETHING SPECIAL, De-Lite, 1982
AS ONE, De-Lite, 1982
KOOL KUTS, De-Lite, 1982
IN THE HEART, De-Lite, 1983
TWICE AS KOOL, De-Lite, 1983
EMERGENCY, De-Lite, 1985
FOREVER, Club, 1986
VICTORY, Club, 1986
THE SINGLES COLLECTION, Club, 1988
SWEAT, Phonogram, 1989
AT THEIR BEST, De-Lite, 1989

LA & BABYFACE Antonio "LA" Reid and Kenny "Babyface" Edmonds were both members of the Cincinnati group, The Deele, with whom they remained for five years. In 1987 they launched out on their own, writing and producing *Rock Steady* for The WHIS-PERS. As a result they were enlisted to work on the second Bobby BROWN LP, *Don't Be Cruel*. Other artists they have worked with include Pebbles, Paula Abdul, Sheena Easton, Perri, Karyn WHITE and, more recently still, Johnny GILL. In 1989 Babyface released a solo LP, *Tender Lover*, which proved that, as a performer in his own right, he may well have a future.

TENDER LOVER, (Babyface), Solar, 1989

LaBELLE, PATTI Patti LaBelle was born Patricia Holt on May 24, 1944, in Philadel-phia. In 1961 she formed The Bluebelles with Cindy Birdsong, whom she had sung with at school in The Ordettes; the line-up was com-pleted by Sarah Dash and Nona HENDRYX,

both of whom had been members of The Del-Capris. After performing locally they were signed by producer Bobby Martin to the New-town label. Their debut, *I Sold My Heart to the Junkman* (USA#15.1962), coincided with the national success of all-girl groups; to empha-sise the point, Martin altered the billing for subsequent records to Patti LaBelle & The Bluebelles. They had to wait until the end of 1963 for their next hit, *Down the Aisle (The Wedding Song)* (USA#37.1963). The following year they were signed to the subsidiary of Cameo, Parkway, where they recorded a cover version of *You'll Never Walk Alone* (USA #34.1964) from the musical *Carousel*. Through-out the latter half of the 1960s they failed to generate much attention, and in 1967, Bird-song left the group to join The SUPREMES. In 1970 they acquired a new manager, Vicki Wickham, who had been involved in the UK TV programme, *Ready Steady Go!* She altered their image by changing the name of the group to LaBelle and securing a fresh recording con-tract with Warner Bros.

Their debut for Warner Bros., *LaBelle*, gen-erated a lot of good reviews, but failed com-mercially. However, Laura NYRO was sufficiently impressed by the group to enlist them as backing vocalists for her LP *It's Gonna Take a Miracle*. The next LaBelle LP, *Moon-shadow*, failed to sell, and their contract with Warner Bros. was not renewed. After another lay-off they signed with Epic and went to New Orleans to record the LP *Nightbirds* (USA #7.1975) with producer Allen TOUSSAINT and the crack session outfit, The Meters (see NEVILLE BROTHERS). It included the single *Lady Marmalade* (USA#1; UK #17.1975), written by Bob Crewe, who had composed most of The Four Seasons' hits, and Kenny Nolan. The next two LPs, *Phoenix* and *Chameleon*, failed to sustain the winning for-mula, and in 1976 the group split up to pursue solo careers.

Patti LaBelle remained with Epic until 1980, recording four LPs, none of them notable successes. In 1981 she was signed to GAMBLE & HUFF's Philadelphia International label. Her debut LP for them, *The Spirit's in It*, was well received critically. The following year she appeared to a rapturous reception on Broadway in the gospel musical, *Your Arm's too Short to Box with God*, with Al GREEN. After another hiatus she recorded the LP *I'm in Love Again* (USA#40.1984). It revitalised her career, prompting Bobby WOMACK to enlist her for a duet on his LP *The Poet II*. In 1985 she signed with MCA, recording *New Attitude* (USA#17.1985) for the soundtrack of the film *Beverly Hills Cop*, starring Eddie Murphy. Her debut LP for MCA, *The Winner in You* (USA#1; UK#30.1986), included a duet with Michael McDonald, *On My Own* (USA#1; UK#2.1986), as well as *Oh, People* (USA#29; UK#26.1986). In 1989 she released the follow-up LP, *Be Yourself*, which included contributions from PRINCE and Narada Michael WALDEN.

I'M IN LOVE AGAIN, Philadelphia International, 1984
THE BEST OF PATTI LaBELLE, Epic, 1986
THE WINNER IN YOU, MCA, 1986
BE YOURSELF, MCA, 1989

LAMBERT, DENNIS In a career spanning approximately three decades, Dennis Lambert has written for or produced almost everyone at some point or another – often in partnership with Brian Holland (see HOLLAND, DOZIER & HOLLAND) or Brian Potter. It is a measure of the esteem in which he is held that he is usually called upon to revitalise flagging careers: *Keeper of the Castle* for The FOUR TOPS in 1972, *Rock 'n' Roll Heaven* for The RIGHTEOUS BROTHERS in 1974, *Don't Look any Further* for Dennis EDWARDS in 1984, *Nightshift* for The COM-

MODORES in 1984, *Pink Cadillac* (1988) and *Miss You Like Crazy* (1989) for Natalie COLE, *Never Been Better* for The O'JAYS in 1989 and *Take Me Through the Night* for Smokey ROBINSON in 1990.

LaVETTE, BETTY Betty LaVette is another of soul's great secrets. She was born in Detroit, Michigan and started to perform on the club and chitlin' circuit, before cutting some sides with Atlantic and then LuPine. In 1965 she recorded the country classic, *Let Me Down Easy*, for the independent Calla label. While her reputation steadily grew she was compelled to rely on the club circuit for her living. In 1969 Lelan Rogers signed her to the Sound Stage Seven subsidiary, Silver Fox, where she recorded a string of tracks like *He Made a Woman Out of Me*, *I'm in Love* and the Joe SOUTH composition *Games People Play*; recorded in Nashville and backed by the nucleus of the DIXIE FLYERS they remain perfect examples of Southern soul.

More years in the doldrums ensued until, in 1979, she returned to Atlantic for the single *Doing the Best I Can*. In 1982, having signed to Motown, two singles were released, *You Seen One You Seen 'em All* and *I Can't Stop*, both taken from the LP *Tell me a Lie*. However, she has recorded little in recent years.

TELL ME A LIE, Motown, 1982
NEARER TO YOU, Charly, 1991

LEE, JACKIE See BOB & EARL

LEE, LAURA Laura Lee started her career as a gospel singer in church in her native Chicago during the late 1950s. As a member of the gospel group The Meditations, she toured constantly. In 1965, she was signed by Chess, who didn't know quite what to do with her, until she was sent down to record at Rick HALL's Fame studios. At Fame she recorded a string of songs like *Dirty Man, Love more than Pride* and *A Man with some Backbone*. The lyrics contained strong assertions of female independence: in the early 1970s Lee, along with Betty WRIGHT and Millie JACKSON, was to become an arch-exponent of that genre. During a spell with one of the HOLLAND, DOZIER & HOLLAND labels, Hot Wax, she recorded tracks like *Rip Off* and *Women's Love Rights* (USA#36.1971); the latter was included on the unjustly neglected LP, *The Two Sides of Laura Lee*. However, during the 1980s she returned to gospel, working occasionally with Al GREEN.

THAT'S HOW IT IS, Chess, 1988

LEIBER & STOLLER. Jerry Leiber was born in Baltimore on April 25, 1933, and Mike Stoller on Long Island on March 13, 1933. Since their first meeting in 1950, their songwriting and production partnership has, like a colossus, bestrode the formative years of contemporary popular music. While many white writers have been able to contribute very successfully to the canon of R&B and soul, few have achieved it with as much panache as Leiber & Stoller. The reason for this has been their ability to capture the vernacular of the street – in other words, the lyrical content was entirely credible within the context of the performer. Throughout their long career, songs like *Hound Dog* for Big Mama THORNTON, *Jailhouse Rock* and *Love Me* for Elvis Presley, *Yakety Yak, Searchin', Poison Ivy, Young Blood* and *Charlie Brown* for The COASTERS, *Kansas City* for Wilbert HARRISON, *There Goes my Baby* and *On Broadway* for The DRIFTERS and *Spanish Harlem* and *Stand by Me* for Ben E. KING have all contributed to the understanding of the term rock 'n' roll.

In 1964 they cofounded the Red Bird label with producer George GOLDNER. The first release was *Chapel of Love* by The DIXIE CUPS: it went to #1 and stayed there for three weeks. After selling their share of the label in 1966 they diversified, working throughout the late 1960s and early 1970s with artists like Peggy Lee, Procol Harum, Stealers Wheel and Elkie Brooks. During the 1980s they have continued to diversify with projects like *Hound Dog*, an animated film feature, and *Yakety Yak*, an autobiographical documentary. In 1969 they acquired the King catalogue from Syd NATHAN's estate but, surprisingly, were unable to capitalise upon this asset and sold it in 1972. In 1980 they assembled the musical, *Only in America*, which included thirty of their more celebrated compositions.

ONLY IN AMERICA, (Various Artists), WEA, 1980

LEWIS, BARBARA Barbara Lewis was born on February 9, 1944, in Detroit. In 1961 she was scouted by Ollie McLaughlin, who had been a DJ with the local radio station in Ann Arbor, Michigan. After discovering Del Shannon, he gave up DJ-ing in preference to production and management. At first Lewis recorded at the Chess studios in Chicago and at the Motown studios in Detroit. The following year she had her first hit with *Hello Stranger* (USA#3.1963), but subsequent records failed to sell. In 1964 she went to New York to be produced by Bert BERNS, obtaining a recording contract with the Atlantic label. Over the next two years she had a further four hits: *Puppy Love* (USA#38.1964), *Baby, I'm Yours* (USA#11.1965), *Make Me Your Baby* (USA#11.1965) and *Make Me Belong to You* (USA#28.1966). However, in 1967, after a few failures, she retired from the music industry.

LEWIS, RAMSEY Ramsey Lewis was born on May 27, 1935 in Chicago. His career started while still at school when he played piano at his local church. By 1955 when he formed his first trio, he had studied classical music at Chicago School of Music and been a member of The Clefs. His first trio was made up by former Clefs, bassist Eldee Young and drummer Isaac Holt, and they were signed by Chess to the subsidiary Cadet. With the success of instrumental groups like BOOKER T & THE MGs, Lewis moved further and further from jazz . In 1965 he had the first of a series of hit singles, *The "In" Crowd* (USA#5.1965); it was followed by *Hang On Sloopy* (USA#11.1965), *A Hard Day's Night* (USA#29.1966) and *Wade In The Water* (USA#19; UK#31.1966). The LPs, *The "In" Crowd* (USA#2.1965), *Hang On Ramsey* (USA#15.1966) and *Wade In The Water* (USA#16.1966), consolidated his appeal.

In 1966, Holt and Young left to form Young–Holt Unlimited, who had hits with *Wack Wack* (USA#40.1967) and *Soulful Strut* (USA#3.1968) on Brunswick. Lewis replaced them with drummer Maurice White and bassist Cleveland Eaton. In 1969, White left to form EARTH, WIND & FIRE. Over the years Lewis has continued to record, his most successful LP being *Sun Goddess* (USA#12.1975), produced by White. *Legacy* (1979) saw him augmenting the basic trio format with woodwind sections and, in 1984, he recorded *The Two of Us*, with Nancy Wilson. However, since the successes of the 1960s his records have lacked fire, settling for an anodyne tunefulness instead.

REUNION, CBS, 1984
HIS GREATEST SIDES, Chess, 1987
KEYS TO THE CITY, CBS, 1987
GREATEST HITS, Chess, 1990

LEWIS, SMILEY During the 1950s Smiley Lewis was one of the most influential R&B artist in New Orleans. Backed by the Dave BARTHOLOMEW Band, he issued a series of records that were just "too black" for mass appeal, and it was left to artists like Fats DOMINO to promote the cause of the "Crescent City".

Lewis was born Overton Amos Lemons on July 5, 1913, in DeQuincy, Louisiana. His career started in the 1930s when he played the clubs first as a soloist and then as the member of the trio he formed. After recording for DeLuxe, he was signed to the Imperial label in 1950, where he remained until 1960, cutting a string of singles that embodied the finer points of New Orleans R&B: *Tee Nah Na, The Bells are Ringing, Blue Monday, I Hear You Knocking, One Night* and *Shame Shame Shame*. In the 1960s, having left Imperial, he recorded for a number of other labels until his death on October 7, 1966.

I SHALL NOT BE MOVED, Official, 1989
NEW ORLEANS BOUNCE: 30 0F HIS BEST, Sequel, 1990

LEWIS, STAN In 1945 Stan Lewis expanded his business in jukeboxes to include a record shop, based on Texas Street, Shreveport, Louisiana. By 1950 the shop had expanded to embrace mail-order and distribution, and in 1951 he started to advertise regularly through the local radio network. In the early 1960s he started his first record label, Jewel, whose first signing was Bobby Charles. In 1965 he formed two further labels, Paula and Ronn, which left the Jewel label free to concentrate upon its roster of blues and gospel artists like Lightnin' Hopkins and Lowell Fulson. While Paula was devoted to pop signings, Ronn was devoted to soul and R&B; among the roster were Ted TAYLOR, Toussaint McCall and Little Johnny Taylor. At first Lewis used the Robin Hood Brian studios in Texas but, with the rapidly increasing profile of Rick HALL's Fame studios, Lewis began to send artists like Taylor off to Fame. By the early 1970s he had all but given up soul and had reverted to recording gospel and country music.

LEWIS, TERRY See JAM, Jimmy, & Terry Lewis

LITTLE ANTHONY & THE IMPERIALS Little Anthony & The Imperials have, in their various incarnations, been key members of the oldies circuit ever since its inception in the late 1960s. However, they have also managed to embrace changing fashions with greater success than many of their contemporaries.

Anthony Gourdine (born in New York on January 8, 1940) became a member of The Duponts in 1955 before leaving to form The Chesters with Tracy Lord, Ernest Wright, Clarence Collins and Glouster Rogers. They were signed in 1958 by Richard BARRETT to the End label, the name of the group being changed to Little Anthony & The Imperials. They were immediately successful with *Tears on my Pillow* (USA#4.1958), *A Prayer and a Jukebox* and *Shimmy, Shimmy Ko-Bop* (USA #24.1960); then Gourdine left for a solo career. In 1963 the group re-formed, with Sammy Strain replacing Lord, and were signed by Teddy Randazzo to the DCP label. Over the next two years they notched up another five hit singles: *I'm on the Outside (Looking In)* (USA #15.1964), *Goin' out of my Head* (USA#6.1964), *Hurt so Bad* (USA#10.1965), *Take me Back* (USA#16.1965) and *I Miss You So* (USA #34.1965). After leaving DCP for the Veep label and then for United Artists, they had a hit

with *Better Use Your Head* (UK#15.1976). However, Gourdine had recommenced his solo career and Strain had left to replace William Powell in The O'JAYS. In 1977 the group once more re-formed, this time for a European tour and a fresh contract with Power Exchange, where they had a hit with *Who's Gonna Love Me?* (UK#17.1977). Since then they have toured extensively on the cabaret and oldies circuits.

OUTSIDE LOOKIN' IN, Liberty, 1984
LITTLE ANTHONY AND THE IMPERIALS, Roulette, 1990

LITTLE DAVID See PORTER, David

LITTLE ESTHER See PHILLIPS, Esther

LITTLE EVA In the career of Eva Boyd (born June 29, 1945, in Bellhaven, North Carolina) there is a perfect example of how the opportunism of hit factories like the Brill Building actually works. She was acting as a babysitter for songwriters GOFFIN & KING when they suggested that she might like to sing a demo of *The Locomotion* (USA#3; UK #2.1962/#10.1974) so that they could present it to Dee Dee SHARP's producer. He didn't like it, but another producer, Don Kirshner, did, and released it on his his newly established Dimension label. Little Eva became a star overnight. Two more hits followed, *Keep Your Hands off My Baby* (USA#12; UK#30.1962) and *Let's Turkey Trot* (USA#20; UK#13.1963), and an uncredited duet with Big Dee Irwin on *Swinging on a Star* (USA#37.1963; UK #6.1964). Since then her career has gone into a complete decline: she has recorded for other labels, but without any success. In recent years, she has been living on welfare benefit and singing gospel. *The Locomotion* remains one of the few records never to have been deleted from either the US or UK catalogues.

L-L-L-L-LOCOMOTION, Decca, 1962

LITTLE MILTON Little Milton's reputation has been built upon his ability to transcend fashion with an almost effortless ease. While he has never been of the mainstream, as a journeyman he has performed and recorded throughout his career. That this career has lasted for over 35 years is proof of his enduring appeal.

He was born Milton Campbell in Inverness, Mississippi, on September 7, 1934, and brought up on gospel in his local church, where he regularly sang. In 1953 he got work with Ike TURNER, which led to a contract with the Sun label. After recording for Sun, he went to Meteor and Bobbin, where he met Oliver Sain, recording *Lonely Man* in 1958. In 1961 he was signed by Leonard CHESS to the Checker label, where he recorded *If Walls could Talk, Blind Man, We're Gonna Make It* (USA #25.1965), *Who's Cheating Who* and *Grits ain't Groceries*. After Chess collapsed, he was signed to Stax, where he remained until they in turn collapsed in 1976, after which he was signed by Henry STONE to Glades, a subsidiary of TK. At Glades, he recorded *Friend of Mine* and *Loving You*, both of which were R&B hits. When TK went out of business in the early 1980s he was signed by MCA. After recording *Age ain't Nothing but a Number* and *Let it be Me*, among others, he was signed to the Malaco label in 1984. Since joining Malaco, he has settled into a comfortable groove of producing very superior blues-oriented LPs like *Playing for Keeps, Annie Mae's Cafe, I Will Survive, Moving to the Country, Back to Back* and *Too Much Pain*, while touring constantly.

RAISE A LITTLE SAND, Red Lightnin', 1982
PLAYING FOR KEEPS, Malaco, 1984
ANNIE MAE'S CAFE, Malaco, 1986
HIS GREATEST HITS, Chess, 1987
LITTLE MILTON SINGS BIG BLUES, Chess, 1987
WE'RE GONNA MAKE IT, Chess, 1987
I WILL SURVIVE, Malaco, 1987
MOVING TO THE COUNTRY, Malaco, 1988
BACK TO BACK, Malaco, 1989
TOO MUCH PAIN, Malaco, 1990

LITTLE RICHARD Of all the performers who lay claim to the crown of rock 'n' roll, none is more worthy of the title than Little Richard: his charismatic performances – with his hair piled high in a pompadour and his face liberally daubed with mascara – were the catalyst of rock 'n' roll.

He was born Richard Wayne Penniman on December 5, 1935 in Macon, Georgia, one of twelve brothers and sisters; his parents, Charles and Leva Mae, ran the Tip In Inn. His career started in 1950 when he started to sing with the B. Brown Orchestra, having spent his childhood singing gospel in church choirs before running away to join Dr West's Medicine Show and then Sugarfoot Sam's Minstrel Show, which was where he learned the art of performing. In 1951 he cut some sides for RCA. In 1953 he moved to Houston where he recorded for Don ROBEY's Peacock Label with the group, The Tempo Toppers. After meeting Lloyd PRICE, he sent a demo to Art RUPE, the owner of Specialty Records in Los Angeles. Following an audition with "Bumps" BLACKWELL, the head of A&R at Specialty, he toured briefly with The Johnny OTIS Show.

In 1955 he started to record at the J&M studios in New Orleans with Blackwell producing. From then until his conversion to religion in October 1957 he made a series of records that changed the face of popular music: *Tutti Frutti* (USA#17.1956; UK #29.1957), *Long Tall Sally* (USA#6.1956; UK-#3.1957), *Rip it Up* (USA#17; UK#30. 1956/#37.1977), *The Girl Can't Help It* (UK #9.1957), *Lucille* (USA#21; UK#10.1957), *Jenny, Jenny* (USA#10; UK#11.1957), *Keep a Knocking* (USA#8; UK#21.1957), *Good Golly Miss Molly* (USA#10; UK#8.1958/#37.1977); *Ooh! My Soul* (USA#31; UK#22.1958), *Baby Face* (UK#2.1959), *By the Light of the Silvery Moon* (UK#17.1959) and *Kansas City* (UK #26.1959). His backing band on these records comprised some of the finest session musicians in the country; it was based around Alvin "Red" Tyler and Lee ALLEN (saxes), Frank Fields (bass), Ernest McLean and Justin Adams (guitars), Earl PALMER (drums) and Huey "Piano" SMITH and Richard himself (piano). (His touring band, The Upsetters, backed him on a couple of his hit singles, however). In 1957, he appeared in two films, *The Girl Can't Help It*, starring Jayne Mansfield, and *Don't Knock the Rock* with Bill Haley. In 1958 he was ordained as a Seventh-Day Adventist minister at Oakwood Theological College in Huntsville, Alabama.

From 1959 until 1962 he recorded gospel songs, including some for Mercury with Quincy JONES producing. In 1962 he returned to the arena with a comeback tour of the UK, where he headlined a concert at the Cavern Club in Liverpool which featured Cilla Black, Gerry & The Pacemakers and The Swinging Blue Jeans. This led to further tours of the UK and Europe the following year with groups like The Beatles, The Rolling Stones and The Everly Brothers. In 1964, he signed with the VeeJay label and re-recorded his greatest hits. This was the first of a series of different recording deals he would do: Modern in 1965, the CBS subsidiary Okeh in 1966, Brunswick in 1968, and Reprise in 1969. In 1972 he reunited with Palmer, Allen and Blackwell to record the LP *The Second Coming*. After the death of his

brother Tony in 1976, he became a fully fledged evangelist, preaching throughout the USA.

Since 1979 his profile as an evangelist and a personality has never been higher, with contributions to a number of films and documentaries, most notably *Down and out in Beverly Hills*, starring Bette Midler and Richard Dreyfus, and *Twins*, starring Arnold Schwarzenegger and Danny DeVito, in which he duetted with Philip BAILEY on the the title song. In 1988 he performed *Rock Island Line* on the Leadbelly and Woody Guthrie tribute LP, *Folkways: A Vision Shared*. Throughout his career, he has exerted such a strong influence upon other musicians that, irrespective of the number of hit records he has had, his presence is evident in the performance of artists from PRINCE to Paul McCartney.

FRIENDS FROM THE BEGINNING, (with Jimi Hendrix), Ember, 1974
NOW, Creole, 1977
HIS BIGGEST HITS, Sonet, 1980
LITTLE RICHARD, Sonet, 1980
SINGS GOSPEL FAVOURITES, Bulldog, 1982
WHOLE LOTTA SHAKIN', Bulldog, 1982
THE REAL THING, Magnum, 1983
GREATEST HITS, CBS, 1984
LUCILLE, CBS/Premier, 1984
THE BEST OF LITTLE RICHARD, Creole, 1984
HERE'S LITTLE RICHARD, Ace, 1985
HIS GREATEST RECORDINGS, Ace, 1985
THE FABULOUS LITTLE RICHARD, Ace, 1985
GOLDEN HIGHLIGHTS, CBS, 1986 20
CLASSIC CUTS, Ace, 1986
OOH! MA SOUL!, Magnum, 1986
ROCKIN' 'N' RAVIN', RCA, 1986
ROCK 'N' ROLL RESURRECTION, Charly, 1986
LIFETIME FRIEND, Warner Bros., 1986
16 ROCK AND ROLL CLASSICS, Arena, 1987
16 GREATEST HITS, Bescol, 1987
LITTLE RICHARD, Deja Vu, 1987
LITTLE RICHARD: THE COLLECTION, Castle, 1987

SLIPPIN', SLIDIN' AND SHAKIN', Charly, 1989
THE SPECIALTY SESSIONS, Ace, 1990
HERE'S LITTLE RICHARD, VOLUME 2, Ace, 1990

WALKING WITH A PANTHER, Def Jam, 1989
MAMA SAID KNOCK YOU OUT!, Def Jam, 1990

L. L. COOL J James Todd Smith was born in Queens, New York City, in 1968. By the time he was 13 he was already a proficient rapper and had started to send demos to record companies. In 1984 Rick Rubin, part-owner and producer of Def Jam Records, was so impressed by L. L. Cool J – which stands for 'Ladies Love Cool James' – that he was signed immediately. His first record, *I Need a Beat*, attracted enough attention to gain him a place on the bill of the New York City Fresh Festival, which was headlined by Run DMC and GRANDMASTER FLASH. As a result of Def Jam's international distribution deal with CBS, his debut LP, *Radio* (USA#46; UK #71.1986), was released in 1986. After two tours, one supporting Run DMC, and the other headlining Def Jam '87, which featured Public Enemy and Eric B, he released the LP, *Bigger and Deffer* (USA#3; UK#54.1987), which included the ballad, *I Need Love* (USA#14; UK#8.1987). It was followed by the Double A-side, *Goin' Back to Cali/Jack the Ripper* (USA#31; UK#37.1988). In 1990, he released the LP, *Mama Said Knock You Out* (UK#49.1990), which seemed to indicate an unhealthy propensity for the mainstream. L. L. Cool J has contributed to the overall acceptance of rap and hip-hop as much any other artist. His later records lack the same vital rawness that set apart his earlier records like *I Can't Live Without My Radio* and *Rock The Bells*, although he has shown a rather too great a reliance upon the machismo of his chosen role.

RADIO, Def Jam, 1986
BIGGER AND DEFFER, Def Jam, 1987

LOVE, ANDREW See JACKSON, Wayne

LOVE, DARLENE Unlike so many of Phil SPECTOR's signings, Darlene Wright was a professional session singer. She was born in Los Angeles in 1938. Her career started in 1958 as a member of The Blossoms. The group recorded in its own right for Capitol, Challenge and Okeh, but their most significant contribution was as backing vocalists. It was in this capacity that she met Spector in 1962 who was so impressed by her voice that he used her as lead vocalist on a string of hits under a variety of guises: *He's a Rebel* and *He's Sure the Boy I Love* by The CRYSTALS; in her own right (under the pseudonym of Darlene Love) on *(Today I Met) the Boy I'm Gonna Marry* (USA#39.1963) and *Wait 'Til My Bobby Gets Home* (USA#26.1963); and, as Bob B. Soxx & The Blue Jeans, which featured Bobby Sheen and Fanita James, *Zip-A-Dee Doo-Dah* (USA#8.1962; UK#45.1963) and *Why Do Lovers Break Each Other's Hearts* (USA #38.1963). After her success with Spector, she returned to session work, singing back-up vocals for Elvis Presley and Dionne WARWICK, among others. During the 1980s she appeared in the musicals, *Carrie* and *Leader of the Pack*, as well as playing a bit part in the film *Lethal Weapon*. In 1989 she released the LP *Paint Another Picture*. Unfortunately, her excellent voice was marred by the age-old problem: indifferent material and careless production.

PAINT ANOTHER PICTURE, CBS, 1989

LOVE UNLIMITED Love Unlimited was formed in the early sixties by Diane Parsons and Linda and Glodean James as The Croonettes in their hometown of San Pedro, California, while they were still at school. By the late 1960s the group had disbanded, but they were reunited when they were introduced to Barry WHITE by a girlfriend of Glodean James, Andrea Sprewell, who was recording an LP with White. White became their manager and producer, signing the group to the Uni label; after their first hit, *Walkin' in the Rain with the One I Love* (USA/UK#14.1972), White formed his own production company and signed the group to the 20th Century label. He and arranger Gene PAGE assembled a group of studio musicians, known collectively as The Love Unlimited Orchestra, who not only backed him on his own records but also became integral to the sound of the group and had hits in their own right with *Love's Theme* (USA#1.1973; UK#10.1974) and *Satin Soul* (USA#22.1975). In 1973 the group released the LP, *Under the Influence of Love Unlimited* (USA#3.1973). A single, *It May be Winter Outside (but in My Heart it's Spring)* (UK #11.1975) followed, and then came *I Belong To You* (USA#27.1975). By the end of 1975 the group had broken up. Glodean James had married White in 1974 and, although she recorded an LP with him in 1980 and there have been rumours of a new version of the group forming, nothing has materialised. Diane Parsons died of cancer in 1985, and Linda James remarried, moving to Switzerland in 1978.

LTD See OSBORNE, Jeffrey

LYMON, FRANKIE, & THE TEEN-AGERS In 1955 Frankie Lymon (born September 30, 1942, in Washington Heights,

New York City) joined the vocal group, The Premiers, which had been formed at his school in the Bronx by Jimmy Merchant (born February 10, 1940), Sherman Garnes (born June 8, 1940), Herman Santiago (born February 18, 1941) and Joe Negroni (born September 9, 1940). They were discovered by Richard BARRETT, a talent scout for George GOLDNER. They were signed to his Gee label and the name of the group was changed to The Teenagers. Their debut, *Why Do Fools Fall in Love?* (USA#7; UK#1.1956), was written by Lymon and produced by Goldner; it was followed by *I Want You to be my Girl* (USA #17.1956). In the wake of their immediate success, the group undertook a gruelling schedule of touring and recording, releasing *I Promise to Remember, The ABC's of Love, I'm not a Juvenile Delinquent* (UK#12.1957) and *Baby, Baby* (UK#4.1957). At the end of 1957 Lymon went solo with *Goody Goody* (USA#22; UK #24.1957). It was his final hit. Their career hit the skids and Goldner went bankrupt. After three years in the wilderness, Lymon returned with a cover of *Little Bitty Pretty One,* but his voice had broken, which effectively removed any vestigial appeal. Throughout the early 1960s, he was racked by heroin addiction, which necessitated several stints in rehabilitation centres. On February 28, 1968, aged 25, with a new contract from Roulette under his belt, he had a celebratory shot of heroin. It was his last.

THE BEST OF FRANKIE LYMON AND THE TEENAGERS, Roulette, 1990

LYNN, BARBARA Barbara Lynn Ozen was born on January 16, 1942, in Beaumont, Texas. She started her career in the late 1950s as a blues singer, playing the Louisiana club circuit where she was scouted by Huey P. MEAUX, who took her to the J&M Studios in New Orleans. Her debut, *You'll Lose a Good Thing* (USA#8.1962), was leased to the Jamie label, as were its successors, *Give Me a Break, You're Gonna Need Me, It's Better to Have it* and *Oh Baby*. In 1965 at the end of the Jamie deal, she recorded her version of MAURICE & MAC's *You Left the Water Running* for Meaux, who had started his own label, Tribe. She remained with Tribe until 1968 and then she signed with Atlantic, releasing the LP *Here is Barbara Lynn* which, despite its lack of commercial success, was one of the most cohesive LPs of the period. She then recorded some sessions at Chips MOMAN's American studios with Spooner OLDHAM producing, including the PENN and Oldham composition, *He ain't Gonna do Right*. In the early 1970s she disappeared into obscurity, but re-emerged in 1988 with *You don't Have to Go* for John Abbey's Ichiban label.

McCLINTON, DELBERT

As a performer, Delbert McClinton's solo career has always been low-key: he has preferred to pursue his calling in the comparative intimacy of the Texas club circuit rather than try to break into the mainstream with constant international touring.

He was born on November 4, 1940, in Lubbock, Texas. Throughout the early 1960s, he was a key figure on the Texas club circuit, achieving a reputation as a harmonica player with his solo on Bruce Chanel's monster hit, *Hey Baby*. In 1964 he joined The Ron-Dels, recording *If You Really Want Me To, I'll Go*, which became a local hit. After moving to the West Coast in 1970, he teamed up with Glen Clark to form the duo, Delbert & Glen. In the mid-1970s, he returned to Texas and recorded two solo LPs for ABC, *Victims of Life's Circumstances* (1975) and *Love Rustler* (1977). He then moved to Capricorn for *Second Wind* (1978) and *Keeper of the Flame* (1979). In 1980,

having signed with Capitol, he hit the big-time with *Giving it up for Your Love* (USA#8.1980), which was extracted from the LP, *The Jealous Kind* (USA#34.1981), produced by Barry BECKETT. During the 1980s he returned to the club circuit, cutting a live LP for the Alligator label, *Live from Austin*, in 1989.

LIVE FROM AUSTIN, Alligator, 1989

McCOY, VAN

Van McCoy's reputation has always been based upon his work with The STYLISTICS and HUGO & LUIGI, when he crested the disco wave with *The Hustle*. However, his career stretched back to the beginning of the 1960s when he was influential as a writer, arranger and producer.

He was born on January 6, 1940, in Washington DC, learning to play the piano when he was four. He joined The Starlighters, who had a contract with George GOLDNER's End label, and then formed his own label, Rockin' Records. In 1961 he was hired by Florence Greenberg to become a producer at Scepter, where he worked with Chuck JACKSON and Maxine BROWN until in 1962 he was hired by LEIBER & STOLLER as an arranger. He worked with them for only a short time, soon being signed by Columbia as a solo artist and writer. Although his own records failed to generate much interest, his compositions for artists like Barbara LEWIS, Ruby & The Romantics, Aretha FRANKLIN and The MARVELETTES increased his reputation; his work as a producer with Gladys KNIGHT & The Pips and PEACHES & HERB was equally successful.

In 1967 he set up his own production company, which he was to maintain until his death; among the artists he worked with were David RUFFIN, Aretha Franklin and Jackie WILSON. However, when Thom BELL stopped working with The Stylistics and Hugo &

Luigi took over the production chores, they enlisted the services of McCoy as arranger and they signed him as a solo artist to their Avco label. At Avco he had a succession of hit singles including *The Hustle* (USA#1; UK#3.1975), *Change with the Times* (UK#36.1975), *Party , Soul Cha Cha* (UK#34.1977), *The Shuffle* (UK #4.1977)and *My Favourite Fantasy*. His most successful LP *Disco Baby* (USA#12; UK #32.1975) became staple fare for DJs throughout the disco boom. His career was cut short by his premature death from a heart attack on July 6, 1979.

HUSTLE TO THE BEST OF VAN McCOY, H&L, 1977

McCRAE, GEORGE Although the disco boom of the mid-1970s was responsible for a considerable amount of execrable dross, it did generate a few records that were excellent. *Rock your Baby* (USA/UK#1.1974) was a case in point. It was written by Howie Casey and Rick Finch of KC & THE SUNSHINE BAND, who, unable to record it themselves brought in George McCrae (born in West Beach, Florida, on October 19, 1944) to provide the vocals. Not only did this single help to kindle the flames of disco, it also helped to establish Henry STONE's TK studios in Florida as a recording mecca. The LP *Rock your Baby* (USA#38.1974) featured an extended version of the title track- a practice which would indirectly lead to the arrival of the twelve-inch single. After its success he went on to cut similar records, but was never able to recapture the magic of the debut. Among them were *I Can't Leave you Alone* (UK#9.1974), *You Can Have it All* (UK#23.1974), *I Get Lifted* (USA#37.1975), *Sing a Happy Song* (UK#38.1975), *It's Been so Long* (UK#4.1975), *I ain't Lyin'* (UK#12.1975) and *Honey* (UK#33.1976). With his wife Gwen who was signed to the Cat label, he recorded

some duets before becoming her manager; however, her biggest hits – like *Lead me On*, *Rockin' Chair* (USA#9.1975) and *All this Love that I'm Giving* (UK#63.1988) – were as a solo artist. After their marriage broke up, George resumed his career but with little success, having just the one hit, *One Step Closer (to Love)* (UK#57.1984). On January 24, 1986, he died of cancer.

THE BEST OF GEORGE McCRAE, JayBoy, 1976
GEORGE McCRAE, TK, 1978
ONE STEP CLOSER TO LOVE, President, 1984
TOGETHER, (with Gwen McCrae), President, 1985

McCRAE, GWEN See McCRAE, George

McDANIELS, GENE Gene McDaniels was born in Kansas on February 12, 1935. In 1960, having played the saxophone in various local gospel groups, he was signed to Liberty by Snuff Garrett. Throughout the early 1960s, he recorded a series of singles like *A Hundred Pounds of Clay* (USA#3.1961), *A Tear* (USA #31.1961), *Tower of Strength* (USA#5; UK #49.1961), *Chip Chip* (USA#10.1962), *Point of no Return* (USA#21.1962) and *Spanish Lace* (USA#31.1962). By the early 1970s, having spent years in obscurity, he recorded the LP, *Outlaw*, for Atlantic; produced by Joel Dorn, it failed to generate much interest but did encourage him to resume his career as a writer and producer. In this capacity he had considerable success when Roberta FLACK recorded his composition *Feel like Making Love* , with Dorn producing; as a producer he has worked with Gladys KNIGHT, among others. Since 1980 he has been running his own studios in Seattle.

McGRIFF, JIMMY Jimmy McGriff's one great contribution to R&B was his version of the Ray CHARLES composition *I've got a Woman* in 1962. This record did much to encourage the use of the Hammond organ within popular music – both Georgie Fame and Booker T. Jones (see BOOKER T & THE MGs) took the hint.

McGriff was born in Philadelphia on April 3, 1936. Initially a bassist, he then switched to the organ, backing visiting musicians on the club circuit . After recording *I've got a Woman* (USA#20.1962) for the Sue label, he released *All about my Girl* and *The Last Minute*. Despite these successes, he returned to playing a much purer form of jazz in a post-bop style for labels like Blue Note, Solid State and Groove Merchant; for the latter he recorded in1972 the LP, *Good Things Don't Happen Every Day* with Junior Parker, as well as collaborating with Hank Crawford for the LP *Soul Survivors*. More recently he has recorded the LP *State Of The Art* (1986) for Fantasy, on which he showcased his virtuosity within a variety of styles.

BLUES FOR MR JIMMY, Stateside, 1986
STATE OF THE ART, Fantasy, 1986
THE STARTING FIVE, Milsetone, 1987

McPHATTER, CLYDE Clyde McPhatter was born on November 13, 1933, in Durham, North Carolina. In 1950 he became lead singer in Billy WARD's group, The Dominoes, who had a contract with Syd NATHAN's Federal label. In 1953 he left the group after a disagreement with Ward, and formed The DRIFTERS at the suggestion of Ahmet ERTEGUN and signed with Atlantic. His eerie tenor voice underpinned the future success of the group, although he was a member for slightly less than a year. In 1954 he was drafted into the army, where he became a forces entertainer, and after his discharge in 1956 he started a solo career.

Between 1956 and 1959 he notched up a string of hits that were superlative examples of soul in its purest form; they included *Treasure of Love* (USA#16; UK#27.1956), *Without Love (There is Nothing)* (USA#19.1957), *Just to Hold My Hand* (USA#26.1957), *A Lover's Question* (USA#6.1958) and *Since You've Been Gone* (USA#38.1959). In 1959 he parted company with Atlantic, and signed with Mercury. At Mercury he had a few more hits like *Ta Ta* (USA#23.1960), *Lover Please* (USA#7.1962) and *Little Bitty Pretty One* (USA#25.1962). In 1962 he was taken to Nashville by Shelby SINGLETON in an abortive attempt to revive his popularity, which was on the decline. However, by the mid-1960s his way of singing had been superseded by the rather more histrionic styles of Otis REDDING and Wilson PICKETT, and his career continued its decline; it was not helped by bouts of alcoholism and drug addiction. On June 13, 1972, he died of heart, kidney and liver disease, aged 39. It was a tragic end to a career that had been so influential in the development of what has come to be termed 'soft-soul', providing inspiration for successive generations of artists like Jackie WILSON, Smokey ROBINSON, Teddy PENDERGRASS and Luther VANDROSS.

BIP BAM, (with The Drifters), Edsel, 1984
ROCK AND CRY, Charly, 1984
CLYDE McPHATTER WITH BILLY WARD AND HIS DOMINOES, King, 1988

MANHATTANS See ALSTON, Gerald

MANN, BARRY, & CYNTHIA WEIL Barry Mann (born February 9, 1939, in New York) and ex-actress, Cynthia Weil (born October 18, 1937 in New York) formed a songwriting partnership that worked for Don

Kirshner's music publishing company, Aldon, in the Brill Building on New York's Broadway. Along with other partnerships like GOFFIN & KING, BARRY & GREENWICH and POMUS & SHUMAN, they provided the bulk of the material published by Kirshner during the early 1960s, with countless titles like *Uptown* and *He's Sure the Boy I Love* for The CRYSTALS, *Walkin' in the Rain* (with Phil SPECTOR) for The RONETTES, *You've Lost that Lovin' Feeling* and *(You're my) Soul and Inspiration* for The RIGHTEOUS BRO-THERS, *Come on Over to My Place, I'll Take You Home* and *On Broadway* (with LEIBER & STOLLER) for The DRIFTERS, *Just Once* for Quincy JONES and James INGRAM and *We Gotta Get Outta this Place* for The Animals. They have continued to this day, but now they have broadened the base of their operation to include filmwork, but like many of their con-temporaries, however, they have been unable to knock out the hits with the same regularity as before.

MARCELS Street-corner singing has been one of the key influences in the formation and development of black music: it evolved into doo-wop in the 1950s and then, in the late 1970s, into rap; along the way it spawned some curious adaptations. The Marcels, who comprised Cornelius Harp, Ronald Mundy, Gene Bricker, Dick Knauss and Fred John-son, were a vocal group from Pittsburg who had cut their teeth on old R&B classics and popular doo-wop standards while working the local club circuit. In 1960 their manager, Julius Kruspir, sent a demo to Stu Phillips at Colpix in New York. The following year they went into the studios and recorded the Rodg-ers & Hart standard, *Blue Moon* (USA/UK #1.1961); their version retained the melody but almost turned it into the subtext to a bass doo-wop part, that was so over-emphasised that it

verged on parody. Nevertheless, Murray the K, the DJ at WINS in New York, was so enamoured of it that he played it 26 times in one night. Although they recorded a number of other standards – *Summertime* (UK#46.1961), *You Are My Sunshine, Heartaches* (USA #7.1961) and *My Melancholy Baby* – none were able to repeat the impact of that first record. Their career had petered out by 1963, but they resurfaced in the 1970s when the oldies circuit picked up momentum.

BLUE MOON, Emus, 1979

MARCHAN, BOBBY When Huey SMITH teamed up with The Clowns in 1957 their lead singer was Bobby Marchan. Mar-chan was a noted eccentric on the New Orleans music scene with a penchant for transvestism. Before joining The Clowns he had a solo hit with *Little Chicken Wah Wah* (1955) for Johnny VINCENT's Ace label. His impassioned falsetto was absolutely perfect for Smith's compositions like *Rockin' Pneumonia and the Boogie Woogie Flu* and *Don't You Just Know It*. In 1959 Marchan left the group to continue his solo career and had a hit with the Big Jay McNeely composition, *There is Some-thing on Your Mind* (USA#31.1960) for Bobby ROBINSON's Fury label. By 1964 he was making regular appearances on the New Orleans club circuit. Furthermore, a contract with Buddy KILLEN's Dial label enabled him to cut sides like *I've Got a Thing Goin' On* and *I Gotta Sit Down and Cry*. After his stint with Dial he was signed by Cameo, where he cut his version of *Rockin' Pneumonia and the Boogie Woogie Flu* and the Joe TEX composition, *Meet Me in Church*. However, in recent years he has recorded seldom, concentrating instead on his live work.

SLY STONE, backed by (out of picture) the Family Stone, at Woodstock (courtesy Warner Bros.).

EARTH, WIND & FIRE became one of the hottest soul acts of the 1970s (courtesy Columbia Records).

Three Funkateers: GEORGE CLINTON (*top left*) (courtesy Paisley Park), BOOTSY COLLINS (*top right*) (courtesy Columbia Records) and RICK JAMES (*bottom*) (courtesy Motown Records).

Three successful solo artists who had been lead vocalists in equally successful groups: MICHAEL JACKSON in The Jackson Five (*top*), TEDDY PENDERGRASS in Harold Melvin & The Blue Notes (*bottom left*) and LUTHER VANDROSS in Luther (*bottom right*) (all courtesy Epic Records).

Opposite

Two soulmen who benefitted from the Music Shoals treatment: BOZ SCAGGS (courtesy Columbia Records) and BOBBY WOMACK (courtesy Motown Records).

During the 1980s, the Malaco label provided a new, creative home for many soul and R&B singers: BOBBY BLAND (*top left*), LITTLE MILTON (*top right*), Z.Z. HILL (*bottom left*), JOHNNIE TAYLOR (*bottom right*) (all courtesy Malaco Records).

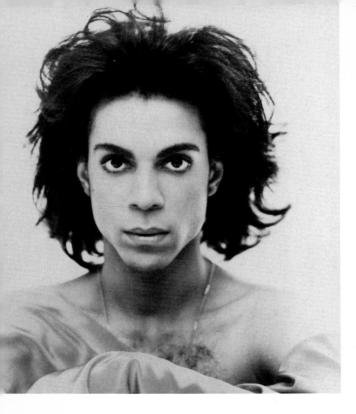

The 'Minneapolis Mafia' seemed to dominate soul in the 1980s: PRINCE (*top left*), (courtesy of Warner Bros.); ALEXANDER O'NEAL (*top right*) (courtesy Epic Records/Eugene Adebari); JIMMY JAM (*bottom left*) (courtesy Epic Records); TERRY LEWIS (*bottom right*) (courtesy Epic Records).

The shape of things to come? TERENCE TRENT D'ARBY (*top left*) (courtesy Columbia Records); JOHNNY GILL AND BOBBY BROWN (*top right*) (courtesy Motown Records); CARON WHEELER (*bottom left*) (courtesy of RCA/BMG/Tessa Hallman & Vicki Jackman); MARIAH CAREY (*bottom right*) (courtesy Columbia Records).

Since the start of his career, in the late 1940s, to the present day, QUINCY JONES has been a guiding influence as a performer, composer, producer and catalyst (courtesy Qwest Records).

MARDIN, ARIF Like Berry GORDY at Motown, Ahmet ERTEGUN at Atlantic has always managed to stay ahead by being prepared to accept and develop the natural progressions in contemporary music. He has achieved this through the simple expedient of surrounding himself with inventive technicians like Jerry WEXLER, Tom DOWD and Arif Mardin.

Mardin was born in Istanbul, Turkey, on March 15, 1932. After leaving his native land in 1962 he settled in New York, where he was hired by Nesuhi Ertegun to write arrangements for the roster of jazz artists at Atlantic. Since then he has honed and refined his skills as a producer, working with artists like The Young Rascals, Aretha FRANKLIN, Donny HATHAWAY, Roberta FLACK, The AVERAGE WHITE BAND, Daryl HALL & John Oates and Brook BENTON. In 1975 he was recruited by The Bee Gees' manager, Robert Stigwood, to revive their flagging career; the subsequent LP, *Main Course*, relaunched them and set the stage for the film soundtrack, *Saturday Night Fever*. Since Atlantic's absorption into Warner Bros., he has continued to broaden the scope of the company, working with artists like Chaka KHAN, Eric Clapton, Scritti Politti, Bette Midler, David Bowie and Rod Stewart.

MARKEYS The Markeys, the Stax house band, were put together out of the group Steve CROPPER formed while still at high school, The Royal Spades. Initially, The Markeys comprised guitarists Charlie Freeman and Cropper, bassist 'Duck' DUNN, drummer Terry Johnson and the horn section of Packy Axton, Wayne JACKSON and Don Nix. In 1961 they had a major hit with *Last Night* (USA#3.1961) on the Satellite label. It was this record that caused Jim STEWART to change the name of the label from Satellite to Stax,

because the success drew the attention of a Californian label, also called Satellite, to the fact that he had inadvertently used their name. By 1962 the success of *Green Onions* by BOOKER T & THE MGs had effectively eclipsed The Markeys, although they continued to function as an umbrella unit within Stax and in due course provided openings for musicians like Andrew Love (see JACKSON, Wayne) and Isaac HAYES, both of whom would later go on to greater celebrity.

DAMN IF I KNOW, Stax, 1990

MARK Vs See PENN, Dan

MARTHA & THE VANDELLAS This group was formed in 1960 by school friends Martha Reeves (born July 18, 1941, in Alabama), Rosalind Ashford (born September 2, 1943, in Detroit), Annette Sterling and Gloria Williams, as The Del-Phis. They secured a recording contract with Chess, but their first single failed to make any impression and so Williams left the group. Reeves got a job as a secretary in the A&R department at Motown and by 1962 had been given the opportunity to use her group, which she had renamed Martha & The Vandellas, as backing vocalists on sessions.

In 1962 they were signed as artists in their own right to the subsidiary label Gordy. Their debut, *I'll Have to Let Him Go,* bombed, but the follow-up, *Come and Get these Memories* (USA#29.1963), was the first of a series of singles that established the group as one of the major stars of the Motown firmament: *Heat Wave* (USA#4.1963), *Quicksand* (USA #11.1963), *Dancing in the Street* (USA#2; UK #4.1964/#4.1969), *Wild One* (USA#34.1964), *Nowhere to Run* (USA#8; UK#26.1964/ #42.1969/#52.1988), *You've Been in Love too*

Long (USA#36.1965), *My Baby Loves Me* (USA#22.1966), *I'm Ready for Love* (USA#9; UK#29.1966), *Jimmy Mack* (USA#10; UK #21.1967/#21.1970), *Love Bug Leave my Heart Alone* (USA#25.1967), *Honey Chile* (USA #11.1967; UK#30.1968), *Forget me Not* (UK #11.1971) and *Bless You* (UK#33.1972).

However, despite their success, Sterling left in 1963 to get married and was replaced by a member of The VELVELETTES, Betty Kelly (born September 16, 1944, in Detroit), who remained with the group until 1968, when she in turn was replaced, by Reeves sister Lois. In 1969 the group split up as a result of Reeves' having a breakdown. They re-formed in 1971, but Ashford stayed out of the picture; her place was taken by Sandra Tilley. The following year when the group broke up once more. Reeves, miffed at Diana ROSS's preferential treatment at Motown, left to start a solo career. Her first solo LP *Martha Reeves* (1974) for her new label MCA was notably unsuccessful, despite being produced by Richard Perry. She left MCA for Arista, recording the LP, *The Rest of my Life* (1976). It failed to sell, as did the follow-up for Fantasy, *We Meet Again* (1978). In 1978 she re-formed the Vandellas and took to the oldies circuit, touring the world constantly.

HEATWAVE, Motown, 1963
ANTHOLOGY, Motown, 1982
GREATEST HITS, Motown, 1982
COMPACT COMMAND PERFORMANCES, Motown, 1987
MARTHA REEVES, The Collection, 1987

MARVELETTES One of the very first Motown groups to break was The Marvelettes. They were a bunch of schoolfriends from one of the housing projects, Inkster, built by Henry Ford to accommodate his workforce. After winning a talent contest, the group – which consisted of Gladys Horton, Georgia

Dobbins, Georgeanna Tillman, Katherine Anderson, Juanita Cowart and Wanda Young – were given the opportunity to audition for Motown.

Their first single, *Please Mr Postman* (USA #1.1961), was written by William Garrett and arranged by Dobbins; it featured Marvin GAYE on drums. Over the next year the group had a run of hits: *Twistin' Postman* (USA #34.1962), *Playboy* (USA#7.1962) and *Beechwood 4- 5789* (USA#17.1962). The success took its toll upon them, individually, as they were compelled to tour extensively. Cowart had a nervous breakdown and Tillman left due to ill-health: she married one of The CONTOURS, Billy Gordon, but died young of sickle-cell anaemia.

For two years the group was allowed to moulder in the Motown wilderness. They finally returned to the charts with *Too Many Fish in the Sea* (USA#25.1964). This was followed by *I'll Keep Holding On* (USA#34.1965), *Don't Mess with Bill* (USA#7.1966), *The Hunter Gets Captured by the Game* (USA#13.1967), *When You're Young and in Love* (USA#23; UK #13.1967) and *My Baby Must be a Magician* (USA#17.1968). In 1967 Horton departed to go with her husband to the West Coast, where he promptly left her. When Motown relocated to Hollywood, Young remained in Detroit. Today, there are so many different versions of the group playing the oldies circuit that, more often than not, the line-up appearing as The Marvelettes contains not a single original member.

ANTHOLOGY, Motown, 1982
COMPACT COMMAND PERFORMANCES, Motown, 1987

MARY JANE GIRLS It was always difficult to tell whether or not The Mary Jane Girls were put together by Rick JAMES to maintain his challenge to PRINCE as the most outrageous performer in the USA. They were formed in 1979 and comprised Joanna McDuffie, Candice Grant, Kim Wuletick and Yvette Marine. After touring extensively with James as part of his revue, they recorded the LP *Mary Jane Girls* (UK#51.1983), which was written and produced by James and included the singles: *Candy Man* (UK#60.1983), *All Night Long* (UK#13.1983) and *Boys* (UK #74.1983). Their next LP, *Only Four You* (USA #18.1985), included another single, *In My House* (USA#7.1985), but it turned out to be their last hit. Their final single, *Walk Like a Man*, merely heralded the end.

MARY JANE GIRLS, Motown, 1983
ONLY FOUR YOU, Motown, 1985

MASON, BARBARA Barbara Mason was born on August 9, 1947, in Philadelphia. She shot to stardom with *Yes I'm Ready* (USA #5.1965) for the independent Arctic label. She seemed assured of a long career when the follow-up *Sad, Sad Girl* (USA#27.1965) consolidated that early success, but unfortunately Arctic went out of business and her career slipped into the doldrums. It was revived in 1973, having signed with Buddah, when she notched up another brace of hit singles, *Give Me Your Love* (USA#31.1973) and *From His Woman to You* (USA#28.1974). During the years of disco supremacy she recorded little, concentrating instead on touring. By the early 1980s she had resumed her recording career with the LP *A Piece of my Life* (1981) on the independent WMOT label. In 1984 she signed with the Streetwave label, recording the singles, *Another Man* (UK#45.1984) and *Don't I Ever Cross Your Mind Sometime*, but neither attracted very much attention. In 1987 she signed with the Jetstar label and released the single *I'll Never*

Love the Same Way Again. Throughout she has remained a popular attraction on the Northern Soul circuit.

A PIECE OF MY LIFE, Jetstar, 1981

MAURICE & MAC Maurice & Mac were arguably one of the great 'lost' soul duo's of the 1960s. Maurice McAlister and McLaurin Green formed one half of Chicago-based group, The Radiants, the other half being Wallace Simpson and Leonard Caston. The group scored with *Voice Your Choice* in 1964. In 1965 Mac went into the army for two years, The Radiants continued initially as a trio but broke up when Caston went to Motown as a writer and producer. In 1967 when Mac came out of the army, he resumed recording with Maurice as a duo for Chess. Chess sent them down to Muscle Shoals where they recorded the PENN & OLDHAM composition, *You Left the Water Runnin'*; with Rick HALL producing, it was a fine example of southern soul but it failed to sell in any quantity. They continued to record, cutting tracks like *Lay It on Me* and *So Much Love*, but nothing could arrest their inexorable descent into obscurity.

MAYFIELD, CURTIS Curtis Mayfield was born in Chicago on June 3, 1942. In 1957 he and his close friend Jerry BUTLER joined the R&B group, The Roosters; the following year the name of the group was changed to The IMPRESSIONS. After a number of records including their biggest hit, *For Your Precious Love*, Butler left. Without him the group folded. Mayfield continued to work as a session guitarist and writer at VeeJay, where he collaborated with Butler to provide songs like *He Will Break Your Heart* and *Find Another Girl*. In 1960 Mayfield re-formed The Impressions. He remained with them until 1970, and during that time they became one of the most consistent black vocal groups in the USA. Throughout, he guided their career, providing the material and production. The culmination was the formation of his own record label, Curtom. From the mid-1960s, the lyrics of his songs were concerned with the quest for racial harmony: titles like *Keep on Pushing; People Get Ready* and *We're a Winner* were clear indications of Mayfield's political stance.

His debut LP, *Curtis* (USA#19.1970), was funkier than anything he had previously done with The Impressions, although he still used string arrangements where appropriate. A single from the LP, *Move on Up* (USA #29.1970; UK#12.1971), belatedly became a hit in the UK, where it is still regarded as a dance-floor classic. The following year he released a double live LP, *Curtis Live!* (USA#21.1971), which was recorded at the Bitter End in New York and contained new material, as well as reworkings of the Impressions' greatest hits. It also featured a much smaller unit than he was accustomed to – just drummer, percussionist and bassist. It was followed by the LP, *Roots* (USA#40.1971). In the wake of the success of the film *Shaft*, Mayfield was asked to compose the score for the film, *Superfly*; this yielded his biggest successes, as the soundtrack LP (USA #1.1972; UK#26.1973) provided him with two hit singles: *Freddie's Dead* (USA#4.1972) and *Superfly* (USA#8.1973). The next LP, *Back to the World* (USA#16.1973), was another exploration of social issues.

In 1973 Chicago's WTTW-TV produced a tribute to Mayfield, featuring current and former line-ups of The Impressions, as well as other artists like Gene CHANDLER and Betty EVERETT. A soundtrack LP, *Curtis in Chicago,* was released and two of its tracks became singles. From 1974 his solo career, which had peaked with *Superfly*, began to play second fiddle to his collaborations with other artists: he produced and played on the soundtrack of the film *Claudine*, featuring Gladys KNIGHT & The Pips; he worked with Donny HATHA-WAY on the LP, *Sweet Exorcist* (USA #39.1974); he collaborated with The STAPLE SINGERS on the soundtrack for the film, *Let's Do it Again*; and he produced two Aretha FRANKLIN LPs, *Sparkle* (1976) and *Almighty Fire* (1978).

In 1979 he sold Curtom to RSO: the ensuing LP, *Heartbeat* (USA#42.1979), was the first in twenty years that he did not produce himself; instead, it was produced by the Philadelphia team of Norman Harris, Ron Tyson and Bunny Sigler. Throughout the 1980s, Mayfield has continued to record LPs at regular intervals, despite the lack of commercial success: *Love is the Place* (1981), *Honesty* (1982) and *We Come in Peace with a Message of Love* (1985). However, through touring the UK and Europe frequently, he has developed a fresh following, which led to a collaboration with the group, The Blow Monkeys, the result was *Celebrate (The Day after You)* (UK#52.1987). In 1988 the Curtom label was revived by the independent Ichiban Records. However, on August 13, 1990, a lighting rig was blown over at an outdoor festival in Brooklyn: it struck Mayfield on the base of the neck, breaking it, and paralysing him from the neck down.

SUPERFLY, Ichiban, 1972
GIVE GET AND TAKE, Buddah, 1976
NEVER SAY YOU CAN'T SURVIVE, Curtom, 1977
SOMETHING TO BELIEVE IN, Curtom, 1980
HONESTY, Epic, 1983

MAYFIELD, PERCY Percy Mayfield was born in Linden, Louisiana, on August 12, 1920. He was brought up in Houston, Texas, moving to Los Angeles in the 1940s, where he started to compose for other people, like Jimmy Witherspoon. However, he was persuaded to cut some of his own material like *Half Awake* and *Two Years of Torture* himself. The success of these enabled him to get a contract with Art RUPE's Specialty label, where he recorded the self-penned *Please Send Me Someone to Love* in 1950. It was followed by other hits like *What a Fool I Was, Cry Baby* and *Lost Love*. After being injured in a road accident, he turned from performing to concentrate again on composition; he continued to record, but with little success.

During the early 1960s he wrote for Ray CHARLES, composing *Hit the Road Jack* among others, and this led to a contract with Charles' Tangerine label. His first LP for Tangerine, *My Jug and I*, spawned a minor hit, *River's Invitation*. He was then signed by Brunswick and by RCA, but LPs like *Weakness is a Thing Called Man* in 1969 were anachronistic and consequently failed to sell in any quantity. After years of obscurity, he returned to live performance in 1982 with a European tour and then a US tour. He died on August 11, 1984.

HIT THE ROAD AGAIN, Timeless, 1985

MY HEART IS ALWAYS SINGING SAD SONGS, Ace, 1985

THE VOICE WITHIN, Route 66, 1988

POET OF THE BLUES, Ace, 1990

MAZE Maze was formed in San Francisco by Frankie Beverly in 1976. Initially the line-up comprised Beverly (vocals and guitar), Vernon Black (guitars), William Bryant (keyboards), Robin Duhe (bass), Wayne Lindsey (keyboards), Roame Lowery (percussion), Ron Smith (guitars), Billy Johnson (drums) and McKinley Williams (percussion). Beverly had gravitated to the West Coast from his native Philadelphia, where he had been a member of the group Raw Soul with Williams and Lowery. Although they had had modest local success, the all-pervasive Philadelphia Sound had swamped any musical distinction and Raw Soul had disbanded.

After touring with Marvin GAYE as the opening act, Maze was signed to Capitol by Larkin Arnold, who had been given the task of expanding the company's roster of black artists. Their style was comparable to that of EARTH, WIND & FIRE, but they were unable to match the commercial success of that group, mainly because they couldn't get a big hit single. Their debut LP, *Maze featuring Frankie Beverly*, established a strong reputation, which was enhanced by a thrilling live show. Their next LP, *Golden Time of Day* (USA #27.1978), showed Beverly continuing to expand his repertoire. It was followed by the LPs *Inspiration* (USA#33.1979) and *Joy and Pain* (USA#31.1980). The following year as if to emphasise the importance of their live work, they released the double LP, *Live in New Orleans* (USA#34.1981).

After more intensive worldwide touring they released the LP, *We are the One* (USA#25; UK #38.1983); it gave them their breakthrough in the UK, where they had always had a loyal following. The next LP, *Can't Stop the Love* (UK#41.1985), included the single *Too Many Games* (UK#36.1985) and consolidated their international standing. It was followed by another double live LP, *Live in Los Angeles* (UK#70.1986), which was little more than a greatest hits package; a single, *I Wanna be with You* (UK#55.1986) was extracted. After a period of rest and recuperation they changed labels, signing with Warner Bros. for the LP *Silky Soul* in 1989, which was consistent with what their fans expected of them. But that big hit single has still eluded them.

MAZE FEATURING FRANKIE BEVERLY, Capitol, 1977

GOLDEN TIME OF THE DAY, Capitol, 1978

INSPIRATION, Capitol, 1979

JOY AND PAIN, Capitol, 1980
LIVE IN NEW ORLEANS, Capitol, 1981
WE ARE ONE, Capitol, 1983
CAN'T STOP THE LOVE, Capitol, 1985
LIVE IN LOS ANGELES, Capitol, 1986
SILKY SOUL, Warner Bros., 1989

MEADE, NORMAN See RAGAVOY, Jerry

MEAUX, HUEY. P Huey P. Meaux was born on March 10, 1929, in Kaplan, Louisiana. His father – an occasional accordionist – raised him on a diet of Tex-Mex and Cajun music. After doing his national service, Meaux opened a barber's shop in Winnie in Texas, but soon turned the shop into a makeshift studio, where he recorded some demos. These came to the attention of Floyd Soileau of Jin Records, who leased *Breaking up is Hard to Do* by Jivin' Gene. After this moderate success, he sold the barber's shop to concentrate upon talent scouting and production, discovering Joe Barry, who recorded *I'm a Fool to Care* (USA#24.1961); it was leased by Soileau to Smash. With the proceeds he set up his own network of labels in Houston: they included Crazy Cajun, Tribe, Teardrop and Jetstream. Among the artists he recorded were Barbara LYNN, Roy HEAD, Doug Sahm, Freddy Fender, T- Bone Walker and Johnny Copeland. His biggest successes came with Doug Sahm's Sir Douglas Quintet in the mid-1960s and Freddy Fender during the 1970s. However, in the late 1960s he was jailed for fourteen months for conspiring to contravene the Mann Act: a girl he had taken to a DJ's convention started to work as a prostitute and then told the police about her activities. During the 1980s, he has dealt less and less with soul, tending to work more with local Texans. In 1986 he appeared as a DJ in the David Byrne (the guiding spirit of Talking Heads) film, *True Stories*.

MEDLEY, BILL See RIGHTEOUS BROTHERS

MELLE MEL Melvin Glover was born in New York City. In 1978 he joined GRANDMASTER FLASH as one of the Three MCs, which, with the addition of Cowboy (Keith Wiggins), Creole (Danny Glover), Mr Ness (Eddie Morris) and Raheim (Guy Williams) evolved into The Furious Five. In 1983, after the departure of Flash for a solo career, Mel and Duke Bootee (Ed Fletcher) released *The Message II*; the following year saw the establishment of the group as Grandmaster Melle Mel & The Furious Five as a result of their contribution to the film *Beat Street*, in the shape of *Beat Street Breakdown Part 1* (UK#42.1984). This record was followed by *We Don't Work for Free* (UK#45.1984), and later the same year he immortalised the Chaka KHAN hit, *I Feel for You*, with the charismatic opening line 'Chakakhanchakakhanchakakhan'. In 1985 he released *Step Off (Part 1)* (UK#8.1985) and then *Pump Me Up* (UK #45.1985). In 1987 Grandmaster Flash rejoined the group for a concert at Madison Square Gardens.

WORK PARTY, Sugarhill, 1984
STEPPING OFF, Sugarhill, 1985

MELVIN, HAROLD, & THE BLUE NOTES Often a group or an artist can work for years, developing a strong local reputation, but never manage to break out into the mainstream until an individual or a group of individuals arrives and transform the ordinary to the excellent. Such has been the case with Harold Melvin & The Blue Notes. They were formed by Melvin in 1956 as an R&B based vocal group; for thirteen years they plied their trade on the club circuit, achieving just the one minor hit in 1960 with *My Hero*.

The fortunes of the group changed radically for the better when their lead singer John Atkins was replaced by Teddy PENDER-GRASS, the drummer in their backing group, The Cadillacs. Another fillip was being signed by local producers GAMBLE & HUFF to their recently established Philadelphia International label in 1969. Over the next six years, they had a string of hits, with Pendergrass' highly distinctive lead vocals providing the finish to the material of Gamble & Huff and Gene McFadden and John Whitehead: *If You Don't Know me by Now* (USA#3.1972; UK #9.1973), *The Love I Lost (Part 1)* (USA #7.1973; UK#21.1974), *Satisfaction Guaranteed (or Take Your Love Back)* (UK#32. 1974), *Bad Luck (Part 1)* (USA#15.1975), *Wake up Everybody* (USA#12.1975; UK#23.1976) and *Don't Leave me this Way* (UK#5.1977).

However, in 1976, when Pendergrass left the group for a solo career (his replacement was David Ebo), they moved to ABC, where they had only one minor hit, *Reaching for the World* (UK#48.1977). Since leaving ABC in 1979 they have recorded for a number of independents like Source and Philly World, achieving modest success in the UK with *Don't Give me Up* (UK #59.1984) and *Today's Your Lucky Day* (UK #66.1984). They have toured the US and Europe constantly.

GREATEST HITS, Philadelphia International, 1985
GOLDEN HIGHLIGHTS OF HAROLD MELVIN, CBS, 1986

MEMPHIS HORNS See JACKSON, Wayne

METERS See NEVILLE BROTHERS

MFSB See WANSEL, Dexter

MICKY & SYLVIA See ROBINSON, Sylvia

MIDNIGHTERS See BALLARD, Hank

MIGHTY SAM Mighty Sam McLain was born in Monroe, Louisiana, in 1941. He was a member of various gospel groups before moving into the secular field, where he recorded with Elgie Brown & The Soul Brothers. He was spotted by the Florida DJ Papa Don Schroeder, while he was performing in the group Dothan Sextet. Schroeder took him to Muscle Shoals to record some tracks; there he was teamed up with Dan PENN and Spooner OLDHAM. The cuts included *I'm a Man, In the Same Old Way, Sweet Dreams* and *Just Like Old Times*. The results were as good as anything to emerge from Muscle Shoals. Schroeder leased the tracks to the Bell subsidiary, Amy, but Mighty Sam was unable to attract any more than an enthusiastic local following and following a couple of singles for Atlantic, he disappeared from sight. He re-emerged in the early 1970s to record some sides at Malaco, including *Mr and Mrs Untrue*. In recent years he has re-emerged once more to record with Hubert Sumlin, Howlin' Wolf's former guitarist.

NOTHING BUT THE TRUTH, Charly, 1988

MIMMS, GARNETT Garnett Mimms was born in Ashland, Virginia on November 26, 1935. Before joining The Enchanters, he was a member of The Deltones and then The Gaynors, which included Howard TATE in its line-up. Apart from Mimms, The Enchanters comprised Charles Boyer, Samuel Bell and Zola Pearnell. They were signed by United Artists and scored immediately with *Cry Baby* (USA#4.1963) and *For Your Precious Love* (USA#26.1963), both produced by Jerry RAGAVOY, although credited to Mimms & The Enchanters. He then left the group to pursue a solo career. In 1966 he had minor hits with *I'll Take Good Care of You* (USA#30.1966) and *It Was Easier to Hurt Her*, which were produced by Ragavoy and featured Dionne WARWICK and Cissy HOUSTON as backing vocalists.

In the UK he had a loyal band of devotees who waited for his every offering with bated breath, but he was unable to convert that enthusiasm into lasting success. In 1967 he embarked on a club tour, backed by a group called The Senate; the tour did little to enhance his reputation and the ensuing live LP, recorded at Brighton Polytechnic, sold only modestly. From 1968 until 1977 very little is known of his activities. He re-emerged with the fashionably funky LP, *Garnett Mimms has it All*; produced by Randy Muller of BRASS CONSTRUCTION; a single from it, *What it Is* (UK#44.1977), gave him his first taste of chart success in the UK, but it was a far cry from the records he once made with The Enchanters and Jerry Ragavoy.

WARM & SOULFUL, Liberty, 1984
ROLL WITH THE PUNCHES, Charly, 1987

MIRACLES See ROBINSON, Smokey, & The Miracles

MITCHELL, WILLIE Willie Mitchell was born in Ashland, Mississippi, in 1928. While still at school he played in Tuff Green's and Al Jackson, Sr's big bands. He was conscripted into the army in 1950 and joined a big band in the Special Services; when he left the army he returned to Memphis and formed his own band. Among those who belonged to it at one time or another were George Coleman, Phineas Newborn, Jr, Lewis Steinberg and Al JACKSON, Jr; the last two were to become the rhythm section of BOOKER T & THE MGs. Apart from playing local clubs, where he had a strong following among young white musicians like Steve CROPPER and 'Duck' DUNN, he became producer at the Home of the Blues record label, working with The FIVE ROYALES.

In 1961 he was invited to record some instrumentals for the Hi label, which had established some sort of track record with artists like Ace Cannon and Bill Black's Combo, both of whom Mitchell worked with as arranger. In 1964, he had his first hit, *20-75* (USA#31.1964), and in 1966 Don ROBEY brought his recent signing, O. V. WRIGHT, to the Hi studios at 1329, South Lauderdale Avenue to work with him. The results were impressive enough to encourage Robey to send Bobby BLAND down to Mitchell. In 1968 Mitchell had another hit with *Soul Serenade* (USA#23; UK#43.1968); the same year he was introduced to and signed Ann PEEBLES and Al GREEN, as well as producing O. V. Wright, Syl JOHNSON and Otis CLAY.

While building a roster of artists he had also put together a house band made up of a combination of session musicians and members of his own band: Mabon Hodges (guitar), Charles Hodges (organ), Leroy Hodges (bass), Al Jackson, Jr (drums), Wayne JACKSON (trumpet), James Mitchell (baritone sax), Andrew Love (see JACKSON, Wayne) (tenor sax), Ed Logan (tenor sax) and Jack Hale (trombone). It was this band that provided the Hi label with the distinctive sound that characterised all its releases, including another minor hit, *The Champion* (UK#47.1976), for Mitchell himself. In 1971 Mitchell became chief executive of the label after the death of the owner, Joe Cuoghi. In 1980 he decided to sell the label to Al Bennett's Cream Organization in Los Angeles. By 1982 he had opened up a fresh label, Waylo, with artists from the halcyon Hi years like Ann Peebles and Otis Clay under contract, as well as signing fresh talent like Lynn White and David Hudson.

THAT DRIVING BEAT, Hi, 1987

MOIR, MONTE See JAM, Jimmy, & Terry Lewis

MOMAN, CHIPS Chips Moman was born in LaGrange, Georgia, in 1936. By 1957, he had gravitated to California as a member of Dorsey Burnette's road group; there he worked as a session guitarist at the Gold Star studios in Los Angeles. In 1959 he became a member of Gene Vincent's group, The Bluecaps, only to leave when they reached Memphis. In Memphis he met up with the owner of the Satellite label, Jim STEWART, and encouraged him to concentrate upon signing R&B acts, rather than country. In 1960 Moman found a disused cinema on East McLemore Avenue and suggested that Stewart should convert it into a recording studio. From its inception the studio became a focal point for the embryonic soul scene, with Moman guiding the creative side of the operation. The first hit, *Gee Whiz*, by Carla THOMAS, was leased to Atlantic. However, subsequent records like *Last Night* by The MARKEYS were released on the Satellite label, until the name was changed to Stax. During the formative years of Stax, Moman's influence coursed through the veins of the operation: producing and playing on early hits like *Gee Whiz, Last Night* and William BELL'S *You Don't Miss Your Water*. In late 1962 Moman left Stax to set up his own studio, American, after a rather bitter argument with Stewart: as a settlement Stewart gave him $3,000, which he used to set up and open the studio at 827, Thomas Street in 1964.

Between 1964 and 1971, Moman's American Studios turned out a succession of hits for artists like James CARR, The Gentrys, Sandy Posey, The Box Tops, Oscar TONEY, Jr, Bobby WOMACK, Joe TEX, Joe SIMON and Elvis Presley. The house band consisted of Reggie Young (guitar), Bobby Emmons and Bobby Wood (keyboards), Tommy COGBILL and Mike Leech (bass) and Gene Chrisman (drums). Quite apart from the excellence of the house band, he tended to attract to his fold similarly creative people, such as Dan PENN and Spooner OLDHAM; with this nucleus he was able to cross the barriers of pop/soul/country with ease and never get hampered by a perceived notion of what artists ought to sound like. Consequently, the "feel" of many of his most successful productions – like *Suspicious Minds* by Elvis Presley – is a curious amalgam of very disparate influences. Although Moman was highly sought-after as a producer, he was also held in great respect as a guitarist by fellow producers like Jerry WEXLER, which resulted in his appearance on sessions for Atlantic at Muscle Shoals by artists like Aretha FRANKLIN and Wilson PICKETT.

In 1972, in a fit of pique, Moman shut down the studio in Memphis and reopened it in Atlanta; his wrath was caused by a reluctance on the part of the musical establishment to give him any credit for his achievements. It turned out to be a false move. In 1975 he moved to Nashville and set up studios on Music Row. This marked the end of his involvement with soul and his return to his first love, country: his midas touch was discernible in the offerings of artists like Waylon Jennings and Willie Nelson. However, such is his restless enthusiasm that he has recently forsaken Nashville and returned to Memphis.

MOONGLOWS   See FUQUA, Harvey

MOORE, DOROTHY   Dorothy Moore was born in Jackson, Mississippi, in 1946. While at Jackson State University she teamed up with Fern Kinney and Patsy McKewen to form The Poppies, who were discovered by the writer/production team of Cliff and Ed Thomas in 1965. Although the group had a minor hit with the Billy Sherrill composition, *Lullaby of Love*, they soon broke up, with Moore pursuing a solo career. Working as a session singer, she had to wait until 1975 before signing with Malaco. Eddie FLOYD heard one of her demos and persuaded Tommy COUCH to release it: *Misty Blue* (USA#3; UK#5.1976), with string arrangements by Wardell QUEZERGUE, guitar overdubs by Jimmy JOHNSON, and Couch and James Stroud producing, was the first hit for the Malaco label. It was followed by *Funny how Time Slips Away* (UK#38.1977), *I Believe You* (USA#27; UK#20.1977), *For Old Time's Sake* and *With Pen in Hand*. The success of the LP, *Misty Blue* (USA#29.1976), encouraged Couch to record more artists from the country soul genre. After a brief sojourn with Epic at the end of the 1970s, Moore returned to Malaco. In recent years she has not been so productive, although she did record the single *We Just Came Apart at the Dreams* in 1985 in Nashville, with Stroud producing, and in 1989, *Time Out for Me* for the Volt label; the latter proving that deep soul is still alive and kicking. By 1990 she had retur-

ned to Malaco after a twelve year absence to record the LP, *Feel the Love*, which continued from where its predecessor had left off.

MISTY BLUE, Malaco, 1976
DOROTHY MOORE, Epic, 1977
ONCE MORE WITH FEELING, CBS, 1979
THE DOROTHY MOORE ALBUM, CBS, 1980
TIME OUT FOR ME, Volt, 1989
FEEL THE LOVE, Malaco, 1990

MORRISON, VAN   The career of Van Morrison seems to loom like a colossus over the music industry – not just because he has had loads of hits, not just because his influence has been profound, but because his iconoclasm has made him unavoidable. For Morrison there are no neat pigeonholes. He has remained his own man, impervious to the machinations of the music business as a whole.

He was born in Belfast on August 31, 1945. He played with Deanie Sands & The Javelins and joined The Monarchs to tour the UK and Europe before forming Them. The group was signed by Decca and teamed with producers Tommy Scott and Bert BERNS with whom they recorded such records as *Baby Please Don't Go* (UK#10.1965), *Gloria, Here Comes the Night* (USA#24; UK#2.1965) and *Mystic Eyes* (USA#33.1965). In 1967 Morrison left Them and signed a solo contract with Berns' Bang label. His first single, *Brown Eyed Girl* (USA#10.1967), was written by Morrison and extracted from the LP *Blowin' Your Mind*. When Berns died of a heart attack in December 1967, Morrison signed with Warner Bros. His first LP for them, *Astral Weeks*, was written and produced by Morrison and featured a host of jazz musicians: the seamless arrangements and the poetic lyricism of the record were perfectly captured in Morrison's phrasing, which seemed to transcend soul, jazz, blues and gospel.

This set the pattern for the rest of his career in that, although he would release singles, the emphasis was on LPs. The follow-up to *Astral Weeks* was *Moondance* (USA#29; UK #32.1970), from which came the single, *Come Running* (USA#39.1970). The same year another LP, *His Band and the Street Choir* (USA#32.1971), was released and included his most successful single, *Domino* (USA#9.1970), as well as *Blue Money* (USA#23.1971) and *Call me up in Dreamland*. His next LP, *Tupelo Honey* (USA#27.1971), included *Wild Night* (USA #28.1971) and was followed by *St Dominic's Preview* (USA#15.1972). *Hard Nose the Highway* (USA#27; UK#22.1973) reflected his inner turmoil as he was getting divorced; the follow-up was the double live LP, *It's too Late to Stop Now*. Featuring his touring band The Caledonia Soul Orchestra, this LP managed to capture the essence of his stage show and paid respect to his influences and heroes. After releasing the LP, *Veedon Fleece* (UK#41.1974), he slipped out of the spotlight for a couple of years, during which he recorded with The CRUSADERS and appeared at The Band's farewell concert, *The Last Waltz*, in 1976.

He returned to recording with the LP *A Period of Transition* (UK#23.1977), which featured pianist DOCTOR JOHN. It was followed by *Wavelength* (USA#28; UK#27.1978), the title track being one of the great evocations of the impact and influence of radio upon its audience. In 1979 he released the LP *Into the Music* (UK#21.1979), which included his first charting single as a solo artist in the UK, *Bright Side of the Road* (UK#63.1978). It was followed by the LP *Common One* (UK#53.1980), which has variously been described as one of his rather more mystically inclined offerings: matters of the spirit have always suffused his music and, together with his pride in Ireland, they form a

subtext critical to the understanding of his work. In 1982 he released the LP *Beautiful Vision* (UK#31.1982); it included *Cleaning Windows,* which has become a staple in his live performances. *Inarticulate Speech of the Heart* (UK#14.1983) followed, and then, as if to assert his birthright, came a live LP recorded in Belfast, *Live at the Grand Opera House* (UK #44.1984). In 1985 he released the LP *A Sense of Wonder* (UK#25.1985), which was followed a year later by *No Guru, No Teacher, No Method* (UK#27.1986). After *Poetic Champions Compose* (UK#26.1987) came *Irish Heartbeat* (UK #18.1988), featuring The Chieftains. In 1989 he released the LP *Avalon Sunset*, which included a duet with Cliff Richard. The following year he released the LP *Enlightenment* (UK#5.1990), which gave him his highest chart placing in the UK.

THEM, Decca, 1965

THEM AGAIN, (Them), Decca, 1966

ASTRAL WEEKS, Warner Bros., 1968

MOONDANCE, Warner Bros., 1970

VAN MORRISON, HIS BAND AND THE STREET CHOIR, Warner Bros., 1970

TUPELO HONEY, Polydor, 1972

ST DOMINIC'S PREVIEW, Polydor, 1972

HARD NOSE THE HIGHWAY, Polydor, 1973

THEM, FEATURING VAN MORRISON, Deram, 1973

T B SHEETS, Bellaphon, 1974

IT'S TOO LATE TO STOP NOW, Polydor, 1974

VEEDON FLEECE, Polydor, 1974

A PERIOD OF TRANSITION, Polydor, 1977

THIS IS WHERE I CAME IN, Bang, 1977

WAVELENGTH, Polydor, 1978

INTO THE MUSIC, Mercury, 1979

COMMON ONE, Mercury, 1980

BEAUTIFUL VISION, Mercury, 1982

INARTICULATE SPEECH OF THE HEART, Mercury, 1983

LIVE AT THE GRAND OPERA HOUSE, Mercury, 1984

A SENSE OF WONDER, Mercury, 1985
NO GURU, NO TEACHER, NO METHOD, Mercury, 1986
THEM: THE COLLECTION, Castle, 1986
POETIC CHAMPIONS COMPOSE, Mercury, 1987
IRISH HEARTBEAT, Mercury, 1988
AVALON SUNSET, Polydor, 1989
THE BEST OF VAN MORRISON, Polydor, 1990
ENLIGHTENMENT, Polydor, 1990

MYSTICS See HOOD, David

NASH, JOHNNY Johnny Nash was born in Houston, Texas, on August 19, 1940. His career started during the 1950s when he began to appear on local television as a result of singing gospel in various churches. He was signed by ABC-Paramount. His first records, *A Teenager Sings the Blues* and *A Very Special Love* (USA#23.1958), showed how hopeless the larger record companies were at recognising the true potential of black music. After his contract with ABC expired he recorded a number of LPs for various labels, before setting up his own, Jad and Joda, with promoter Danny Sims. In 1967 they moved to Jamaica, where he set about adapting reggae to US tastes. The results were a number of anodyne pop-soul reggae-influenced hits like *Hold me Tight* (USA/UK#5.1968), *You Got Soul* (UK#6.1968) and *Cupid* (USA#39.1970; UK#6.1969). In 1972, he was signed to the Epic label, where he recorded titles like *I Can See Clearly Now* (USA#1; UK#5.1972), *Stir it Up* (USA #12.1973; UK#13.1972), *There are More Questions than Answers* (UK#9.1972), *Tears on my Pillow* (UK#1.1975), *Let's be Friends* (UK #42.1975) and *(What a) Wonderful World* (UK#25.1976). During the 1980s he recorded his version of *Rock me Baby* (UK#47.1985). Perhaps his single greatest contribution was to sign Bob Marley to a publishing contract, thereby giving exposure to one of the most original performers of the 1970s.

I CAN SEE CLEARLY NOW, CBS, 1974
TEARS ON MY PILLOW, CBS, 1975
THE JOHNNY NASH ALBUM, CBS, 1980
STIR IT UP, Hallmark, 1981
GOLDEN HIGHLIGHTS, CBS, 1986
HERE AGAIN, London, 1986

NATHAN, SYD Syd Nathan was born April 27, 1904, in Cincinnati, Ohio. After selling furniture, he opened a record shop in 1938. In 1944 he founded the King label. Although the label was started to record country and western, he quickly diversified when he saw the potential in the gospel and R&B markets. In 1947 he appointed Henry GLOVER musical director for the label, with Ralph BASS in place as the head of A&R and of the subsidiary, Federal. Nathan built a roster of artists by making a practice of regular exploratory field trip down to the South in search of fresh talent, a custom that would be emulated in later years by the Bihari Brothers at Modern, Art RUPE at Specialty, Leonard CHESS and Ahmet ERTEGUN and Herb ABRAMSON at Atlantic. It proved to be a wildly successful policy for Nathan, enabling him to sign artists like Billy WARD & The Dominoes, Little Willie JOHN, Hank BALLARD & The Midnighters, The FIVE ROYALES and James BROWN. Nathan died in 1968, shortly after his death, James Brown signed with Polydor, taking with him his entire catalogue of recordings, something that is hard to imagine happening had Nathan lived.

NEVILLE, AARON See NEVILLE BROTHERS

NEVILLE, ART See NEVILLE BRO-THERS

NEVILLE BROTHERS The Neville Bro-thers have gradually built upon the reputation of The Meters with a succession of LPs that pay tribute to their origins but are as adventurous as anything being currently recorded.

They were born and brought up in New Orleans and originally comprised Aaron (vocals, born January 24, 1941), Art (vocals and piano, born December 17, 1938), Charles (sax, born December 28, 1939) and Cyril (vocals and percussion, born January 10, 1950). In 1954 Art joined a local R&B group, The Hawketts, and they recorded *Mardi Gras Mambo* for Chess, which was a local hit. In 1957 Art joined Lee Diamond's band and signed a solo deal with Specialty, recording a handful of singles. When he left The Hawketts, his replacement was his brother, Aaron. By 1959 Art had joined the navy and Aaron was serving six months in prison for stealing a car. In 1960 Aaron signed a solo deal with Allen TOUSSAINT at Minit, where his first record, *Over You*, reached #21 on the R&B charts. When Art was discharged from the navy he returned to The Hawketts briefly before cut-ting *All These Things* for the local Instant label in 1962; later that year he formed The Neville Sounds with Aaron and Cyril, and then signed to Minit as a solo artist. Meanwhile Charles had moved to New York to become a member of Joey Dee & The Starliters.

By 1966 Aaron had signed with the Parlo label, scoring the following year with *Tell it Like it Is* (USA#2.1967). He started a nation-wide tour, backed by The Neville Sounds. However, the follow-up, *She Took You for a Ride*, was only a minor hit and Parlo went out of business soon afterwards. In 1968 Aaron and Cyril left The Neville Sounds to form The Soul Machine; Art, with the remainder of the group, "Ziggy" Modeliste (drums), George Porter (bass) and Leo Nocentelli (guitar) became known as The Meters. Between 1968 and 1970 Toussaint and Marshall Sehorn used The Meters as the resident house band at the Sea-Saint studios in New Orleans. Fur-thermore, Toussaint and Sehorn decided to record the group in their own right as an instru-mental group, emulating the success of BOOKER T & THE MGs. It proved to be a wise move as they had a succession of hit singles: *Sophisticated Lady* (USA#34.1969), *Cissy Strut* (USA#23.1969), *Ease Back* (USA #61.1969), *Look-Ka Py Py* (USA#56.1970) and *Chicken Strut* (USA#50.1970).

In 1972 the group signed to Reprise and recorded the LP *Cabbage Alley*. Although their recording career as a group was on the wane they were still in demand as session musicians, backing artists like DOCTOR JOHN, LaBELLE, Robert PALMER and Toussaint, himself. They continued to record, cutting LPs like *Rejuvenation* (1974), *Fire on the Bayou* (1975) and *Trick Bag* (1976). In 1975 Cyril joined the group and was followed by Aaron and Charles for the recording of the LP *The Wild Tchipitoulas* with George and Amos Landry. However, in 1977 they parted com-pany with Toussaint and teamed up with pro-ducer David Rubinson for the LP *New Directions*; legal problems with Toussaint ensued and the group broke up. The four bro-thers remained together, forming The Neville Brothers.

In 1978, after signing with Capitol, they released their first LP *The Neville Brothers*, which was produced by Jack Nitzsche. It failed to sell and they changed labels, moving to A&M. At A&M they released *Fiyo on the Bayou* in 1981; this also failed to sell, but it created a buzz about the group with people like Keith Richards singing its praises. In 1984 they released the live LP *Neville-ization*, which included versions of songs like *Tell it Like it Is*.

Their next LP *Uptown* (1987) was over-produced and represented a small step backwards for the group. In 1989 *Yellow Moon*, produced by Daniel Lanois, lived up to all that had been said about the group; it included the single *Don't Know Much* (USA/UK#2.1990), which was a duet between Aaron and Linda Ronstadt, and a strikingly soulful reworking of the Bob Dylan composition, *God on Our Side*. In 1990 they appeared at The Nelson Mandela concert in London, celebrating his release from jail. Later the same year they toured the UK extensively and released the LP *Brother's Keeper*, which proved that *Yellow Moon* was no trick of the tail.

THE WILD TCHIPITOULAS, Island, 1976

FIYO ON THE BAYOU, Demon, 1981

NEVILLE-IZATION, Demon, 1984

HUMDINGER, (Aaron Neville), Stateside, 1986

MAKE ME STRONG, (Aaron Neville), Charly, 1986

ORCHID IN THE STORM, (Aaron Neville), Demon, 1986

MARDI GRAS ROCK 'N' ROLL, (Art Neville), Ace, 1986

STRUTTIN', (The Meters), Charly, 1987

YELLOW MOON, A&M, 1989

SHOW ME THE WAY, (Aaron Neville), Charly, 1989

LEGACY: A HISTORY OF THE NEVILLE BROTHERS, (Art & Aaron Neville), Charly, 1990

BROTHER'S KEEPER, A&M, 1990

LIVE AT TIPITINA'S, Essential, 1990

GOOD OLD FUNKY MUSIC, (The Meters), Special Delivery, 1990

TELL IT LIKE IT IS, (Aaron Neville), Ace, 1990

MY GREATEST GIFT, (Aaron Neville), Rounder, 1991

FUNKY CIRCLE, (The Meters), Charly, 1991

NEW EDITION See BROWN, Bobby

NEW YORK CITY PLAYERS See CAMEO

NYRO, LAURA It was Laura Nyro's misfortune that her emergence coincided with a vogue for singer-songwriters, because she was overlooked amid the plethora while many with far less talent achieved considerable celebrity. Her skill as a composer was peerless among her contemporaries, as she was able to utilise a degree of harmonic invention that had hitherto been confined to jazz.

She was born in New York on October 18, 1947; her father was a jazz trumpeter who encouraged her interest in composition. She made her debut with the LP *More than a Discovery* in 1966, having been signed by Verve. It included compositions that were covered by The Fifth Dimension, Blood, Sweat & Tears and Barbra Streisand. In 1968 her manager, David Geffen, signed her to Columbia, where she recorded a series of LPs: *Eli and the Thirteenth Confession, New York Tendaberry* (USA #32.1969), *Christmas and the Beads of Sweat* and *It's Gonna Take a Miracle*. Each was highly idiosyncratic, illustrating the broad expanse of her influences: *Christmas and the Beads of Sweat* was produced by Arif MARDIN and featured contributions from Alice Coltrane and Duane ALLMAN, while *It's Gonna Take a Miracle* included cover versions of songs like The CRYSTALS' *Da Doo Ron Ron* and MARTHA & THE VANDELLAS' *Dancing in the Streets* with backing vocals supplied by LaBELLE. In 1975 she released the LP *Smile*, which chronicled her emotional turmoil and general disgust with the music industry. However, later LPs like *Nested* in 1978 and *Mother's Spiritual* in 1984 showed that she had not lost any of her earlier flair. Her live work has always been erratic – the live LP *Season of Light* (1977) bore all the hallmarks of one who is not remotely interested in what they're doing – but in 1989 *Live at the Bottom Line*, showed her to be back, and in excellent fettle.

IMPRESSIONS, CBS, 1980

OATES, JOHN See HALL, Daryl, & John Oates

OCEAN, BILLY Billy Ocean was born Leslie Sebastian Charles on January 21, 1950, in Trinidad. In 1959 he moved to the UK with the rest of his family. On leaving school he worked in the rag trade as a cutter, but started to perform in an East End pub with The Shades of Midnight. In 1974 he released his first single under the name of Scorched Earth; it failed and so he got a job at Ford Motors in Dagenham, Essex, on the night shift, so that he could concentrate upon his writing and recording during the day. The following year he was signed to Dick Leahy's GTO label. His first single failed, but the second, *Love Really Hurts without You* (USA#22; UK#2.1976), established him. Then came *L.O.D (Love on Delivery)* (UK#19.1976) and *Stop Me (If You've Heard it Before)* (UK#12.1976). The next year he met up with Laurie Jay, who became his manager, and recorded *Red Light Spells Danger* (UK#2.1977). He then had a couple of comparatively lean years, although La Toya Jackson recorded two of his compositions for her debut LP. In 1982 Leahy sold GTO to Epic and with his career approaching the doldrums, Ocean signed with Jive in 1984.

His first record with his new producer, Keith Diamond, was *European Queen (No More Love on the Run)*, retitled *Caribbean Queen* (USA#1; UK#6.1984) and became an international dance-floor smash. The ensuing LP, *Suddenly* (USA/UK#9.1984), featured two more singles, *Loverboy* (USA#2; UK#13.1985) and *Suddenly* (USA/UK#4.1985). In 1985 he recorded *When the Going Gets Tough, the Tough Get Going* (USA#2.1985; UK#1.1986) for the soundtrack of the film, *The Jewel of the Nile*, which starred Michael Douglas and Kathleen Turner. His next LP, *Love Zone* (USA#6; UK#2.1986), featured the singles *There'll be Sad Songs (to Make You Cry)* (USA#1; UK#12.1986), *Love Zone* (USA#10; UK#49.1986); *Love is Forever* (USA#16.1986; UK#34.1987) and *Bittersweet* (UK#44.1986). In 1988 the LP *Tear Down these Walls* (USA#18; UK#3.1988) included another batch of singles: *Get outta my Dreams (Get into my Car)* (USA#1; UK#3.1988), *Calypso Crazy* (UK#35.1988) and *The Colour of Love* (USA#17; UK#65.1988). The same year he embarked on a world tour.

NIGHTS (I FEEL LIKE GETTIN' DOWN), Epic, 1981
INNER FEELINGS, Epic, 1982
SUDDENLY, Jive, 1984
BILLY OCEAN, Epic, 1985
IN MOTION, MFP, 1986
LOVE ZONE, Jive, 1986
TEAR DOWN THESE WALLS, Jive, 1988
GREATEST HITS, Jive, 1989

OHIO PLAYERS The Ohio Players were formed as The Ohio Untouchables in Dayton in 1959, although the group went through a number of changes in personnel. In 1962 they were the backing band for The FALCONS on their minor hit *I Found a Love*, which led them to becoming the house band at Compass records; this, in turn, enabled them to acquire a contract with Capitol. The resulting LP, *Observations In Time*, was not a commercial success and Capitol allowed their contract to expire.

By 1971 the group had managed to stem the ebb and flow of personnel and now consisted of Leroy 'Sugarfoot' Bonner (guitar and vocals), Billy Beck (keyboards), Clarence Satchell (saxophones and flute), Marvin 'Merv' Pierce (trumpet), Ralph 'Pee Wee' Middlebrooks (trumpet), Marshall Jones (bass) and Jimmy 'Diamond' Williams (drums and percussion). Furthermore, their style of funk had become fashionable, and so they were able to sign a recording contract with the Detroit label,

Westbound. Their first LP for Westbound, *Pain*, was only moderately successful, but the single *Pain* (USA#64.1972) put them on the map. They consolidated this success with a novelty record, *Funky Worm* (USA#15.1973), taken from *Pleasure* (USA#64.1973); the sexist connotations of the LP's cover photograph had the desired effect of establishing a graphic, if not a musical, identity for the group. Their next LP, *Ecstasy* (USA#70.1973), was their last record for Westbound.

With a contract for Mercury under their belts they were able to establish themselves as one of the country's premier funk outfits with four hits in succession: *Skintight* (USA #13.1974), *Fire* (USA#1.1974), *Sweet Sticky Thing* (USA#33.1975) and *Love Rollercoaster* (USA#1.1975). The LPs were equally successful: *Skintight* (USA#11.1974), *Fire* (USA #1.1974), *Honey* (USA#2.1975) and *Contradiction* (USA#12.1976). They were unable to match their US success in the UK. Despite their considerable popularity in clubs, they had just the one UK hit, *Who'd She Coo* (USA#18; UK#43.1976). By the end of 1976 their brand of funk had been superseded by the disco fad. Although they continued to record, the results became less commercially successful, until by the early 1980s they were concentrating upon touring and on participating in community projects in their hometown of Dayton, taking only occasional trips to the studio.

FIRE, Mercury, 1975
GOLD, Mercury, 1976
OHIO PLAYERS, Capitol, 1977
TENDERNESS, Epic, 1981
GRADUATION, Air City, 1985

O'JAYS The O'Jays exemplify the journeyman soul group. Despite changes in personnel, producers and fashion, they have retained their own identity in a career that has spanned five decades.

The nucleus of the group – Eddie Levert (born June 16, 1942, in Canton, Ohio), Walter Williams (born August 25, 1942, in Canton, Ohio) and William Powell (born in 1941 in Canton, Ohio) – formed as The Mascots in 1958, while they were all at McKinley High School in Canton. The line-up was completed by Bobby Massey and Bill Isles. In 1961 they recorded *Miracles* for the Wayco label and were introduced to Cleveland DJ Eddie O'Jay, after whom they named the group, as a gesture of gratitude for his help in developing their stage act.

In 1963 having recorded a few singles for King, they released *Lonely Drifter* (USA #93.1963) for the Imperial label under the watchful eye of producer/arranger H. B. BARNUM, it was the first of a series of singles for the label, including *Lipstick Traces (on a Cigarette)* (USA#48.1965). Although the major breakthrough eluded them they were much sought-after as session singers, backing artists like Nat 'King' Cole and The RONETTES. After the departure of Isles in 1966, they were switched from Imperial to its subsidiary, Minit, in 1968; they then moved to the Bell label and scored with the Thom BELL production, *I'll be Sweeter Tomorrow (than I was Today)* (USA#68.1968).

In 1969, they left the Bell label and were signed to the Chess-distributed Neptune label by producers GAMBLE & HUFF. Their debut for Neptune, *One Night Affair* (USA #68.1969), was followed by *Deeper (in Love with You)* (USA#64.1970). The collapse of Chess left them without a recording contract until, in 1972, they were signed to Gamble & Huff's label Philadelphia International. From 1972, despite having pared down to a trio after the departure of Massey for a career in record production, they became one of the jewels in the

Philadelphia crown, with hits like *Backstabbers* (USA#3; UK#14.1972), *Love Train* (USA#1; UK#9.1973), *Put Your Hands Together* (USA #10.1974), *For the Love of Money* (USA #9.1974), *I Love Music* (USA#5; UK#13.1976/ #38.1978), *Darlin' Darlin' Baby (Sweet Tender Love)* (UK#24.1977) and *Used ta be my Girl* (USA#4; UK#12.1978). In 1976, Powell left the group due to illness (he died of cancer on May 26, 1977); his replacement was the Brooklyn-born, Sammy Strain, formerly a member of LITTLE ANTHONY & THE IMPERIALS.

Throughout, their LPs, many of which contained critiques of social conditions, consistently breached the upper echelons of the US charts: *Backstabbers* (USA#10.1972), *Ship Ahoy* (USA#11.1974), *Live in London* (USA #17.1974), *Survival* (USA#11.1975), *A Family Reunion* (USA#7.1975), *So Full of Love* (USA #6.1978) and *Identify Yourself* (USA#16.1979). The 1980s saw a marked decline in their output, as they tended to concentrate on touring irrespective of the position of their latest record in the charts. This professionalism has permeated their career and enabled them to continue recording with the best technicians and musicians available. In 1987, following a new deal with the EMI Manhattan label, they released the LP *Let me Touch You*, which reunited them with Gamble & Huff and Thom Bell. It was followed in 1989 by the LP *Serious*, which was produced by Levert and Dennis LAMBERT.

MESSAGE IN THE MUSIC, Philadelphia International, 1976
COLLECTOR'S ITEMS: GREATEST HITS, Philadelphia International, 1978
IDENTIFY YOURSELF, Philadelphia International, 1979
THE YEAR 2000, Philadelphia International, 1980
PEACE, Phoenix, 1981
WHEN WILL I SEE YOU AGAIN, Philadelphia International, 1983
LOVE AND MORE, Philadelphia International, 1984
GREATEST HITS, Philadelphia International, 1984
WORKING ON YOUR CASE, Stateside, 1985
LET ME TOUCH YOU, Manhattan, 1987
FROM THE BEGINNING, Chess, 1988
SERIOUS, Manhattan, 1989

OLDHAM, SPOONER While it was Rick HALL's tenacity that launched the Fame studios, it was the contribution of session musicians like Lindon 'Spooner' Oldham and Dan PENN that turned the dream into a reality. Oldham had played piano in a variety of high-school bands before going to the University of North Alabama. After meeting Hall he started to collaborate with Penn, and together they wrote a number of classics like *Sweet Inspiration* and *I'm Your Puppet*. After bassist Norbert PUTNAM, guitarist David BRIGGS and drummer Jerry CARRIGAN left Fame in 1964, Oldham became a regular member of the house band, whose other members were Jimmy JOHNSON (guitar), Junior Lowe (bass) and Roger HAWKINS (drums). Until 1967, when he was lured to Memphis by Penn and Chips MOMAN, Oldham played on most of the hits to be recorded at Fame and Quin IVY's Quinvy studios, backing artists like Aretha FRANKLIN, Percy SLEDGE, Wilson PICKETT and Joe TEX. When he joined Penn at Moman's American studios in Memphis, they wrote and produced such hits as *The Letter* and *Cry Like a Baby* for The Box Tops. By 1970, Oldham had lost interest, through years of continuous playing, and had moved to the West Coast.

O'NEAL, ALEXANDER In 1978 Alexander O'Neal linked up with his future producers, Jimmy JAM & Terry Lewis, to form Flyte Time in his native Minneapolis and PRINCE asked them to become his backing band. It was the first step in a process that made Minneapolis one of the most influential recording centres of the 1980s. O'Neal was born in 1954. Although he was considered good enough to play football professionally, he settled on a career in music. By the time he linked up with Jam & Lewis, he had worked the club circuit for six years. His association with Prince was short-lived and he started up his own group, the Secret.

In 1984, with Jam & Lewis, writing and producing, in association with Flyte Time colleague Monte Moir (see JAM, Jimmy & Terry Lewis), he recorded his debut LP, *Alexander O'Neal* (UK#19.1985), for the Tabu label, which was an arm of the Jam & Lewis operation. It included the singles *If You Were Here Tonight* (UK#13.1986) and *A Broken Heart Can Mend* (UK#53.1986). He was teamed with Cherrelle for the duet, *Saturday Love* (UK#6.1985), which was written and produced by Jam & Lewis. After a period of hospitalization for drug and alcohol addiction he released his follow-up, *Hearsay* (USA#29; UK#4.1987), which included a slew of singles: *Fake* (USA#25; UK#33.1987), *Criticize* (UK#4.1987), *Never Knew Love Like this Before* (USA#28; UK#26.1988) another duet with Cherrelle, *The Lovers* (UK#28.1988) and *What Can I Say to Make You Love Me* (UK#27.1988). In November 1988 a seasonally inspired offering, *My Gift to You*, was released, as was a remixed version of his second LP under the title of *Hearsay all Mixed Up*. He also guested on Cherrelle's LP, *Affair*. In 1991 he released the LP *All True Man* (UK#2.1991), written and produced by Jam & Lewis; it represented O'Neal's coming of age as a performer, showing his adeptness at handling a variety of styles.

ALEXANDER O'NEAL, Tabu, 1985
HEARSAY, Tabu, 1987
HEARSAY ALL MIXED UP, Tabu, 1988
MY GIFT TO YOU, Tabu, 1988
ALL TRUE MAN, Tabu, 1991

OSBORNE, JEFFREY In 1970 Jeffrey Osborne (born March 9, 1948, in Providence, Rhode Island) joined the ten- piece funk outfit, LTD (Love, Togetherness and Devotion). For four years they toured the club circuit before signing with A&M. Their first two LPs, *Love, Togetherness and Devotion* and *Gettin' Down*, failed to make any impression. Their breakthrough came with *Love Ballad* (USA#20.1976) from the LP, *Love to the World*. Their next LP, *Something to Love* (USA#21.1978), featured the single *(Every Time I Turn Around) Back in Love Again* (USA#4.1977). Their next three LPs, *Together-ness* (USA#18.1978), *Devotion* (USA#29,1979) and *Shine On* (USA#28.1980), kept up the momentum with *Shine On* (USA#40.1981) being released as a single. After one more LP, *Love Magic*, the group split up and Osborne embarked on a solo career, remaining with A&M.

His debut solo LP, *Jeffrey Osborne*, was produced by George DUKE and featured *I Really Don't Need no Light* (USA#39.1982) and *On the Wings of Love* (USA#29.1982; UK#11.1984). The follow-up LP, *Stay with Me Tonight* (USA#25; UK#56.1984), included the singles, *Don't You Get so Mad* (USA#25.1984) and *Stay with Me Tonight* (USA#30; UK#18.1984). His third LP, *Don't Stop* (1984), followed a duet with Joyce Kennedy on *The Last Time I Made Love* (USA#40.1984) that was featured on her debut LP, *Lookin' for Trouble,* which Osborne produced. In 1986 the LP *Emotional* (USA#26.1986) included the singles *You Should be Mine (The Woo Woo Song)* (USA#13.1986) and *Soweto* (UK#44.1986). It featured a variety of producers among them George Duke, Michael Masser, Richard Perry and Rod Temperton (see HEATWAVE). In 1988 he returned, after a lay-off of two years with the LP, *One Love, One Dream*, co-written by Bruce Roberts. After collaborating with Dionne WARWICK on the single Love Power (1990) he signed with Arista. His first LP for his new label, *Only Human*, saw him retreading familiar territory.

SOMETHING TO LOVE, (LTD), A&M, 1978
TOGETHERNESS, (LTD), A&M, 1978
JEFFREY OSBORNE, A&M, 1982
STAY WITH ME TONIGHT, A&M, 1983
DON'T STOP, A&M, 1984
EMOTIONAL, A&M, 1986
ONE LOVE, ONE DREAM, A&M, 1988
ONLY HUMAN, Arista, 1991

OTIS, JOHNNY Throughout the 1950s The Johnny Otis Show provided a springboard for a crop of artists to further and develop their careers.

Otis was born John Veliotes in Vallejo, California, on December 28, 1921. Throughout the 1930s and early 1940s he toured the West Coast and the South with a number of bands (including Louis Jordan's), playing drums, vibes or piano. In 1945 he formed his own first band, which included people like Jimmy Rushing and Bill Doggett. In 1948 he opened the Barrelhouse Club in the Watts District of Los Angeles, where he could not only provide a showcase for his own band but also feature new talent – artists like Etta JAMES, T-Bone Walker, Lowell Fulson, The Robins (see COASTERS), Esther PHILLIPS and Charles Brown. The success of the club enabled him to take the show on the road as The Johnny Otis Show. As a scout for Syd NATHAN's King label, he discovered artists like Jackie WILSON, Little Willie JOHN and Hank BALLARD & The Midnighters. In 1953, he prevailed upon LEIBER & STOLL-ER to write a song for Big Mama THORNTON: the result was *Hound Dog*. In addition, he worked for Don ROBEY's Duke label, where his band backed artists like Bobby BLAND and Johnny ACE .

In 1957 he was signed by Capitol and released a number of singles like *Ma! He's Making Eyes at Me* (UK#2.1958), *Bye Bye Baby* (UK #20.1958) and *Willie and the Hand Jive* (USA #9.1958). Although there was a strong novelty element to some of his hits, this did not detract from the fact that as a catalyst for fresh talent, he was invaluable. Throughout the 1960s, he continued touring and began to campaign for the Democratic party. In 1969 he recorded the LP *Cold Shot* which featured his son Shuggie. The following year he played the Monterey Jazz Festival, which was recorded and released by Epic: it featured veterans like Ivory Joe HUNTER, Esther Phillips, Eddie 'Cleanhead' Vinson, as well Shuggie Otis, who had started a solo career with the LP *Here Comes Shuggie Otis* the same year.

In 1974 Otis launched his own label, Blues Spectrum, but it wasn't a great commercial success. In 1981 he signed with the Alligator label, recording *The New Johnny Otis Show*. During the 1980s he has effectively retired from the music business, concentrating instead on his post of pastor at the Landmark Community Church in Los Angles.

LIVE AT MONTEREY, Edsel, 1970
ROCK AND ROLL HIT PARADE, Flyright, 1979
THE NEW JOHNNY OTIS SHOW, Alligator, 1982
GREAT RHYTHM AND BLUES, VOLUME 3, Bulldog, 1982
THE JOHNNY OTIS SHOW, Capitol, 1983
THE ORIGINAL JOHNNY OTIS SHOW, Savoy, 1985

PAGE, GENE In the wake of Barry WHITE's success in the early 1970s, Gene

Page became the doyen of arrangers by virtue of having worked with White. His career had started as a result of winning a scholarship to the Brooklyn Conservatory in New York, which enabled him to get work as a studio arranger. Under the auspices of Phil SPECTOR he arranged *You've Lost that Lovin' Feeling* for The RIGHTEOUS BROTHERS. His next major achievement was the arrangement for *The 'In' Crowd* by Dobie GRAY. His skill encouraged Motown to secure his services for the Marvin GAYE LP *Hello Broadway* and was the beginning of a sporadic liaison that lasted until the late 1970s, with Page providing the arrangements for *Come Get to This* (1973) and *Got to Give it Up* (1977).

However, he really made his mark with the string arrangements for all of White's hits, like *Never Gonna Give You Up* and *You're my First, my Last, my Everything*. Furthermore, he participated in White's shows as conductor of the LOVE UNLIMITED Orchestra. As a result he was encouraged to record under his own name. However, his solo albums proved to be little more than excuses for him to flex his cerebral muscles. Since then he has continued to work with Diana ROSS, Deniece WILLIAMS, Betty EVERETT and Manhattan Transfer.

PALMER, EARL Throughout the 1950s Earl Palmer was the drummer at the J&M Studio in New Orleans. As a member of Dave BARTHOLOMEW's Band he backed artists like Fats DOMINO, Lloyd PRICE, LITTLE RICHARD, Larry WILLIAMS, PROFESSOR LONGHAIR, Smiley LEWIS and SHIRLEY & LEE. The economy of his drumming was critical to the development of what came to be known as rock'n'roll. In the early 1960s he moved to the West Coast and picked up where he had left off, playing sessions for producers like Phil SPECTOR and Harold Battiste.

PALMER, ROBERT Robert Palmer was born on January 19,1949 in Batley, Yorkshire. He made his musical debut in a local group, Mandrake Paddle Steamer, before heading south to replace Jess Roden in The Alan Bown Set in 1969. After recording one single with them, in 1970 he joined the jazz-oriented group DADA, which, after making the LP *Dada* for Atco, broke up. The nucleus of Dada went on to form Vinegar Joe, who stayed together for two years and established a loyal following, although their records, released by the Island label were commercially disastrous. Palmer then embarked on a solo career; he remained signed to Island.

In 1974, he recorded the LP, *Sneakin' Sally through the Alley*, with guitarist Lowell George and The Meters (see NEVILLE BROTHERS). The sinuous funk of The Meters and the choice of material by writers like Allen TOUSSAINT and Lowell George provided the perfect settings for Palmer's voice. Although the LP failed to make significant inroads in the charts, it set him up as a cult hero of sorts. The follow-up, *Pressure Drop* (1975), featured Little Feat as well as string arrangements by Gene PAGE. Once again it was held up by the cognoscenti as a model of blue-eyed soul, but sales were modest. In 1976, having moved to Nassau, Bahamas, he started to record with the crack rhythm section of Sly & Robbie at Compass Point studios. The result was the LP *Some People Can do what They Like* (UK#46.1976). It was followed by the LP *Double Fun*, which included the single *Every Kinda People* (USA#16; UK#53.1978). His next LP, *Secrets* (USA#19; UK#54.1979) kept up the momentum in the USA; a single, *Bad Case of Loving You (Doctor, Doctor)* (USA#14.1979), was extracted from it.

The 1980s saw a marked increase in his popularity in the UK, with the LP *Clues* (UK #31.1980) and a live LP, *Maybe it's Live* (UK #32.1982), both charting. The latter, recorded at the Dominion Theatre in London, featured also a studio recording of The Persuaders' composition, *Some Guys Have all the Luck (UK#16.1982)*. *His next LP, Pride* (UK #37.1983), was followed by a collaboration with Andy and John Taylor, Tony Thompson and producer Bernard EDWARDS of CHIC under the name of The Power Station. After completing the project, he recorded the LP *Riptide* (USA#8; UK#5.1986), which included the singles *Addicted to Love* (USA#1; UK#5.1986), *Hyperactive* (USA#33.1986) and *I Didn't Mean to Turn You On* (USA#2; UK#9.1986).

In 1988, having moved to Switzerland, he left the Island label and signed with the EMI subsidiary, Manhattan. His debut LP for Manhattan, *Heavy Nova* (USA#25; UK#17.1988), featured the single, *Simply Irresistible* (USA#20; UK#44.1988). The following year he toured intermittently and was featured on the UB40 World Tour. In 1990 he released the double LP, *Don't Explain*, which included a bunch of covers of songs by Bob Dylan, Rodgers & Hammerstein and Mose Allison, among others, as well as arrangements by Teo Macero, who produced some of the Miles Davis' LPs of the late 1960s and early 1970s.

SNEAKIN' SALLY THROUGH THE ALLEY, Island, 1974

PRESSURE DROP, Island, 1975

SOME PEOPLE CAN DO WHAT THEY LIKE, Island, 1976

DOUBLE FUN, Island, 1978

SECRETS, Island, 1979

CLUES, Island, 1980

MAYBE IT'S LIVE, Island, 1982

PRIDE, Island, 1983

RIPTIDE, Island, 1985

THE EARLY YEARS, See For Miles, 1987

HEAVY NOVA, Manhattan, 1988

ADDICTIONS: (THE BEST OF ......), VOLUME 1, Island, 1990

DON'T EXPLAIN, Manhattan, 1990

PARAMOUNTS See KNIGHT, Robert

PARIS, MICA Mica Paris has in a very short period of time become one of the stalwarts of the British soul scene. She was born in London, of Jamaican parents, and started to sing gospel in the group The Spirit of Watts when she was sixteen. Such was the impact of the group that she came to the attention of Mark Rogers of Hollywood Beyond, who enlisted her services as a vocalist in that group's touring unit. After meeting Paul JOHNSON and Style Council bassist Paul Powell, she was signed to the Island subsidiary 4th & Broadway. Her debut LP, *So Good* (UK#6.1988), included the singles *My One Temptation* (UK#7.1988), *Like Dreamers Do* (UK#26.1988) and *Breathe some Life into Me* (UK#26.1988), as well as contributions from Johnson, Will DOWNING and Courtney Pine. A duet with Downing on *Where is the Love?*, the Roberta FLACK and Donny HATHAWAY original, followed. Her second LP, *Contribution*, teamed her with a host of fashionable contributors like Rakim and Danny D, and featured material from such notables as PRINCE. It seems unfortunate that her own personal touch lacks a clear identity of its own.

SO GOOD, 4th & Broadway, 1988

CONTRIBUTION, 4th & Broadway, 1990

PARKER, Jr, RAY Ray Parker was born on May 1, 1954, in Detroit, Michigan. By the time he was sixteen, he had got a job at the Motown Studios and at HOLLAND, DOZIER & HOLLAND's studios in Detroit as a guitarist, where among the artists he worked with was Stevie WONDER. As a result of this felicitous contact, he joined Wonder's touring band and, in 1973, moved to Los Angeles and took up session work with artists like Barry WHITE, Boz SCAGGS and Patti LaBELLE. In his spare time he composed; his first hit was *You Got the Love* for Rufus (see KHAN, Chaka) in 1974. In 1977 he opened his own recording studio, Ameraycan and secured a recording contract with Arista after he had submitted a demo.

He also assembled a group, Raydio, made up of colleagues from Detroit: Charles Fearing (guitar), Vincent Bonham (keyboards), Arnell Carmichael (keyboards), Jerry Knight (bass) and Larry Tolbert (drums). Their debut single, *Jack and Jill* (USA#8; UK#11.1978), was followed by *Is this Love a Thing?* (UK#27.1978), both being extracted from the LP *Raydio* (USA#27.1978). Their second LP, *Rock On*, included *You Can't Change That* (USA #9.1979). Their next LPs, *Two Places at the Same Time* (USA#33.1980) and *A Woman Needs Love* (USA#13.1981), were credited to Ray Parker, Jr & Raydio. However the title track of the former was released as a single (USA#30.1980), while the latter included two singles *A Woman Needs Love (Just Like You Do)* (USA#4.1981) and *That Old Song* (USA #21.1981). They proved to be his final records with the group, which he disbanded in favour of a solo career.

The title track of his debut LP, *The Other Woman* (USA#11.1982), was extracted as a single (USA#4.1982), as were *Let Me Go* (USA#38.1982) and *Bad Boy* (USA#35.1983). His next LP, *Woman out of Control* (USA #30.1984), featured *I Still Can't Get Over Loving You* (USA#12.1984). The same year he was asked to write and record a theme song for the film, *Ghostbusters* (USA#1; UK#2.1984/ #6.1986); unfortunately, Huey Lewis sued him, claiming he had plagiarised his composition, *I Want a New Drug,* the court agreed. His own LP *Ghostbusters* was adumbrated by the original film soundtrack, but another single *Jamie* (USA#14.1985) was extracted from it. His next

LP, *Sex and the Single Man,* included the hit single *Girls Have More Fun* (USA#34.1985; UK#46.1986). In 1987 he was signed by the Geffen label, for whom his debut single, *I Don't Think Man Should Sleep Alone* (UK#13.1987), was extracted from the LP, *After Dark* (UK #40.1987). In 1989 he appeared in the film *Ghostbusters II.*

ROCK ON, (Raydio), Arista, 1979
TWO PLACES AT THE SAME TIME, (with Raydio), Arista, 1980
A WOMAN NEEDS LOVE, (with Raydio), Arista, 1981
THE OTHER WOMAN, Arista, 1982
THE VERY BEST OF RAY PARKER JR, Arista, 1983
WOMAN OUT OF CONTROL, Arista, 1984
RAY PARKER'S GHOSTBUSTERS, Arista, 1985
SEX AND THE SINGLE MAN, Arista, 1985
AFTER DARK, Geffen, 1987

PARKER, ROBERT Saxophonist Robert Parker has been a stalwart of the New Orleans recording scene since the early 1960s. He began his career as a session musician, then started to record in his own right for the independent Nola label. He achieved his biggest hit with *Barefootin'* (USA#7; UK #24.1966), which was produced by Allen TOUSSAINT and arranged by Wardell QUEZERGUE. Its success prompted him to record a whole string of singles like *Get ta Steppin'* and *Let's Go Baby (Where the Action is)*, all of which have proved hardy perennials on the dance-floor. However, after his brief flirtation with success, he returned to the New Orleans club circuit, reappearing only to record the novelty record *Disco Doctor*, in the mid-1970s. In recent years, he has been able to capitalise upon his cult status by touring the UK and Europe, where *Barefootin'* has become a classic of the genre.

PARLIAMENT See CLINTON, George

PAUL, BILLY Billy Paul was born Paul Williams on December 1, 1934, in Philadelphia. He made his debut in 1945 singing on the local radio station. Throughout the early 1950s, while studying music at Temple University, he developed his style playing the local jazz clubs. After recording with Tadd Dameron in 1955, he joined the army to do his national service; on his return he became an occasional member of Harold MELVIN & The Blue Notes. In 1967 he was signed by Kenny Gamble (see GAMBLE & HUFF) to the Neptune label. His first LP, *Feelin' Good at the Cadillac Club*, a collection of standards, was followed by *Ebony Woman* (1970); in both his background in jazz was evident. The Neptune label folded when Chess went out of business, but Gamble & Huff then signed him to the Philadelphia International label, which they set up shortly after the demise of Neptune.

Throughout the early 1970s Paul had a number of hits, particularly in the UK, where his relaxed style found great appeal with the Johnny Mathis audience. *Me and Mrs Jones* (USA#1.1972; UK#12.1973), nominally a tale about adultery and was considered by some to be slightly risqué, was extracted from the LP *360 Degrees of Billy Paul* (USA#17.1973). Among his other singles were *Thanks for Saving my Life* (USA#37; UK#33.1974), *Let's make a Baby* (UK#30.1976), *Let 'em In* (UK#26.1977), *Your Song* (UK#37.1977), *Only the Strong Survive* (UK#33.1977) and *Bring the Family Back* (UK#51.1979). When Philadelphia International finally closed, Paul stopped recording until 1985. He returned with the LP *Lately*, on the Total Experience label, and in 1988 he recorded the LP *Wide Open* for Ichiban.

WHEN LOVE IS NEW, Philadelphia International, 1976

ONLY THE STRONG SURVIVE, Philadelphia International, 1977
GREATEST HITS, Philadelphia International, 1983
LATELY, Total Experience, 1985
WIDE OPEN, Ichiban, 1988
THE SOUND OF PHILADELPHIA, Blatant, 1989

PAUL, CLARENCE Clarence Paul, born in 1928, was one of Motown's most sterling operatives in their formative years. After joining Motown in 1960 he began to collaborate with Henry Cosby, forming a writing and production partnership. Their biggest assignment was to look after Stevie WONDER; with Cosby he wrote, produced and arranged songs like *Uptight* and *Fingertips*. He also collaborated with Marvin GAYE, cowriting his first hit, *Hitch Hike*. Due to a lack of credit and appreciation he left the company in 1968.

PEACHES & HERB Peaches & Herb was formed in 1966 in Washington DC by Herb Fame and Francine Barker. Fame was Herbert Feemster in 1942 and Barker was born Francine Hurd in 1947. Before forming the duo Fame was a member of the vocal group, The Dreamtones, which he left for a solo career, and Barker was a member of another vocal group, Sweet Things. The duo was signed by the CBS subsidary Date for whom they had a succession of hit singles: *Let's Fall in Love* (USA#21.1967), *Close Your Eyes* (USA #8.1967), *For Your Love* (USA#20.1967), *Love is Strange* (USA#13.1967) and *Two Little Kids* (USA#31.1968).

In 1968 Marlene Mack replaced Barker for a year, and in 1978 Barker left for good to be replaced by Linda Greene. In the intervening years they played the club and cabaret circuit, but their records were unable to compete with the ubiquitous thump of disco. In 1979 they were signed by Polydor, where they notched up some more hit singles including *Shake Your*

Groove Thing (USA#5; UK#26.1979), *Reunited* (USA#1; UK#4.1979) and *I Pledge my Love* (USA#19.1980). Two LPs were released during this period, *Hot!* (USA#2.1979) and *Twice the Fire* (USA#31.1979), which slotted into the vogue for romantic ballads. However, after releasing a few rather unsuccessful LPs they returned to the cabaret circuit.

WELL WORTH THE WAIT, Polydor, 1980
SAYING SOMETHING, Polydor, 1982

PEASTON, DAVID Since his debut LP, *Introducing David Peaston*, in 1989, David Peaston has been lionised by those 'in the know' as the male equivalent of Anita BAKER. This similarity is arguably due to the fact that they share the same writer and producer, Michael Powell, rather than to any latent artistic similarities. Prior to recording his debut, he worked as a school teacher in Brooklyn and sang in various gospel groups; he contributed vocals to the Lester Bowie LP *All the Magic*, in 1983, with his sister Fontella BASS, Bowie's wife. He was discovered having hit a year-long winning streak at the Apollo Theatre amateur nights, which resulted in an appearance on the TV series, *Showtime at the Apollo*, in 1987. After signing with Geffen his first LP was released to unanimous critical approval.

INTRODUCING DAVID PEASTON, Geffen, 1989

PEEBLES, ANN Always one of the great stylists of Southern soul, she has never had the opportunity (or, perhaps, incentive) to break out and achieve the lasting success that is her due, despite the high esteem in which she is held by her contemporaries and fans alike.

Ann Peebles was born in St Louis on April 27, 1947. From 1955 she was a member of the local church choir, which was directed by her father Perry. In 1968 she was introduced to Willie MITCHELL, the chief producer at Hi records in Memphis, by Gene 'Bowlegs' Miller, a session musician at Stax. She was put under contract to Hi and her first record, *Walk Away*, became an R&B hit. Her first national hit came in 1970, with *Part Time Love* (USA #45.1970); it was followed by another R&B hit, *I Feel Like Breaking up Somebody's Home*. However, her version of *Slipped Stumbled and Fell in Love* seemed to define as well as anything that Al GREEN sang the sound of Hi. She had to wait until 1973, for her major breakthrough with *I Can't Stand the Rain* (USA#38.1973; UK#41.1974), which she wrote with her husband Don Bryant. It was followed by her version of the Earl Randle composition, *I'm Gonna Tear Your Playhouse Down*.

In 1977, after the sale of the Hi label to Al Bennett's Cream Organization, singles like *Old Man with Young Ideas* and *If You've Got the Time, I've Got the Love* seemed to lack the chutzpah of her previous outings under Mitchell and she gradually disappeared from sight. When Mitchell set up the Waylo label Peebles became one of the initial signings. In 1988 she made her debut for Waylo with the LP *Call Me*.

I'M GONNA TEAR YOUR PLAYHOUSE DOWN, Hi, 1974
99 LBS, Hi, 1988
GREATEST HITS, Hi, 1988
CALL ME, Waylo, 1989

PENDERGRASS, TEDDY As his mother was a nightclub performer, it was predictable that Teddy Pendergrass (born March 26, 1950, in Philadelphia) should become a singer. Through the church's and his mother's encouragement, he was thoroughly grounded in gospel music, joining The Cadillacs as a drummer. He got his first real break in 1969 when the group was recruited by Harold

MELVIN to back The Blue Notes. The following year Pendergrass became lead vocalist of The Blue Notes when John Atkins left. Throughout the 1970s his vocals were the crucial factor in a string of hits for the group, although the songs of GAMBLE & HUFF and McFadden & Whitehead were so well crafted that he would have been hard-pressed not to deliver the goods. In 1976 he left the group to concentrate upon a solo career; however, he remained signed to Gamble & Huff's Philadelphia International label.

His solo career was kicked off by the release of the LP *Teddy Pendergrass*, which featured the singles, *I Don't Love you Anymore* and *The Whole Town's Laughing at Me* (UK#44.1977). It was followed by a US tour with The Teddy Bear Orchestra during which he started to offer Barry WHITE serious competition as 'Lurve Man #1' with large slices of his performances dedicated to the ladies in the audience. His next LP, *Life is a Song Worth Singing* (USA #11.1978), featured the single *Close the Door* (USA#25.1978). The succeeding four years saw him issue a string of LPs that, despite the sugary sentiments and the developing sense of self-parody in the narcissistic posturings of his concerts, were perfect vehicles for his superb voice: *Teddy* (USA#5.1979), *Teddy Live! Coast to Coast* (USA#33.1980), *TP* (USA#14.1980) and *It's Time for Love* (USA#19.1981). In 1981 he duetted with Stephanie Mills on her single *Two Hearts* (USA#40; UK#49.1981). The following year he appeared in the film, *Soup for One*, performing *Dream Girl* on the soundtrack, which was produced by Bernard EDWARDS and Nile RODGERS.

On March 18, 1982, his Rolls Royce skidded across the road and crashed. The injuries he sustained put an end to his career for two years, as he was paralysed from the neck down. When he returned, he was signed to the Asylum label. His debut for them, *Love Language* (USA #38.1984), included a duet with Whitney HOUSTON on *Hold Me* (UK#4.1986). As a whole, the LP showed that his balladeering instincts were undimmed, as did the follow-ups, *Working it Back* and *Joy*, the latter included the single *Joy* (UK#58.1988). In 1990 he released the LP *Truly Blessed*, which contained few surprises.

TEDDY PENDERGRASS, Philadelphia International, 1977
LIFE IS A SONG WORTH SINGING, Philadelphia International, 1978
TEDDY, Philadelphia International, 1979
TP, Philadelphia International, 1980
IT'S TIME FOR LOVE, Philadelphia International, 1981
THIS ONE'S FOR YOU, Philadelphia International, 1982
HEAVEN ONLY KNOWS, Philadelphia International, 1983
GREATEST HITS, Philadelphia International, 1984
LOVE LANGUAGE, Asylum, 1984
WORKING IT BACK, Asylum, 1985
JOY, Asylum, 1988
TEDDY PENDERGRASS, Blatant, 1989
TRULY BLESSED, Elektra, 1990

PENN, DAN Wallace Daniel Pennington was born on November 16, 1941, in Vernon, Alabama. He became a guitarist and vocalist in a local group, Benny Cagle & The Rhythm Swingsters, which included Billy Sherrill, who was to become a leading light in Nashville as a writer and producer. He met Rick HALL, who was a member of another local group with a tremendous reputation, The Fairlanes, and started to sing with them. His big break as a songwriter came in 1960, when Conway Twitty recorded one of his songs, *Is a Bluebird Blue?*. He formed The Mark Vs – later known as Dan Penn & The Pallbearers – with Norbert PUTNAM, David BRIGGS and Jerry CARRIGAN, and they were to become the nucleus of the Muscle Shoals house band after providing the backing for Rick Hall's first hit, *You Better Move On* by Arthur ALEXANDER. Hall, having started the Fame Studios with the proceeds from the Alexander record, gave Penn a job as a writer and producer.

Penn formed a partnership with the keyboardist and writer Spooner OLDHAM. Among their collaborations was *I'm Your Puppet*, released by James & Bobby PURIFY. In 1966 he teamed up with Chips MOMAN, who had opened his own studios in Memphis, and together they wrote such classics as *Dark End of the Street* and *Do Right Woman, Do Right Man*. In 1967 Oldham left Hall to join Penn and Moman in Memphis, and together they wrote and produced *Cry Like a Baby* and *The Letter* for The Box Tops. Throughout, Penn's compositions have been recorded by artists like Aretha FRANKLIN, Otis REDDING, Clarence CARTER and Elvis Presley.

In 1971 Penn established his own studio, Beautiful Sounds, recording an LP *Nobody's Fool* for Bell; it contained flashes of brilliance, but was otherwise a peculiar offering from one with such finely developed instincts when it came to cutting records. In recent years, as a born-again Christian, he has concentrated his energies upon gospel music.

PERETTI, HUGO   See HUGO & LUIGI

PHILLIPS, ESTHER   One of the great underrated vocalists of our time, Esther Phillips had an intuitive knack for interpreting songs that had been made famous by others so that they became (almost) her own. Had it not been for her continual problems with drug addiction – which ultimately sent her to an early grave – she would surely have attained much wider recognition.

She was born Esther Mae Jones on December 23, 1935, in Galveston, Texas. During childhood she moved to Los Angeles, where she sang in church choirs and at talent shows. When she was thirteen she was spotted by Johnny OTIS who recruited her to be a member of his revue and to perform at his club under the name Little Esther. Between 1948 and 1954 she had R&B hits like *Double Crossing Blues, Cupid's Boogie, Mistrusting Blues* and *Ring-a-Ding-Doo* for labels like Savoy, Modern and Federal. From 1953 until the early 1960s, she lived in Texas and recorded very little, but in 1962 she was signed by Lelan Rogers to the Lenox label, for whom she recorded *Release Me* (USA#8.1962) in Nashville; it was leased to Atlantic. She started to tour once again and appeared at The Newport Jazz Festival in 1966, but her career was interrupted by three years of rehabilitation for her drug addiction. In 1969 she recorded briefly for Roulette and appeared at the Monterey Jazz Festival; the following year she appeared at Monterey again, this time with the Johnny Otis Show.

In 1972 she was signed to Creed Taylor's Kudu label, where she cut a string of LPs like *From a Whisper to a Scream, Alone Again Naturally* and *What a Difference a Day Makes* (USA#32.1975). What set these LPs apart from those of her contemporaries was her ability to work alongside jazz musicians like Joe Beck, Eric Gale, Joe Farrell, Hank Crawford and Freddie Hubbard and yet impose her own style upon the recordings, never allowing herself to be swamped by the excellence of the sidemen. The LP *From a Whisper to a Scream* (1972) has acquired a reputation as being one of the great lost classics. She had only one hit single, *What a Difference a Day Makes* (USA#20; UK #6.1975), a reworking of the Dinah Washington song, but her version of the maudlin Gilbert O'Sullivan composition, *Alone Again Naturally*, was a moving assertion of resigned independence, illustrating her ability to turn a song on its head. Towards the end of the 1970s she was signed by Mercury, but her career was plagued by illness and just plain bad luck. On August 7, 1984, she died in Los Angeles.

WHAT A DIFFERENCE A DAY MAKES, CTI (France), 1975
ESTHER PHILLIPS, Kudu, 1978
HERE'S ESTHER – ARE YOU READY?, Mercury, 1979
GOOD BLACK IS HARD TO CRACK, Mercury, 1981
COMPLETE SAVOY RECORDINGS, Savoy, 1987
A WAY TO SAY GOODBYE, Muse, 1987
I PAID MY DUES, (Little Esther), Sing, 1989
BETTER BEWARE, (Little Esther), Charly, 1990

PICKETT, WILSON The career of Wilson Pickett has been like the curate's egg – good in parts. This has been due to a lack of continuity: despite remaining with Atlantic for over seven years, he was never given the opportunity to get settled with any one group of musicians or any one writer, always being shunted to and from whichever studio happened to be in vogue. Consequently he never had the opportunity to establish his skills as a writer in partnership with anyone on a regular basis. While he has a reputation for being 'difficult', the music industry has always thrived upon 'difficult' artists.

He was born in Prattville, Alabama, on March 18, 1941. In 1961, having moved to Detroit in 1955 and sung in various gospel groups, he joined The FALCONS as lead vocalist. Their producer, Robert Bateman, encouraged him to start a solo career and recommended that he contact Lloyd PRICE, the owner of the Double L label. For Price he recorded three singles, all of them becoming minor hits, including *If You Need Me*, which was his own composition written with Bateman; it was covered by Solomon BURKE, who got the bigger hit, and not surprisingly this has always been a source of irritation to Pickett.

In 1965 his contract was bought by Jerry WEXLER and he was signed to the Atlantic label. After he had released two singles, Wexler took him down to the Stax Studios in Memphis. His first single from there, *In the Midnight Hour* (USA#21; UK#12.1965), was written with Steve CROPPER; it was followed by *Don't Fight It* (UK#29.1965), *634-5789* (USA#13; UK#36.1966) and *Ninety Nine And a Half (Won't Do)*. His next records were recorded at the Fame Studios in Muscle Shoals. They included *Land of a Thousand Dances* (USA#6; UK#22.1966), *Mustang Sally* (USA#23; UK#28.1967), *Everybody Needs Somebody to Love* (USA#29.1967), *I Found a Love* (USA#32.1967) – a revival of The Falcons hit – and *Funky Broadway* (USA#8; UK#43.1967). He then returned to Memphis, this time to Chips MOMAN's American studios, where he recorded *Stag-O-Lee* (USA#22.1967), *She's Lookin' Good* (USA#15.1968) and *I'm a Midnight Mover* (USA#24; UK#38.1968). His next hit was a cover of the Lennon/McCartney composition *Hey Jude* (USA#23; UK#16.1969), featuring guitarist Duane ALLMAN; it was recorded at Muscle Shoals and was the first of a number of rock- oriented tracks that did him little credit. In 1970 he was teamed with GAMBLE & HUFF at the Sigma Sound Studios in Philadelphia for *(Get Me Back on Time) Engine Number 9* (USA #14.1970) and *Don't Let the Green Grass Fool You* (USA#17.1971). His final hits for Atlantic, *Don't Knock my Love* (USA#13.1971) and *Fire and Water* (USA#24.1972) were recorded at Atlantic South in Florida with Brad Shapiro and Dave Crawford.

The following year he was signed by RCA, where he remained until 1976, recording a series of very ordinary LPs, including *Mr*

Magic Man (1973). In 1978 he attempted to recapture his former glory with the LP, *A Funky Situation*, produced by Rick HALL for the Big Tree label. In 1979, he was signed by EMI America, but both of the ensuing LPs – *I Want You* (1979) and *Right Track* (1981) – failed to make any impression. However, his career has always revolved around his live appearances, and his popularity in the USA and Europe has made him a constant attraction. In 1988 he was signed by Motown for the LP *American Soul Man*.

THE RIGHT TRACK, EMI America, 1981
THE BEST OF WILSON PICKETT, Atlantic, 1982
AMERICAN SOUL MAN, Motown, 1988

PLATTERS Of all the doo-wop groups that were formed in the 1950s, none have endured as well as The Platters. They were formed in 1953 by Tony Williams, David Lynch, Herb Reed and Alex Hodge in Los Angeles. While working the local club circuit they met Buck Ram, the manager and producer of The Penguins, who signed them to his management company. Ram recruited Zola Taylor of The Teen Queens and Paul Robi as a replacement for Hodge (who had a disagreement with the police and was compelled to leave). He obtained a contract for the group with the King subsidiary, Federal, but the group failed to make any headway until The Penguins struck with the single *Earth Angel*. Consequently Mercury Records started to take an interest in the group, since the deal had been that Mercury couldn't have one without the other.

In 1955 The Platters had a hit for Mercury, *Only You* (USA#5.1955; UK#5.1956), and this was the first of a string that lasted until 1961, including *The Great Pretender* (USA#1.1955), *(You've Got) The Magic Touch* (USA#4.1956),

My Prayer (USA#1; UK#4.1956), *You'll Never Never Know* (USA#11.1956; UK#23.1957), *On my Word of Honour* (USA#20.1957), *I'm Sorry* (USA#11; UK#18.1957), *My Dream* (USA#24.1957), *Twilight Time* (USA#1; UK#3.1958), *Smoke Gets in Your Eyes* (USA #1.1958; UK#1.1959), *Enchanted* (USA #12.1959), *Harbour Lights* (USA#8; UK #11.1960), *To Each his Own* (USA#21.1960), *If I Didn't Care* (USA#30.1961) and *I'll Never Smile Again* (USA#25.1961).

In 1961 Williams left the group for a solo career, signing with Reprise; he was replaced by Sonny Turner. The following year, both Taylor and Robi left to pursue solo careers, to be replaced by two former members of The FLAMINGOS, Sandra Dawn and Nate Nelson. With the departure of Williams, whose dulcet tones had distinguished the group from others, their sound became more commonplace, but the demand on the cabaret circuit was as strong as ever. In 1966, having left Mercury for Musicor, they had a hit with *I Love You 1,000 Times* (USA#31.1966); the next year they scored once again with *With this Ring* (USA#14.1967). Since the late 1960s they have remained a big draw on the oldies and cabaret circuits internationally.

THE PLATTERS COLLECTION, Pickwick, 1977
ENCORE OF GOLDEN HITS, Mercury, 1980
THE GREAT PRETENDER, Mercury, 1981
GOLDEN HITS, Phoenix, 1982
JUKE BOX GIANTS, Audio Fidelity, 1982
THE EARLY YEARS, Bulldog, 1982
PLATTERAMA, Mercury, 1982
20 GREATEST HITS, Mercury, 1983
THE MORE I SEE YOU, Pickwick, 1983
20 GOLDEN PIECES, Bulldog, 1984
BEST OF THE PLATTERS, Creole, 1984
MUSIC FOR THE MILLIONS, Phonogram, 1984
COLLECTION, Deja Vu, 1986
GOLDEN HITS, Mercury, 1986
20 GREATEST HITS, Bescol, 1987

POINTER SISTERS The Pointer Sisters were formed by Bonnie (born July 11, 1950) and June Pointer (born 1954) in 1969 in East Oakland, California, where they had been born and raised as daughters of a minister. Their upbringing was steeped in gospel music, which they drew upon as they began to perform on the local club circuit. By the end of the year another sibling, Anita (born January 23, 1948), had left her secretarial job and joined them. In 1971 they caught the eye of promoter Bill Graham, who started to manage them; also the producer David Rubinson began to hire them as backing vocalists for artists like Boz SCAGGS and Taj Mahal. The following year yet another sibling, Ruth (born 1946), was tempted into the line-up, and they were signed to Atlantic. They recorded only one single for Atlantic, *Don't Try to Take the Fifth* (1972), produced by Wardell QUEZERGUE. It failed to make any waves and they parted company first with Atlantic and then with Graham.

They were signed by Rubinson to the ABC subsidiary, Blue Thumb, who produced their eponymous debut LP (USA#13.1973), which featured *Yes We Can Can* (USA#11.1973), the Allen TOUSSAINT composition. Another single, a rousing version of the Willie Dixon composition, *Wang Dang Doodle*, emphasised their versatility. The next two LPs, *That's a Plenty* and *Live at the Opera House*, were not as successful commercially, but the former included a gorgeous country-style composition, *Fairy Tale* (USA#13.1974), written by Anita and Bonnie, which charted in the US C&W charts and led to a performance at Nashville's Grand Ole Opry. After a further two LPs, *Steppin'* (USA#22.1975), including the single *How Long (Betcha Got a Chick on the Side)* (USA#20.1975), and *Having a Party,* they left Blue Thumb, suing them for unpaid royalties, and signed with producer Richard Perry's Planet label in 1979. The previous year, Bonnie

had left to launch a solo career, being signed by Motown.

With Perry ensconced as their producer, they moved into a phase of their career during which their output was more pop-oriented than it had been to date. Their debut single was a reworking of the Bruce Springsteen composition *Fire* (USA#2; UK#34.1979), from the LP *Energy* (USA#13.1979). The next single from the same LP was a Toussaint composition, *Happiness* (USA#30.1979). Meanwhile, Bonnie had revived two old Motown hits: The ELGINS' *Heaven Must Have Sent You* (USA #11.1979) and The FOUR TOPS' *I Can't Help Myself* (USA#40.1980). After the LP *Priority* (1979), they released the LP *Special Things* (USA#34.1980), featuring *He's So Shy* (USA #3.1980). Their next LP, *Black and White* (USA#12; UK#21.1981), was crucial to the widening of their popularity, particularly in the UK, where their reputation had never been reflected by their record sales. Two singles were extracted from the LP: *Slow Hand* (USA#2; UK#10.1981) and *Should I Do It?* (USA#13; UK#50.1981). Another LP, *So Excited,* followed. It included *American Music* (USA#16.1982) and *I'm so Excited* (USA#30.1982). Then came the LP, *Break Out* (USA#8; UK#9.1984), which contained five singles: *I Need You* (UK #25.1984), *Automatic* (USA#5; UK#2.1984), *Jump (for my Love)* (USA#3; UK#6.1984), a remixed version of *I'm so Excited* (USA#9; UK#11.1984) and *Neutron Dance* (USA#6; UK#31.1985). Their next LP, *Contact* (USA#25; UK#34.1985), included *Dare Me* (USA#11; UK#17.1985). *Hot Together* (1986) showed that they needed to rethink their strategy, as the formula was beginning to wear thin.

Since 1987 they have tended to keep a lower profile, contributing just *Be There*, on the soundtrack of the film *Beverly Hills Cop II*, and their version of *Santa Claus is Coming to Town* to the Special Olympics charity LP, *A Very*

Special Christmas. In 1990, having signed to Motown, they released the LP *Right Rhythm*; much of it had been recorded at PRINCE' Paisley Park studios under the watchful eye of Prince's bassist, Levi Seacer, Jr, who played most of the instruments.

PRIORITY, Planet, 1979
SPECIAL THINGS, Planet, 1980
RETROSPECT, MCA, 1981
SO EXCITED, RCA, 1982
BREAK OUT, Planet, 1984
CONTACT, RCA, 1986
HOT TOGETHER, RCA, 1987
THE COLLECTION, Castle, 1988
RIGHT RHYTHM, Motown, 1990

POMUS, JEROME 'DOC' The songwriting team of 'Doc' Pomus and Mort SHUMAN lasted from 1958 until 1965, and during that time they wrote a string of songs that did much to crystallise the essence of rock'n' roll. Like LEIBER & STOLLER they were adept at getting to the heart of black music.

Jerome Pomus was born in New York on June 27, 1925; throughout the early 1950s he wrote for artists like Joe Turner, Ray CHARLES, The COASTERS and The Crowns (who became The DRIFTERS) as well as recording occasionally under his own name. In 1958 he met up with Shuman and formed a songwriting partnership. They obtained work with the publishers Hill & Range, and their material was recorded by Bobby Darin, Dion, Elvis Presley and The Drifters: the songs they wrote for the latter included *Save the Last Dance for Me*, *I Count the Tears*, *This Magic Moment* and *Sweets for My Sweet*. Pomus also cowrote with Phil SPECTOR during this time. In 1965 his partnership with Shuman was severed when he was badly hurt in a fall that left him partially paralysed. Over the next ten years

or so Pomus remained out of the business, until in 1978 he started to work with DOCTOR JOHN on the LPs, *City Lights* (1978) and *Tango Palace* (1979). During the 1980s, he worked with Shuman on the B. B. KING LP. *There must be a Better World Somewhere*, 'Dee' died in New York, 14 March 1991.

PORTER, DAVID When Stax opened its doors (initially as Satellite) it became a meeting place for aspiring musicians, both black and white. David Porter was one of the earliest recruits. He had been born in Memphis on November 21, 1941, and had gone to the Booker T. Washington High School. At first he recorded for Savoy as Little David and then for Hi as Kenny Cain. By 1964 he had become an insurance salesman, which was how he linked up with Isaac HAYES – he was trying to sell him a policy. Their songwriting and production partnership didn't really coalesce until Jerry WEXLER brought SAM & DAVE to the Stax Studios. From 1965 until 1969 they created a string of hits for the duo, including *Hold On, I'm Comin'*, *I Thank You* and *Soul Man*. However, the partnership disintegrated with the success of Hayes' solo career. Although Porter started to record once again as a solo artist for the Stax subsidiary Enterprise, his career never assumed the staggering proportions as that of his former colleague. In 1979 he made an abortive attempt to relaunch Stax with the backing of the Fantasy label. To this day he has continued to write and produce, but his success has been limited.

PRESTON, BILLY Although it took the combined efforts of The Beatles and The Rolling Stones to establish Billy Preston as a household name, his reputation as a musician started as early as 1956, when he played W. C. Handy in the film *St Louis Blues* .

He was born on September 9, 1946, in Houston, Texas, but moved to Los Angeles in the late 1940s. After playing with various gospel groups, including the Cogic Singers, he became a member of LITTLE RICHARD's band in 1962. In 1964 he recorded briefly for Sam COOKE's Sar label, which enabled him to secure a regular slot on the TV Show, *Shindig*, where he replaced Leon Russell. Throughout he was developing his style as an organist in the mode of Jimmy Smith and Jimmy McGRIFF. The funky instrumental *Billy's Bag* never charted, but became a classic of the genre, with McGriff's, *I've Got a Woman*. While working on *Shindig*, he met Ray CHARLES and joined his band, with which he remained for three years. More session work followed, including some with The Beatles, which led to his signing a contract with their recently established Apple label. His first single, *That's the Way God Planned It* (UK#11.1969), showed that his style of playing had not dated and that his vocals were very strong.

At the end of his contract with Apple he signed with A&M in 1971, where he remained for the next six years, notching up a number of hits: *Outta Space* (USA#2; UK#44.1972), *Will it Go Round in Circles* (USA#1.1973), *Space Race* (USA#4.1973), *Nothing from Nothing* (USA#1.1974) and *Struttin'* (USA#22.1975). His success with A&M made him one of the most sought-after session musicians in the country, working with Quincy JONES, Aretha FRANKLIN, The Rolling Stones, SLY & THE FAMILY STONE and Barbra Streisand.

In 1977 he was signed by Motown, where he was teamed with SYREETA for the LP *Fast Break*, it included *With You I'm Born Again* (USA#4.1980; UK#2.1979) and *It Will Come in Time* (UK#47.1980). The LP was an affirmation of his total commitment to Christianity, and subsequent releases veered increasingly towards gospel in its purest form, culminating in the gospel LP *Behold* in 1982. Since then he has been devoting his time to spiritual commitments, although he has recorded the occasional single.

FASTBREAK, (with Syreeta), Motown, 1979
LATE AT NIGHT, Motown, 1979
THE WAY I AM, Motown, 1981
BILLY PRESTON AND SYREETA, Motown, 1981
BEHOLD, Myrrh, 1982
PRESSIN' ON, Motown, 1982
THE COLLECTION, Castle, 1989

PRICE, LLOYD In 1952 Art RUPE signed Lloyd Price to his Specialty label, after recording *Lawdy Miss Clawdy* at the J&M Studios in New Orleans. Price was born in Kenner, Louisiana, on March 9, 1934. His career started in 1950, when he led his own group, performing jingles and the like for the radio station, WBOK, in New Orleans. In 1953 he was drafted into the US Army, where he formed a group that toured Japan and Southeast Asia entertaining the forces.

After three years, he was discharged and formed the Kent record company. His debut, the self-penned *Just Because* (USA#29.1957), was leased to ABC-Paramount, as were subsequent releases until 1963: *Stagger Lee* (USA#1; UK#7.1959), *Where Were You (on our Wedding Day)?* (USA#23; UK#15.1959), *Personality* (USA#2; UK#9.1959), *I'm Gonna Get Married* (USA#3; UK#23.1959), *Come into My Heart* (USA#20.1959), *Lady Luck* (USA#14; UK #45.1960), *No Ifs, No Ands* (USA#40.1960) and *Question* (USA#19.1960).

In 1963 he set up another label, Double L, and signed Wilson PICKETT. Price's final major hit was his version of the Errol Garner composition *Misty* (USA#21.1963), which was to become the inspiration for the Clint Eastwood film, *Play Misty for Me*. Since then his chart success has been negligible, but his entrepeneurial efforts have seen him dabbling in all sorts of enterprises, including opening a club and another record label, Turntable, in 1969 in New York.

JUKE BOX GIANTS, Audio Fidelity, 1982
LAWDY MISS CLAWDY, Ace, 1985

PRIMES See TEMPTATIONS

PRINCE One of the most prodigiously talented performers to emerge in the 1980s was Prince. What has set him apart from others has been his all-round ability: writing, producing, performing – and even directing his own films. There are few areas in which he has not dabbled.

He was born Prince Rogers Nelson on June 7, 1958, in Minneapolis, Minnesota; his father was a jazz pianist in the Prince Roger Trio and his mother did the occasional turn as vocalist for the group. In 1965 his parents split up and he started to devote more and more of his energies to music. In 1970, having run away from home, he was befriended by Andre Anderson, who was to become Andre CYMONE; eventually Prince moved in with the Anderson family. Throughout the early 1970s, he honed his skills as a writer and arranger for a school group, Grand Central, which featured Prince, Cymone on bass, Linda Anderson on keyboards and Charles Smith, a cousin of Prince's, on drums. When he went to Minneapolis High School in 1973, the name of the group was changed to Champagne. Smith left, to be replaced by Morris Day. These early beginnings formed the basis of the Minneapolis Sound as other like-minded individuals like Terry Lewis (see JAM, Jimmy & Terry Lewis), Alexander O'NEAL and Jellybean Johnson of Flyte Tyme, among others, gravitated towards Prince.

By 1978 he had secured a recording contract with Warner Bros. The debut LP, *For You*, was a portent of things to come as he played everything himself and wrote all of the material, causing him to be dubbed 'The New Stevie WONDER'. The group he formed for touring purposes comprised Cymone (bass), Gayle Chapman and Matt Fink (keyboards), Bobby Z (drums) and Dez Dickerson (guitar). The follow-up, *Prince* (US#22.1979), included *I Wanna be Your Lover* (USA#11.1979; UK #41.1980). Gayle Chapman left the group to be replaced by Lisa Coleman. In 1980 he released the LP *Dirty Mind*, in which the influences of Sly Stone (see SLY & THE FAMILY STONE), Jimi HENDRIX and James BROWN were all fused into a distinctive style of his own that has characterised all his subsequent work.

After touring the UK in 1981, Cymone left the group to pursue a solo career, and Prince, under the pseudonym of Jamie Starr, contributed all the songs to the debut LP by Time (see JAM, Jimmy & Terry Lewis). His next LP, *Controversy* (USA#21.1981), seemed to lack the impact of its predecessor, but he went out on tour with Time in support. The following year he released the LP *1999* (USA#9.1982; UK#30.1984), and followed it up with a tour of the USA. The tour comprised Prince & The Revolution, Time and the all-girl trio, Vanity 6 (Brenda Bennett, Dee Dee Winters and Susan Moonsie). Three singles were taken from the LP: *1999* (USA#12; UK#25.1983/#2.1985), *Little Red Corvette* (USA#6; UK#34.1983/ #2.1985) and *Delirious* (USA#8.1983). At the end of the tour Dickerson left the group and was replaced by Wendy Melvoin, who formed a songwriting partnership with Coleman, as WENDY & LISA.

The next project was the film *Purple Rain*, the

soundtrack of which (USA#1; UK#7.1984) included five singles: *When Doves Cry* (USA#1; UK#4.1984), *Let's Go Crazy* (USA#1.1984; UK#7.1985), *Purple Rain* (USA#2; UK #8.1984), *I Would Die for U* (USA#8; UK #58.1984) and *Take me with U* (USA#25.1985). The extraordinary success of the soundtrack almost overshadowed the success of the film itself, which opened up to rave reviews and took over $60 million at the box office in its first two months. More significantly, it did not represent a compromise on Prince's part: he was still doing what he had always been doing, but his expertise had increased vastly and he was able to blend funk and rock into a sound that was suddenly acceptable to the masses. After the opening of the film, he undertook another tour of the USA featuring Sheila E.

At the end of the tour in 1985 he launched his own record label, Paisley Park, based at his studios in Minneapolis, the Warehouse, which became the nerve centre of all his operations. His first LP for it, *Around the World in a Day* (USA#1; UK#5.1985), showed no concessions. However, as with his former records, irrespective of how outrageous the arrangements might be his pop sensibility remained unassailable. Three singles were taken from it: *Raspberry Beret* (USA#2; UK#25.1985), *Paisley Park* (UK#18.1985) and *Pop Life* (USA#7; UK #60.1985). His next project was the film *Under the Cherry Moon*, which was shot in France; halfway through filming he assumed the director's mantle. The soundtrack LP, *Parade – Music from Under the Cherry Moon* (USA#3; UK#4.1986), included another bunch of singles: *Kiss* (USA#1; UK#6.1986), *Girls and Boys* (UK#11.1986), *Anotherloverholenyohead* (UK#36.1986) and *Mountains* (USA#23; UK #45.1986).

After another tour, he disbanded The Revolution, only to re-form it the following year to include Fink, hornman Eric Leeds, singers Cat Glover and Sheila E, guitarist Mico Weaver,

bassist Levi Seacer Jr and keyboardist Boni Boyer. His next LP, *Sign o' the Times* (USA#6; UK#4.1987), featured four singles: *Sign o' the Times* (USA#3; UK#10.1987), *If I was Your Girlfriend* (UK#20.1987), *U Got the Look* (USA#2; UK#11.1987) – a duet with Sheena Easton – and *I Could never Take the Place of Your Man* (USA#10; UK#29.1987). It was followed by rumours of another LP, known as *The Black Album*, copies of which slipped onto the bootleg market after its commercial release had been revoked by WEA. His next LP, *Lovesexy* (USA#11; UK#1.1988), featured *Alphabet Street* (USA#8; UK#9.1988), *Glam Slam* (UK#29.1988) and *I Wish U Heaven* (UK#24.1988). In 1989 he contributed songs for the film, *Batman* (USA/UK#1.1989), starring Jack Nicholson, *Batdance* (USA#1.1989) was another monster workout, showing he could simulate sampling himself as well as any DJ could. Another film soundtrack followed, *Graffiti Bridge* (UK#1.1990), which had two singles taken from it: *Thieves in the Temple* (UK#7.1990) and *Melody Cool*, featuring Mavis Staples (see STAPLE SINGERS).

Throughout, Prince has collaborated with other artists like Miles Davis and duetted with Madonna, Sheena Easton and others, as well as signing Mavis Staples and George CLINTON to his Paisley Park label. Furthermore, his songs have been recorded by artists like Chaka KHAN, The Bangles, Cyndi Lauper, Sinead O'Connor and Sheena Easton.

FOR YOU, Warner Bros., 1978

PRINCE, Warner Bros., 1979

DIRTY MIND, Warner Bros., 1980

CONTROVERSY, Warner Bros., 1981

1999, Warner Bros., 1982

PURPLE RAIN, Warner Bros., 1984

AROUND THE WORLD IN A DAY, Paisley Park, 1985

PARADE – MUSIC FROM UNDER THE CHERRY MOON, Paisley Park, 1986

SIGN O' THE TIMES, Paisley Park, 1987
LOVESEXY, Paisley Park, 1988
BATMAN, Warner Bros., 1989
GRAFFITI BRIDGE, Paisley Park, 1990

MARDI GRAS IN NEW ORLEANS, Nighthawk, 1982
HOUSE PARTY NEW ORLEANS STYLE, Rounder, 1987

PROFESSOR LONGHAIR Henry Roeland Byrd was born on December 19, 1918, in Bogalusa, Louisiana. He started his career as a street entertainer and then in the late 1940s graduated to playing the piano on the New Orleans club circuit with his group The Four Hairs, who became The Shuffling Hungarians. From the late 1940s through the early 1950s he recorded with a succession of labels including Mercury, Federal and Atlantic. His rolling style influenced a whole generation of pianists like Fats DOMINO, Huey 'Piano' SMITH and Allen TOUSSAINT, but recognition eluded him until the early 1970s when DOCTOR JOHN recorded the LP *Gumbo*, on which he played songs like *Tipitina*, one of the Professor's most celebrated offerings.

The Professor became a regular attraction at the New Orleans Jazz Festival from 1971, and began to record once again. His LPs included *Rock 'n' Roll Gumbo* (1974), *Live on the Queen Mary* (1975) and *The Last Mardi Gras* (1978). In 1978 he toured the UK. One of his concerts was recorded and released posthumously by the JSP label as *The London Concert*. In 1987 Rounder finally issued some recordings made in 1971/72 as the LP *House Party New Orleans Style*, which featured bluesman Snooks Eaglin. Although his records often gave the impression of being afterthoughts, his live performances – where his penchant for bizarre costumes was given full expression – encapsulated the spirit of New Orleans at its most unpredictable.

LIVE ON THE QUEEN MARY, Stateside, 1978
CRAWFISH SIESTA, Sonet, 1980
THE COMPLETE LONDON CONCERT, JSP, 1981

PURIFY, JAMES & BOBBY James Purify was teamed with his cousin, Robert Dickey, by the Florida DJ Papa Don Schroeder while they were members of the group Dothan Sextet. Their most enduring contribution was their version of the Dan PENN and Spooner OLDHAM composition, *I'm Your Puppet* (USA#6.1966), which was recorded at Muscle Shoals. After this initial success, Schroeder took them to Memphis to record at Chips MOMAN's American studios, where they notched up another three hits: *Wish You Didn't Have to Go* (USA#38.1967), *Shake a Tail Feather* (USA#25.1967) and *Let Love Come between Us* (USA#23.1967). It was their misfortune that, being a duo, they invited comparison with SAM & DAVE, in which they didn't come out too well. In 1976, armed with a fresh contract with Mercury, they had two hits in the UK, a remake of *I'm Your Puppet* (UK#12.1976) and *Morning Glory* (UK#27.1976), after which they returned to the anonymity of the club circuit.

100 PERCENT PURIFIED SOUL, Charly, 1988

PUTNAM, NORBERT By 1961, Norbert Putnam was ensconced as bassist in the Mark Vs, who became the house band at the Fame Studios in Muscle Shoals. He contributed to records by Arthur ALEXANDER, Jimmy HUGHES, Tommy Roe, Ray Stevens and The TAMS. In 1964 he was lured to Nashville by David BRIGGS and Jerry CARRIGAN, where they set up the Quadrafonic studios.

Since then he has recorded with a whole host of artists, including Elvis Presley and Kris Kristofferson.

QUEZERGUE, WARDELL Wardell Quezergue, a creole, came to prominence in the mid-1960s as an arranger in New Orleans, working on titles like *Chapel of Love* by The DIXIE CUPS and *Barefootin'* by Robert PARKER. In 1970 he went to Malaco in Jackson to record *Funky Thing* by The Unemployed. Such was its success that the next time he went to Malaco, he took a bus load of musicians that he'd been working with in New Orleans. One of them was KING FLOYD. Under the aegis of Tommy COUCH and Quezergue, Floyd cut *What Our Love Needs* and *Groove Me* for Couch's Chimneyville label. Quezergue next success for the fledgling Malaco label was his production of *Mr Big Stuff* by Jean KNIGHT; Malaco leased it out for distribution by Stax. Quezergue continued to work with Malaco, arranging *Misty Blue* for Dorothy MOORE. Among his other projects was producing a single, *Don't Try to Take the Fifth* (1972), for The POINTER SISTERS. He went on to produce the LP *Ted Taylor 1976* for the Alarm label, which had been set up by Stewart Madison and Jerry Strickland. To this day he has continued to work in and around New Orleans.

RAGAVOY, JERRY A master of the grand production, Jerry Ragavoy had the breadth of vision to harness lavish string arrangements within the context of deep soul. Artists like Lorraine ELLISON, Erma FRANKLIN, Garnett MIMMS, Howard TATE and Irma THOMAS were all worthy benefactors of his dramatic approach.

He was born in Philadelphia in 1935. After forming the Grand label with Herb Slotkin in 1954 to release records by The Castelles, whom he had discovered, he left the label to study composition and piano. He worked as an arranger with Claudine Clark, and then he produced his first hit for The Majors, *A Wonderful Dream* (USA#22.1962). This led to a partnership with Bert BERNS: they wrote and produced *Cry Baby* for Mimms, for whom Ragavoy also produced *I'll Take Good Care of You* and *For your Precious Love* . He went on to produce *Time is on my Side* for Irma Thomas. In 1964, he became head of A&R for Warner Bros. in New York, where he produced Linda JONES and Lorraine Ellison for the subsidiary, Loma. Among his achievements at Loma included the production of Ellison's magnum opus *Stay with me Baby*. He continued to work as a freelance, writing for and producing Howard Tate for the Verve label and, in 1967, Erma Franklin for the Shout label. In 1969 he established his own label (an error of judgement) and the Hit Factory recording studios, but apart from sessions with Tate for Atlantic in 1972, Dionne WARWICK in 1975 and Major Harris (see DELFONICS) in 1978, he has not been as successful as he was during the 1960s.

RAWLS, LOU Lou Rawls, in common with any number of performers, has consistently aimed for the cabaret circuit, with the result that his performances have been totally devoid of oomph. This is a very considerable shame, because his gospel roots and his jazz-inflected phrasing indicate that, were he to stretch himself by using demanding material and working with sympathetic producers, he could make some very fine records. Since signing to Blue Note in 1988 he has shown that he might do just that in the near future.

He was born in Chicago on December 1, 1937. While still at school he sang in the gospel groups The Highway QCs and The Soul Stirrers, where he met Sam COOKE (for whom, in 1962, he would provide backing vocals on *Bring it on Home to Me*). Upon completing his stint in the army, he moved to Los Angeles, where he became a member of The Pilgrim Travellers in 1958. His career was then interrupted by a car accident. After his recovery he recorded for a number of local labels, like Shardee and Candix, with Herb Alpert and Lou Adler producing. In 1961, he was signed by Capitol.

At Capitol his style was moulded to appeal to the fans of one of the compay's biggest acts, Nat 'King' Cole. Initially the ploy failed to work, but by the mid-1960s, Rawls had established himself with a succession of singles: *Love is a Hurtin' Thing* (USA#13.1966), *Dead End Street* (USA#29.1967) and *Your Good Thing (is About to End)* (USA#18.1969). LPs like *Live!* (USA#4.1966), *Soulin'* (USA#7.1966), *Carryin' On* (USA#20.1967), *Too Much* (USA#18.1967) and *That's Lou* (USA#29.1967) did much to guarantee him a regular slot on the cabaret circuit.

By 1970 his style had become dated, and he moved to MGM, where he remained until 1975, having just the one hit, *A Natural Man* (USA#17.1971). He was then signed by GAMBLE & HUFF to the Philadelphia International label. His first offering was the LP *All Things in Time* (USA#7.1976), which included *You'll Never Find Another Love Like Mine* (USA#2; UK#10.1976). This single was followed by other R&B hits like *See You when I Get There*, *Lady Love* (USA#24.1978) and *Let me be Good to You*. In 1982, he moved to the Epic label where he recorded LPs like *Now is the Time* (1982), *When the Night Comes* (1983), *Close Company* (1984) and *Love All your Blues Away* (1986).

In 1988 he was signed to the revived Blue Note label for the LP *At Last*, which featured a host of jazz musicians, like George Benson, Stanley Turrentine, Cornell Dupree and Richard Tee, among others, and was his most cohesive effort for many a long year. In 1990 he released the follow-up for Blue Note, *It's Supposed to be Fun*, which confirmed the promise of its predecessor

STORMY MONDAY, (with Les McCann), See For Miles, 1961

UNMISTAKABLY LOU, Philadelphia International, 1977

THE BEST OF LOU RAWLS, Capitol, 1979

LET ME BE GOOD TO YOU, Philadelphia International, 1979

SHADES OF BLUE, Philadelphia International, 1981

SOUL SERENADE, Stateside, 1985

CLASSIC SOUL, Blue Moon, 1986

LOVE ALL YOUR BLUES AWAY, Epic, 1986

AT LAST, Blue Note, 1989

IT'S SUPPOSED TO BE FUN, Blue Note, 1990

RAYDIO See PARKER, Jr, Ray

REBENNACK, MAC See DOCTOR JOHN

REDDING, OTIS On December 10, 1967, the plane carrying Otis Redding and his band, The BARKAYS, to a concert in the Mid-West crashed into Lake Monoma, near Madison, Wisconsin. Ben Cauley of The Barkays was the sole survivor. It was (almost) three years to the day since Redding's idol, Sam COOKE, had been shot in a Los Angeles motel. In those three years, Redding had become the embodiment of soul although, ironically, he had never sold a vast number of records. All that was to change with the posthumous release of *(Sittin' on the) Dock of the Bay* (USA#1; UK#3.1967).

He was born in Dawson, Georgia on September 9, 1941. His career started in 1959 when he started to appear with a local group, Johnny JENKINS & The Pinetoppers, doing imitations of LITTLE RICHARD. His first record was a version of *Shout Bamalama* for the Confederate label; it was followed by *Gettin' Hip* for the Alshire label. Both records failed to sell, but they aroused the interest of Jenkins' manager, Phil WALDEN, who became Redding's manager as well. In October 1962 he was allowed to record a couple of demos at the newly established Stax studios in Memphis as there was still some studio time available after a Jenkins session. He cut *Hey Hey Baby* and *These Arms Of Mine* (USA#85.1963), backed by Jenkins on guitar, Steve CROPPER on piano, Lewis Steinberg on bass and Al JACKSON on drums. Jim STEWART signed him to Stax on the strength of the session.

The follow-up, *Pain in My Heart* (USA #61.1963), an adaptation of an Irma THOMAS song, *Ruler of My Heart*, coincided with his appearance at the prestigious Apollo Theatre in Harlem. Over the next two years he built upon his reputation with a series of singles, including *I've Been Loving You too Long* (USA#21.1965) and *Respect* (USA#35.1966). However, he failed to make any impression upon the UK charts until Atlantic lifted his version of the Smokey ROBINSON composition *My Girl* (UK#11.1965) from the LP *Otis Blue* (UK#6.1966/#7.1967). It was an LP of great maturity, combining his two greatest assets: a natural sense of timing and an emotional urgency. Some of the credit for the cohesiveness of the sound was due to the unflagging efforts of the backing band, BOOKER T & THE MGs. His next single was his version of *Satisfaction* (USA#31; UK #33.1966), in which he came perilously close to self-parody. The same year, he toured the UK and Europe, which prompted ATV in the UK to devote an entire edition of *Ready Steady Go!* to a specially staged concert – which had one of the biggest studio audiences of all time, to judge by the number of people nowadays who claim to have been there!

In August 1966, he set up his own label and production company, Jotis. His first signing was Arthur CONLEY, whose first record *Sweet Soul Music*, written and produced by Redding, sold over a million copies. In January 1967 *Try a Little Tenderness* (USA#25; UK #47.1967), from the LP *The Dictionary of Soul* (UK#23.1967), was released; it was the perfect distillation of all the vital ingredients of soul. Next came a collection of duets with Carla THOMAS on the LP *King & Queen* (USA#36; UK#18.1967). The single from it, *Tramp* (USA#26; UK#18.1967), was a reworking of the Lowell Fulson song and was clearly intended as a novelty item. Their version of *Knock on Wood* (USA#30; UK#35.1967) showed that, in Thomas and Redding, Stax had a duo that could match any combination Motown might dream up.

On June 16 he took part in the Monterey Pop Festival in a calculated effort by Al BELL to win over the young, white middle-class rock audience. The ploy succeeded, but Redding was unable to reap the full rewards as within six months he was dead.

OTIS BLUE, Atlantic, 1965

LOVE MAN, Atlantic, 1969

THE BEST OF OTIS REDDING, Atlantic, 1972

THE HISTORY OF OTIS REDDING, Atlantic, 1974

PURE OTIS, Atlantic, 1979

THE DOCK OF THE BAY, Atlantic, 1987

THE OTIS REDDING STORY, Atlantic, 1988

OTIS REDDING LIVE: RECORDED IN JULY 1965, Traditional Line, 1991

REEVES, MARTHA, & THE VANDELLAS See MARTHA & THE VANDELLAS

REVOLUTION See PRINCE

REYNOLDS, L.J. See DRAMATICS

RICHBOURG, JOHN The influence of John Richbourg in the development of Southern soul was crucial. For it was Richbourg (along with fellow DJs Hoss Allen and Zenas Sears) who, through his radio programmes, brought the emergent synthesis of gospel and R&B – soul – to the attention of white audiences. Impressionable youngsters like Dan PENN, Steve CROPPER and Rick HALL developed their taste for R&B through listening to his programmes.

Richbourg was born near Charleston, South Carolina. During the 1930s he played character roles for radio dramas. By 1940 he had returned to Charleston, where he got a job as a DJ on the local radio station WTMA. After his stint with WTMA, he moved to WLAC in Nashville, taking over Ernie Young's 1–3 am slot (Young was to start the Excello label). The success of his radio programmes enabled him to gain access to artists and producers, and in 1955 he started his own Rich label. Throughout the late 1950s he guided the careers of Roscoe Shelton and Lattimore Brown, both of whom were signed to Excello.

In 1963 he was hired by Fred FOSTER to set up the Monument soul subsidiary, Sound Stage Seven. Richbourg took all of his artists down to either Muscle Shoals, Stax or American. Among the artists he produced were Shelton, Brown, Joe SIMON, Sam Baker and Ella Washington. Despite the fact that his productions failed to cross over into the mainstream, he cut some very fine records like Washington's *I Can't Afford to Lose Him*, Simon's *Let's Do it Over* and Shelton's *Strain on My Heart* and *It's Such a Sad Sad World*. In 1970

Richbourg parted company with Foster, who had set up a fresh deal with CBS. He set up the Seventy Seven label in 1972, but, apart from Ann Sexton, there was little he could do to stop it from going out of business in 1977. In 1973 he retired from WLAC. With the changes in musical tastes he retired from the music industry, falling ill with cancer soon after. In 1985 a benefit was organised in Nashville, featuring B. B. KING, Joe Simon, The COASTERS, among others. He died in 1986.

RICHIE, LIONEL Lionel Brockman Richie was born on June 20, 1949 in Tuskegee, Alabama. In 1967, while studying economics at the Tuskegee Institute, he formed The Mighty Mystics, who combined with The Jays to become The COMMODORES. Throughout the late 1960s and early 1970s the group toured, developing a reputation for their live act. In 1971 they signed with the Motown label on the instigation of Suzanne DePasse. They had to wait until 1974 before they had their first hit with *Machine Gun*. Throughout the latter half of the 1970s they became one of the biggest selling acts in the USA, due in part to Richie's talent as a songwriter. In 1980 country singer, Kenny Rogers had a #1 hit with the Richie composition *Lady*; in 1981, Richie was approached by film director Franco Zeffirelli to write the theme song to the film *Endless Love* (USA#1; UK#7.1981), which he performed as a duet with Diana ROSS. As a result of such successes he embarked on a solo career in 1982.

His first solo LP, *Lionel Richie* (USA#3; UK#9.1982), was produced by James Carmichael and included three hit singles: *Truly* (USA#1; UK#6.1982), *You Are* (USA#4; UK#43.1983) and *My Love* (USA#5; UK#70.1983). The follow-up, *Can't Slow Down* (USA/UK#1.1983), provided him with another five hit singles: *All Night Long (All Night)* (USA#1; UK#2.1983), *Running with the*

Night (USA#7; UK#9.1983), *Hello* (USA/UK #1.1984), *Stuck on You* (USA#3; UK#12.1984) and *Penny Lover* (USA#8; UK#18.1984).

In 1984, with his solo career booming, he signed an $8.5 million sponsorship deal with Pepsi-Cola and was invited to participate in the closing ceremony of the Los Angeles Olympics; he performed *All Night Long,* having added an extra verse to mark the occasion. Later the same year he wrote a tribute to Marvin GAYE, *Missing You,* for Diana Ross. In 1985 he co-wrote with Michael JACKSON, *We are the World,* for USA for Africa, a supergroup formed by Quincy JONES to raise funds for famine relief. In December that year he released *Say You, Say Me* (USA#1; UK#8.1985), which was featured in the film *White Nights,* starring Mikhail Baryshnikov and Gregory Hines and won a 1986 Oscar for Best Original Song.

His third solo LP, *Dancing on the Ceiling* (USA#1; UK#2.1986), continued his run of success, providing him with another four hit singles: *Dancing On The Ceiling* (USA#2; UK#7.1986), *Love Will Conquer All* (USA#9; UK#45.1986), *Ballerina Girl* (USA#7; UK-#17.1986) and *Se La* (USA#20; UK #43.1987). At the end of 1987, he embarked upon a three-month world tour. Since then he has been recording the follow-up to *Dancing on the Ceiling.*

LIONEL RICHIE, Motown, 1982
CAN'T SLOW DOWN, Motown, 1983
GREAT LOVE SONGS BY LIONEL RICHIE, (with The Commodores), Motown, 1986
DANCING ON THE CEILING, Motown, 1986

RIGHTEOUS BROTHERS In 1962 The Righteous Brothers were formed by Bill Medley and Bobby Hatfield. Medley (born September 19, 1940, in Santa Ana, California) had been a member of The Paramours, who had had a regional hit with *There She Goes.* Hatfield (born August 10, 1940, at Beaver Dam, Wisconsin) had been a member of The Variations, as well as recording *Hot Tamales* as a solo artist. As both had been under contract to the Moonglow label, they were obliged to release their first three singles together, *Little Latin Lupe Lu, Koko Joe* and *My Babe,* through that label.

In 1964 Phil SPECTOR saw them in a concert package at the Cow Palace in San Francisco and did a deal with Moonglow, enabling them to be signed to his Philles label. They remained with Spector until 1966, during which time they recorded a string of singles that were object lessons in production techniques: *You've Lost that Lovin' Feeling* (USA/UK #1.1964/ UK#10.1969/#42.1977), *Just Once in my Life* (USA#9.1965), *Unchained Melody* (USA#4; UK#14.1965; USA/UK #1.1990) and *Ebb Tide* (USA#5; UK#48.1965).

In 1966 Spector sold their contract to the MGM subsidiary Verve for $1 million. Their debut under the new deal was *(You're My) Soul and Inspiration* (USA#1; UK#15.1966), written and produced by Medley. More singles followed: *He* (USA#18.1966), *Go Ahead and Cry* (USA#30.1966), *White Cliffs of Dover* (UK#21.1966) and *Islands in the Sun* (UK #36.1966). The following year Medley left to pursue the obligatory solo career and was replaced by former Knickerbocker, Jimmy Walker; in 1970, having had no appreciable further success, the duo split up. In 1974, having pursued their individual projects, Hatfield and Medley re-formed and were teamed with producers Dennis LAMBERT and Brian Potter for the macabre *Rock 'n' Roll Heaven* (USA#3.1974) on the Capitol subsidiary, Haven. It was followed by two more singles, *Give it to the People* (USA#20.1974) and *Dream On* (USA#32.1974).

After the murder of Medley's wife Karen, in 1976, he left the group and the music business altogether; however, in 1981 he resumed his solo career, recording an LP *Right Here and Now*, with Richard Perry producing. In 1987 he was teamed with Jennifer Warnes for *(I've Had) the Time of my Life* (USA#1; UK #6.1987), which was featured on the soundtrack to the film *Dirty Dancing;* the following year he revived *He Ain't Heavy, He's my Brother* (UK#25.1988) for the soundtrack of the film *Rambo III*. Since then he has concentrated upon running his club, *Medleys*, in Los Angeles, which he opened in 1982. In 1990 *Unchained Melody* was featured on the soundtrack of the film *Ghost*. It became a hit all over again in the USA and the UK, with two separate versions of the song being released, one a reissue and the other a reissue of a re-recorded version. As a result, *You've Lost that Lovin' Feeling* and *The Time of My Life* were also reissued and achieved spectacular sales.

GREATEST HITS, MGM, 1983
THE VERY BEST OF THE RIGHTEOUS BRO-
THERS, Verve, 1990

RILEY, TEDDY Teddy Riley was born in Harlem in 1967. In just a few short years he has become one of the most sought after, of the new up-and-coming producers. His career started in 1981, when he produced his own group, Kids at Work. In 1984 he produced Kool Moe Dee's debut LP and then arranged the single, *The Show,* for Doug E. Fresh & The Get Fresh Crew. Since then he has worked with Bobby BROWN, Boy George, James INGRAM and The WINANS. He has shown an artful ability to combine the traditions of gospel disciplines with the immediacy of contemporary production techniques, which would seem to indicate that he may well survive changes in fashion to become one of the most significant producers of the 1990s.

ROBEY, DON Don Robey was born in Houston, Texas, in 1904 and became in due course the owner of a record store and night club. He founded his first record label, Peacock, in 1949; named after his club, The Bronze Peacock, it was formed to record Clarence 'Gatemouth' Brown. In 1952 he acquired the Duke label from James Mattias, a DJ at the Memphis radio station WDIA.

While he was not a well liked man, he built up a roster of artists that included Johnny ACE, Junior Parker, Bobby BLAND, LITTLE RICHARD, O.V. WRIGHT and Big Mama THORNTON, as well as an equally strong list of gospel artists. The fact that he bought songwriting credits (under the name of 'Deadric Malone') did not endear him to anyone but, on the plus side, he was willing to take chances by recording young artists. He was fortunate in having a staff producer and arranger Joe Scott, who more than anyone else imbued each record with an instantly recognisable 'sound', the guitar-work of Mel Brown being a particular trademark. Furthermore, in Evelyn Johnson, who ran his booking agency Buffalo, he was able to ensure that records were always supported by tours.

In 1973 Robey sold his record company, which by now comprised four labels – Duke, Peacock, Songbird and Backbeat – and his publishing interests to ABC-Dunhill for over $1 million. He died on June 16, 1975.

ROBINS See COASTERS

ROBINSON, BOBBY From his record shop on 125th Street in Harlem, Bobby Robinson became owner of one of the most successful of the small independent labels. He established his first label, Robin, in 1951; it became Red Robin in 1953 and attracted the attention of the emergent doo-wop groups as well as blues musicians like Sonny Terry & Brownie McGhee.

By the beginning of the 1960s he had labels like Fury, Enjoy, Everlast and Fire. His great skill lay in his ability of recognizing the potential of specific songs and recording the artists involved on a per-record basis, so that he could reap the full benefit of their successes without getting embroiled in costly contractual obligations. Among the artists he recorded were KING CURTIS, Wilbert HARRISON, Lee DORSEY and Gladys KNIGHT & The Pips. By the mid-1960s, his entrepreneurial style had been superseded by the larger companies. In the late 1970s he was one of the first to recognise the potential of rap, signing GRANDMASTER FLASH to the revived Enjoy label. Throughout all this he has kept the shop running, which has become a mecca for record buyers.

ROBINSON, SMOKEY, & THE MIRACLES It is a measure of the esteem in which he is held that William 'Smokey' Robinson has remained one of the stalwarts of Motown ever since its inception. While his reputation has always appeared to be based upon his skills as a songwriter and performer, as a producer and arranger he has never been afraid to take chances and, like Phil SPECTOR, has used production techniques that have at first seemed to be out of context but, his unerring feeling for music, have usually proved him right. Where Berry GORDY was (and is) a record man, Robinson is the supreme craftsman. This does not mean he

has never made a duff record – he has made plenty – but with Robinson there is a vein of integrity that has coursed through everything he has put his hand to. Although Motown and Gordy have been the object of some vilification over the years, Robinson has remained staunchly loyal and got on with the job of making records.

He was born on February 19, 1940, in Detroit. While at Northern High School in 1954 he assembled a vocal group from among his friends: Warren Moore (born Detroit on November 19, 1939), Bobby Rogers (born Detroit on February 19, 1940), Emerson Rogers, who left to join the army shortly after, Ronnie White (born Detroit on April 5, 1939) and guitarist Marvin Tarplin; when Emerson Rogers left the group he was replaced by his sister Claudette Rogers (she was to become Robinson's wife). Throughout the mid-1950s, as The Matadors and then The Miracles, they developed a reputation on the club circuit. In 1957 they were introduced to Gordy, who was writing for Jackie WILSON as well as holding down a job at the Ford car works; he helped them to get a recording contract with the End label, which was owned by George GOLDNER, and gave Robinson lots of tips about structure in songwriting. The Miracles' debut in 1958, *Got a Job*, was written by Robinson with Gordy and his partner Billy Davis. It was followed by *I Cry*. Both generated local interest but not much else. The following year they recorded *Bad Girl*, which was leased to Chess and peaked at #93.

In 1960 Gordy set up Motown. Their debut for the new label, *Way over There*, failed to do anything. The follow-up, *Shop Around* (USA #2.1961), was Motown's first monster hit and set the stage for Robinson and the rest of the group just as much as it did for Motown itself. While Robinson was the nominal leader of the group, being the arranger and producer, the songwriting was often a joint activity with each member contributing in some way. Over the next ten years, they strung together a series of hits that put them in the vanguard of the Motown organisation: *What's so Good about Goodbye?* (USA#35.1962), *I'll Try Something New* (USA#39.1962), *You've Really Got a Hold on Me* (USA#8.1963), *A Love She Can Count On* (USA#31.1963), *Mickey's Monkey* (USA #8.1963), *I Gotta Dance to Keep from Crying* (USA#35.1964), *I Like it Like That* (USA #27.1964), *That's what Love is Made of* (USA #35.1964), *Oooh Baby Baby* (USA#16.1965), *The Tracks of my Tears* (USA#16.1965; UK #9.1969), *My Girl has Gone* (USA#14.1965), *Going to A-Go-Go* (USA#11; UK#44.1966), *(Come 'Round Here) I'm the One you Need* (USA#17; UK#45.1966/#13.1971), *The Love I Saw in You was Just a Mirage* (USA#20.1967), *More Love* (USA#23.1967), *I Second that Emotion* (USA#4; UK#27.1967), *If You Can Want* (USA#11; UK#50.1968), *Yester Love* (USA#31.1968), *Special Occasion* (USA #26.1968), *Baby, Baby Don't Cry* (USA #8.1969), *Abraham, Martin and John* (USA#33.1969), *Doggone Right* (USA #32.1969), *Point it Out* (USA#37.1969), *The Tears of a Clown* (USA/UK#1.1970/#34.1976) and *I Don't Blame You at All* (USA#18; UK #11.1971).

Although Robinson had his own group to work with he was also instrumental in developing the careers of other Motown artists like The MARVELETTES, The TEMPTATIONS, Marvin GAYE and Mary WELLS. In 1972 he embarked upon the much-vaunted solo career that had been in the pipeline since 1970. His replacement was William Griffin, but without Robinson The Miracles were able to manage only two more hits: *Do it Baby* (USA#13.1974) and *Love Machine (Part 1)* (USA#1; UK #3.1976).

Since launching his solo career, Robinson has not attained the same degree of consistency that he had with The Miracles: musical tastes have expanded to encompass many more influences and yet, every so often, he has come up with a composition like *Just my Soul Responding* or *Being with You* which makes the years fall away so that it could be 1965 all over again: *Just my Soul Responding* (UK#35.1974), *Baby Come Close* (USA#27.1974), *Baby that's Back-atcha* (USA#26.1975), *The Agony and the Ecstasy* (USA#36.1975), *Cruisin'* (USA #4.1979), *Let me be the Clock* (USA#31.1980), *Being with You* (USA#2; UK#1.1982), *Tell Me Tomorrow, Part 1* (USA#33; UK#51.1982), *Just To See Her* (USA#8; UK#52.1987) and *One Heartbeat* (USA#10.1987). His LPs have proved as successful as his singles: *A Quiet Storm* (USA#36.1975), *Where There's Smoke* (USA#17.1980), *Warm Thoughts* (USA #14.1980), *Being with You* (USA#10; UK #17.1981), *Yes It's You Lady* (USA#33.1982) and *One Heartbeat* (USA#26.1987). More recently, *Love, Smokey* (1990), showed an over reliance on other producers like George DUKE and Dennis LAMBERT.

In 1981 *American Bandstand* paid tribute to him with the Smokey Robinson 25th Anniversary Special and in 1983, he was reunited with The Miracles for the NBC-TV Special celebrating the 25th Anniversary of Motown. In all probability he will be there for the 50th Anniversary as well.

GOING TO A-GO-GO, Motown, 1966

THE TEARS OF A CLOWN, Motown, 1967

SMOKEY, (Smokey Robinson), Motown, 1973

PURE SMOKEY,(Smokey Robinson), Motown, 1974

WHERE THERE'S SMOKE, (Smokey Robinson), Motown, 1979

WARM THOUGHTS, (Smokey Robinson), Motown, 1980

BEING WITH YOU, (Smokey Robison), Motown, 1981

ANTHOLOGY, Motown, 1982

HOT SMOKEY, (Smokey Robinson), Motown, 1982

YES IT'S YOU LADY, (Smokey Robinson), 1982

BLAME IT ON LOVE AND ALL THE GREAT HITS, (Smokey Robinson), Motown, 1983
SMOKEY ROBINSON AND THE MIRACLES, Motown, 1983
THE SMOKEY ROBINSON STORY, K-Tel, 1983
TOUCH THE SKY, (Smokey Robinson), Motown 1983
18 GREATEST HITS, Motown, 1984
ESSAR, (Smokey Robinson), Motown, 1984
SMOKE SIGNALS, (Smokey Robinson), Motown, 1986
COMPACT COMMAND PERFORMANCES, Motown, 1987
ONE HEARTBEAT, (Smokey Robinson), Motown, 1987
LOVE, SMOKEY, (Smokey Robinson), Motown, 1990
THE TRACKS OF MY TEARS: THE BEST OF SMOKEY ROBINSON, Din, 1991

ROBINSON, SYLVIA Sylvia Robinson has over the past 30 years been one of the more eclectic personalities to emerge. As Sylvia Vanderpol, she teamed up with guitarist Micky Baker in 1957 and recorded *Love is Strange* (USA#11.1957) under the name of Micky & Sylvia, which had been given to them by Bo DIDDLEY's wife, Ethel Smith, ostensibly the song's writer. Despite its success, Baker split up the partnership because he loathed touring.

In 1971 Sylvia and her husband, Joe Robinson, set up the All Platinum Label and set about building a roster of artists, which included Shirley Goodman (see SHIRLEY & LEE), Retta Young and The Moments. In 1973 Sylvia released *Pillow Talk* (USA#3; UK #14.1973) for the Vibration label, a subsidiary of All Platinum. However, by 1979 All Platinum was in total disarray due to the decline in the disco market, where they had had most of their successes. At a party in a Harlem disco she heard three young black guys rapping through a microphone, she signed them up as The

Sugarhill Gang and released their *Rapper's Delight* (USA#36.1980; UK#3.1979). Over the next five years, she ran Sugarhill, the most successful rap-oriented label in the USA with a roster of artists that included GRANDMASTER FLASH, MELLE MEL and The Furious Five. By the end of the eighties, with the proliferation of competition in the market place for rap – most notably from the majors, ever willing to move onto the ground broken by the independents – Sugarhill was absorbed into MCA.

RODGERS, NILE Nile Rodgers was born in New York City on September 19, 1952. In 1970, he started running into Bernard EDWARDS at clubs. By 1972 they had formed The Big Apple Band, which toured the clubs providing backup for singers and vocal groups. In 1973 the name of the group was changed to CHIC. Throughout the latter half of the 1970s, Chic were responsible for some of the most sophisticated dance-oriented records to appear on the market. As a result Rodgers and Edwards, the creative impetus of Chic, became increasingly sought-after as producers, and together they worked with a variety of artists including SISTER SLEDGE in 1979, Sheila B. Devotion and Diana ROSS in 1980 and Debbie Harry in 1981.

After the demise of Chic in 1983, Rodgers launched a solo career with the LP, *Adventures in the Land of the Good Groove*; it failed to chart but attracted a cult following of sorts in clubs. He then produced David Bowie's LP *Let's Dance* and, in 1984, Madonna's LP *Like a Virgin*, both of which were hugely successful. In 1984 he joined The Honeydrippers, which consisted of Robert Plant, Jeff Beck and Jimmy Page; the resulting LP, *The Honeydrippers, Volume 1* (USA#4; UK#56.1984), provided the group with two hit singles, *Sea of Love* (USA#3; UK#56.1985) and *Rockin' at Mid-*

night (USA#25.1985). In 1987 he formed the trio Outloud with Philippe Saisse and Felicia Collins. In 1989 he coproduced the LP by The B52s, which revived their flagging career.

ROMEOS   See GAMBLE & HUFF

RONETTES   The Ronettes came together out of a perfectly natural desire for teenagers to have fun. Sisters Ronnie (Veronica, born August 10, 1943) and Estelle Bennett (born July 22, 1944) with their cousin Nedra Talley (born January 27, 1946) used to frequent the Peppermint Lounge in their native New York City; they were such good dancers that they got hired as a featured attraction. This led to them being employed as The Dolly Sisters by DJ Clay Cole for his 'Twist Package Tour', and then by DJ Murray the K, which enabled them to secure a contract with the Colpix label. Their debut, *I Want a Boy*, credited them as Ronnie & The Relatives; for subsequent releases they became The Ronettes.

In 1963 they were introduced to Phil SPEC-TOR; with him taking over the production duties, they became the archetypal girl group. Unlike other successful girl groups like The SHIRELLES, The MARVELETTES and The CRYSTALS, though, their image was carefully cultivated: the beehive hair-dos, the tight skirts and the chewing-gum were totally at odds with the girl next-door image fostered by most image builders. Their success was instantaneous: *Be my Baby* (USA#2; UK#4.1963), *Baby, I Love You* (USA#24; UK#11.1964), *(The Best Part of) Breaking Up* (USA#39; UK #43.1964), *Do I Love You?* (USA#34; UK #35.1964) and *Walking in the Rain* (USA #23.1964). Although the material, penned by such stalwarts of the Brill Building as Barry MANN & Cynthia Weil, Pete Anders, Vinnie Poncia and Spector himself, was of a very

high calibre, the records were not as commercially successful as some of Spector's other productions due to the increasing sophistication of his production techniques, which rather confused the US record-buying public. The exemplar of this was to be Ike & Tina TURNER's *River Deep, Mountain High*, which bombed in the USA but was very successful elsewhere.

By 1965 their career had effectively finished. Ronnie married Spector, and the other two members left to get married in 1966. In 1969 Ronnie, with Spector producing, recorded *You Came, You Saw, You Conquered*, which failed to chart, as did *Try Some, Buy Some* (1971), released on The Beatles' Apple label. A contract with Buddah and two further singles failed to deliver the goods. In 1976, having divorced Spector in 1974, she recorded the Billy Joel song, *Say Goodbye to Hollywood*, backed by Bruce Springsteen's group, The E Street Band. In 1979 she finally cut a solo LP, *Siren*, which was a bit of a hodge-podge of various styles: punk, soul and heavy-metal. In 1987 the LP *Unfinished Business*, recorded for CBS, showed that while the spirit was certainly willing, the material was well below par; as a result it sank without trace. In 1991 she came back into the public eye with the publication of her autobiography *Be my Baby*.

THE RONETTES SING THEIR GREATEST HITS, Phil Spector International, 1975
UNFINISHED BUSINESS, (Ronnie Spector), CBS, 1987

ROSE ROYCE   This group was formed by Motown producer Norman WHITFIELD in 1973 as Total Concept Unlimited to back artists like Edwin STARR; it consisted of Kenyi Chiba Brown (guitar), Kenny Copeland (horns), Freddie Dunn (horns), Henry Garner (drums), Juke Jobe (bass),

Michael Moore (horns), Mike Nash (keyboards) and Terral Santiel (percussion). When Starr left Motown they became the road band for The UNDISPUTED TRUTH and The TEMPTATIONS. In 1976, when Whitfield left Motown to set up his own operation, Whitfield Records, he took the group with him, recruiting vocalist Gwen Dickey to its ranks and changing the name to Rose Royce.

Whitfield's first big coup was to secure the contract to write the score for the film *Car Wash* (USA#14.1977). He had Rose Royce perform the music, bringing in to the group Melvin Ragin (guitar) and Ben Wilbur and Mark David (keyboards), with The POINTER SISTERS providing additional vocals. The title song, *Car Wash* (USA#1; UK#9.1976), was followed by *Put your Money where your Mouth is* (UK#44.1977) and *I Wanna Get next to You* (USA#10; UK#14.1977), the latter emphasising the ethereal quality of Dickey's voice.

Their group's next LP, *In Full Bloom* (USA#9; UK#18.1977), included the singles *Do Your Dance* (USA#39; UK#30.1977), *Wishing on a Star* (UK#3.1978) and *It Makes you Feel like Dancing* (UK#16.1978). It was followed by the LP *Strikes Again!* (USA#28; UK#7.1978), which featured *Love don't Live here Anymore* (USA#32; UK#2.1979). Although in the USA, their popularity began to wane, in the UK they continued to chart with titles like *Is it Love You're After?* (UK#13.1979) and *Ooh Boy* (UK#46.1980). In 1981 Dickey left the group and Whitfield terminated his association with it; since then the group has lost the distinctive touch that set it apart from other funk-oriented combos, although they have had odd successes with titles like *Magic Touch* (UK#43.1984), taken from the LP *Music Magic* (UK#69.1984), on Morgan Khan's Streetwave label.

THE BEST OF CAR WASH, MCA, 1977
IN FULL BLOOM, Whitfield, 1977

RAINBOW CONNECTION IV, Whitfield, 1979
GREATEST HITS, Whitfield, 1980
GOLDEN TOUCH, Warner Bros., 1981
STRONGER THAN EVER, Epic, 1982
IS IT LOVE YOU'RE AFTER, Blatant, 1989

ROSS, DIANA The career of Diana Ross has spanned the global warming to and acceptance of Black US culture. This has represented one of the single biggest steps taken in US society since the end of World War Two. Her career has been inextricably tied up with the development of Motown into the single largest black-owned conglomerate in the USA. So, while her music today tends to owe much to the M-o-R ethos, her contribution as one of the icons of the 1960s and 1970s overrides any subsequent doubts about the intrinsic value of her achievements.

She was born in Detroit on March 26, 1944. After joining The Primettes in 1959, the group changed their name to the SUPREMES; she remained with them for eleven years before launching her own solo career in 1970. Over the next eleven years she notched up a series of hits for Motown: *Reach Out and Touch (Somebody's Hand)* (USA#20; UK#33.1970), *Ain't No Mountain High Enough* (USA#1; UK#6.1970), *Remember Me* (USA#16; UK#7.1971), *I'm Still Waiting* (UK#1.1971), *Reach out I'll be There* (USA#29.1971), *Surrender* (USA#38; UK#10.1971), *Doobedood'n Doobe Doobedood'n Doobe* (UK#12.1972), *Good Morning Heartache* (USA#34.1973), *Touch me in the Morning* (USA#1; UK#9.1973), *All of my Life* (UK#9.1974), *Last Time I Saw Him* (USA#14; UK#35.1974), *Love Me* (UK#38.1974), *Sorry Doesn't Always Make it Right* (UK#23.1975), *Theme from Mahogany (Do You Know Where You're Going To?)* (USA#1.1975; UK#5.1976), *Love Hangover* (USA#1; UK#10.1976), *One Love in my Lifetime* (USA#25.1976), *I Thought it Took a Little Time*

(UK#32.1976), *Gettin' Ready for Love* (USA#27; UK#23.1977), *Lovin', Livin' and Givin'* (UK#54.1979), *The Boss* (USA#19; UK #40.1979), *No One Gets the Prize* (UK #59.1979), *It's my House* (UK#32.1979), *Upside Down* (USA#1; UK#2.1980), *My Old Piano* (UK#5.1980), *I'm Coming Out* (USA#5; UK #13.1980), *It's my Turn* (USA#9.1980; UK #16.1981); *One More Chance* (UK#49.1981) and *Cryin' my Heart for You* (UK#58.1981).

During the 1970s she starred in three films, and performed songs on the soundtrack LPs: *Lady Sings the Blues* (USA#1.1972; UK #50.1973), a biography of Billie Holiday; *Mahogany* (USA#19.1975), featuring a score written by Michael Masser with Gerry Goffin (see GOFFIN & KING); and *The Wiz* (USA #40.1978), a remake of the Judy Garland film *The Wizard of Oz*, with Ross starring in the Judy Garland role and Michael JACKSON appearing as the Scarecrow. However, none of these parts seemed to fulfil her potential as an actress.

Among her other projects were an LP of duets with Marvin GAYE, *Diana and Marvin* (USA#26; UK#6.1974), which included *You're a Special Part of Me* (USA#12.1973), *You are Everything* (UK#5.1974), *Stop Look Listen (to Your Heart)* (UK#25.1974) and *My Mistake was to Love You* (USA#19.1974), and the duetted title song, with Lionel RICHIE, for the Franco Zefferelli film *Endless Love* (USA#1; UK#7.1981), starring Brooke Shields.

In 1981 she left Motown, signing with RCA in the USA and Capitol for the rest of the world. Her first single under this arrangement was a reworking of the Frankie LYMON composition, *Why do Fools Fall in Love?* (USA#7; UK#4.1981). It was followed by another string of hits: *Mirror, Mirror* (USA#8; UK#36.1982), *Work that Body* (UK#7.1982), *It's Never too Late* (UK#41.1982), *Muscles* (USA#10; UK #15.1982), *So Close* (USA#40; UK#43.1983), *Pieces of Ice* (USA#31; UK#46.1983), *Touch by*

Touch (UK#47.1984), *Swept Away* (USA #19.1984), *Missing You* (USA#10.1985), *Chain Reaction* (UK#1.1986), *Experience* (UK #47.1986), *Dirty Looks* (UK#49.1987) and *Mr Lee* (UK#58.1988). She reunited briefly with Mary Wilson and Cindy Birdsong for The Supremes' appearance on the NBC TV Special celebrating Motown's 25th Anniversary.

Throughout her career she has been able to call upon the services of some of the more creative forces at large in the music industry, like Berry GORDY, HOLLAND, DOZIER & HOLLAND, ASHFORD & SIMPSON, Michael Jackson, Nile RODGERS, Bernard EDWARDS, Daryl HALL and Tom DOWD. Doubtless she will continue to do so, even if these talents are not granted as free a hand as is perhaps desirable.

DIANA ROSS, Motown, 1970
EVERYTHING IS EVERYTHING, Motown, 1971
DIANA (TV SPECIAL), Motown, 1971
I'M STILL WAITING, Motown, 1971
SURRENDER, Motown, 1971
GREATEST HITS, Motown, 1972
TOUCH ME IN THE MORNING, Motown, 1973
DIANA AND MARVIN, (with Marvin Gaye), Motown, 1973
LADY SINGS THE BLUES, (Original Soundtrack), Motown, 1973
LAST TIME I SAW HIM, Motown, 1974
LIVE AT CAESAR'S PALACE, Motown, 1974
MAHOGANY, (Original Soundtrack), Motown, 1975
GREATEST HITS, VOLUME 2, Motown, 1976
BABY IT'S ME, Motown, 1977
AN EVENING WITH DIANA ROSS, Motown, 1977
THE BOSS, Motown, 1979
20 GOLDEN GREATS, Motown 1979
DIANA, Motown, 1980
TO LOVE AGAIN, Motown, 1981
WHY DO FOOLS FALL IN LOVE, Capitol, 1981
ALL THE GREATEST HITS, Motown, 1981
DIANA ROSS, Motown, 1982
DIANA'S DUETS, Motown, 1982

SILK ELECTRIC, Capitol, 1982
LOVE SONGS, Telstar, 1982
THE VERY BEST OF DIANA ROSS, Motown, 1983
PORTRAIT, Telstar, 1983
SWEPT AWAY, Capitol, 1984
EATEN ALIVE, Capitol, 1985 14
GREATEST HITS, Motown, 1986
RED HOT RHYTHM 'N' BLUES, EMI, 1987
WORKIN' OVERTIME, EMI, 1989
GREATEST HITS LIVE, EMI, 1990

ROYAL SPADES See MARKEYS

RUFFIN, DAVID From 1962 until 1968 the voice of David Ruffin, lead singer of The TEMPTATIONS, graced some of the most soulful records to emanate from Motown. He was born in Meridian, Mississippi, on January 18, 1941. He left The Temptations after a disagreement over their musical direction and embarked upon a solo career. It was indicative of the autocratic regime Berry GORDY ran at Motown that, from the moment Ruffin severed his relationship with the group his career effectively ground to a halt: he had just one significant hit, ironically titled *My Whole World Ended (the Moment You Left Me)* (USA #9.1969). After a number of duets with his brother, Jimmy RUFFIN, including a version of *Stand by Me*, he had to wait six years before scoring another hit, *Walk Away from Love* (USA#9.1975; UK#10.1976). In 1982 he was invited to participate with Eddie KENDRICKS and The Temptations in a reunion concert; an LP, *Reunion*, and a brief tour ensued.

His reinstatement as one of the great soul singers has been due to the ministrations of Daryl HALL & John Oates, who invited both Ruffin and Kendricks to appear with them at the reopening of the Apollo. The resulting LP, *Live at the Apollo with David Ruffin and Eddie*

Kendricks (USA#21; UK#32.1985), also provided them with a hit single, *A Nite Live at the Apollo* (USA#20; UK#58.1985). In 1987 Ruffin and Kendricks signed with RCA as a duo. The eponymous debut LP showed that Ruffin's voice could still bring the house down.

LIVE AT THE APOLLO WITH DAVID RUFFIN AND EDDIE KENDRICKS, RCA, 1985
RUFFIN AND KENDRICKS, RCA, 1987

RUFFIN, JIMMY Jimmy Ruffin was born in Colinsville, Mississippi on May 7, 1939. In 1961 he was recommended by a member of the Motown group The CONTOURS to Berry GORDY, who signed him to the subsidiary Miracle. In 1963 he was asked to join The TEMPTATIONS but he declined and continued to sing backing vocals. In 1966, having been moved to another subsidiary label, Soul, he was given the opportunity to record *What Becomes of the Brokenhearted?* (USA#7; UK#10.1966/#4.1974). Written and produced by William 'Mickey' STEVENSON and William Weatherspoon, it showed that, while his voice was nowhere near as impressive as that of his brother, David RUFFIN, once the Motown machinery cranked into gear it could create hit records out of nowhere. Over the next five years, he had a number of hit singles, particularly in the UK, including *I've Passed this Way Before* (USA#17;UK#29.1967/#33.1969), *Farewell is a Lonely Sound* (UK#8.1970/#30.1974), *I'll Say Forever my Love* (UK #7.1970) and *It's Wonderful* (UK#6.1970).

His contract with Motown expired in 1971, although they would continue to reissue his records periodically. In 1974 he signed with Polydor, but was unable to recapture his chart-winning ways until 1980, when he signed with RSO Records and recorded *Hold on to my Love* (USA#10; UK#7.1980), written and produced by Robin Gibb of The Bee Gees. An LP entitled *Sunrise* followed. For the next five years he toured constantly, especially in the UK, where he had a large following on the cabaret circuit. He emerged briefly in 1984 to participate in Paul Weller's Council Collective. The resulting single, *Soul Deep*, reached #24 in the UK. He recorded briefly for EMI in 1985, but was quickly dropped due to a dearth of suitable material. Since then he has resumed touring.

20 GOLDEN CLASSICS, Motown, 1981

RUFUS   See KHAN, Chaka

RUPE, ART   In 1946 Art Rupe founded the Specialty label in Los Angeles. He was born in Pittsburgh in 1919 and moved out to the West Coast in the early 1940s, where he studied at UCLA. After leaving UCLA he had an abortive stab at film production before joining the Premier Record label. In 1944 he established the Jukebox label, which would be the basis of Specialty. Rupe was quick to capitalize upon the urgent need for 'race' music, signing artists like Roy Milton and Joe Liggins.

By 1950 he had expanded to take in the very lucrative gospel market, signing The Soul Stirrers and The Swan Silvertones. In 1952 he went to New Orleans with his A&R director Bumps BLACKWELL, where, at the suggestion of Dave BARTHOLOMEW, they signed Lloyd PRICE. With Blackwell, Rupe went on to record other artists like LITTLE RICHARD, Larry WILLIAMS and Sam COOKE. All of whom contributed to the popularisation of R&B and its hybrids, soul and rock'n'roll. However, Rupe closed down Specialty in 1959 to concentrate upon his other interests in oil and property. He revived the label briefly during the 1960s to instigate a series of reissues.

RUSSELL, BERT   See BERNS, Bert

SADE   Of all UK-based soul singers, Sade is the one who has most successfully managed to evolve a style of her own. While not wildly original, her subtle blend of jazz and soul, reminiscent of Curtis MAYFIELD's solo work of the early 1970s, has set her apart from most of her competitors.

She was born Helen Folasade Adu on January 16, 1959, in Ibadan, Nigeria. In 1963 she moved to Clacton, Essex, where she was brought up. While studying fashion design at St Martins School Of Art in London, she worked at the music venue the Rainbow Theatre. In 1980 she joined her first group, Arriva, which became the nucleus of Pride, featuring saxophonist Stewart Matthewman, bassist Paul Denman and keyboardist Andrew Hale. Although nominally a funk band, their ability to integrate Latin rhythms was critical to their initial success.

Sade was signed by Epic in 1983 with Pride remaining in place as her group. Her debut LP, *Diamond Life* (USA#5.1985; UK#2.1984), included three hit singles: *Your Love is King*(UK#6.1984), *When am I Gonna Make a Living?* (UK#36.1984) and *Smooth Operator* (USA#5.1985; UK#19.1984). The follow-up, *Promise* (USA/UK#1.1985), included another three singles: *The Sweetest Taboo* (USA#5; UK#31.1985), *Never as Good as the First Time* (USA#20.1985) and *Is it a Crime?* (UK #49.1986). After an appearance in 1987 in the film *Absolute Beginners* , to the soundtrack of which she contributed *Killer Blow*, she moved to Spain, where she started to prepare her third LP, *Stronger than Pride* (USA#7; UK#3.1988);

this featured the singles *Love is Stronger than Pride* (UK#44.1988) and *Paradise* (UK #29.1988) and was followed by a world tour at the end of 1988.

DIAMOND LIFE, Epic, 1984
PROMISE, Epic, 1985
STRONGER THAN PRIDE, Epic,1988

SALT 'N' PEPA Salt 'n' Pepa – Cheryl James and Sandy Denton, respectively – have become two of the most respected female rappers to emerge. Abetted by producer Hurby "Luv Bug" Azor and DJ Spinderella, their imaginative use of language, which has eschewed the common themes of hip hop, has placed them just beyond the mainstream of rappers.

They made their debut in 1987 with the LP *Hot Cool and Vicious*. Their first successful single, *Push It* (UK#2.1988), from their second LP, *A Salt with a Deadly Pepa*, was coupled with *Tramp*, from their debut LP, and both were massive dance-floor hits. The follow-up, *Shake Your Thang* (UK#22.1988), while being another dance-floor filler, demonstrated their ability to keep their sense of humour. Their version of *Twist and Shout* (UK#4.1988) turned a classic song on its head, deconstructed it and came up with a mix that James BROWN would have been proud of. With their most recent LP, *Black's Magic*, they have adopted a fresh approach, leaving behind commercial raps, in favour of a more socially aware theme. Never ones for navel searching, they have maintained their sense of humour with titles like *Negro with an Ego*, all of which they produced themselves.

HOT COOL AND VICIOUS, Champion, 1987
A SALT WITH A DEADLY PEPA, London, 1988
BLACKS' MAGIC, Next Plateau, 1990

SAM & DAVE Sam Moore was born on October 12, 1935, in Miami, Florida. One evening in 1958, when he was performing on stage at the King of Hearts Club in Miami, David Prater (born May 9, 1937 in Ocilla, Georgia) climbed on stage and started to sing with him. The audience liked what they heard, and thus one of soul music's better duos came into being. In 1960 they were signed by the Roulette label, with Henry GLOVER producing, but had little success until, in 1965, at the end of their contract, they were signed by Jerry WEXLER to Atlantic.

Wexler arranged for them to record at the prestigious Stax studios in Memphis with the provision that all of their records would be issued on Stax under licence from Atlantic. Jim STEWART teamed them up with the writing and production team of Isaac HAYES and David PORTER. Over the next three years they released a steady stream of hits: *Hold on I'm Coming* (USA#21.1966), *Soothe Me* (UK#35.1967), *Soul Man* (USA#2; UK#24.1967), *I Thank You* (USA#9; UK #34.1968) and *Soul Sister Brown Sugar* (UK #15.1969).

In 1970 the duo broke up to pursue solo careers. Moore remained with Atlantic while Prater signed with Henry STONE's Alston, but neither was able to recreate the success they had enjoyed as a duo. Over the years they periodically reformed for touring purposes but, as the relationship had never been harmonious, the intervals between reunions became increasingly protracted until in 1981 they parted for good. In 1987 Moore re-recorded *Soul Man* (UK#30.1987) with Lou Reed. Prater was arrested for selling crack to an undercover policeman; on April 9, 1988, he was killed when his car crashed into a tree in Syracuse, Georgia. Moore has continued to re-form the duo (with substitutes, naturally) and has carved a niche for himself on the strength of a few seminal singles on the 'oldies' circuit.

BEST OF SAM & DAVE, Atlantic, 1982
CAN'T STAND UP FOR FALLING DOWN, Edsel, 1984
HOLD ON I'M COMING, Platinum, 1985
GREATEST HITS, Showcase, 1986

SAMPLE, JOE   Joe Sample (born February 1, 1939 in Houston, Texas) was a founder member of The CRUSADERS. Throughout his career he has worked with artists like B. B. KING, Bobby BLAND, Bobby WOMACK, Quincy JONES, Randy CRAWFORD, Joe Cocker and Steve Winwood.

In 1978 he released his first solo LP for ABC, *Rainbow Seeker* (USA#62.1978); it was followed by *Carmel* (USA#56.1979). Both were fine examples of his virtuosity and his instinctive flair for composition. His first LP for MCA, *Voices in the Rain* (USA#65.1981), was followed by *The Hunter* (1983) and *Oasis* (1985). In 1986 he collaborated with session guitarist David T. Walker on the LP *Swing Street Cafe*, and in 1987 he released the solo LP, *Roles*. In 1990, armed with a contract from Warner Bros., he recorded the LP *Ashes to Ashes*, which saw him returning to his jazz origins. Throughout he has continued to be the guiding force of The Crusaders.

RAINBOW SEEKER, ABC, 1978
CARMEL, ABC, 1979
VOICES IN THE RAIN, MCA, 1981
THE HUNTER, MCA, 1983
OASIS, MCA, 1985
SWING STREET CAFE, (with David T. Walker), MCA, 1986
ROLES, MCA, 1987
ASHES TO ASHES, Warner Bros., 1990

SANBORN, DAVID   David Sanborn has managed to overcome the restrictions of session work to establish himself as a performer in his own right. Unlike many saxophonists, who move from session work to solo careers, he has shown himself to be an innovative composer, this has given his records a distinctive flavour and enabled him to pick up a string of Grammy awards for his LPs.

He was born in Tampa, Florida on July 30, 1945. After moving to St Louis he contracted polio, part of his physiotherapy was learning to play the alto saxophone. During the 1960s he played in local R&B clubs and studied at North Western University before in 1967 moving to the West Coast, where he joined The Paul Butterfield Blues Band and played on sessions. Throughout the early 1970s, he was employed by artists like Stevie WONDER, Bruce Springsteen, David Bowie, Paul Simon, James BROWN, Gil Evans and B. B. KING.

In 1975, he launched his solo career with the LP *Taking Off*. It was followed by *Sanborn* (1976), *Promise me the Moon* (1977), *Heart to Heart* (1978), *Hideaway* (1980), *Voyeur* (1981) – for which he won his first Grammy Award for Best R&B Instrumental Performance – *As We Speak* (1982), *Backstreet* (1983), *Straight to the Heart* (1984), *Double Vision* (1986), *A Change of Heart* (UK#86.1987) and *Close Up* (1988). In the process he has been featured on the TV programme *Late Night with David Letterman*, and been given his own networked radio programme, *The Jazz Show*, which was briefly syndicated to Jazz FM in the UK. And he still does session work.

HIDEAWAY, Warner Bros., 1980
VOYEUR, Warner Bros., 1981
AS WE SPEAK, Warner Bros., 1982
BACKSTREET, Warner Bros., 1983
STRAIGHT TO THE HEART, Warner Bros., 1984
A CHANGE OF HEART, Warner Bros., 1987
CLOSE UP, Reprise, 1988

SCAGGS, BOZ William Royce Scaggs was born in Ohio on June 8, 1944. His family moved to Dallas, Texas, when he was a child. While still at school he met Steve Miller and joined his group, The Marksmen, as vocalist. Together they attended the University of Wisconsin and joined a local R&B group, The Ardells. In 1963 he went back to Texas and formed The Wigs with guitarist John Andrew, bassist Bob Arthur and drummer George Rains. By 1964 the group had split up and Scaggs had moved to Europe. The following year he settled in Stockholm and recorded the LP *Boz* for Polydor, its lack of success was due to the fact that it was only released in Sweden. Over the next two years he continued to travel the world before he returned to San Francisco, where he joined The Steve Miller Band. In 1967 the group backed Chuck BERRY at the the Fillmore; the performance was recorded and released as an LP *Live at the Fillmore*. Their first two LPs, *Children of the Future* and *Sailor*, were recorded in the UK with Glyn Johns producing; Scaggs left the group on completion of the sessions because of 'musical differences' with Miller.

In 1969 Jann Wenner, editor of *Rolling Stone*, effected an introduction for Scaggs to Atlantic. The resulting LP, *Boz Scaggs*, was recorded at Muscle Shoals Sound studios with session musicians like Duane ALLMAN, Barry BECKETT, Roger HAWKINS, Eddie HINTON, David HOOD and Jimmy JOHNSON. While it failed to sell in any great quantity, it attracted a lot of attention critically and started a fashion among the rock fraternity for travelling down to Muscle Shoals to record; furthermore, it confounded the popular conception that white men couldn't sing the blues. However, Atlantic were unimpressed by the sales and dropped him. The following year, having returned to San Francisco, he formed The Boz Scaggs Band and secured a deal with CBS.

The group's debut LP, *Moments* (1971), showed just how far he had strayed from the traditional path pursued by white musicians in paying homage to their influences. The follow-up, *Boz Scaggs and Band* (1972), was recorded in London and was much more rock-oriented than its two predecessors, but the timbre of his voice combined with the quality of his material left no doubt as to where his heart lay. His next LP, *My Time*, marked a return to the overt R&B style of his earlier efforts. After touring he broke up his band to form a new group: the line-up was Les Dudek (guitar), Tom Rutley (bass), Rick Schlosser (drums), Jack Schroer (horns) and Jimmy Young (keyboards).

His first LP with the new band was *Slow Dancer*, produced by Johnny BRISTOL and arranged by H. B. BARNUM; it featured lushly textured arrangements that were reminiscent of Thom BELL's work and the emergent Philadelphia Sound than that of Motown, with which both Bristol and Barnum had been associated. His next LP, *Silk Degrees* (USA #2.1976; UK#20.1977), represented the big commercial breakthrough that he had been threatening for so long. It was produced by Joe Wissert and arranged by David Paich, and featured session musicians like Jeff and Steve Porcaro (both of whom would later form Toto with Paich). Four of the tracks were issued as singles: *It's Over* (USA#38.1976), *Lowdown* (USA#3; UK#28.1976), *What Can I Say* (UK #10.1977) and *Lido Shuffle* (USA#11; UK #13.1977); furthermore, Rita Coolidge had her biggest hit with a cover of the track *We're All Alone*. His next LP, *Down Two then Left* (USA#11; UK#55.1977), featured the same team of musicians as its predecessor, but included only one hit single, *Hollywood* (UK #33.1978).

After an interval of three years he released the LP *Middle Man* (USA#8; UK#52.1980). It included the four hit singles: *Breakdown Dead Ahead* (USA#15.1980), *Jo Jo* (USA#17.1980),

Look what You've Done to Me (USA#14.1980) and *Miss Sun* (USA#14.1981), a duet with Lisa Dal Bello. However, he then retired from the music business to concentrate upon running the restaurant he had opened in San Francisco. He remained out of the public eye until 1988, when he recorded the LP *Other Roads*, on which he was backed by members of Toto; it included the single, *Heart of Mine* (USA #35.1988). The same year he opened a jazz club in San Francisco, which has become a mecca for visiting musicians.

BOZ SCAGGS, Atlantic, 1969
BOZ SCAGGGS AND BAND, CBS, 1971
SLOW DANCER, CBS, 1974
SILK DEGREES, CBS, 1976
DOWN TWO THEN LEFT, CBS, 1977
MIDDLE MAN, CBS, 1980
HITS, CBS, 1981
OTHER ROADS, CBS, 1988

SCOTT, CALVIN See CARTER, Clarence

SHALAMAR Shalamar was at first an agglomeration of session singers and musicians created by producers Dick Griffey and Simon Soussan for a rather dubious disco medley of Motown hits entitled *Uptown Festival* (USA#25; UK#30.1977). With the success of the ensuing LP, *Uptown Festival* (USA #8.1977), Griffey, a producer on the TV series *Soul Train*, formed his own record label, Solar, and recruited Jody WATLEY (born in Chicago on January 30, 1959), Jeffrey Daniel (born in Los Angeles on August 24, 1955) and Gerald Brown turning Shalamar into a proper group.

They were teamed with producer Leon Sylvers for the LP *Disco Gardens*, which included the single *Take that to the Bank* (UK#20.1979). Brown left the group and was replaced as lead singer by Howard Hewett (born in Akron, Ohio, on October 1, 1955). Their next LP, *Big Fun* (USA#23.1980), included the singles *The Second Time Around* (USA#9.1980; UK #45.1979), *Right in the Socket* (UK#44.1980) and *I Owe you One* (UK#13.1980). It was followed by *Three for Love* (USA#40.1981), which included the singles *Full of Fire* and *Make that Move* (UK#30.1981). The next LP was *Go for It*, and then came *Friends* (USA#35.1982; UK #6.1983), which contained four hit singles: *I Can Make You Feel Good* (UK#7.1982), *A Night to Remember* (UK#5.1982), *There it Is* (UK#5.1982) and *Friends* (UK#12.1982). The next LP, *The Look* (USA#38; UK#7.1983), included yet another brace of singles, *Dead Giveaway* (USA#22; UK#8.1983) and *Over and Over* (UK#23.1983).

In 1984, Daniel moved to the UK to host the TV programme *Soul Train*, which was being launched there, and Watley left to pursue a solo career. They were replaced Delisa Davis and Micki Free. However, despite contributions to various film soundtracks, like those for *Footloose* and *Beverly Hills Cop*, the popularity of the group continued to decline until, in 1986, Hewett left to go solo; he was replaced by the former LA Rams footballer Sidney Justin, but the group broke up shortly afterwards. Hewett's solo career was launched amid much hoo-ha: he had signed a contract with Elektra and gathered such stellar session musicians together as Wilton FELDER, Stanley Clarke and George DUKE for his debut LP, *Commit to Love*. However, the single extracted from it, *I'm For Real*, aroused only modest interest. In 1990 the group re-formed and released the LP *Wake Up*.

THREE FOR LOVE, Solar, 1980
GO FOR IT, Solar, 1981
FRIENDS, Solar, 1982
GREATEST HITS, Solar, 1982
HEARTBREAK, Solar, 1985

GREATEST HITS, Stylus, 1986
CIRCUMSTANTIAL EVIDENCE, Solar, 1987
COMMIT TO LOVE, (Howard Hewett), Elektra, 1987
WAKE UP, Epic, 1990

SHEMWELL, SYLVIA See HOUSTON, Cissy

SHIRELLES The Shirelles were formed at school in Passaic, New Jersey, in 1957, where they were known as The Poquellos; they were Shirley Owens (born June 10, 1941), Addi Harris (born January 22, 1940), Doris Coley (born August 2, 1941) and Beverly Lee (born August 3, 1941). In 1958 they were persuaded by a schoolfriend, Mary Jane Greenberg, to audition a song they had written, *I Met Him on a Sunday* (USA#50.1958), for her mother, Florence, who owned the Tiara label. It was leased to Decca and became their first hit.

After a brace of flops for Decca, Florence Greenberg formed Scepter Records with writer/ producer Luther DIXON, and in 1959 the group recorded their version of The FIVE ROYALES' composition, *Dedicated to the One I Love* (USA#83.1959/#3.1961). Their next releases failed to strike a chord with the public, apart from *Tonight's the Night* (USA#39.1960). The follow-up, *Will You Love Me Tomorrow?* (USA#1; UK#4.1961), written by GOFFIN & KING, represented the first time an all-girl group had hit the #1 spot in the USA. Accordingly, throughout the country, soon no school was complete without at least one all-girl vocal group. After the successful reissue of *Dedicated to the One I Love*, they recorded a string of hit singles, that provided a blueprint for other producers to emulate: *Mama Said* (USA#4.1961), *Baby it's You* (USA#8.1962), *Soldier Boy* (USA#1; UK#23.1962) and *Foolish Little Girl* (USA#4; UK#38.1963).

In 1964 there started a legal tussle between the group and Scepter that would not be resolved until 1967; it concerned their earnings, which had not been paid into their individual trust funds as originally agreed. By the time they were free to record elsewhere their popularity had faded, and recording contracts with Mercury, Bell and RCA, among others, could not revitalise their flagging career. Ever since the beginning, they have toured constantly, which they do to this day on the oldies circuit – although it is rumoured that each of the three surviving members fronts her own version of The Shirelles. On June 10, 1982, Harris collapsed and died of a heart attack after a performance in Atlanta; she was 42.

JUKE BOX GIANTS, Audio Fidelity, 1982
SOULFULLY YOURS, Kent, 1984
SHA LA LA, Ace, 1985
LOST AND FOUND, Ace, 1987
21 GREATEST HITS, Bescol, 1987
GREATEST HITS, Ace, 1987
THE COLLECTION, Castle, 1990

SHIRLEY & COMPANY See SHIRLEY & LEE

SHIRLEY & LEE Shirley Pixley was born in New Orleans on June 19, 1936, as was Leonard Lee on June 29, 1935. After recording a demo at the J&M studios they were signed to the Aladdin label. Their debut single *I'm Gone* (1952) was a big R&B hit; it was the first of a series of records including *Rock all Night, Rockin' with the Clock, Feel so Good, Let the Good Times Roll* (USA#20.1956) and *I Feel Good* (USA#38.1957), all produced by Dave BARTHOLOMEW and featuring a studio band that included Lee ALLEN and Earl PALMER. After the collapse of Aladdin, they recorded for Imperial before separating in

1963. Shirley, having married to become Shirley Goodman, moved to Los Angeles where she worked as a session singer with Jesse Hill, a pianist from New Orleans, who had had a hit in his own right with *Ooh Poo Pah Do* (USA #28.1960), produced Allen TOUSSAINT. In 1975 she was recruited by Sylvia ROBINSON to record *Shame Shame Shame* (USA#12; UK #6.1975) under the name Shirley & Company; it became one of the year's biggest disco hits. On October 26, 1976, after years of obscurity, Lee died in New Orleans.

THE BEST OF SHIRLEY AND LEE, Ace, 1982
Y'ALL READY NOW?, (Jesse Hill), Charly, 1989

SHOWMEN See CHAIRMEN OF THE BOARD

SHUMAN, MORT From 1958 until 1965 the songwriting partnership of 'Doc' POMUS and Mort Shuman (born in New York on November 12, 1936) was rivalled only by that of LEIBER & STOLLER as one of the most successful and penetrating to emerge from the Brill Building. After joining the publishers Hill & Range they wrote for artists like Bobby Darin, Elvis Presley, The DRIFTERS, Ben E. KING, Gene McDANIELS and Gary 'U S' Bonds.

After the partnership broke up, following a fall that left Pomus confined to a wheelchair, Shuman teamed up with Kenny Lynch, a UK writer and singer, to pen hits for UK artists like The Small Faces. He then collaborated with producer Jerry RAGAVOY in 1966 on sessions with Howard TATE, which resulted in *Get it While you Can,* among others. After moving to Paris he worked with Johnny Halliday and then produced, wrote and starred in a musical based on the life of songwriter, Jacques Brel. As a result, he became something of a cult

figure in France, which enabled him to record as a solo artist. In 1981 he and the late Pomus wrote most of the B. B. KING LP *There must be a Better World Somewhere*, and in 1988 he returned to the theatre, this time in the UK, where he teamed up with Don Black for the musical *Budgie*.

SIMON, JOE Those who dismiss the significance of country music in soul need look no further than Joe Simon to see the process in action. However, rather than dominating his style country music has remained a subliminal influence on his work.

He was born in Simmesport, Louisiana, on September 2, 1943. After moving to California in 1958 he sang gospel with The Goldentones, who recorded for the Hush label. In 1962 he recorded *My Adorable One*, which became a local hit and was picked up by Veejay, who put him under contract. After meeting John RICHBOURG of WLAC in Nashville, he was taken over to the Fame Studios, where he recorded the PENN/ OLDHAM composition, *Let's Do it Over*. On the collapse of VeeJay, he was signed by Richbourg to Fred FOSTER's Sound Stage Seven label. Over the next four years he recorded songs like *Teenager's Prayer, Nine Pound Steel,(You Keep Me) Hanging On* (USA #25.1968), *No Sad Songs* and *The Chokin' Kind* (USA#13.1969).

In 1970 he was signed to the Spring label, where he recorded *Your Time to Cry* (USA #40.1971) before being packed off to Philadelphia producers GAMBLE & HUFF, recording *Drowning in a Sea of Love* (USA #11.1971) and *The Power of Love* (USA #11.1972). In 1973 he recorded the LP *Simon Country*, before Spring dispatched him to disco-producer Raeford Gerald for *Step by Step* (USA#37; UK#14.1973) and *Get Down, Get Down (on the Floor)* (USA#8.1975), and enlisted him to compose the *Theme from Cleopatra Jones* (USA#18.1973). In 1981 he was produced by country singer Porter Wagoner on the LP *Glad You Came my Way* for the Posse label. It was followed by *Mr Right* (1986), which was recorded in Nashville for the Compleat label.

THE SOUNDS OF SIMON, Westbound, 1971
SIMON COUNTRY, Westbound, 1973
MR RIGHT, Compleat, 1986
LOOKIN' BACK: 1966–70, Charly, 1988

SIMONE, NINA Despite a propensity for controversy and her outspoken militancy towards any who might step on her toes, Nina Simone has a breadth of vision that has enabled her to embrace any style she wishes with the same degree of commitment and expertise.

She was born Eunice Waymon on February 21, 1933 in Tryon, North Carolina. Although raised on gospel, she studied music at the Juilliard School of Music in New York, becoming a teacher of piano before cutting her first records for the Bethlehem label. Her debut hit was a version of *I Loves You, Porgy* (USA #18.1959) from Gershwin's *Porgy And Bess*. This was followed by *My Baby just Cares for Me* (UK#5.1987), which has over the years acquired cult status in the UK through constant playing in clubs and occasional use in commercials.

In 1960, she signed with the Colpix label (a subsidiary of Screen Gems, the music publishers) where her virtuosity stood out on a series of records – some blues and R&B standards, some self-written – like *The Other Woman, Trouble in Mind, I Put a Spell on You* (UK#49.1965/#28. 1969) and *Don't Let me be Misunderstood*. From then on her audiences were substantially better in the UK and France, where LPs like *I Put a Spell on You* (UK#18.1965) were eagerly awaited by aficionados.

The latter half of the sixties saw her signing to RCA and aligning herself with the Civil Rights Movement alongside other notables like James BROWN. Her outspoken views and the militancy of her rhetoric alienated her from the mainstream, and consequently RCA never gave her records the promotion they deserved. Such was the intensity of her work that harmless songs like *Ain't Got No – I Got Life* (UK #2.1968), from the musical *Hair*, The Bee Gees composition, *To Love Somebody* (UK#5.1969) and the George Harrison song *Here Comes The Sun* acquired a whole different meaning, when set in the context of the rest of her output like *Backlash Blues, Why? (The King of Love is Dead), Old Jim Crow* and *Young, Gifted and Black*. To this day, her recording of *Young, Gifted and Black* has been overshadowed by the Aretha FRANKLIN and Bob & Marcia versions.

In 1972 she recorded her last LP for RCA, *Is it Finished?*. In 1978 she returned with the LP *Baltimore* for the CTI label. Once again her ability to make a song her own was evident in her version of the title track, a Randy Newman composition. In 1980 she was signed to the EMI subsidary Manhattan for the LP, *Cry Before I Go*. Another gap followed until 1986, when she recorded *Nina's Back*. Both picked up sales, but gave the impression that she was doing something else while recording them. Throughout her career, live recordings of her concert and club performances have formed the cornerstone of her output with *Nina at Newport* (USA#23.1961), *Live at the Carnegie Hall* and *Live at Ronnie Scott's* being excellent examples of what to expect from a Nina Simone performance.

AT NEWPORT, Official, 1961
BALTIMORE, CTI, 1978

CRY BEFORE I GO, Manhattan, 1980
HERE COMES THE SUN, RCA, 1980
BLACK SOUL, RCA (Germany), 1983
OUR LOVE, Barclay (France), 1983
A PORTRAIT OF NINA SIMONE, Musidisc (France), 1983
THE ARTISTRY OF NINA SIMONE, RCA, 1984
BACKLASH, Star Jazz, 1984
THE BEST OF NINA SIMONE, Philips, 1984
FODDER ON MY WINGS, IMS, 1984
MY BABY JUST CARES FOR ME, Charly, 1985
NINA SIMONE SINGS THE BLUES, RCA, 1985
REPLAY ON NINA SIMONE, Sierra, 1985
MAGIC MOMENTS, RCA, 1986
NINA'S BACK, Jungle Freud, 1986
LIVE AT VINE STREET, Verve, 1987
THE AMAZING NINA SIMONE, Official, 1988
LIVE AT RONNIE SCOTT'S, Essential, 1989

SIMPSON, VALERIE See ASHFORD & SIMPSON

SINGLETON, SHELBY Shelby Singleton was born in Waskom, Texas, on December 16, 1931. In the mid-1950s he became a promotion man for Mercury. By 1960 he had become a producer, collaborating with Brook BENTON, Bruce Chanel and Clyde McPHATTER. In 1962 he was promoted to label director of the Mercury subsidiary, Smash; he went on to become a vice-president of Mercury, signing artists like Jerry Lee Lewis and Charlie Rich.

In 1966, he resigned to form his own labels: the country specialist label, Plantation, and the soul specialist labels, Silver Fox and S S S International. Among the artists he signed were Johnny ADAMS, Big Al DOWNING, the duo Peggy Scott & Jojo Benson and Betty LaVETTE. Throughout, he built up a catalogue of songs with up to thirty writers under contract. In 1969, he acquired the Sun catalogue and, by the mid-1970s, he had stopped recording soul to concentrate upon his publishing interests and to maximise the full potential of the Sun catalogue.

SISTER SLEDGE The group Sister Sledge comprised four sisters from Philadelphia, Debbie, Joni, Kathy and Kim. From childhood they all sang gospel in the neighbourhood church. They made their debut in 1971 for the Money Back label, recording *Time will Tell* as well as providing backing vocals for GAMBLE & HUFF recording sessions. In 1973 they were signed by Atlantic to its subsidiary, Cotillion, where, produced initially by Tony Bell, they recorded *The Weathermen* and *Mama Never Told Me* (UK #20.1975).

After two unsuccessful LPs, *Circle of Love* and *Together*, they were teamed with Nile RODGERS and Bernard EDWARDS of CHIC, who produced a string of hit singles for them; these were featured on the LP, *We are Family* (USA#3; UK#7.1979), which has become one of the most enduring testaments to the skill of Rodgers and Edwards: *He's the Greatest Dancer* (USA#9; UK#6.1979), *We are Family* (USA#2; UK#6.1979/#33.1984), *Lost in Music* (UK#17.1979/#4.1984) and *Thinking of You* (UK#11.1984). After *Love Somebody Today* (USA#31.1980), which included *Got to Love Somebody* (UK#34.1980), they recorded *All American Girls*, with Narada Michael WALDEN producing; the title track (UK #41.1981) was released as a single. The following year they covered the Mary WELLS hit, *My Guy* (USA#23.1982).

After a lull in their career, they released the LP *When the Boys Meet the Girls* (UK #19.1985), featuring the singles *Frankie* (UK #1.1985) and *Dancing on the Jagged Edge*

(UK#50.1985). In 1988 they contributed *Here to Stay* to the soundtrack of the film *Playing for Keeps*.

WE ARE FAMILY, Atlantic, 1979
LOVE SOMEBODY TODAY, Atlantic, 1980
WHEN THE BOYS MEET THE GIRLS, Atlantic, 1985
GREATEST HITS, Atlantic, 1986
GREATEST HITS, (with Chic), Telstar, 1987

SLEDGE, PERCY In 1965 Percy Sledge turned up at Quin IVY's Quinvy studios in Muscle Shoals and recorded *When a Man Loves a Woman*. None of these factors were particularly odd in themselves: the peculiarity lay in the fact that an unknown artist should make a record that would shape the perception of southern soul and establish Muscle Shoals as a recording Mecca.

Sledge was born in Leighton, Alabama in 1940. After leaving school he worked as a hospital orderly in Colbert County and sang occasionally with the gospel group The Singing Clouds (which included his cousin Jimmy HUGHES) and a local group, The Esquires. At Christmas 1965 they recorded *When a Man Loves a Woman* (USA#1; UK#4.1966/#2.1987); the backing band was Spooner OLDHAM (keyboards), Marlin GREENE (guitar), Junior Lowe (bass) and Roger HAWKINS (drums), and the session was engineered by Jimmy JOHNSON. It was the first of a series of hits for Sledge, which included *Warm and Tender Love* (USA#17; UK#34.1966), *It Tears Me Up* (USA#20.1966), *Love me Tender* (USA #40.1967) and *Take Time to Know Her* (USA #11.1968). He continued to record for Ivy and Atlantic until 1973, when he cut the LP *I'll be Your Everything* for Phil WALDEN's Capricorn label.

After years of obscurity, during which he toured on the chitlin' circuit and recorded occasionally but was unable to capitalise upon his earlier success, he was re-discovered in 1987 when his biggest hit was revived as the soundtrack for a commercial for jeans in the UK. The single was reissued and became a hit all over again. Since then he has toured the UK and Europe regularly and, in 1987, he recorded a country LP for Monument, *Wanted Again*.

GREATEST HITS, K-Tel, 1984
WARM AND TENDER LOVE, Blue Moon, 1986
THE BEST OF PERCY SLEDGE, Atlantic, 1987
GREATEST HITS, MCS, 1987
PERCY!, Charly, 1987
WANTED AGAIN, Demon, 1989

SLY & THE FAMILY STONE Sly Stone was born Sylvester Stewart in Dallas, Texas, on March 15, 1944, however, and soon thereafter his family moved to Vallejo, California. By the time he was nineteen he was a producer for the Autumn label, owned by DJ Tom Donahue, working with artists like The Beau Brummels and Bobby FREEMAN. After attending radio school he got a job as a DJ at the San Francisco station KSOL, and started his own group, The Stoners, which included trumpeter Cynthia Robinson. In 1966 he formed The Family Stone, which included Robinson, Sly's brother Freddie (guitar; born June 5, 1946), sister Rosemary (piano and vocals; born March 21, 1945), cousin Larry GRAHAM (bass), Greg Errico (drums) and Jerry Martini (horns). What set the group apart from others was that Sly was prepared to experiment; having assimilated the influences of the fledgling psychedelic movement of San Francisco and, combined with his native flair for programming music at KSOL, he was able to put together a hybrid that owed as much to soul and R&B as white rock'n'roll. The fact that this hybrid was a reflection of what was happening on the streets was pivotal to his success. It has continued to exert a strong influence upon artists like PRINCE, George CLINTON, Run DMC and Public Enemy.

He secured a contract with Epic. The group's debut LP, *A Whole New Thing*, proved to be too esoteric, but the follow-up, *Dance to the Music*, showed that they could be commercial if push came to shove. The title track, *Dance to the Music* (USA#8; UK#7.1968), quickly set the charts alight and created one of those audible buzzes that heralds the arrival of a new group, who are a bit special. The next LP, *Life*, was modestly successful, but the follow-up, *Stand* (USA#13.1969), included a number of tracks that were striking in both their lyrical conviction and their melodic immediacy: *Everyday People* (USA#1; UK#36.1969), *Sing a Simple Song, Stand!* (USA#22.1969) and *I Want to Take you Higher* (USA#38.1970). Two more singles followed – *Hot Fun in the Summertime* (USA#2.1969) and *Thank You (Falettinme be Mice Elf Agin)* coupled with *Everybody Is A Star* (USA#1.1970) – from an LP that never materialised entitled *The Incredible and Unpredictable Sly and the Family Stone*.

In 1971 he released the LP, *There's a Riot Goin' On* (USA#1.1971; UK#31.1972), which included the singles *Family Affair* (USA #1.1971; UK#15.1972) and *Running Away* (USA#23; UK#17.1972). It was one of the most pessimistic LPs of the era: the brutal suppression of the black civil rights activists, culminating in the shooting of George Jackson, was an issue that made it a profoundly uncomfortable record to have around at a time when confidence in the Nixon administration was ebbing fast and the spirit of the 1960s, with all the hopes and aspirations that had been entailed, had disappeared down the drain.

In 1972 Larry Graham left to form his own group and was replaced by Rusty Allen; Greg Errico likewise left, and was replaced by Andy Newmark and hornman Pat Ricco joined. The next LP, *Fresh* (USA#7.1973), was an altoge-

ther lighter affair, containing a single hit, *If You Want me to Stay* (USA#12.1973). It was followed by *Small Talk* (USA#15.1974), which contained *Time for Living* (USA#32.1974). Despite the apparent optimism implicit in the titles, both were lack-lustre efforts signalling, if not retreat, tacit acceptance. By 1976 Sly was filing for bankruptcy; the latter half of the 1970s and the early 1980s saw him locked into a fierce battle with drug problems, which were only partly resolved when Bobby WOMACK persuaded him to get treatment and invited him to go out on tour with him. In the interim, however, he recorded the LPs *Back on the Right Track* (1979) and *Ain't but the One Way* (1983). Since then there have been occasional rumours that he will record again, but all that has materialised has been a duetted cover, with former Motel members Martha Davis, of the Joan Armatrading song *Love and Affection*, for the soundtrack of the film *Soul Man*.

GREATEST HITS, Epic, 1970
THERE'S A RIOT GOIN' ON, Edsel, 1971
FRESH, Edsel, 1973
AIN'T BUT THE ONE WAY, Warner Bros., 1983

SMITH, ARLENE See CHANTELS

SMITH, HUEY "PIANO" The rolling boogie-woogie piano style of Huey Smith has become a trademark sound of New Orleans R&B. Not that Smith was its originator: like Fats DOMINO he adapted it from the early jazz styles of the 1920s and placed it in a contemporary setting.

He was born on January 26, 1934, in New Orleans. In 1949 he joined Guitar Slim's trio as pianist, a position which enabled him to secure regular session work at Cosimo Matassa's J&M studios backing artists like LITTLE RICHARD, Smiley LEWIS and Lloyd

PRICE. A meeting with Johnny VINCENT gave him the opportunity to record under his own name. As his vocals lacked confidence, he formed The Clowns: Bobby MARCHAN, Gerri Hall, Eugene Francis and Billy Roosevelt. With The Clowns, he had a series of hits including *Rockin' Pneumonia and the Boogie Woogie Flu* (1957), *Don't You just Know It* (USA#9.1958) and *High Blood Pressure* (1958). After Marchan left The Clowns, Smith embarked on a solo career.

Smith was signed by Imperial in 1960, but failed to attract anything more than local attention. Throughout the 1960s he toured with three different groups – The Pitta Pats, The Hueys and The Clowns – and recorded for the Instant label. After a brief spell with the Atlantic subsidiary Cotillion in 1970, he retired with the proceeds of a commercial for Coca-Cola and became a Jehovah's Witness.

ROCKIN' PNEUMONIA AND THE BOOGIE WOOGIE FLU, Ace, 1979
'TWAS THE NIGHT BEFORE CHRISTMAS, Ace, 1979
SOMEWHERE THERE'S HONEY FROM THE GRIZZLY, Ace, 1984
THE IMPERIAL SIDES: 1960/61, Pathe Marconi, 1984
PITTA PATTIN', Charly, 1989

SOS BAND The SOS Band (the name of the group stands for the Sounds of Success) were formed around the vocals of Mary Davis in the late 1970s in Atlanta. They failed to attract any attention until they were signed by Jimmy JAM and Terry Lewis to their Tabu label. With the combined efforts of Jam & Lewis behind them they had a string of hits during the 1980s: *Take Your Time (Do it Right), Part 1* (USA#3; UK#51.1980), *Groovin' (That's what we're Doin')* (UK#71.1983), *Just be Good to Me* (UK#13.1984), *Just the Way You Like It* (UK#32.1984), *Weekend Girl* (UK#51.1984), *The Finest* (UK#17.1986), *Borrowed Love* (UK#50.1986) and *No Lies* (UK#64.1987).

In 1989 Davis left for a solo career, her replacement was Chandra Culley. Their first LP *Diamonds in the Raw*, without Davis or producers Jam & Lewis, showed the extent of their reliance on them. While it was good, solid stuff it lacked the immediacy of their previous outings and Culley was no match for the departed Davis. Davis made her solo debut with *Separate Ways* (1990), produced by LA & BABYFACE. While it signally failed to create a spectacular impression it showed that she does possess a gorgeous voice.

JUST THE WAU YOU LIKE IT, Tabu, 1984
S O S, Tabu, 1984
SANDS OF TIME, Tabu, 1986
ON THE RISE, Tabu, 1986
DIAMONDS IN THE RAW, Tabu, 1989
SEPARATE WAYS, Mary Davis, Tabu, 1990

SOUL CLAN See BURKE, SOLOMON

SOUL MACHINE See NEVILLE BROTHERS

SOUL II SOUL Since their emergence in 1989 Soul II Soul, under the guidance of Jazzie B (born as Beresford Romeo), have established themselves as one of the major contributors to the profile of UK-bred soul music. A loose collective in every sense, consisting of musicians, DJs and designers, they have developed a sound that is based on the principles of rap and hip-hop, but readily identifiable from their counterparts by the use of their own original material.

Their first LP, *Club Classics Volume One* (USA/UK#1.1989), became the soundtrack to the summer of 1989; written and produced by Jazzie B and Nellee Hooper and featuring a trio of female vocalists, Caron WHEELER, Rose Windross and Do'reen Waddell, it included the singles *Back to Life* (USA/UK #1.1989) and *Keep on Moving* (UK#1.1989). As a result of their success Jazzie B expanded the base of the operation to include shops, clothing and their own record label. In 1990 the second LP, *Volume 2 1990 – A New Decade* (UK #1.1990), was released to much media attention and featured Caron Wheeler's replacement, Marcie Lewis. In 1991 the launch was announced of the Funki Dred record label, which was to be distributed by Motown.

CLUB CLASSICS, VOLUME I, Ten, 1989
VOLUME 2, 1990 – A NEW DECADE, Ten, 1990

SOUTH, JOE Joe South was born on February 28, 1940, in Atlanta, Georgia. By the time he was eleven he had become a very proficient guitarist and, in 1958, he had a minor novelty hit with a take-off of the Sheb Wooley hit *The Purple-People Eater* with steel guitarist Pete Drake. After becoming a DJ, he continued to record intermittently as a session musician until he met up with Bill Lowery, who was beginning to assemble a roster of artists which included The TAMS and Tommy Roe; two of the biggest hits he wrote were *What Kind of Fool (Do You Think I Am)?* and *Untie Me* for The Tams. As the Atlanta music scene was in its infancy, Lowery had taken his charges up to Rick HALL's studios in Muscle Shoals. The success of the Muscle Shoals sessions encouraged Lowery to set up his own label in Atlanta.

In 1965 South started to work with Billy Joe Royal. Royal, a native of Atlanta, had a series of hits with South's compositions: *Down in the Boondocks, I Knew You When, I've Got to be*

Somebody and *Hush*. Meanwhile, his reputation as a session musician grew, being used by Bob Dylan and Simon & Garfunkel. In 1968, he signed a contract with Capitol as a solo artist. His first LP, *Introspect* (1969), was and still is an exemplar of country-soul; it included *Games People Play* (USA#12; UK#6.1969) and *Rose Garden*, which has been covered by artists like Lynn Anderson – who had the hit – and Elvis Presley. His next LP, *Don't it Make You Want to go Home?*, included *Walk a Mile in my Shoes* (USA#12.1970); the title track was covered by Brook BENTON. After cutting the LP *So the Seeds are Growing* (1971), his brother Tommy died. South retired and moved to Hawaii, where he stayed until 1975.

On his return, he went back into the studios and recorded the LPs, *Midnight Rainbows* (1975) and *To Have, to Hold and to Let Go* (1976), for the Island label; he was backed by various members of the Atlanta Rhythm Section. However, neither was successful, which discouraged him from further attempts.

INTROSPECT, See For Miles, 1986

SPECTOR, PHIL While there have been many producers, who have exerted a major influence upon the development of soul music and the ways of treating it, none of has enjoyed such a high profile as Phil Spector.

He was born on December 26, 1940 in the Bronx. He first came to prominence as a member of The Teddybears with *To Know Him is to Love Him* (USA#1.1958), an emblematic piece of teenage *angst* if ever there was one. By 1961, having recorded for the Imperial label and worked as a producer with Lee Hazelwood in Los Angeles, he moved to New York, where he became an assistant to LEIBER & STOLLER and wrote with Gene Pitney. That same year he set up his own label, Philles, with Lester Sill. His innovative approach to production, which paid scant attention to cost or feasibility, provided a backdrop for Brill Building writers like Ellie GREENWICH, Jeff BARRY, Cynthia Weil and Barry MANN to explore the whole gamut of teenage emotion. The vehicles were groups like The CRYSTALS and The RONETTES and session singers, like Darlene LOVE, – all were more or less interchangeable, The Ronettes being the only group that had a clear identity of its own. The full extent of the impersonality was exemplified by a 1963 Christmas LP, *A Christmas Gift for You* (USA #6.1972), in which he unleashed all his technological wizardry on standards like *White Christmas*. Spector was always assisted by having the cream of the session fraternity – drummers Hal Blaine and Earl PALMER, bassist Joe Osborne, pianist Leon Russell and co-ordinator/saxophonist Steve Douglas, among others – to implement his grandiose schemes.

Later productions, known as the Wall of Sound, with The RIGHTEOUS BROTHERS and Ike & Tina TURNER set the stage for him until, in 1966, when *River Deep, Mountain High* by Ike & Tina Turner bombed in the USA he retired from production work seriously miffed.

In 1969 he tried to relaunch the career of his wife, Ronnie, the former Ronette, by setting up the Phil Spector International label, through A&M. His only real success was with *Black Pearl* (USA#13.1969) by Sonny Charles and The Checkmates. As such, his new label was not a great success, but it gave him the necessary impetus to revive his career and led to an association with the disintegrating Beatles, particularly John Lennon and George Harrison; both of whom he worked with on their various solo projects for the Apple label. In later years he produced The Ramones, Leonard Cohen and Cher. In recent years, he has been marshalling the publishing rights of his extensive catalogue.

ECHOES OF THE SIXTIES, Phil Spector International, 1977
PHIL SPECTOR'S CHRISTMAS ALBUM, Phil Spector International, 1979
THE WALL OF SOUND, Phil Spector International, 1981
PHIL SPECTOR: EARLY PRODUCTIONS 1958–61, Rhino, 1984

SPECTOR, RONNIE See RONETTES

SPELLMAN, BENNY See K-DOE, Ernie

SPINNERS See DETROIT SPINNERS

STAPLE SINGERS The Staple Singers have been, for almost 40 years, one of the more idiosyncratic groups , in that their style has been adapted to cater to the perceived notions of whoever was producing them at the time.

They were formed as a family gospel quartet in 1951 in Chicago by Roebuck 'Pops' Staples (born December 28, 1915, in Winoma, Misissippi), with his son Pervis (born 1935, in Drew, Mississippi) and his two daughters Mavis (born 1940, in Chicago, Illinois) and Cleotha (born 1934, in Drew, Mississippi). Pops became a blues guitarist while still a teenager. In 1935 he joined the gospel group The Gold Trumpets before moving to Chicago in 1936. He joined The Trumpet Jubilees, and for five years they played the gospel circuit. In 1951 he formed The Staple Singers and they recorded for the independent United label in 1953. In 1956, having signed to the Veejay label, they scored a monster gospel hit with *Uncloudy Day*. However, in 1959 Pervis left the group to join the army and was replaced by another sibling, Yvonne. The group left Veejay in 1962 and were signed by Epic. Their style began to veer more towards R&B and country-soul, due to the influence of producers like Larry WILLIAMS and Billy Sherrill. They had a couple of minor hits, *Why (am I Treated So Bad)* and *For what it's Worth*.

In 1968 they signed to Stax, where they were teamed with Steve CROPPER. The most successful aspect of the Stax connection was that Mavis was able to record an LP, *Only for the Lonely* (1970), on the Volt subsidiary, with Don Davis producing; it included a minor hit, *I Have Learned to Live without You*. Al BELL took over the production duties and they scored with *Heavy Makes You Happy (Sha-Na-Boom-Boom)* (USA#27.1971); written by Jeff BARRY and Bobby Bloom, it was completely at odds with anything they had ever recorded before. An eponymously titled LP made a small dent in the lower reaches of the charts. Towards the end of the year, Bell took the group over to Muscle Shoals Sound studios, where they were teamed with the crack session squad of Barry BECKETT, Roger HAWKINS and the rest of the gang. They scored their second major hit, *Respect Yourself* (USA #12.1971), which was written by Luther INGRAM and Mack Rice. It was a particularly trite piece of philosophising, but somehow it seemed to capture the mood of the era. An LP followed, *Bealtitude: Respect Yourself* (USA#19.1972); another single was extracted, *I'll Take You There* (USA#1; UK#30.1972), and then two more followed, *This World* (USA #38.1972) and *Oh La De Da* (USA#33.1973). Much of the material was written by Homer BANKS and Carl Hampton and Bettye Crutcher and Mack Rice. The next LP, *Be What You Are*, included the singles *If You're Ready (Come Go with Me)* (USA#9.1973; UK #34.1974) and *Touch a Hand, Make a Friend* (USA#23.1974). Their final LP before the demise of Stax, *City in the Sky* (1975), was

again quietly successful, but couldn't halt the inexorable decline of the label into bankruptcy and closure.

They were signed by Curtis MAYFIELD to his Curtom label and recorded the title song for the film *Let's Do it Again* (USA#1.1976) on the soundtrack LP (USA#20.1976) of the same name, produced by Mayfield and arranged by Donny HATHAWAY; a further single, *New Orleans*, was extracted. Their next LP, *Pass it On* (1977), was marred by indifferent material. They performed at The Band's farewell concert, which was filmed by Martin Scorsese. After leaving Curtom they were signed by 20th Century records, which they left after recording one LP, *Hold on to Your Dream* (1981). In 1983 Mavis collaborated with HOLLAND, DOZIER & HOLLAND for the LP *Love Gone Bad*. In 1984 the group signed with Epic for the LP *Turning Point*, which included a version of *Slippery People*, a Talking Heads composition. Once again this showed what chameleons the group were: a substantial dance- floor hit and one of the most authoritative grooves of the year. The following year, another LP, *The Staple Singers*, was released to almost unanimous disinterest. In 1988, Mavis relaunched her on-off solo career by signing with PRINCE's Paisley Park label. The resulting LP, *Time Waits for No One*, was written and produced by Prince with Al Bell. In 1990, Mavis was featured on the soundtrack of the Prince film *Graffiti Bridge* singing *Melody Cool*.

STAPLE SINGERS, Stax, 1971
BEALTITUDE: RESPECT YOURSELF, Stax, 1971
HOLD ON TO YOUR DREAMS, 20th Century, 1981
AT THEIR BEST, Stax, 1982
THE STAPLE SINGERS, Audio Fidelity, 1984
STAPLE SINGERS, Epic, 1985
PRAY ON, New Cross, 1986
WE'LL GET OVER, Stax, 1987
TIME WAITS FOR NO ONE, (Mavis Staples), Paisley Park, 1989

STAPLES, MAVIS See STAPLE SINGERS

STARR, EDWIN Edwin Starr was born Charles Hatcher in Nashville on January 21, 1942. After moving to Detroit, where he built up his live act on the club circuit, he was signed to Eddie Wingate's locally based Ric-Tic label. At Ric-Tic Wingate used the Motown session musicians The Funk Brothers (see JAMERSON, James) to back his artists, which accounted for the propulsive machine gun-like delivery of his first hit, *Agent Double-O Soul* (USA#21.1965). This was followed by *Stop her on Sight (S.O.S)* (UK#35.1966/#11.1968) and *Headline News* (UK#39.1966/#11.1968). Although Berry GORDY had recognised the indelible signature of The Funk Brothers on Starr's initial outings for the label, when *Stop her on Sight* came out, he decided he liked Starr's voice enough to buy the company and its roster of artists; but not before *Headline News* had been released.

Once under the wing of Motown, Starr worked with a variety of producers until being teamed with Norman WHITFIELD in 1969. After *Twenty Five Miles* (USA#6; UK #36.1969) he recorded the Barrett STRONG and Norman Whitfield composition *War* (USA#1; UK#3.1970); the whole production was a seething mass of fuzz guitars, with Starr's vocals urging them onwards and The Funk Brothers providing the most rock solid rhythm tracks that anyone could hope to find. It was followed by *Stop the War Now* (USA#26; UK #33.1971) and *You Set my Soul on Fire*. When Motown moved to Los Angeles, Starr stayed in Detroit and played the club circuit before signing with the 20th Century label, where he had some success in the UK with *Contact* (UK #6.1979) and *H.A.P.P.Y. Radio* (UK#9.1979) until being dropped in the early 1980s.

Throughout that decade he has continued to record for smaller independent labels – gaining a minor hit with *It ain't Fair* (UK#56.1985) – and to tour constantly, particularly in the UK, where his following has always been strong.

25 MILES, Motown, 1969
WAR AND PEACE, Motown, 1970
20 GREATEST MOTOWN HITS, Motown, 1981
THE HITS OF EDWIN STARR, Motown, 1987

STARR, JAMIE See PRINCE

STATON, CANDI The career of Candi Staton remains something of an enigma. Whenever she has recorded, she has come up with great records: during the disco era, for example, she cut one of the best records of the genre, *Young Hearts Run Free*. However, her career has been bedevilled by an apparent total indifference of the record companies.

She was born in 1943 in Hanceville, Alabama. Her career as a singer started in her local church. By the mid-1960s she had become a member of a touring gospel group, The Jewel Trio, and was married with four children. In 1967 she stopped singing gospel on being booked to appear at the 27–28 Club in Birmingham, Alabama, having auditioned with the Dan PENN and Chips MOMAN composition, *Do Right Woman – Do Right Man*. While working at the club she met Clarence CARTER, who introduced her to Rick HALL. Hall signed her immediately to his Fame label and she started to record a whole string of country songs like *Another Man's Woman, In the Ghetto* and *Stand by Your Man* (USA#24.1970), as well as rather more traditional examples of Southern soul by writers like George JACKSON and Carter. (She was married to Carter for a short time).

After divorcing Carter and leaving Fame, she was signed by Warner Bros., who teamed her with the Miami-based producer Dave Crawford for the LP, *Young Hearts Run Free* (UK#34.1976). As a result she notched up five further hits: *Young Hearts Run Free* (USA#20; UK#2.1976/#47.1986), *Destiny* (UK#41.1976), *Nights on Broadway* (UK#6.1977), *Honest I Do Love You* (UK#48.1978) and *Victim*. However, by the end of the 1970s her career had gone awry. Despite brief spells with Crawford's label, LA, and Sylvia ROBINSON's Sugarhill label in the early 1980s, when she cut a version of *Suspicious Minds* (UK#31.1982), she went back to singing gospel, cutting the LP *Make Me an Instrument* for the Myrrh label in 1985.

CANDI STATON, Warner Bros., 1980
SUSPICIOUS MINDS, Sugarhill, 1982
MAKE ME AN INSTRUMENT, Myrrh, 1985
TELL IT LIKE IT IS, (with Bettye Swann), Stateside, 1986

STEVENSON, WILLIAM William "Mickey" Stevenson was another of Berry GORDY's talented honchos, who, as A&R director of Motown, could get the best out of any artist that fell into his lap. He could also write songs with almost anyone, including Marvin GAYE, Ivy Hunter, Barrett STRONG and Clarence PAUL. Among the records in which he had a hand in the production were *Uptight (Everything's Alright)* by Stevie WONDER, *What Becomes of the Broken Hearted?* by Jimmy RUFFIN, *It Takes Two* by Gaye and Kim Weston, *Dancing in the Streets* by MARTHA & THE VANDELLAS, *Stubborn Kind of Fellow* and *Hitch Hike* by Gaye. When he left in 1968 to take up an appointment with MGM he took his wife, Kim Weston, with him. As often happens, he never got the same opportunites again.

STEWART, BILLY Billy Stewart's reputation was based on one song, *Summertime*, the George Gershwin standard; so outrageous was Stewart's version that it has become a classic. However, prior to its success, he penned a number of songs that were very superior soulful items, but this talent as a writer was soon eclipsed when it was recognised that his treatment of standards had a certain novelty value.

Stewart's career started as a member of The Rainbows, which included in its line-up, Marvin GAYE and Don COVAY. After the group disbanded Stewart settled on a solo career. He was signed by Chess where he had a run of hits, including *I Do Love You* (USA #26.1965), *Sitting in the Park* (USA#24.1965), *Summertime* (USA#10; UK#39.1966) and *Secret Love* (USA#29.1966). The success of *Summertime* typecast him and he became a regular attraction on the nightclub circuit, where his larger than life personality (matching his 300-pound frame) became very popular. It was while touring that he was killed in a car crash on January 17, 1970, aged 32.

STEWART, JIM In 1961 Jim Stewart founded the Stax label. Throughout the 1960s the name Stax was synonymous with soul and R&B. While Motown – their counterpart – seemed to be more adept at penetrating the white mainstream, Stax aimed at the black markets, despite the fact that Stewart was white, as were most of the producers and session musicians.

Stewart was born in Middleton, Tennessee in 1930. After graduating from Memphis State University he went into banking, but played the fiddle in a country-swing band in his sparetime. In 1957 he recorded the country tune Blue Rose. The following year, he and his sister Estelle Axton formed their own record label, Satellite. In 1958 Chips MOMAN, a session guitarist, teamed up with Stewart and produced most of the records that were issued by Satellite. In 1960 Moman spotted an old cinema called the Capitol on East McLemore Avenue, Memphis; Stewart rented it for $100 a month. He knew that in order to survive it was necessary to have the cooperation of the local radio stations. He approached John RICHBOURG of the Nashville station, WLAC, which had a predominantly black audience, and made over to him a percentage of the royalties of a song he had written. The song was *Cause I Love You*, recorded by Carla THOMAS, the daughter of Rufus THOMAS, who was a DJ on the Memphis station, WDIA; Rufus persuaded another DJ, Dick Cole of WLDK, to play the record. After it had sold fifteeen thousand copies locally it came to the attention of Jerry WEXLER, who leased it from Stewart for $1000 for national release on the Atlantic label; this was the first money Stewart had earned for Stax. The record featured, as session musicians, Steve CROPPER on guitar and, on baritone sax, Booker T. Jones (see BOOKER T & THE MGS), who became pivotal to the Stax 'sound'. That year they changed the name of the label from Satellite to Stax: the name 'Stax' was derived from the first two letters of the names Stewart and Axton.

Throughout the early 1960s he set about establishing the company; signings like William BELL and Otis REDDING began to develop the reputation of the label. In 1965 he enlisted the services of Al BELL, as head of promotion. With Bell in place he had a man who was quite prepared to use his blackness in the same way as Motown's Berry GORDY: to inspire racial loyalty. By 1968 Stax had accumulated a roster of artists – like Eddie FLOYD, SAM & DAVE, Johnnie TAYLOR, Carla Thomas, Albert KING and Rufus Thomas – that was the envy of many of the major companies, although the loss of Otis Redding in 1967 was a major blow.

In 1968 Stewart signed a deal with Gulf & Western, the owners of Paramount Records. It was the first of a series of decisions that signalled the beginning of the end for Stax. As part of the deal Stax was required to deliver 27 LPs to Paramount to cement it. That they were able to fulfil this commitment within a month showed an admirable proficiency, even though the quality was variable. The biggest seller was *Hot Buttered Soul* by Isaac HAYES. In 1972 Stewart sold his share of the company to Bell, but remained as president.

Since 1972 Stewart has gradually slipped out of sight. The demise of Stax in 1976 spelt the end of his effective involvement in the music business, although he was briefly associated with the Houston-based Connection label in 1983, when he produced a minor hit for Margie Joseph. While Stewart was much criticized for the apparent excesses at Stax, it has to be remembered that it was he, who was responsible for developing the careers of a host of artists that, without his input, would not have flourished as they did.

STONE, HENRY Throughout the 1970s Henry Stone's TK group of labels – Alston, TK, Cat and Glades – represented a serious challenge to the sway held by Motown. With records like George McCRAE's *Rock Your Baby* they managed to breast the tide of disco, establishing Miami as one of the fashionable recording centres in the USA.

Henry Stone opened his first record shop in Miami, Florida, during the 1950s. This enabled him to establish Tone distributors and the record label, Alston, which was licensed for national distribution by Atlantic. One of the first and most successful signings was Betty WRIGHT, who scored with *Clean Up Woman* in 1971, featuring the crisp economical guitar work of session musician, Willie 'Beaver' Hale (born in Forrest City, Arkansas on August 15, 1944), which was as critical to the sound of the early records for the label as Steve CROPPER's had been at Stax. However, Hale's attempt at starting a solo career, under the name of Little Beaver, was met with only limited success.

Stone's biggest success was the signing of Harry Casey, who teamed up with Richard Finch, an engineer at the TK Studios, to form KC & THE SUNSHINE BAND. Not only did they define, through their own records, the sound of Miami they also formed the nucleus of the TK house band. They also wrote for and produced other artists, like McCrae and Wright. Among the other artists signed to the labels were Timmy Thomas and LITTLE MILTON. The national success of KC & The Sunshine Band and McCrae enabled Stone to negotiate a worldwide distribution deal with CBS in 1978. By 1981, with disco slipping out of fashion TK went bankrupt.

STONE, JESSE When Atlantic was set up in 1947 by Ahmet ERTEGUN and Herb ABRAMSON, they were shrewd enough to enlist Jesse Stone. He was born on November 16, 1901, in Atchison, Kansas. His career started as a child, when he had been in Vaudeville. During the 1920s, he worked around Kansas City as a pianist and vocalist. As a result of meeting Duke Ellington, he got work at the Cotton Club, which led to a multipurpose position at the Apollo. By 1942 one of his compositions, *Idaho*, had been recorded by Benny Goodman. In 1944 he joined Al Greene's National label as an arranger, where he met Abramson. Greene's notion of saleable black music was still governed by the perceived stereotype of what had always been acceptable: he was unwilling to take chances with new artists and new sounds.

In 1947, armed with Ertegun's money, Atlantic came into being and one of Stone's briefs was to seek out fresh talent by going down to the South on field trips. While Stone proved to be more than adept at unearthing talent, he also wrote hits, many under his pseudonym of Charles Calhoun, like *Money Honey* for The DRIFTERS and *Shake, Rattle and Roll* for Big Joe Turner. As an arranger, working with artists like Ray CHARLES, Ruth BROWN and The CLOVERS, he brought R&B out of the closet and into the twentieth century, banging the door behind it. After leaving Atlantic in 1955, he worked for Aladdin until its collapse in 1956, when he set up the publishing company Roosevelt Music. He retired to Florida in 1983.

STONE, SLY See SLY & THE FAMILY STONE

STRONG, BARRETT In partnership with producer Norman WHITFIELD, Barrett Strong contributed some of the most important songs to emanate from Motown in the latter half of the 1960s.

He was born in Mississippi on February 5, 1941. After moving to Detroit in the 1950s he started to write and gained a contract as an artist with Gwen Gordy's Anna label, later assimilated into Motown. His first hit, *Money* (USA#23.1960), was also his last as a performer; it had the added distinctions of being written by Berry GORDY and being the debut hit for the fledgling Motown Corporation.

It wasn't until he teamed up with Whitfield in 1967 that he really came into his own, cowriting hits like *I Heard it Through the Grapevine* for Gladys KNIGHT & The Pips and Marvin GAYE, *War* for Edwin STARR, *I Wish it Would Rain, Just my Imagination* and *Papa was a Rolling Stone* for The TEMPTATIONS and *Smiling Faces Sometimes* for The UNDISPUTED TRUTH. Quite apart from his work at Motown he collaborated with The

DELLS. By the time Whitfield left Motown in 1975 to form his own label, Strong had effectively disappeared from the picture.

STYLISTICS The Stylistics were formed in 1968 in Philadelphia by Russell Tompkins, Jr, Airron Love and James Smith of The Monarchs and Herb Murrell and James Smith of The Percussions. Their debut, *You're a Big Girl Now*, was released by the local Sebring label in 1969 and was a big hit locally. They remained with the label until HUGO & LUIGI's Avco Embassy signed them up in 1971.

They were teamed with Thom BELL and lyricist Linda Creed at GAMBLE & HUFF's Sigma Sound studios in Philadelphia. Over the next three years this partnership provided them with a string of hit singles that were as responsible as anything else that Gamble & Huff did for the creation of the genre known as Philly-Soul: *Stop, Look, Listen (to Your Heart)* (USA #39.1971), *You are Everything* (USA#9.1971), *Betcha by Golly Wow* (USA#3; UK#13.1972), *People Make the World go Round* (USA #25.1972), *I'm Stone in Love with You* (USA#10; UK#9.1972), *Break Up To Make Up* (USA#5; UK#34.1973), *Peek-a-Boo* (UK #35.1973), *You'll Never Get to Heaven (if You Break my Heart)* (USA#23.1973; UK #24.1976), *Rockin' Roll Baby* (USA#14; UK #6.1973) and *You Make me Feel Brand New* (USA/UK#2.1974).

In mid-1974 they parted company with Bell and Creed and label owners Hugo & Luigi, with arranger Van McCOY, took over the production chores. While there was no earthly reason why this change should have made a significant difference to their fortunes, the fact remains that the quality of their subsequent material could not hold a candle to what they had done previously. In the USA, their popularity declined dramatically, but in the UK it increased quite considerably, as their succes-

sion of UK hits show: *Let's Put it all Together* (USA#18; UK#9.1974), *Star on a TV Show* (UK#12.1975), *Sing Baby Sing* (UK#3.1975), *Can't Give you Anything (but my Love)* (UK#1. 1975), *Na Na is the Saddest Word* (UK#5.1975), *Funky Weekend* (UK#10.1976), *Can't Help Falling in Love* (UK#4.1976), *16 Bars* (UK #7.1976) and *$7000 and You* (UK#24.1977).

By the beginning of 1978 their popularity even in the UK was on the wane, as their style had been superseded by the disco fever, that was sweeping the land. After leaving Hugo & Luigi in 1979, they were signed by Mercury. In 1980 they returned to Philadelphia, where they signed with Gamble & Huff's TSOP label and recorded a number of LPs: *Hurry up this Way again* (1980), *Closer than Close* (1981) and *1982*. Since then they have become regulars on the cabaret circuit where their innocuous style has a devoted following among the blue-rinse brigade. In 1985 they were signed by Virgin for the LP *Some Things Never Change*.

HURRY UP THIS WAY AGAIN, Philadelphia International, 1980
ALL ABOUT LOVE, Contour, 1981
THE GREAT LOVE HITS, Contour, 1983
THE VERY BEST OF THE STYLISTICS, H & L, 1983
SOME THINGS NEVER CHANGE, Virgin, 1985

SUMMER, DONNA The disco phenomenon of the late 1970s did have some positive aspects: while much of what was produced was rubbish, a few performers were able to respond to the limitations of the genre and contribute some very high quality performances. Donna Summer is a perfect example.

She was born LaDonna Gaines on December 31, 1948, in Boston, Massachusetts. In 1968, having sung with local rock bands, she auditioned for a part in the Broadway production of *Hair*; she was offered a principal role in the German production in Munich. For the next five years she remained in Europe, appearing in Austrian productions of *Porgy and Bess* and *Showboat*, as well as doing odd bits of session work, modelling and appearing in a German production of *Godspell*. In 1971 she married Austrian actor Helmut Sommer; the marriage only lasted until 1976, but she kept the name, anglicising it to Summer.

In 1973, while singing on sessions at Musicland studios in Munich, she met studio owners Giorgio Moroder and Pete Bellotte, who signed her to their Oasis label. Her first two singles, *Hostage* and *Ladies of the Night*, were very successful in Europe. Her next single was *Love to Love you Baby* (USA#2.1975; UK #4.1976); it was picked up and licensed by Neil Bogart of the Casablanca label, and became one of the key records of the disco era, the seventeen-minute version being a staple in the collection of any aspiring DJ. For the next three years she was the unchallenged Queen Of Disco, with a string of singles: *Could it be Magic* (UK#40.1976), *Winter Melody* (UK#27.1976), *I Feel Love* (USA#6; UK#1.1977/#21.1982), *Down Deep Inside* – theme from the film, *The Deep* – (UK#5.1977), *I Remember Yesterday* (UK#14.1977), *Love's Unkind* (UK#3.1977), *I Love You* (USA#37.1978; UK#10.1977), *Rumour has it* (UK#19.1978), *Back in Love Again* (UK#29.1978) and *Last Dance* (USA#3; UK#51.1978).

By the end of 1978, the emphasis in her records was shifting from the disco-synth groove that had characterised her earlier work towards a more rock-oriented style; it was not that she eschewed the trademark thumping drums of disco, but more that the guitar came to be featured much more prominently in the mix. Her choice of material, like her reworking of the Richard Harris hit, *MacArthur Park* (USA#1; UK#5.1978), the first step in the transition, indicated her gradual distancing from disco. There followed *Heaven Knows* (USA#4; UK#34.1979), *Hot Stuff* (USA#1; UK #11.1979), *Bad Girls* (USA#1; UK#14.1979), *Dim all the Lights* (USA#2; UK#29.1979), *On the Radio* (USA#5; UK#32.1980) and *Sunset People* (UK#46.1980). Throughout, her LPs exhibited a growing maturity and coherence, from the protracted disco-groove of her earliest efforts, like *Love to Love you Baby* (USA#11; UK#16.1975) and *A Love Trilogy* (USA#21; UK#41.1976) to the live LP *Live and More* (USA#1; UK#16.1978) and *Bad Girls* (USA#1; UK#23.1979).

In 1980, as if to confirm this change in direction, she slapped a $10 million suit on her manager, Joyce Bogart, and her husband, Neil, for 'fraud, undue influence and misrepresentation'. They let her leave the Casablanca label and she signed with David Geffen's Geffen label. She continued to notch up hits: *The Wanderer* (USA#3; UK#48.1980), *Walk Away* (USA#36.1980), *Cold Love* (USA#33; UK #44.1981), *Who do you Think you're Foolin'* (USA#40.1981), *Love is in Control (Finger on the Trigger)* (USA#10.1982), *State Of Independence* (UK#14.1982), *The Woman in Me* (USA#33; UK#62.1983), *She Works Hard for the Money* (USA#3; UK#25.1983), *Unconditional Love* (UK#14.1983), *Stop Look and Listen* (UK#57.1984), *There Goes my Baby* (USA#21.1984), *Dinner with Gershwin* (UK #13.1987) and *All Systems Go* (UK#54.1988).

In 1982, she collaborated with producer Quincy JONES for the LP *Donna Summer* (UK#13.1982); it featured contributions from a whole galaxy of stars like Michael JACKSON, Stevie WONDER, Lionel RICHIE, Dionne WARWICK and James INGRAM, as well as the cream of the Los Angeles session musician fraternity. In 1984, she took a sabbatical from the music business to concentrate upon her family and her religious activities and, although in 1987 she toured Europe and released the LP *All Systems Go*, she had shown a marked indifference to the rigours of developing her career any further. However, in 1989 she released the LP *Another Place and Time,* which included the single *This Time I Know it's for Real*; produced by the UK Svengalis Stock, Aitken & Waterman, .

I REMEMBER YESTERDAY, Casablanca, 1977
ONCE UPON A TIME, Casablanca, 1978
LIVE AND MORE, Casablanca, 1978
BAD GIRLS, Casablanca, 1979
ON THE RADIO, Casablanca, 1980
WALK AWAY, Casablanca, 1980
DONNA SUMMER, Warner Bros., 1982
GREATEST HITS: Volume 1, Casablanca, 1982
GREATEST HITS: Volume 2, Casablanca, 1982
SHE WORKS HARD FOR THE MONEY, Mercury, 1983
CATS WITHOUT CLAWS, Warner Bros., 1984
THE SUMMER COLLECTION, Mercury, 1985,
I LOVE TO DANCE, Perfect, 1987
ALL SYSTEMS GO, Warner Bros., 1987
ANOTHER PLACE AND TIME, Warner Bros., 1989
THE BEST OF DONNA SUMMER, East West, 1990.

SUPREMES One of the greatest misconceptions about Berry GORDY was that, in his quest to conquer the white market, he was prepared to sacrifice the basic principle of soul music – emotion – to achieve that end. It was because of his tireless championing of The Supremes, particularly of Diana Ross, that this criticism gained currency. What has always been ignored was that Gordy was, first and foremost, a record man: he had started Motown not just to have complete control of his artists but also to ensure that the records bearing his name were not swamped with lush arrangements (as had happened when he was a writer for Jackie WILSON) so that their dramatic impact was often lost. The success of The Supremes was due to the efficiency of the machinery he established: the precision of James JAMERSON and Benny BENJAMIN

behind each record and the ingenious flair of the songwriting and production partnership of HOLLAND, DOZIER & HOLLAND were the ingredients behind the success of The Supremes. The fact that they were great records and caught the imagination of the white audiences was an added good fortune.

The Primettes were formed in 1959 by Milton Jenkins, the manager of The Primes (see TEMPTATIONS). Their line-up was Mary Wilson (born in Greenville, Mississippi, on March 6, 1944), Florence Ballard (born in Detroit on June 30, 1943) and Betty Anderson; later that year they were joined by Diana Ross. In 1960 Anderson was replaced by Barbara Martin, and the group was signed to the local LuPine label, and then by Gordy to Motown. Gordy asked them to change the name of the group and Ballard came up with The Supremes, a move which prompted Martin to leave.

Their earliest records, written by either Smokey ROBINSON or Gordy, failed to ignite popular opinion successful until, in 1964, they started their partnership with Holland, Dozier & Holland with *When the Lovelight Starts Shining through his Eyes* (USA#23.1964). The follow-up, *Run, Run, Run,* failed to set the charts alight, but the next record, *Where Did Our Love Go* (USA#1; UK#3.1964) set the ball rolling. Over the next four years their partnership with Holland, Dozier & Holland notched up an unprecedented sequence of hits for an all-girl group: *Baby Love* (USA/UK#1.1964/ #12.1974), *Come and See about Me* (USA #1.1964; UK#27.1965), *Stop! In the Name of Love* (USA#1; UK#7.1965), *Back in my Arms Again* (USA#11; UK#40.1965), *I Hear a Symphony* (USA#1; UK#39.1965), *My World is Empty without You* (USA#5.1966), *Love is Like an Itching in my Heart* (USA#9.1966), *You can't Hurry Love* (USA#1; UK#3.1966), *You Keep me Hangin' On* (USA#1; UK#8.1966), *Love is Here and Now You're Gone* (USA#1; UK

#17.1966), *The Happening* (USA#1; UK #6.1967), *Reflections* (USA#2; UK#5.1967), *In and Out of Love* (USA#9; UK#13.1967) and *Forever Came Today* (USA/UK#28.1968).

The partnership was broken when Holland, Dozier & Holland left Motown to establish their own labels. However, their departure was not the only problem for the group: Ballard was fired (she died, in poverty, of a heart attack on February 22, 1976, aged 32), as she had become unreliable owing to the increasing dominance of Diana Ross, which had turned both Ballard and Wilson into little more than backing vocalists. She was replaced by Cindy Birdsong born in Camden, New Jersey, on December 15, 1939), a former member of Patti LaBELLE's group, The Bluebelles. Furthermore, Ross had managed to get the billing of the group changed to Diana Ross & The Supremes, much to Wilson's chagrin.

The Supremes were then teamed with a variety of writers and producers like ASHFORD & SIMPSON and Johnny BRISTOL, but no one was able to capture the unique quality that had characterised their earlier hits. Nevertheless, they still notched up hits with enviable regularity: *Some Things You Never Get Used To* (USA#30; UK#34.1968), *Love Child* (USA#1; UK#15.1968), *I'm Livin' in Shame* (USA#10; UK#14.1969), *The Composer* (USA #27.1969), *No Matter What Sign you Are* (USA#31; UK#37.1969) and *Someday We'll be Together* (USA#1; UK#13.1969). In 1968 they were teamed with The Temptations for the LP, *Diana Ross and The Supremes Join The Temptations* (USA#2.1968; UK#1.1969), which featured the single, *I'm Gonna Make you Love Me* (USA#2; UK#3.1968). It was followed by a soundtrack for a TV Special, *TCB.* (USA#1; UK#11.1969), including their version of the Smokey Robinson & The Miracles song, *I'll Try Something New* (USA#25.1969).

On January 14, 1970, Ross left the group to be replaced by Jean Terrell (born in Texas, on November 26,1944). Although, the distinctive voice of Ross was gone, it did not stop the new line-up from having hits: *Up the Ladder to the Roof* (USA#10; UK#6.1970), *Everybody's Got the Right to Love* (USA#21.1970), *Stoned Love* (USA#7.1970; UK#3.1971), *Nathan Jones* (USA#16; UK#5.1971), *Floy Joy* (USA#16; UK#9.1972), *Automatically Sunshine* (USA #37; UK#10.1972) and *Bad Weather* (UK #37.1973). At the end of 1970 they were teamed with another bastion of Motown, The FOUR TOPS, for the LP *The Magnificent Seven* (UK#6.1971), which featured the revival of *River Deep, Mountain High* (USA#14; UK#11.1970).

In 1972 Birdsong left to devote more energy to her family, and was replaced by Lynda Lawrence, who remained until 1976. In 1973 Terrell left to be replaced by Scherrie Payne. In 1976, they had a hit with *I'm Gonna Let my Heart do the Walking* (USA#37.1976); at the end of 1976, Wilson left the group and they broke up soon after. Since then there have been occasional reunions; in 1983 Ross, Wilson and Birdsong got together for Motown's 25th Anniversary concert, which was followed by a US tour on the oldies circuit. In 1984, Wilson published her autobiography, *Dreamgirl: My Life As A Supreme*. More recently, Terrell, Payne and Lawrence have recorded for the Motor City label, including the storming *Back by Popular Demand*, why it failed to emerge as a single is a bit of a mystery.

WHERE DID OUR LOVE GO, Motown, 1964
WE REMEMBER SAM COOKE, Motown, 1965
MORE HITS BY THE SUPREMES, Motown, 1965
AT THE COPA, Motown, 1965
I HEAR A SYMPHONY, Motown, 1966
THE SUPREMES A-GO-GO, Motown, 1966
REFLECTIONS, Motown, 1968
DIANA ROSS AND THE SUPREMES JOIN THE TEMPTATIONS, Motown, 1968
LOVE CHILD, Motown, 1968

TCB, (with The Temptations), Motown, 1969
LET THE SUNSHINE IN, Motown, 1969
CREAM OF THE CROP, Motown, 1969
20 GOLDEN GREATS, Motown, 1977
EARLY YEARS: 1961–1964, Motown, 1981
MOTOWN SPECIAL, Motown, 1981
ANTHOLOGY, Motown, 1986
20 GREATEST HITS, Motown, 1986
25th ANNIVERSARY, Motown, 1986

SWEET INSPIRATIONS See HOUS-
TON, Cissy

SYREETA Rita Wright was born in
Pittsburg. Her singing career started when she
was three, but began to crystallise when she
joined the choir of the Mather Academy in
South Carolina. She remained there for four
years, during which time she began to perform
locally. She went on to win talent contests and
an eventual audition with producer Brian
Holland (see HOLLAND, DOZIER & HOL-
LAND) who signed her to Motown. Her
debut, *I Can't Give Back the Love*, was written
by ASHFORD & SIMPSON. Although she
continued recording, with little success, she
started to write her own material, which came
to the attention of Stevie WONDER.

In 1970 she married Wonder, having collaborated with him on his LPs, *Signed Sealed Delivered*, *Where I'm Coming From* and *Music of my
Mind*. Although the marriage broke up in 1972,
her 1974 LP was called *Stevie Wonder Presents
Syreeta*; it included the single *Spinnin' and Spinnin'*, which became a big turntable hit. Despite
her domestic separation from Wonder, she has
continued work with him, contributing to his
LP *Journey through the Secret Life of Plants*.

After collaborating with G. C. Cameron,
formerly a member of The DETROIT SPIN-
NERS, on the LP *Rich Love Poor Love*, she
released the LP *Syreeta*, produced by Richard

Perry. It was followed by a collaboration with
Billy PRESTON on the LP *Billy Preston &
Syreeta*; it included the ballad, *With You I'm Born
Again* (USA#4.1980; UK#2.1979). It was followed by another solo set, *Set My Love in Motion*
(1981). Her most recent offering was *Spell*
(1983), produced by Jermaine JACKSON and
including contributions from Stevie Wonder.

STEVIE WONDER PRESENTS SYREETA,
Motown, 1974
SYREETA, Motown, 1980
THE BEST OF SYREETA, Motown, 1981
SET MY LOVE IN MOTION, Motown, 1981

TAMS The Tams were born and brought up
in Atlanta, Georgia. The line-up comprised
Charles Pope (born August 7, 1948), Joseph
Pope (born November 6, 1933), Robert Smith
(born March 18, 1936), Floyd Ashton (born
November 15, 1933) and Horace Rey (born
April 13, 1934). They knocked around the local
club circuit during the late 1950s, recording *The
Valley of Love* for the Swan label.

In 1962 they linked up with music publisher,
Bill 'King William' Lowery, who became their
manager and took them to the newly established Fame studios in Muscle Shoals, where they
recorded *Untie Me* for the Arlen label, while
this single certainly didn't set the world on fire,
it was enough to attract the attention of ABC-
Paramount, who put them under contract.
Their next record, *What Kind of Fool (Do You
Think I Am?)* (USA#9.1964), was written by
Joe SOUTH. Major chart success was to elude
them in the UK until the early seventies when
titles like *Be Young, Be Foolish, Be Happy* (UK-
#32.1970) and *Hey Girl Don't Bother Me* (UK-
#1.1971) were re-issued. They disappeared
from sight until 1987, when they re-emerged
with the sensitively titled *There ain't Nothing
like Shagging* (UK#21.1987). Obscurity and the
chitlin' circuit beckoned.

TARPLIN, MARV See ROBINSON, Smokey, & The Miracles

TATE, HOWARD Howard Tate was born in 1943 in Macon, Georgia, but grew up in Philadelphia, where he sang in a number of gospel groups before joining Bill Doggett's Band. He next joined the R&B group, The Gaynors, which numbered Garnett MIMMS among its personnel. While he was primarily a guitarist, his powerful voice appealed to Jerry RAGAVOY, who decided to produce some sessions for him. The resulting LP, *Get it While You Can*, featured *Ain't Nobody Home, Look at Granny Run Run* and *Part Time Love*, all of which achieved some reputation amongst aficionados. However, his career was erratic. He recorded for Lloyd PRICE's Turntable label towards the end of the 1960s and was then reunited with Ragavoy for the LP *Burglar* (1972) for Atlantic. Since then he has recorded for other labels on odd occasions like Epic, but without achieving any lasting success – or, indeed, approaching the quality of the early Ragavoy sessions.

GET IT WHILE YOU CAN, Verve, 1966

TAVARES During the latter half of the 1970s Tavares were one of the few groups to accomodate disco without any loss of face. They comprised five brothers Ralph, Antone 'Chubby', Feliciano 'Butch', Arthur 'Pooch' and Perry Lee 'Tiny' Tavares – from New Bedford, Massachusetts. In 1964 they were formed as Chubby & The Turnpikes and worked on the local club circuit until 1969, when they changed their name to Tavares.

After signing with Capitol, they had their first hit with *Check it Out* (USA#35.1973), a Johnny BRISTOL production, but it wasn't until 1975 their teaming up with Freddie Perren, a former Motown producer from Philadelphia, that their style finally coalesced.

Over the next three years they notched up a succession of hits that were eminently danceable, but each managing to rise above the plethora of anonymous disco pap that was then the norm: *Remember what I Told you to Forget* (USA#25.1975), *It Only Takes a Minute* (USA#10.1975; UK#46.1986), *Heaven Must be Missing an Angel* (USA#15; UK#4.1976/#12.1986), *Don't Take Away the Music* (USA#34; UK#4.1976), *Mighty Power of Love* (UK#25.1977), *Whodunit* (USA#22; UK#5.1977), *One Step Away* (UK#16.1977), *The Ghost of Love* (UK#29.1978), *More than a Woman* (USA#32; UK#7.1978) and *Slow Train to Paradise* (UK#62.1978). During this period the LPs *In the City* (USA#26.1976) and *Sky High!* (USA#24; UK#22.1976) briefly managed to sustain the momentum, enabling them to rival The O'JAYS for consistency.

In 1982, they moved to RCA from Capitol after a lean spell and scored with *A Penny for your Thoughts* (USA#33.1982), but in general they have tended since the late 1970s to ply their trade on the international club circuit, where their popularity has proved to be enduring. In 1986 *Heaven Must be Missing an Angel* and *It Only Takes a Minute* were reissued in the UK and became hits all over again.

THE BEST OF TAVARES, Fame, 1978
LOVE UPRISING, Capitol, 1981
NEW DIRECTIONS, RCA, 1982
THE VERY BEST OF TAVARES, Capitol, 1986

TAYLOR, JOHNNIE Johnnie Taylor was born on May 5, 1938 in Crawfordsville, Arkansas. In 1954 he joined the doo-wop group The Five Echoes, who recorded one single for the Chance label. He then joined the gospel group The Highway QCs, where he remained until he was selected by Sam COOKE to be his replacement in The Soul Stirrers. In 1959 he left the group to embark on a short-lived career as a preacher before, in 1962, signing to the Sar label, which had been started by Cooke and J. W. ALEXANDER. Although he scored with *Rome wasn't Built in a Day,* his career was interrupted by the death of Cooke in 1964.

In 1966 he moved back to Memphis and signed with the Stax label, where from 1968 until 1974 he had a string of hits: *Who's Making Love* (USA#5.1968), *Take Care of your Homework* (USA#20.1969), *Testify (I Wanna)* (USA#36.1969), *Steal Away* (USA#37.1970), *I Am Somebody, Part 2* (USA#39.1970), *Jody's Got Your Girl and Gone* (USA#28.1971), *I Believe in You* (USA#11.1973), *Cheaper to Keep Her* (USA#15.1973) and *We're Getting Careless with our Love* (USA#34.1974). Taylor was able to combine the raw grittiness of Southern soul with the sophistication of Northern soul that producer Don Davis had brought with him from his former employers in Detroit, Motown. Additionally, Taylor had the benefit of material from local songwriters like Homer BANKS, Bettye Crutcher, Raymond Jackson and George JACKSON, whose songs were as impressive as anything that Stax had previously been associated with. All these elements, combined with the flair of the session musicians went a long way in establishing Taylor as one of the brightest stars in the Stax firmament – that is, until the company went out of business in 1976.

After the demise of Stax he was signed by Columbia Records and recorded *Disco Lady* (USA#1; UK#25.1976), which was featured on the LP *Eargasm* (USA#5.1976), produced by Don Davis. While it was a pale imitation of his earlier work with Stax, it was his most successful single and was, reputedly, the inspiration for Marvin GAYE's *Got to Give it Up.* Three further LPs for Columbia followed,

Rated Extraordinaire (1977), *Disco 9000* (1977) and *Ever Ready* (1978). After spending a couple of years touring, he signed with the Beverly Glen label in Los Angeles in 1982, recording the LP *Just Ain't Good Enough* with arrangements by Gene PAGE. In 1984, he signed with the Malaco label in Jackson, Mississippi, where he has recorded a series of LPs that are as good as anything he has ever done. With Malaco owners Tommy COUCH and Wolf Stephenson producing, and session musicians like David HOOD, Roger HAWKINS, Jimmy JOHNSON and Pete Carr backing him, he has found a home, not unlike Stax in its halcyon days, and has continued to show his ability to adapt to any style he chooses.

EVER READY, CBS, 1978

THIS IS YOUR NIGHT, Malaco, 1984

WALL TO WALL, Malaco, 1986

LOVERBOY, Malaco,1987

20 GREATEST HITS, London, 1987

SOMEBODY'S GETTIN' IT, Charly, 1988

IN CONTROL, Malaco, 1988

CRAZY 'BOUT YOU, Malaco, 1989

TAYLOR, TED Ted Taylor, a native of Oklahoma, started his career singing in church. By the early 1960s he had moved from gospel to secular singing. He was signed to the Okeh label and was recorded in Nashville by Billy Sherrill. Among the sides he cut were *Stay Away from my Baby* and *(Love is like a) Ramblin' Rose.* After signing to Stan LEWIS' Ronn label in 1965, where he recorded the LP *Shades of Blue,* he joined the trek to Fame in Muscle Shoals, where he cut the LP *You Dig It* in 1967; his emotional falsetto was perfectly complemented by Rick HALL's house band. The follow-up, *Taylor Made,* fared less well as the arrangements sounded a bit like Norman WHITFIELD out-takes. However he became increasingly bogged down at Ronn and left the label in the early 1970s when his career went into the doldrums. It was briefly revived when he recorded the LP *Ted Taylor 1976*, for the Alarm label, which had been set up by Stewart Madison and Jerry Strickland; the LP was produced by Wardell QUEZERGUE. However, since then he has recorded less and less.

TEMPERTON, ROD See HEATWAVE

TEMPTATIONS The Temptations were responsible for some of the most powerful records to emerge from the Motown studios during the 1960s and early 1970s. While they were undoubtedly fortunate in having excellent writers and perceptive producers to work with, plus the Motown house band, the voices of David RUFFIN, Eddie KENDRICKS and Dennis EDWARDS lifted the records into another dimension.

At first, the group, known as The Elgins, was an amalgamation of two other groups, The Primes and The Distants. The former comprised Kendricks, Paul Williams (born July 2, 1939) and Cal Osborne and came from their hometown of Birmingham, Alabama. The latter comprised Melvin Franklin (born as David English on October 12, 1942 in Montgomery, Alabama), Otis Williams – (born as Otis Miles on October 30, 1939 in Texarkana, Texas), Richard Street (born on October 5, 1942 in Detroit), Albert Harrell and Eldridge Bryant. Both Harrell and Street left The Distants after the failure of the single, *Come On*, on the Northern label; they were replaced by Kendricks and Williams. In 1961, The Elgins were signed by Berry GORDY to the fledgling Motown label, and changed the name to The Temptations for their first single, *Oh Mother of Mine*, which failed to sell, as did the follow-up. Bryant promptly left the group and was replaced by David Ruffin.

In 1962 they started their collaboration with the writer and producer Smokey ROBINSON. The partnership lasted the best part of four years and generated some of the most emotive performances to emanate from Motown, including *The Way you Do the Things you Do* (USA#11.1964), *My Girl* (USA#1; UK#43. 1965), *It's Growing* (USA#18; UK#45.1965), *Since I Lost my Baby* (USA#17.1965), *Get Ready* (USA#29.1966; UK#10.1970) and *My Baby* (USA#18.1965).

Under Robinson's successors, Norman WHITFIELD and Eddie Holland (see HOLLAND, DOZIER & HOLLAND), they continued to notch up hits including *Ain't too Proud to Beg* (USA#13; UK#21.1966), *Beauty is only Skin Deep* (USA#3; UK#18.1966) and *(I Know) I'm Losing You* (USA#8.1966; UK #19.1967). In 1967, following Eddie Holland's departure from Motown, Whitfield became their sole producer and formed a songwriting partnership with Barrett STRONG, which provided the group with a succession of hits that lasted into the mid- 1970s including: *All I Need* (USA#8.1967), *You're my Everything* (USA#6; UK#26.1967), *I Wish it Would Rain* (USA#4; UK#45.1968), *Cloud Nine* (USA #6.1968; UK#15.1969), *Run away Child, Running Wild* (USA #6.1969), *I Can't Get Next to You* (USA#1.1969; UK#13.1970), *Psychedelic Shack* (USA#7; UK#33.1970), *Ball of Confusion* (USA#3; UK#7.1970), *Just my Imagination (Running away with Me)* (USA#1; UK #8.1971), *Papa was a Rolling Stone* (USA #1.1972; UK#14.1973/#31.1987), *Law of the Land* (UK#41.1973), *Masterpiece* (USA #7.1973), *The Plastic Man* (USA#40.1973), *Hey Girl (I Like Your Style)* (USA#35.1973), *Let Your Hair Down* (USA#27.1974).

Throughout their collaborations with Whitfield they released a series of ground breaking LPs, including *Gettin' Ready* (USA#12; UK#40.1966), *With a Lot o' Soul* (USA#7; UK#19.1967), *The Temptations In a*

Mellow Mood (USA#13.1968), *Wish it Would Rain* (USA#13.1968), *Live at the Copa* (USA #15.1969), *Cloud Nine* (USA#4; UK#32.1969), *Puzzle People* (USA#5; UK#20.1969), *Psychedelic Shack* (USA#5.1969; UK#56.1970), *Sky's the Limit* (USA#16.1971), *Solid Rock* (USA#24; UK#34.1972), *All Directions* (USA #2; UK#19.1972), *Masterpiece*(USA#7; UK #28.1973) and *1990* (USA#19.1974). They were also teamed with Diana ROSS & The SUPREMES for a series of LPs, including the soundtrack LP for a TV special, *TCB (Taking Care of Business)* (USA#1; UK#11.1969).

However, despite the commercial success, the group underwent a series of changes in personnel. In July 1968 Ruffin left the group to pursue a solo career; he was replaced by Dennis Edwards. Kendricks followed his example three years later, and Paul Williams was compelled to leave through ill-health in 1971. (He committed suicide on August 17, 1973, at the age of 34). They were replaced by former member Richard Street and by Damon Harris (born July 3, 1950, in Baltimore, Maryland), who remained with the group until 1977 when he was replaced by Glenn Leonard (born 1948, in Washington DC). In 1978 Edwards left the group to pursue a solo career, he was replaced by Louis Price (born 1953, in Detroit, Illinois).

After Whitfield's departure from Motown they were teamed with producer Jeffrey Bowen. Despite a gradual decrease in the sales of their singles their LPs sustained their popularity: *A Song for You* (USA#13.1975), *House Party* (USA#40.1975) and *Wings of Love* (USA#29.1976). In 1978 they signed with Atlantic, where they recorded two LPs before Gordy tempted them back to Motown. In 1980 Edwards returned; he was followed in 1982 by Kendricks and Ruffin to record an LP, *Reunion* (USA#37.1982), produced by Rick JAMES, and to participate in a tour. The next year the writer and producer Ron Tyson, who had written most of the material for the debut Atlantic LP, *Hear to Tempt You*, in 1978, joined the group and took part in Motown's 25th. Anniversary Show on NBC TV. In 1984 Edwards left again, this time being replaced by Ali Ollie Woodsin (born 1951 in Detroit, Michigan), who was the lead vocalist on the single, *Treat her Like a Lady* (USA#48.1985; UK#12.1984). By 1987 Edwards had returned to the group once more for the LP *Together Again*. He left shortly after. In 1989 they released the LP *Special*.

In spite of the volatile line-up, their years of treading the boards, combined with a profusion of immaculate material and their sheer professionalism, has ensured that The Temptations can keep on going as long as they want to.

SING SMOKEY, Motown,1965
GETTIN' READY, Motown, 1966
WITH A LOT O' SOUL, Motown, 1967
CLOUD NINE, Motown, 1969
LIVE AT THE COPA, Motown, 1969
PUZZLE PEOPLE, Motown, 1969
DIANA ROSS AND THE SUPREMES JOIN THE TEMPTATIONS, Motown, 1968
TCB, (with Diana Ross & The Supremes), Motown, 1969
PSYCHEDELIC SHACK, Motown, 1970
ALL DIRECTIONS, Motown, 1972
MASTERPIECE, Motown, 1973
A SONG FOR YOU, Motown, 1975
POWER, Motown, 1980
THE TEMPTATIONS, Motown, 1981
20 GOLDEN GREATS, Motown, 1981
ANTHOLOGY, VOLUMES 1 & 2, Motown, 1981
SURFACE THRILLS, Motown, 1983
BACK TO BASICS, Motown, 1984
TRULY FOR YOU, Motown, 1984
ALL THE MILLION SELLERS, Motown, 1984
17 GREATEST HITS, Motown, 1985
TOUCH ME, Motown, 1985
25th ANNIVERSARY, Motown, 1986
TO BE CONTINUED, Motown, 1986
BEST OF THE TEMPTATIONS, Motown, 1986

TOGETHER AGAIN, Motown, 1987
SPECIAL, Motown, 1989

TERRELL, TAMMI Of all the Motown duos formed with Marvin GAYE, the one with Tammi Terrell has proved the most enduring. She was born Tammy Montgomery in Philadelphia in 1947. She cut her first single, *I Cried*, in 1966, produced by James BROWN. Brown then featured her in his Famous Flames revue. She was then teamed with Marvin Gaye.

Her partnership with Gaye lasted for two years, during that time they recorded a string of hits, most of which were written by ASHFORD & SIMPSON: *Ain't No Mountain High Enough* (USA#19.1967), *Your Precious Love* (USA#5.1967), *If I Could Build my Whole World around You* (USA#10; UK#41.1967), *Ain't Nothing Like the Real Thing* (USA#8; UK#34.1968), *You're All I Need to Get By* (USA#7; UK#19.1968), *Keep on Loving Me Honey* (USA#24.1968), *You Ain't Livin' til You're Lovin'* (UK#21.1969), *Good Lovin' ain't Easy to Come By* (USA#30; UK#26.1969) and *The Onion Song* (UK#9.1969). The partnership was brought to an abrupt halt by her death on March 16, 1970, due to a brain tumour.

UNITED, (with Marvin Gaye), Motown, 1982
GREATEST HITS, (with Marvin Gaye), Motown, 1982

TEX, JOE Joe Tex achieved eminence in the 1960s as one of the band of artists who recorded through the Atlantic label. However, his foremost achievement was in writing not only for himself, but also for other distinguished tunesmiths like Jerry BUTLER and James BROWN.

He was born Joseph Arrington in Rogers, Texas, on August 8, 1933. He was vocalist in a succession of gospel groups, having sung while at school. In 1955 he cut some sides for a series of labels, including King, Ace and Anna before in 1961 linking up with Buddy KILLEN, a song publisher from Nashville, who formed the Dial label would guide Tex's career for the rest of his life. After three years of trying to cut a hit record, Killen, having established a distribution deal with Jerry WEXLER at Atlantic, took him to the Fame studios in Muscle Shoals. The result was *Hold what You've Got* (USA#5.1964), the first of a string of hits that included *I Want To (Do Everything for You)* (USA#23.1965), *A Sweet Woman like You* (USA#29.1966), *S.Y.S.L.J.F.M. (The Letter Song)* (USA#39.1966), *Show Me* (USA#35.1967), *Skinny Legs and All* (USA#10.1967) and *Men are Gettin' Scarce* (USA#33.1968). In 1968 Tex participated in the debut of The Soul Clan (see BURKE, Solomon), which proved to be a case of too little, too late – commercially, at least.

By the early 1970s, the deal with Atlantic had expired and Tex's brand of soul, which vacillated between the odd novelty item like *Skinny Legs and All* and the overtly sententious like *A Sweet Woman Like You,* had been superseded by the urban funk of SLY & THE FAMILY STONE, Marvin GAYE and Curtis MAYFIELD. However, in 1972 he notched up his biggest hit with *I Gotcha* (USA#2.1972), the LP of the same name (USA#17.1972) was his most commercially successful. After this he converted to Islam, becoming Joseph Hazziez, and over the next five years devoted his time to preaching.

His return to recording in 1977 was the disco-inflected novelty item, *Ain't Gonna Bump no More (with no Big Fat Woman)* (USA#12; UK#2.1977); it was his one and only hit in the UK. In 1981 he participated in the reunion concert of The Soul Clan. On August 13, 1982, he died of a heart attack, aged 49.

THE BEST OF JOE TEX, Atlantic, 1984
DIFFERENT STROKES, Charly, 1989
STONE SOUL COUNTRY, Charly, 1989
THE VERY BEST OF JOE TEX, Charly, 1989

THOMAS, CARLA Carla Thomas was born in Memphis on December 21, 1942. Her father, Rufus THOMAS, was a DJ and had his own group, The Bearcats, and so her career started virtually from birth. In 1960, her association with Satellite (Stax) began when she recorded the duet *'Cause I Love You* with her father. It was followed by *Gee Whiz (Look at his Eyes)* (USA#10.1961), produced by Chips MOMAN, which provided the springboard whereby Stax could achieve their later prosperity.

Throughout the mid-1960s she was an integral part of Stax, touring constantly. In 1966 she had her final hit as a soloist, *B-A-B-Y* (USA #14.1966), although she would continue to hit the R&B charts. In 1967 she duetted with Otis REDDING on the LP, *King & Queen* (USA#36; UK#18.1967), from which two singles were taken, *Tramp* (USA#26; UK #18.1967) and *Knock on Wood* (USA#30; UK #35.1967). Her association with Stax lasted right up to its demise in 1976. For some time she has recorded less and less, preferring to tour instead.

MEMPHIS QUEEN, Stax, 1990

THOMAS, IRMA Irma Thomas was born in Panchatla, Louisiana. Her career started in the late 1950s with the New Orleans-based Ronn label; in 1962 she moved on to the Minit label, where she recorded *Ruler of my Heart* and *It's Raining* with Allen TOUSSAINT producing. After switching to Imperial she cut her biggest hit, *Wish Someone Would Care* (USA#17.1964), produced and arranged by H. B. BARNUM, and *Time is on my Side*, cowritten and produced by Jerry RAGAVOY. Unfortunately for her, *Ruler of my Heart* was adapted to *Pain in my Heart* by Otis REDDING, and *Time is on my Side* was popularised by The Rolling Stones. In 1967, having signed with Chess, she went to Rick HALL's Fame studios, where with the Muscle Shoals house band she recorded songs like *I've Been Loving You too Long*, *Yours until Tomorrow* and *A Woman will do Wrong*, these breathy ballads failed to change her fortune, but were worthy additions to her extensive repertoire.

In the early 1970s she recorded the LP *In Between Tears*, with Swamp Dogg (aka Jerry Williams) producing, for Phil WALDEN's Capricorn label. For the remainder of the 1970s she continued to ply her trade on the chitlin' circuit, recording for independent labels in and around New Orleans as well as making the occasional festival appearance. In 1979 she released the LP *The Soul Queen of New Orleans*. During the 1980s, having signed with Rounder, she has recorded more frequently with the LPs *The New Rules* (1986), *The Way I Feel* (1988) and a live LP *Simply the Best* (1991), recorded in San Francisco. She still remains criminally underrated, however.

IRMA THOMAS SINGS, Bandy, 1979
THE SOUL QUEEN OF NEW ORLEANS, Maison De Soul, 1979
WISH SOMEONE WOULD CARE, Flyover, 1979
TIME IS ON MY SIDE, Kent, 1985
THE NEW RULES, Rounder, 1986
BREAKAWAY, Stateside, 1987
THE WAY I FEEL, Demon, 1988
SOMETHING GOOD: THE MUSCLE SHOALS SESSIONS, Chess, 1990
SIMPLY THE BEST, Network, 1991

THOMAS, RUFUS The name Rufus Thomas has been synonymous with the term "soul music" ever since the term started being bandied about in the 1960s. Although his better known contributions were half a dozen or so novelty songs, based on dance crazes, which he recorded for Stax during the 1960s and 1970s, through these novelty items he did much to dissipate the preconceptions held by many that soul was purely a secular version of gospel and thus "too heavy" for general consumption. In short, he was one of soul music's first and best PR men: his willingness to tour constantly and his penchant for daft stage costumes were contributing factors.

He was born on March 28, 1917, in Collierville, Texas. He started his career as a comedian with The Rabbit Foot Minstrels before becoming a DJ on the Memphis station, WDIA, a position he would retain well into the 1970s; as a result of this position he started to run talent shows where artists like B. B. KING, Bobby BLAND, Ike TURNER and Johnny ACE first attracted attention. After recording during the 1940s, he cut *Bearcat* for Sam Phillips' Sun label in 1953; thereafter his touring band was known as The Bearcats. Throughout the 1950s he continued to record for lesser-known Memphis labels like Meteor while concentrating on talent scouting for his radio show.

In 1960 he approached Jim STEWART, the owner of the fledgling Satellite label, with the idea that he and his daughter Carla THOMAS should duet on one of his own compositions, *'Cause I Love You*. The local success of the record came to the attention of Atlantic's Jerry WEXLER. Through his radio contacts Thomas was instrumental in the early successes of Satellite (later, Stax). His first solo hit, *Walking the Dog* (USA#10.1963), was followed by a string of dance-floor epics: *Can your Monkey do the Dog?*, *Do the Funky Chicken* (USA#28; UK#18.1970), *Do the Push and Pull* (USA #25.1971), *Breakdown* (USA#31.1971) and *Do the Funky Penguin*. He wasn't confined to

novelty items, as is confirmed by his interpretations of songs like *Fine and Mellow* and *Did you Ever Love a Woman?*.

Since the 1970s, having been poorly represented by Stax, he recorded the LP *If There Were no Music*, for an independent label. After years of touring, he finally recorded *Rappin' Rufus* for the Ichiban label in 1986.

JUMP BACK, Edsel, 1984
RAPPIN' RUFUS, Ichiban, 1986

THORNTON, BIG MAMA The career of Big Mama Thornton has, seemingly, revolved around one incident: in 1953 she recorded the first version of the LEIBER & STOLLER composition *Hound Dog*. This helped to launch the careers of Leiber & Stoller into a level of influence then unprecedented in the albeit short history of record production. Moreover Elvis Presley heard the song and liked it so much that he did his own version.

She was born Willie Mae Thornton on December 11, 1926, in Montgomery, Alabama. She toured the South during the 1940s as a multi-talented entertainer , eventually settling in Houston, Texas, where she was signed by Don ROBEY to his Peacock label. She was spotted by Johnny OTIS, who featured her in his 1952 revue before Leiber & Stoller produced *Hound Dog*. Throughout the 1950s she toured with other Duke-Peacock artists like Junior Parker, Clarence 'Gatemouth' Brown, Johnny ACE and Bobby BLAND. In 1957 she moved to Los Angeles, where she performed regularly on the club circuit; by the mid-1960s, she had become a fixture also on the university circuit, where her raucous, rocking style increasingly appealed to the young, white middle-class audiences.

The immediacy of her style was never entirely satisfactorily captured on record, but the LP *Big Mama Thornton, Volume 2* (1966), for the Arhoolie label, on which she was teamed with the Muddy Waters Band, was one of the better efforts. Throughout the 1970s and 1980s she recorded less and less. The LP *Sassy Mama* (1975) for Sam Charters' Vanguard label was one of the few high spots, although a number of her live performances were often recorded for release. After years of declining health, brought on by her rigorous regimen of touring, she died on July 25, 1984, in Los Angeles.

BIG MAMA THORNTON AND THE CHICAGO BLUES BAND, Arhoolie, 1981
IN EUROPE, Arhoolie, 1981
QUIT SNOOPIN' AROUND MY DOOR, Ace, 1986
BALL & CHAIN, Arhoolie, 1987
THE ORIGINAL HOUND DOG, Ace, 1990

TIME   See JAM, Jimmy, & Terry Lewis

TONEY, Jr, OSCAR   Oscar Toney was born in Selma, Alabama, in 1939, but grew up in the environs of Macon, where he sang in various gospel groups until he formed The Searchers with whom in 1957 he recorded some sides, including *Yvonne* and *Little Wonder* , for the local Max label. Despite the involvement of Bobby Smith, one of Otis REDDING's earliest sponsors, who leased some sides to the King label, his big break was not to come until 1964, when MIGHTY SAM suggested that he should join The Dothan Sextet who needed a replacement for James Purify. As a result he met up with Papa Don SCHROEDER, who was beginning to assemble his own roster of artists.

His sojourn with The Sextet was brief, as Schroeder swiftly set his solo career in motion with an extraordinarily powerful rendition of the Jerry BUTLER composition *For Your Precious Love* (USA#23.1967). This single

proved to be his biggest hit. He went on to record some cracking versions of classics like the Chips MOMAN and Dan PENN compositions, *Dark End of the Street* and *Do Right Woman, Do Right Man*. However, by the end of the decade he had lapsed into semi-obscurity, despite having been signed by Phil WALDEN to his embryonic Capricorn label, where he cut some notable sides like *Down on my Knees*, but his cause was not helped by Walden's increasing interest in developing his white rock-oriented artists. Toney therefore began to revert more to gospel, which had always been the strongest influence in his style of singing.

TOUSSAINT, ALLEN   Throughout the early 1960s Allen Toussaint wrote, produced and played on a number of definitive hits from New Orleans. He was born on January 14, 1938, in New Orleans. A member of Snooks Eaglin's band before joining SHIRLEY & LEE's touring band, he was then hired by Dave BARTHOLOMEW as a session pianist and arranger. In 1959 he was hired by Joe Banashak of the Minit label: he became the house-producer and arranger, working with Ernie K-DOE, Aaron Neville (see NEVILLE BROTHERS), Smiley LEWIS, Chris KENNER and Irma THOMAS. After doing his national service between 1963 and 1965, he teamed up with Marshall Sehorn to mastermind the revitalised career of Lee DORSEY.

Throughout the 1970s, he continued writing for and producing other artists like The Meters (see NEVILLE BROTHERS), DOCTOR JOHN, Robert PALMER and LaBELLE. In 1971 he wrote the horn arrangements for The Band's New Year's Eve concert that was recorded as *Rock of Ages*. The same year he launched his own solo career with the LP *Toussaint*, for the Wand label. It was followed by *Southern Nights* and *Motion*, both for Warner Bros., the former was a most impressive homage to the legacy of New Orleans music.

During the 1980s he has been involved with The NEVILLE BROTHERS as well as producing Etta JAMES; furthermore, he has written the musical *Stagger Lee*, which was produced off- Broadway, and supervised the soundtrack of the Louis Malle film *Pretty Baby*, which starred Brooke Shields. In 1983, he released the LP *With the Stokes* for the independent Bandy label.

SOUTHERN NIGHTS, Edsel, 1974
WITH THE STOKES, Bandy, 1984
FROM A WHIPER TO A SCREAM, Kent, 1985
THE WILD SOUND OF NEW ORLEANS BY TOUSAN, Edsel, 1988

TRESVANT, RALPH See BROWN, Bobby

TROY, DORIS Doris Troy was born in New York as Doris Payne. Her father was a minister and so she was brought up singing in his church choir; this led to her joining a succession of gospel groups. By the late fifties she had joined The Halos, a jazz group, and in 1959, she started to apply herself to songwriting, where she scored with a minor hit for Dee CLARK, *How About That?*. Despite this success she started to sing on sessions, cutting demos and providing back-up vocals for artists like Solomon BURKE, Maxine BROWN and Chuck JACKSON, as well as forming The Gospelaires with Dionne WARWICK, Dee Dee WARWICK and Cissy HOUSTON.

In 1963 she was spotted by James BROWN at the Apollo Theatre in Harlem where she was working as an usherette. After cutting some sides as a member of the duo Jay & Dee she was introduced to producer Artie Ripp. Together they cut *Just one Look* (USA#10.1963), which

she had written in tandem with Gregory Carroll; it was followed by *Whatcha Gonna Do About It?* (UK#37.1964/#38.1965), whose success in the UK prompted her to move there. Despite the lack of further chart success there, she teamed up with Madeleine BELL and became one of the most sought-after session singers on the circuit. By the end of the 1960s, she had been signed to The Beatles' fledgling Apple label, for whom she recorded an eponymously titled LP and a brace of singles. Although none of them set the charts afire, they certainly consolidated her reputation as a vocalist, enabling her to continue as a session singer as well as bringing her employment as a vocalist on commercials and the like. In 1985, she returned to New York, where she went back to her roots by working in gospel groups.

TUCKER, TOMMY Robert Higgenbotham was born in Springfield, Ohio, in 1934. His early career was spent playing in a variety of pick-up groups, who backed such visiting luminaries as Roland Kirk and Eddie 'Cleanhead' Vinson. It wasn't until 1959 that he started a solo career under the name of Tommy Tucker recording for Willie MITCHELL's Hi label in Memphis. He was unable at first to achieve any chart success.

In 1964 he was discovered in Asbury Park, New Jersey, by Herb ABRAMSON, who became his manager. Tucker recorded the self-penned *Hi-Heel Sneakers* (USA#11; UK #23.1964), which Abramson leased to Checker, the Chess subsidiary; despite speculation about the bizarre lyrical content it has become a standard, with artists like Stevie WONDER, Roland Kirk, Elvis Presley, Jerry Lee Lewis and Jose Feliciano all recording their own versions. Although Abramson continued to manage him, Tucker was unable to repeat his success and returned to obscurity *via* the chitlin' circuit. In 1982, he died of food-poisoning, aged 48.

THE ROCKS IS MY PILLOW, THE COLD GROUND IS MY BED, Red Lightnin', 1982
MOTHER TUCKER, Red Lightnin', 1984
MEMPHIS BAD BOY, Zu Zazz. 1989.

TURNER, IKE & TINA Of all the R&B bandleaders of the 1950s, few were more autocratic than Ike Turner. He was born on November 5, 1931, in Clarksdale, Mississippi. He formed his first band, The Kings of Rhythm, while he was still at school and acted as a talent scout for the Modern label. He participated in one of the first big hits of the rock 'n' roll era, *Rocket 88* (1951), by saxophonist Jackie Brenston; it was recorded at the Sun studios in Memphis and became a big hit in the R&B charts. His role as Modern's talent scout enabled him to secure session work, backing artists like B. B. KING, Howlin' Wolf, Johnny ACE and other artists whom he had recruited. In 1956 he met Annie Mae Bullock while he and his band were performing at a club in East St Louis. She became the band's vocalist, and in 1958 they were married. Thus the name Tina TURNER came into being.

Their first record, *A Fool in Love* (USA #27.1960), came about by mistake when the session singer, who was booked to sing Ike's song failed to show up and so Tina stepped into the breach. The following year they notched up their first top twenty hit with *It's Gonna Work out Fine* (USA#14.1961). During the next five years they established a reputation for being one of the most exciting and entertaining live acts in the country: billed as 'The Ike & Tina Turner Revue', the act featured not only Tina but also a trio of female backing vocalists, The Ikettes, which included at various times in its lne-up, P.P. Arnold, Bonnie Bramlett and Claudia Linnear; they had two hit singles in their own right, *I'm Blue (The Gong-Gong Song)* (USA#19.1962) and *Peaches and Cream* (USA#36.1965); produced by Ike, these were leased to Atco and Modern, respectively.

Their first major international success came in 1966, when they were enlisted by Phil SPECTOR to record some songs by Brill Building writers Jeff BARRY and Ellie GREENWICH. The single from the sessions *River Deep, Mountain High* (UK#3.1966/#33.1969) was a big hit all over the world, yet failed to register in the USA. However, they were chosen to support The Rolling Stones on their forthcoming US Tour. The decision highlighted their growing popularity among young white audiences.

In 1969 they signed with the Blue Thumb label, a subsidiary of Minit, for whom they recorded two LPs, *Outta Season* and *The Hunter*. The following year they released the LP *Come Together*, the title track of which, a Lennon & McCartney composition, was released as a single. Another cover version followed, *I Wanna Take You Higher* (USA #34.1970), a Sly Stone (see SLY & THE FAMILY STONE) song, which was to become an integral part of their live act. In 1971 they released the LP *Workin' Together*, which featured their version of the John Fogerty song *Proud Mary* (USA#4.1971). Then came the double live LP *Live at the Carnegie Hall/What you See is what You Get* (USA#25.1971). Their final hit as a duo was *Nutbush City Limits* (USA#22; UK#4.1973).

In 1976 Tina walked out on Ike and divorced him, claiming that he had persistently beaten her up throughout their years of marriage. Her precipitous departure spelt the effective end of Ike's career. Despite periodic attempts to relaunch it, he has spent most of his time entangled with the law for a variety of offences, including income tax evasion, drug violations, and even the rigging of electronic devices to avoid paying for use of the telephone. However being a decent chap has never been a necessary qualification for making good records. In 1990 he stated that he intended to sue Tina for $70 million, as her success had come about as a direct result of using his name!

FINGERPOPPIN': THE WARNER BROTHERS YEARS, Edsel, 1965

LIVE!, Edsel, 1965

RIVER DEEP, MOUNTAIN HIGH, Pickwick, 1966

THE FANTASTIC IKE AND TINA, Sunset, 1974

BLACK ANGEL, Musidisc, 1976

BLACK BEAUTY, Musidisc, 1977

SOUL SELLERS, Liberty, 1979

THE KINGS OF RHYTHM, VOLUME ONE, Ace, 1980

THE KINGS OF RHYTHM: FROM COBRA AND ARTISTIC 1958–59, Flyright, 1981

JUKE BOX GIANTS, Audio Fidelity, 1982

I'M TORE UP, (The Kings of Rhythm), Red Lightnin',1982

ROCK ME BABY, Bulldog, 1982

SO FINE, Happy Bird (Germany), 1983

NICE AND ROUGH, Liberty, 1984

TOUGH ENOUGH, Liberty, 1984

HEY! HEY!, (Kings of Rhythm), Red Lightnin', 1984

THE SOUL OF IKE AND TINA, Kent, 1984

HER MAN......HIS WOMAN, Stateside, 1985

THE KINGS OF RHYTHM, VOLUME TWO, Ace, 1985

KINGS OF RHYTHM, Flyright, 1986

ROCKIN' BLUES, (Kings of Rhythm), Stateside, 1986

THE DYNAMIC DUO, Ace, 1986

GOLDEN EMPIRE, Spartan, 1986

THE BEST OF IKE AND TINA TURNER, United Artists, 1987

THE IKE AND TINA SESSIONS, Kent, 1987

TURNER, TINA Tina Turner was born Annie Mae Bullock on November 26, 1939. Prior to her acrimonious split from her husband Ike TURNER in 1976, she had been chosen to costar in the film *Tommy* as the Acid

Queen, and as a result she recorded a solo LP, *The Acid Queen*. Although this had been commercially unsuccessful, the experience prompted her to launch a solo career in earnest. For the next four years she supported herself and her four children by playing the cabaret circuit, until in 1980 she met the Australian promoter Roger Davis, who started to book her into rather more salubrious venues than those to which she had become accustomed; consequently he became her manager.

In 1981 she played support for The Rolling Stones and was asked by Ian Craig Marsh and Martyn Ware of Heaven 17 to record a cover version of The TEMPTATIONS song *Ball of Confusion* for the LP *Music of Quality and Distinction* for The British Electric Foundation. Her participation in the project had the desired effect, and she was signed by Capitol. Her first single was a cover of the AL GREEN song, *Let's Stay Together* (USA#26; UK#6.1983), and was included on her first Capitol LP, *Private Dancer* (USA#3; UK#2.1984). This LP spawned a clutch of hit singles including the poignant *What's Love Got to Do with It?* (USA#1; UK#3.1984) and *Better be Good to Me* (USA#5; UK#45.1984) and Private Dancer (USA#7; UK#26.1984); moreover, it established her internationally as a solo performer.

In 1985 she appeared in the film *Mad Max 3: Beyond the Thunderdome*, and performed the theme song, *We Don't Need Another Hero* (USA#2; UK#3.1985). Later that year she duetted with Bryan Adams on the single *It's only Love* (USA#15; UK#29.1985). Her next LP *Break Every Rule* (USA#4; UK#2.1986); this too included a bunch singles: *Typical Male* (USA#2; UK#33.1986), *Two People* (USA#30; UK#43.1986), *What You See is what You Get* (UK#30.1987) and *Break Every Rule* (UK #43.1987). In 1987 she embarked upon a world tour to promote the LP and cut a live LP *Break Every Rule Live*, which was recorded in the Club Zero in Paris and included her version of the Robert PALMER song, *Addicted to Love*.

In 1989 she released the LP, *Foreign Affair* (USA#3; UK#2.1989), which has, like its predecessors, sold by the truckload. In 1989/90, she embarked upon another global tour to promote the LP. Recently she commented that she felt that she was primarily a rock rather than soul singer, her choice of material has always tended to bear out that assertion. Irrespective of the finer points of category, she is still one of the great performers of our time.

ACID QUEEN, MFP/EMI, 1975
GOES COUNTRY, Connoisseur, 1977
PRIVATE DANCER, Capitol, 1984
BREAK EVERY RULE, Capitol, 1986
BREAK EVERY RULE: LIVE, Capitol, 1986
FOREIGN AFFAIR, Capitol, 1989.

TWO MEN, A DRUM MACHINE & A TRUMPET see FINE YOUNG CANNIBALS

TYMES The Tymes were formed in Philadelphia in 1956, as The Latineers by Donald Banks, Albert Berry, Norman Burnett and George Hilliard. For the next few years they worked the local club circuit, developing their stage act. In 1960 George Williams joined the group as lead vocalist and they changed their name to The Tymes. Another three years elapsed before they were spotted on a talent show sponsored by the radio station WDAS and signed by Cameo-Parkway.

Their first release, *So Much in Love* (USA#1; UK#21.1963), was based upon a half-completed composition by Williams, but was rearranged by producer Billy Jackson and arranger Roy Straigis. Their first LP, *So Much in Love* (USA#15.1963), featured another single, a revival of the Johnny Mathis hit, *Wonderful! Wonderful!* (USA#7.1963); it was follow-ed by *Somewhere* (USA#19.1964). However, their succeeding releases failed to capture the popular imagination as their style of singing had been superseded by Motown, Atlantic and, of course, British Groups like The Beatles and The Animals.

In 1965, as Cameo-Parkway was in deep financial trouble, they established their own label; called Winchester, it was set up with the help of Leon Huff (see GAMBLE & HUFF) among others. After two records the label folded and they were signed by MGM, only to be dropped by them after releasing two records. In 1968 they were signed by CBS and cut a dramatic reworking of *People* (USA#39; UK#16.1968), from the Broadway musical, *Funny Girl*; it had been a big hit for Barbra Streisand. However, the following year they were dropped by CBS.

For the next three years they concentrated on updating their image; also Hilliard left the group. In 1972 their producer Billy Jackson, financed some sessions for them at Gamble & Huff's Sigma Sound studios in Philadelphia. Gamble & Huff were unimpressed by their efforts and refused to sign the group to their Philadelphia International label, but RCA picked up the half-finished tapes and signed them. Their debut for RCA, *You Little Trustmaker* (USA#12; UK#18.1974), was written by Jackson; the follow-up, *Miss Grace* (UK#1.1974), was massive everywhere except the USA and, once again, they lost their momentum. In 1976, they had two more modest hits with *God's Gonna Punish You* (UK #41.1976) and *It's Cool*, but once more their style was, in the process, of becoming outdated. Since that time, rumour has it that they are still together, touring the cabaret circuit in the USA and Europe.

UNDISPUTED TRUTH The Undisputed Truth was formed by Billie Rae Calvin and

Brenda Evans at the suggestion of Norman WHITFIELD, who was enjoying immense success with The TEMPTATIONS. After providing backing vocals for some of Whitfield's productions, he offered them a management contract and augmented the line-up with Joe Harris, signing them to the Motown subsidiary, Gordy. (Harris had been raised in Detroit and, after he had achieved some prominence in baseball, he formed his own group to supplement his income; this group gradually evolved into The Stone Soul Children but, by the end of the 1960s, had disbanded). Their brand of post-psychedelic funk found its most successful expression in the new group's single *Smiling Faces Sometimes* (USA#3.1971), which came from the LP *The Undisputed Truth*. Although their second LP, *Face to Face with the Truth*, failed to consolidate their earlier success, they developed a strong live act with ROSE ROYCE as their touring band. When their contract with Gordy expired they were signed to Warner Bros., where they had a minor hit with *You + Me = Love* (UK#43.1977). After touring and without having had any more hit records, the group separated in the early 1980s.

UPCHURCH, PHIL Although in recent years Phil Upchurch has been primarily a session guitarist with artists like George Benson, Grover WASHINGTON, The CRUSADERS and Bo DIDDLEY, he, like Jimmy McGRIFF, achieved some eminence with a dance floor hit in the early sixties, *You Can't Sit Down*.

He was born in Chicago and learnt to play the guitar while at school. After playing in various local groups he obtained work at the Chess studios as a bassist. Throughout the late 1950s and early 1960s, in partnership with Maurice White (see EARTH, WIND & FIRE), he backed artists like Howlin' Wolf, The DELLS, Gene CHANDLER, Jerry BUTLER and

Muddy Waters. Consequently he got the opportunity to record the instrumental *You Can't Sit Down* (USA#29.1961; UK#39.1966); its success encouraged further instrumentals from him, but they failed to register. Through the late 1960s, he recorded a number of jazz LPs for a variety of different labels.

In the early 1970s he signed to the Blue Thumb label and recorded LPs like *Darkness, Darkness* (1972) and *Lovin' Feeling* (1973); both were produced by Tommy LiPuma. He also played on sessions for other Blue Thumb signings like The Crusaders and Ben Sidran. In 1975, he was signed by Creed Taylor to the Kudu label, where he cut the LP *Upchurch Tennyson*, with pianist and vocalist Tennyson Stephens. In 1985 he cut the LP *Companions* for the independent Palladin label. In recent years he has recorded less and less under his own name and tended to concentrate on session work.

COMPANIONS, Palladin, 1985

VALENTINOS   See WOMACK, Bobby

VANDROSS, LUTHER During the 1980s Luther Ronzoni Vandross has emerged as one of the premier stylists in a genre that has been worked to death: ballads. His pre-eminence has been due to his all- round ability: performing, writing and producing. Furthermore, he has shown himself to be adept at selecting complementary artists and technicians to work alongside him, like bandleader and arranger Nat Adderley, Jr, arranger, bassist and cowriter Marcus Miller, and engineer Ray Bardani. These collaborators, as well as an excellent touring band, have enabled him to outshine many of his competitors.

He was born on April 20, 1951, in New York; his mother had been a gospel singer, his father a big band vocalist and his sister a member of the doo-wop vocal group The Crests. He formed his own group when he was school in the early 1970s with guitarist Carlos Alomar and keyboardist Robin Clark. After the group split up he studied music briefly. In 1974, both he and Clark were invited to Sigma Sound studios in Philadelphia by Alomar, who was working with David Bowie on the *Young Americans* LP. Bowie asked Vandross to put together the vocal arrangements and provide backing vocals on the sessions; in addition Bowie recorded *Fascination*, which had been written by Vandross.

The following year he was invited by Bowie to open for him on the *Young Americans* tour and was then introduced by Bowie to Bette Midler, who recruited him to sing on the LP *Songs for the New Depression*, which was being produced by Arif MARDIN. Mardin began to use him on most of his productions with artists like Carly Simon, Chaka KHAN and The AVERAGE WHITE BAND.

The following year Vandross put together his own group, Luther, who were signed by the Atlantic subsidiary Cotillion; however their style was completely at odds with the prevailing disco trend and the group broke up after a couple of LPs, *Luther* and *This Close to You*. Vandross started singing jingles for commercials. In 1978, however, Quincy JONES asked him to provide some vocals for the LP *Sounds .... and Stuff Like That!!,* and as a result Nile RODGERS and Bernard EDWARDS asked him to provide backing vocals for CHIC and SISTER SLEDGE. That, in turn, led to an invitation to be the lead vocalist on the debut LP by the group CHANGE. All this activity prompted Epic to sign him, giving him complete artistic freedom.

His first LP, *Never Too Much* (USA#19.1981; UK#41.1987), was a classy affair showing that it was quite possible to record an LP full of ballads without swamping it with treacly arrangements and overworked standards; the title track was released as a single (USA #33.1981; UK#44.1983). The following year he produced the Aretha FRANKLIN LP, *Jump to It,* and managed to extract from her performances of a quality that had not been heard since her earliest days at Atlantic. His own next LP, *Forever, for Always, for Love* (USA#20. 1982; UK#23.1987), confirmed the promise of the debut. (In the UK Epic selected tracks from his first two LPs *Never Too Much* and*Forever, for Always, for Love* to make up his debut LP *Luther Vandross.* Both LPs were released in their entirety in 1986 and 1987 respectively).

In 1983 he produced the Dionne WARWICK LP *How Many Times Can we Say Goodbye?,* duetting with her on the title track, which was released as a single (USA#27.1983). His third LP, *Busy Body* (USA#32.1983; UK #42.1984), was followed by *The Night I Fell in Love* (USA/UK#19.1985), which included *'Til my Baby Comes Home* (USA#29.1985). His next two LPs, *Give me the Reason* (USA#14; UK#9.1986) and *Any Love* (USA#9; UK-#3.1988), were not dramatically different from his previous outings, but they consolidated his reputation internationally, giving rise to a number of hit singles: *Give me the Reason* (UK-#60.1986/#26.1988), *See Me* (UK#60.1987), *I Really Didn't Mean It* (UK#16.1987), *Stop to Love* (USA#15; UK#24.1987), *So Amazing* (UK#33.1987), *I Gave it Up (When I Fell in Love)* (UK#28.1988) and *Any Love* (UK-#31.1988). In 1990 he toured the UK, playing at Wembley on five consecutive nights, all of which had been sold out months in advance.

NEVER TOO MUCH, Epic, 1981
LUTHER VANDROSS, Epic, 1982
FOREVER, FOR ALWAYS, FOR LOVE, Epic, 1982
BUSY BODY, Epic, 1983
THE NIGHT I FELL IN LOVE, Epic, 1985

GIVE ME THE REASON, Epic, 1986
ANY LOVE, Epic, 1988

VANITY 6   See PRINCE

VELVELETTES   The Velvelettes were discovered by Robert Bullock, a nephew of Berry GORDY, while they were performing at a dance at Western Michigan University. The group had been formed by sisters Carolyn and Milly Gill, Bertha and Norma Barbee and Betty Kelley while they were all still at school. After auditioning for Motown, they were assigned to writer and producer Norman WHITFIELD; soon afterwards Kelley left to join MARTHA & THE VANDELLAS. With Whitfield The Velvelettes recorded *There he Goes, Needle in a Haystack, He was Really Saying Something* and *These Things will Keep me Loving You* (UK#34.1971). Since the expiry of their contract in 1969 they have ceased recording, although they have continued to perform locally.

VINCENT, JOHNNY   Johnny Vincent was born Vincent Imbragulio. Prior to the formation of Ace in 1955 he worked as a distributor in the late 1940s before being employed on by Art RUPE as Specialty's Head of A&R for the Southern states in 1952. Upon the formation of Ace in Jackson, he contracted Specialty artists like Huey 'Piano'' SMITH and Earl KING to the label, producing hits like *Rockin' Pneumonia and the Boogie Woogie Flu* and *Don't You Just Know It* for Smith and *Those Lonely, Lonely Nights* for King. These early successes prompted him to sign artists like Frankie FORD and Jimmy Clanton, whose records were aimed firmly at the white pop markets. By the early 1960s Vincent's career as a producer was over, but his fast-talking entrepeneurial zeal encouraged Tommy COUCH, who had rented office space from him, to set up what was to become the Malaco label.

WALDEN, NARADA MICHAEL   Narada Michael Walden was born on April 23, 1952. He came to prominence in the mid-1970s when he was employed as a drummer to work with artists like Jeff Beck, John McLaughlin, Herbie Hancock, Chick Corea and Weather Report. He made his own solo recording debut in 1977 with *Garden of Love Light*, which was produced by Tom DOWD. He enjoyed great success in the 1980s with a number of dance-oriented compositions like *Tonight I'm Alright* (UK#34.1980), *I Shoulda Loved Ya* (UK#8.1980) and *Divine Emotions* (UK#8.1988). However, his greatest contribution has been as a writer and producer for other artists like Aretha FRANKLIN, The FOUR TOPS, Natalie COLE, Whitney HOUSTON and SISTER SLEDGE. This particular facet of his career began with Stacy Lattishaw's 1980 hit, *Jump to the Beat,* and culminated with the Aretha Franklin and George Michael duet, *I Knew You were Waiting for Me*. He has continued to record as a solo artist.

AWAKENING, Atlantic, 1979
VICTORY, Atlantic, 1980
NATURE OF THINGS, Atlantic, 1985

WALDEN, PHIL   Phil Walden was born in Macon, Georgia, in 1940. After leaving Mercer University, he set up Phil Walden & Associates as a booking agency for local dances and fraternity hops. One of his first acts was Johnny JENKINS & The Pinetoppers. By 1961, he had taken over as Otis REDDING's manager and started a management agency, a role he would maintain for the rest of Redding's life. As Redding was signed to Stax, this set-up enabled Walden to book most of the other Stax artists, like SAM & DAVE, Eddie FLOYD and Carla THOMAS, through his booking agency. After Redding's death in 1967, Walden started the Capricorn label at the suggestion of Jerry WEXLER, with Duane ALLMAN and his group The Allman Brothers Band among the first signings. Other artists to be taken on included Arthur CONLEY, The Marshall Tucker Band, Johnny Jenkins, Percy SLEDGE, Eddie HINTON, Wet Willie and Elvin Bishop. Despite the initial success of the label, it went bankrupt in 1978. Many of Walden's critics have claimed that, after Allman's death and the success of the group, he was interested only in finding another group to emulate that success rather than in concentrating upon the vast reservoir of talent that was there waiting to be employed.

WALKER, JUNIOR, & THE ALL-STARS One of the superb (if possibly apocryphal) tales of how a group's name came into being has it that Junior Walker was playing a gig in a club with his group when an enthusiastic member of the audience leapt to his feet and shouted: 'These guys are all stars!'. Never was a truer word uttered. The strength of the group was that, of all the Motown artists, their sound was the least polished. Walker's honking sax and strained vocals were the antithesis of the slick professionalism of, say, The FOUR TOPS. In a way, the group provided an affirmation of Motown's very real commitment to black music in all its variegated forms.

They were formed by Walker (born Autry DeWalt II in 1942 in Blythesville, Arkansas), who had moved to South Bend, Indiana; by the time he enlisted school-friends guitarist Willie Woods, organist Vic Thomas and drummer James Graves. They started to play on the club circuit, where they were spotted by Johnny BRISTOL, who recommended them to Harvey FUQUA. Fuqua signed them to his Harvey label but, despite a number of releases, they could not break out. When Fuqua sold his roster of artists to Berry GORDY the group was assigned to the Motown subsidiary Soul, where they were teamed with producers HOLLAND, DOZIER & HOLLAND and then, in 1969, to Johnny Bristol. Their first hit single, *Shotgun* (USA#3.1965), was a Walker composition, based on a dance called *The Shotgun*. It was first in a string of hits over the next eight years: *Do the Boomerang* (USA#36.1965), *Shake and Fingerpop* (USA#29.1965), *Road Runner* (USA#20. 1966; UK#12.1969), *How Sweet it is (to be Loved by You)* (USA#18; UK#22.1966), *Pucker up Buttercup* (USA#31.1967), *Come See About Me* (USA#24.1967), *Hip City* (USA#31.1968), *What Does it Take (to Win your Love)* (USA#4; UK#13.1969), *These Eyes* (USA#16.1969), *Gotta Hold on to this Feeling* (USA#21.1970), *Do You See my Love (for you Growing)* (USA#32.1970), *Walk in the Night* (UK#16.1972), *Take Me Girl I'm Ready* (UK#16.1973) and *Way Back Home* (UK#35.1973).

Throughout the latter half of the 1970s, Walker became another victim of the disco era. Although he left Motown for Warner Bros., where he recorded the LP *Back Street Boogie* in 1980, he has been unable to repeat his former success, despite contributing a searing solo to Foreigner's 1981 hit, *Urgent*. In 1982, he returned to Motown and recorded the LP *Blow the House Down*, which failed to score. However, he has continued to tour constantly, and his stage show remains one of the few perks of Western civilisation.

SHOTGUN, Motown, 1965
ROAD RUNNER, Motown, 1966

ANTHOLOGY, Motown, 1981
JUNIOR WALKER'S GREATEST HITS, Motown, 1982
BLOW THE HOUSE DOWN, Motown, 1983
COMPACT COMMAND PERFORMANCES, Motown, 1987

WANSEL, DEXTER When GAMBLE & HUFF set up the Philadelphia International label in 1971 they folowed Berry GORDY's example of not only gathering together a roster of artists – like The O'JAYS and Harold MELVIN & The Blue Notes – but also recruiting in-house musicians, writers and arrangers. The house band was known as MFSB (Mother, Father, Sister, Brother) and the principal arranger was Dexter Wansel.

A native of Philadelphia, Wansel worked with Gamble & Huff throughout the early 1970s, arranging a whole string of hits for Melvin and The O'Jays, as well as *TSOP (The Sound of Philadelphia)* (USA#1; UK#22.1974) and *Sexy* (UK#37.1975) for MFSB. After Teddy PENDERGRASS embarked on a solo career, Wansel became his musical director. In 1978 he launched his own solo career with the LP, *Voyager*, which included the single *All Night Long* (UK#59.1978). Despite its success in the UK, he was unable to sustain his momentum with later LPs like *Life on Mars,* and he returned to arranging and session work. In 1986, having signed with the Virgin subsidiary Ten, he resumed his solo career with the LP *Captured*.

VOYAGER, Philadelphia International, 1978
CAPTURED, Ten, 1986

WAR War were one of the few groups that came to prominence in the early 1970s who managed to brave the disco years and emerge with not a stain upon their character. Their blend of jazz, funk, salsa, rock and soul managed to coexist with even the most execrable rubbish and had that uncanny ability of making everything sound better than it probably was. Furthermore, while their lyrics expressed a social awareness they managed to avoid the growing vocabulary of cliche that was already beginning to sound tired by the mid-1970s.

The nucleus of the group was formed as The Creators in Long Beach, California, in 1960; it then became Night Shift. By 1969, it comprised Lonnie Jordan (keyboards and vocals; born November 21, 1948, in San Diego), Howard Scott (guitar and vocals; born March 15, 1946, in San Pedro), Charles Miller (horns and clarinet; born June 2, 1939, in Olathe, Kansas), Harold Brown (drums and percussion; born March 17, 1946, in Long Beach), Peter Rosen (bass) and former LA Rams footballer, Deacon Jones (vocals). Eric Burdon, former lead singer of The Animals, Lee Oskar (harmonica; born Oskar Levetin Hansen on March 24, 1948, in Copenhagen, Denmark) and producer Jerry Goldstein were looking for a group to back Burdon. They saw the group and they all decided to join forces, with Burdon replacing Jones. Later the same year Rosen died of a drug overdose and was replaced by Morris 'B.B.' Dickerson (born August 3, 1949, in Torrance, California); the line-up was augmented still further by Thomas 'Papa Dee' Allen (keyboards and vocals; born July 18, 1931, in Wilmington, Delaware).

As Eric Burdon was signed to MGM, the group continued with him under the same contract and as the mood of the time was all sweetness and light, the group was christened War. In 1970, after touring the USA, Europe and the UK (where they jammed with Jimi HENDRIX at Ronnie Scott's Club in London) they released the LP *Eric Burdon Declares War* (USA#18.1970); it contained the single *Spill the Wine* (USA#3.1970). The following year they released a double LP, *The Black Man's Burdon* (UK#34.1971), and undertook another European tour. Midway through it Burdon, who was suffering from acute exhaustion, left the group to continue the tour alone. Upon completion of the tour they decided against teaming up with Burdon again and negotiated a fresh contract with United Artists.

Their debut LP without Burdon, *War*, attracted some benevolent notices but caused few ripples. The follow-up, however, *All Day Music* (USA#16.1971), included two hit singles, *All Day Music* (USA#35.1971) and *Slippin' into Darkness* (USA#16.1972). In 1973 the group and producer Jerry Goldstein formed their own production company, Far Out. Their first LP under this new deal was *The World is a Ghetto* (USA#1.1973); the title track, *The World is a Ghetto* (USA#7.1973) and *The Cisco Kid* (USA#2.1973), were both released as singles. The next LP, *Deliver the Word* (USA#6.1973), included two singles, *Gypsy Man* (USA#8.1973) and *Me and Baby Brother* (USA#15.1974; UK#21.1976). Their live performances were pivotal to their success and the double live LP, *War Live!* (USA#13.1974), went someway towards capturing the spontaneity of their shows; the instrumental *Ballero* (USA#33.1974) was extracted as a single. Their next studio LP, *Why Can't We Be Friends?* (USA#8.1975), included their first hit single in the UK, *Low Rider* (USA#7.1975; UK #12.1976).

In 1976 Oskar launched a parallel solo career with the LP *Lee Oskar* (USA#29.1976), and the group issued the single, *Summer* (USA#7. 1976). In 1977 they released their final LP with United Artists. Entitled *Platinum Jazz* (USA#23.1977), it was arguably their least commercial set to date, but that didn't stop it from earning a gold disc. They established a new deal with MCA for their production company, and their first LP under this new set-up, *Galaxy* (USA#15.1978), included two singles,

Galaxy (USA#39; UK#14.1978) and *Hey Senorita* (UK#40.1978). The same year they recruited another vocalist, Alice Tweed Smyth, but bassist Dickerson left to be replaced by Luther Rabb. Meanwhile, Oskar released his second solo LP, *Before the Rain*, which was a modest commercial success. After providing the soundtrack for the film *Youngblood*, they released the LP *The Music Band*, and then supplemented their line-up with Pat Rizzo (horns) and Ron Hammond (percussion). Although by 1980 their popularity had passed its peak, *The Music Band 2* showed no inclination to hop onto the disco bandwagon. The following year Oskar released another solo LP, *My Road Our Road*. In 1982 they changed labels once more, this time signing with RCA. Two more LPs followed, *Outlaw* (1982) and *Life (Is So Strange)* (1983). By the mid-1980s the group and Goldstein were leasing their material to independent labels without any great degree of success. However, while past their best, they have left an admirable legacy which has stood the test of time remarkably well.

WAR LIVE!, MCA, 1974
OUTLAW, RCA, 1982
WAR GIVE YOU ...... THE FREEDOM TO ROCK, War, 1985
ON FIRE, Thunderbolt, 1987

WARD, BILLY, & THE DOMINOES

The Dominoes were formed by pianist and arranger Billy Ward in 1950. They were signed by Ralph BASS to the King subsidiary, Federal. From 1950 to1953 their lead singer was Clyde McPHATTER; when he was fired he was replaced by Jackie WILSON.

Throughout the 1950s they had a string of hits including *Sixty Minute Man* (USA #17.1951), *St Therese of the Roses* (USA #13.1956), *Star Dust* (USA#12; UK#13.1957) and *Deep Purple* (USA#20; UK#30.1957).

More important than their success is the fact that records like *Have Mercy Baby* and *Do Something for Me* had a considerable impact on the black music of the 1950s: the unbridled salacity of the performances were pivotal to the secularisation of the various gospel styles, and thereby sowed the seeds of soul.

CLYDE McPHATTER WITH BILLY WARD AND HIS DOMINOES, King, 1988
BILLY WARD AND HIS DOMINOES, (with Clyde McPhatter and Jackie Wilson), King, 1988
SIXTY MINUTE MAN, Charly, 1990

WARE, LEON Leon Ware was born in Detroit and educated at Northern High School. He was raised on gospel, singing in church choirs from an early age, and by the time he was eleven he had joined his first group, The Romeos, which included Lamont Dozier (see HOLLAND, DOZIER & HOLLAND) and Ty Hunter, latterly of The Originals. Through these associations he began to pick up work as a freelance arranger and composer: among the artists he wrote for were The RIGHTEOUS BROTHERS, The ISLEY BROTHERS, Ike & Tina TURNER and Kim Weston. In 1972, with Diana ROSS' brother Arthur, he wrote *I Wanna be Where you Are* for Michael JACKSON and in 1974 he cowrote and performed *Body Heat* and *If I Ever Lose this Heaven* on the Quincy JONES LP *Body Heat*. As a result, he became a staff writer and producer at Motown, where his biggest achievement was as a writer and arranger of the Marvin GAYE LP *I Want You*.

In 1977 Ware launched his own solo career with the LP *Musical Massage,* on which Marvin Gaye contributed backing vocals. Throughout the 1980s he has continued releasing solo LPs intermittently, having signed to Elektra. However, his principal contribution has remained as a producer and arranger.

ROCKING YOU ETERNALLY, Elektra, 1981
LEON WARE, Elektra, 1982

WARWICK, DEE DEE Throughout her career Dee Dee Warwick has been overshadowd by her more famous sister, Dionne WARWICK, and as a result has been unjustly neglected. During the 1950s she was a member of the gospel group, The Drinkard Singers, which included her sister in its lineup. In the early 1960s, she sang back-up vocals with her sister, Cissy HOUSTON and Doris TROY. After recording for LEIBER & STOLLER's Tiger label, she recorded her version of the Betty EVERETT hit, *You're No Good* for Jubilee in 1964. It was followed by a spell with Mercury, where she cut *I'm Gonna Make you Love Me* (which was covered in 1969 by The SUPREMES with The TEMPTATIONS) and *Foolish Fool*. After signing with Atlantic subsidiary Atco in 1970, she recorded a peerless version of *Suspicious Minds*. However, despite further releases on various labels like RCA, Private Stock and Buddah, she has been unable to establish any real continuity in her career.

WARWICK, DIONNE Throughout a career that has spanned thirty years, Dionne Warwick has never received the critical plaudits that have been showered upon lesser artists: the overt pop sensibilities of her first producers, Burt Bacharach and Hal David, have stigmatised all her subsequent work, branding her erroneously as just another balladeer rooted in the glitz of the Las Vegas cabaret circuit. Her work with Thom BELL and Linda Creed showed her to be Dinah Washington's natural successor, but all too often in recent years she has been landed with producers who have not been simpatico, and as a result her records have been either overproduced or marred by horrendous material or both, and this has conspired to disguise the unique qualities of her voice.

She was born Marie Dionne Warwick on December 12, 1940, in East Orange, New Jersey. By the time she was six she was singing in the church choir. She then joined the gospel group The Drinkard Singers. In 1960 while studying music in Hartford, Connecticut, she formed The Gospelaires with her sister Dee Dee WARWICK, her cousin Cissy HOUSTON and Doris TROY, In addition to playing the gospel circuit, they started to provide backing vocals on sessions. In 1961, while working on a DRIFTERS session, she met Burt Bacharach, who suggested that she might like to record some demos of his songs. One of the demos was picked up by Luther DIXON at Scepter Records for The SHIRELLES.

By 1962, she was ensconced at Scepter, providing back-up vocals for artists like Maxine BROWN, Chuck JACKSON and Tommy HUNT, and later the same year she was signed to the label as a solo artist. Her debut, *Don't Make me Over* (USA#21.1963) was written by Bacharach and his partner, Hal David, as were most of her early hits: *Anyone who had a Heart* (USA#8; UK#42.1964), *Walk on By* (USA#6; UK#9.1964), *You'll Never Get to Heaven (if you Break my Heart)* (USA#34; UK#20.1964), *Reach out for Me* (USA#20; UK#23.1964), *You Can Have Him* (UK #37.1965), *Are You There (with Another Girl)?* (USA#39.1966), *Message to Michael* (USA#8. 1966), *Trains and Boats and Planes* (USA#22.1966), *I Just don't Know What to do with Myself* (USA#26.1966), *Alfie* (USA#15.1967), *The Windows of the World* (USA#32.1967), *I Say a Little Prayer* (USA# 4.1967), *Theme from the Valley of the Dolls* (USA#2; UK#28.1968), *Do You Know the Way to San Jose?* (USA#10; UK#8.1968), *Who is Gonna Love Me?* (USA#33.1968), *Promises, Promises* (USA#19.1968), *This Girl's in Love with You* (USA#7.1969), *The April Fools* (USA#37.1969), *You've Lost that Lovin' Feeling* (USA#16.1969), *I'll Never Fall in Love Again* (USA#6.1970), *Let me Go to Him* (USA #32.1970) and *Make it Easy on Yourself* (USA #37.1970).

In 1971 she left Scepter and signed with Warner Bros. Her first LP, *Dionne*, marked the end of her collaboration with Bacharach & David, who stopped working together as a team; she promptly sued them for breach of contract. Her next LP, *Just Being Myself* (1973), was produced by the former Motown production team of HOLLAND, DOZIER & HOLLAND; it was a commercial disaster. It was followed by a duet with The DETROIT SPINNERS, *Then Came You* (USA#1; UK#29.1974), produced by Thom BELL; this record proved to her countless detractors that when presented with good material her phrasing and timing were just as suitable for uptempo productions as for ballads. Her next LP, *Track of the Cat* (1976), was written and produced by Bell and his cowriter Linda Creed.

During the next three years she toured with Isaac HAYES, recording the double live LP, *A Man and a Woman*, which was composed of a number of duets, and then went on the lucrative night club circuit. In 1979 she was signed by Clive DAVIS to his Arista label. Her debut LP for Arista, *Dionne* (USA#12.1979), produced by Barry Manilow, included the singles, *I'll Never Love this Way Again* (USA#5.1979; UK#62.1983) and *Deja Vu* (USA#15.1980) and marked her return to the mainstream. Her public profile was consolidated still further by her appearance as host on the TV pop show *Solid Gold*. Another LP, *No Night so Long* (USA#23.1980), followed; the title track (USA#23.1980) was released as a single. The following year she recorded another double live LP, *Hot! Live and Otherwise*; one of the sides consisted of studio performances, mostly written and produced by Michael Masser. In 1982 the LP *Friends In Love* was released; it included a duet with Johnny Mathis. It was followed by collaborations with Barry Gibb of The Bee Gees, together with his regular team of Karl Richardson and Albhy Galuten. The resulting LP, *Heartbreaker* (USA#25; UK#3.1982), featured the singles *Heartbreaker* (USA#10.1983; UK#2.1982) and *All the Love in the World* (UK#10.1982).

Towards the end of 1983 she recorded a duet with producer Luther VANDROSS, *How Many Times Can we Say Goodbye* (USA #27.1983), which was included on the LP *So Amazing* (UK#60.1983). Since 1984 she has been collaborating with other artists: participation in the recording of the USA For Africa single in 1985, *We are the World* ; a single, *That's what Friends are For* (USA#1. 1986; UK#16.1985), which included additional vocals by Stevie WONDER, Gladys KNIGHT and Elton John, from the LP *Friends* (USA#12.1985); and the LP *Reservation for Two*, which contained duets with Smokey ROBINSON, Howard Hewett – formerly of SHALAMAR – and June Pointer of The POINTER SISTERS, from which the single, *Love Power* (USA#12; UK#67.1987), with Jeffrey OSBORNE, was taken. Despite her increasing pre-eminence as a cabaret performer, she has much potential yet to be realised. If the 1990 LP *Dionne Warwick sings Cole Porter* is anything to go by, this is a situation about which she is little concerned .

COLLECTION, Pickwick, 1976
DIONNE, Arista, 1979
NO NIGHT SO LONG, Arista, 1980
HOT! LIVE AND OTHERWISE, Arista, 1981
20 GOLDEN PIECES, Bulldog, 1982
FRIENDS IN LOVE, Arista, 1982
GOLDEN HITS, VOLUME 1, Phoenix, 1982
GOLDEN HITS, VOLUME 2, Phoenix, 1982

HEARTBREAKER, Arista, 1983
SO AMAZING, Arista, 1983
ANTHOLOGY: 1962–1971, Rhino, 1985
THIS GIRL'S IN LOVE, Cambra, 1985
WITHOUT YOUR LOVE, Arista, 1985
FRIENDS, Arista, 1985
DIONNE WARWICK CLASSICS, K-Tel, 1986
16 GOLDEN CLASSICS, Castle, 1986
20 GREATEST HITS, Bescol, 1987
RESERVATIONS FOR TWO, Arista, 1987
WALK ON BY AND OTHER FAVOURITES, Charly, 1989
DIONNE WARWICK SINGS COLE PORTER, Arista, 1990

WASHINGTON, Jr, GROVER The dual success of Marvin GAYE and Stevie WONDER at the end of the 1960s broke down many of the musical barriers that had existed between jazz and soul, forming a hybrid known as jazz-funk. The bi-products of this hybrid were a plethora of instrumentalists who had previously been confined to doing session work or playing in small groups on the club circuit and who now found that the compositional talents of Gaye and Wonder, among others, provided an endless source of material.

One of the most successful exponents of the genre was saxophonist Grover Washington. He was born in Buffalo on December 12, 1943; his father was a saxophonist. He joined his first group, The Four Clefs, in 1959. After moving to Philadelphia in the early 1960s he started to play in local clubs, where he came to the attention of organist Charles Earland, with whom he made his recording debut.

In 1971 he was signed by Creed Taylor to the Kudu label, which Taylor had established after his departure from Verve. Taylor built up a roster of artists including Hank Crawford, Freddie Hubbard and Esther PHILLIPS, each of whom contributed to one another's records, thus creating a real sense of urgency and unity. Washington made his debut with the LP *Inner City Blues* (1972). It was followed by *All the King's Horses* (1973). In 1975, the LP *Mister Magic* (USA#10.1975) provided the breakthrough; consolidation followed with *Feels so Good* (USA#10.1975) and *A Secret Place* (USA#31.1977). In 1977 he recorded a double LP entitled *Live at the Bijou* (USA #11.1977). In the following year Kudu, suffering from cashflow problems, was taken over by the label's distributors, Motown. Washington's first LP for Motown was *Reed Seed* (USA#35.1978).

In 1978 he signed also with Elektra, on the understanding that he would deliver alternate LPs for both labels. His debut for Elektra, *Paradise* (USA#24.1979), was followed by *Skylarkin'* (USA #24.1980) for Motown. In 1980 he recorded his most successful LP, *Winelight* (USA#5; UK#34.1981), featuring vocals by Bill WITHERS on the single *Just the Two of Us* (USA#2; UK#34.1981). With subsequent releases he continued to emulate the example set by The CRUSADERS by engaging guest vocalists like Patti LaBELLE and Jean Carne. In 1984, following the LPs *Come Morning* (USA#28.1982; UK#98.1981) and *The Best is yet to Come*, he released a live LP with the jazz group Weather Report. Recorded at and entitled *The Playboy Jazz Festival*, it wasn't as successful commercially as some of his previous efforts, but reperesented a pleasant departure from the anodyne sophistication of his later recordings.

In 1985 Bruce Lundvall, who masterminded the renaissance of the jazz label Blue Note, teamed him with guitarist Kenny Burrell, bassist Ron Carter and percussionist Jack DeJohnette for *Togethering*; this LP once again demonstrated his intention to be taken seriously as a jazz musician. However, since he signed with CBS in 1986, his LPs like *Strawberry Moon* (1987), *Then and Now* (1988) and *Time*

out of Mind (1989) have suffered from a lack of incisiveness and direction.

INNER CITY BLUES, Motown, 1972
ALL THE KING'S HORSES, Motown, 1973
MISTER MAGIC, Motown, 1975
FEELS SO GOOD, Motown, 1975
A SECRET PLACE, Motown, 1977
LIVE AT THE BIJOU, Motown, 1977
REED SEED, Motown, 1978
PARADISE, Elektra, 1979
SKYLARKIN', Motown, 1980
WINELIGHT, Elektra, 1980
BADDEST, Motown, 1981
COME MORNING, Elektra, 1981
ANTHOLOGY, Motown, 1982
THE BEST IS YET TO COME, Elektra, 1983
GREATEST PERFORMANCES, Motown, 1983
PLAYBOY JAZZ FESTIVAL, (with Weather Report), Elektra, 1984
INSIDE MOVES, Elektra, 1984
AT HIS BEST, Motown, 1985
TOGETHERING, (with Kenny Burrell, Ron Carter & Jack DeJohnette), Blue Note, 1985
STRAWBERRY MOON, CBS, 1987
THEN AND NOW, CBS, 1988
TIME OUT OF MIND, CBS, 1989

WATLEY, JODY Jody Watley was a dancer on the TV programme *Soul Train* before being recruited in 1978 by Dick Griffey to become a member of SHALAMAR. For the next six years, she was the key member of the group: when she and Jeffrey Daniel left in 1984, it broke up shortly afterwards. This indicates that, despite Shalamar's beginnings as a manufactured studio group, both Watley and Daniel were fundamental in establishing its identity – they were not just pretty faces that fitted the bill!

Watley was born in Chicago on January 30, 1959, and moved to Los Angeles in 1974. Her first solo LP, *Jody Watley* (USA#4;

UK#62.1987), was produced by Bernard EDWARDS and Andre CYMONE, among others and featured a number of singles including *Looking for a New Love* (USA#2; UK#13.1987) and *Don't You Want Me* (UK#55.1987). Her second LP, *Larger than Life* has been reasonably successful commercially despite, perhaps, placing an over reliance on her own abilities as a writer. Her producer, Cymone, of the later LP created a backdrop for her voice that made it sound like just another product of the Minneapolis Method; this method will pall if too many more female vocalists believe that sounding 'nasty" is the passport to superstardom.

JODY WATLEY, MCA, 1987
LARGER THAN LIFE, MCA, 1989
YOU WANNA DANCE WITH ME?, MCA, 1990

WATSON, JOHNNY 'GUITAR'
Johnny 'Guitar' Watson has, since 1952, been one of the more idiosyncratic performers to emerge from Texas. Echoes of his influence resound in the work of artists like Steve Miller and Joe Ely, but Watson himself has pursued a line enabling him to transcend fashion, even his mid-1970s ventures into disco territory demonstrated this quality.

He was born on February 3, 1935, in Houston, Texas. After moving to Los Angeles in 1950 he joined The Chuck Higgins Band as pianist, and came to the attention of Ralph BASS. He was signed to the Federal label as Young John Watson, recording *Highway 60* and *Space Guitar*. In 1955 he moved from Federal to Modern, where he was dubbed 'Guitar' Watson by Joe Bihari. Although major chart success eluded him, he built up a strong reputation with his performances on the club circuit, where he employed such novel techniques as playing the guitar with his teeth and using feed-back. After a stint wth the King label, he was signed to the CBS subsidiary Okeh by erstwhile producer Larry WILLIAMS. The two of them started to tour and record together, most notably adding lyrics to the Joe Zawinul composition *Mercy Mercy Mercy*. Although they couldn't compete with SAM & DAVE as a duo, their combined experience enabled them to provide a very entertaining live act, which was captured on record as *The Larry Williams Show* (1965) when they toured the UK.

In 1972 he was signed by Fantasy, cutting the LPs *Listen* (1973) and *I Don't Want to be Alone, Stranger* (1976); from the latter the single *I Don't Want to be a Lone Ranger* was extracted. After signing with the DJM label, he recorded the LP *Ain't That a Bitch?*, which included the single *I Need It* (UK#35.1976). This was followed by the single *A Real Mother for Ya* (UK#44.1977), from the LP (USA#20.1977) of the same name. Later LPs for DJM, like *Johnny and the Family Clone* failed to consolidate his streak of success and he signed to A & M, recording the LP *That's what Time it Is* (1982). Although it failed to sell, it showed that his ardour was undimmed and his imagination still just as active. In recent years, he has recorded less and less, playing the Los Angeles club circuit (principally) and cutting the odd LP like *Strike on Computers* for Polygram.

THE LARRY WILLIAMS SHOW, Edsel, 1965
AIN'T THAT A BITCH?, DJM, 1976
A REAL MOTHER FOR YA, DJM, 1977
FUNK BEYOND THE CALL OF DUTY, DJM, 1978
GIANT, DJM, 1979
WHAT THE HELL IS THIS?, DJM, 1979
LOVE JONES, DJM, 1980
JOHNNY AND THE FAMILY CLONE, DJM, 1981
THE VERY BEST OF JOHNNY "GUITAR" WATSON, DJM, 1981
THE GANGSTER IS BLACK, Red Lightnin', 1982
HIT THE HIGHWAY, Ace, 1983

STRIKE ON COMPUTERS, Polygram, 1987
THREE HOURS PAST MIDNIGHT, Ace, 1987

GREATEST HITS, Motown, 1964
MARY WELLS SINGS MY GUY, Motown, 1982
TWENTY TWO GREATEST HITS, Motown, 1987

WEIL, CYNTHIA   See MANN, Barry, & Cynthia Weil

WELLS, MARY   With Mary Wells, Berry GORDY created his first real star. She was born in Detroit on May 13, 1943. After being signed to Motown in 1959, she recorded a series of singles (most written and produced by Smokey ROBINSON) that came close to defining the parameters of the Motown Sound itself: *I Don't Want to Take a Chance* (USA#33.1961), *The One who Really Loves You* (USA#8.1962), *You Beat me to the Punch* (USA#9.1962), *Two Lovers* (USA#7.1962), *Laughing Boy* (USA#15.1963), *Your Old Stand By* (USA#40.1963), *You Lost the Sweetest Boy* (USA#22. 1963), *What's Easy for Two is so Hard for One* (USA#29.1964) and *My Guy* (USA#1; UK#5. 1964/#14.1972). After her success as a solo artist, she was teamed with Marvin GAYE for the LP *Together,* which featured the single *Once upon a Time* (USA#19; UK#50.1964).

At the peak of her popularity, her aspirations as an actress got the better of her. She left Motown and moved to Los Angeles. She was signed by Fox's record division, 20th Century, but her debut single, *Use your Head* (USA#34.1965), was only modestly successful. During the 1970s she was briefly married to Cecil Womack (later to achieve fame as half of WOMACK & WOMACK). She recorded for a succession of labels like Atlantic, Epic and Jubilee, but so far has been unable to arrest the seemingly inexorable decline of her career. In recent years, she has resumed recording, but with little success.

WENDY & LISA   The duo of Wendy & Lisa was formed when both were members of PRINCE's group The Revolution. Keyboardist Lisa Coleman, daughter of session musician Gary Coleman, joined The Revolution in 1980, and Wendy Melvoin, daughter of another session musician, Mike Melvoin, joined in 1983 as the replacement for guitarist Dez Dickerson. At first they merely wrote together, contributing, among others, *Mountains* (USA#23; UK#45.1986) to *Parade,* but in 1986 they embarked upon a career as a duo, being signed by Virgin. Their debut LP, *Wendy and Lisa* (UK#84.1987), included the minor hit *Waterfall* (UK#66.1987). It was followed in 1988 by *Side Show,* the title track of which was released as a single (UK#49.1988), and then *Fruit at the Bottom* (1989). In 1990 they released the LP *Eroica* (UK#32.1990).

WENDY AND LISA, Virgin, 1987
SIDE SHOW, Virgin, 1988
FRUIT AT THE BOTTOM, Virgin, 1989
EROICA, Virgin, 1990

WE THREE   See BANKS, Homer

WEXLER, JERRY   Ahmet ERTEGUN and Herb ABRAMSON set up Atlantic in 1947 to service an area of the market that was then being under exploited: black music. However, both of them were creative, and part of their creativity revolved around their ability to spot talent and to enlist the assistance of like-minded honchos like Tom DOWD and Arif MARDIN. When Abramson enlisted in the army, his replacement was Jerry Wexler (born in 1918, in New York City).

Wexler's background was in promotion and advertising. His arrival heralded a new era in Atlantic's short history. He was able to apply the skills of the marketplace to the company. With the assistance of Jesse STONE, he was able to play the field, choosing individual producers like LEIBER & STOLLER to come in and work with Atlantic's roster of acts. This particular skill paid dividends during the 1960s when he travelled the studios of the Deep South, teaming recent signings with whichever studio happened to be flavour of the month. Had it not been for his adaptability, SAM & DAVE might not have worked with Isaac HAYES and David PORTER at Stax, or Aretha FRANKLIN might not have recorded at Muscle Shoals. Thus, although his business acumen was as sharp as a razor, he also possessed the instincts of a record man through and through.

Among the productions he instigated were: *Soul on Fire* and *I Cried a Tear* by LaVern BAKER, *Just out of Reach (of my Two Open Arms)* by Solomon BURKE, *What'd I Say?* and *(Night Time is) the Right Time* by Ray CHARLES, *Sh-Boom* by The Chords, *One Mint Julep* and *Blue Velvet* by The CLOVERS, *Money Honey* by The DRIFTERS, *I Never Loved a Man (the Way I Love You), Do Right Woman – Do Right Man, Respect, Baby I Love You, A Natural Woman, Chain of Fools, Think, (Sweet Sweet Baby) Since You've been Gone, The House that Jack Built, Don't Play that Song, Rock Steady* and *Brand New Me* by Aretha Franklin, *Since I Met you Baby* by Ivory Joe HUNTER, *Don't Play that Song (You Lied)* by Ben E. KING, *A Lover's Question* and *Without Love (There is Nothing)* by Clyde McPHATTER, *In the Midnight Hour, Land of a 1,000 Dances* and *Funky Broadway* by Wilson PICKETT and *Shake, Rattle and Roll* by Big Joe Turner. Quite apart from his writing and production work, he was instrumental in licensing labels like Stax, Dial and Alston to Atlantic, which resulted in hits for artists like Joe TEX, Betty WRIGHT and Otis REDDING.

By the end of the 1960s, having provided Barry BECKETT, Roger HAWKINS, David HOOD and Jimmy JOHNSON with a loan to set up the Muscle Shoals Sound studios at 3614, Jackson Highway, he instigated the purchase of Criteria studios in Miami – now known as Atlantic South – and became less involved in the overall running of the label, preferring to remain in the background. Like Ertegun, he has assumed an almost mythical status within the international music industry.

WHEELER, CARON Caron Wheeler shot to prominence in 1989 as lead singer of SOUL II SOUL, having sung as a session vocalist since 1979. Such was the success of their first LP *Club Classics, Volume 1*, that she was signed by RCA as a solo artist. Her debut LP *UK Blak* showed that she has the ability to perpetuate what she started with Soul II Soul.

UK BLAK, RCA, 1990

WHISPERS The Whispers were formed in Los Angeles in 1964 by Walter and Wallace Scott, Gordy Harmon, Marcus Hutson and Nicholas Caldwell. They started to record in 1964 for the Dore label, although, they failed to achieve any great degree of success until 1979, when they were signed to Dick Griffey's Solar label. For the first fifteen years they had recorded for a succession of labels and built up their reputation on the club circuit. In 1973 Harmon had left the group, to be replaced by Leavil Degree; in 1977, following an appearance on the TV series *Soul Train*, they had been signed by the show's producer, Griffey, to the Soul Train label.

When Griffey left to set up Solar he took The Whispers with him, and they finally broke through into the mainstream with a number of hit singles: *And the Beat Goes On* (USA#19; UK#2.1980/#45.1987), *Lady* (USA#28; UK#55.1980), *My Girl* (UK#26.1980), *It's a Love Thing* (USA#28; UK#9.1981), *I Can Make it Better* (UK#44.1981), *Contagious* (UK#56.1985), *Rock Steady* (UK#38.1987) and *Special F/X* (UK#69.1987). The success of the singles was matched by an increased interest in the LPs, enabling them to establish themselves as one of the most consistent vocal groups of the mid-1980s: *The Whispers* (USA#6.1980), *Imagination* (USA#23; UK#42.1981), *Love is where you Find It* (USA#35.1982), *Love for Love* (USA #37.1983) and *Just Gets Better with Time* (UK#63.1987). In 1990 they moved from Solar to Capitol, where their debut LP, *More of the Night*, attempted in places to update their sound. Their past track record and their slick live act has guaranteed them a loyal following on the club and cabaret circuit in the USA and Europe.

THIS KIND OF LOVIN', Solar, 1981
THE BEST OF THE WHISPERS, Solar, 1982
SO GOOD, MCA, 1985
JUST GETS BETTER WITH TIME, MCA, 1987
MORE OF THE NIGHT, Capitol, 1990

WHITE, BARRY The considerable girth of Barry White loomed into prominence in the early 1970s with a series of hits that slotted neatly into the transitional stage between the lush, overstated arrangements of Isaac HAYES and the emergence of disco. His propensity for extolling the virtues of his nimble prowess in the bedroom was exceeded only by his ability to churn out singles in the manageable three- to four-minute format, in contrast to Hayes' seeming inability to make a statement in less than fifteen minutes. So, despite nicknames like 'the Walrus of Love', 'the Lurve Man' and 'the Sultan of Bedroom Soul', he established a genre that would crystallise with the emergence of a whole breed of artists like Alexander O'NEAL, Freddie JACKSON, Luther VANDROSS, Teddy PENDER-GRASS and Peabo BRYSON. What has set him apart has been the fact that, whether as a producer, musician or performer, he is a record man primarily.

He was born in Galveston, Texas, on September 12, 1944, but moved out to Los Angeles as a child. Throughout his childhood he was something of a rogue, getting into scrapes with the authorities – although he also sang in the church choir and taught himself to play a variety of instruments. After spending four months in a penal institution (for tyre theft), he changed tack by joining a local R&B group, The Upfronts. Despite their lack of success, he secured session work for small independent labels like Ebb, Class and Rampart. Among his earliest claims to fame was that he provided the arrangements for *Harlem Shuffle* by BOB & EARL and *The Duck* by Jackie Lee. In 1967, he secured a position in A&R with the Mustang label, where he discovered Felice Taylor and LOVE UNLIMITED. By 1972 he had become the producer and manager of Love Unlimited whom he had signed to the Uni label. Having set up his own production company, he secured a deal with 20th Century records for himself and the group.

In 1973 he released his first record under his own name, *I'm Gonna Give You Just a Little Bit More* (USA#3; UK#23.1973). A succession of hits followed over the next five years. Written and produced by White himself, they often had arrangements by Gene PAGE: *I've Got so Much to Give* (USA#32.1973), *Never, Never*

Gonna Give Ya Up (USA#7.1973; UK #14.1974), *Can't Get Enough of Your Love, Babe* (USA#1; UK#8.1974), *You're the First, the Last, My Everything* (USA#2; UK#1.1974), *What am I Gonna do with You* (USA#8; UK #5.1975), *I'll do for You Anything You Want me To* (USA#40; UK#20.1975), *Let the Music Play* (USA#32.1976; UK#9. 1975), *You See the Trouble with Me* (UK#2.1976), *Baby We Better Try to Get it Together* (UK#15.1976), *Don't Make Me Wait too Long* (UK#17.1976), *I'm Qualified to Satisfy* (UK#37.1977), *It's Ecstasy when You Lay Down next to Me* (USA#4; UK #40.1977), *Oh What a Night for Dancing* (USA #24.1978), *Just the Way you Are* (UK#12.1978) and *Sha La La Means I Love You* (UK #55.1979). His LPs featured extended versions of the singles: *I've Got so Much to Give* (USA #16.1973), *Stone Gon'* (USA#20.1974), *Can't Get Enough* (USA#1; UK#4.1974), *Just Another Way to Say I Love You* (USA#17; UK #12.1975), *Let the Music Play* (UK#22.1976), *Barry White Sings for Someone You Love* (USA #8.1977) and *Barry White the Man* (USA #36.1978; UK #46.1979).

In 1979 he set up his own record label, Unlimited Gold, distributed by CBS, but this ultimately, failed to consolidate his previous achievements, although his stature as a performer ensured that he was able to tour on the lucrative cabaret circuit. In 1987 he signed with A&M, installing a new recording studio at his home in Sherman Oaks, California, and assembling a new backing group. Despite his new contemporary stripped-down sound he has not been able to achieve the same degree of success as in former years. One exception has been the single *Sho' You Right* (UK#14. 1987), from the LP *The Right Night and Barry White* (UK #74.1987). This was followed in 1989 by the LP *The Man is Back*.

GREATEST HITS, 20th Century, 1975
THE MESSAGE IS LOVE, Unlimited Gold, 1979

BARRY WHITE'S SHEET MUSIC, Unlimited Gold, 1980
DEDICATED, Unlimited Gold, 1983
HEART AND SOUL, K-Tel, 1985
THE RIGHT NIGHT AND BARRY WHITE, Breakout, 1987
THE COLLECTION, Mercury, 1988
THE MAN IS BACK, A&M, 1989

WHITE, KARYN Karyn White was born in Los Angeles and throughout her childhood she sang in the local church where her mother was choirmistress. She graduated to appearing in talent contests, in one of which she was spotted and recruited for the group Legacy in 1984. In 1986 she was enlisted for his LP *Private Passion* by keyboardist Jeff Lorber to provide the vocal parts for the track *Facts Of Love*, which was a big dance-floor hit as a single. A duet with the former Tower of Power vocalist Michael Jeffreys, *Black and White*, from the same LP was equally successful. Over the next two years she was one of the most sought-after session vocalists in the business, working with Ray PARKER, Julio Iglesias and The COMMODORES. In 1987 she secured a solo contract with Warner Bros. Her eponymously titled debut LP, was produced by LA & BABYFACE, and failed to set the charts alight, but the extracted single, *The Way you Love Me*, performed very creditably.

KARYN WHITE, Warner Bros., 1988

WHITE, MAURICE See EARTH, WIND & FIRE

WHITFIELD, NORMAN Norman Whitfield's contribution to Motown was twofold. First, in partnership with Barrett STRONG he wrote songs like *I Heard it*

Through the Grapevine, War and *Cloud Nine*. Lyrically these represented a departure for Motown from the tales of teenage *angst* that had inspired most of the company's other writers, establishing a precedent for occasionally writing songs whose lyrics were overtly critical of the conditions in which black Americans were expected to live. Second, as a producer, he made LPs that weren't the standard hodge-podge collection of recent singles strung together and padded out with filler tracks, but were by contrast well constructed musical statements, with individual tracks lasting as long as nine or ten minutes. Despite the fact that some of these statements may now sound a trifle overblown, this practice opened the door for other Motown artists like Marvin GAYE and Stevie WONDER (as well as Isaac HAYES at Stax) to get away from the standard two- or three-minute single format and construct their records around what they wanted to say, in musical terms, as opposed to having to adhere to a marketable length. This factor was crucial to the development of Motown as a company that could market LPs, as well as singles. In the longer term, it contributed to the development of the twelve-inch single.

Whitfield was born in 1943 in New York. He was employed by the Thelma label before joining Motown as a writer in 1962. After working with The MARVELETTES, among others, he formed a songwritng partnership with Strong in 1967. They struck gold immediately with *I Heard it Through the Grapevine* for Gladys KNIGHT & The Pips, which was later covered by Marvin Gaye. When HOLLAND, DOZIER & HOLLAND left Motown, Whitfield and Strong became Motown's principal production team. Throughout the late 1960s and early 1970s, Whitfield and Strong produced a succession of hits for The TEMPTATIONS, Gaye and Edwin STARR.

In 1976 he left Motown to set up his own label, Whitfield, with The UNDISPUTED TRUTH. However, that group's touring band, ROSE ROYCE, with vocalist Gwen Dickey, proved to be the label's main asset, with a succession of hits including *Love don't Live here Anymore*. In 1981, he sold the label off and retired from the music business. In 1988, as if to emphasize the esteem in which Whitfield was held by younger musicians and producers, the group S-Express lifted the opening riff of the Rose Royce hit, *Is it Love you're After?* for their first single *Theme from S-Express*; this became one of the biggest dance-floor fillers of the year, as well as topping the charts in the UK.

WILLIAMS, DENIECE Deniece Chandler was born in Gary, Indiana, on June 3, 1951. As a child she sang in the choir at church. In 1967, after meeting a rep from a local record label, Toddlin' Town, she released a series of singles. In 1971 these records brought her to the attention of Stevie WONDER who auditioned her for his backing group, Wonderlove. She remained with Wonderlove until 1975, contributing backing vocals to some of Wonder's most influential LPs.

In 1975 she signed to CBS as a result of the intervention of Maurice White (see EARTH, WIND & FIRE) , who produced her first LP, *This is Niecy* (USA#33.1976; UK#31.1977); it included the singles, *Free* (USA#25.1976; UK#1.1977) and *That's what Friends are For* (UK#8.1977). Her second LP, *Songbird*, couldn't match the success of its predecessor. In 1978 she teamed up with Johnny Mathis for the single, *Too Much, Too Little, Too Late* (USA#1; UK#3.1978). An LP together, *That's what Friends are For* (USA#19; UK#16.1978), followed. In 1979 White signed her to his ARC label, for whom her first LP was *When Love Comes Calling*, produced by Ray PARKER. It was followed by *My Melody* and *Niecy* (USA

#20.1982), both written and produced by Thom BELL, the latter featured the single, *It's Gonna Take a Miracle* (USA#10. 1982).

In 1983 she returned to CBS and released the LP *I'm So Proud*. After another duet with Johnny Mathis she recorded *Let's Hear it for the Boy* (USA#1; UK#2.1984), which was featured on the soundtrack of the film *Footloose*. Since 1984, she has continued releasing LPs at regular intervals, including a gospel LP, *So Glad I Know*. For the most part these records have suffered from a paucity of good material – a problem that did not affect her gospel record, on which she sounded a lot more confident than in her pop- oriented outings.

THIS IS NIECY, CBS, 1977

THAT'S WHAT FRIENDS ARE FOR, (with Johnny Mathis), CBS, 1978

I'M SO PROUD, CBS, 1983

HOT ON THE TRAIL, CBS, 1986

SO GLAD I KNOW, Bird, 1986

WATER UNDER THE BRIDGE, CBS, 1987

AS GOOD AS IT GETS, CBS, 1988

WILLIAMS, LARRY At one point in his career Larry Williams was seen as the pretender to LITTLE RICHARD's throne. However, this phase was very short-lived, and was due more to the efforts of producer Bumps BLACKWELL and the J&M Studios house band, all of whom worked on Little Richard's records, than to any inherent quality of Williams'. And whereas Little Richard became a minister of the church, Williams flourished as a pimp and a dealer until, on January 2, 1980, being found shot dead in his Cadillac in the garage of his house in Laurel Canyon, California.

He was born in New Orleans on May 10, 1935. After moving to San Francisco in 1953 he formed The Lemon Drops as well as playing sessions with Percy MAYFIELD and Lloyd PRICE. By 1955 he had returned to New Orleans with Price and signed with Art RUPE's Specialty label, where he notched up a string of hits including *Short Fat Fannie* (USA#5; UK#21.1957), *Bony Moronie* (USA #14. 1957; UK#11.1958), *Slow Down* and *Dizzy Miss Lizzy*. In 1959 he was busted for possession of drugs, with the result that he disappeared from public view for a time.

He returned in 1964 and teamed up with Johnny 'Guitar' WATSON; together they toured the UK in a revue called The Larry Williams Show, which was recorded by Mike Vernon for release as an LP. On his return to the USA, he got work with the Okeh label as a producer, where he recorded some tracks with Little Richard and also formed a duo with Watson in 1967, cutting *Mercy Mercy Mercy*, an instrumental to which he and Watson added lyrics. However, he returned to the lowlife, where, according to critic Dave Marsh, he was very successful. In 1978 he recorded a comeback LP for Fantasy entitled *That Larry Williams*.

THE LARRY WILLIAMS SHOW, (with Johnny 'Guitar' Watson), Edsel, 1965

ALACAZAM, Ace, 1987

BAD BOY, Ace, 1990

WILLIAMS, MAURICE, & THE ZODIACS The career of Maurice Williams and his group, The Zodiacs (Willie Bennett, Henry Gaston and Charles Thomas) has been built on the success of just one record, *Stay*, which despite – or, perhaps, because of – the very basicness of its mix remains one of the finest examples of the vocal group genre.

Williams was born in Lancaster, North Carolina, on April 26, 1938. He formed his first group, The Charms, in 1955, changed their name to The Gladiolas (so as to avoid confusion with Otis WILLIAMS' group of the same name) and signed to the Excello label; they had a minor hit with the Williams composition, *Little Darlin'*, but it was covered by The Diamonds, whose version became one of the classic records of the era. After changing their name to The Royal Charms and then, even more prosaically, to The Excellos, they moved to New York, signed with the Herald label and became The Zodiacs.

As Maurice Williams & The Zodiacs they released another Williams composition, *Stay* (USA#1. 1960; UK#14. 1961), whose falsetto vocal part is guaranteed to send a shiver up the sturdiest spine. However, subsequent records like *May I?* failed to consolidate their success, and they disbanded in 1963. Williams made an abortive attempt to go solo. When the oldies circuit picked up momentum in the late 1960s he re-formed the group for touring purposes.

THE BEST OF MAURICE WILLIAMS AND THE ZODIACS, Herald, 1979

WILLIAMS, OTIS   There has been a tendency to understate this considerable influence of country music on the development of soul. One of the more overt exponents of country-soul was Otis Williams. Raised in Cincinnati, he formed The Charms in 1953. The group were signed by Henry GLOVER to the De-Luxe label, a subsidiary of King, where it had hits with *Hearts of Stone* (USA #15.1954), *Ling, Ting, Tong* (USA#26.1955) and *Ivory Tower* (USA#11.1956). Despite these hits, Williams was much more committed to country music, although neither Syd NATHAN nor Glover would allow him to follow his instincts. In 1960, having left The Charms, he formed The Midnight Cowboys and, after some solo sides for Epic, he recorded for the independent labels, Power Pak and Stop. With steel guitarist Pete Drake producing, he recorded songs by Tom T. Hall, Marty Robbins and Jimmie Rodgers, among others, before disappearing into obscurity.

WILLIS, CHUCK   Chuck Willis was born in Atlanta, Georgia on January 31, 1928. He made his debut in a talent show hosted by his future manager, DJ Zenas Sears. In 1946 he became a vocalist in Ron Mays' Band and then Red McAllister's; this background as a big-band vocalist was to prove pivotal to his development, as it enabled him to adapt his style to almost any type of arrangement. After signing with the Okeh label in 1951, his versatility became clear when he had his first hit with the ballad *My Story* (1952); it was backed by his version of the Louis Jordan hit *Caldonia*. Over the next five years he had a string of R&B hits including *Going to the River* (1953), *Change my Mind* and *I Feel so Bad* (1954).

In 1956 he was signed to Atlantic, where he was teamed with arranger Jesse STONE, Sears being credited with the production. His first hit for Atlantic was a rearranged version of the blues standard *C.C.Rider* (USA#12.1957). Dick Clark picked it up and used it to promote a new dance called 'the Stroll' on his TV show *American Bandstand*. Willis was immediately dubbed 'King of the Stroll', as well as the 'Sheikh of Rock 'n' Roll'. The follow-up, *Betty and Dupree* (USA#33 1958), was less successful, but the double A-side, *What am I Living for?* (USA#9.1958) and *Hang up my Rock 'n' Roll Shoes* (USA#24.1958), was a superlative combination of blues, soul and rock'n'roll: the former track, being a soulful epic, was given greater poignancy by his death before it hit the charts; the latter, charting in the wake of his death, set out as a paean to teenage insurrection but, with hindsight, it was perhaps an intimation of mortality.

His death on April 10, 1958, in Atlanta was the result of bleeding stomach ulcers, possibly brought on by a car accident which caused internal bleeding. Whatever the root cause, he refused to be operated upon until it was too late. In recent years, his reputation as a writer has grown through the appearance of cover versions of his compositions by artists like The Band and Wilbert HARRISON. His own records, sadly, remain neglected.

WILSON, JACKIE   While the 1950s were a decade of change and discovery, they were also a time when, because rock'n'roll was in its infancy, the music business was still populated by producers and arrangers who just could not get to grips with the changing criteria. As a result, the talents of a vast number of artists were wasted. Jackie Wilson was one of the great lost heroes of soul. So often his talent was squandered upon schlock material and his voice submerged beneath treacly arrangements.

Thus in 1967, after years of semi-obscurity, he was given *Higher and Higher* to record. The result was a piece of genius: his mellifluous phrasing demonstrated what an articulate performer he was and that given appropriate material he was a match for soul's most revered artists. A collaboration with Count Basie followed – nothing intrinsically wrong with that, of course, but it showed just how far the powers-that-be were missing the point: the man who had proven that he was the personification of soul was having to record songs like the standard *For Once in my Life,* complete with full orchestral accompaniment, when he should have been being packed off to Memphis or Muscle Shoals. His career consequently foundered yet again and with only the odd hit to sustain him, he was reduced to playing the oldies circuit. In 1975 he collapsed on stage, hitting his head and went him into a coma from which he never properly recovered. He remained under care until January 21, 1984,

when he finally died, aged 49. Despite the number of benefits played on his behalf, he was buried in a pauper's grave.

He was born Jack Leroy Wilson on June 9, 1934, in Detroit, Michigan. While at school he seemed to be heading for a boxing career, winning the American Amateur Golden Gloves Welterweight Title, but his mother dissuaded him, advising him to concentrate upon singing career instead. He sang with The Ever Ready Gospel Singers before joining the vocal group The Thrillers, which included Hank BALLARD. In 1951 he was spotted at a talent contest by Johnny OTIS, who recommended him to Billy WARD, who enlisted him as a backing vocalist in The Dominoes, and two years later made him lead vocalist when Clyde McPHATTER was fired. Wilson remained with Ward for three years, recording for Syd NATHAN's King label. In many ways his years with Ward were a harbinger of his later career: the only big hit the group had during his tenure was a peculiarly inappropriate reworking of *St Therese of the Roses.*

In 1957 he left The Dominoes to start a solo career at the behest of his future manager, Al Green; he was signed to the Decca subsidiary Brunswick. His solo debut, *Reet Petite* (UK #6.1957/#1.1986), was written by Berry GORDY and Wilson's cousin Billy Davis, under the pseudonym of Tyran Carlo. It was the first of a number of hits penned by that songwriting team: *To be Loved* (USA#22; UK #23.1958), *Lonely Teardrops* (USA#7.1958), *That's Why (I Love You So)* (USA#13.1959) and *I'll be Satisfied* (USA#20.1959). When Gordy started to put Motown together, he stopped writing for Wilson. The death of Green meant a change of management, too, with Nat Tarnopol, Green's former assistant, taking over. Throughout the early 1960s Tarnopol guided Wilson's career towards the glitz of Vegas and Hollywood. The results were extraordinary (and heart-breaking): adaptations from classical pieces like *Night* (USA #4.1960, from *My Heart at thy Sweet Voice* from *Samson and Delilah* by Saint-Saens), *Alone at Last* (USA#8; UK#50.1960, from the *Piano Concerto #1 in B flat* by Tchaikovsky) and *My Empty Arms* (USA#9.1961, from *On with the Motley* from *Il Pagliacci* by Leoncavallo), as well as *(You Were Made for) All My Love* (USA#12.1960), *Please Tell Me Why* (USA#20.1961), *I'm Comin' on Back to You* (USA#19.1961), *Years From Now* (USA #37.1961) and *The Greatest Hurt* (USA #34.1961). Despite some of these extraordinary aberrations he still managed to leaven the dross with some real stormers like *Doggin' Around* (USA#15.1960) and *Baby Workout* (USA #5.1963). His stature as a performer was matched only by his profile as a sex symbol: the latter caused him to be shot in the stomach by a rampant fan, Juanita Jones, while he was trying to disarm her after she had broken into his New York apartment.

From 1963, apart from a duet with LaVern BAKER, he continued to record very ordinary material until being teamed in 1966 with writer/producer Carl Davis, for *Whispers* (USA#11.1966), it showed what could be done when he had halfway decent material.Two more aberrations followed before he recorded *(Your Love Keeps Lifting me) Higher and Higher* (USA#6.1967; UK#11.1969/#25.1975/ #15.1987). The following year, with Count Basie, he recorded the LP, *Manufacturers of Soul*, which included versions of *For Your Precious Love* and *Chain Gang*. His next hit, *I Get the Sweetest Feeling* (USA#34.1968; UK#9.1972/ #25.1975/#3.1987), was co-written by arranger Van McCOY and apart from the odd minor hit was his final notable success. In 1986, his first single *Reet Petite* was reissued in the UK, becoming the Christmas #1 and selling over 700,000 copies. The follow-up, *I Get the Sweetest Feeling*, climbed to #3 the following year.

THE SOUL YEARS, Kent, 1985
REET PETITE, Ace, 1985
HIGHER AND HIGHER, Kent, 1986
THE SOUL YEARS, VOLUME 2, Kent, 1986
THE VERY BEST OF JACKIE WILSON, Ace, 1987

WILSON, RONNIE   See GAP BAND

WINANS   The Winans are four brothers: Calvin, Marvin, Michael and Ronald. Initially they were a gospel group, but in 1982, they signed with the Light label, recording two LPs, *The Winans* (1982) and *Tomorrow* (1984), both of which were critically lauded. In 1984 they were signed to Quincy JONES' label, Qwest, for whom their first LP was *Let my People Go* (1985), it was followed in 1987 by *Decisions*, which featured duets with Anita BAKER and Michael MacDonald. The same year they collaborated with Michael JACKSON on the track *Man in the Mirror* from his LP *Bad*. In 1990 they released the LP, *Return*, which was produced in part by Teddy RILEY and Michael J. Powell. Ever since their inception, they have remained true to their gospel roots. The group has gradually accumulated a committed following.

THE WINANS, Light, 1982
TOMORROW, Light, 1984
LET MY PEOPLE GO, Qwest, 1985
DECISIONS, Qwest, 1987
RETURN, Qwest, 1990

WITHERS, BILL   Bill Withers was born in Slab Fork, West Virginia, on July 4, 1938. After leaving school he enlisted in the US Navy, in which he remained for nine years. On leaving he did a variety of jobs, working at Ford, IBM and after moving to California, Lockheed. Once on the West Coast he started to pool his resources to make demos of some of the songs he had written in his spare time. In 1970, he met Booker T. Jones (see BOOKER T & THE MGs), who had got a job as a staff producer at A&M after leaving Stax in 1969. Booker T was sufficiently impressed by the quality of his material to get him a deal with the Sussex label.

His debut LP, *Just I Am* (USA#39.1971), included *Ain't no Sunshine* (USA#3.1971), which was later covered by Michael JACKSON. His wistful vocal style owed more to the blues than to soul and seemed to complement the contemporary popularity of writers like Joni Mitchell, Carole King (see GOFFIN & KING) and James Taylor. His follow-up, *Still Bill* (USA#4.1972), was self-produced and contained *Lean on Me* (USA#1; UK#18.1972), *Use Me* (USA#2.1972) and *Kissing my Love* (USA#31.1973). The full intimacy of his style was demonstrated to particularly good effect on the double live LP, recorded at the Carnegie Hall; despite having had only moderate success it remains one of the better examples of his work, illustrating his versatility within a range of styles. In 1974 he released the LP *'Justments* which, apart from a compilation LP, was his final effort for Sussex (subsequently the label went out of business). The lack of success of *'Justments* was due more to the gradual falling out of favour of the whole singer/ songwriter category, in which he had always been loosely bracketed.

After the demise of Sussex he was signed by CBS. His first two LPs for the label, *Making Music* (1975) and *Naked and Warm* (1976), were both lost in the disco euphoria. His next LP, *Menagerie* (USA#39; UK#27.1978), contained the single *Lovely Day* (USA#30; UK#7.1977/#4.1988); the loose languid airiness of the song evoked all the feelings of summer in much the same way as had *Just my Imagination* by The TEMPTATIONS in 1971. Over the next couple of years his solo recording

career was relatively quiet, but he was a featured vocalist on the track *Soul Shadows* from The CRUSADERS' LP, *Rhapsody and Blue* in 1980; the following year he fulfilled the same function on *Just the Two of Us* (USA#2; UK#34.1981) from the Grover WASHINGTON LP *Winelight*, and in 1984, he was guest vocalist on *In the Name of Love* from the Ralph McDonald LP *Universal Rhythm*. The following year, he returned to recording in his own right with the LP *Watching You, Watching Me* (UK#60.1985). In 1988 *Lovely Day* was remixed by the DJ Ben Leibrand and became a hit all over again in the UK.

MENAGERIE, CBS, 1978
GREATEST HITS, CBS, 1981
WATCHING YOU, WATCHING ME, CBS, 1985

WOMACK, BOBBY Bobby Womack has for almost three decades been at the core of the development of soul, from his earliest associations with Sam COOKE right up to the present day, with a succession of LPs during the 1980s which, despite occasional lapses, seem to possess the one vital ingredient of soul: emotion.

He was born in Cleveland, Ohio, on March 5, 1944. In 1959, with his brothers Cecil, Curtis, Harris and Friendly, he formed The Womack Brothers and started to tour on the gospel circuit, where he met Sam Cooke, who recruited him as a guitarist in his touring band. (Cecil and Cooke's daughter Linda would later become WOMACK & WOMACK). When Cooke and J. W. ALEXANDER set up the Sar label, among their first signings were The Valentinos, as The Womack Brothers had become; they released three singles, *Lookin' for a Love*, *I'll Make it Alright* and *It's all over Now*, but their career was interrupted by the death of Cooke, which prompted Alexander to wind up the Sar label.

In 1965, having signed to first Chess and then Atlantic, the group began to break up as Bobby started to work as a session guitarist at Chips MOMAN's American studios and then at Fame in Muscle Shoals, where he worked with artists like Wilson PICKETT, KING CURTIS, Aretha FRANKLIN, Ray CHARLES, Dusty Springfield and The Box Tops.

In 1968 he was signed to the Liberty subsidiary Minit, where, despite his evident ability as a songwriter – he had written titles like *It's all over Now* for The Valentinos and *I'm a Midnight Mover* for Wilson Pickett – he covered titles like *Fly me to the Moon* and *California Dreamin'*, The Mamas & The Papas hit. In 1971, after the assimilation of Liberty into United Artists, he scored his first major hit with *That's the Way I Feel about 'Cha* (USA#27.1972) from the LP *Communication*. It was followed by *Woman's Gotta Have It*, a cover of the Neil Diamond song *Sweet Caroline* and *Harry Hippie* (USA#31.1972). The next year he wrote the score for the Anthony Quinn film *Across 110th Street*, and recorded the first of a number of LPs at Muscle Shoals Sound studios, *Facts of Life* (USA#37.1973), which included *Nobody Wants you When you're Down and Out* (USA#29.1973). The title song (USA#10.1974) of the next LP, *Lookin' for a Love*, provided him with his biggest hit single. *I Don't Know what the World is Coming to* was released the following year. In 1976 he released *Safety Zone* and the country LP *B.W. Goes C & W*; the latter was his final LP for United Artists who dropped him. The same year he signed with CBS, releasing *Home Is Where The Heart Is,* which was his final LP at Muscle Shoals. In 1978 he released the LP *Pieces*. However, both LPs failed to sell and, what with the murder of his brother Harry, to whom the song *Harry Hippie* had been dedicated, he stopped recording for a couple of years.

In 1980 he was approached by Wilton FELDER to provide the vocals for Felder's LP *Inherit the Wind*. The title track (UK#39.1980) gave him his first hit in the UK. The association with Felder had a galvanising effect upon his career. He signed with Otis Smith's Beverly Glen label, and the ensuing LP, *The Poet* (USA#29.1981), was one of the great soul LPs of the 1980s. However, he had to sue Smith to get royalties, and for the next two years he was locked in a bitter legal dispute over contractual obligations. The follow-up, *The Poet II,* was released by Motown; it included a duet with Patti LaBELLE and the single *Tell Me Why* (UK#60.1984). After organizing a benefit tour for his old friend Sly Stone (see SLY & THE FAMILY STONE) he was recruited once again by Felder for his LP *Secrets*, which featured a duet between Womack and Altrina Grayson,*(No Matter How High I Get) I'll Still be Looking Up to You*. He was then signed by MCA; his first LP for them *So Many Rivers* (UK#28.1985), featured the single *I Wish He Didn't Trust me so Much* (UK#64.1985). In 1986 he returned to Memphis to record the LP *Womagic*, with Chips Moman and all the rest of his former cohorts from the American studios, including Reggie Young. Although repackaged as *The Last Soul Man,* the LP failed to attract much attention in either format.

THE WOMACK LIVE!, Charly, 1971

COMMUNICATION, Charly, 1972

UNDERSTANDING, Charly, 1972

THE FACTS OF LIFE, Charly, 1973

LOOKING FOR A LOVE AGAIN, Edsel, 1974

I DON'T KNOW WHAT THE WORLD IS COMING TO, Charly, 1975

SAFETY ZONE, Charly, 1976

B.W GOES C.W, Charly, 1976

HOME IS WHERE THE HEART IS, Edsel, 1976

THE POET, Motown, 1981

THE POET II, Motown, 1984

BOBBY WOMACK AND THE VALENTINOS, Chess, 1984

SOMEBODY SPECIAL, Liberty, 1984

SO MANY RIVERS, MCA,1985,
THE PREACHER, Stateside, 1986
THE LAST SOUL MAN, MCA, 1987
WOMACK WINNERS, Charly, 1988
WOMACK IN MEMPHIS, Charly, 1990
THE MIDNIGHT MOVER, Charly, 1990

WOMACK & WOMACK Cecil and Linda Womack got their first recording contract as a duo with Elektra in 1983, by which time neither of them were exactly strangers to recording. Cecil's career had started in 1959 when, with his brothers Curtis, Friendly, Harry and Bobby WOMACK, he had formed The Womack Brothers. After meeting up with Sam COOKE, while touring on the gospel circuit, they were signed to his fledgling label, Sar, as The Valentinos. Cooke's subsequent death left them without a recording contract. Although signed by Chess, the group broke up as Bobby's solo career picked up momentum. After marrying and divorcing Mary WELLS, Cecil married Linda Cooke, Sam's daughter, and started to play on sessions and to write.

Their first LP together, *Love Wars* (UK#45.1984), was an immediate success; it contained the singles *Love Wars* (UK#14.1984) and *Baby I'm Scared of You* (UK#72.1984), and was produced by Stewart Levine. The follow-up, *Radio M.U.S.C. Man* (UK#56.1985), lacked the immediacy of their debut. They changed labels, moving to EMI'S Manhattan label for the LP, *Star Bright*, which included the single *Soul Love/Soul Man* (UK#58.1986) but once again seemed a bit lack-lustre. The following year they were signed by Island Records supremo Chris Blackwell to the subsidiary, 4th & Broadway. Blackwell took over the production chores and was musical director of the ensuing LP, *Conscience*, which included the singles *Teardrops* (UK#3.1988) and *Life's just a*

Ballgame (UK#32.1988). In 1990 they changed labels once more and signed with Arista, recording the LP *Family Spirit*.

Although their LPs and singles have been successful, it seems that the couple's apparent personal happiness and the cosiness of family life has knocked the stuffing out of their music: the endless philosophising becomes a mite wearing after a while.

WOMACK & WOMACK, Elektra, 1983
RADIO M.U.S.C. MAN, Elektra, 1985
STAR BRIGHT, Manhattan, 1987
CONSCIENCE, 4th & Broadway, 1988
FAMILY SPIRIT, Arista, 1991

WONDER, STEVIE One of the biggest problems in writing about any field of popular music is the frequency with which terms like 'major artist' are bandied around. In some cases the terms are warranted within the broader view of contemporary music as a whole; in other cases they constitute a personal view. With Stevie Wonder such terms are irrelevant, because irrespective of personal musical taste, his impact upon contemporary music is as inescapable as it is considerable. There are few performers whose instinctive understanding of music has had as far-reaching consequences, not just because of the degree of his commercial success, but also because he has been of his ground-breaking musical techniques. His ability to harness the most up-to-date technology within the context of the popular song has often been overshadowed by the outpourings of those who have used that same technology for its own sake alone. With Wonder, by contrast, his musicianship has enabled him to maximise its potential rather than be enslaved by it.

Steveland Morris Judkins was born on May 13, 1950, in Saginaw, Michigan. After singing in the church choir he was introduced to Berry

GORDY and Brian Holland (see HOLLAND, DOZIER & HOLLAND) by Ronnie White of The Miracles (see ROBINSON, Smokey, & The Miracles) in 1960. He was signed immediately and for the next two years he was groomed for stardom. His first single, credited to Little Stevie Wonder, was entitled *I Call it Pretty Music (but the Old People Call it the Blues)*. It featured Marvin GAYE on drums. After its commercial failure he was teamed up with The SUPREMES, The Miracles, Marvin Gaye and Mary WELLS for one of the Motown package tours. His first LP, the live *12 Year Old Genius* (USA#1.1963), featured the single *Fingertips, Part 2* (USA #1.1963). Due to his success he had to enrol at the Michigan School for the Blind to continue his education. After a couple of modest hits, he released *Hey Harmonica Man* (USA#29. 1964); as he had attained the age of fourteen, he now dropped the 'Little' from his professional name. In early 1965, the Motortown Revue hit London. As well as Wonder the package included MARTHA & THE VANDELLAS, The Supremes, The TEMPTATIONS and The Miracles. The tour coincided with the launch in the UK of the Tamla Motown label, which had previously been licensed to other labels for distribution.

The following year, Wonder had his first hit in the UK with *Uptight (Everything's Alright)* (USA #1; UK#14.1966), produced by William STEVENSON, Clarence PAUL and Henry Cosby. Over the next five years his stature as one of Motown's most significant acts was consolidated by a string of hits and he was increasingly allowed greater artistic control over his work, collaborating principally with Clarence Paul: *Nothing's too Good for my Baby* (USA#20.1966), *Blowin' in the Wind* (USA#9; UK#36.1966), *A Place in the Sun* (USA#9.1966; UK#20.1967), *Travellin' Man* (USA#32.1967), *I Was Made to Love Her* (USA#2; UK#5.1967), *I'm Wonderin'* (USA#12; UK #22.1967), *Shoo-*

Be-Doo-Be-Doo-Da-Dey (USA#9; UK#46. 1968), *You Met Your Match* (USA#35.1968), *For Once in my Life* (USA#2; UK#3.1968), *My Cherie Amour* (USA/UK#4. 1969), *Yester-Me, Yester-You, Yester-Day* (USA#7; UK#2.1969), *Never had a Dream Come True* (USA#26; UK#6.1970), *Signed, Sealed, Delivered, I'm Yours* (USA#3; UK#15.1970) and *Heaven Help us All* (USA#9; UK#29.1970). His musical prowess grew in stature with each LP, culminating in the underrated *Signed, Sealed & Delivered* (USA#25.1970).

In 1971, having reached the age of seniority, he set up his own production company, Taurus, and his own publishing company, Black Bull, both of which were licensed through Motown.This move enabled him to gain complete artistic control over his recorded output. He shifted the emphasis in his recording from singles to LPs; he still had as many hit singles as before, but they were tracks originally written as segments of LPs. These changes represented a notable departure and a supreme article of faith in Wonder on the part of Motown, who had always relied more on the sales of singles than of LPs. After recording a cover of the Lennon-McCartney composition *We Can Work it Out* (USA#13; UK#27.1971), he recorded *If you Really Love Me* (USA#8; UK#20.1971), which he had written with his wife SYREETA. These were followed by the LP *Music from my Mind* (USA#21.1972), recorded with synthesiser experts, Malcolm Cecil and Robert Margouleff. The sophistication of the arrangements and the practical application of synths were a real eye-opener, proving that synths could be used constructively rather than just as gimmicks. The next LP, *Talking Book* (USA#3; UK#16.1973), included *Superstition* (USA#1; UK#11.1973) and *You are the Sunshine of my Life* (USA#1; UK#7.1973), the former having been written for guitarist Jeff Beck and the latter now a 'standard' – which is just another way of saying that it has since been massacred by countless other singers. Later that year he was hospitalised after being seriously injured in a road accident in North Carolina. His follow-up LP was *Innervisions* (USA#4; UK#8.1973), which included *Higher Ground* (USA#4; UK#29.1973), *Livin' for the City* (USA#8.1973; UK#15.1974), *He's Misstra Know it All* (UK#10.1974) and *Don't You Worry about a Thing* (USA#16.1974). After releasing the LP *Fulfillingness' First Finale* (USA#1; UK#5.1974), which included *You Haven't Done Nothing* (USA#1; UK#30.1974) with vocal support from The Jackson Five (see JACKSONS) and *Boogie on Reggae Woman* (USA#3.1974; UK#12. 1975), he embarked upon a US Tour.

In 1975 he was awarded a NARM Presidential award for his Contributions to American Music. While his stature as an artist grew, his activities on behalf of the community increased – headlining a concert in Washington celebrating 'Human Kindness Day', playing (with Isaac HAYES and Bob Dylan) a benefit concert in aid of boxer 'Hurricane Carter', opening a Stevie Wonder Home for Blind and Retarded Children, and so on.

In 1976 he released the double LP, *Songs in the Key of Life* (USA#1; UK#2.1976), which showed once again his adeptness at handling 'serious' topics without being trite while at the same time being able to pen memorable melodies. Several hit singles were extracted: *I Wish* (USA#1.1977; UK#5.1976), *Sir Duke* (USA#1; UK#2.1977), *Another Star* (USA#32; UK#29.1977) and *As* (USA#36.1978). The following year he released another double LP, *Journey through the Secret Life of Plants* (USA#4; UK#8.1979). A soundtrack for a documentary film, it contained the singles *Send One Your Love* (USA#4; UK#52.1979) and *Black Orchid* (UK#63.1980). His next LP, *Hotter than July* (USA#3; UK#2.1980), contained the singles *Master Blaster (Jammin')*

(USA#5; UK#2.1980), *I Ain't Gonna Stand for It* (USA#11; UK#10.1981), *Lately* (UK#3. 1981) and *Happy Birthday* (UK#2.1981), the latter was used by him in the lobbying for recognition of Martin Luther King's Birthday, January 15, as a national holiday (his wish was finally granted in 1986). His next singles, *That Girl* (USA#4; UK#39.1982), *Do I Do* (USA#13; UK#10.1982) and *Ribbon in the Sky* (UK#45.1982), were taken from the greatest hits compilation, *Original Musiquarium I* (USA#4; UK#8.1982), which featured odd slices of new material.

A duet with Paul McCartney, *Ebony and Ivory* (USA/UK#1.1982), gave further proof – as if it were needed – that he was one of the most sought after collaborators in the world of contemporary music. After duets with other artists like Charlene and Elton John he recorded the soundtrack for the film *The Woman in Red* (USA#4; UK#2.1984), starring Gene Wilder and Gilda Radner, and featuring contributions from Dionne WARWICK as well as the single, *I Just Called to Say I Love You* (USA/UK#1.1984). This was his first solo #1 in the UK and won him an Oscar for Best Song at the following year's Academy Awards. Also from the soundtrack came *Love Light in Flight* (UK#44.1984). After being given the freedom of the city of Detroit, he recorded *Don't Drive Drunk* (UK#62.1985) and then participated in the recording of *We are the World*, an all-star recording on behalf of famine relief in Ethiopia. His next LP, *In Square Circle* (USA/UK#5.1985), featured the singles *Part-Time Lover* (USA#1; UK#5.1985), *Go Home* (USA#10.1986; UK#67. 1985), *Overjoyed* (USA#24; UK#17.1986) and *Stranger on the Shore of Love* (UK#55.1987).

After undertaking a US tour, he collaborated on the recording of an anti-drug song, *Stop, Don't Pass Go* with Nile RODGERS and Quincy JONES. This was followed by a European and UK Tour. His next LP, *Characters*

(USA#17; UK#33.1987), included the single *Skeletons* (USA#19; UK#59. 1987) and a duet with Michael JACKSON on *Get It* (UK#37.1988). In 1988 he appeared at the Nelson Mandela Birthday Concert in London and recorded a duet with Julio Igleias, *My Love*. After further extensive touring, he released the single *Keep Our Love Alive* (1990) from the forthcoming LP *Conversation Pieces*.

RECORDED LIVE – THE 12 YEAR OLD GENIUS, Motown, 1963
UPTIGHT EVERYTHING'S ALRIGHT, Motown, 1966
DOWN TO EARTH, Motown, 1967
I WAS MADE TO LOVE HER, Motown, 1967
GREATEST HITS, Motown, 1968
SOMEDAY AT CHRISTMAS, Motown, 1968
FOR ONCE IN MY LIFE, Motown, 1969
MY CHERIE AMOUR, Motown, 1969
LIVE AT THE TALK OF THE TOWN, Motown, 1970
SIGNED SEALED DELIVERED, Motown, 1970
WHERE I'M COMING FROM, Motown, 1971
GREATEST HITS, VOLUME 2, Motown, 1971
MUSIC FROM MY MIND, Motown, 1972
TALKING BOOK, Motown, 1972
INNERVISIONS, Motown, 1973
FULFILLINGNESS' FIRST FINALE, Motown, 1974
ANTHOLOGY, Motown, 1977
JOURNEY THROUGH THE SECRET LIFE OF PLANTS, Motown, 1979
HOTTER THAN JULY, Motown, 1980
THE JAZZ SOUL OF LITTLE STEVIE, Motown, 1982
TRIBUTE TO UNCLE RAY, Motown, 1982
WITH A SONG IN MY HEART, Motown, 1982
ORIGINAL MUSIQUARIUM I, Motown, 1982
LOVE SONGS, Telstar, 1984
THE WOMAN IN RED, Motown, 1984
IN SQUARE CIRCLE, Motown, 1985
THE ESSENTIAL STEVIE WONDER, Motown, 1987
CHARACTERS, Motown, 1987

WRIGHT, BETTY Betty Wright was born in Miami, Florida, on December 21, 1953, to a large family. She cut her first gospel record in 1966 with The Echoes of Joy. After recording with a succession of independent labels, she was signed by Henry STONE to his Alston label, where she remained until 1981, notching up a string of hits including *Girls Can't do what the Guys Do* (USA#3.1968), *He's Bad Bad Bad, Clean Up Woman* (USA#6.1971), *The Baby Sitter, Secretary, Shoorah Shoorah* (UK#27.1975) and *Where is the Love* (UK#25.1975). Of all the singles, *Clean Up Woman*, featuring guitarist Willie 'Beaver' Hale (see STONE, Henry), was the most influential: a cautionary tale it sparked off a whole sub-genre chronicling 'man's intrinisic dishonesty when it comes to women', a theme taken up by Millie JACKSON, Laura LEE and Shirley BROWN, among others. In 1978 she released the LP *Betty Wright Live* (USA#26.1978).

However, in 1981 she was signed by Epic; the ensuing LP, *Betty Wright*, featured a contribution from Stevie WONDER. During the 1980s she hosted some chat shows for the local Miami TV network, before returning to recording with the single *Pain* (UK#42.1986) and the LPs, *Mother Wit* (1988) and *4U2NJOY* (1989).

WRIGHT BACK AT YOU, Epic, 1983
4U2NJOY, Jetstar, 1989

WRIGHT, O.V Overton Vertis Wright (born in Leno, Tennessee, on October 9, 1939) was one of the great gospel singers to move into secular music. He started to sing professionally when he was six. By 1963 he had been a member of such prestigious gospel groups as The Highway QCs, The Harmony Echoes and The Sunset Travellers; the latter were under contract to Don ROBEY's Duke label. He and James CARR were taken to meet Quinton CLAUNCH, the owner of the Goldwax label, by their manager Roosevelt Jamison. (Wright and Carr had met Jamison when they were members of The Harmony Echoes, who used to rehearse at the rear of the Interstate Blood Bank where Jamison worked as a medical technician). When Robey heard that Wright had recorded *That's how Strong my Love Is* for Goldwax, he promptly slapped an injunction on him to prevent him from recording for anyone other than Duke.

After the implementation of his contract with Robey, Wright was sent to record at the Hi Studios, with Willie MITCHELL producing. There he recorded some of the finest performances of his career, *Eight Men, Four Women, A Nickel and a Nail* and *I'll Take Care of You*. At the end of the 1960s, he signed with the Hi label, where he remained until his death on November 16, 1980, from a heart attack, brought on by drug abuse.

THE WRIGHT STUFF, Hi, 1987
LIVE, Hi, 1990
THAT'S HOW STRONG MY LOVE IS, Hi, 1991

ZODIACS   See WILLIAMS, Maurice.

ACKNOWLEDGEMENTS

The writing and compilation of this particular tome has not been without its problems. There are certain key people who have been pivotal in keeping me at it. Chrissy Pierce has never been less than whole-hearted in her support and encouragement and her sense of humour has been essential in helping me keep a sense of proportion.

Graham Fletcher has always been enthusiastic and objective in equal measure. Christopher Fagg at Cassell was the vital catalyst. Stuart Booth, the commissioning editor, has brought his appreciation of the music to bear and has been remarkably tolerant of my vagaries. Paul Barnett, the copy editor, wrestled manfully with my erratic syntax and beat it into shape. Pete Nickols added his expertise.

Record companies have also been immensely solicitous, especially Nicky Denaro, Gordon Frewin and Judith Weaterston at Motown (UK), Jonathan Morrish of Sony Music (UK) and Julian De Takats at Malaco. Cliff White handed me helpful hints without hesitation. Many more, who are too numerous to mention, contributed ideas and wisdom.

H.G.

BIBLIOGRAPHY

The number of books that have influenced me are too numerous to mention; the following represent a cross-section:

Alan Betrock, *Girl Groups: The Story Of A Sound,* Delilah, New York, 1982

Ray Charles, with David Ritz, *Brother Ray,* Dial Press, New York, 1978

Nik Cohn, *WopBopaLooBopLopBamBoom,* Paladin, London, 1972

Tony Cummings, *The Sound Of Philadelphia,* Methuen, London, 1975

Fred Dellar, R. Thompson & Douglas Green, *The Illustrated Encyclopaedia Of Country Music,* Salamander, London, 1977

Paul Gambaccini, Tim Rice and Jo Rice, *British Hit Singles,* GRR Publications, London, 1989

Paul Gambaccini, Tim Rice and Jo Rice, *British Hit Albums,* GRR Publications, London, 1988

Nelson George, *Where Did Our Love Go? The Rise and Fall of The Motown Sound,* Omnibus, London, 1985

Nelson George, *The Death of Rhythm & Blues,* Omnibus, London, 1988

Charlie Gillett, *The Sound Of The City,* Souvenir, London, 1970

Charlie Gillett, *Making Tracks: Atlantic Records And The Growth Of A Multi-Billion Dollar Industry,* Souvenir, London, 1974

Charlotte Greig, *Will You Still Love Me Tomorrow?,* Virago, London, 1989

Peter Guralnick, *Sweet Soul Music,* Virgin, London, 1986

Peter Guralnick, *Feel Like Going Home,* Omnibus, London, 1981

Phil Hardy & Dave Laing, *The Faber Companion To 20th Century Popular Music,* Faber, London, 1990

Gerri Hirshey, *Nowhere To Run,* Macmillan, London, 1984

Ian Hoare, Clive Anderson, Tony Cummings, Simon Frith, *The Soul Book,* Methuen, London,1975

Barney Hoskyns, *Say It One Time For The Broken Hearted: The Country Side Of Southern Soul,* Fontana, London, 1987

Leroi Jones, *Black Music,* William Morrow & Co., New York, 1968

Greil Marcus, *Mystery Train,* Omnibus, London, 1979

Dave Marsh, *The Heart Of Rock And Soul,* Penguin, London, 1989

Bill Millar, *The Coasters,* Star Books, London, 1974

Bill Millar, *The Drifters,* Studio Vista, London, 1971

Charles Shaar Murray, *Crosstown Traffic,* Faber, London, 1989

David Ritz, *Divided Soul: The Life Of Marvin Gaye,* Grafton, London, 1986

Charles Sawyer, *B.B. King: The Authorised Biography,* Blandford, Poole, 1981

Alan Warner, *Who Sang What In Rock 'n' Roll,* Blandford, London, 1990

Joel Whitburn, *The Billboard Book of US Top 40 Hits,* Billboard Publications, 1986

Joel Whitburn, *The Billboard Book of US Top 40 Albums,* Billboard Publications, 1987

Richard Williams, *The Sound Of Phil Spector: Out Of His Head,* Abacus, London, 1974

Mary Wilson, *Dreamgirl: My Life As A Supreme,* Sidgwick & Jackson, London, 1987

AUG.